To my parents, who gave me life and taught me what to do with it.

Microsoft*Press

Programming the

Microsoft®

Windows®
Driver
Model

Walter Oney

PUBLISHED BY
Microsoft Press
A Division of Microsoft Corporation
One Microsoft Way
Redmond, Washington 98052-6399

Library of Congress Cataloging-in-Publication Data
Oney, Walter.
    Programming the Microsoft Windows Driver Model
        p.   cm.
    Includes index.
    ISBN 0-7356-0588-2
    1. Microsoft Windows NT device drivers (Computer programs)
    2. Computer programming.   I. Title.
    QA76.76.D49O54 1999
    005.7'126--dc21   99-33878
                                                              CIP

Printed and bound in the United States of America.

1 2 3 4 5 6 7 8 9   QMQM   4 3 2 1 0 9

Distributed in Canada by Penguin Books Canada Limited.

A CIP catalogue record for this book is available from the British Library.

Microsoft Press books are available through booksellers and distributors worldwide. For further information about international editions, contact your local Microsoft Corporation office or contact Microsoft Press International directly at fax (425) 936-7329. Visit our Web site at mspress.microsoft.com.

Acquisitions Editor: Ben Ryan
Project Editor: Devon Musgrave
Technical Editor: Robert Lyon

Contents

Foreword

The Windows Driver Model traces its roots several years back to an OS called Windows for Workgroups 3.10. At that time we were struggling with support for the myriad of different SCSI controllers, and I was gazing longingly at the assortment of miniports that the Windows NT team had created. It didn't take long to realize that it would take less effort to re-create the necessary image loader and execution environment that the miniports expected than it would to rewrite and debug all of those miniports in some sort of VxD form.

Unfortunately Windows for Workgroups 3.10 ended up shipping without support for SCSI miniports, due mainly to peripheral issues such as solid ASPI (Advanced SCSI Programming Interface) compatibility. However, the groundwork to share the same executable driver images across the Windows and Windows NT operating systems was in place and would see the light of day in Windows 95, which could share both SCSI and NDIS miniport binaries with Windows NT.

The potential benefits of a shared driver model are significant. For driver developers interested in supporting both platforms, a shared driver model can cut the driver development and testing costs almost in half. For Microsoft, a shared model means easier migration from Windows 9x to Windows 2000 and future releases of this platform. And for the end user, a larger variety of more stable drivers would be available for both platform families.

The next logical step, then, was to create a driver model with the ability to share general purpose drivers across both platforms. But what form should it take? Three requirements were immediately obvious: it must be multiprocessor-capable, it must be processor-independent, and it must support Plug and Play (PnP). Fortunately, the Windows NT 4.0 driver model met the first two requirements, and it seemed clear that the next major release of Windows NT would support PnP as well. As a result, WDM can be considered a proper subset of what is now the Windows NT driver model.

The potential benefits of a shared driver model can be realized today for many classes of devices, and choosing the WDM driver model will continue to pay dividends in the future. For example, a correctly written WDM driver requires only a recompile before functioning in an NT 64-bit environment prototype.

WDM will continue to evolve as new platforms and device classes are supported. Future versions of Windows 9x and Windows 2000 will contain upwardly revised WDM execution environments. Fortunately, WDM is designed to be "backward compatible," meaning that WDM drivers written according to the Windows 2000 DDK and designed to work for the intended environment will continue to work in subsequent WDM environments.

There is a lot to WDM, and in this book Walter does an excellent job of offering an in-depth tour of every aspect as well as the philosophy of the Windows Driver Model.

Forrest Foltz
Architect, Windows Development
Microsoft Corporation

Acknowledgments

I'm indebted to many people who helped make this book a reality. Devon Musgrave, Robert Lyon, and the rest of the team at Microsoft Press performed yeoman service in turning a rugged WinWord manuscript into the polished work you're holding in your hands. I know that Ben Ryan, the Acquisitions Editor for this project, logs countless hours and frequent flyer miles searching for great authors and sizzling new books; well, better luck next time. Microsoft's Sandy Spinrad, in just one of his many aspects, ably assisted by locating technical information, hardware for testing, up-to-date releases, and much of the other research material on which I relied. Many members of the Windows 2000 and Windows 98 base teams reviewed this material and deserve personal mention, but they've requested anonymity; they and I know who they are, at least. My seminar students and the online community helped in many large and small ways by asking thought-provoking questions or sharing hard-won insights. Finally, I want to thank my wife, Marty, who's always there when the going gets tough.

Walter Oney
http://www.oneysoft.com

Chapter 1

Introduction

Souvenir shops in many of the cities I visit sell posters depicting the world from the local perspective. Landmarks and famous watering holes appear prominently in the foreground. The background features the rest of the planet in progressively less detail, confirming that the natives are less impressed by, say, the pyramids in Giza or the Great Wall of China than by some busy downtown street corner. From the same sort of insular perspective, a Microsoft Windows 2000 or Microsoft Windows 98 system consists of an operating system and a collection of device drivers for whatever hardware the end user chooses to populate the system with from one moment to the next. This book is all about the drivers and the nearby detail.

AN OVERVIEW OF THE OPERATING SYSTEMS

The Windows Driver Model (WDM) provides a framework for device drivers that operate in two operating systems—Windows 98 and Windows 2000. Although to the end user these two systems are very similar, they work very differently on the inside. In this section, I'll present a brief overview of the two systems.

Windows 2000 Overview

Figure 1-1 is my perspective poster of the Windows 2000 operating system, wherein I emphasize the features that are important to people who write device drivers. Software executes either in *user mode* (untrusted and restricted to authorized activities only) or in *kernel mode* (fully trusted and able to do anything). A user-mode program that wants to, say, read some data from a device would call an application programming interface (API) such as **ReadFile**. A subsystem module such as KERNEL32.DLL implements this API by invoking some sort of platform-dependent system service interface to reach a kernel-mode support routine. In the case of a call to ReadFile, the mechanism involves making a user-mode call to an entry point named **NtReadFile** in a system dynamic-link library (DLL) named—redundantly, I've always thought—NTDLL.DLL. The user-mode NtReadFile function uses the system service interface to reach a kernel-mode routine that's also named NtReadFile.

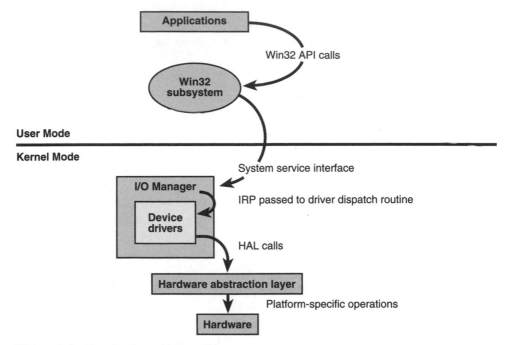

Figure 1-1. *The Windows 2000 architecture.*

We often say that NtReadFile is part of a system component that we call the I/O Manager. The term *I/O Manager* is perhaps a little misleading because there isn't any single executable module with that name. We need a name to use when discussing the "cloud" of operating system services that surrounds our own driver, though, and this name is the one we usually pick.

Many routines serve a purpose similar to NtReadFile. They operate in kernel mode to service an application's request to interact with a device in some way. They all validate their parameters, thereby ensuring that they don't inadvertently allow a security breach by performing an operation or accessing some data that the user-mode program wouldn't have been able to perform or access by itself. They then create a data structure called an I/O request packet (IRP) that they pass to an entry point in some device driver. In the case of an original ReadFile call, NtReadFile would create an IRP with a *major function code* of IRP_MJ_READ (a constant in a DDK [Device Driver Kit] header file). Processing details at this point can differ, but a likely scenario is for a routine like NtReadFile to return to the user-mode caller with an indication that the operation described by the IRP hasn't finished yet. The user-mode program might continue about its business and then wait for the operation to finish, or it might wait immediately. Either way, the device driver proceeds independently of the application to service the request.

A device driver might eventually need to actually access its hardware to perform an IRP. In the case of an IRP_MJ_READ to a programmed I/O (PIO) sort of device, the access might take the form of a read operation directed to an I/O port or a memory register implemented by the device. Drivers, even though they execute in kernel mode and can therefore talk directly to their hardware, use facilities provided by the hardware abstraction layer (HAL) to access hardware. A read operation might involve calling READ_PORT_UCHAR to read a single data byte from an I/O port. The HAL routine uses a platform-dependent method to actually perform the operation. On an Intel x86 computer, the HAL would use the IN instruction; on an Alpha, it would perform a memory fetch.

After a driver has finished with an I/O operation, it *completes* the IRP by calling a particular kernel-mode service routine. Completion is the last act in processing an IRP, and it allows the waiting application to resume execution.

Windows 98 Overview

Figure 1-2 shows one way of thinking about Windows 98. The operating system kernel is called the Virtual Machine Manager (VMM) because its main job is to create one or more "virtual" machines that share the hardware of a single physical machine. The original purpose of a virtual device driver (VxD) in Microsoft Windows 3.0 was to virtualize a specific device to help the VMM create the fiction that each virtual machine had a full complement of hardware. The same VMM architecture introduced with Windows 3.0 is in Windows 98 today but with a bunch of accretions to handle new hardware and 32-bit applications.

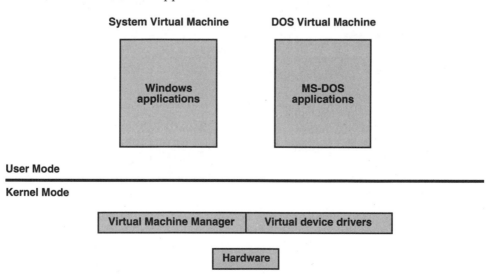

Figure 1-2. *The Windows 98 architecture.*

Windows 98 doesn't handle I/O operations in quite as orderly a way as Windows 2000. There are major differences in how Windows 98 handles operations directed to disks, to communication ports, to keyboards, and so on. Windows 98 also services 32-bit and 16-bit applications in fundamentally different ways. See Figure 1-3.

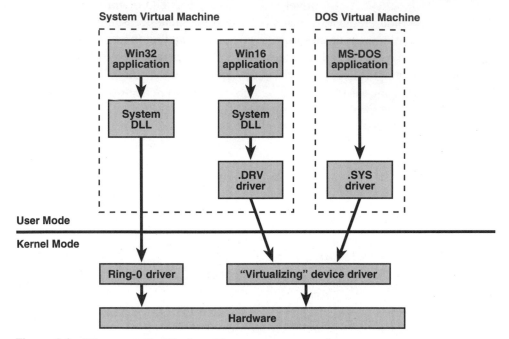

Figure 1-3. *I/O requests in Windows 98.*

The left column of Figure 1-3 shows how 32-bit applications get I/O done for them. An application calls a Win32 API such as ReadFile, which a system DLL like KERNEL32.DLL services. But applications can only use ReadFile for reading disk files, communication ports, and devices that have WDM drivers. For any other kind of device, an application must use some ad hoc mechanism based on **DeviceIoControl**. The system DLL contains different code than its Windows 2000 counterpart, too. The user-mode implementation of ReadFile, for example, validates parameters—a step done in kernel mode on Windows 2000—and uses one or another special mechanism to reach a kernel-mode driver. There's one special mechanism for disk files, another for serial ports, another for WDM devices, and so on. The mechanisms all use software interrupt 30h to make the transition from user mode to kernel mode, but they're otherwise completely different.

The middle column of Figure 1-3 shows how 16-bit Windows-based applications (Win16 applications) perform I/O. The right column illustrates the control flow for DOS-based applications. In both cases, the user-mode program calls directly or indirectly on the services of a user-mode driver that, in principle, could stand alone by itself on a bare machine. Win16 programs perform serial port I/O by indirectly calling a 16-bit DLL named COMM.DRV, for example. (Up until Microsoft Windows 95, COMM.DRV was a stand-alone driver that hooked IRQ 3 and 4 and issued IN and OUT instructions to talk directly to the serial chip.) A virtual communications device (VCD) driver intercepts the port I/O operations to guard against having two different virtual machines access the same port simultaneously. In a weird way of thinking about the process, you might say that these user-mode drivers use an "API" interface based on interception of I/O operations. "Virtualizing" drivers like VCD service these pseudo-API calls by simulating the operation of hardware.

Whereas all kernel-mode I/O operations in Windows 2000 use a common data structure (the IRP), no such uniformity exists in Windows 98 even once an application's request reaches kernel mode. Drivers of serial ports conform to a port driver function-calling paradigm orchestrated by VCOMM.VXD. Disk drivers, on the other hand, participate in a packet-driven layered architecture implemented by IOS.VXD. Other device classes use still other means.

When it comes to WDM drivers, however, the interior architecture of Windows 98 is necessarily very similar to that of Windows 2000. A system module (NTKERN.VXD) contains Windows-specific implementations of a great many Microsoft Windows NT kernel support functions. NTKERN.VXD creates IRPs and sends them to WDM drivers in just about the same way as Windows 2000. WDM drivers almost cannot tell the difference between the two environments, in fact.

WINDOWS 2000 DRIVERS

Many kinds of drivers form a complete Windows 2000 system. Figure 1-4 diagrams several of them.

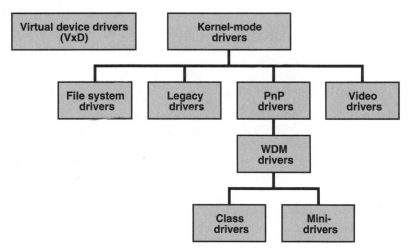

Figure 1-4. *Types of device drivers in Windows 2000.*

■ A *virtual device driver* (VDD) is a user-mode component that allows DOS-based applications to access hardware on x86 platforms. A VDD relies on the I/O permission mask to trap port access, and it essentially simulates the operation of hardware for the benefit of applications that were originally programmed to talk directly to hardware on a bare machine. Although this kind of driver shares a name and a purpose with a kind of driver used in Windows 98, it's a different animal altogether. We use the acronym VDD for this kind of driver and the acronym VxD for the Windows 98 driver to distinguish the two.

■ The category of *kernel-mode drivers* includes many subcategories. A *PnP driver* is a kernel-mode driver that understands the Plug and Play (PnP) protocols of Windows 2000. To be perfectly accurate, this book concerns PnP drivers and nothing else.

■ A *WDM driver* is a PnP driver that also understands power management protocols and is source-compatible with both Windows 98 and Windows 2000. Within the category of WDM drivers, you can also distinguish between *class drivers,* which manage a device belonging to some well-defined class of device, and *minidrivers,* which supply vendor-specific help to a class driver.

■ *Video drivers* are kernel-mode drivers for displays and printers—devices whose primary characteristic is that they render visual data.

■ *File system drivers* implement the standard PC file system model (which includes the concept of a hierarchical directory structure containing named files) on local hard disks or over network connections.

■ *Legacy device drivers* are kernel-mode drivers that directly control a hardware device without help from other drivers. This category essentially includes drivers for earlier versions of Windows NT that are running without change in Windows 2000.

Not all the distinctions implied by this classification scheme are important all of the time. As I remarked in my previous book, *Systems Programming for Windows 95* (Microsoft Press, 1996), you have not stumbled into a nest of pedants by buying my book. In particular, I'm not always going to carefully distinguish between WDM drivers and PnP drivers in the rigorous way implied by the preceding taxonomy. The distinction is a phenomenological one based on whether a given driver runs both in Windows 2000 and Windows 98. Without necessarily using the technically exact term, I'll be very careful to discuss system dependencies when they come up hereafter.

Attributes of Kernel-Mode Drivers

Kernel-mode drivers share a number of general attributes, as suggested by the list of attributes (drawn from the introductory chapters of the Windows 2000 Device Driver Kit) that I describe in the following sections. (Note that throughout this book, I'll often refer to just the "DDK," meaning the Windows 2000 DDK. If I need to discuss another DDK, I'll give its specific name.)

Portable

Kernel-mode drivers should be source-portable across all Windows NT platforms. WDM drivers are, by definition, source-portable between Windows 98 and Windows 2000 as well. To achieve portability, you should write your driver entirely in C, using language elements specified by the ANSI C standard. You should avoid using implementation-defined or vendor-specific features of the language, and you should avoid using run-time library functions that aren't already exported by the operating system kernel (concerning which, see Chapter 3). If you can't avoid platform dependencies in your code, you should isolate them with conditional compilation directives. If you follow all of these guidelines, you'll be able to recompile and relink your source code to produce a driver that will "just work" on any new Windows NT platform.

In many cases, it will be possible to achieve binary compatibility for a WDM driver between Windows 98 and the 32-bit Intel x86 Windows 2000 operating system. You achieve source compatibility merely by restricting yourself to using the subset of kernel-mode support functions declared in WDM.H. There are some areas in which the two operating systems behave differently in a way that matters to a device driver, however, and I'll discuss these areas in various parts of the book.

Configurable

A kernel-mode driver should avoid hard-coded assumptions about device characteristics or system settings that can differ from one platform to another. It's easiest to illustrate this abstract and lofty goal with a couple of examples. On an x86-based PC, a standard serial port uses a particular interrupt request line and set of eight I/O ports whose numeric values haven't changed in over 20 years. Hard-coding these values into a driver makes it not configurable. In Chapter 8, I'll discuss two power management features—idle detection and system wake-up—that an end user should be able to control; a driver that always uses particular idle timeout constants or that always arms its device's wake-up feature would not allow for that kind of control. The driver would therefore not be configurable in the sense we're discussing.

Achieving configurability requires, first of all, that you avoid coding direct references to hardware, even within platform-specific conditional compilation blocks. Call on the facilities of the HAL or of a lower-level bus driver instead. You can also implement a standard or custom control interface to allow control-panel applications to communicate end user wishes. Better yet, you can support Web-Based Enterprise Management (WBEM) controls that allow users and administrators to configure hardware features in a distributed enterprise environment. (See Chapter 10.) Finally, you can use the registry database as a repository for configuration information that ought to persist from one session to the next.

Preemptible and Interruptible

Windows 2000 and Windows 98 are multitasking operating systems that apportion use of a CPU among an arbitrary number of threads. Much of the time, driver subroutines execute in an environment in which they can be preempted to allow another thread to execute on the same CPU. Thread preemption depends on a thread priority scheme and on using the system clock to allocate CPU time in slices to threads having the same priority.

Windows 2000 also incorporates an interrupt prioritization concept known as interrupt request level (IRQL). I'll discuss IRQL in detail in Chapter 4, but the following summary will be useful for now. You can think of a CPU as having an IRQL register that records the level at which the CPU is currently executing. Three IRQL values have major significance for device drivers: PASSIVE_LEVEL (numerically equal to 0), DISPATCH_LEVEL (numerically equal to 2), and the so-called device IRQL (or DIRQL, numerically equal to a value higher than 2) at which a particular device's interrupt service routine executes. Most of the time, a CPU executes at PASSIVE_LEVEL. All user-mode code runs at PASSIVE_LEVEL, and many of the activities a driver performs also occur at PASSIVE_LEVEL. While a CPU is at PASSIVE_LEVEL, the current thread can be preempted by any other thread that has a higher thread priority or by expiration of its own time slice. Once a CPU's IRQL is above PASSIVE_LEVEL, however, thread preemption no longer occurs. The CPU executes in the context of whatever thread was current when the IRQL was most recently raised above PASSIVE_LEVEL.

You can think of the IRQ levels above PASSIVE_LEVEL as a priority scheme for interrupts. This is a different sort of priority than that which governs thread preemption because, as I just remarked, no thread preemption occurs above PASSIVE_LEVEL. But an activity running at any IRQL can be interrupted to perform an activity at a higher IRQL. Consequently, a driver must anticipate that it might lose control at any moment while the system performs some more essential task.

Multiprocessor-Safe

Windows 2000 can run on computers with one or more than one CPU. Windows 2000 uses a *symmetric multiprocessor* model, in which all CPUs are considered equal. System tasks and user-mode programs can execute on any CPU, and all CPUs have equal access to memory. The existence of multiple CPUs poses a difficult synchronization problem for device drivers because code executing on two or more CPUs might simultaneously need to access shared data or shared hardware resources. The Windows 2000 kernel provides a synchronization object called a *spin lock* that drivers can use to avoid destructive interference in such situations. (See Chapter 4.)

Object-Based

The Windows 2000 kernel is *object-based* in the sense that many of the data structures used by device drivers and kernel routines have common features that a centralized *Object Manager* component controls. These features include names, reference counts, security attributes, and so on. Internally, the kernel contains *method routines* for performing common object management tasks such as opening and closing objects or parsing object names.

Kernel components export service routines that drivers use to manipulate certain kinds of object or certain fields within objects. Some kernel objects—the kernel interrupt object, for example—are completely opaque in that the DDK headers don't declare the members of the data structure. Other kernel objects—such as the device object or the driver object—are *partially opaque*: the DDK headers declare all the members of the structure, but documentation describes only certain accessible members and cautions driver writers not to access or modify other members directly. Support routines exist to access and modify those opaque fields that must be indirectly available to drivers. Partially opaque objects are analogous to C++ classes, which can have public members accessible to anyone and private or protected members accessible only via method functions.

Packet-Driven

The I/O Manager and device drivers use the I/O request packet to manage the details of I/O operations. Some kernel-mode component creates an IRP to perform an operation on a device or to send an instruction or query to a driver. The I/O Manager sends the IRP to one or more of the subroutines that a driver exports. Generally, each driver subroutine performs a discrete amount of work on the IRP and returns back to the I/O Manager. Eventually, some driver subroutine completes the IRP, whereupon the I/O Manager destroys the IRP and reports the ending status back to the originator of the request.

Asynchronous

Windows 2000 allows applications and drivers to initiate operations and continue processing while the operations progress. Consequently, drivers ordinarily process time-consuming operations in an asynchronous way. That is, a driver accepts an IRP, initializes whatever state information it requires to manage the operation, and then returns to its caller after arranging for the IRP to be performed and completed in the future. The caller can then decide whether or not to wait for the IRP to finish.

As a multitasking operating system, Windows 2000 schedules threads for execution on the available processors according to eligibility and priority. The asynchronous operations a driver needs to perform for handling an I/O request often occur in the context of some unpredictable thread, the identification of which can differ from one invocation of the driver's asynchronous processing routines to the next. We use the term *arbitrary thread context* to describe the situation in which a driver doesn't know (or care) which thread happens to be current as it performs its work. Drivers should avoid blocking arbitrary threads, and this stricture generally results in a driver architecture that responds to hardware events by performing discrete operations and then returning.

The Windows Driver Model

In the Windows Driver Model, each hardware device has at least two device drivers. One of these drivers, which we call the *function driver,* is what you've always thought of as being "the" device driver. It understands all the details about how to make the hardware work. It's responsible for initiating I/O operations, for handling the interrupts that occur when those operations finish, and for providing a way for the end user to exercise whatever control over the device might be appropriate.

We call the other of the two drivers that every device has the *bus driver.* It's responsible for managing the connection between the hardware and the computer. For example, the bus driver for the PCI (Peripheral Component Interconnect) bus is the software component that actually detects that your card is plugged in to a PCI slot and determines what requirements your card has for I/O-mapped or memory-mapped connections with the host. It's also the software that turns the flow of electrical current to your card's slot on or off.

Some devices have more than two drivers. We use the generic term *filter driver* to describe these other drivers. Some filter drivers simply watch as the function driver performs I/O. More often, a software or hardware vendor supplies a filter driver to modify the behavior of an existing function driver in some way. "Upper" filter drivers see IRPs before the function driver, and they have the chance to support additional features that the function driver doesn't know about. Sometimes an upper filter can perform a workaround for a bug or other deficiency in the function driver or the hardware. "Lower" filter drivers see IRPs that the function driver is trying to send to the bus driver. In some cases, such as when the device is attached to a universal serial bus (USB), a lower filter can modify the stream of bus operations that the function driver is trying to perform.

A WDM function driver is often composed of two separate executable files. One file, the *class driver,* understands how to handle all of the WDM protocols that the operating system uses (and some of them can be very complicated) and how to manage the basic features of an entire class of devices. A class driver for the class of USB cameras is one example. The other file, called the *minidriver,* contains functions that the class driver uses to manage the vendor-specific features of a particular instance of that class. The combination of class plus minidriver adds up to a complete function driver.

A useful way to think of a complete driver is as a container for a collection of subroutines that the operating system calls to perform various operations on an IRP. Figure 1-5 illustrates this concept. Some routines, such as the **DriverEntry** and **AddDevice** routines, as well as dispatch functions for a few types of IRP, will be present in every such container. Drivers that need to queue requests—and most do—might have a **StartIo** routine. Drivers that perform direct memory access (DMA) transfers will have an **AdapterControl** routine. Drivers for devices that generate hardware interrupts—again, most do—will have an interrupt service routine (ISR) and a deferred procedure call (DPC) routine. Most drivers will have dispatch functions for several types of IRP besides the three that are required. One of your jobs as the author of a WDM driver, therefore, is to select the functions that need to be included in your particular container.

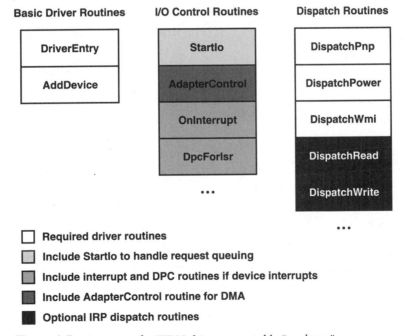

Figure 1-5. *Contents of a WDM driver executable "package."*

SAMPLE CODE

The companion disc contains a great many sample drivers and test programs. I crafted each sample with a view toward illustrating a particular issue or technique that the text discusses. Each of the samples is, therefore, a "toy" that you can't just ship after changing a few lines of code. I wrote the samples this way on purpose. Over the years, I've observed that programmer-authors tend to build samples that illustrate their prowess at overcoming complexity rather than samples that teach beginners how to solve basic problems, so I won't do that to you. Chapters 7 and 11 have some drivers that work with "real" hardware, namely development boards from the makers of a PCI chip set and a USB chip set. Apart from that, however, all the drivers are for nonexistent hardware.

In nearly every case, I built a simple user-mode test program that you can use to explore the operation of the sample driver. These test programs are truly tiny: they contain just a few lines of code and are concerned only with whatever point the driver sample attempts to illustrate. Once again, I think it's better to give you a simple way to exercise the driver code that I assume you're really interested in instead of trying to show off every MFC programming trick I ever learned.

You're free to use all of the sample code in this book in your own projects without paying me or anyone else a royalty. (Of course, you must consult the detailed license agreement at the end of the book—this paraphrase is not intended to override that agreement in any way.) There are few cases in which I ask that you get my permission before redistributing one of my sample modules as a freestanding piece of software, however; these include GENERIC.SYS (discussed in Appendix B) and WDMSTUB.VXD (discussed in Appendix A). I'll gladly give permission, but I will need to ask your company to agree to some conditions designed to ensure that if a bunch of readers all decide to ship copies of these modules along with their production drivers, end users receive up-to-date and reliable versions. See the companion disc for more information on redistribution.

The Companion Disc

The CD-ROM that comes with this book contains the complete source code and an executable copy of each sample. It also contains a few utility programs that you might find useful in your own work. Open the file WDMBOOK.HTM in your Web browser for an index to the samples and an explanation of how to use these tools.

The setup program on the disc gives you the option to install all of the samples on your own disk or to leave them on the CD-ROM. However, setup will not install any kernel-mode components on your system. Setup will ask your permission to add some environment variables to your AUTOEXEC.BAT file. The build procedure for the samples relies on these environment variables. They will be correctly set the next time you reboot your Windows 2000 or Windows 98 computer. Setup will also install the necessary registry entries to define a SAMPLE class of device, to which each of the sample drivers belongs.

If your computer runs both Windows 2000 and Windows 98, I recommend performing a full install under one OS and a compact install under the other. Additionally, I recommend allowing the setup program to modify your AUTOEXEC.BAT under just one OS. If you follow these suggestions, setup will be able to make necessary changes in both registry databases but will copy the sample code only one time. (Note that Windows 2000 interprets your AUTOEXEC.BAT file at startup time to set environment variables. That's why the setup program needs to modify this file.)

Each sample includes an HTML file that explains (very briefly) what the sample does, how to build it, and how to test it. I recommend that you read the file before trying to install the sample, because some of the samples have unusual installation requirements. Once you've installed a sample driver, you'll find that the Device Manager has an extra property page from which you can view the same HTML file. (See Figure 1-6.)

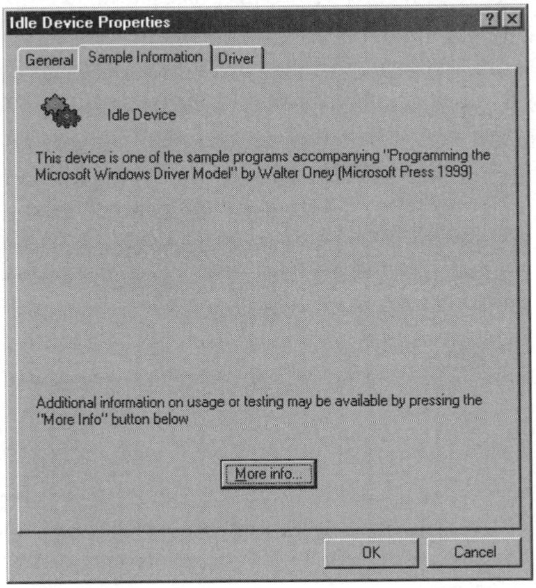

Figure 1-6. *A custom Device Manager property page for sample drivers.*

How the Samples Were Created

There's a good reason why my sample drivers look like they all came out of a cookie cutter: they did. Faced with so many samples to write, I decided to write a custom application wizard. The wizard functionality in Microsoft Visual C++ version 6.0 is almost up to snuff for building a WDM driver project, so I elected to depend on it.

The wizard is named WDMWIZ.AWX, and you'll find it on the companion disc. I've documented how to use it in Appendix C. Use it, if you wish, to construct the skeletons for your own drivers. But be wary that this wizard is not of product grade—it's intended to help you learn about writing drivers rather than to replace or compete with a commercial toolkit. Be aware, too, that you need to change a few project settings by hand because the wizard support is only *almost* what's needed. Refer to the WDMBOOK.HTM in the root directory of the companion disc for more information.

Installing the Windows 2000 Device Driver Kit provides you with Start menu commands for opening a "checked build" environment and a "free build" environment. Each environment is a command prompt with a collection of environment variables set in a particular way to dovetail with a command line–based method of building drivers. This method relies on a utility named BUILD.EXE that comes with the DDK and on the existence of a file named SOURCES that describes a driver project. I've provided a SOURCES file for each project so that you can use this method for building a driver if you want to.

I personally prefer using the Microsoft Visual Studio environment for driver projects. I used to advocate using BUILD.EXE because I was afraid that Microsoft might change some important compile or link option in such a way that any approach based on an integrated development environment (IDE) would break. Something like this happened during the Windows 2000 beta period, in fact. (Somebody decided to change the decade-old structure of library files, and I had to change a slew of project settings.) I guess I think the productivity improvement I gain by using modern IDE-based tools is significant enough that I'll run the risk of having to make similar changes in the future.

GENERIC.SYS

A WDM driver contains a great deal of code that you could call boilerplate for handling Plug and Play and power management. This code is long. It's boring. It's easy to get wrong. My samples all rely on what amounts to a kernel-mode DLL named GENERIC.SYS. WDMWIZ.AWX will build a project that uses GENERIC.SYS or that doesn't, as you specify. Appendix B details the support functions that GENERIC.SYS exports in case you want to use them yourself.

ORGANIZATION OF THIS BOOK

After teaching driver programming seminars to hundreds of students over the past several years, I've come to understand that people learn things in fundamentally different ways. Some people like to learn a great deal of theory about something and then learn how to apply that theory to practical problems. Other people like to learn practical things first and then learn the general theory. I'd call the former approach deductive and the latter approach inductive. I personally prefer an inductive approach, and I've organized this book to suit that style of learning.

My aim is to explain how to write device drivers. Broadly speaking, I wanted to provide the minimum background you'll need to write an actual driver and then move on to more specialized topics. That "minimum background" is pretty extensive, however; it consumes six chapters. Once past Chapter 7, you'll be reading about topics that are important but not necessarily on the fall line that leads straight downhill to a working driver.

Chapter 2, "Basic Structure of a WDM Driver," explains the basic data structures that Windows 2000 uses to manage I/O devices and the basic way your driver relates to those data structures. I'll discuss the driver object and the device object. I'll also discuss how you write two of the subroutines—the DriverEntry and AddDevice routines—that every WDM driver package contains.

Chapter 3, "Basic Programming Techniques," describes the most important service functions you can call on to perform mundane programming tasks. In that chapter, I'll discuss error handling, memory management, and a few other miscellaneous tasks.

Chapter 4, "Synchronization," discusses how your driver can synchronize access to shared data in the multitasking, multiprocessor world of Windows 2000. You'll learn the details about IRQL and about various synchronization primitives that the operating system offers for your use.

Chapter 5, "The I/O Request Packet," introduces the subject of input/output programming, which of course is the real reason for this book. I'll explain where I/O request packets come from, and I'll give an overview of what drivers do with them when they follow what I call the "standard model" for IRP processing. I'll also discuss the knotty subject of IRP cancellation, wherein accurate reasoning about synchronization problems becomes crucial.

Chapter 6, "Plug and Play," concerns just one type of I/O request packet, namely IRP_MJ_PNP. The Plug and Play Manager component of the operating system sends you this IRP to give you details about your device's configuration and to notify you of important events in the life of your device. Being a good PnP citizen implies that many drivers can't use the "standard model" for IRP processing. I'll therefore describe an object I named a DEVQUEUE that you can use to queue and dequeue IRPs appropriately when PnP events are occurring all around you.

Chapter 7, "Reading and Writing Data," is where we finally get to write driver code that performs I/O operations. I'll discuss how you obtain configuration information from the PnP Manager and how you use that information to prepare your driver for "substantive" IRPs that read and write data. I'll present two simple driver sample programs as well: one for dealing with a PIO device and one for dealing with a bus-mastering DMA device.

Chapter 8, "Power Management," describes how your driver participates in power management. I think you'll find, as I did, that power management is pretty complicated. Unfortunately, you have to participate in the system's power management protocols or else the system as a whole won't work right. Worse yet, the system will sometimes present a dialog box that identifies *you* as the culprit if you don't do the right things. Luckily, the community of driver writers already has a grand tradition of cutting and pasting, and that will save you.

Chapter 9, "Specialized Topics," contains a discussion of filter drivers, error logging, I/O control operations, and system threads.

Chapter 10, "Windows Management Instrumentation," concerns a scheme for enterprisewide computer management in which your driver can and should participate. I'll explain how you can provide statistical and performance data for use by monitoring applications, how you can respond to standard WBEM controls, and how you can alert controlling applications of important events when they occur.

Chapter 11, "The Universal Serial Bus," describes how to write drivers for USB devices.

Chapter 12, "Installing Device Drivers," tells you how to arrange for your driver to get installed onto end user systems. You'll learn the basics of writing an INF file to control installation, and you'll also learn some interesting and useful things to do with the system registry.

Appendix A, "Coping with Windows 98 Incompatibilities," explains a VxD-based scheme that will allow you to deploy the same driver binary on both Windows 2000 and Windows 98 platforms. The basic problem you now have to solve—and the basic reason a distinction exists between PnP drivers and WDM drivers—is that Windows 2000 was finished after Windows 98 and predictably exports some service routine that Windows 98 either doesn't export or doesn't implement in quite the same way. You can solve this problem with a short VxD that I'll show you.

Appendix B, "Using GENERIC.SYS," describes the public interface to my GENERIC.SYS library. Most of my sample drivers use GENERIC.SYS, and you might need to consult this documentation to fully understand how the samples work.

Appendix C, "Using WDMWIZ.AWX," describes how to use my Visual C++ application wizard to build a driver. I repeat that WDMWIZ.AWX is not intended to take the place of a commercial toolkit. Among other things, that means that it's not easy enough to use that you can dispense with documentation.

Note on Errors

This book is as accurate as I could make it. Let's face it, though: when writing about a complex technology with many new elements, it's impossible to be 100 percent right. In addition, WDM will inevitably change over the next few months as the Windows 2000 beta period winds down to a retail release. My publisher and I have a plan to deal with this. To deal with errors, I'll publish an errata page at my Web site (*http://www.oneysoft.com*). I hope friendly readers will email me comments that I can post there.

OTHER RESOURCES

This book should not be the only source of information you use to learn about driver programming. It emphasizes the features that I think are important; but you might need information I don't provide, or you might have a different way of learning than I do. I don't explain how the operating system works except insofar as it bears on what I think one needs to know to effectively write drivers. If you're a deductive learner, or if you simply want more theoretical background, you might want to consult one of the additional resources listed below. If you're standing in a bookstore right now trying to decide which book to buy, my advice is to buy all of them: a wise craftsperson never skimps on his or her tools. Besides, books on specialized subjects like driver writing often go out of print before their useful life expires.

Books Specifically About Driver Development

Art Baker, *The Windows NT Device Driver Book: A Guide for Programmers* (Prentice Hall, 1997).

Chris Cant, *Writing Windows WDM Device Drivers* (R&D Press, 1999).

Edward N. Dekker and Joseph M. Newcomer, *Developing Windows NT Device Drivers: A Programmer's Handbook* (Addison-Wesley, 1999).

Rajeev Nagar, *Windows NT File System Internals: A Developer's Guide* (O'Reilly & Associates, 1997).

Peter G. Viscarola and W. Anthony Mason, *Windows NT Device Driver Development* (Macmillan, 1998).

Dekker and Newcomer's book went to press as the Beta 2 release of Windows 2000 appeared and contains just two chapters on WDM drivers. My publishing schedule was such that I wasn't able to look at Chris Cant's book. Nagar's book, while nominally concerned with file system drivers, contains a great deal of material that's generally applicable to writing kernel-mode drivers of any kind. I don't believe in trying to evaluate another book on the same subject as my own, inasmuch as you'd have a perfect right to doubt my objectivity, so I simply present this list for you to use as you wish.

Another Useful Book

David A. Solomon, *Inside Windows NT, Second Edition* (Microsoft Press, 1998).

Magazines

Microsoft Systems Journal occasionally has articles of interest to driver developers. *Windows Developer Journal* usually has at least one relevant article in each issue.

Newsgroup

The *comp.os.ms-windows.programmer.nt.kernel-mode* newsgroup provides a forum for technical discussion on kernel-mode programming issues. This is the place to go for support from your peers.

Seminars

I conduct public and on-site seminars on WDM programming. Visit my Web site at *http://www.oneysoft.com* for more information and schedules. Most other authors in this subject area conduct seminars as well. This is how we pay our bills. Once again, I won't presume to offer any evaluation. And I'm sure you'll forgive me for not giving explicit pointers to information about my competition!

WARNING

For expository purposes, this book presents fragments of driver code without error checking and without all of the special case checks that are necessary in a working driver. I'm following the precept that it's better to explain complicated subjects in a step-by-step manner without inundating you with too much detail too soon. I promise not to lie to you, but I won't always be telling the whole, ugly truth either.

The sample drivers on the companion disc, on the other hand, do have all of the error checking and other stuff that production drivers need. Please refer to the disc, therefore, before incorporating something in your own code.

Chapter 2

Basic Structure of a WDM Driver

In the first chapter, I described the basic architecture of the Microsoft Windows 2000 and Microsoft Windows 98 operating systems. I introduced the idea that a device driver is a container for a collection of subroutines that the operating system can call upon to carry out various activities related to a hardware device. This chapter is about the basic contents of one of those driver containers. I'll discuss how device drivers are layered and how that layering comes about. I'll also discuss the DriverEntry and AddDevice functions that every WDM driver includes. In later chapters, I'll tell you about the other types of subroutines that will be part of the driver for your device.

DEVICE AND DRIVER LAYERING

The Windows Driver Model formalizes a layering of drivers, as illustrated in Figure 2-1. A stack of *device objects* appears at the left of the figure. The device objects are data structures that the system creates to help software manage hardware. Many of these data structures can exist for a single piece of physical hardware. The lowest-level device object in a stack is called the *physical device object,* or PDO for short. Somewhere in the middle of a device object stack is an object called the *functional device object,* or FDO. Above and below the FDO there might be a collection of *filter device objects*. Filter device objects above the FDO are called *upper filters,* whereas filter device objects below the FDO (but still above the PDO) are called *lower filters*.

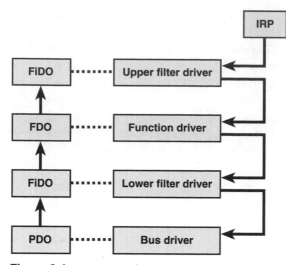

Figure 2-1. *Layering of device objects and drivers in the WDM.*

AN ACRONYM FOR FILTER DEVICE OBJECTS?

In an industry known for its prolific use of acronyms, it seems odd that the term *filter device object* has no official abbreviation. FDO is taken—as I've said, it refers to the functional device object that belongs to the real driver for the device. Once upon a time, Microsoft was using the acronym FiDO to describe these objects. This acronym suffers from a slight lack of specificity in that you can't immediately tell whether you're talking about an upper or a lower filter. There may have been other reasons why the term fell into disfavor as something appropriate to sober discussion about a serious new technology, however. My seminar students have been quick to point out, for example, that the FiDO at the top of any given stack is, of course, the "top dog."

Being a sometime cat owner and thus unoffended by canine allusions, and not being a total slave to prevailing convention, I'll use the acronym FiDO in this book as a generic way of describing filter device objects. I guess driver programming (or at least this book) is going to the dogs.

The Plug and Play (PnP) Manager component of the operating system constructs the stack of device objects at the behest of device drivers. For our purposes in this book, we can use the generic term *bus* to describe a piece of hardware to which devices connect electronically. This is a pretty broad definition. Not only does it include things like the PCI (Peripheral Component Interconnect) bus, but it also includes a SCSI (Small Computer System Interface) adapter, a parallel port, a serial port, a USB (universal serial bus) hub, and so on—anything, in fact, that can have multiple devices plugged into it. One responsibility of the driver for a bus is to enumerate the devices attached to the bus and to create PDOs for each of them. The PnP Manager begins painting the picture in Figure 2-1, then, by creating a PDO because some bus driver has detected some actual hardware.

Having created a PDO, the PnP Manager consults the registry database to find the filter and function drivers that occupy the middle of the figure. The setup program is responsible for many of these registry entries, and the INF files that control hardware installation are responsible for others. The registry entries define the order in which the drivers will appear in the stack, so the PnP Manager begins by loading the lowest-level filter driver and calling its AddDevice function. This function creates a FiDO, thus establishing the horizontal link between a FiDO and a driver. AddDevice then connects the PDO to the FiDO; that's where the line connecting the two device objects comes from. The PnP Manager proceeds upward, loading and calling each lower filter, the function driver, and each upper filter, until the stack is complete.

The purpose for the layering becomes apparent when you consider the flow of I/O requests diagrammed on the right-hand side of Figure 2-1. Each request for an operation affecting a device uses an I/O request packet (IRP). IRPs are normally sent to the topmost driver for the device and can percolate down the stack to the other drivers. At each level, the driver decides what to do with the IRP. Sometimes, a driver will do nothing except pass the IRP down. Other times, a driver might completely handle the IRP without passing it down. Still other times, a driver might process the IRP *and* pass it down, or vice versa. It all depends on the device and the exact semantics of the IRP. I'll explain in a later sidebar how it comes to pass that drivers can send IRPs down even though device objects are linked upward from the PDO.

The various drivers that occupy the stack for a single piece of hardware perform different roles. The function driver manages the device, represented by the FDO. The bus driver manages the connection between the device and the computer, represented by the PDO. Because of the close relationship between driver software and device object, I'll sometimes use the term *FDO driver* to mean the function driver and the term *PDO driver* to refer to the bus driver. The filter drivers, if they even exist, monitor or modify the stream of IRPs.

One of my seminar students, on seeing a diagram similar to Figure 2-1, was misled (I won't say by which teacher, who also wrote this book) into thinking of C++ and class inheritance. A perfectly reasonable way of designing an architecture for device drivers would be to define base classes from which programmers could derive progressively more specialized classes. In such a scheme, you could have a set of abstract classes that manage different sorts of PDOs, and you could derive FDO drivers from them. The system would send IRPs to virtual functions, some of which would be handled by the base class in the PDO driver and some of which would be handled by the derived class in the FDO driver. WDM doesn't work this way, though. The PDO driver performs completely different jobs from the FDO driver. The FDO driver "delegates" certain work to the PDO driver by passing IRPs down to it, but the relationship is more like being peers in a bucket brigade (and we won't discuss the contents of the metaphorical buckets!) than like being hierarchically related.

How the System Loads Drivers

Having presented this much description of device layering in the WDM, it's time for me to be a bit more precise. To begin with, there's an obvious chicken-and-egg problem with what I've described. I said that the bus driver creates the PDO, but I also said that the PnP Manager loads drivers based on registry entries for a PDO that already exists. So where does the bus driver come from? I'll explain that in the next section. The registry database plays a crucial role in the process of loading drivers and configuring devices, so I'll explain which registry keys are relevant and what they contain.

Recursive Enumeration

In the first instance, the PnP Manager has a built-in "driver" for a "root" bus that doesn't actually exist. The root bus conceptually connects the computer to all hardware that can't electronically announce its presence—including the primary hardware bus (such as PCI). The root bus driver gets information about the computer from the registry, which was initialized by the Windows 2000 Setup program. Setup got the information by running an elaborate hardware detection program and by asking the end user suitable questions. Consequently, the root bus driver knows enough to create a PDO for the primary bus.

The function driver for the primary bus can then *enumerate* its own hardware electronically. The PCI bus, for example, provides a way of accessing a special configuration space for each attached device, and the configuration space contains a description of the device and its resource requirements. When a bus driver enumerates hardware, it acts in the guise of an ordinary function driver. Having detected a piece of hardware, however, the driver switches roles: it becomes a bus driver and creates a new PDO for the detected hardware. The PnP Manager then loads drivers for this device PDO, as previously discussed. It might happen that the function driver for the device enumerates still more hardware, in which case the whole process repeats recursively. The end result will be a tree like that shown in Figure 2-2, wherein a bus device stack branches into other device stacks for the hardware attached to that bus.

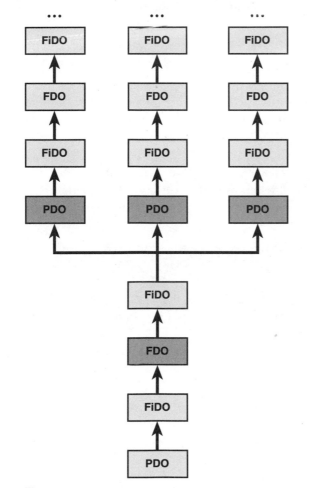

Figure 2-2. *Layering of recursively enumerated devices.*

The Role of the Registry

Three different registry keys bear on configuration. These are called the *hardware key,* the *class key,* and the *service key.* To be clear, these are not the proper names of specific subkeys: they are generic names of three keys whose pathnames depend on the device to which they belong. Broadly speaking, the hardware key contains information about a single device, the class key concerns all devices of the same type, and the service keys contains information about drivers. People sometimes use the name "instance key" to refer to the hardware key and "software key" to refer to the service key. The multiplicity of names derives from the fact that Windows 95/98 and Windows 2000 were written (mostly) by different people.

The Hardware (Instance) Keys Device hardware keys appear in the \System\ CurrentControlSet\Enum subkey of the local machine branch of the registry. You normally can't look inside this key because the system grants access to the System account only. In other words, kernel-mode programs and user-mode services running in the System account can read from and write to the Enum key and its subkeys, but not even an administrator can do so. To see what's inside Enum, you can run REGEDT32.EXE from an administrator-privilege account and change the security settings. Figure 2-3 illustrates the hardware key for one of the sample devices that accompanies this book (namely, the USB42 sample I'll discuss in Chapter 11, "The Universal Serial Bus").

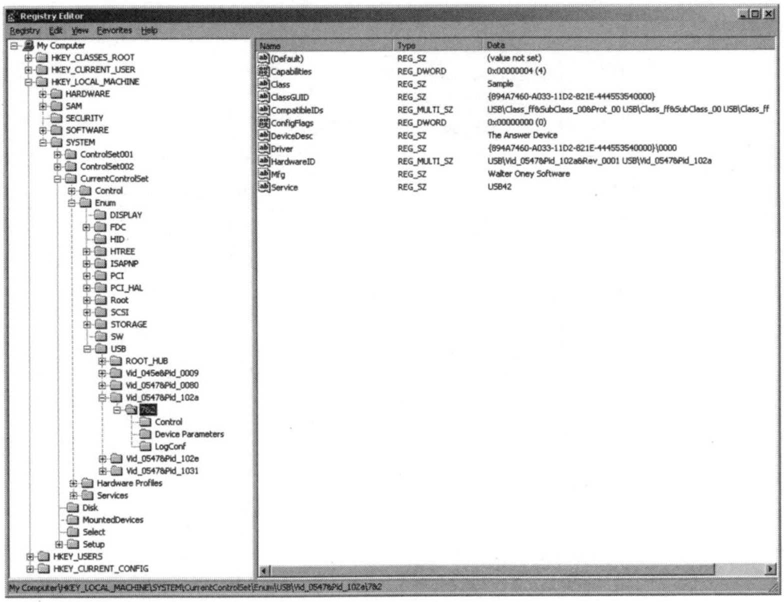

Figure 2-3. *A hardware key in the registry.*

HOW REGISTRY KEYS ARE NAMED

The naming of the very top level of the registry key hierarchy is confusing for the first-time visitor. When you use Win32 API functions to access the registry in user mode, you identify the top level with one of the predefined handle constants, such as HKEY_CLASSES_ROOT, HKEY_CURRENT_USER, HKEY_LOCAL_MACHINE, and a few others. The REGEDIT.EXE registry editor applet uses these same names, as shown in Figure 2-3. Sometimes, in writing about registry access, the length of these keywords induces one to use abbreviations like HKCR, HKCU, HKLM, and so on.

In point of fact, HKCR is an alias for HKLM\Software\Classes, and HKCU is an alias for one of the subkeys of HKEY_USERS. The targets of these two aliases depend on which session context you're dealing with.

In kernel mode, however, you use a different naming scheme, based on the kernel namespace. (I'll discuss this namespace a bit further on in this chapter.) The top levels are named \Registry\User and \Registry\Machine. The Machine branch, which is the same branch that user mode knows as HKLM, is where you can find all information relevant to device drivers. Unless otherwise indicated, therefore, you should assume that a particular registry key referred to in the text can be found in \Registry\Machine.

The subkeys on the first level below the Enum key correspond to the different bus enumerators in the system. The description of all past or present USB devices is in the …\Enum\USB subkey. I've expanded the key for the USB42 sample to show you how the device's hardware ID (vendor 0574, product 102A) has turned into the name of a key (Vid_0547&Pid_102A) and how a particular instance of the device that has that ID appears as a further subkey named 7&2. The 7&2 key is the hardware, or instance, key for this device.

Some of the values in the hardware key provide descriptive information that user-mode components such as the Device Manager can use. (You reach the Device Manager from the Management Console or, more easily, from the Hardware tab of the property sheet you get when you right-click the My Computer desktop icon and select Properties.) Figure 2-4 shows how the Device Manager portrays the properties of USB42. Refer to the sidebar "Accessing Device Keys from User Mode" for an indication of how the Device Manager can gather this information even though it can't, by itself, get past the normal security block to the Enum key.

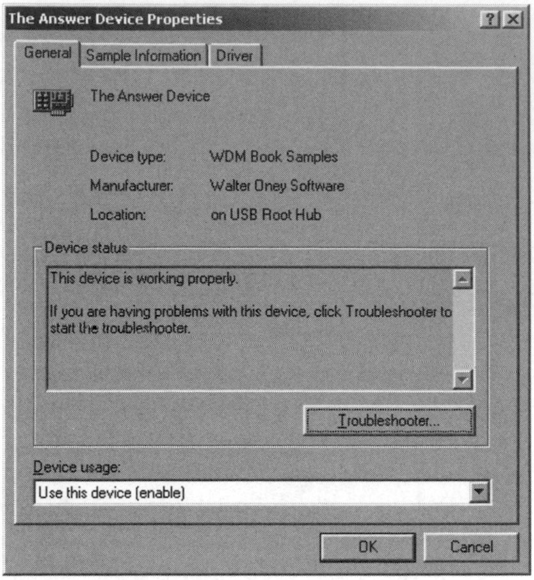

Figure 2-4. *The Device Manager properties display for a device.*

ACCESSING DEVICE KEYS FROM USER MODE

Applications often need to access information about hardware devices. To make this possible without tempting fate by exposing the crucial Enum key to inadvertent (or not-so-inadvertent) tampering, Microsoft provides the CFGMGR32 set of APIs. The header file and library for this API is part of the Windows 2000 DDK, and the functions in the API set work both in Windows 2000 and Windows 98. The API is currently documented in a DOC file that's part of the Microsoft Windows NT version 4.0 (!) DDK.

To give you one example, let's suppose you knew the name of a device's hardware key somehow. One of the ways you could know is by enumerating all "device instances" starting from the device root by recursively calling **CM_Locate_DevNode**, **CM_Get_Child**, and **CM_Get_Sibling**. Here's a short fragment of code illustrating how to read the **Manufacturer** value from the corresponding hardware key:

```
#include <cfgmgr32.h>
...
LPTSTR lpszDevnodeName;
```

(continued)

continued

```
DEVNODE dn;
CONFIGRET cr = CM_Locate_DevNode(&dn, lpszDevnodeName,
  CM_LOCATE_DEVNODE_NORMAL);
if (cr != CR_SUCCESS)
  <handle error>
TCHAR buffer[_MAX_PATH];
DWORD size = sizeof(buffer);
cr = CM_Get_DevInstRegistry_Property(dn, CM_DRP_MFG, NULL,
  buffer, size, 0);
```

The **lpszDevnodeName** is a string like "USB\Vid_0547&Pid_102A\7&2" whose relationship to the hardware key name should now be obvious. I use code just like this fragment to gather some of the information in the DEVVIEW applet I'll tell you about presently.

The hardware key also contains several values that identify the class of device to which the device belongs and the drivers for the device. **ClassGUID** is the ASCII representation of a *globally unique identifier* (GUID) that uniquely identifies a device class; in effect, it's a pointer to the class key for this device. **Service** is a pointer to the service key. Optional values (which USB42 doesn't have) named **LowerFilters** and **UpperFilters**, if present, would identify the service names for any lower or upper filter drivers, respectively.

Finally, a hardware key might have overriding values named **Security**, **Exclusive**, **DeviceType**, and **DeviceCharacteristics** that force the device object the driver will create to have certain attributes. I'll discuss the importance of these overrides later on when I tell you how to create a device object.

Most of the values in the hardware key get there automatically as part of the setup process or because the system recognizes new hardware (or gets told it about via the Hardware Wizard) sometime after initial setup. Some of the values get there because the INF file that's used to install the hardware directs that they be put there. I'll discuss INF files when I talk about how to plan for installation in Chapter 12, "Installing Device Drivers."

The Class Keys The class keys for all classes of device appear in the HKLM\ System\CurrentControlSet\Control\Class key. Their key names are GUIDs assigned by Microsoft. Figure 2-5 illustrates the class key for SAMPLE devices, which is the class to which the USB42 sample and all the other sample drivers in this book belong.

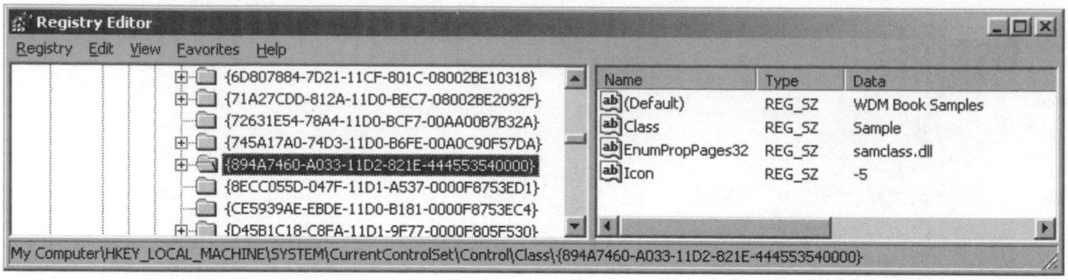

Figure 2-5. *A class key in the registry.*

The USB class isn't particularly interesting as it lacks some of the optional values that might be there, such as these:

■ **LowerFilters** and **UpperFilters**, if present, specify filter drivers for all devices of this class.

■ **Security**, **Exclusive**, **DeviceType**, and **DeviceCharacteristics**, if present in a Properties subkey of the class key, specify values that override default settings of certain device object parameters for all devices of this class. These overrides have less precedence than the ones (if any) in the hardware key. System administrators will eventually be able to set up these overrides through the Management Console.

Each device also has its own subkey below the class key. The name of this key is the **Driver** value in the device's hardware key. Refer to Figure 2-6 for an illustration of the contents of this subkey, the purpose of which is to correlate all these registry entries with the INF file used to install the device.

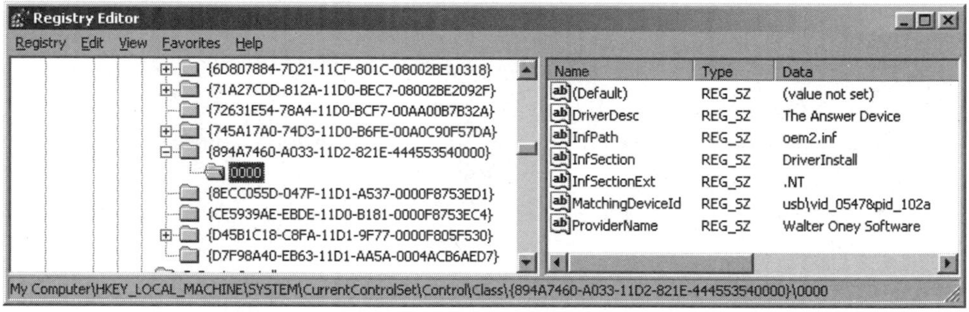

Figure 2-6. *A device-specific subkey of the device's class key in the registry.*

The Service (Software) Keys   The last key that's important for a device driver is the service key. It indicates where the driver's executable file is on disk and contains some other parameters that govern the way the driver is loaded. Service keys appear in the HKLM\System\CurrentControlSet\Services key. Refer to Figure 2-7 for USB42's service key.

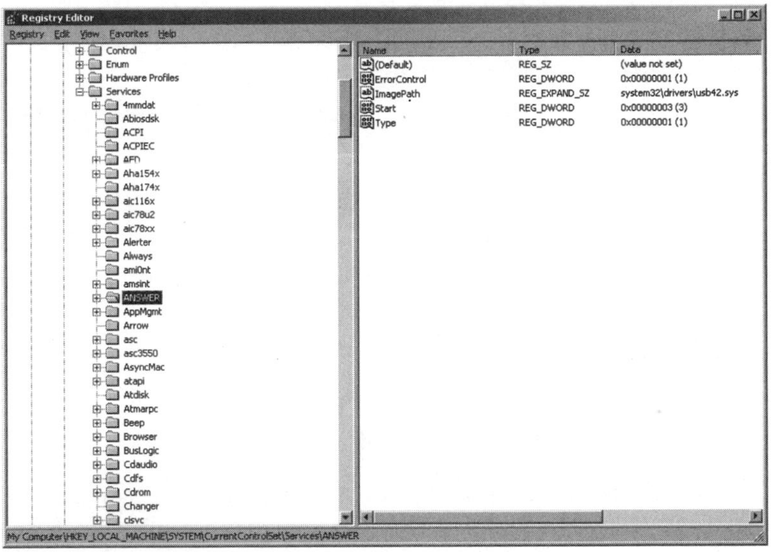

Figure 2-7. *A service key in the registry.*

It's not my purpose to rehash all the possible settings in the service key, which is splendidly documented in several places, including under the heading "Service Install" in the Platform Software Development Kit (SDK). In this particular case, the values have the following significance:

- **ImagePath** indicates that the executable file for the driver is named USB42.SYS and can be found in %SystemRoot%\system32\drivers. Note that the registry setting in this case is a relative pathname starting from the system root directory.

- **Type** (1) indicates that this entry describes a kernel-mode driver.

- **Start** (3) indicates that the system should load this driver when it's needed to support a newly arrived device. (This numeric value corresponds to the SERVICE_DEMAND_START constant in a call to CreateService. When applied to a kernel-mode driver, it has the meaning I just described—it's not necessary to explicitly call StartService or issue a NET START command to start the driver.)

- **ErrorControl** (1) indicates that a failure to load this driver should cause the system to log the error and display a message box.

Order of Driver Loading

When the PnP Manager encounters a new device, it opens the hardware and class keys and proceeds to load drivers in the following order:

1. Any lower filter drivers specified in the hardware key for the device. Since the LowerFilters value is of type REG_MULTI_SZ, it can specify more than one driver. They're loaded in the order in which they appear in the value's data string.

2. Any lower filter drivers specified in the class key. Again, these are loaded in the order in which they appear in the LowerFilters value's data string.

3. The driver specified by the Service value in the hardware key.

4. Any upper filter drivers specified in the hardware key, in the order in which they appear in the UpperFilters data string.

5. Any upper filter drivers specified in the class key, in the order in which they appear in the UpperFilters data string.

When I say the system "loads" a driver, I mean that it maps the driver's image into virtual memory, fixes up relocatable references, and calls the driver's main entry point. The main entry point is usually named DriverEntry. I'll describe the DriverEntry function a bit further on in this chapter. It might turn out that a particular driver is already present in memory, in which case nothing happens at the load stage except incrementing a reference count that will preserve the image in memory for however long some device needs it.

You might have noticed that the loading of upper and lower filters belonging to the class and to the device instance isn't neatly nested as you might have expected. Before I knew the facts, I guessed that device-level filters would be closer to the function driver than class-level filters. As we'll see later on, it's not very important in what order the loading occurs. However, the system calls the drivers' AddDevice functions (another topic I'll discuss in considerable detail shortly) in the same order in which the PnP Manager loads the drivers. Consequently, the device object stack will mirror this order, with possibly unexpected results.

How Device Objects Interrelate

The tree of device object stacks shown in Figure 2-2 doesn't imply that IRPs necessarily flow from a PDO to the top FiDO for the next lower branch of the tree. In fact, the driver for one stack's PDO is the FDO driver for the next lower branch, as illustrated by the shading in the figure. When the driver receives an IRP in its PDO role, it will do *something* to perform the IRP, but that might not involve sending the same, or even any other, IRP to the devices in the stack it occupies while performing its FDO role.

Conversely, when a bus driver receives an IRP in its FDO role, it might or might not need to send some IRPs to one or more of the devices for which it acts as PDO.

A few examples should clarify the relationship between FiDOs, FDOs, and PDOs. The first example concerns a read operation directed to a device that happens to be on a secondary PCI bus that itself attaches to the main bus through a PCI-to-PCI bridge chip. To keep things simple, let's suppose that there's one FiDO for this device, as illustrated in Figure 2-8. You'll learn in later chapters that a read request turns into an IRP with a major function code of IRP_MJ_READ. Such a request would flow first to the upper FiDO and then to the function driver for the device. (That driver is the one for the device object marked FDO_{dev} in the figure.) The function driver calls the hardware abstraction layer (HAL) directly to perform its work, so none of the other drivers in the figure will see the IRP.

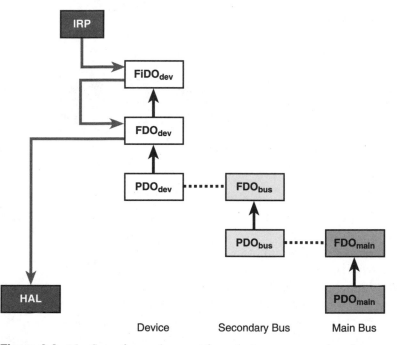

Figure 2-8. *The flow of a read request for a device on a secondary bus.*

A variation on the first example is shown in Figure 2-9. Here we have a read request for a device plugged into a USB hub that itself is plugged into the host controller. The complete device tree therefore contains stacks for the device, for the hub, and for the host controller. The IRP_MJ_READ flows through the FiDO to the function driver, which then sends one or more IRPs of a different kind downward to its own PDO. The PDO driver for a USB device is USBHUB.SYS, and it forwards the IRPs to the topmost driver in the host controller device stack, skipping the two-driver stack for the USB hub in the middle of the figure.

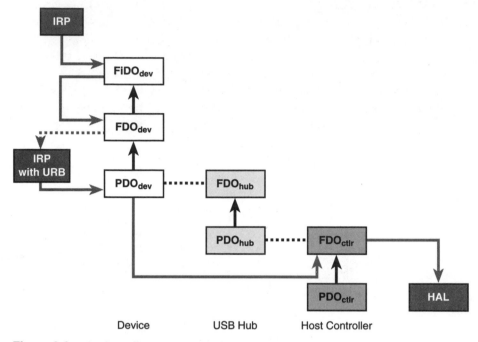

Device   USB Hub   Host Controller

Figure 2-9. *The flow of a read request for a USB device.*

The third example is similar to the first, except that the IRP in question is a notification concerning whether a disk drive on a PCI bus will or will not be used as the repository for a system paging file. You'll learn in Chapter 6, "Plug and Play," that this notification takes the form of an IRP_MJ_PNP request with the minor function code IRP_MN_DEVICE_USAGE_NOTIFICATION. In this case, the FiDO driver will pass the request to the FDO_{dev} driver, which will take note of it and pass it further down the stack to the PDO_{dev} driver. This particular notification has implications about how other I/O requests that concern the PnP system or power management will be handled, so the PDO_{dev} driver sends an identical notification to the stack within which it's the FDO_{bus}, as illustrated in Figure 2-10. (Not all bus drivers work this way, but the PCI bus does.)

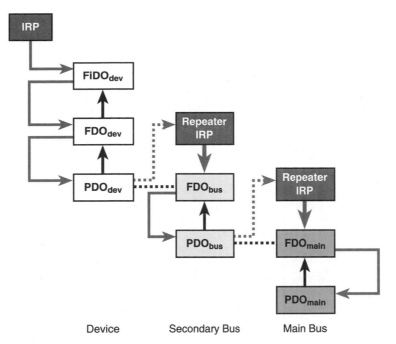

Figure 2-10. *The flow of a device usage notification.*

Examining the Device Stack

To better visualize the way device objects and drivers are layered, it helps to have a tool. I wrote the DEVVIEW utility, which you'll find on the companion disc, for this purpose. I'll be describing other uses for DEVVIEW in this chapter, but the feature that concerns us now is its ability to display the device objects that are used to manage hardware devices. With the so-called Answer device plugged into my USB hub, I ran DEVVIEW and generated the two screen shots shown in Figure 2-11 and Figure 2-12.

This particular device uses only two device objects. The PDO is managed by USBHUB.SYS, whereas the FDO is managed by USB42.SYS (the image for the Answer device). In the first of these screen shots, you can see other information about the PDO. Based on our exploration of the registry keys associated with USB42, it should now be clear where that information came from.

It's worth experimenting with DEVVIEW on your own system to see how various drivers are layered for the hardware you own.

Figure 2-11. *DEVVIEW information about USB42's PDO.*

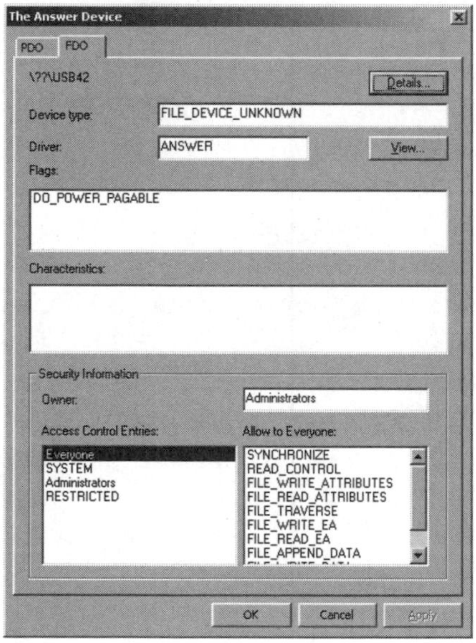

Figure 2-12. *DEVVIEW information about USB42's FDO.*

Driver Objects

The I/O Manager uses a *driver object* data structure to represent each device driver. See Figure 2-13. Like many of the data structures we'll be discussing, the driver object is *partially opaque*. This means that you and I are only supposed to directly access or change certain fields in the structure, even though the DDK headers declare the entire structure. I've shown the opaque fields of the driver object in the figure with a gray background. These opaque fields are analogous to the private and protected members of a C++ class, and the accessible fields are analogous to public members.

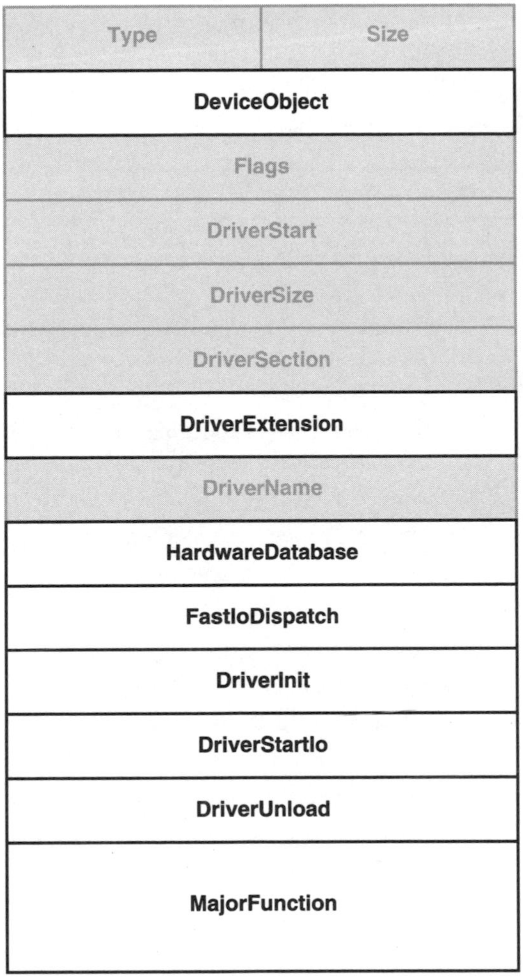

Type	Size
DeviceObject	
Flags	
DriverStart	
DriverSize	
DriverSection	
DriverExtension	
DriverName	
HardwareDatabase	
FastIoDispatch	
DriverInit	
DriverStartIo	
DriverUnload	
MajorFunction	

Figure 2-13. *The DRIVER_OBJECT data structure.*

The DDK headers declare the driver object, and all other kernel-mode data structures for that matter, in a stylized way, as this excerpt from WDM.H illustrates:

```
typedef struct _DRIVER_OBJECT {
  CSHORT Type;
  CSHORT Size;
  ...
  } DRIVER_OBJECT, *PDRIVER_OBJECT;
```

That is, the header declares a structure with a type name of DRIVER_OBJECT. It also declares a pointer type (PDRIVER_OBJECT) and assigns a structure tag (_DRIVER_ OBJECT). This declaration pattern appears many places in the DDK, and I won't mention it again. The headers also declare a small set of type names (like CSHORT) to describe the atomic data types used in kernel mode. Table 2-1 lists some of these names. CSHORT, for example, means "signed short integer used as a cardinal number."

Type Name	Description
PVOID, PVOID64	Generic pointers (default precision and 64-bit precision)
NTAPI	Used with service function declarations to force use of __stdcall calling convention on x86 architectures
VOID	Equivalent to "void"
CHAR, PCHAR	8-bit character, pointer to same (signed or not according to compiler default)
UCHAR, PUCHAR	Unsigned 8-bit character, pointer to same
SCHAR, PSCHAR	Signed 8-bit character, pointer to same
SHORT, PSHORT	Signed 16-bit integer, pointer to same
USHORT, PUSHORT	Unsigned 16-bit integer, pointer to same
LONG, PLONG	Signed 32-bit integer, pointer to same
ULONG, PULONG	Unsigned 32-bit integer, pointer to same
WCHAR, PWSTR	Wide (Unicode) character or string
PCWSTR	Pointer to constant Unicode string
NTSTATUS	Status code (typed as signed long integer)
LARGE_INTEGER	Signed 64-bit integer
ULARGE_INTEGER	Unsigned 64-bit integer
PSZ, PCSZ	Pointer to ASCIIZ (single-byte) string or constant string
BOOLEAN, PBOOLEAN	TRUE or FALSE (equivalent to UCHAR)

Table 2-1. *Common type names for kernel-mode drivers.*

NOTE ON 64-BIT TYPES

The DDK headers contain type names that will make it relatively painless for driver authors to compile the same source code for either 32-bit or 64-bit Intel platforms. For example, instead of blithely assuming that a long integer and a pointer are the same size, you should declare variables that might be either a LONG_PTR or a ULONG_PTR. Such a variable can hold either a long (or unsigned long) or a pointer to something. Also, for example, declare an integer that can count as high as a pointer might span as a SIZE_T—you'll get a 64-bit integer on a 64-bit platform. These and other 32/64 typedefs are in the DDK header file named BASETSD.H.

I'll briefly discuss the accessible fields of the driver object structure now.

DeviceObject (PDEVICE_OBJECT) anchors a list of device object data structures, one for each of the devices managed by the driver. The I/O Manager links the device objects together and maintains this field. The DriverUnload function of a non-WDM driver would use this field to traverse the list of device objects in order to delete them. A WDM driver probably doesn't have any particular need to use this field.

DriverExtension (PDRIVER_EXTENSION) points to a small substructure within which only the **AddDevice** (PDRIVER_ADD_DEVICE) member is accessible to the likes of us. (See Figure 2-14.) AddDevice is a pointer to a function within the driver that creates device objects; this function is rather a big deal, and I'll discuss it at length later in this chapter.

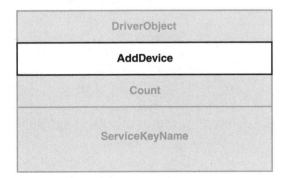

Figure 2-14. *The DRIVER_EXTENSION data structure.*

HardwareDatabase (PUNICODE_STRING) describes a string that names a hardware database registry key for the device. This is a name like "\Registry\Machine\ Hardware\Description\System" and names the registry key within which resource allocation information resides. WDM drivers have no need to access the information below this key because the PnP Manager performs resource allocation automatically. The name is stored in Unicode. (In fact, all kernel-mode string data uses Unicode.) I'll discuss the format and the use of the UNICODE_STRING data structure in the next chapter.

FastIoDispatch (PFAST_IO_DISPATCH) points to a table of function pointers that file system and network drivers export. How these functions are used is beyond the scope of this book. If you're interested in learning more about file system drivers, consult Rajeev Nagar's *Windows NT File System Internals: A Developer's Guide* (O'Reilly & Associates, 1997).

DriverStartIo (PDRIVER_STARTIO) points to a function in your driver that processes I/O requests that the I/O Manager has serialized for you. I'll discuss request queuing in general and the use of this routine in particular in Chapter 5, "The I/O Request Packet."

DriverUnload (PDRIVER_UNLOAD) points to a cleanup function in your driver. I'll discuss this function a bit further on in connection with DriverEntry, but you might as well know now that a WDM driver probably doesn't have any significant cleanup to do anyway.

MajorFunction (array of PDRIVER_DISPATCH) is a table of pointers to functions in your driver that handle each of the roughly two dozen types of I/O request. This table is also something of a big deal, as you might guess, because it defines how I/O requests make it into your code.

Device Objects

Figure 2-15 illustrates the format of a *device object* and uses the same shading convention for opaque fields that I used in the preceding discussion of driver objects. As the author of a WDM driver, you will create some of these objects by calling **IoCreateDevice**, but the I/O Manager will be responsible for managing them.

DriverObject (PDRIVER_OBJECT) points to the object describing the driver associated with this device object, usually the one that called IoCreateDevice to create it. Filter drivers sometimes need to use this pointer to find the driver object for a device they're filtering so that they can inspect entries in the MajorFunction table.

NextDevice (PDEVICE_OBJECT) points to the next device object that belongs to the same driver as this one. This field is the one that links device objects together starting from the driver object's DeviceObject member. There's probably no reason for a WDM driver to use this field.

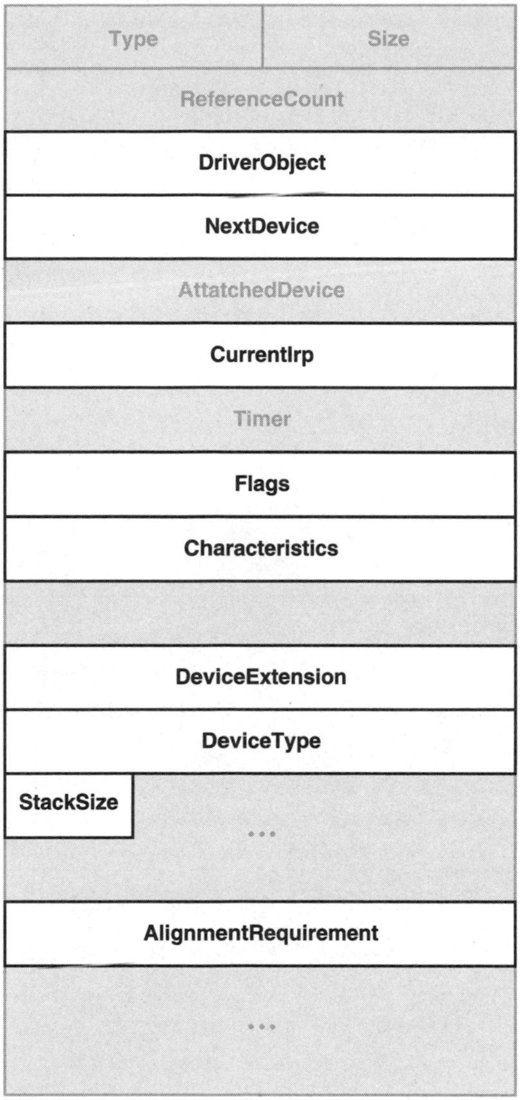

Type	Size
ReferenceCount	
DriverObject	
NextDevice	
AttatchedDevice	
CurrentIrp	
Timer	
Flags	
Characteristics	
DeviceExtension	
DeviceType	
StackSize	•••
AlignmentRequirement	
•••	

Figure 2-15. *The DEVICE_OBJECT data structure.*

CurrentIrp (PIRP) points to the I/O request packet most recently sent to the corresponding driver's StartIo function. I'll have more to say about the CurrentIrp field in Chapter 5 when I discuss cancel routines.

Flags (ULONG) contains a collection of flag bits. Table 2-2 lists the bits that are accessible to driver writers.

Flag	Description
DO_BUFFERED_IO	Reads and writes use the buffered method (system copy buffer) for accessing user-mode data
DO_EXCLUSIVE	Only one thread at a time allowed to open a handle
DO_DIRECT_IO	Reads and writes use the direct method (memory descriptor list) for accessing user-mode data
DO_DEVICE_INITIALIZING	Device object not initialized yet
DO_POWER_PAGABLE	IRP_MJ_PNP must be handled at PASSIVE_LEVEL
DO_POWER_INRUSH	Device requires large in-rush of current during power-on
DO_POWER_NOOP	Device doesn't participate in power management

Table 2-2. *Accessible flags in a DEVICE_OBJECT data structure.*

Characteristics (ULONG) is another collection of flag bits describing various optional characteristics of the device. (See Table 2-3.) The I/O Manager initializes these flags based on an argument to IoCreateDevice. Filter drivers propagate them upward in the device stack.

Flag	Description
FILE_REMOVABLE_MEDIA	Media can be removed from device
FILE_READ_ONLY_DEVICE	Media can only be read, not written
FILE_FLOPPY_DISKETTE	Device is a floppy disk drive
FILE_WRITE_ONCE_MEDIA	Media can be written once
FILE_REMOTE_DEVICE	Device accessible through network connection
FILE_DEVICE_IS_MOUNTED	Physical media is present in device
FILE_DEVICE_SECURE_OPEN	Check security on device object during open operations

Table 2-3. *Characteristics flags in a DEVICE_OBJECT data structure.*

DeviceExtension (PVOID) points to a data structure *you* define that will hold per-instance information about the device. The I/O Manager allocates space for the structure, but its name and contents are entirely up to you. A common convention is to declare a structure with the type name DEVICE_EXTENSION. To access it given a pointer (for example, **fdo**) to the device object, use a statement like this one:

```
PDEVICE_EXTENSION pdx = (PDEVICE_EXTENSION) fdo->DeviceExtension;
```

It happens to be true (now, anyway) that the device extension immediately follows the device object in memory. It would be a bad idea to rely on this always being true, though, especially when the documented method of following the DeviceExtension pointer will always work.

DeviceType (DEVICE_TYPE) is an enumeration constant describing what type of device this is. The I/O Manager initializes this member based on an argument to IoCreateDevice. Filter drivers might conceivably need to inspect it. At the date of this writing, there are roughly 50 possible values for this member. (See Table 2-4.)

Device Type	Default Security
FILE_DEVICE_BEEP	Public Open Unrestricted
FILE_DEVICE_CD_ROM	Modified Public Default Unrestricted
FILE_DEVICE_CD_ROM_FILE_SYSTEM	Public Default Unrestricted
FILE_DEVICE_CONTROLLER	Public Open Unrestricted
FILE_DEVICE_DATALINK	Public Open Unrestricted
FILE_DEVICE_DFS	Public Open Unrestricted
FILE_DEVICE_DISK	Modified Public Default Unrestricted
FILE_DEVICE_DISK_FILE_SYSTEM	Public Default Unrestricted
FILE_DEVICE_FILE_SYSTEM	Public Default Unrestricted
FILE_DEVICE_INPORT_PORT	Public Open Unrestricted
FILE_DEVICE_KEYBOARD	Public Open Unrestricted
FILE_DEVICE_MAILSLOT	Public Open Unrestricted
FILE_DEVICE_MIDI_IN	Public Open Unrestricted
FILE_DEVICE_MIDI_OUT	Public Open Unrestricted
FILE_DEVICE_MOUSE	Public Open Unrestricted
FILE_DEVICE_MULTI_UNC_PROVIDER	Public Open Unrestricted
FILE_DEVICE_NAMED_PIPE	Public Open Unrestricted
FILE_DEVICE_NETWORK	Modified Public Default Unrestricted
FILE_DEVICE_NETWORK_BROWSER	Public Open Unrestricted

Table 2-4. *Device type codes and default security.*   *(continued)*

continued

Device Type	Default Security
FILE_DEVICE_NETWORK_FILE_SYSTEM	Modified Public Default Unrestricted
FILE_DEVICE_NULL	Public Open Unrestricted
FILE_DEVICE_PARALLEL_PORT	Public Open Unrestricted
FILE_DEVICE_PHYSICAL_NETCARD	Public Open Unrestricted
FILE_DEVICE_PRINTER	Public Open Unrestricted
FILE_DEVICE_SCANNER	Public Open Unrestricted
FILE_DEVICE_SERIAL_MOUSE_PORT	Public Open Unrestricted
FILE_DEVICE_SERIAL_PORT	Public Open Unrestricted
FILE_DEVICE_SCREEN	Public Open Unrestricted
FILE_DEVICE_SOUND	Public Open Unrestricted
FILE_DEVICE_STREAMS	Public Open Unrestricted
FILE_DEVICE_TAPE	Public Open Unrestricted
FILE_DEVICE_TAPE_FILE_SYSTEM	Public Default Unrestricted
FILE_DEVICE_TRANSPORT	Public Open Unrestricted
FILE_DEVICE_UNKNOWN	Public Open Unrestricted
FILE_DEVICE_VIDEO	Public Open Unrestricted
FILE_DEVICE_VIRTUAL_DISK	Modified Public Default Unrestricted
FILE_DEVICE_WAVE_IN	Public Open Unrestricted
FILE_DEVICE_WAVE_OUT	Public Open Unrestricted
FILE_DEVICE_8042_PORT	Public Open Unrestricted
FILE_DEVICE_NETWORK_REDIRECTOR	Public Open Unrestricted
FILE_DEVICE_BATTERY	Public Open Unrestricted
FILE_DEVICE_BUS_EXTENDER	Public Open Unrestricted
FILE_DEVICE_MODEM	Public Open Unrestricted
FILE_DEVICE_VDM	Public Open Unrestricted
FILE_DEVICE_MASS_STORAGE	Modified Public Default Unrestricted
FILE_DEVICE_SMB	Public Open Unrestricted
FILE_DEVICE_KS	Public Open Unrestricted
FILE_DEVICE_CHANGER	Public Open Unrestricted
FILE_DEVICE_SMARTCARD	Public Open Unrestricted
FILE_DEVICE_ACPI	Public Open Unrestricted
FILE_DEVICE_DVD	Public Open Unrestricted
FILE_DEVICE_FULLSCREEN_VIDEO	Public Open Unrestricted

(continued)

continued

Device Type	Default Security
FILE_DEVICE_DFS_FILE_SYSTEM	Public Open Unrestricted
FILE_DEVICE_DFS_VOLUME	Public Open Unrestricted
FILE_DEVICE_SERENUM	Public Open Unrestricted
FILE_DEVICE_TERMSRV	Public Open Unrestricted
FILE_DEVICE_KSEC	Public Open Unrestricted

StackSize (CCHAR) counts the number of device objects starting from this one and descending all the way to the PDO. The purpose of this field is to inform interested parties about how many stack locations should be created for an IRP that will be sent first to this device's driver. WDM drivers don't normally need to modify this value, however, because the support routines they use for building the device stack do so automatically.

HOW THE DEVICE STACK IS IMPLEMENTED

In the textual discussion of the DEVICE_OBJECT, I indicated that there's a NextDevice field that horizontally links together all the devices belonging to a particular driver, but I didn't describe the method that links device objects into a vertical stack from the uppermost FiDO through the FDO and from the lower FiDOs to the PDO. The opaque field **AttachedDevice** performs this office. Starting with the PDO, each device object points to the object immediately above it. There is no documented downward pointer—drivers must keep track on their own of what's underneath them. (In fact, **IoAttachDeviceToDeviceStack** does set up a downward pointer in a structure for which the DDK doesn't have a complete declaration. It would be unwise to try to reverse-engineer that structure because it's subject to change at any time.)

The AttachedDevice field is purposely not documented because its proper use requires synchronization with code that might be deleting device objects from memory. You and I are allowed to call **IoGetAttachedDeviceReference** to find the topmost device object in a given stack and to increment a reference count that will prevent that object from being prematurely removed from memory. If you wanted to work your way down to the PDO, you could send your own device an IRP_MJ_PNP request with the minor function code IRP_MN_QUERY_DEVICE_RELATIONS and a **Type** parameter of **TargetDeviceRelation**.

(continued)

continued

The PDO's driver will answer by returning the address of the PDO. This IRP is supposedly reserved for use by the operating system, though, so you really shouldn't be issuing it on your own. Instead, you need to remember the PDO address when you first create the device object.

Similarly, to know what device object is immediately underneath you, you need to save a pointer when you first add your object to the stack. Since each of the drivers in a stack will have its own unknowable way of implementing the downward pointers used for IRP dispatching, it's not practical to alter the device stack once the stack has been created.

THE DRIVERENTRY ROUTINE

In the preceding section, I said that the PnP Manager loads the drivers needed for hardware and calls their AddDevice functions. A given driver might be used for more than one piece of similar hardware, and there's some global initialization that the driver needs to perform only once when it's loaded for the first time. That global initialization is the responsibility of the **DriverEntry** routine.

DriverEntry is the name conventionally given to the main entry point to a kernel-mode driver. The I/O Manager calls the routine as follows:

```
extern "C" NTSTATUS DriverEntry(IN PDRIVER_OBJECT DriverObject,
  IN PUNICODE_STRING RegistryPath)
  {
  ...
  }
```

> **NOTE** You call the main entry point to a kernel-mode driver "DriverEntry" because the build script—if you use standard procedures—will instruct the linker that DriverEntry is the entry point, and it's best to make your code match this assumption (or else to change the build script, but why bother?).

Before I describe the code you'd write inside DriverEntry, I want to mention a few things about the function prototype itself. Unbeknownst to you and I (unless we look carefully at the compiler options used in the build script), kernel-mode functions and the functions in your driver use the **__stdcall** calling convention when compiled for an x86 computer. This shouldn't affect any of your programming, but it's something to bear in mind when you're debugging. I used the **extern "C"** directive because, as a rule, I package my code in a C++ compilation unit—mostly to gain the freedom to declare variables wherever I please instead of only immediately after left braces. This directive suppresses the normal C++ decoration of the external name so that the linker can find this function. Thus, an x86 compile produces a function whose external name is **_DriverEntry@8**.

Another point about the prototype of DriverEntry is those "IN" keywords. **IN**, **OUT**, and **INOUT** are all noise words that the DDK defines as empty strings. By original intention, they perform a documentation function. That is, when you see an IN parameter, you're supposed to infer that it's purely input to your function. An OUT parameter is output by your function, while an INOUT parameter is used for both input and output. As it happens, the DDK headers don't really use these keywords intuitively, and there's not a great deal of point to them. To give you just one example out of many: DriverEntry claims that the DriverObject pointer is IN; indeed, you don't change the pointer, but you will assuredly change the object to which it poin

The last general thing I want you to notice about the prototype is that it declares this function as returning an NTSTATUS value. NTSTATUS is actually just a long integer, but you want to use the typedef name NTSTATUS instead of LONG so that people understand your code better. A great many kernel-mode support routines return NTSTATUS status codes, and you'll find a list of them in the DDK header NTSTATUS.H. I'll have a bit more to say about status codes in the next chapter; for now, just be aware that your DriverEntry function will be returning a status code when it finishes.

Overview of DriverEntry

The first argument to DriverEntry is a pointer to a barely initialized driver object that represents your driver. A WDM driver's DriverEntry function will finish initializing this object and return. Non-WDM drivers have a great deal of extra work to do—they must also detect the hardware for which they're responsible, create device objects to represent the hardware, and do all the configuration and initialization required to make the hardware fully functional. The relatively arduous detection and configuration steps are handled automatically for WDM drivers by the PnP Manager, as I'll discuss in Chapter 6. If you want to know how a non-WDM driver initializes itself, consult Art Baker's *The Windows NT Device Driver Book* (Prentice Hall, 1997) and Viscarola and Mason's *Windows NT Device Driver Development* (Macmillan, 1998).

The second argument to DriverEntry is the name of the service key in the registry. This string is not persistent—you must copy it if you plan to use it later.

A WDM driver's main job in DriverEntry is to fill in the various function pointers in the driver object. These pointers indicate to the operating system where to find the subroutines you've decided to place in your driver container. They include these pointer members of the driver object:

■   **DriverUnload**   Set this to point to whatever cleanup routine you create. The I/O Manager will call this routine just prior to unloading the driver.

Most of the time, a WDM driver doesn't allocate any resources during DriverEntry, so it doesn't need to clean anything up.

- **DriverExtension->AddDevice**   Set this to point to your AddDevice function. The PnP Manager will call AddDevice once for each hardware instance you're responsible for. Since AddDevice is so important to the way WDM drivers work, I've devoted the next main section ("The AddDevice Routine") of this chapter to explaining what it does.

- **DriverStartIo**   If your driver uses the standard method of queuing I/O requests, you'd set this member of the driver object to point to your StartIo routine. Don't worry (yet, that is) if you don't understand what I mean by the "standard" queuing method; all will become clear in Chapter 5, where you'll discover that many drivers do use it.

- **MajorFunction**   The I/O Manager initializes this vector of function pointers to point to a dummy dispatch function that fails every request. You're presumably going to be handling certain types of IRPs—otherwise, your driver is basically going to be deaf and dumb—so you'd set at least some of these pointers to your own dispatch functions. Chapter 5 discusses IRPs and dispatch functions in detail. For now, all you need to know is that you *must* handle three kinds of IRPs and that you'll *probably* be handling several other kinds as well.

A nearly complete DriverEntry routine would, then, look like this:

```
extern "C" NTSTATUS DriverEntry(IN PDRIVER_OBJECT DriverObject,
  IN PUNICODE_STRING RegistryPath)
  {
  DriverObject->DriverUnload = DriverUnload;
  DriverObject->DriverExtension->AddDevice = AddDevice;
  DriverObject->DriverStartIo = StartIo;
  DriverObject->MajorFunction[IRP_MJ_PNP] = DispatchPnp;
  DriverObject->MajorFunction[IRP_MJ_POWER] = DispatchPower;
  DriverObject->MajorFunction[IRP_MJ_SYSTEM_CONTROL] = DispatchWmi;
  ...
  servkey.Buffer = (PWSTR) ExAllocatePool(PagedPool,
    RegistryPath->Length + sizeof(WCHAR));
  if (!servkey.Buffer)
    return STATUS_INSUFFICIENT_RESOURCES;
  servkey.MaximumLength = RegistryPath->Length + sizeof(WCHAR);
  RtlCopyUnicodeString(&servkey, RegistryPath);
  return STATUS_SUCCESS;
  }
```

1. These three statements set the function pointers for entry points elsewhere in the driver. I elected to give them simple names indicative of their function: DriverUnload, AddDevice, and StartIo.

2. Every WDM driver must handle PNP, POWER, and SYSTEM_CONTROL I/O requests; this is where you'd specify your dispatch functions for these requests. What's now IRP_MJ_SYSTEM_CONTROL was called IRP_MJ_WMI in some early beta releases of the Windows 2000 DDK, which is why I called my dispatch function **DispatchWmi**.

3. In place of this ellipsis, you'd have code to set several additional MajorFunction pointers.

4. If you ever need to access the service registry key elsewhere in your driver, it's a good idea to make a copy of the **RegistryPath** string here. If you're going to be acting as a WMI (Windows Management Instrumentation) provider (as I discuss in Chapter 10, "Windows Management Instrumentation"), you'll need to have this string around, for example. I've assumed that you declared a global variable named **servkey** as a UNICODE_STRING elsewhere. I'll explain the mechanics of working with Unicode strings in the next chapter.

5. Returning STATUS_SUCCESS is how you indicate success. If you were to discover something wrong, you'd return an error code chosen from the standard set in NTSTATUS.H or from a set of error codes that you define yourself. STATUS_SUCCESS happens to be numerically 0.

DriverUnload

The purpose of a WDM driver's **DriverUnload** function is to clean up after any global initialization that DriverEntry might have done. There's almost nothing to do. If you made a copy of the RegistryPath string in DriverEntry, though, DriverUnload would be the place to release the memory used for the copy:

```
VOID DriverUnload(PDRIVER_OBJECT DriverObject)
  {
  RtlFreeUnicodeString(&servkey);
  }
```

If your DriverEntry routine returns a failure status, the system does not call your DriverUnload routine. Therefore, if DriverEntry generates any side effects that need cleaning up prior to returning an error status, DriverEntry has to perform the cleanup.

Driver Reinitialization Routine

The I/O Manager provides a service function, **IoRegisterDriverReinitialization**, that solves a peculiar problem for non-WDM drivers, and I want to explain what it does so you'll know why you don't need to worry about it. Non-WDM drivers need to enumerate their hardware at DriverEntry time. It might happen that a non-WDM driver must load and initialize before all possible instances of its own hardware have been identified. This is true for mouse and keyboard devices, for example. But, if DriverEntry is supposed to enumerate all the mice or keyboards and create device objects for them, these drivers can't do their work properly if their DriverEntry routine runs too soon. They use IoRegisterDriverReinitialization to register a routine that the I/O Manager will call back the next time someone detects new hardware. The reinitialization routine can then try again and, potentially, register itself for even later callbacks.

WDM drivers shouldn't need to register reinitialization routines because they don't rely on their own resources to detect hardware. The PnP Manager will automatically match up newly arrived hardware to the right WDM driver and call that driver's AddDevice routine (the subject of the next section) to do all the necessary initialization work.

THE ADDDEVICE ROUTINE

In the preceding main section, I showed how you initialize a WDM driver when it's first loaded. In general, though, a driver might be called upon to manage more than one actual device. In the WDM architecture, a driver has a special **AddDevice** function that the PnP Manager can call for each such device. The function has the following prototype:

```
NTSTATUS AddDevice(PDRIVER_OBJECT DriverObject, PDEVICE_OBJECT pdo)
  {
  }
```

The **DriverObject** argument points to the same driver object that you initialized in your DriverEntry routine. The **pdo** argument is the address of the physical device object at the bottom of the device stack, even if there are already filter drivers below.

The basic responsibility of AddDevice in a function driver is to create a device object and link it into the stack rooted in this PDO. The steps involved are as follows:

1. Call IoCreateDevice to create a device object and an instance of your own device extension object.

2. Register one or more device interfaces so that applications know about the existence of your device. Alternatively, give the device object a name and then create a symbolic link.

3. Next initialize your device extension and the Flags member of the device object.

4. Call IoAttachDeviceToDeviceStack to put your new device object into the stack.

Now I'll explain these steps in more detail.

Creating a Device Object

You create a device object by calling **IoCreateDevice**. For example:

```
PDEVICE_OBJECT fdo;
NTSTATUS status = IoCreateDevice(DriverObject,
  sizeof(DEVICE_EXTENSION), NULL,
  FILE_DEVICE_UNKNOWN, FILE_DEVICE_SECURE_OPEN, FALSE, &fdo);
```

The first argument (**DriverObject**) is the same value supplied to AddDevice as the first argument. This argument establishes the connection between your driver and the new device object, thereby allowing the I/O Manager to send you IRPs intended for the device. The second argument is the size of your device extension structure. As I discussed earlier in this chapter, the I/O Manager allocates this much additional memory and sets the DeviceExtension pointer in the device object to point to it.

The third argument, which is **NULL** in this example, can be the address of a UNICODE_STRING providing a name for the device object. Deciding whether to name your device object and which name to give it requires some thought, and I'll describe these surprisingly complex considerations a bit further on in the section, "Should I Name My Device Object?"

The fourth argument (**FILE_DEVICE_UNKNOWN**) is one of the device types listed in Table 2-4. Whatever value you specify here can be overridden by an entry in the device's hardware key or class key. If both keys have an override, the hardware key has precedence. For devices that fit into one of the established categories, specify the right value in one of these places because some details about the interaction between your driver and the surrounding system depend on it. In addition, the default security settings for your device object depend on this device type.

The fifth argument (**0**) provides the Characteristics flag for the device object. (See Table 2-3 on page 40.) These flags are relevant mostly for mass storage devices. The undocumented flag bit FILE_AUTOGENERATED_DEVICE_NAME is for internal use only—the DDK documenters didn't simply forget to mention it. Whatever value you specify here can be overridden by an entry in the device's hardware key or class key. If both keys have an override, the hardware key has precedence.

The sixth argument to IoCreateDevice (**FALSE** in my example) indicates whether the device is *exclusive*. The I/O Manager allows only one handle to be opened by normal means to an exclusive device. Whatever value you specify here can be overridden by an entry in the device's hardware key or class key. If both keys have an override, the hardware key has precedence.

> **NOTE** The exclusivity attribute matters only for whatever named device object is the target of an open request. If you follow Microsoft's recommended guidelines for WDM drivers, you won't give your device object a name. Open requests will then target the PDO, but the PDO will *not* usually be marked exclusive because the bus driver usually has no way of knowing whether you need your device to be exclusive. The only time the PDO will be marked exclusive is when there's an **Exclusive** override in the device's hardware key or class key's Properties subkey. You're best advised, therefore, to avoid relying on the exclusive attribute altogether. Instead, make your IRP_MJ_CREATE handler reject open requests that would violate whatever restriction you require.

The last argument (**&fdo**) points to a location where IoCreateDevice will store the address of the device object it creates.

If IoCreateDevice fails for some reason, it returns a status code and does not alter the PDEVICE_OBJECT described by the last argument. If it succeeds, it returns a successful status code and sets the PDEVICE_OBJECT pointer. You can then proceed to initialize your device extension and do the other work associated with creating a new device object. Should you discover an error after this point, you should release the device object and return a status code. The code to accomplish these tasks would be something like this:

```
NTSTATUS status = IoCreateDevice(...);
if (!NT_SUCCESS(status))
  return status;
...
if (<some other error discovered>)
  {
  IoDeleteDevice(fdo);
  return status;
  }
```

I'll explain the NTSTATUS status codes and the NT_SUCCESS macro in the next chapter.

Naming Devices

Windows NT uses a centralized Object Manager to manage many of its internal data structures, including the driver and device objects I've been talking about. David Solomon presents a fairly complete explanation of the Windows NT Object Manager and namespace in Chapter 3, "System Mechanisms," of *Inside Windows NT, Second Edition* (Microsoft Press, 1998). Objects have names, which the Object Manager maintains in a hierarchical namespace. Figure 2-16 is a screen shot of my DEVVIEW application showing the top level of the name hierarchy. The objects displayed as folders in this screen shot are *directory objects,* which can contain subdirectories and "regular" objects. The objects displayed with other icons are examples of these regular objects. (In this respect, DEVVIEW is similar to the WINOBJ utility that you'll find in the BIN\WINNT directory of the Platform SDK. WINOBJ can't give you information about device objects and drivers, though, which is why I wrote DEVVIEW in the first place.)

Figure 2-16. *Using DEVVIEW to view the namespace.*

Device objects can have names that conventionally live in the \Device directory. Names for devices serve two purposes in Windows 2000. Giving your device object a name allows other kernel-mode components to find it by calling service functions like **IoGetDeviceObjectPointer**. Having found your device object, they can send you IRPs.

The other purpose of naming a device object is to allow applications to open handles to the device so *they* can send you IRPs. An application uses the standard **CreateFile** API to open a handle, whereupon it can use **ReadFile**, **WriteFile**, and **DeviceIoControl** to talk to you. The pathname an application uses to open a device handle begins with the prefix \\.\ rather than with a standard Universal Naming Convention (UNC) name such as C:\MYFILE.CPP or \\FRED\C-Drive\HISFILE.CPP. Internally, the I/O Manager converts this prefix into **\??** before commencing a name search. To provide a mechanism for connecting names in the **\??** directory to objects whose names are elsewhere (such as in the \Device directory), the Object Manager implements an object called a *symbolic link.*

Symbolic Links

A symbolic link is a little bit like a desktop shortcut in that it points to some other entity that's the real object of attention. Symbolic links are mainly used in Windows NT to connect the leading portion of DOS-style names to devices. Figure 2-17 shows a portion of the \?? directory, which includes a number of symbolic links. Notice, for example, that C: and other drive letters in the DOS file-naming scheme are actually links to objects whose names are in the \Device directory. These links allow the Object Manager to "jump" somewhere else in the namespace as it parses through a name. So, if I call CreateFile with the name C:\MYFILE.CPP, the Object Manager will take this path to open the file:

1. Kernel-mode code initially sees the name \??\C:\MYFILE.CPP. The Object Manager looks up "??" in the root directory and finds a directory object with that name.

2. The Object Manager now looks up "C:" in the \?? directory. It finds a symbolic link by that name, so it forms the *new* kernel-mode pathname \Device\HarddiskVolume1\MYFILE.CPP and parses that.

3. Working with the new pathname, the Object Manager looks up "Device" in the root directory and finds a directory object.

4. The Object Manager looks up "HarddiskVolume1" in the \Device directory. It finds a device object by that name.

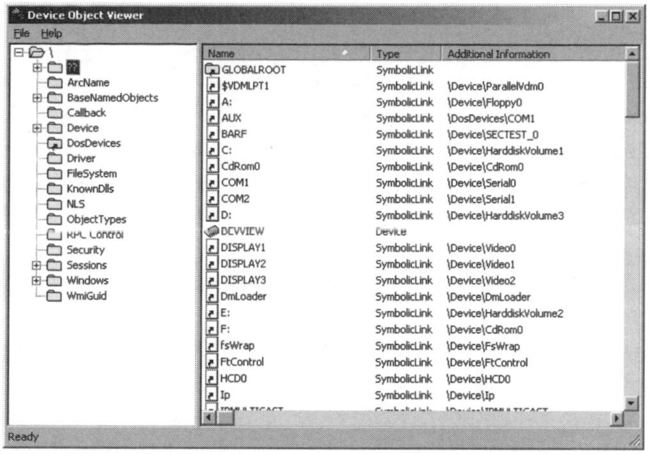

Figure 2-17. *The \?? directory with several symbolic links.*

At this point in the process, the Object Manager will create an IRP that it will send to the driver(s) for HarddiskVolume1. The IRP will eventually cause some file system driver or another to locate and open a disk file. Describing how a file system driver works is beyond the scope of this book. If we were dealing with a device name like COM1, the driver that ends up receiving the IRP would be the driver for \Device\Serial0. How a device driver handles an open request is definitely within the scope of this book, and I'll be discussing it in this chapter (in the section "Should I Name My Device Object?") and in Chapter 5 when I'll talk about IRP processing in general.

A user-mode program can create a symbolic link by calling **DefineDosDevice**, as in this example:

```
BOOL okay = DefineDosDevice(DDD_RAW_TARGET_PATH,
  "barf", "\\Device\\SECTEST_0");
```

You can see the aftermath of a call like this one in Figure 2-17, by the way.

You can create a symbolic link in a WDM driver by calling **IoCreate-SymbolicLink**,

```
IoCreateSymbolicLink(linkname, targname);
```

where **linkname** is the name of the symbolic link you want to create and **targname** is the name to which you're linking. Incidentally, the Object Manager doesn't care whether targname is the name of any existing object: someone who tries to access an object by using a link that points to an undefined name simply receives an error. If you want to allow user-mode programs to override your link and point it somewhere else, you should call **IoCreateUnprotectedSymbolicLink** instead.

ARC NAMES

In the Advanced RISC Computing (ARC) architecture, there is a concept known as *ARC naming* that Windows 2000 relies on. You can see ARC names at work in the BOOT.INI file in the root directory of your boot drive. Here's what my copy of that file looked like at one point in the development of this book:

```
[boot loader]
timeout=30
default=c:\
[operating systems]
C:\="Microsoft Windows 98"
scsi(0)disk(1)rdisk(0)partition(1)\BETA2F="Win2k Beta-2 (Free Build)"
  /fastdetect /noguiboot
scsi(0)disk(1)rdisk(0)partition(1)\WINNT="Win2K Beta-3 (Free Build)"
  /fastdetect /noguiboot
```

On an Intel platform, ARC names like scsi(0)disk(1)rdisk(0)partition(1) are symbolic links within the kernel's \ArcName directory that point—eventually, that is, if you resolve all the links in the way—to regular device objects. DEVVIEW will show you these links on your own system.

Drivers for mass-storage devices other than hard disks should call **IoAssignArcName** during initialization to set up one of these links. The I/O Manager automatically creates the ARC names for hard disk devices, since these are needed to boot the system in the first place.

Should I Name My Device Object?

Deciding whether to give your device object a name requires, as I said earlier, a little thought. If you give your object a name, it will be possible for any kernel-mode program to try to open a handle to your device. Furthermore, it will be possible for any kernel-mode or user-mode program to create a symbolic link to your device object and to use the symbolic link to try to open a handle. You might or might not want to allow these actions.

The primary consideration in deciding whether to name your device object is security. When someone opens a handle to a named object, the Object Manager verifies that they have permission to do so. When IoCreateDevice creates a device object for you, it assigns a default security descriptor based on the device type you specify as the fourth argument. There are three basic categories that the I/O Manager uses to select a security descriptor. (Refer to the second column in Table 2-4 on pages 41–43.)

- Most file system device objects (that is, disk, CD-ROM, file, and tape) receive the "public default unrestricted" access control list (ACL). This list gives just SYNCHRONIZE, READ_CONTROL, FILE_READ_ATTRIBUTES, and FILE_TRAVERSE access to everyone except the System account and all administrators. File system device objects, by the way, exist only so that there can be a target for a CreateFile call that will open a handle to a file managed by the file system.

- Disk devices and network file system objects receive the same ACL as the file system objects with some modifications. For example, everyone gets full access to a named floppy disk device object, and administrators get sufficient rights to run ScanDisk. (User-mode network provider DLLs need greater access to the device object for their corresponding file system driver, which is why network file systems are treated differently than other file systems.)

- All other device objects receive the "public open unrestricted" ACL, which allows anyone with a handle to the device to do pretty much anything.

You can see that anyone will be able to access a nondisk device for both reading and writing if the driver gives the device object a name at the time when it calls IoCreateDevice. This is because the default security allows nearly full access *and because there is no security check at all associated with creating a symbolic link*—the security checks happen at open time, based on the named object's security descriptor. This is true even if other device objects in the same stack have more restrictive security.

DEVVIEW will show you the security attributes of the device objects it displays. You can see the operation of the default rules I just described by examining a file system, a disk device, and any other random device.

The PDO also receives a default security descriptor, but it's possible to override it with a security descriptor stored in the hardware key or in the Properties subkey of the class key. (The hardware key has precedence if both keys specify a descriptor.) Even lacking a specific security override, if either the hardware key or the class key's Properties subkey overrides the device type or characteristics specification, the I/O Manager constructs a *new* default security descriptor based on the new type. The I/O Manager does not, however, override the security setting for any of the other device objects above the PDO. Consequently, for the overrides (and the administrative actions that set them up) to have any effect, you should not name your device object. Don't despair though—applications can still access your device by means of a *registered interface,* which I'll discuss very shortly.

You need to know about one last security concern. As the Object Manager parses its way through an object name, it needs only FILE_TRAVERSE access to the intermediate components of the name. It only performs a full security check on the object named by the final component. So, suppose you had a device object reachable under the name \Device\SECTEST_0 or by the symbolic link \??\SecurityTest_0. A user-mode application that tries to open \\.\SecurityTest_0 for writing will be blocked if the object security has been set up to deny write access. But if the application tries to open a name like \\.\SecurityTest_0\ExtraStuff that has additional name qualifications, the open request will make it all the way to the device driver (in the form of an IRP_MJ_CREATE I/O request) if the user merely has FILE_TRAVERSE permission, which is routinely granted. The I/O Manager expects the device driver to deal with the additional name components and to perform any required security checks with regard to them.

To avoid the security concern I just described, you can supply the flag FILE_DEVICE_SECURE_OPEN in the device characteristics argument to IoCreateDevice. This flag causes Windows 2000 to verify that someone has the right to open a handle to a device even if additional name components are present.

The Device Name

If you decide to name the device object, you would normally put the name in the \Device branch of the namespace. To give it a name, you have to create a UNICODE_STRING structure to hold the name, and you have to specify that string as an argument to IoCreateDevice:

```
UNICODE_STRING devname;
RtlInitUnicodeString(&devname, L"\\Device\\Simple0");
IoCreateDevice(DriverObject, sizeof(DEVICE_EXTENSION), &devname, ...);
```

I'll discuss the usage of **RtlInitUnicodeString** in the next chapter.

Conventionally, drivers assign their device objects a name by concatenating a string naming their device type ("Simple" in this fragment) with a zero-based integer denoting an instance of that type. In general, you don't want to hard-code a name like I just did—you want to compose it dynamically using string-manipulation functions like the following:

```
UNICODE_STRING devname;
static LONG lastindex = -1;
LONG devindex = InterlockedIncrement(&lastindex);
WCHAR name[32];
```

```
_snwprintf(name, arraysize(name), L"\\Device\\SIMPLE%2.2d", devindex);
RtlInitUnicodeString(&devname, name);
IoCreateDevice(...);
```

I'll explain the various service functions used in this fragment in the next couple of chapters. The instance number you derive for private device types might as well be a static variable, as shown in the previous fragment.

NOTES ON DEVICE NAMING

If all you wanted to do was to provide a quick-and-dirty way for an application to open a handle to your device during development, you could perfectly well assign the device object a name in the \?? branch. For a production driver, however, you're better advised to do what the text suggests and name the device object with a \Device directory name.

The \?? directory used to be named \DosDevices. In fact, \DosDevices will still work, but it itself is a symbolic link to \??. The change was made to move the often-searched directory of user-mode names to the front of the alphabetical list of directories. *See the "Windows 98 Compatibility Notes" section at the end of this chapter for an important caution about using \?? in your names.*

In previous versions of Windows NT, drivers for certain classes of devices (notably disks, tapes, serial ports, and parallel ports) called **IoGetConfigurationInformation** to obtain a pointer to a global table containing counts of devices in each of these special classes. A driver would use the current value of the counter to compose a name like Harddisk0, Tape1, and so on, and would also increment the counter. WDM drivers don't need to use this service function or the table it returns, however. Constructing names for the devices in these classes is now the responsibility of a Microsoft type-specific class driver (such as DISK.SYS).

Device Interfaces

The older method of naming I just discussed—naming your device object and creating a symbolic link name that applications can use—has two major problems. We've already discussed the security implications of giving your device object a name. In addition, the author of an application that wants to access your device has to know the scheme you adopted to name your devices. If you're the only one writing the applications that will be accessing your hardware, that's not much of a problem. But if many different companies will be writing applications for your hardware, and especially if many hardware companies are making similar devices, devising a suitable naming scheme is difficult. Finally, many naming schemes rely on the language spoken by the programmer, which isn't necessarily a good choice in an increasingly global economy. (My favorite example involves an American chef who tells a German diner he's eating a "gift" [poison], whereupon the diner, only incompletely realizing the linguistic difficulty, calls the chef a "schmuck" [jewelry].)

To solve these problems, WDM introduces a new naming scheme for devices that is language-neutral, easily extensible, usable in an environment with many hardware and software vendors, and easily documented. The scheme relies on the concept of a *device interface,* which is basically a specification for how software can access hardware. A device interface is uniquely identified by a 128-bit GUID. You can generate GUIDs by running the Platform SDK utilities UUIDGEN or GUIDGEN—both utilities generate the same kind of number, but they output the result in different formats. The idea is that some industry group gets together to define a standard way of accessing a certain kind of hardware. As part of the standard-making process, someone runs GUIDGEN and publishes the resulting GUID as the identifier that will be forever after associated with that interface standard.

MORE ABOUT GUIDS

The GUIDs used to identify software interfaces are the same kind of unique identifier that's used in the Component Object Model (COM) to identify COM interfaces and in the Open Software Foundation (OSF) Distributed Computing Environment (DCE) to identify the target of a remote procedure call (RPC). For an explanation of how GUIDs are generated so as to be statistically unique, see page 66 of Kraig Brockschmidt's *Inside OLE, Second Edition* (Microsoft Press, 1995), which contains a further reference to the original algorithm specification by the OSF. I found the relevant portion of the OSF specification online at *http://www.opengroup.org/onlinepubs/9629399/apdxa.htm.*

The mechanics of creating a GUID for use in a device driver involve running either UUIDGEN or GUIDGEN and then capturing the resulting identifier in a header file. GUIDGEN is easier to use because it allows you to choose to format the GUID for use with the DEFINE_GUID macro and to copy the resulting string onto the clipboard. Figure 2-18 shows the GUIDGEN window. You can paste its output into a header file to end up with this:

```
// {CAF53C68-A94C-11d2-BB4A-00C04FA330A6}
DEFINE_GUID( <<name>>,
0xcaf53c68, 0xa94c, 0x11d2, 0xbb, 0x4a, 0x0, 0xc0, 0x4f, 0xa3, 0x30, 0xa6);
```

You then replace the *<<name>>* with something more mnemonic like GUID_SIMPLE and include the definition in your driver and applications.

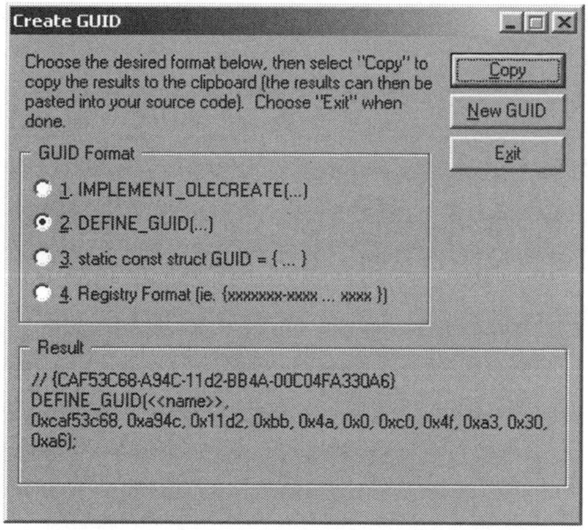

Figure 2-18. *Using GUIDGEN to generate a GUID.*

I think of an interface as being analogous to the protein markers that populate the surface of living cells. An application desiring to access a particular kind of device has its own protein markers that fit like a key into the markers exhibited by conforming device drivers. See Figure 2-19.

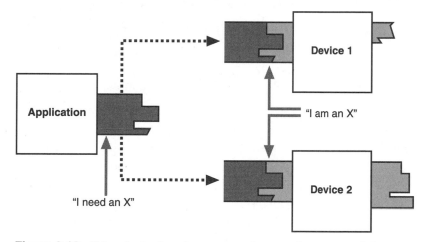

Figure 2-19. *Using device interfaces to match up applications and devices.*

Registering a Device Interface   A function driver's AddDevice function should register one or more device interfaces by calling **IoRegisterDeviceInterface**, as shown here:

```
1    #include <initguid.h>
2    #include "guids.h"
     ...
```

(continued)

```
NTSTATUS AddDevice(...)
  {
  ...
  IoRegisterDeviceInterface(pdo, &GUID_SIMPLE, NULL, &pdx->ifname);
  ...
  }
```

3

1. We're about to include a header (GUIDS.H) that contains one or more DEFINE_GUID macros. DEFINE_GUID normally declares an external variable. Somewhere in the driver, though, we have to actually reserve initialized storage for every GUID we're going to reference. The system header file INITGUID.H works some preprocessor magic to make DEFINE_ GUID reserve the storage even if the definition of the DEFINE_GUID macro happens to be in one of the precompiled header files.

2. I'm assuming here that I put the GUID definitions I want to reference into a separate header file. This would be a good idea, inasmuch as user-mode code will also need to include these definitions and will *not* want to include a bunch of extraneous kernel-mode declarations relevant only to our driver.

3. The first argument to IoRegisterDeviceInterface must be the address of the PDO for your device. The second argument identifies the GUID associated with your interface, and the third argument specifies additional qualified names that further subdivide your interface. Only Microsoft code uses this name subdivision scheme. The last argument is the address of a UNICODE_STRING structure that will receive the name of a symbolic link that resolves to this device object.

The return value from IoRegisterDeviceInterface is a Unicode string that applications will be able to determine without knowing anything special about how you coded your driver and will then be able to use in opening a handle to the device. The name is pretty ugly, by the way; here's an example that I generated for one of my sample devices in Windows 98: \DosDevices\0000000000000007#{CAF53 C68-A94C-11d2-BB4A-00C04FA330A6}. (You can call it 007 once you get to know it better.)

All that registration actually does is create the symbolic link name and save it in the registry. Later on, in response to the IRP_MN_START_DEVICE Plug and Play request we'll discuss in Chapter 6, you'll make the following call to **IoSet-DeviceInterfaceState** to "enable" the interface:

```
IoSetDeviceInterfaceState(&pdx->ifname, TRUE);
```

In response to this call, the I/O Manager creates an actual symbolic link *object* pointing to the PDO for your device. You'll make a matching call to disable the interface at a still later time (just call IoSetDeviceInterfaceState with a FALSE argument), whereupon the I/O Manager will delete the symbolic link object while preserving the registry entry that contains the name. In other words, the name persists and will always be associated with this particular instance of your device; the symbolic link object comes and goes with the hardware.

Since the interface name ends up pointing to the PDO, the PDO's security descriptor ends up controlling whether people can access your device. That's good, because it's the PDO's security that an administrator can control through the Management Console.

Enumerating Device Interfaces   Both kernel-mode and user-mode code can locate all the devices that happen to support an interface in which they're interested. I'm going to explain how to enumerate all the devices for a particular interface in user mode. The enumeration code is so tedious to write that I eventually wrote a C++ class to make my own life simpler. You'll find this code in the DEVICELIST.CPP and DEVICELIST.H files that are part of the WDMIDLE sample in Chapter 8, "Power Management." These files declare and implement a **CDeviceList** class, which contains an array of **CDeviceListEntry** objects. These two classes have the following declaration:

```
class CDeviceListEntry
{
public:
  CDeviceListEntry(LPCTSTR linkname, LPCTSTR friendlyname);
  CDeviceListEntry(){}
  CString m_linkname;
  CString m_friendlyname;
};

class CDeviceList
{
public:
  CDeviceList(const GUID& guid);
  ~CDeviceList();
  GUID m_guid;
  CArray<CDeviceListEntry, CDeviceListEntry&> m_list;
  int Initialize();
};
```

The classes rely on the **CString** class and **CArray** template class that are part of the Microsoft Foundation Classes (MFC) framework. The constructors for these two classes simply copy their arguments into the obvious data members:

```
CDeviceList::CDeviceList(const GUID& guid)
  {
  m_guid = guid;
  }
```

continued

61

```
CDeviceListEntry::CDeviceListEntry(LPCTSTR linkname,
  LPCTSTR friendlyname)
  {
  m_linkname = linkname;
  m_friendlyname = friendlyname;
  }
```

All the interesting work occurs in the **CDeviceList::Initialize** function. The executive overview of what it does is this: it will enumerate all of the devices that expose the interface whose GUID was supplied to the constructor. For each such device, it will determine a "friendly" name that we're willing to show to an unsuspecting end user. Finally, it will return the number of devices it found. Here's the code for this function:

```
int CDeviceList::Initialize()
  {
  HDEVINFO info = SetupDiGetClassDevs(&m_guid, NULL, NULL,
    DIGCF_PRESENT | DIGCF_INTERFACEDEVICE);
  if (info == INVALID_HANDLE_VALUE)
    return 0;
  SP_INTERFACE_DEVICE_DATA ifdata;
  ifdata.cbSize = sizeof(ifdata);
  DWORD devindex;
  for (devindex = 0;
    SetupDiEnumDeviceInterfaces(info, NULL, &m_guid,
    devindex, &ifdata); ++devindex)
    {
    DWORD needed;
    SetupDiGetDeviceInterfaceDetail(info, &ifdata, NULL, 0,
      &needed, NULL);

    PSP_INTERFACE_DEVICE_DETAIL_DATA detail =
      (PSP_INTERFACE_DEVICE_DETAIL_DATA) malloc(needed);
    detail->cbSize = sizeof(SP_INTERFACE_DEVICE_DETAIL_DATA);
    SP_DEVINFO_DATA did = {sizeof(SP_DEVINFO_DATA)};
    SetupDiGetDeviceInterfaceDetail(info, &ifdata, detail,
      needed, NULL, &did));

    TCHAR fname[256];
    if (!SetupDiGetDeviceRegistryProperty(info, &did, SPDRP_FRIENDLYNAME,
        NULL, (PBYTE) fname, sizeof(fname), NULL)
      && !SetupDiGetDeviceRegistryProperty(info, &did, SPDRP_DEVICEDESC,
        NULL, (PBYTE) fname, sizeof(fname), NULL))
      _tcsncpy(fname, detail->DevicePath, 256);
```

```
5      CDeviceListEntry e(detail->DevicePath, fname);
       free((PVOID) detail);

       m_list.Add(e);
       }

   SetupDiDestroyDeviceInfoList(info);
   return m_list.GetSize();
   }
```

1. This statement opens an enumeration handle that we can use to find all devices that have registered an interface that uses the same GUID.

2. Here we call **SetupDiEnumDeviceInterfaces** in a loop to find each device.

3. The only two items of information we need are the "detail" information about the interface and information about the device instance. The detail is just the symbolic name for the device. Since it's variable in length, we make two calls to **SetupDiGetDeviceInterfaceDetail**. The first call determines the length. The second call retrieves the name.

4. We obtain a "friendly" name for the device from the registry by asking for either the **FriendlyName** or the **DeviceDesc**.

5. We create a temporary instance named **e** of the CDeviceListEntry class, using the device's symbolic name as both the link name and the friendly name.

FRIENDLY NAMES

You might be wondering how the registry comes to have a FriendlyName for a device. The INF file you use to install your device driver—see Chapter 12—can have an HW section that specifies registry parameters for the device. You should normally provide a FriendlyName as one of these parameters.

Other Global Device Initialization

You need to take some other steps during AddDevice to initialize your device object. I'm going to describe these steps in the order you should do them, which isn't exactly the same order as their respective logical importance. I want to emphasize that the code snippets in this section are even more fragmented than usual—I'm going to show only enough of the entire AddDevice routine to establish the surrounding context for the small pieces I'm trying to illustrate.

Initializing the Device Extension

The content and management of the device extension are entirely up to you. The data members you place in this structure will obviously depend on the details of your hardware and on how you go about programming the device. Most drivers would need a few items placed there, however, as illustrated in the following fragment of a declaration:

```
typedef struct _DEVICE_EXTENSION {
  PDEVICE_OBJECT DeviceObject;
  PDEVICE_OBJECT LowerDeviceObject;
  PDEVICE_OBJECT Pdo;
  UNICODE_STRING ifname;
  IO_REMOVE_LOCK RemoveLock;
  DEVSTATE devstate;
  DEVSTATE prevstate;
  POWERSTATE powerstate;
  DEVICE_POWER_STATE devpower;
  SYSTEM_POWER_STATE syspower;
  DEVICE_CAPABILITIES devcaps;
  ...
} DEVICE_EXTENSION, *PDEVICE_EXTENSION;
```

1. I find it easiest to mimic the pattern of structure declaration used in the official DDK, so I declared this device extension as a structure with a tag as well as a type and pointer-to-type name.

2. You already know that you locate your device extension by following the **DeviceExtension** pointer from the device object. It's also useful in several situations to be able to go the other way—to find the device object given a pointer to the extension. The reason is that the logical argument to certain functions is the device extension itself (since that's where all of the per-instance information about your device resides). Hence, I find it useful to have this **DeviceObject** pointer.

3. I'll mention in a few paragraphs that you need to record the address of the device object immediately below yours when you call IoAttachDevice-ToDeviceStack, and **LowerDeviceObject** is the place to do that.

4. A few service routines require the address of the PDO instead of some higher device object in the same stack. It's very difficult to locate the PDO, so the easiest way to satisfy the requirement of those functions is to record the PDO address in a member of the device extension that you initialize during AddDevice.

5. Whichever method (symbolic link or device interface) you use to name your device, you'll want an easy way to remember the name you assign. In this fragment, I've declared a Unicode string member named **ifname** to record a device interface name. If you were going to use a symbolic link name instead of a device interface, it would make sense to give this member a more mnemonic name, such as "linkname."

6. I'll discuss in Chapter 6 a synchronization problem affecting how you decide when it's safe to remove this device object by calling **IoDeleteDevice**. The solution to that problem involves using an IO_REMOVE_LOCK object that needs to be allocated in your device extension as shown here. AddDevice needs to initialize that object.

7. You'll probably need a device extension variable to keep track of the current Plug and Play state and current power states of your device. DEVSTATE and POWERSTATE are enumerations that I'm assuming you've declared elsewhere in your own header file. I'll discuss the use of all these state variables in later chapters.

8. Another part of power management involves remembering some capability settings that the system initializes by means of an IRP. The **devcaps** structure in the device extension is where I save those settings in my sample drivers.

The initialization statements in AddDevice (with emphasis on the parts involving the device extension) would be as follows:

```
NTSTATUS AddDevice(...)
  {
  PDEVICE_OBJECT fdo;
  IoCreateDevice(..., sizeof(DEVICE_EXTENSION), ..., &fdo);
  PDEVICE_EXTENSION pdx = (PDEVICE_EXTENSION) fdo->DeviceExtension;
  pdx->DeviceObject = fdo;
  pdx->Pdo = pdo;
  IoInitializeRemoveLock(&pdx->RemoveLock, ...);
  pdx->devstate = STOPPED;
  pdx->powerstate = POWERON;
  pdx->devpower = PowerDeviceD0;
  pdx->syspower = PowerSystemWorking;
  IoRegisterDeviceInterface(..., &pdx->ifname);
  pdx->LowerDeviceObject = IoAttachDeviceToDeviceStack(...);
  }
```

Initializing the Default DPC Object

Many devices signal completion of operations by means of an interrupt. As you'll learn when I discuss interrupt handling in Chapter 7, "Reading and Writing Data," there are strict limits on what your interrupt service routine (ISR) can do. In particular, an ISR isn't allowed to call the routine (**IoCompleteRequest**) that signals completion of an IRP, but that's exactly one of the steps you're likely to want to take. You utilize a *deferred procedure call* (DPC) to get around the limitations. Your device object contains a subsidiary DPC object that can be used for scheduling your particular DPC routine, and you need to initialize it shortly after creating the device object:

```
NTSTATUS AddDevice(...)
  {
  IoCreateDevice(...);
  IoInitializeDpcRequest(fdo, DpcForIsr);
  }
```

Setting the Buffer Alignment Mask

Devices which perform direct memory access (DMA) transfers work directly with data buffers in memory. The HAL might require that buffers used for DMA be aligned to some particular boundary, and your device might require still more stringent alignment. The **AlignmentRequirement** field of the device object expresses the restriction—it is a bit mask equal to one less that the required address boundary. You can round an arbitrary address down to this boundary with this statement:

```
PVOID address = ...;
SIZE_T ar = fdo->AlignmentRequirement;
address = (PVOID) ((SIZE_T) address & ~ar);
```

You round an arbitrary address *up* to the next alignment boundary like this:

```
PVOID address = ...;
SIZE_T ar = fdo->AlignmentRequirement;
address = (PVOID) (((SIZE_T) address + ar) & ~ar);
```

In these two code fragments, I used **SIZE_T** casts to transform the pointer (which may be 32 bits or 64 bits wide, depending on the platform for which you're compiling) into an integer wide enough to span the same range as the pointer.

IoCreateDevice sets the AlignmentRequirement field of the new device object equal to whatever the HAL requires. For example, the HAL for Intel x86 chips has no alignment requirement, so AlignmentRequirement is 0 initially. If your device requires a more stringent alignment for the data buffers it works with (say, because you have bus-mastering DMA capability with a special alignment requirement), you want to override the default setting. For example:

```
if (MYDEVICE_ALIGNMENT - 1 > fdo->AlignmentRequirement)
  fdo->AlignmentRequirement = MYDEVICE_ALIGNMENT - 1;
```

I've assumed here that elsewhere in your driver is a manifest constant named MYDEVICE_ALIGNMENT that equals a power of two and represents the required alignment of your device's data buffers.

Miscellaneous Objects

Your device might well use other objects that need to be initialized during AddDevice. Such objects might include a controller object, various synchronization objects, various queue anchors, scatter/gather list buffers, and so on. I'll discuss these objects, and the fact that initialization during AddDevice would be appropriate, in various other parts of the book.

Initializing the Device Flags

Two of the flag bits in your device object need to be initialized during AddDevice and never changed thereafter: the DO_BUFFERED_IO and DO_DIRECT_IO flags. You can set one (but only one) of these bits to declare once and for all how you want to handle memory buffers coming from user mode as part of read and write requests. (I'll explain in Chapter 7 what the difference between these two buffering methods is and why you'd want to pick one or the other.) The reason you have to make this important choice during AddDevice is that any upper filter drivers that load after you will be copying your flag settings and it's the setting of the bits in the topmost device object that's actually important. Were you to change your mind after the filter drivers load, they probably wouldn't know about the change.

Three of the flag bits in the device object pertain to power management. In contrast to the two buffering flags, these three can be changed at any time. I'll discuss them in greater detail in Chapter 8, but here's a preview. DO_POWER_PAGABLE means that the Power Manager must send you IRP_MJ_POWER requests at interrupt request level (IRQL) DISPATCH_LEVEL. (If you don't understand all of the concepts in the preceding sentence, don't worry—I'll completely explain all of them in later chapters.) DO_POWER_INRUSH means that your device draws a large amount of current when powering on, such that the Power Manager should make sure that no other in-rush device is powering up simultaneously. DO_POWER_NOOP means that you don't participate in power management in the first place and is only an appropriate setting for WDM drivers that don't manage any hardware.

Setting the Initial Power State

Most devices start life in the fully powered state. If you know the initial state of your device, you should tell the Power Manager:

```
POWER_STATE state;
state.DeviceState = PowerDeviceD0;
PoSetPowerState(fdo, DevicePowerState, state);
```

See Chapter 8 for much more detail about power management.

Building the Device Stack

Each filter and function driver has the responsibility of building up the stack of device objects, starting from the PDO and working upward. You accomplish your part of this work with a call to IoAttachDeviceToDeviceStack:

```
NTSTATUS AddDevice(..., PDEVICE_OBJECT pdo)
  {
  PDEVICE_OBJECT fdo;
  IoCreateDevice(..., &fdo);
  pdx->LowerDeviceObject = IoAttachDeviceToDeviceStack(fdo, pdo);
  }
```

The first argument to IoAttachDeviceToDeviceStack (**fdo**) is the address of your own newly created device object. The second argument is the address of the PDO. The second argument to AddDevice is this address. The return value is the address of whatever device object is immediately underneath yours, which can be the PDO or the address of some lower filter device object.

Clear DO_DEVICE_INITIALIZING

Pretty much the last thing you do in AddDevice should be to clear the DO_DEVICE_INITIALIZING flag in your driver object:

```
fdo->Flags &= ~DO_DEVICE_INITIALIZING;
```

While this flag is set, the I/O Manager will refuse to attach other device objects to yours or to open a handle to your device. You have to clear the flag because your device object initially arrives in the world with the flag set. In previous releases of Windows NT, most drivers created all of their device objects during DriverEntry. When DriverEntry returns, the I/O Manager automatically traverses the list of device objects linked from the driver object and clears this flag. Since you're creating *your* device object long after DriverEntry returns, however, this automatic flag clearing won't occur, and you must do it yourself.

WINDOWS 98 COMPATIBILITY NOTES

Windows 98 handles some of the details surrounding device object creation and driver loading differently than Windows 98. This section explains the differences that might affect your driver.

Differences in DriverEntry Call

As I indicated earlier, the DriverEntry routine receives a UNICODE_STRING argument naming the service key for the driver. In Windows 2000, the string is a full registry path of the form "\Registry\Machine\System\CurrentControlSet\Services*xxx*" (where "*xxx*" is the name of the service entry for your driver). In Windows 98, however, the string is of the form "System\CurrentControlSet\Services*<classname>**<instance-#>*" (where *<classname>* is the class name of your device and *<instance-#>* is an instance number like 0000 indicating which device of that class you happen to be). You can open the key in either environment by calling **ZwOpenKey**, however.

Differences in Registry Organization

Windows 98 uses a slightly different scheme for organizing the registry entries for devices than Windows 2000 does. The following short explanation will make better sense if you come back to it after reading the material on driver installation in Chapter 12.

■ The hardware key is below HKLM\Enum and isn't protected in any way (because Windows 98 doesn't have a security system). There is no **Service** value; instead, there's a **Driver** value that supplies the final two components of the name of the service key. The **LowerFilters** and **UpperFilters** values are treated as binary because the Windows 98 registry doesn't have a MULTI_SZ type, and the values use 8-bit characters to name driver image files (with the .SYS extension) rather than services.

■ The class key is below HKLM\System\CurrentControlSet\Services\Class.

■ The service key is a child of the class key. The entries in the service key include a **DevLoader** value pointing to NTKERN.VXD and an **NTMPDriver** value naming your driver image (with the .SYS extension), which must reside in %SystemRoot%\System32\Drivers.

The \?? Directory

Windows 98 doesn't understand the directory name **\??**. Consequently, you need to put symbolic link names in the \DosDevices directory. You can use \DosDevices in Windows NT also, because it is a symbolic link to the \?? directory.

Unimplemented Device Types

Original Windows 98 doesn't support creating device objects for mass storage devices. These are devices with types FILE_DEVICE_DISK, FILE_DEVICE_TAPE, FILE_DEVICE_CD_ROM, and FILE_DEVICE_VIRTUAL_DISK. You can call IoCreateDevice, and it will even return with a status code of STATUS_SUCCESS, but it won't have actually created a device object or modified the PDEVICE_OBJECT variable whose address you gave as the last argument.

The reason this functionality isn't available is that Windows 98 disk drivers must use the I/O Supervisor architecture invented for Windows 95. Why IoCreateDevice fails so silently is a bit of a puzzle, though.

Chapter 3

Basic Programming Techniques

Writing a WDM driver is fundamentally an exercise in software engineering. Whatever the requirements of your particular hardware, you will combine various elements to form a program. In the previous chapter, I described the basic structure of a WDM driver, and I showed you two of its elements—DriverEntry and AddDevice—in detail. In this chapter, I'll focus on the even more basic topic of how you call upon the large body of kernel-mode support routines that the operating system exposes for your use. I'll discuss error handling, memory and data structure management, registry and file access, and a few other topics. I'll round out the chapter with a short discussion of the steps you can take to help debug your driver.

THE KERNEL-MODE PROGRAMMING ENVIRONMENT

Figure 3-1 (on page 73) illustrates some of the components that make up the Microsoft Windows NT operating system. Each component exports service functions whose names begin with a particular two-letter prefix:

■   The I/O Manager (prefix **Io**) contains many service functions that drivers use, and I'll be discussing them all throughout this book.

■ The Process Structure module (prefix **Ps**) creates and manages kernel-mode threads. An ordinary WDM driver might use an independent thread to repeatedly poll a device incapable of generating interrupts.

■ The Memory Manager (prefix **Mm**) controls the page tables that define the mapping of virtual addresses onto physical memory.

■ The executive (prefix **Ex**) supplies heap management and synchronization services. I'll discuss the heap management service functions in this chapter. The next chapter covers the synchronization services.

■ The Object Manager (prefix **Ob**) provides centralized control over the many data objects with which Windows NT works. WDM drivers rely on the Object Manager only for keeping a reference count that prevents an object from disappearing while someone is still using it.

■ The Security Reference Monitor (prefix **Se**) allows file system drivers to perform security checks. Someone else has usually dealt with security concerns by the time an I/O request reaches a WDM driver, so I won't be discussing these functions in this book.

■ The so-called run-time library component (prefix **Rtl**) contains utility routines, such as list and string management routines, that kernel-mode drivers can use instead of regular ANSI standard library routines. For the most part, the operation of these functions is obvious from their names, and you would pretty much know how to use them in a program if you just were aware of them. I'll describe a few of them in this chapter.

■ Windows NT implements user-mode calls to the Win32 subsystem in kernel mode with routines whose names begin with the **Zw** prefix. The Microsoft Windows 2000 DDK exposes just a few of these functions for use by drivers, including functions for accessing files and the registry. I'll discuss those functions in this chapter.

■ The Windows NT kernel (prefix **Ke**) is where all the low-level synchronization of activities between threads and processors occurs. I'll discuss the Ke*Xxx* functions in the next chapter.

■ The very bottom layer of the operating system, on which the support sandwich rests, is the hardware abstraction layer (or HAL, prefix **Hal**). All the operating system's knowledge of how the computer is actually wired together reposes in the HAL. The HAL understands how interrupts work on a particular platform, how to implement spin locks, how to address I/O and memory-mapped devices, and so on. Instead of talking directly to their hardware, WDM drivers call functions in the HAL to do it. The driver ends up being platform-independent and bus-independent.

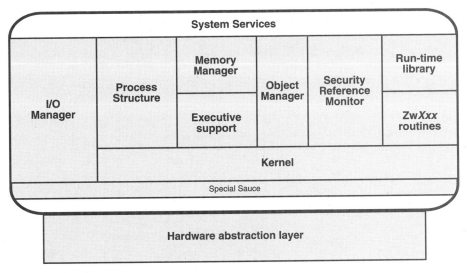

Figure 3-1. *Overview of kernel-mode support routines.*

Using Standard Run-Time Library Functions

Historically, the Windows NT architects have preferred that drivers not use the run-time libraries supplied by vendors of C compilers. In part, the initial disapproval arose from simple timing. Windows NT was designed at a time when there was no ANSI standard for what functions belonged in a standard library and when many compiler vendors existed, each with its own idea of what might be cool to include and its own unique quality standards. Another factor is that standard run-time library routines sometimes rely on initialization that can only happen in a user-mode application and are sometimes implemented in a thread-unsafe or multiprocessor-unsafe way.

Until now, the official rule has been that kernel-mode drivers should call only functions specifically documented in the DDK. Rather than call **wcscmp**, for example, one should call **RtlCompareUnicodeString**. It's been a pretty open secret, however, that the standard import library that one uses to build a driver (NTOSKRNL.LIB) defines many of the functions declared by application header files such as STRING.H, STDIO.H, STDLIB.H, and CTYPES.H. So why not call them? In fact, there's no reason not to call them, provided you understand all the implications. Don't, for example, switch to always calling **memcpy** instead of **RtlCopyBytes**, because there's a subtle difference between the two. (RtlCopyBytes is guaranteed to proceed byte by byte instead of in larger chunks, which can matter on particular RISC [reduced instruction set computing] platforms.)

A Caution About Side Effects

Many of the support "functions" that you use in a driver are defined as macros in the DDK header files. We were all taught to avoid using expressions that have side effects (that is, expressions that alter the state of the computer in some persistent way) as arguments to macros for the obvious reason that the macro can invoke the argument more or less than exactly once. Consider, for example, the following code:

```
int a = 2, b = 42, c;
c = min(a++, b);
```

What's the value of **a** afterward? (For that matter, what's the value of **c**?) Take a look at a plausible implementation of **min** as a macro:

```
#define min(x,y) (((x) < (y)) ? (x) : (y))
```

If you substitute **a++** for **x**, you can see that **a** will equal 4 because the expression **a++** gets executed twice. The value of the "function" **min** will be 3 instead of the expected 2 because the second invocation of **a++** delivers the value.

You basically can't tell when the DDK will use a macro and when it will declare a real external function. Sometimes, a particular service function will be a macro for some platforms and a function call for other platforms. Furthermore, Microsoft is free to change its mind in the future. Consequently, you should follow this rule when programming a WDM driver:

> Never use an expression that has side effects as an argument to a kernel-mode service function.

ERROR HANDLING

To err is human, to recover is part of software engineering. Exceptional conditions are always arising in programs. Some of them start with program bugs, either in our own code or in the user-mode applications that invoke our code. Some of them relate to system load or the instantaneous state of hardware. Whatever the cause, unusual circumstances demand a flexible response from our code. In this section, I'll describe three aspects of error handling: status codes, structured exception handling, and bug checks. In general, kernel-mode support routines report unexpected errors by returning a status code, whereas they report expected variations in normal flow by returning a Boolean or numeric value other than a formal status code. Structured exception handling offers a standardized way to clean up after really unexpected events, such as dividing by zero or dereferencing an invalid pointer, or to avoid the system crash that normally ensues after such an event. A *bug check* is the internal name for a catastrophic failure for which a system shutdown is the only cure.

Status Codes

Kernel-mode support routines (and your code too, for that matter) indicate success or failure by returning a status code to their caller. An NTSTATUS value is a 32-bit integer composed of several subfields, as illustrated in Figure 3-2. The high-order two bits denote the severity of the condition being reported—success, information, warning, or error. The customer bit is, I believe, a vestige of the 1960s when IBM reserved customer fields for local modification of its mainframe operating systems. I can't think of a current use for a customer field. The facility code indicates which system component originated the message and basically serves to decouple development groups from each other when it comes to assigning numbers to codes. The remainder of the status code—16 bits' worth—indicates the exact condition being reported.

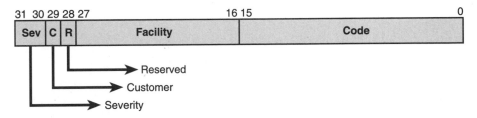

Figure 3-2. *Format of an NTSTATUS code.*

You should always check the status returns from routines that provide them. I'm going to break this rule frequently in some of the code fragments I show you because including all the necessary error handling code often obscures the expository purpose of the fragment. But don't you emulate this sloppy practice!

If the high-order bit of a status code is zero, any number of the remaining bits could be set and the code would still indicate success. Consequently, never just compare status codes to zero to see if you're dealing with success—instead, use the NT_SUCCESS macro:

```
NTSTATUS status = SomeFunction(...);
if (!NT_SUCCESS(status))
  {
  <handle error>
  }
```

Not only do you want to test the status codes you receive from routines you call, but you also want to return status codes to the routines that call you. In the preceding chapter, I dealt with two driver subroutines—**DriverEntry** and **AddDevice**—that are both defined as returning NTSTATUS codes. As I discussed, you want to return NT_SUCCESS as the success indicator from these routines. If something goes wrong, you often want to return an appropriate status code, which is sometimes the same value that a routine returned to you.

As an example, here are some initial steps in the AddDevice function, with all the error checking left in:

```
NTSTATUS AddDevice(PDRIVER_OBJECT DriverObject, PDEVICE_OBJECT pdo)
  {
  NTSTATUS status;
  PDEVICE_OBJECT fdo;
  status = IoCreateDevice(DriverObject, sizeof(DEVICE_EXTENSION),
    NULL, FILE_DEVICE_UNKNOWN, 0, FALSE, &fdo);
  if (!NT_SUCCESS(status))
    {
    KdPrint(("IoCreateDevice failed - %X\n", status));
    return status;
    }
  PDEVICE_EXTENSION pdx = (PDEVICE_EXTENSION) fdo->DeviceExtension;
  pdx->DeviceObject = fdo;
  pdx->Pdo = pdo;
  pdx->state = STOPPED;
  IoInitializeRemoveLock(&pdx->RemoveLock, 0, 0, 255);
  status = IoRegisterDeviceInterface(pdo, &GUID_SIMPLE, NULL,
    &pdx->ifname);
  if (!NT_SUCCESS(status))
    {
    KdPrint(("IoRegisterDeviceInterface failed - %X\n", status));
    IoDeleteDevice(fdo);
    return status;
    }
  ...
  }
```

1. If **IoCreateDevice** fails, we'll simply return the same status code it gave us. Note the use of the NT_SUCCESS macro as described in the text.

2. It's sometimes a good idea, especially while debugging a driver, to print any error status you discover. I'll discuss the exact usage of **KdPrint** later in this chapter (in the "Making Debugging Easier" section).

3. **IoInitializeRemoveLock**, discussed in Chapter 6, "Plug and Play," is a VOID function, meaning that it can't fail. Consequently, there's no need to check a status code.

4. Should **IoRegisterDeviceInterface** fail, we have some cleanup to do before we return to our caller; namely, we must call **IoDeleteDevice** to destroy the device object we just created.

You don't always have to fail calls that lead to errors in the routines you call, of course. Sometimes you can ignore an error. For example, in Chapter 8, "Power Management," I'll tell you about a power management I/O request with the subtype IRP_MN_POWER_SEQUENCE that you can use as an optimization to avoid unnecessary state restoration during a power-up operation. Not only is it optional whether you use this request, but it's also optional for the bus driver to implement it. Therefore, if that request should fail, you should just go about your business. Similarly, you can ignore an error from **IoAllocateErrorLogEntry** because the inability to add an entry to the error log isn't at all critical.

Structured Exception Handling

Windows NT provides a method of handling exceptional conditions that helps you avoid potential system crashes. Closely integrated with the compiler's code generator, *structured exception handling* lets you easily place a guard on sections of your code and invoke exception handlers when something goes wrong in the guarded section. Structured exception handling also lets you easily provide cleanup statements that you can be sure will always execute no matter how control leaves a guarded section of code.

Very few of my seminar students have been familiar with structured exceptions, so I'm going to explain some of the basics here. You can write better, more bulletproof code if you use these facilities. In many situations, the parameters that you receive in a WDM driver have been thoroughly vetted by other code and won't cause you to generate inadvertent exceptions. Good taste may, therefore, be the only impetus for you to use the stuff I'm describing in this section. As a general rule, though, you *always* want to protect direct references to user-mode virtual memory with a structured exception frame. Such references occur when you call **MmProbeAndLockPages**, **ProbeForRead**, and **ProbeForWrite**, and perhaps at other times.

> **NOTE** The structured exception mechanism will let you avoid a system crash when kernel-mode code accesses an invalid user-mode address. It will *not* catch other processor exceptions, such as division by zero or attempts to access invalid kernel-mode addresses. In this respect, the whole facility is less universal in kernel mode than in user mode.

Kernel-mode programs use structured exceptions by establishing *exception frames* on the same stack that's used for argument passing, subroutine calling, and automatic variables. I'm not going to describe the mechanics of this process in detail because it differs from one Windows NT platform to another. The mechanism is the same as the one that user-mode programs use, though, and there are a couple of places you can look for implementation details. See, for example, Matt Pietrek's article "A Crash Course on the Depths of Win32 Structured Exception Handling" in *Microsoft Systems Journal* (January 1997). And Jeff Richter discusses the subject in *Programming Applications for Microsoft Windows, Fourth Edition* (Microsoft Press, 1999).

When an exception arises, the operating system scans the stack of exception frames looking for a handler. Refer to Figure 3-3 for a flowchart depicting the logic. In effect, each exception frame designates a filter function that the system calls to answer the question, "Can you handle this exception?" When the system finds a handler, it unwinds the exception and execution stacks in parallel to restore the context of the handler. The unwinding process involves calling the same set of filter functions with an argument that indicates, in effect, "We're unwinding now; if you answered *yes* the last time, take over now!" There's always a default handler in place that crashes the system if no one else fields the exception.

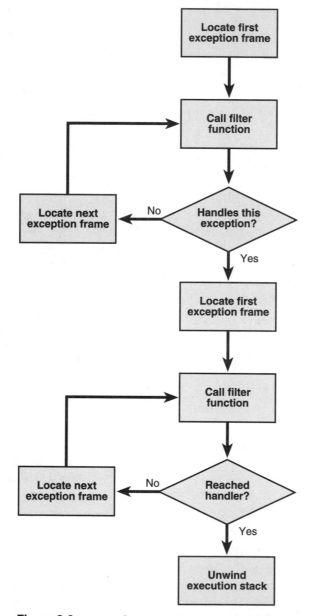

Figure 3-3. *Logic of structured exception handling.*

When you use the Microsoft compiler, you can use Microsoft extensions to the C/C++ language that hide some of the complexities of working with the raw operating system primitives. In particular, you use the __**try** statement to designate a compound statement as the *guarded body* for an exception frame, and you use either the __**finally** statement to establish a *termination handler* or the __**except** statement to establish an *exception handler*. Run-time library routines interact with the operating system's raw exception mechanisms to produce the effects that I'll describe in the following sections.

> **NOTE** It's better to always spell the words __**try**, __**finally**, and __**except** with leading underscores. In C compilation units, the DDK header file WARNING.H defines macros spelled **try**, **finally**, and **except** to be the words with underscores. DDK sample programs use those macro names rather than the underscored names. The problem this can create for you is that in a C++ compilation unit **try** is a statement verb that pairs with **catch** to invoke a completely different exception mechanism that's part of the C++ language. C++ exceptions don't work in a driver unless you manage to duplicate some infrastructure from the run-time library. Microsoft would prefer you not do that because of the increased size of your driver and the memory pool overhead associated with handling the **throw** verb.

Try-Finally Blocks

It's easiest to begin explaining structured exception handling by describing the *try-finally* block, which you can use to provide cleanup code:

```
__try
  {
  <guarded body>
  }
__finally
  {
  <termination handler>
  }
```

In this fragment of pseudocode, the guarded body is a series of statements and subroutine calls that expresses some main idea in your program. In general, these statements have side effects. If there are no side effects, there's no particular point to using a try-finally block because there's nothing to clean up. The termination handler contains statements that undo some or all of the side effects that the guarded body might leave behind.

Semantically, the try-finally block works as follows. First, the computer executes the guarded body. When control leaves the guarded body *for any reason,* the computer executes the termination handler. See Figure 3-4.

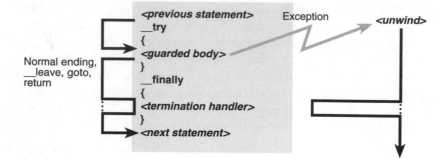

Figure 3-4. *Flow of control in a try-finally block.*

Here's one simple illustration:

```
LONG counter = 0;
__try
  {
  ++counter;
  }
__finally
  {
  --counter;
  }
KdPrint(("%d\n", counter));
```

First, the guarded body executes and increments the **counter** variable from 0 to 1. When control "drops through" the right-brace at the end of the guarded body, the termination handler executes and decrements **counter** back to 0. The value printed will therefore be 0.

Here's a slightly more complicated variation:

```
VOID RandomFunction(PLONG pcounter)
  {
  __try
    {
    ++*pcounter;
    return;
    }
  __finally
    {
    --*pcounter;
    }
  }
```

The net result of this function is no change to the integer at the end of the **pcounter** pointer: whenever control leaves the guarded body *for any reason,* including a **return** statement or a **goto,** the termination handler executes. Here the guarded body increments the counter and performs a return. Next the cleanup code executes and decrements the counter. Then the subroutine actually returns.

One final example should cement the idea of a try-finally block:

```
static LONG counter = 0;
__try
  {
  ++counter;
  BadActor();
  }
__finally
  {
  --counter;
  }
```

Here I'm supposing that we call a function, **BadActor**, that will raise some sort of exception that triggers a stack unwind. As part of the process of unwinding the execution and exception stacks, the operating system will invoke our cleanup code to restore the counter to its previous value. The system then continues unwinding the stack, so whatever code we have after the **__finally** block won't get executed.

Try-Except Blocks

The other way to use structured exception handling involves a *try-except* block:

```
__try
  {
  <guarded body>
  }
__except(<filter expression>)
  {
  <exception handler>
  }
```

The guarded body in a try-except block is code that might fail by generating an exception. Perhaps you're going to call a kernel-mode service function like MmProbeAndLockPages that uses pointers derived from user mode without explicit validity checking. Perhaps you have other reasons. In any case, if you manage to get all the way through the guarded body without an error, control continues after the exception handler code. You'll think of this case as being the normal one. If an exception arises in your code or in any of the subroutines you call, however, the operating system will unwind the execution stack, evaluating the filter expressions in __except statements. These expressions yield one of the following values:

- EXCEPTION_EXECUTE_HANDLER is numerically equal to 1 and tells the operating system to transfer control to your exception handler. If your handler falls through the ending right-brace, control continues within your program at the statement immediately following that right-brace. (I've seen Platform SDK documentation to the effect that control returns to the point of the exception, but that's not correct.)

- EXCEPTION_CONTINUE_SEARCH is numerically equal to 0 and tells the operating system that you can't handle the exception. The system keeps scanning up the stack looking for another handler. If no one has provided a handler for the exception, a system crash will occur.

- EXCEPTION_CONTINUE_EXECUTION is numerically equal to −1 and tells the operating system to return to the point where the exception was raised. I'll have a bit more to say about this expression value a little further on.

Take a look at Figure 3-5 for the possible control paths within and around a try-except block.

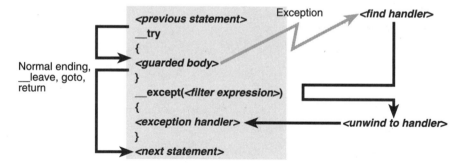

Figure 3-5. *Flow of control in a try-except block.*

For example, you could protect yourself from receiving an invalid pointer by using code like the following. (See the SEHTEST sample on the companion disc.)

```
PVOID p = (PVOID) 1;
__try
  {
  KdPrint(("About to generate exception\n"));
  ProbeForWrite(p, 4, 4);
  KdPrint(("You shouldn't see this message\n"));
  }
```

```
__except(EXCEPTION_EXECUTE_HANDLER)
  {
  KdPrint(("Exception was caught\n"));
  }
KdPrint(("Program kept control after exception\n"));
```

ProbeForWrite tests a data area for validity. In this example, it will raise an exception because the pointer argument we supply is not aligned to a 4-byte boundary. The exception handler gains control. Control then flows to the next statement after the exception handler and continues within your program.

In the preceding example, had you returned the value EXCEPTION_CONTINUE_ SEARCH, the operating system would have continued unwinding the stack looking for an exception handler. Neither your exception handler code nor the code following it would have been executed: either the system would have crashed or some higher-level handler would have taken over.

You should not return EXCEPTION_CONTINUE_EXECUTION in kernel mode because you have no way to alter the conditions that caused the exception in order to allow a retry to occur.

Note that you cannot trap arithmetic exceptions, page faults, actual references through invalid pointers, and the like by using structured exceptions. You just have to write your code so as not to generate such exceptions.

Exception Filter Expressions

You might be wondering how to perform any sort of involved error detection or correction when all you're allowed to do is evaluate an expression that yields one of three integer values. You could use the C/C++ comma operator to string expressions together:

```
__except(expr-1, ... EXCEPTION_CONTINUE_SEARCH){}
```

RAW EXCEPTION HANDLING VS. MICROSOFT SYNTAX

The statements __**try**, __**except**, and __**finally** are Microsoft extensions to the C language that simplify use of the underlying raw exception handling mechanism that the operating system provides. In the flowchart in Figure 3-3 on page 78, I illustrated *two* calls to each filter function—one for locating the exception handler and the other for stack unwinding. The run-time library contains the actual filter function that the operating system calls. When you use __try, __except, and __finally, you're talking to other run-time library functions that work with that filter function and the operating system to yield the simpler model I've been describing. In particular, the *filter expression* that you use in an __except clause gets evaluated only once per exception.

The comma operator basically discards whatever value is on its left side and evaluates its right side. The value that's left over after this computational game of musical chairs (with just one chair!) is the value of the expression.

You could use the C/C++ conditional operator to perform some more involved calculation:

```
__except(<some-expr>
    ? EXCEPTION_EXECUTE_HANDLER
    : EXCEPTION_CONTINUE_SEARCH)
```

If the *some_expr* expression is TRUE, you execute your own handler. Otherwise, you tell the operating system to keep looking for another handler above you in the stack.

Finally, it should be obvious that you could just write a subroutine whose return value is one of the EXCEPTION_*Xxx* values:

```
LONG EvaluateException()
  {
  if (<some-expr>)
    return EXCEPTION_EXECUTE_HANDLER;
  else
    return EXCEPTION_CONTINUE_SEARCH;
  }


...
__except(EvaluateException())
...
```

For any of these expression formats to do you any good, you need access to more information about the exception. There are two functions you can call when evaluating an __except expression that will supply the information you need. Both functions actually have intrinsic implementations in the Microsoft compiler and can be used only at the specific times indicated:

- **GetExceptionCode()** returns the numeric code for the current exception. This value is an NTSTATUS value that you can compare with manifest constants in NTSTATUS.H if you want to. This function is available in an __except expression and within the exception handler code that follows the __except clause.

- **GetExceptionInformation()** returns the address of an EXCEPTION_POINTERS structure that, in turn, allows you to learn all the details about the exception, such as where it occurred, what the machine registers contained at the time, and so on. This function is available only within an __except expression.

NOTE The scope rules for names that appear in try-except and try-finally blocks are the same as elsewhere in the C/C++ language. In particular, if you declare variables within the scope of the compound statement that follows __try, those names are not visible in a filter expression, exception handler, or termination handler. Documentation to the contrary that you might have seen in the Platform SDK or on MSDN is incorrect. For what it's worth, the stack frame containing any local variables declared within the scope of the guarded body still exists at the time the filter expression is evaluated. So, if you had a pointer (presumably declared at some outer scope) to a variable declared within the guarded body, you could safely dereference it in a filter expression.

Because of the restrictions on how you can use these two expressions in your program, you'd probably want to use them in a function call to some filter function, like this:

```
LONG EvaluateException(NTSTATUS status, PEXCEPTION_POINTERS xp)
  {
  ...
  }
...
__except(EvaluateException(GetExceptionCode(),
  GetExceptionInformation()))
...
```

Raising Exceptions

Program bugs are one way you can (inadvertently) raise exceptions that invoke the structured exception handling mechanism. Application programmers are familiar with the Win32 API function **RaiseException**, which allows you to generate an arbitrary exception on your own. In WDM drivers, you can call the routines listed in Table 3-1. I'm not going to give you a specific example of calling these functions because of the following rule:

Only raise an exception in nonarbitrary thread context when you know there's an exception handler above you and you otherwise really know what you're doing.

Service Function	Description
ExRaiseStatus	Raise exception with specified status code
ExRaiseAccessViolation	Raise STATUS_ACCESS_VIOLATION
ExRaiseDatatypeMisalignment	Raise STATUS_DATATYPE_MISALIGNMENT

Table 3-1. *Service functions for raising exceptions.*

In particular, raising exceptions is not a good way to tell your callers information that you discover in the ordinary course of executing. It's far better to return a status code, even though that leads to apparently more unreadable code. You should eschew exceptions because the stack-unwinding mechanism is very expensive. Even the cost of establishing exception frames is significant and something to avoid when you can.

Some Real-World Examples

Notwithstanding the expense of setting up and tearing down exception frames, you have to use structured exception syntax in an ordinary driver in particular situations. And on some other occasions when time isn't of the essence, you might as well use this mechanism because you'll end up with a better program.

One of the times you must set up an exception handler is when you call **MmProbeAndLockPages** to lock the pages for a memory descriptor list (MDL) you've created. This wouldn't be a frequent problem for a WDM driver, because you typically deal with MDLs for which someone else has already done the probe-and-lock step. But you're allowed to define I/O control (IOCTL) operations that use the METHOD_NEITHER buffering method, and you might therefore need to write code like the following:

```
PMDL mdl = MmCreateMdl(...);
__try
  {
  MmProbeAndLockPages(mdl, ...);
  }
__except(EXCEPTION_EXECUTE_HANDLER)
  {
  NTSTATUS status = GetExceptionCode();
  ExFreePool((PVOID) mdl);
  return CompleteRequest(Irp, status, 0);
  }
```

(**CompleteRequest** is a helper function I use to handle the mechanics of completing I/O requests. Chapter 5, "The I/O Request Packet," explains all about I/O requests and what it means to complete one. **ExFreePool** is a kernel-mode service routine that releases a memory block, such as the one that **MmCreateMdl** creates. I'll discuss ExFreePool later in this chapter in "Releasing a Memory Block.")

For another real-world example, consider the code I showed you earlier in this chapter for dealing with errors in your AddDevice function. As you progress through the function, you keep accumulating side effects that all have to be undone if you discover an error. You could use structured exception handling to make the function more maintainable. I'm omitting a bunch of stuff in this example to emphasize the error-handling aspects:

```
NTSTATUS AddDevice(...)
  {
  NTSTATUS status = STATUS_UNSUCCESSFUL;
  PDEVICE_OBJECT fdo;
```

```
PDEVICE_EXTENSION pdx;
status = IoCreateDevice(..., &fdo);
if (!NT_SUCCESS(status))
  return status;
__try
  {
  pdx = (PDEVICE_EXTENSION) fdo->DeviceExtension;
  ...
  IoInitializeRemoveLock(&pdx->RemoveLock, ...);
  status = IoRegisterDeviceInterface(..., &pdx->ifname);
  if (!NT_SUCCESS(status))
    return status;
  ...
  }
__finally
  {
  if (!NT_SUCCESS(status))
    {
    ...
    if (pdx->ifname.Buffer)
      RtlFreeUnicodeString(&pdx->ifname);
    IoDeleteDevice(fdo);
    }
  }
return status;
}
```

The key idea here is that whenever we discover an error status from some service function, we just execute a **return status** statement. (See the next sidebar for a description of a more efficient technique.) The return status statement triggers execution of the termination handler, which undoes each of the side effects that have accumulated so far. For this technique to work properly, you have to do two things. Since the termination handler is always executed, even by the normal ending of the guarded body, you have to know when to undo side effects and when not to undo them. Here we test the **status** variable. If it's a success code of some kind, we don't do any cleanup. Otherwise, we undo everything. The second thing you have to do is provide a way to know which side effects need to be cleaned up. We dealt with that concern by initializing all the side-effect variables to NULL. If we never succeed in registering a device interface, there won't be a string in **pdx->ifname** to release. And so on.

The biggest advantage of a try-finally block in a situation like that I just showed you is that your code is easier to modify. You can put any statement at all—even one which returns a status code and leaves behind a side effect if it succeeds—in between, say, the call to **IoCreateDevice** and the call to **IoRegisterDeviceInterface**. All you need do to ensure proper cleanup is add a compensating statement inside the termination handler. The alternative—having explicit cleanup code after every test of the status code—is prone to error because you must remember to add a new cleanup statement in every place where you might exit the subroutine.

THE __LEAVE STATEMENT

Microsoft added the __**leave** statement to the C/C++ language to deal with an efficiency problem that arises in routines like the AddDevice example in the text. If you issue a normal return inside a __try block, you trigger the expensive unwinding mechanism that the operating system uses for exception handling. The __leave statement, however, just transfers control to the termination handler and, thereafter, to the statement following the termination handler. It's much faster than return because it doesn't cause any unwinding. In this case, we always want to execute the termination handler and then return a status code. Since the code we want to execute in both success and failure cases is the same (namely, **return status**), we should use __**leave** instead of **return**.

So, suppose we needed to allocate a block of memory for some auxiliary purpose. We could just insert a few statements in AddDevice like so (with the new parts in boldface):

```
NTSTATUS AddDevice(...)
  {
  NTSTATUS status = STATUS_UNSUCCESSFUL;
  PDEVICE_OBJECT fdo;
  PDEVICE_EXTENSION pdx;
  status = IoCreateDevice(..., &fdo);
  if (!NT_SUCCESS(status))
    return status;
  __try
    {
    pdx = (PDEVICE_EXTENSION) fdo->DeviceExtension;
    ...
    pdx->DeviceDescriptor = (PUSB_DEVICE_DESCRIPTOR)
      ExAllocatePool(NonPagedPool, sizeof(USB_DEVICE_DESCRIPTOR));
    if (!pdx->DeviceDescriptor)
      return STATUS_INSUFFICIENT_RESOURCES;
    IoInitializeRemoveLock(&pdx->RemoveLock, ...);
    status = IoRegisterDeviceInterface(..., &pdx->ifname);
    if (!NT_SUCCESS(status))
      return status;
    ...
    }
```

```
__finally
  {
  if (!NT_SUCCESS(status))
    {
    ...
    if (pdx->ifname.Buffer)
      RtlFreeUnicodeString(&pdx->ifname);
    if (pdx->DeviceDescriptor)
      ExFreePool((PVOID) pdx->DeviceDescriptor);
    IoDeleteDevice(fdo);
    }
  }
return status;
}
```

Without using structured exceptions, you'd need to go through the rest of the program and add a call to ExFreePool to every code sequence that returns an error.

Bug Checks

Unrecoverable errors in kernel mode manifest themselves in the so-called *blue screen of death* (BSOD) that's all too familiar to driver programmers. Figure 3-6 is an example (hand-painted because there's no screen capture software running when one of these occurs!). Internally, these errors are called bug checks after the service function you use to diagnose their occurrence: **KeBugCheckEx**. The main feature of a bug check is that the system shuts itself down in as orderly a way as possible and presents the BSOD. Once the BSOD appears, the system is dead and must be rebooted.

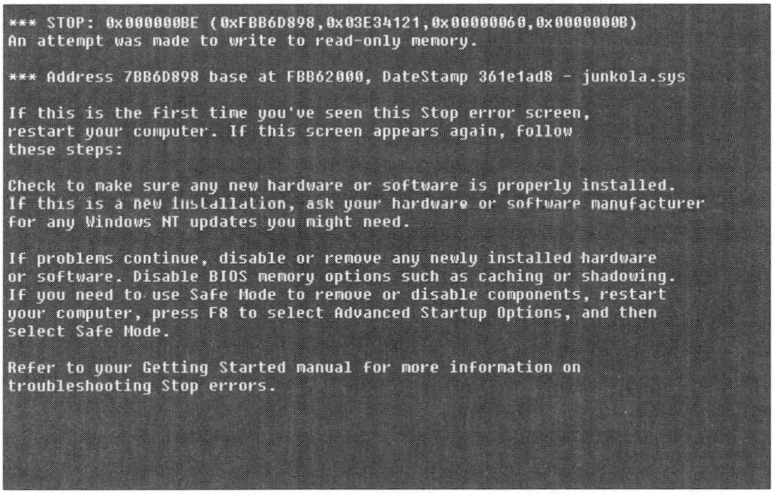

```
*** STOP: 0x000000BE (0xFBB6D898,0x03E34121,0x00000060,0x0000000B)
An attempt was made to write to read-only memory.

*** Address 7BB6D898 base at FBB62000, DateStamp 361e1ad8 - junkola.sys

If this is the first time you've seen this Stop error screen,
restart your computer. If this screen appears again, follow
these steps:

Check to make sure any new hardware or software is properly installed.
If this is a new installation, ask your hardware or software manufacturer
for any Windows NT updates you might need.

If problems continue, disable or remove any newly installed hardware
or software. Disable BIOS memory options such as caching or shadowing.
If you need to use Safe Mode to remove or disable components, restart
your computer, press F8 to select Advanced Startup Options, and then
select Safe Mode.

Refer to your Getting Started manual for more information on
troubleshooting Stop errors.
```

Figure 3-6. *The "blue screen of death."*

You call KeBugCheckEx like this:

```
KeBugCheckEx(bugcode, info1, info2, info3, info4);
```

where **bugcode** is a numeric value identifying the cause of the error, and **info1**, **info2**, and so on are integer parameters that will appear in the BSOD display to help some programmer understand the details of the error. This function does not return (!).

I'm not going to describe here how to interpret the information in a BSOD or in a crash dump. Section 17.3 in Art Baker's *The Windows NT Device Driver Book* (Prentice Hall, 1997) is one place you can go for more information. Microsoft's own bugcheck codes appear in BUGCODES.H (one of the DDK headers); a fuller explanation of the codes and their various parameters can be found in Knowledge Base article Q103059, "Descriptions of Bug Codes for Windows NT," which is available on MSDN, among other places.

You can certainly create your own bugcheck codes if you want. The Microsoft values are simple integers beginning with 1 (APC_INDEX_MISMATCH) and (currently) extending through 0xDE (POOL_CORRUPTION_IN_FILE_AREA) along with a few others. To create your own bugcheck code, define an integer constant as if it were STATUS_SEVERITY_SUCCESS status code, but supply either the customer flag or a nonzero facility code. For example:

```
#define MY_BUGCHECK_CODE 0x002A0001
...
KeBugCheckEx(MY_BUGCHECK_CODE, 0, 0, 0, 0);
```

You use a nonzero facility code (42 in this example) or the customer flag (which I left zero in this example) so that you can tell your own codes from the ones Microsoft uses.

Now that I've told you *how* to generate your own BSOD, let me tell you *when* to do it: never. Or, at most, in the checked build of your driver for use during your own internal debugging. You and I are unlikely to write a driver that will discover an error so serious that taking down the system is the only solution. It would be far better to log the error (using the error-logging facilities I'll describe in Chapter 9, "Specialized Topics") and return a status code.

MEMORY MANAGEMENT

In this section, I'll discuss the topic of memory management. Windows 2000 divides the available virtual address space in several ways. One division—a very firm one based on security and integrity concerns—is between user-mode addresses and kernel-mode addresses. Another division, which is almost but not quite coextensive with the first, is between paged and nonpaged memory. All user-mode addresses and some kernel-mode addresses reference page frames that the Memory Manager swaps to and from the disk over time, while some kernel-mode addresses always reference the same page frames in physical memory. Since Windows 2000 allows portions of drivers to be paged, I'll explain how you control the pagability of your driver at the time you build your driver and at run time.

Windows 2000 provides several methods for managing memory. I'll describe two basic service functions—ExAllocatePool and ExFreePool—that you use for allocating and releasing randomly sized blocks from a heap. I'll also describe the primitives that you use for organizing memory blocks into linked lists of structures. Finally, I'll describe the concept of a *lookaside list*, which allows you to efficiently allocate and release blocks that are all the same size.

User-Mode and Kernel-Mode Address Spaces

Windows NT and Microsoft Windows 98 run on computers that support a virtual address space, wherein virtual addresses are mapped either to physical memory or (conceptually, anyway) to page frames within a swap file on disk. To grossly simplify matters, you can think of the virtual address space as being divided into two parts: a kernel-mode part and a user-mode part. See Figure 3-7.

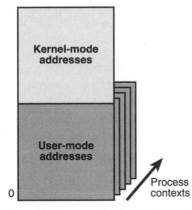

Figure 3-7. *User-mode and kernel-mode portions of the address space.*

Each user-mode process has its own address context, which maps the user-mode virtual addresses to a unique collection of physical page frames. In other words, the meaning of any particular virtual address changes from one moment to the next as the Windows NT scheduler switches from a thread in one process to a thread in another process. Part of the work in switching threads is to change the page tables used by a processor so that they refer to the incoming thread's process context.

NOTE If you're familiar with the Alpha and you're a stickler for accuracy, you'll know that Alphas don't have *page tables*. They have something different called *translation buffers* that map virtual page addresses to physical page addresses. To me, this is a distinction without a difference—on a par with saying that *The Odyssey* was written by a different Homer than the one historians used to think wrote it. But someone would have sent me an email pointing this out if I didn't say it first.

It's generally unlikely that a WDM driver will execute in the same thread context as the initiator of the I/O requests it handles. We say that we're running "in arbitrary thread context" if we don't know for sure to which process the current user-mode address context belongs. In arbitrary thread context, we simply can't use a virtual address that belongs to user mode because we can't have any idea to what physical memory it might point. In view of this uncertainty, we generally obey the following rule inside a driver program:

Never (well, hardly ever) directly reference user-mode memory.

In other words, don't take an address that a user-mode application provides and treat that address as a pointer that we can directly dereference. I'll discuss in later chapters a few techniques for accessing data buffers that originate in user mode. All we need to know right now, though, is that we're (nearly) always going to be using kernel-mode virtual addresses whenever we want to access the computer's memory.

How Big Is a Page?

In a virtual memory system, the operating system organizes physical memory and the swap file into like-sized page frames. In a WDM driver, you can use the manifest constant PAGE_SIZE to tell you how big a page is. In some Windows NT computers, a page is 4096 bytes long; in others, it's 8192 bytes long. There's a related constant named PAGE_SHIFT that equals the page size as a power of two. That is:

```
PAGE_SIZE == 1 << PAGE_SHIFT
```

For your convenience, you can use a few preprocessor macros in your code when you're working with the size of a page:

- ROUND_TO_PAGES rounds a size in bytes to the next higher page boundary. For example, ROUND_TO_PAGES(1) is 4096 on a 4 KB–page computer.

- BYTES_TO_PAGES determines how many pages are required to hold a given number of bytes beginning at the start of a page. For example, BYTES_TO_PAGES(42) would be 1 on all platforms, and BYTES_TO_PAGES(5000) would be 2 on some platforms and 1 on others.

- BYTE_OFFSET returns the byte offset portion of a virtual address. That is, it calculates the starting offset within some page frame of a given address. On a 4 KB–page computer, BYTE_OFFSET(0x12345678) would be 0x678.

- PAGE_ALIGN rounds a virtual address down to a page boundary. On a 4 KB–page computer, PAGE_ALIGN(0x12345678) would be 0x12345000.

- ADDRESS_AND_SIZE_TO_SPAN_PAGES returns the number of page frames occupied by a specified number of bytes beginning at a specified virtual address. For example, ADDRESS_AND_SIZE_TO_SPAN_PAGES(0x12345FFF, 2) is 2 on a 4 KB–page machine because the two bytes span a page boundary.

Paged and Nonpaged Memory

The whole point of a virtual memory system is that you can have a virtual address space that's much bigger than the amount of physical memory on the computer. To accomplish this feat, the Memory Manager needs to swap page frames in and out of physical memory. Certain parts of the operating system can't be paged, though, because they're needed to support the Memory Manager itself. The most obvious example of something that must always be resident in memory is the code that handles page faults (the exceptions that occur when a page frame isn't physically present when needed) and the data structures used by the page fault handler. But the category of "must be resident" stuff is much broader than that.

Windows NT divides the kernel-mode address space into paged and nonpaged memory pools. (The user-mode address space is always pagable.) Things that must always be resident are in the nonpaged pool; things that can come and go on demand are in the paged pool. Windows NT provides a simple rule for deciding whether your code and the data it uses must be resident. I'll elaborate on the rule in the next chapter, but here it is anyway:

Code executing at or above interrupt request level (IRQL) DISPATCH_LEVEL cannot cause page faults.

You can use the PAGED_CODE preprocessor macro (declared in WDM.H) to help you discover violations of this rule in the checked build of your driver. For example:

```
NTSTATUS DispatchPower(PDEVICE_OBJECT fdo, PIRP Irp)
  {
  PAGED_CODE()
  ...
  }
```

PAGED_CODE contains conditional compilation. In the checked-build environment, it prints a message and generates an assertion failure if the current IRQL is too high. In the free-build environment, it doesn't do anything. If you were to test your driver in a situation where the page containing **DispatchPower** happened fortuitously to be in memory, you would never discover that it had been called at an elevated IRQL. PAGED_CODE will detect the problem even so. A bug check would occur if the page happened to not be present, so you would certainly learn about the problem then!

THE DRIVER VERIFIER

The Driver Verifier feature of Windows 2000 helps you debug many features of your driver, including the placement of programs into sections, your use of the memory heap, and so on. This feature was still in flux at press time, so I can't say much more about it here. But notice that the PAGED_CODE macro spots a problem only in the checked build of your driver that exists at the point where you invoke it. The Driver Verifier can diagnose a problem arising anywhere in a function, even with the free build of the driver.

Compile-Time Control of Pagability

Given that some parts of your driver must always be resident and some parts can be paged, you need a way to control the assignment of your code and data to the paged and nonpaged pools. You accomplish part of this job by instructing the compiler how to apportion your code and data among various sections. The run-time loader uses the names of the sections to put parts of your driver in the places you intend. You can also accomplish parts of this job at run time by calling various Memory Manager routines that I'll discuss in the next section.

> **NOTE** Win32 executable files, including kernel-mode drivers, are internally composed of one or more *sections.* A section can contain code or data and, generally speaking, has additional attributes such as being readable, writable, sharable, executable, and so on. A section is also the smallest unit that you can designate when you're specifying pagability. When loading a driver image, the system puts sections whose literal names begin with "page" or ".eda" (the start of ".edata") into the paged pool unless the **DisablePagingExecutive** value in the HKLM\System\CurrentControlSet\Control\Session Manager\Memory Management key happens to be set (in which case no driver paging occurs). In one of the little twists of fate that affect us all from time to time, running Soft-Ice/W on Windows 2000 requires you to disable kernel paging in this way. This certainly makes it harder to find bugs caused by misplacement of driver code or data into the paged pool! If you use this debugger, I recommend that you religiously use the PAGED_CODE macro *and* the Driver Verifier.

The traditional way of telling the compiler to put code into a particular section is to use the **alloc_text** pragma. Since not every compiler will necessarily support the pragma, the DDK headers either define or don't define the constant ALLOC_PRAGMA to tell you whether to use the pragma. You can then invoke the pragma to specify the section placement of individual subroutines in your driver, as follows:

```
#ifdef ALLOC_PRAGMA
  #pragma alloc_text(PAGE, AddDevice)
  #pragma alloc_text(PAGE, DispatchPnp)
  ...
#endif
```

These statements serve to place the **AddDevice** and **DispatchPnp** functions into the paged pool.

The Microsoft C/C++ compiler places two annoying restrictions on using alloc_text:

■ The pragma must follow the declaration of a function but precede the definition. One way to obey this rule is to declare all the functions in your driver in a standard header file and invoke alloc_text at the start of the source file that contains a given function but after you include that header.

■ The pragma can be used only with functions that have C-linkage. In other words, it won't work for class member functions or for functions in a C++ source file that you didn't declare using **extern "C"**.

To control the placement of data variables, you use a different pragma under control of a different preprocessor macro symbol:

```
#ifdef ALLOC_DATA_PRAGMA
  #pragma data_seg("PAGE")
#endif
```

The **data_seg** pragma causes all static data variables declared in a source module after the appearance of the pragma to go into the paged pool. You'll notice that this pragma differs in a fundamental way from alloc_text. A pagable section starts where **#pragma data_seg("PAGE")** appears and ends where a countervailing **#pragma data_seg()** appears. Alloc_text, on the other hand, applies to a specific function.

Think twice before putting some of your data into a pagable section, because you might actually be making things worse. The smallest unit that can be paged is PAGE_SIZE long. It's probably silly to put just a few bytes into a pagable section. You'll end up using an entire page worth of memory. Consider, too, that a data page is often "dirty" (that is, changed since it was fetched from disk) and would need to be rewritten to disk before its physical page frame could be reused for another purpose.

MORE ABOUT SECTION PLACEMENT

In general, I find it more convenient to specify the section placement of whole blocks of code by using the Microsoft **code_seg** pragma, which works the same way as data_seg, only for code. That is, you can tell the Microsoft compiler to start putting functions into the paged pool like this:

```
#pragma code_seg("PAGE")
NTSTATUS AddDevice(...){...}
NTSTATUS DispatchPnp(...){...}
```

The **AddDevice** and **DispatchPnp** functions would both end up in the paged pool. You can check to see whether you're compiling with the Microsoft compiler by testing the existence of the predefined preprocessor macro **_MSC_VER**.

To revert to the default code section, just code **#pragma code_seg** with no argument:

```
#pragma code_seg()
```

Similarly, to revert to the regular nonpaged data section, code **#pragma data_seg** with no argument:

```
#pragma data_seg()
```

This sidebar is also the logical place to mention that you can also direct code into the INIT section if it's not needed once your driver finishes initializing. For example:

```
#pragma alloc_text(INIT, DriverEntry)
```

This statement forces the **DriverEntry** function into the INIT section. The system will release the memory it occupies when it returns. This small savings is not very important in the grand scheme of things because a WDM driver's DriverEntry function doesn't do much work. Previous Windows NT drivers had large DriverEntry functions that had to create device objects, locate resources, configure devices, and so on. For them, using this feature offered significant memory savings.

You can use the DUMPBIN utility that comes with Microsoft Visual C++ to easily see how much of your driver is initially pagable. Your marketing department might even want to crow about how much less nonpaged memory you use than your competitors.

Run-Time Control of Pagability

Table 3-2 lists the service functions you can use at run time to fine-tune the pagability of your driver in various situations. The purpose of these routines is to let you release the physical memory that would otherwise be tied up by your code and data during periods when it won't be needed. In Chapter 8, for example, I'll discuss how you can register your device with the Power Manager so that you're automatically powered down after a period of inactivity. Powering down might be a good time to release your locked pages.

Service Function	Description
MmLockPagableCodeSection	Lock a code section given an address inside it
MmLockPagableDataSection	Lock a data section given an address inside it
MmLockPagableSectionByHandle	Lock a code section by using a handle from a previous MmLockPagableCodeSection call (Windows 2000 only)
MmPageEntireDriver	Unlock all pages belonging to driver
MmResetDriverPaging	Restore compile-time pagability attributes for entire driver
MmUnlockPagableImageSection	Unlock a locked code or data section

Table 3-2. *Routines for dynamically locking and unlocking driver pages.*

I'm going to describe one way to use these functions to control the pagability of code in your driver. You might want to read the DDK descriptions to learn about other ways to use them. First distribute subroutines in your driver into separately named code sections, like this:

```
#pragma alloc_text(PAGEIDLE, DispatchRead)
#pragma alloc_text(PAGEIDLE, DispatchWrite)
...
```

That is, define a section name beginning with "PAGE" and ending in any four-character suffix you please. Then use the alloc_text pragma to place some group of your own routines into that special section. You can have as many special pagable sections as you want, but your logistical problems will grow as you subdivide your driver in this way.

During initialization (say, in **DriverEntry**), lock your pagable sections like this:

```
PVOID hPageIdleSection;
NTSTATUS DriverEntry(...)
  {
  hPageIdleSection = MmLockPagableCodeSection((PVOID) DispatchRead);
  }
```

When you call **MmLockPagableCodeSection**, you specify any address at all within the section you're trying to lock. The real purpose of making this call during DriverEntry is to obtain the handle value it returns, which I've shown you saving in a global variable named **hPageIdleSection**. You'll use that handle much later on, when you decide you don't need a particular section in memory for a while:

```
MmUnlockPagableImageSection(hPageIdleSection);
```

This call will unlock the pages containing the PAGEIDLE section and allow them to move in and out of memory on demand. If you later discover that you need those pages back again, you make this call:

```
MmLockPagableSectionByHandle(hPageIdleSection);
```

Following this call, the PAGEIDLE section will once again be in nonpaged memory (but not necessarily the same physical memory as previously). *Note that this function call is available to you only in Windows 2000, and then only if you've included NTDDK.H instead of WDM.H. In other situations, you will have to call MmLockPagableCodeSection again.*

You can do something similar to place data objects into pagable sections:

```
PVOID hPageDataSection;

#pragma data_seg("PAGE")
ULONG ulSomething;
#pragma data_seg()

hPageDataSection = MmLockPagableDataSection((PVOID) &ulSomething);

MmUnlockPagableImageSection(hPageDataSection);

MmLockPagableSectionByHandle(hPageDataSection);
```

I've played fast and loose with my syntax here—these statements would appear in widely disparate parts of your driver.

The key idea behind the Memory Manager service functions I just described is that you initially lock a section containing one or more pages and obtain a handle for use in subsequent calls. You can then unlock the pages in a particular section by calling **MmUnlockPagableImageSection** and passing the corresponding handle. Relocking the section later on requires a call to **MmLockPagableSectionByHandle**.

A quick shortcut is available if you're sure that *none* of your driver will need to be resident for a while. **MmPageEntireDriver** will mark all the sections in a driver's image as being pagable. Conversely, **MmResetDriverPaging** will restore the compile-time pagability attributes for the entire driver. To call these routines, you just need the address of some piece of code or data in the driver. For example:

```
MmPageEntireDriver((PVOID) DriverEntry);
...
MmResetDriverPaging((PVOID) DriverEntry);
```

You need to exercise care when using any of the Memory Manager routines I've just described if your device uses an interrupt. Spurious interrupts have been known to happen, and it will be very difficult for anyone to discover that the reason for some random crash is that the system tried to call your missing interrupt service routine (ISR) to handle one. The rule stated in the DDK is that you simply mustn't page your ISR or any deferred procedure call (DPC) routine it might schedule after connecting your interrupt.

Heap Allocator

The basic heap allocation service function in kernel mode used to be **ExAllocatePool**. This service is still the one referred to in most discussions of heap allocation and used by sample drivers. You call it like this:

```
PVOID p = ExAllocatePool(type, nbytes);
```

The **type** argument is one of the POOL_TYPE enumeration constants described in Table 3-3, and **nbytes** is the number of bytes you want to allocate. The return value is a kernel-mode virtual address pointer to the allocated memory block. Unless you specify either **NonPagedPoolMustSucceed** or **NonPagedPoolCacheAlignedMustS** for the pool type, you can receive back a NULL pointer if enough memory isn't available to satisfy your request. If you specify either of those two must-succeed types, lack of memory will cause a bug check with the code MUST_SUCCEED_POOL_EMPTY.

> **NOTE** Drivers should not allocate memory using one of the "must succeed" specifiers. This is because they can fail whatever operation is underway with a status code if memory is unavailable. Causing a system crash in a low-memory situation is not something a driver should do. Furthermore, only a limited pool of "must succeed" memory exists in the entire system, and the operating system might not be able to allocate memory needed to keep the computer running if drivers tie up some. In fact, Microsoft wishes they had never documented the must-succeed options in the DDK to begin with.

Pool Type	Description
NonPagedPool	Allocate from the nonpaged pool of memory
PagedPool	Allocate from the paged pool of memory
NonPagedPoolMustSucceed	Allocate from the nonpaged pool; bugcheck if unable to do so
NonPagedPoolCacheAligned	Allocate from the nonpaged pool and ensure that memory is aligned with the CPU cache
NonPagedPoolCacheAlignedMustS	Like NonPagedPoolCacheAligned, but bugcheck if unable to allocate
PagedPoolCacheAligned	Allocate from the paged pool of memory and ensure that memory is aligned with the CPU cache

Table 3-3. *Pool type arguments for ExAllocatePool.*

The most basic decision you must make when you call ExAllocatePool is whether the allocated memory block should be swapped out of memory. That choice depends simply on which parts of your driver will need to access the memory block. If you will be using a memory block at or above DISPATCH_LEVEL, you must allocate it from the nonpaged pool. If you'll always use the memory block below DISPATCH_LEVEL, you can allocate from the paged or nonpaged pool as you choose.

The memory block you receive will be aligned to at least an 8-byte boundary. If you place an instance of some structure into the allocated memory, members to which the compiler assigns an offset divisible by 4 or 8 will therefore occupy an address divisible by 4 or 8, too. On some RISC platforms, of course, you must have doubleword and quadword values aligned in this way. For performance reasons, you might want to be sure that the memory block will fit in the fewest possible number of processor cache lines. You can specify one of the *Xxx*CacheAligned type codes to achieve that result. If you ask for at least a page's worth of memory, the block will start on a page boundary.

Releasing a Memory Block

To release a memory block you previously allocated with ExAllocatePool, you call **ExFreePool**:

```
ExFreePool((PVOID) p);
```

You do need to keep track somehow of the memory you've allocated from the pool in order to release it when it's no longer needed. No one else will do that for you. You must sometimes closely read the DDK documentation of the functions you call with an eye toward memory ownership. For example, in the AddDevice function I showed you in the previous chapter, there's a call to IoRegisterDeviceInterface.

That function has a side effect: it allocates a memory block to hold the string that names the interface. *You* are responsible for releasing that memory later on.

It should go without saying that you need to be extra careful when accessing memory you've allocated from the free storage pools in kernel mode. Since driver code executes in the most privileged mode possible for the processor, there's almost no protection from wild stores.

ExAllocatePoolWithTag

I said that **ExAllocatePool** *used* to be the standard way to allocate memory from a kernel-mode heap. For some time, there has been a variant of ExAllocatePool named **ExAllocatePoolWithTag** that provides a useful extra feature. For reasons I'll explain presently, you should prefer to use this variant in new drivers even though neither I nor the authors of the DDK samples currently do. This is a clear case of "do as I [actually the people inside Microsoft who make wishes about how programmers use the DDK] say, not as I do."

When you use ExAllocatePoolWithTag, the system allocates 4 more bytes of memory than you asked for and returns you a pointer that's 4 bytes into that block. The tag occupies the initial 4 bytes and therefore precedes the pointer you receive. The tag will be visible to you when you examine memory blocks while debugging or while poring over a crash dump, and it can help you identify the source of a memory block that's involved in some problem or another. For example:

```
PVOID p = ExAllocatePoolWithTag(PagedPool, 42, 'KNUJ');
```

Here, I used a 32-bit integer constant as the tag value. On a little-endian computer like an x86, the bytes that compose this value will be reversed in memory to spell out a common word in the English language.

Pool tags are also useful as a way of controlling certain features of the Driver Verifier. Please consult the DDK documentation for more information.

It turns out that you're using ExAllocatePoolWithTag even when you think you're calling ExAllocatePool. The declarations of memory allocation functions in wdm.h are under control of a preprocessor macro named POOL_TAGGING. WDM.H (and NTDDK.H too, for that matter) unconditionally defines POOL_TAGGING, with the result that the without-tag functions are actually macro'ed to the equivalent with-tag functions with a tag value of **' mdW'** (that is, a space followed by the mirror image of "Wdm"). If POOL_TAGGING were not to be defined in some future release of the DDK, the with-tag functions would be macro'ed to the without-tag versions. Microsoft has no current plans to change the setting of POOL_TAGGING.

Because of the POOL_TAGGING macros, when you write a call to ExAllocate-Pool in your program, you end up calling ExAllocatePoolWithTag, but the tag you specify is too generic to be of much help. As it turns out, even if you managed to call ExAllocatePool by some subterfuge or another, ExAllocatePool internally calls ExAllocatePoolWithTag with a tag value of **'enoN'** (that is, "None"). Since you can't get away from memory tagging, you might as well explicitly call ExAllocatePool-WithTag and specify a usefully unique tag of your own devising. In fact, Microsoft strongly encourages you to do this.

Variations on ExAllocatePool

Although ExAllocatePoolWithTag is the function you should use for heap allocation, you would use some variations in special circumstances:

- **ExAllocatePoolWithQuota** allocates a memory block and charges the current thread's scheduling quota. This function is for use by file system drivers and other drivers running in a nonarbitrary thread context for allocating memory that belongs to the current thread.

- **ExAllocatePoolWithQuotaTag** allocates a block with a tag *and* charges the current thread's quota.

Linked Lists

Windows NT makes extensive use of linked lists as a way of organizing collections of similar data structures. In this chapter, I'll discuss the basic service functions you use to manage doubly-linked and singly-linked lists. Separate service functions allow you to share linked lists between threads and across multiple processors; I'll describe those functions in the next chapter after I've explained the synchronization primitives on which they depend.

Whether you organize data structures into a doubly-linked or a singly-linked list, you normally embed a linking substructure—either a LIST_ENTRY or a SINGLE_LIST_ENTRY—into your own data structure. You also reserve a list head element somewhere that uses the same structure as the linking element. For example:

```
typedef struct _TWOWAY
  {
  ...
  LIST_ENTRY linkfield;
  ...
  } TWOWAY, *PTWOWAY;

LIST_ENTRY DoubleHead;

typedef struct _ONEWAY
  {
  ...
  SINGLE_LIST_ENTRY linkfield;
  ...
  } ONEWAY, *PONEWAY;
```

```
SINGLE_LIST_ENTRY SingleHead;
```

When you call one of the list-management service functions, you always work with the linking field or the list head—never directly with the containing structures themselves. So, suppose you've got a pointer (**pdElement**) to one of your TWOWAY structures. To put that structure onto a list, you'd reference the embedded linking field like this:

```
InsertTailList(&DoubleHead, &pdElement->linkfield);
```

Similarly, when you retrieve an element from a list, you're really getting the address of the embedded linking field. To recover the address of the containing structure, you can use the **CONTAINING_RECORD** macro. (See Figure 3-8.)

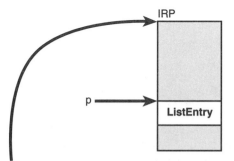

(PIRP) CONTAINING_RECORD(p, IRP, ListEntry)

Figure 3-8. *The CONTAINING_RECORD macro.*

So, if you wanted to process and discard all the elements in a singly-linked list, your code would look something like this:

```
PSINGLE_LIST_ENTRY psLink = PopEntryList(&SingleHead);
while (psLink)
  {
  PONEWAY psElement = (PONEWAY) CONTAINING_RECORD(psLink,
    ONEWAY, linkfield);
  ...
  ExFreePool(psElement);
  psLink = PopEntryList(&SingleHead);
  }
```

Just before the start of this loop, and again after every iteration, you retrieve the current first element of the list by calling **PopEntryList**. PopEntryList returns the address of the linking field within a ONEWAY structure, or else it returns NULL to signify that the list is empty. Don't just indiscriminately use CONTAINING_RECORD to develop an element address that you then test for NULL—you need to test the link field address that PopEntryList returns!

Doubly-Linked Lists

A doubly-linked list links its elements both backward and forward in a circular fashion. See Figure 3-9. That is, starting with any element, you can proceed forward or backward in a circle and get back to the same element. The key feature of a doubly-linked list is that you can add or remove elements anywhere in the list.

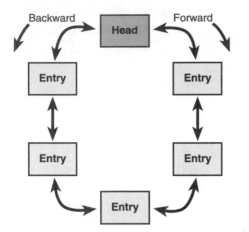

Figure 3-9. *Topology of a doubly-linked list.*

Table 3-4 lists the service functions you use to manage a doubly-linked list.

Service Function or Macro	*Description*
InitializeListHead	Initialize the LIST_ENTRY at the head of the list
InsertHeadList	Insert element at the beginning
InsertTailList	Insert element at the end
IsListEmpty	Is list empty?
RemoveEntryList	Remove element
RemoveHeadList	Remove first element
RemoveTailList	Remove last element

Table 3-4. *Service functions for use with doubly-linked lists.*

Here is a fragment of a fictitious program to illustrate how to use some of these functions:

```
typedef struct _TWOWAY {
  ...
  LIST_ENTRY linkfield;
  ...
  } TWOWAY, *PTWOWAY;
```

```
      LIST_ENTRY DoubleHead;
1     InitializeListHead(&DoubleHead);
      ASSERT(IsListEmpty(&DoubleHead));

      PTWOWAY pdElement = (PTWOWAY) ExAllocatePool(PagedPool,
        sizeof(TWOWAY));
2     InsertTailList(&DoubleHead, &pdElement->linkfield);
      ...
3     if (!IsListEmpty(&DoubleHead))
        {
4       PLIST_ENTRY pdLink = RemoveHeadList(&DoubleHead);
        pdElement = CONTAINING_RECORD(pdLink, TWOWAY, linkfield);
        ...
        ExFreePool(pdElement);
        }
```

1. **InitializeListHead** initializes a LIST_ENTRY to point (both backward and forward) to itself. That configuration indicates that the list is empty.

2. **InsertTailList** puts an element at the end of the list. Notice that you specify the address of the embedded linking field instead of your own TWOWAY structure. You could call **InsertHeadList** to put the element at the beginning of the list instead of the end. By supplying the address of the link field in some existing TWOWAY structure, you could put the new element either just before or just after the existing one.

3. Recall that an empty doubly-linked list has the list head pointing to itself, both backward and forward. Use **IsListEmpty** to simplify making this check. The return value from **Remove*Xxx*List** will never be NULL!

4. **RemoveHeadList** removes the element at the head of the list and gives you back the address of the linking field inside it. **RemoveTailList** does the same thing, just with the element at the end of the list instead.

It's important to know the exact way RemoveHeadList and RemoveTailList are implemented if you want to avoid errors. For example, consider the following innocent looking statement.

```
if (<some-expr>)
  pdLink = RemoveHeadList(&DoubleHead);
```

What I obviously intended with this construction was to conditionally extract the first element from a list. *C'est raisonnable, n'est-ce pas?* But no, when you debug this later on, you find that elements keep mysteriously disappearing from the list. You discover that **pdLink** gets updated only when the **if** expression is TRUE but that RemoveHeadList seems to get called even when the expression is FALSE.

Mon dieu! What's going on here? Well, RemoveHeadList is really a macro that expands into multiple statements. Here's what the compiler really sees in the above statement:

```
if (<some-expr>)
  pdLink = (&DoubleHead)->Flink;
{{
PLIST_ENTRY _EX_Blink;
PLIST_ENTRY _EX_Flink;
_EX_Flink = ((&DoubleHead)->Flink)->Flink;
_EX_Blink = ((&DoubleHead)->Flink)->Blink;
_EX_Blink->Flink = _EX_Flink;
_EX_Flink->Blink = _EX_Blink;
}}
```

Aha! Now the reason for the mysterious disappearance of list elements becomes clear. The TRUE branch of the **if** statement consists of just the single statement **pdLink = (&DoubleHead)->Flink** that stores a pointer to the first element. The logic that removes a list element stands alone outside the scope of the **if** statement and is therefore always executed. Both RemoveHeadList and RemoveTailList amount to an expression plus a compound statement, and you dare not use either of them in a spot where the syntax requires an expression or statement alone. *Zut alors!*

The other list-manipulation macros don't have this problem, by the way. The difficulty with RemoveHeadList and RemoveTailList arises because they have to return a value and do some list manipulation. The other macros do only one or the other, and they're syntactically safe when used as intended.

Singly-Linked Lists

A singly-linked list links its elements in only one direction, as illustrated in Figure 3-10. Windows NT uses singly-linked lists to implement pushdown stacks, as suggested by the names of the service routines in Table 3-5. Just as was true for doubly-linked lists, these "functions" are actually implemented as macros in WDM.H, and similar cautions apply. **PushEntryList** and **PopEntryList** generate multiple statements, so you can use them only on the right side of an equal sign in a context where the compiler is expecting multiple statements.

Service Function or Macro	Description
PushEntryList	Add element to top of list
PopEntryList	Remove topmost element

Table 3-5. *Service functions for use with singly-linked lists.*

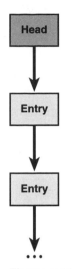

Figure 3-10. *Topology of a singly-linked list.*

The following pseudofunction illustrates how to manipulate a singly-linked list:

```
typedef struct _ONEWAY {
...
SINGLE_LIST_ENTRY linkfield;
} ONEWAY, *PONEWAY;

SINGLE_LIST_ENTRY SingleHead;
SingleHead.Next = NULL;

PONEWAY psElement = (PONEWAY) ExAllocatePool(PagedPool,
  sizeof(ONEWAY));
PushEntryList(&SingleHead, &psElement->linkfield);

SINGLE_LIST_ENTRY psLink = PopEntryList(&SingleHead);
if (psLink)
   {
   psElement = CONTAINING_RECORD(psLink, ONEWAY, linkfield);
   ...
   ExFreePool(psElement);
   }
```

1. Instead of invoking a service function to initialize the head of a singly-linked list, just set the **Next** field to NULL. Note also the absence of a service function for testing whether this list is empty; just test Next yourself.

2. **PushEntryList** puts an element at the head of the list, which is the only part of the list that's directly accessible. Notice that you specify the address of the embedded linking field instead of your own ONEWAY structure.

3. **PopEntryList** removes the first entry from the list and gives you back a pointer to the link field inside it. Unlike doubly-linked lists, a NULL value indicates that the list is empty. In fact, there's no counterpart to IsListEmpty for use with a singly-linked list.

Lookaside Lists

Even employing the best possible algorithms, a heap manager that deals with randomly sized blocks of memory will require some scarce processor time to coalesce adjacent free blocks from time to time. Figure 3-11 illustrates how, when something returns block B to the heap at a time when blocks A and C are already free, the heap manager can combine blocks A, B, and C to form a single large block. The large block is then available to satisfy some later request for a block bigger than any of the original three components.

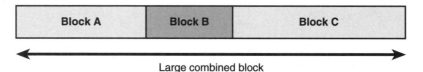

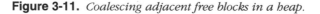

Large combined block

Figure 3-11. *Coalescing adjacent free blocks in a heap.*

If you know you're always going to be working with fixed-size blocks of memory, you can craft a much more efficient scheme for managing a heap. You could, for example, preallocate a large block of memory that you subdivide into pieces of the given fixed size. Then you could devise some scheme for knowing which blocks are free and which are in use, as suggested by Figure 3-12. Returning a block to such a heap merely involves marking it as free—you don't need to coalesce it with adjacent blocks because you never need to satisfy randomly sized requests.

Merely allocating a large block that you subdivide might not be the best way to implement a fixed-size heap, though. In general, it's hard to guess how much memory to preallocate. If you guess too high, you'll be wasting memory. If you guess too low, your algorithm will either fail when it runs out (bad!) or make too frequent trips to a surrounding random heap manager to get space for more blocks (better). Microsoft has created the *lookaside list* object and a set of adaptive algorithms to deal with these shortcomings.

☑ Block in use
☐ Block free

Figure 3-12. *A heap containing fixed-size blocks.*

Figure 3-13 illustrates the concept of a lookaside list. Imagine that you had a glass that you could (somehow—the laws of physics don't exactly make this easy!) balance upright in a swimming pool. The glass represents the lookaside list object. When you initialize the object, you tell the system how big the memory blocks (water drops, in this analogy) are that you'll be working with. In earlier versions of Windows NT, you could also specify the capacity of the glass, but the operating system now determines that adaptively. To allocate a memory block, the system first tries to remove one from the list (remove a water drop from the glass). If there are no more, the system dips into the surrounding memory pool. Conversely, to return a memory block, the system first tries to put it back onto the list (add a water drop to the glass). But if the list is full, the block goes back into the pool using the regular heap manager routine (the drop slops over into the swimming pool).

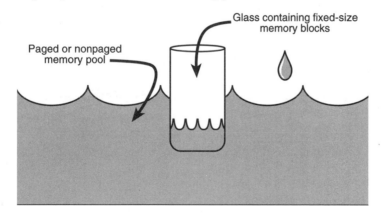

Glass containing fixed-size
memory blocks

Paged or nonpaged
memory pool

Figure 3-13. *Lookaside lists.*

The system periodically adjusts the depths of all lookaside lists based on actual usage. The details of the algorithm aren't really important, and they're subject to change in any case. Basically (in the current release, anyway), the system will reduce the depth of lookaside lists that haven't been accessed recently or that aren't forcing pool access at least 5 percent of the time. The depth never goes below 4, however, which is also the initial depth of a new list.

Table 3-6 lists the eight service functions that you use when you work with a lookaside list. There are really two sets of four functions, one set for a lookaside list that manages paged memory (the **Ex*Xxx*PagedLookasideList** set) and another for a lookaside list that manages nonpaged memory (the **Ex*Xxx*NPagedLookasideList** set). The first thing you must do is reserve nonpaged memory for a PAGED_LOOKASIDE_LIST or an NPAGED_LOOKASIDE_LIST object. These objects are similar. The paged variety uses a FAST_MUTEX for synchronization, whereas the nonpaged variety uses a spin lock. (See the next chapter for a discussion of both of these synchronization objects.) Even the paged variety of object needs to be in nonpaged memory because the system might access it at an elevated IRQL.

Service Function	Description
ExInitializeNPagedLookasideList ExInitializePagedLookasideList	Initialize a lookaside list
ExAllocateFromNPagedLookasideList ExAllocateFromPagedLookasideList	Allocate a fixed-size block
ExFreeToNPagedLookasideList ExFreeToPagedLookasideList	Release a block back to a lookaside list
ExDeleteNPagedLookasideList ExDeletePagedLookasideList	Destroy a lookaside list

Table 3-6. *Service functions for lookaside lists.*

After reserving storage for the lookaside list object somewhere, you call the appropriate initialization routine:

```
PPAGED_LOOKASIDE_LIST pagedlist;
PNPAGED_LOOKASIDE_LIST nonpagedlist;

ExInitializePagedLookasideList(pagedlist, Allocate, Free,
  0, blocksize, tag, 0);
ExInitializeNPagedLookasideList(nonpagedlist, Allocate, Free,
  0, blocksize, tag, 0);
```

(The only difference between the two examples is the spelling of the function name and the first argument.)

The first argument to either of these functions points to the [N]PAGED_ LOOKASIDE_LIST object for which you've already reserved space. **Allocate** and **Free** are pointers to routines you can write to allocate or release memory from a random heap. You can use NULL for either or both of these parameters, in which case ExAllocatePoolWithTag and ExFreePool will be used, respectively. The **blocksize** parameter is the size of the memory blocks you will be allocating from the list, and **tag** is the 32-bit tag value you want placed in front of each such block. (Look back to the section entitled "Variations on ExAllocatePool" for an explanation of the tagging concept.) The two zero arguments are placeholders for values that you supplied in previous versions of Windows NT but which the system now determines on its own; these values are flags to control the type of allocation and the depth of the lookaside list.

To allocate a memory block from the list, call the appropriate **AllocateFrom** function:

```
PVOID p = ExAllocateFromPagedLookasideList(pagedlist);
PVOID q = ExAllocateFromNPagedLookasideList(nonpagedlist);
```

To put a block back onto the list, call the appropriate **FreeTo** function:

```
ExFreeToPagedLookasideList(pagedlist, p);
ExFreeToNPagedLookasideList(nonpagedlist, q);
```

Finally, to destroy a list, call the appropriate **Delete** function:

```
ExDeletePagedLookasidelist(pagedlist);
ExDeleteNPagedLookasidelist(nonpagedlist);
```

It's a common mistake to forget to delete a lookaside list. You won't be making such a mistake of course, but you might need to advise one of your coworkers about how to avoid it(!). You can tell him or her, "Be sure to do that before your lookaside list passes out of scope. If you created a lookaside list during AddDevice, for example, you probably put the object into your device object and want to delete the list before you call **IoDeleteDevice**. If you created a lookaside list during DriverEntry, you probably put the object into a global variable and want to delete the list before you return from your **DriverUnload** routine."

STRING HANDLING

WDM drivers can work with string data in any of four formats:

- A Unicode string, normally described by a UNICODE_STRING structure, contains 16-bit characters. Unicode has sufficient code points to accommodate the language scripts used on this planet (and on at least one other—see *http://www.indigo.ie/egt/standards/csur/klingon.html*).

■ An ANSI string, normally described by an ANSI_STRING structure, contains 8-bit characters. A variant is an OEM_STRING, which also describes a string of 8-bit characters. The difference between the two is that an OEM string has characters whose graphic depends on the current code page, whereas an ANSI string has characters whose graphic is independent of code page. WDM drivers would not normally deal with OEM strings because they would have to originate in user mode, and some other kernel-mode component will have already translated them into Unicode strings by the time the driver sees them.

■ A null-terminated string of characters. You can express constants using normal C syntax, such as **"Hello, world!"** Strings employ 8-bit characters of type CHAR, which are assumed to be from the ANSI character set. The characters in string constants originate in whatever editor you used to create your source code. If you use an editor that relies on the then-current code page to display graphics in the editing window, be aware that some characters might have a different meaning when treated as part of the Windows ANSI character set.

■ A null-terminated string of wide characters (type WCHAR). You can express wide string constants using normal C syntax, such as **L"Goodbye, cruel world!"** Such strings look like Unicode constants, but, being ultimately derived from some text editor or another, actually use only the ASCII and Latin1 code points (0020-007F and 00A0-00FF) that correspond to the Windows ANSI set.

The UNICODE_STRING and ANSI_STRING data structures both have the layout depicted in Figure 3-14. The **Buffer** field of either structure points to a data area elsewhere in memory that contains the string data. **MaximumLength** gives the length of the buffer area, and **Length** provides the (current) length of the string without regard to any null terminator that might be present. Both length fields are *in bytes,* even for the UNICODE_STRING structure.

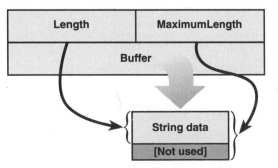

Figure 3-14. *The UNICODE_STRING and ANSI_STRING structures.*

Table 3-7 lists the service functions that you can use for working with Unicode and ANSI strings. I've listed them side by side because there's a fair amount of duplication. I've also listed some functions from the standard C run-time library that are available in kernel mode for manipulating regular C-style strings. The standard DDK headers include declarations of these functions, and the libraries with which you link drivers contain them, so there's no particular reason not to use them even though they've never been documented in the DDK as being available.

Operation	ANSI String Function	Unicode String Function
Length	strlen	wcslen
Concatenate	strcat, strncat	wcscat, wcsncat, RtlAppendUnicodeStringToString, RtlAppendUnicodeToString
Copy	strcpy, strncpy, RtlCopyString	wcscpy, wcsncpy, RtlCopyUnicodeString
Reverse	_strrev	_wcsrev
Compare	strcmp, strncmp, _stricmp, _strnicmp, RtlCompareString, RtlEqualString	wcscmp, wcsncmp, _wcsicmp, _wcsnicmp, RtlCompareUnicodeString, RtlEqualUnicodeString, RtlPrefixUnicodeString
Initialize	_strset, _strnset, RtlInitAnsiString, RtlInitString	_wcsnset, RtlInitUnicodeString
Search	strchr, strrchr, strspn, strstr	wcschr, wcsrchr, wcsspn, wcsstr
Upper/ lowercase	_strlwr, _strupr, RtlUpperString	_wcslwr, _wcsupr, RtlUpcaseUnicodeString
Character	isdigit, islower, isprint, isspace, isupper, isxdigit, tolower, toupper, RtlUpperChar	towlower, towupper, RtlUpcaseUnicodeChar
Format	sprintf, vsprintf, _snprintf, _vsnprintf	swprintf, _snwprintf
String conversion	atoi, atol, _itoa	_itow, RtlIntegerToUnicodeString, RtlUnicodeStringToInteger
Type conversion	RtlAnsiStringToUnicodeSize, RtlAnsiStringToUnicodeString	RtlUnicodeStringToAnsiString
Memory release	RtlFreeAnsiString	RtlFreeUnicodeString

Table 3-7. *Functions for string manipulation.*

Many more **Rtl**Xxx functions are exported by the system DLLs, but I've listed the ones for which the DDK header files (and the SDK headers they include) define prototypes. These are the only ones we should use in drivers.

Allocating and Releasing String Buffers

I'm not going to describe the string manipulation functions in detail because the DDK documentation does this perfectly well and you already know, based on your general programming experience, how to put functions like this together to get your work done. But I do want to discuss a problem that can rear up and bite you if you don't look out for it.

You often define UNICODE_STRING (or ANSI_STRING) structures as automatic variables or as parts of your own device extension. The string buffers to which these structures point usually occupy dynamically allocated memory, but you'll sometimes want to work with string constants, too. Keeping track of who owns the memory to which a particular UNICODE_STRING or ANSI_STRING structure points can be a bit of a problem. Consider the following fragment of a function:

```
UNICODE_STRING foo;
if (bArriving)
  RtlInitUnicodeString(&foo, L"Hello, world!");
else
  RtlAnsiStringToUnicodeString(&foo, "Goodbye, cruel world!", TRUE);
...
RtlFreeUnicodeString(&foo); // ← don't do this!
```

In one case, we initialize **foo.Length**, **foo.MaximumLength**, and **foo.Buffer** to describe a wide character string constant in our driver. In another case, we ask the system (by means of the TRUE third argument to **RtlAnsiStringToUnicodeString**) to allocate memory for the Unicode translation of an ANSI string. In the first case, it's a mistake to call **RtlFreeUnicodeString** because it will unconditionally try to release a memory block that's part of our code or data. In the second case, it's mandatory to call RtlFreeUnicodeString eventually if we want to avoid a memory leak.

Data Blobs

I've borrowed the term *data blob* from the world of database management to describe a random collection of bytes that you want to manipulate somehow. Table 3-8 lists the functions (including some from the standard run-time library) that you can call in kernel mode for that purpose. Once again, I'm going to assume that you can figure out how to use these functions (based on their largely mnemonic names). I need to point out a few nonobvious facts, however:

■ The difference between a memory "copy" and a memory "move" is whether the implementation can tolerate an overlap between the target and source. A move operation is more general in that it works correctly whether or not there's an overlap. The copy operation is faster because it assumes it can perform a left-to-right copy (which won't work if the target overlaps the right portion of the source).

■ The difference between a "byte" and a "memory" operation is in the granularity of the operation. A byte operation is guaranteed to proceed byte by byte. A memory operation can use larger chunks internally, provided all the chunks add up to the specified number of bytes. If this distinction is meaningless on a particular platform (as is true for x86 computers), the byte operations are actually macro'ed to the corresponding memory operations. Thus, **RtlCopyBytes** is a different function than **RtlCopyMemory** on an Alpha but is #define'd equal to RtlCopyMemory on a 32-bit Intel.

Service Function or Macro	Description
memchr	Find a byte in a blob
memcpy, RtlCopyBytes, RtlCopyMemory	Copy bytes, assuming no overlap
memmove, RtlMoveMemory	Copy bytes when there might be an overlap
memsct, RtlFillBytes, RtlFillMemory	Fill blob with given value
memcmp, RtlCompareMemory, RtlEqualMemory	Compare one blob to another
memset, RtlZeroBytes, RtlZeroMemory	Zero-fill a blob

Table 3-8. *Service functions for working with blobs of data.*

MISCELLANEOUS PROGRAMMING TECHNIQUES

In the remainder of this chapter, I'm going to discuss some miscellaneous topics that might be useful in various parts of your driver. I'll begin by describing how you access the registry database, which is where you can find various configuration and control information that might affect your code or your hardware. I'll go on to describe how you access disk files and other named devices. A few words will suffice to describe how you can perform floating-point calculations in a WDM driver. Finally, I'll describe a few of the features you can embed in your driver to make it easier to debug your driver in the unlikely event (☺) it shouldn't work correctly the first time you try it out.

Accessing the Registry

Windows NT and Windows 98 record configuration and other important information in a database called the *registry*. WDM drivers can call the functions listed in Table 3-9 to access the registry. If you've done user-mode programming involving registry access, you might be able to guess how to use these functions in a driver. I found the kernel-mode support functions sufficiently different, however, that I think it's worth describing how you might use them.

Service Function	Description
IoOpenDeviceRegistryKey	Open special key associated with a PDO
IoOpenDeviceInterfaceRegistryKey	Open a registry key associated with a registered device interface
RtlDeleteRegistryValue	Delete a registry value
RtlQueryRegistryValues	Read several values from the registry
RtlWriteRegistryValue	Write a value to the registry
ZwClose	Close handle to a registry key
ZwCreateKey	Create a registry key
ZwDeleteKey	Delete a registry key
ZwEnumerateKey	Enumerate subkeys
ZwEnumerateValueKey	Enumerate values within a registry key
ZwFlushKey	Commit registry changes to disk
ZwOpenKey	Open a registry key
ZwQueryKey	Get information about a registry key
ZwQueryValueKey	Get a value within a registry key
ZwSetValueKey	Set a value within a registry key

Table 3-9. *Service functions for registry access.*

In this section, I'll discuss, among other things, the **Zw***Xxx* family of routines and **RtlDeleteRegistryValue**, which provide the basic registry functionality that suffices for most WDM drivers.

Opening a Registry Key

Before you can interrogate values in the registry, you need to open the key that contains them. You use **ZwOpenKey** to open an existing key. You use **ZwCreateKey** either to open an existing key or to create a new key. Either function requires you to first initialize an OBJECT_ATTRIBUTES structure with the name of the key and (perhaps) other information. The OBJECT_ATTRIBUTES structure has the following declaration:

```
typedef struct _OBJECT_ATTRIBUTES {
  ULONG Length;
  HANDLE RootDirectory;
  PUNICODE_STRING ObjectName;
  ULONG Attributes;
  PVOID SecurityDescriptor;
  PVOID SecurityQualityOfService;
  } OBJECT_ATTRIBUTES;
```

Rather than initialize an instance of this structure by hand, it's easiest to use the macro **InitializeObjectAttributes**, which I'm about to show you.

Suppose, for example, that we wanted to open the service key for our driver. The I/O Manager gives us the name of this key as a parameter to DriverEntry. So, we could write code like the following:

```
NTSTATUS DriverEntry(PDRIVER_OBJECT DriverObject,
  PUNICODE_STRING RegistryPath)
  {
  ...
  OBJECT_ATTRIBUTES oa;
  InitializeObjectAttributes(&oa, RegistryPath, 0, NULL, NULL);
  HANDLE hkey;
  status = ZwOpenKey(&hkey, KEY_READ, &oa);
  if (NT_SUCCESS(status))
    {
    ...
    ZwClose(hkey);
    }
  ...
  }
```

1. We're initializing the object attributes structure with the registry pathname supplied to us by the I/O Manager and with a NULL security descriptor. ZwOpenKey will ignore the security descriptor anyway—you can specify security attributes only when you create a key for the first time.

2. **ZwOpenKey** will open the key for reading and store the resulting handle in our **hkey** variable.

3. **ZwClose** is a generic routine for closing a handle to a kernel-mode object. Here, we use it to close the handle we have to the registry key.

Even though we often refer to the registry as being a database, it doesn't have all of the attributes that have come to be associated with real databases. It doesn't allow for committing or rolling back changes, for example. Furthermore, the access rights you specify when you open a key (KEY_READ in the previous example) are for security checking rather than for the prevention of incompatible sharing. That is, two different processes can have the same key open after specifying write access (for example). The system does guard against destructive writes that occur simultaneously with reads, however, and it does guarantee that a key won't be deleted while someone has an open handle to it.

Other Ways to Open Registry Keys

In addition to ZwOpenKey, Windows 2000 provides two other functions for opening registry keys.

IoOpenDeviceRegistryKey allows you to open one of the special registry keys associated with a device object:

```
HANDLE hkey;
status = IoOpenDeviceRegistryKey(pdo, flag, access, &hkey);
```

where **pdo** is the address of the physical device object (PDO) at the bottom of your particular driver stack, **flag** is an indicator for which special key you want to open (see Table 3-10), and **access** is an access mask such as KEY_READ.

Flag Value	Selected Registry Key
PLUGPLAY_REGKEY_DEVICE	The hardware (instance) subkey of the Enum key
PLUGPLAY_REGKEY_DRIVER	The software (service) key

Table 3-10. *Registry key codes for IoOpenDeviceRegistryKey.*

IoOpenDeviceInterfaceRegistryKey opens the key associated with an instance of a registered device interface:

```
HANDLE hkey;
status = IoOpenDeviceInterfaceRegistryKey(linkname, access, &hkey);
```

where **linkname** is the symbolic link name of the registered interface and **access** is an access mask like KEY_READ.

The interface registry key is a subkey of HKLM\System\CurrentControlSet\Control\DeviceClasses that persists from one session to the next. It's a good place to store parameter information that you want to share with user-mode programs, because user-mode code can call **SetupDiOpenDeviceInterfaceRegKey** to gain access to the same key.

In Chapter 12, "Installing Device Drivers," I'll discuss how your installation script can insert values into the hardware and interface keys, and how application programs can access these values.

Getting and Setting Values

Usually, you open a registry key because you want to retrieve a value from the database. The basic function you use for that purpose is **ZwQueryValueKey**. For example, to retrieve the **ImagePath** value in the driver's service key—I don't actually know why you'd want to know this, but that's not my department—you could use the following code:

```
UNICODE_STRING valname;
RtlInitUnicodeString(&valname, L"ImagePath");
size = 0;
status = ZwQueryValueKey(hkey, &valname, KeyValuePartialInformation,
  NULL, 0, &size);
if (status == STATUS_OBJECT_NOT_FOUND || size == 0)
  <handle error>;
PKEY_VALUE_PARTIAL_INFORMATION vpip = (PKEY_VALUE_PARTIAL_INFORMATION)
  ExAllocatePool(PagedPool, size);
if (!vpip)
  <handle error>;
status = ZwQueryValueKey(hkey, &valname, KeyValuePartialInformation,
  vpip, size, &size);
if (!NT_SUCCESS(status))
  <handle error>;
<do something with vpip->Data>
ExFreePool(vpip);
```

Here, we make two calls to ZwQueryValueKey. The purpose of the first call is to determine how much space we need to allocate for the KEY_VALUE_PARTIAL_ INFORMATION structure we're trying to retrieve. The second call retrieves the information. I left the error checking in this code fragment because the errors didn't work out in practice the way I expected them to. In particular, I initially guessed that the first call to ZwQueryValueKey would return STATUS_BUFFER_TOO_SMALL if I passed it a NULL buffer pointer. It didn't do that, though. The important failure code is STATUS_OBJECT_NAME_NOT_FOUND, which indicates that the value doesn't actually exist. Hence, I test for that value only. If there's some other error that prevents ZwQueryValueKey from working, the second call will uncover it.

The so-called "partial" information structure you retrieve in this way contains the value's data and a description of its data type:

```
typedef struct _KEY_VALUE_PARTIAL_INFORMATION {
    ULONG    TitleIndex;
    ULONG    Type;
```

(continued)

```
    ULONG    DataLength;
    UCHAR    Data[1];
} KEY_VALUE_PARTIAL_INFORMATION,
  *PKEY_VALUE_PARTIAL_INFORMATION;
```

Type is one of the registry data types listed in Table 3-11. (Additional data types are possible but not interesting to device drivers.) **DataLength** is the length of the data value, and **Data** is the data itself. **TitleIndex** has no relevance to drivers. Here are some useful facts to know about the various data types:

■ REG_DWORD is a 32-bit unsigned integer in whatever format (big-endian or little-endian) is natural for the platform.

■ REG_SZ describes a null-terminated Unicode string value. The null terminator is included in the DataLength·count.

■ To expand a REG_EXPAND_SZ value by substituting environment variables, you should use **RtlQueryRegistryValues** as your method of interrogating the registry. The internal routines for accessing environment variables aren't documented or exposed for use by drivers.

■ RtlQueryRegistryValues is also a good way to interrogate REG_MULTI_SZ values, in that it will call your designated callback routine once for each of the potentially many strings.

NOTE RtlQueryRegistryValues is a complex routine for which I'm not providing an example here. The DDK samples contain several drivers that use it.

Data Type Constant	Description
REG_BINARY	Variable-length binary data
REG_DWORD	Unsigned long integer in natural format for the platform
REG_DWORD_BIG_ENDIAN	Unsigned long integer in big-endian format
REG_EXPAND_SZ	Null-terminated Unicode string containing %-escapes for environment variable names
REG_MULTI_SZ	One or more null-terminated Unicode strings, followed by an extra null
REG_SZ	Null-terminated Unicode string

Table 3-11. *Types of registry values useful to WDM drivers.*

To set a registry value, you must have KEY_SET_VALUE access to the parent key. I used KEY_READ earlier, which wouldn't give you such access. You could use

KEY_WRITE or KEY_ALL_ACCESS, although you thereby gain more than the necessary permission. Then call **ZwSetValueKey**. For example:

```
RtlInitUnicodeString(&valname, L"TheAnswer");
ULONG value = 42;
ZwSetValueKey(hkey, &valname, 0, REG_DWORD, &value, sizeof(value));
```

Deleting Subkeys or Values

To delete a value in an open key, you can use **RtlDeleteRegistryValue** in the following special way:

```
RtlDeleteRegistryValue(RTL_REGISTRY_HANDLE, (PCWSTR) hkey, L"TheAnswer");
```

RtlDeleteRegistryValue is a general service function whose first argument can designate one of several special places in the registry. When you use RTL_REGISTRY_HANDLE, as I did in this example, you indicate that you've already got an open handle to the key within which you want to delete a value. You specify the key (with a cast to make the compiler happy) as the second argument. The third and final argument is the null-terminated Unicode name of the value you want to delete. This is one time when you don't have to create a UNICODE_STRING structure to describe the string.

You can delete only those keys that you've opened with at least DELETE permission (which you get with KEY_ALL_ACCESS). You call **ZwDeleteKey**:

```
ZwDeleteKey(hkey);
```

The key lives on until all handles are closed, but subsequent attempts to open a new handle to the key or to access the key by using any currently open handle will fail with STATUS_KEY_DELETED. Since *you* have an open handle at this point, you must be sure to call ZwClose sometime. (The DDK documentation entry for ZwDeleteKey says the handle becomes invalid. It doesn't—you must still close it by calling ZwClose.)

Enumerating Subkeys or Values

A complicated activity you can carry out with an open registry key is to enumerate the elements (subkeys and values) that the key contains. To do this, you'll first call **ZwQueryKey** to determine a few facts about the subkeys and values, such as their number, the length of the largest name, and so on. ZwQueryKey has an argument that indicates which of three types of information you want to retrieve about the key. These types are named basic, node, and full. To prepare for an enumeration, you'd be interested first in the full information:

```
typedef struct _KEY_FULL_INFORMATION {
    LARGE_INTEGER LastWriteTime;
    ULONG    TitleIndex;
    ULONG    ClassOffset;
```

(continued)

```
    ULONG    ClassLength;
    ULONG    SubKeys;
    ULONG    MaxNameLen;
    ULONG    MaxClassLen;
    ULONG    Values;
    ULONG    MaxValueNameLen;
    ULONG    MaxValueDataLen;
    WCHAR    Class[1];
} KEY_FULL_INFORMATION, *PKEY_FULL_INFORMATION;
```

This structure is actually of variable length, since **Class[0]** is just the first character of the class name. It's customary to make one call to find out how big a buffer you need to allocate and a second call to get the data, as follows:

```
ULONG size;
ZwQueryKey(hkey, KeyFullInformation, NULL, 0, &size);
PKEY_FULL_INFORMATION fip = (PKEY_FULL_INFORMATION)
  ExAllocatePool(PagedPool, size);
ZwQueryKey(hkey, 0, KeyFullInformation, bip, size, &size);
```

Were you now interested in the subkeys of your registry key, you could perform the following loop calling **ZwEnumerateKey**:

```
for (ULONG i = 0; i < fip->SubKeys; ++i)
  {
  ZwEnumerateKey(hkey, i, KeyBasicInformation, NULL, 0, &size);
  PKEY_BASIC_INFORMATION bip = (PKEY_BASIC_INFORMATION)
    ExAllocatePool(PagedPool, size);
  ZwEnumerateKey(hkey, i, KeyBasicInformation, bip, size, &size);
  <do something with bip->Name>
  ExFreePool(bip);
  }
```

The key fact you discover about each subkey is its name, which shows up as a counted Unicode string in the KEY_BASIC_INFORMATION structure you retrieve inside the loop:

```
typedef struct _KEY_BASIC_INFORMATION {
    LARGE_INTEGER LastWriteTime;
    ULONG    Type;
    ULONG    NameLength;
    WCHAR    Name[1];
} KEY_BASIC_INFORMATION, *PKEY_BASIC_INFORMATION;
```

The name isn't null-terminated; you must use the **NameLength** member of the structure to determine its length. Don't forget that the length is in bytes! The name isn't the full registry path either: it's the just the name of the subkey within whatever key contains it. This is actually lucky, because you can easily open a subkey given its name and an open handle to its parent key.

To accomplish an enumeration of the values in an open key, employ the following method:

```
ULONG maxlen = fip->MaxValueNameLen +
  sizeof(KEY_VALUE_BASIC_INFORMATION);
PKEY_VALUE_BASIC_INFORMATION vip = (PKEY_VALUE_BASIC_INFORMATION)
  ExAllocatePool(PagedPool, maxlen);
for (ULONG i = 0; i < fip->Values; ++i)
  {
  ZwEnumerateValueKey(hkey, i, KeyValueBasicInformation, vip,
    maxlen, &size);
  <do something with vip->Name>
  }
ExFreePool(vip);
```

Allocate space for the largest possible KEY_VALUE_BASIC_INFORMATION structure that you'll ever retrieve based on the **MaxValueNameLen** member of the KEY_FULL_INFORMATION structure. Inside the loop, you'll want to do something with the name of the value, which comes to you as a counted Unicode string in this structure:

```
typedef struct _KEY_VALUE_BASIC_INFORMATION {
    ULONG    TitleIndex;
    ULONG    Type;
    ULONG    NameLength;
    WCHAR    Name[1];
} KEY_VALUE_BASIC_INFORMATION, *PKEY_VALUE_BASIC_INFORMATION;
```

Once again, having the name of the value and an open handle to its parent key is just what you need to retrieve the value, as shown in the previous section.

There are variations on ZwQueryKey and on these two enumeration functions that I haven't discussed. You can, for example, obtain full information about a subkey when you call ZwEnumerateKey. I showed you only how to get the basic information that includes the name. You can retrieve data values only, or names *plus* data values, from **ZwEnumerateValueKey**. I showed you only how to get the name of a value.

Accessing Files

It's sometimes useful to be able to read and write regular disk files from inside a WDM driver. Perhaps you need to download a large amount of microcode to your hardware, or perhaps you need to create your own extensive log of information for some purpose. There's a set of Zw*Xxx* routines to help you do these things.

The first step in accessing a disk file is to open a handle by calling **ZwCreateFile**. The full description of this function in the DDK is relatively complex because of all the ways in which it can be used. I'm going to show you two simple scenarios, however, that are useful if you just want to read or write a file whose name you already know.

Opening an Existing File for Reading

To open an existing file so that you can read it, follow this example:

```
NTSTATUS status;
OBJECT_ATTRIBUTES oa;
IO_STATUS_BLOCK iostatus;
HANDLE hfile;              // ← the output from this process
PUNICODE_STRING pathname;  // ← you've been given this

InitializeObjectAttributes(&oa, pathname, OBJ_CASE_INSENSITIVE,
  NULL, NULL);
status = ZwCreateFile(&hfile, GENERIC_READ, &oa, &iostatus,
  NULL, 0, FILE_SHARE_READ, FILE_OPEN,
  FILE_SYNCHRONOUS_IO_NONALERT, NULL, 0);
```

Creating or Rewriting a File

To create a new file, or to open and truncate to zero length an existing file, replace the call to ZwCreateFile in the previous fragment with this one:

```
status = ZwCreateFile(&hfile, GENERIC_WRITE, &oa, &iostatus,
  NULL, FILE_ATTRIBUTE_NORMAL, 0, FILE_OVERWRITE_IF,
  FILE_SYNCHRONOUS_IO_NONALERT, NULL, 0);
```

In these fragments, we set up an Object Attributes structure whose main purpose is to point to the full pathname of the file we're about to open. We specify the OBJ_CASE_INSENSITIVE attribute because the Win32 file system model does not treat case as significant in a pathname. Then we call ZwCreateFile to open the handle.

The first argument to ZwCreateFile (**&hfile**) is the address of the HANDLE variable where ZwCreateFile will return the handle it creates. The second argument (**GENERIC_READ** or **GENERIC_WRITE**) specifies the access we need to the handle to perform either reading or writing. The third argument (**&oa**) is the address of the OBJECT_ATTRIBUTES structure containing the name of the file. The fourth argument points to an IO_STATUS_BLOCK that will receive a disposition code indicating how ZwCreateFile actually implemented the operation we asked it to perform. When we open a read-only handle to an existing file, we expect the Status field of this structure to end up equal to FILE_OPENED. When we open a write-only handle, we expect it to end up equal to FILE_OVERWRITTEN or FILE_CREATED, depending on whether the file did or did not already exist. The fifth argument (**NULL**) can be a pointer to a 64-bit integer that specifies the initial allocation size for the file. This argument matters only when you create or overwrite a file, and omitting it as I did here means that the file grows from zero length as you write data. The sixth argument (**0** or **FILE_ATTRIBUTE_NORMAL**) specifies file attribute flags for any new file that you happen to create. The seventh argument (**FILE_SHARE_READ** or **0**) specifies how the file can be shared by other threads. If you're opening for input, you can probably tolerate having other threads read the file simultaneously. If you're opening for sequential output, you probably don't want other threads trying to access the file at all.

The eighth argument (**FILE_OPEN** or **FILE_OVERWRITE_IF**) indicates how to proceed if the file either already exists or doesn't. In the read-only case, I specified FILE_OPEN because I expected to open an existing file and wanted a failure if the file didn't exist. In the write-only case, I specified FILE_OVERWRITE_IF because I wanted to overwrite any existing file by the same name or create a brand new file as necessary. The ninth argument (**FILE_SYNCHRONOUS_IO_NONALERT**) specifies additional flag bits to govern the open operation and the subsequent use of the handle. In this case, I indicated that I'm going to be doing synchronous I/O operations (wherein I expect the read or write function not to return until the I/O is complete). The tenth and eleventh arguments (**NULL** and **0**) are, respectively, an optional pointer to a buffer for extended attributes and the length of that buffer.

You expect ZwCreateFile to return STATUS_SUCCESS and to set the handle variable. You can then carry out whatever read or write operations you please by calling **ZwReadFile** or **ZwWriteFile**, and then you close the handle by calling **ZwClose**:

```
ZwClose(hfile);
```

You can perform synchronous or asynchronous reads and writes, depending on the flags you specified to ZwCreateFile. In the simple scenarios I've outlined, you would do synchronous operations that don't return until they've completed. For example:

```
PVOID buffer;
ULONG bufsize;
status = ZwReadFile(hfile, NULL, NULL, NULL, &iostatus, buffer,
  bufsize, NULL, NULL);
```

-or-

```
status = ZwWriteFile(hfile, NULL, NULL, NULL, &iostatus, buffer,
  bufsize, NULL, NULL);
```

These calls are analogous to a nonoverlapped **ReadFile** or **WriteFile** call from user mode. When the function returns, you might be interested in **iostatus.Information**, which will hold the number of bytes transferred by the operation.

If you plan to read an entire file into a memory buffer, you would probably want to call **ZwQueryInformationFile** to determine the total length of the file:

```
FILE_STANDARD_INFORMATION si;
ZwQueryInformationFile(hfile, &iostatus, &si, sizeof(si),
  FileStandardInformation);
ULONG length = si.EndOfFile.LowPart;
```

TIMING OF FILE OPERATIONS

You'll be likely to want to read a disk file in a WDM driver while you're initializing your device in response to an IRP_MN_START_DEVICE request. (See Chapter 6.) Depending on where your device falls in the initialization sequence, you might or might not have access to files using normal pathnames like \??\C:\dir\file.ext. To be safe, put your data files into some directory below the system root directory and use a filename like \SystemRoot\dir\file.ext. The SystemRoot branch of the namespace is always accessible, since the operating system has to be able to read disk files to start up.

Floating-Point Calculations

There are times when integer arithmetic just isn't sufficient to get your job done and you need to perform floating-point calculations. On an Intel processor, the math coprocessor is also where Multimedia Extensions (MMX) instructions execute. Historically, there have been two problems with drivers carrying out floating-point calculations. The operating system will emulate a missing coprocessor, but the emulation is expensive and normally requires a processor exception to trigger it. Handling exceptions, especially at elevated IRQLs, can be difficult in kernel mode. Additionally, on computers that have hardware coprocessors, the CPU architecture might require a separate, expensive operation to save and restore the coprocessor state during context switches. Therefore, conventional wisdom has forbidden kernel-mode drivers from using floating-point calculations.

Windows 2000 and Windows 98 provide a way around past difficulties. First of all, a system thread—see Chapter 9—running at or below DISPATCH_LEVEL is free to use the math coprocessor all it wants. In addition, a driver running in an arbitrary thread context at or below DISPATCH_LEVEL can use these two system calls to bracket its use of the math coprocessor:

```
ASSERT(KeGetCurrentIrql() <= DISPATCH_LEVEL);
KFLOATING_SAVE FloatSave;
NTSTATUS status = KeSaveFloatingPointState(&FloatSave);
if (NT_SUCCESS(status))
  {
  ...
  KeRestoreFloatingPointState(&FloatSave);
  }
```

These calls, which must be paired as shown here, save and restore the "nonvolatile" state of the math coprocessor for the current CPU—that is, all the state information that persists beyond a single operation. This state information includes registers, control words, and so on. In some CPU architectures, no actual work might occur because the architecture inherently allows any process to perform floating-point operations. In other architectures, the work involved in saving and restoring state information can be quite substantial. For this reason, Microsoft recommends that you avoid using floating-point calculations in a kernel-mode driver unless necessary.

What happens when you call **KeSaveFloatingPointState** depends, as I said, on the CPU architecture. To give you an idea, on an Intel-architecture processor, this function saves the entire floating-point state by executing an FSAVE instruction. It can save the state information either in a context block associated with the current thread or in an area of dynamically allocated memory. It uses the opaque **FloatSave** area to record "meta" information about the saved state to allow **KeRestoreFloatingPointState** to correctly restore the state later.

KeSaveFloatingPointState will fail with STATUS_ILLEGAL_FLOAT_CONTEXT if there's no real coprocessor present. (All CPUs of a multi-CPU computer must have coprocessors, or else none of them may, by the way.) Your driver will therefore need alternative code to carry out whatever calculations you had in mind, or else you'll want to decline to load (by failing DriverEntry) if the computer doesn't have a coprocessor.

Making Debugging Easier

My drivers always have bugs. Maybe you're as unlucky as I am. If so, you'll find yourself spending lots of time with a debugger trying to figure out what your code is doing or not doing correctly or incorrectly. I won't discuss the potentially divisive subject of which debugger is best or the noncontroversial but artistic subject of how to debug a driver. But you can do some things in your driver code that will make your life easier.

When you build your driver, you select either the "checked" or the "free" build environment. (Readers may now thank me for not making a bad joke about how the opposite of "checked" ought really to be named "striped" or something like that.) In the checked build environment, the preprocessor symbol DBG equals 1, whereas it equals 0 in the free build environment. So, one of the things you can do in your own code is to provide additional code that will take effect only in the checked build:

```
#if DBG
  <extra debugging code>
#endif
```

One of the most useful debugging techniques ever invented is to simply print messages from time to time. I used to do this when I was first learning to program (in FORTRAN on a computer made out of vacuum tubes, no less), and I still do it today. **DbgPrint** is a kernel-mode service routine you can call to display a formatted message in whatever output window your debugger provides. Another way to see the output from DbgPrint calls is to download the DbgView utility from *http://www.sysinternals.com*. Instead of directly referencing DbgPrint in your code, it's often easier to use the macro named **KdPrint**, which calls DbgPrint if DBG is true and generates no code at all if DBG is false:

```
KdPrint(("KeReadProgrammersMind failed with code %X\n", status));
```

You use two sets of parentheses with KdPrint because of the way it's defined. The first argument is a string with %-escapes where you want to substitute values. The second, third, and following arguments provide the values to go with the %-escapes. The macro expands into a call to DbgPrint, which internally uses the standard run-time library routine **_vsnprintf** to format the string. You can, therefore, use the same set of %-escape codes that are available to application programs that call this routine.

Another useful debugging technique relies on the **ASSERT** macro:

```
ASSERT(1 + 1 == 2);
```

In the checked build of your driver, ASSERT generates code to evaluate the Boolean expression. If the expression is false, ASSERT will try to halt execution in the debugger so that you can see what's going on. If the expression is true, your program continues executing normally.

If you debug with Soft-Ice/W from Compuware (formerly Nu-Mega Technologies, Inc.), the ASSERT macro in the DDK isn't as useful as it might be. First of all, it relies on calling **RtlAssert**, which does nothing in the free version of the operating system. (You should test your driver in the checked build, but you can debug it perfectly well in the free build.) Second, if it does generate a debug exception, it does so inside RtlAssert rather than in the execution context of your code, which makes it more difficult for you to inspect local variables. You can replace the DDK ASSERT macro (for x86 only, which is the only place Soft-Ice/W currently runs anyway) to overcome these problems as follows:

```
#if DBG && defined(_X86_)
#undef ASSERT
#define ASSERT(e) if(!(e)){DbgPrint("Assertion failure in "\
   __)FILE__) ", line %d: " #e "\n", __LINE__);\
   _asm int 1\
   }
#endif
```

Also remember to issue the Soft-Ice/W command **i1here on** so that the INT 1 traps from your ASSERT macros actually cause the debugger to halt. A possible disadvantage to replacing ASSERT like this is that you will bugcheck even in the free build of the operating system if you're not running a debugger when one of these ASSERTs fails.

WINDOWS 98 COMPATIBILITY NOTES

The Zw*Xxx* routines for accessing disk files don't work in the retail release of Windows 98 because of two basic problems—one from the architecture of Windows and the other from what looks like an ordinary bug.

The first problem with file access has to do with the order in which Windows 98 initializes various virtual device drivers. The Configuration Manager (CONFIGMG.VXD) initializes before the Installable File System Manager (IFSMGR.VXD). WDM drivers for devices that exist at startup time receive their IRP_MN_START_DEVICE requests during CONFIGMG's initialization phase. But, since IFSMGR hasn't initialized at that point, it's not possible to perform file I/O operations by using ZwCreateFile and the other functions discussed earlier in the chapter. Furthermore, there's no way for a WDM driver to defer handling IRP_MN_START_DEVICE until file system functionality becomes available. If you don't have a debugger like Soft-Ice/W running, the symptom you will see is a blue screen complaining of a Windows Protection Error while initializing CONFIGMG.

The second and more crippling problem with file access has to do with the validity checking that ZwReadFile, ZwWriteFile, and ZwQueryInformationFile do on their arguments. If you supply an IO_STATUS_BLOCK in kernel-mode memory (and there's basically no way to do anything else), these functions probe a virtual address that doesn't exist. The resulting page fault gets caught by a structured exception handler and results in you getting back STATUS_ACCESS_VIOLATION even when you've done everything right. There is no workaround for this problem in the July 1998 retail release of Windows 98.

The FILEIO sample on the companion disc illustrates a way past these Windows 98 difficulties. FILEIO makes a run-time decision whether to call the Zw*Xxx* functions or instead to call VxD services to perform file operations.

Chapter 4

Synchronization

Microsoft Windows 2000 is a multitasking operating system that can run in a symmetric multiprocessor environment. It's not my purpose here to provide a rigorous description of the multitasking capabilities of Microsoft Windows NT; one good place to get more information is David Solomon's *Inside Windows NT, Second Edition* (Microsoft Press, 1998). All we need to understand as driver writers is that our code executes in the context of one *thread* or another (and the thread context can change from one invocation of our code to another) and that the exigencies of multitasking can yank control away from us at practically any moment. Furthermore, true simultaneous execution of multiple threads is possible on a multiprocessor machine. In general, we need to assume two worst-case scenarios:

- The operating system can preempt any subroutine at any moment for an arbitrarily long period of time, so we cannot be sure of completing critical tasks without interference or delay.

- Even if we take steps to prevent preemption, code executing simultaneously on another CPU in the same computer can interfere with our code—it's even possible that the exact same set of instructions belonging to one of our programs could be executing in parallel in the context of two different threads.

Windows NT allows you to solve these general synchronization problems by using the *interrupt request level* (IRQL) priority scheme and by claiming and releasing *spin locks* around critical code sections. IRQL avoids destructive preemption on a single CPU, while spin locks forestall interference among CPUs.

AN ARCHETYPAL SYNCHRONIZATION PROBLEM

A hackneyed example will motivate this discussion. Suppose your driver had a static integer variable that you used for some purpose, say to count the number of I/O requests that were currently outstanding:

```
static LONG lActiveRequests;
```

Suppose further that you increment this variable when you receive a request and decrement it when you later complete the request:

```
NTSTATUS DispatchPnp(PDEVICE_OBJECT fdo, PIRP Irp)
  {
  ++lActiveRequests;
  ... // process PNP request
  --lActiveRequests;
  }
```

I'm sure you recognize already that a counter like this one ought not to be a static variable: it should be a member of your device extension so that each device object has its own unique counter. Bear with me and pretend that your driver only ever manages a single device. To make the example more meaningful, suppose finally that a function in your driver would be called when it was time to delete your device object. You might want to defer the operation until no more requests were outstanding, so you might insert a test of the counter:

```
NTSTATUS HandleRemoveDevice(PDEVICE_OBJECT fdo, PIRP Irp)
  {
  if (lActiveRequests)
    <wait for all requests to complete>
  IoDeleteDevice(fdo);
  }
```

This example describes a real problem, by the way, which we'll tackle in Chapter 6, "Plug and Play," in our discussion of Plug and Play (PnP) requests. The I/O Manager can try to remove one of our devices at a time when requests are active, and we need to guard against that by keeping some sort of counter. I'll show you in Chapter 6 how to use **IoAcquireRemoveLock** and some related functions to solve the problem.

A horrible synchronization problem lurks in the code fragments I just showed you, but it becomes apparent only if you look behind the increment and decrement operations inside **DispatchPnp**. On an x86 processor, the compiler might implement them using these instructions:

```
; ++lActiveRequests;
  mov eax, lActiveRequests
  add eax, 1
  mov lActiveRequests, eax

  ...
```

```
; --lActiveRequests;
  mov eax, lActiveRequests
  sub eax, 1
  mov lActiveRequests, eax
```

To expose the synchronization problem, let's consider first what might go wrong on a single CPU. Imagine two threads that are both trying to advance through DispatchPnp at roughly the same time. We know they're not both executing truly simultaneously because we have only a single CPU for them to share. But imagine that one of the threads is executing near the end of the function and manages to load the current contents of **lActiveRequests** into the EAX register just before it gets preempted by the other thread. Suppose that lActiveRequests equals 2 at that instant. As part of the thread switch, the operating system saves the EAX register (containing the value 2) as part of the outgoing thread's context image somewhere in main memory.

Now imagine that the other thread manages to get past the incrementing code at the beginning of DispatchPnp. It will increment lActiveRequests from 2 to 3 (because the first thread never got to update the variable). If this other thread gets preempted by the first thread, the operating system will restore the first thread's context, which includes the value 2 in the EAX register. The first thread now proceeds to subtract one from EAX and store the result back into lActiveRequests. At this point, lActiveRequests contains the value 1, which is incorrect. Somewhere down the road, we may prematurely delete our device object because we've effectively lost track of one I/O request.

Solving this particular problem is very easy on an x86 computer—we just replace the load/add/store and load/subtract/store instruction sequences with atomic instructions:

```
; ++lActiveRequests;
  inc lActiveRequests
  ...
; --lActiveRequests;
  dec lActiveRequests
```

On an Intel x86, the INC and DEC instructions cannot be interrupted, so there will never be a case where a thread could be preempted in the middle of updating the counter. As it stands, though, this code still isn't safe in a multiprocessor environment because INC and DEC are implemented in several microcode steps. It's possible for two different CPUs to be executing their microcode just slightly out of step such that one of them ends up updating a stale value. The multi-CPU problem can also be avoided in the x86 architecture by using a LOCK prefix:

```
; ++lActiveRequests;
  lock inc lActiveRequests
  ...
; --lActiveRequests;
  lock dec lActiveRequests
```

The LOCK instruction prefix locks out all other CPUs while the microcode for the current instruction executes, thereby guaranteeing data integrity.

Not all synchronization problems have such an easy solution, unfortunately. The point of this example isn't to demonstrate how to solve one simple problem on one of the platforms where Windows NT runs, but rather to illustrate the two sources of difficulty: preemption of one thread by another in the middle of a state change and simultaneous execution of conflicting state-change operations. As we'll see in the remainder of this chapter, we can avoid preemption by using the IRQL priority scheme, and we can prevent simultaneous execution by judiciously using spin locks.

INTERRUPT REQUEST LEVEL

Windows NT assigns a priority level known as the *interrupt request level* to each hardware interrupt and to a select few software events. IRQLs provide a synchronization method for activities on a single CPU based on the following rule:

Once a CPU is executing at an IRQL above PASSIVE_LEVEL, an activity on that CPU can be preempted only by an activity that executes at a higher IRQL.

Figure 4-1 illustrates the range of IRQL values for the x86 platform. (In general, the numeric values of IRQL depend on which platform you're talking about.) User-mode programs execute at PASSIVE_LEVEL and are therefore preemptable by any activity that executes at an elevated IRQL. Many of the functions in a device driver also execute at PASSIVE_LEVEL. The **DriverEntry** and **AddDevice** routines discussed in Chapter 2, "Basic Structure of a WDM Driver," are in this category, as are most of the I/O request packet (IRP) dispatch routines that I'll discuss in ensuing chapters.

Certain common driver routines execute at DISPATCH_LEVEL, which is higher than PASSIVE_LEVEL. These include the **StartIo** routine, deferred procedure call (DPC) routines, and many others. What they have in common is a need to access fields in the device object and device extension without interference from driver dispatch routines and each other. When one of these routines is running, the rule stated earlier guarantees that no thread can preempt it to execute a driver dispatch routine because the dispatch routine runs at a lower IRQL. Furthermore, no thread could preempt it to run another of these special routines because that other routine would run at the same IRQL. The rule, once again, is that preemption is allowed to run only an activity at a *higher* IRQL.

> **NOTE** *Dispatch routine* and *DISPATCH_LEVEL* have unfortunately similar names. Dispatch routines are so called because the I/O Manager dispatches I/O requests to them. DISPATCH_LEVEL is so called because it's the IRQL at which the kernel's thread dispatcher originally ran when deciding which thread to run next. (The thread dispatcher now usually runs at SYNCH_LEVEL, if you care.)

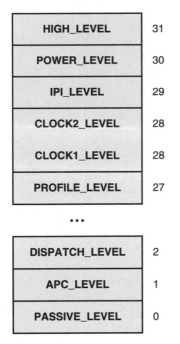

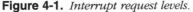

Figure 4-1. *Interrupt request levels.*

Between DISPATCH_LEVEL and PROFILE_LEVEL is room for various hardware interrupt levels. In general, each device that generates interrupts has an IRQL that defines its interrupt priority vis-à-vis other devices. A WDM driver discovers the IRQL for its interrupt when it receives an IRP_MJ_PNP request with the minor function code IRP_MN_START_DEVICE. The device's interrupt level is one of the many items of configuration information passed as a parameter to this request. We often refer to this level as the *device IRQL*, or DIRQL for short. DIRQL is not a single request level. Rather, it is the IRQL for the interrupt associated with whichever device is under discussion at the time.

The other IRQL levels have meanings that sometimes depend on the particular CPU architecture. Since those levels are used internally by the Windows NT kernel, their meanings aren't especially germane to the job of writing a device driver. The purpose of APC_LEVEL, for example, is to allow the system to schedule an *asynchronous procedure call* (APC), which I'll describe in detail later in this chapter, for a particular thread without interference from some other thread on the same CPU. Operations that occur at HIGH_LEVEL include taking a memory snapshot just prior to hibernating the computer, processing a bug check, handling a totally spurious interrupt, and others. I'm not going to attempt to provide an exhaustive list here because, as I said, you and I don't really need to know all the details.

IRQL in Operation

To illustrate the importance of IRQL, refer to Figure 4-2, which illustrates a possible time sequence of events on a single CPU. At the beginning of the sequence, the CPU is executing at PASSIVE_LEVEL. At time t_1, an interrupt arrives whose service routine executes at IRQL−1, one of the levels between DISPATCH_LEVEL and PROFILE_LEVEL. Then, at time t_2, another interrupt arrives whose service routine executes at IRQL−2, which is less than IRQL−1. Because of the preemption rule already discussed, the CPU continues servicing the first interrupt. When the first interrupt service routine completes at time t_3, it might request a DPC. DPC routines execute at DISPATCH_LEVEL. Consequently, the highest priority pending activity is the service routine for the second interrupt, which therefore executes next. When it finishes at t_4, assuming nothing else has occurred in the meantime, the DPC will run at DISPATCH_LEVEL. When the DPC routine finishes at t_5, IRQL can drop back to PASSIVE_LEVEL.

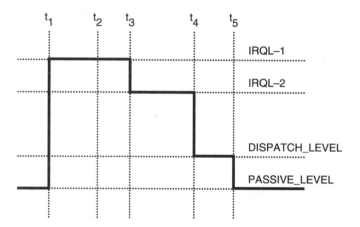

Figure 4-2. *Interrupt priority in action.*

The Basic Synchronization Rule

You can take advantage of IRQL's synchronizing effects by following this rule:

Always access shared data at the same elevated IRQL.

In other words, whenever and wherever your code will access a data object that it shares with some other code, make sure that you execute at some specified IRQL above PASSIVE_LEVEL. Once above PASSIVE_LEVEL, the operating system won't allow preemption by another activity at the same IRQL, so you thereby forestall potential interference. Following this rule isn't sufficient to protect data on a multiprocessor machine, however, so you often need to take the additional precaution of acquiring a spin lock, as described in "Spin Locks" later in this chapter. If you only had to worry about operations on a single CPU, IRQL might be the only synchronizing concept you'd need to use, but the reality is that all WDM drivers must be designed to run on multiprocessor systems.

IRQL Compared with Thread Priorities

Thread priority is a very different concept than IRQL. Thread priority controls the actions of the scheduler in deciding when to preempt running threads and what thread to start running next. No thread switching occurs at or above DISPATCH_LEVEL, however. Whatever thread is active at the time IRQL rises to DISPATCH_LEVEL remains active at least until IRQL drops below DISPATCH_LEVEL. The only "priority" that means anything at elevated IRQL is IRQL itself, and it controls which programs can execute rather than the thread context within which they execute.

IRQL and Paging

One consequence of running at elevated IRQL is that the system becomes incapable of servicing page faults. The rule this fact implies is simply stated:

Code executing at or above DISPATCH_LEVEL must not cause page faults.

One implication of this rule is that any of the subroutines in your driver that execute at or above DISPATCH_LEVEL must be in nonpaged memory. Furthermore, all the data you access in such a subroutine must also be in nonpaged memory. Finally, as IRQL rises, fewer and fewer kernel-mode support routines are available for your use.

The DDK documentation explicitly states the IRQL restrictions on support routines. For example, the entry for **KeWaitForSingleObject** indicates two restrictions:

1. The caller must be running at or below DISPATCH_LEVEL.

2. If a nonzero timeout period is specified in the call, the caller must be running strictly below DISPATCH_LEVEL.

Reading between the lines, what is being said here is this: if the call to KeWaitForSingleObject might conceivably block for any period of time (that is, you've specified a nonzero timeout), you must be below DISPATCH_LEVEL, where thread blocking is permitted. If all you want to do is check to see if an event has been signalled, however, you can be at DISPATCH_LEVEL. You cannot call this routine at all from an interrupt service routine or other routine running above DISPATCH_LEVEL.

Implicitly Controlling IRQL

Most of the time, the system calls the routines in your driver at the correct IRQL for the activities you're supposed to carry out. Although I haven't discussed many of these routines in detail, I want to give you an example of what I mean. Your first encounter with a new I/O request is when the I/O Manager calls one of your dispatch routines to process an IRP. The call occurs at PASSIVE_LEVEL because you might need to block the calling thread and you might need to call any support routine at all. You can't block a thread at a higher IRQL, of course, and PASSIVE_LEVEL is the only level at which there are no restrictions on the support routines you can call.

If your dispatch routine queues the IRP by calling **IoStartPacket**, your next encounter with the request will be when the I/O Manager calls your StartIo routine. This call occurs at DISPATCH_LEVEL because the system needs to access the queue of I/O requests without interference from the other routines that are inserting and removing IRPs from the queue. Remember the rule stated earlier: always access shared data objects at the same (elevated) IRQL. Since every routine that accesses the IRP queue does so at DISPATCH_LEVEL, it's not possible (on a single CPU, that is) for anyone to be interrupted in the middle of an operation on the queue.

Later on, your device might generate an interrupt, whereupon your interrupt service routine will be called at DIRQL. It's likely that some registers in your device can't safely be shared. If you only access those registers at DIRQL, you can be sure that no one can interfere with your interrupt service routine (ISR) on a single-CPU computer. If other parts of your driver need to access these crucial hardware registers, you would guarantee that those other parts execute only at DIRQL. The **KeSynchronizeExecution** service function helps you enforce that rule, and I'll discuss it in Chapter 7, "Reading and Writing Data," in connection with interrupt handling.

Still later, you might arrange to have a DPC routine called. DPC routines execute at DISPATCH_LEVEL because, among other things, they need to access your IRP queue to remove the next request from a queue and pass it to your StartIo routine. You call the **IoStartNextPacket** service routine to extract the next request from the queue, and it must be called at DISPATCH_LEVEL. It might call your StartIo routine before returning. Notice how neatly the IRQL requirements dovetail here: queue access, the call to IoStartNextPacket, and the possible call to StartIo are all required to occur at DISPATCH_LEVEL, and that's the level at which the system calls the DPC routine.

Although it's possible for you to explicitly control IRQL (and I'll explain how in the next section), there's seldom any reason to do so because of the correspondence between your needs and the level at which the system calls you. Consequently, you don't need to get hung up on which IRQL you're executing at from moment to moment: it's almost surely the correct level for the work you're supposed to do right then.

Explicitly Controlling IRQL

When necessary, you can raise and subsequently lower the IRQL on the current processor by calling **KeRaiseIrql** and **KeLowerIrql**. For example, from within a routine running at PASSIVE_LEVEL:

```
1   KIRQL oldirql;
2   ASSERT(KeGetCurrentIrql() <= DISPATCH_LEVEL);
3   KeRaiseIrql(DISPATCH_LEVEL, &oldirql);
    ...
4   KeLowerIrql(oldirql);
```

1. KIRQL is the typedef name for an integer that holds an IRQL value. We'll need a variable to hold the current IRQL, so we declare it this way.

2. This ASSERT expresses a necessary condition for calling KeRaiseIrql: the new IRQL must be greater than or equal to the current level. If this relation isn't true, KeRaiseIrql will bugcheck (that is, report a fatal error via a blue screen of death).

3. KeRaiseIrql raises the current IRQL to the level specified by the first argument. It also saves the current IRQL at the location pointed to by the second argument. In this example, we're raising IRQL to DISPATCH_LEVEL and saving the current level in **oldirql**.

4. After executing whatever code we desired to execute at elevated IRQL, we lower the request level back to its previous value by calling KeLowerIrql and specifying the oldirql value previously returned by KeRaiseIrql.

The DDK documentation says that you must call KeLowerIrql with the same value returned by the immediately preceding call to KeRaiseIrql. This is true in the larger sense that you *should* restore IRQL to what it was before you raised it. Otherwise, various assumptions made by code you call later or by the code which called you can later turn out to be incorrect. This statement in the documentation isn't true in the exact sense, however, because the only rule that KeLowerIrql actually applies is that the new IRQL must be less than or equal to the current one.

It's a mistake (and a big one!) to lower IRQL below whatever it was when some system routine called your driver, even if you raise it back before returning. Such a break in synchronization might allow some activity to preempt you and interfere with a data object that your caller assumed would remain inviolate.

You can use a special routine if you want to raise the IRQL to DISPATCH_LEVEL:

```
KIRQL oldirql = KeRaiseIrqlToDpcLevel();
...
KeLowerIrql(oldirql);
```

The advantage of using this service call is that you don't need to know or remember that DISPATCH_LEVEL is the level you're aiming for. In addition, since **KeRaiseIrqlToDpcLevel** returns the current IRQL as its value, this function is slightly more convenient to use than KeRaiseIrql.

SPIN LOCKS

Since IRQL is a per-CPU concept, it doesn't help you safeguard data against interference by code running on another processor in the same multiprocessor computer. A primitive object known as a *spin lock* serves that purpose. To acquire a spin lock, code on one CPU executes an atomic operation that tests and then sets some memory variable in such a way that no other CPU can access the variable until the operation completes. If the test indicates that the lock was previously free, the program continues. If the test indicates that the lock was previously busy, the program repeats the test-and-set in a tight loop: it "spins." Eventually the owner releases the lock by resetting the variable, whereupon one of the waiting CPUs' test-and-set operations will report the lock as free.

Two facts about spin locks are probably obvious but still worth stating. First of all, if a CPU already owns a spin lock and tries to obtain it a second time, the CPU will deadlock. No usage counter or owner identifier is associated with a spin lock; the lock is either owned by somebody or not. If you try to acquire it when it's owned, you will wait until the owner releases it. If your CPU happens to already be the owner, the code which would release the lock can never execute because you're spinning in a tight loop testing and setting the lock variable.

The second fact about spin locks is that no useful work occurs on a CPU that's waiting for a spin lock. Therefore, to avoid harming performance, you need to minimize the amount of work you do while holding a spin lock that some other CPU is likely to want.

There's another important fact about spin locks that's not obvious but still pretty important: you can only request a spin lock when you're running at or below DISPATCH_LEVEL, and the kernel will raise the IRQL to DISPATCH_LEVEL for the duration of your ownership of the lock. Internally, the kernel is able to acquire spin locks at an IRQL higher than DISPATCH_LEVEL, but you and I are unable to accomplish that feat.

Working with Spin Locks

To use a spin lock explicitly, allocate storage for a KSPIN_LOCK object in nonpaged memory. Then call **KeInitializeSpinLock** to initialize the object. Later, while running at or below DISPATCH_LEVEL, acquire the lock, perform the work that needs to be protected from interference, and then release the lock. For example, suppose that your device extension contains a spin lock named **QLock** that you use for guarding access to a special IRP queue you've set up. You'd initialize this lock in your AddDevice function:

```
typedef struct _DEVICE_EXTENSION {
  ...
  KSPIN_LOCK QLock;
  } DEVICE_EXTENSION, *PDEVICE_EXTENSION;

  ...
```

```
NTSTATUS AddDevice(...)
    {
    ...
    PDEVICE_EXTENSION pdx = ...;
    KeInitializeSpinLock(&pdx->QLock);
    ...
    }
```

Elsewhere in your driver, say in the dispatch function for some type of IRP, you could claim (and quickly release) the lock around some queue manipulation that you needed to perform. Note that this function must be in nonpaged memory because it executes for some period of time at an elevated IRQL.

```
NTSTATUS DispatchSomething(...)
    {
    KIRQL oldirql;
    PDEVICE_EXTENSION pdx = ...;
    KeAcquireSpinLock(&pdx->QLock, &oldirql);
    ...
    KeReleaseSpinLock(&pdx->QLock, oldirql);
    }
```

1. When **KeAcquireSpinLock** acquires the spin lock, it also raises IRQL to DISPATCH_LEVEL and returns the current (that is, preacquisition) level to us wherever the second argument points.

2. When **KeReleaseSpinLock** releases the spin lock, it also lowers IRQL back to the value specified in the second argument.

If you know you're already executing at DISPATCH_LEVEL, you can save a little time by calling two special routines. This technique is appropriate, for example, in DPC, StartIo, and other driver routines that execute at DISPATCH_LEVEL:

```
KeAcquireSpinLockAtDpcLevel(&pdx->QLock);
...
KeReleaseSpinLockFromDpcLevel(&pdx->QLock);
```

KERNEL DISPATCHER OBJECTS

The Windows NT kernel provides five types of synchronization objects that you can use to control the flow of nonarbitrary threads. See Table 4-1 for a summary of these *kernel dispatcher object* types and their uses. At any moment, one of these objects is in one of two states: *signalled* or *not-signalled*. At times when it's permissible for you to block a thread in whose context you're running, you can wait for one or more objects to reach the signalled state by calling **KeWaitForSingleObject** or **KeWaitForMultipleObjects**. The kernel also provides routines for initializing and controlling the state of each of these objects.

Object	Data Type	Description
Event	KEVENT	Blocks a thread until some other thread detects that an event has occurred
Semaphore	KSEMAPHORE	Used instead of an event when an arbitrary number of wait calls can be satisfied
Mutex	KMUTEX	Excludes other threads from executing a particular section of code
Timer	KTIMER	Delays execution of a thread for some period of time
Thread	KTHREAD	Blocks one thread until another thread terminates

Table 4-1. *Kernel dispatcher objects.*

In the next few sections, I'll describe how to use the kernel dispatcher objects. I'll start by explaining when you can block a thread by calling one of the wait primitives, and then I'll discuss the support routines that you use with each of the object types. I'll finish this section by discussing the related concepts of thread alerts and asynchronous procedure call delivery.

How and When You Can Block

To understand when and how it's permissible for a WDM driver to block a thread on a kernel dispatcher object, you have to know some basic facts about threads. In general, whatever thread was executing at the time of a software or hardware interrupt continues to be the "current" thread while the kernel processes the interrupt. We speak of executing kernel-mode code "in the context" of this current thread. In response to interrupts of various kinds, the Windows NT scheduler might decide to switch threads, of course, in which case a new thread becomes "current."

We use the terms *arbitrary thread context* and *nonarbitrary thread context* to describe the precision with which we can know the thread in whose context we're currently operating in a driver subroutine. If we know that we're in the context of the thread which initiated an I/O request, the context is not arbitrary. Most of the time, however, a WDM driver can't know this fact because chance usually controls which thread is active when the interrupt occurs that results in the driver being called. When applications issue I/O requests, they cause a transition from user mode to kernel mode. The I/O Manager routines that create an IRP and send it to a driver dispatch routine continue to operate in this nonarbitrary thread context, as does the first dispatch routine to see the IRP. We use the term *highest-level driver* to describe the driver whose dispatch routine first receives the IRP.

As a general rule, only the highest-level driver for a given device can know for sure that it's operating in a nonarbitrary thread context. This is because driver dispatch routines often put requests onto queues and return back to their callers. Queued requests are then removed from their queues and forwarded to lower-level drivers from within callback routines that execute later. Once a dispatch routine pends a request, all subsequent processing of that request must occur in arbitrary thread context.

Having explained these facts about thread context, we can state a simple rule about when it's okay to block a thread:

Block only the thread that originated the request you're working on.

To follow this rule, you generally have to be the highest-level driver for the device that's getting sent the IRP. One important exception occurs for requests like IRP_MN_START_DEVICE—see Chapter 6—that all drivers process in a synchronous way. That is, drivers don't queue or pend certain requests. When you receive one of these requests, you can trace the call/return stack directly back to the originator of the request. As we'll see in Chapter 6, it's not only okay for you to block the thread in which you process these requests, but blocking and waiting is the prescribed way to handle them.

One more rule should be obvious from the fact that thread switching doesn't occur at elevated IRQL:

You can't block a thread if you're executing at or above DISPATCH_LEVEL.

As a practical matter, this rule means that you must be in your DriverEntry or AddDevice function to block the current thread, or else in a driver dispatch function. All of these functions execute at PASSIVE_LEVEL. I'm hard-pressed to think of why you might need to block to finish DriverEntry or AddDevice, even, because those functions merely initialize data structures for downstream use.

Waiting on a Single Dispatcher Object

You call KeWaitForSingleObject as illustrated in the following example:

```
ASSERT(KeGetCurrentIrql() <= DISPATCH_LEVEL);
LARGE_INTEGER timeout;
NTSTATUS status = KeWaitForSingleObject(object, WaitReason,
  WaitMode, Alertable, &timeout);
```

As suggested by the ASSERT, you must be executing at or below DISPATCH_LEVEL to even call this service routine.

In this call, **object** points to the object on which you wish to wait. While this argument is typed as a PVOID, it should be a pointer to one of the dispatcher objects listed in Table 4-1. The object must be in nonpaged memory—for example, in a device extension structure or other data area allocated from the nonpaged pool. For most purposes, the execution stack can be considered nonpaged.

WaitReason is a purely advisory value chosen from the KWAIT_REASON enumeration. No code in the kernel actually cares what value you supply here, so long as you don't specify **WrQueue**. (Internally, scheduler code bases some decisions on whether a thread is currently blocked for this "reason.") The reason a thread is blocked is saved in an opaque data structure, though. If you knew more about that data structure and were trying to debug a deadlock of some kind, you could perhaps gain clues from the reason code. The bottom line: always specify **Executive** for this parameter; there's no reason to say anything else.

WaitMode is one of the two values of the MODE enumeration: **KernelMode** or **UserMode**. **Alertable** is a simple Boolean value. Unlike WaitReason, these parameters *do* make a difference to the way the system behaves, by controlling whether the wait can be terminated early in order to deliver asynchronous procedure calls of various kinds. I'll explain these interactions in more detail in "Thread Alerts and APCs" later in this chapter. Waiting in user mode also authorizes the Memory Manager to swap your thread's kernel-mode stack out. You'll see examples in this book and elsewhere where drivers create event objects, for instance, as automatic variables. A bug check would result if some other thread were to call **KeSetEvent** at elevated IRQL at a time when the event object was absent from memory. The bottom line: you should probably always wait in KernelMode and specify FALSE for the alertable parameter.

The last parameter to KeWaitForSingleObject is the address of a 64-bit timeout value, expressed in 100-nanosecond units. A positive number for the timeout is an absolute timestamp relative to the same January 1, 1601, epoch of the system clock. You can determine the current time by calling **KeQuerySystemTime**. A negative number is an interval relative to the current time. If you specify an absolute time, a subsequent change to the system clock alters the duration of the timeout you might experience. That is, the timeout doesn't expire until the system clock equals or exceeds whatever absolute value you specify. In contrast, if you specify a relative timeout, the duration of the timeout you experience is unaffected by changes in the system clock.

WHY JANUARY 1, 1601?

Years ago when I was first learning the Win32 API, I was bemused by the choice of January 1, 1601, as the origin for the timestamps in Windows NT. I understood the reason for this choice when I had occasion to write a set of conversion routines. Everyone knows that years divisible by four are leap years. Many people know that century years (such as 1900) are exceptions—they're not leap years even though they're divisible by 4. A few people know that every fourth century year (such as 1600 and 2000) is an exception to the exception—they *are* leap years. January 1, 1601 was the start of a 400-year cycle that ends in a leap

(continued)

---

continued

year. If you base timestamps on this origin, it's possible to write programs that convert a Windows NT timestamp into a conventional representation of the date (and vice versa) without doing any jumps.

Specifying a zero timeout causes KeWaitForSingleObject to return immediately with a status code indicating whether the object is in the signalled state. *If you're executing at DISPATCH_LEVEL, you* must *specify a zero timeout because blocking is not allowed.* Each kernel dispatcher object offers a **KeReadState***Xxx* service function that allows you to determine the state of the object. Reading the state is not completely equivalent to waiting for zero time, however: when KeWaitForSingleObject discovers that the wait is satisfied, it performs the side effects that the particular object requires. In contrast, reading the state of the object does not perform the side effects, even if the object is already signalled and a wait would be satisfied if it were requested right now.

Specifying a NULL pointer for the timeout parameter is okay and indicates an infinite wait.

The return value indicates one of several possible results. STATUS_SUCCESS is the result you expect and indicates that the wait was satisfied. That is, either the object was in the signalled state when you made the call to KeWaitForSingleObject, or else the object was in the not-signalled state and later became signalled. When the wait is satisfied in this way, there may be side effects that need to be performed on the object. The nature of these side effects depends on the type of the object, and I'll explain them later in this chapter in connection with discussing each type of object. (For example, a synchronization type of event will be reset after your wait is satisfied.)

A return value of STATUS_TIMEOUT indicates that the specified timeout occurred without the object reaching the signalled state. If you specify a zero timeout, KeWaitForSingleObject returns immediately with either this code (indicating that the object is not-signalled) or STATUS_SUCCESS (indicating that the object is signalled). This return value is not possible if you specify a NULL timeout parameter pointer, because you thereby request an infinite wait.

Two other return values are possible. STATUS_ALERTED and STATUS_USER_APC mean that the wait has terminated without the object having been signalled because the thread has received an alert or a user-mode APC, respectively. I'll discuss these concepts a bit further on in "Thread Alerts and APCs."

Waiting on Multiple Dispatcher Objects

KeWaitForMultipleObjects is a companion function to KeWaitForSingleObject that you use when you want to wait for one or all of several dispatcher objects simultaneously. Call this function as in the example at the top of the following page.

```
ASSERT(KeGetCurrentIrql() <= DISPATCH_LEVEL);
LARGE_INTEGER timeout;
NTSTATUS status = KeWaitForMultipleObjects(count, objects,
  WaitType, WaitReason, WaitMode, Alertable, &timeout,waitblocks);
```

Here, **objects** is the address of an array of pointers to dispatcher objects, and **count** is the number of pointers in the array. The count must be less than or equal to the value MAXIMUM_WAIT_OBJECTS, which currently equals 64. The array, as well as each of the objects to which the elements of the array point, must be in nonpaged memory. **WaitType** is one of the enumeration values **WaitAll** or **WaitAny** and specifies whether you want to wait until all of the objects are simultaneously in the signalled state or whether, instead, you want to wait until any one of the objects is signalled.

The **waitblocks** argument points to an array of KWAIT_BLOCK structures that the kernel will use to administer the wait operation. You don't need to initialize these structures in any way—the kernel just needs to know where the storage is for the group of wait blocks that it will use to record the status of each of the objects during the pendency of the wait. If you're waiting for a small number of objects (specifically, a number no bigger than THREAD_WAIT_OBJECTS, which currently equals 3), you can supply NULL for this parameter. If you supply NULL, KeWaitForMultipleObjects uses a preallocated array of wait blocks that lives in the thread object. If you're waiting for more objects than this, you must provide nonpaged memory that's at least **count * sizeof(KWAIT_BLOCK)** bytes in length.

The remaining arguments to KeWaitForMultipleObjects are the same as the corresponding arguments to KeWaitForSingleObject, and most return codes have the same meaning.

If you specify **WaitAll**, the return value STATUS_SUCCESS indicates that all the objects managed to reach the signalled state simultaneously. If you specify **WaitAny**, the return value is numerically equal to the **objects** array index of the single object that satisfied the wait. If more than one of the objects happens to be signalled, you'll be told about one of them—maybe the lowest numbered of all the ones that are signalled at that moment, but maybe some other one. You can think of this value being STATUS_WAIT_0 plus the array index. You can perform the usual NT_SUCCESS test of the returned status before extracting the array index from the status code:

```
NTSTATUS status = KeWaitForMultipleObjects(...);
if (NT_SUCCESS(status))
  {
  ULONG iSignalled = (ULONG) status - (ULONG) STATUS_WAIT_0;
  ...
  }
```

When KeWaitForMultipleObjects returns a success code, it also performs the side effects required by the object(s) that satisfied the wait. If more than one object is signalled but you specified WaitAny, only the one that's deemed to satisfy the wait has its side effects performed.

Kernel Events

You use the service functions listed in Table 4-2 to work with kernel event objects. To initialize an event object, first reserve nonpaged storage for an object of type KEVENT and then call **KeInitializeEvent**:

```
ASSERT(KeGetCurrentIrql() == PASSIVE_LEVEL;
KeInitializeEvent(event, EventType, initialstate);
```

Event is the address of the event object. **EventType** is one of the enumeration values **NotificationEvent** or **SynchronizationEvent.** A notification event has the characteristic that, when it is set to the signalled state, it stays signalled until it is explicitly reset to the not-signalled state. Furthermore, all threads that wait on a notification event are released when the event is signalled. This is like a manual-reset event in user mode. A synchronization event, on the other hand, gets reset to the not-signalled state as soon as a single thread gets released. This is what happens in user mode when someone calls **SetEvent** on an auto-reset event object. The only side effect performed on an event object by KeWait*Xxx* is to reset a synchronization event to not-signalled. Finally, **initialstate** is TRUE to specify that the initial state of the event is to be signalled and FALSE to specify that the initial state is to be not-signalled.

Service Function	Description
KeClearEvent	Sets event to not-signalled, don't report previous state
KeInitializeEvent	Initializes event object
KeReadStateEvent	Determines current state of event
KeResetEvent	Sets event to not-signalled, return previous state
KeSetEvent	Sets event to signalled, return previous state

Table 4-2. *Service functions for use with kernel event objects.*

NOTE In this series of sections on synchronization primitives, I'm repeating the IRQL restrictions that the DDK documentation describes. In the current release of Microsoft Windows 2000, the DDK is sometimes more restrictive than the OS actually is. For example, KeClearEvent can be called at any IRQL, not just at or below DISPATCH_LEVEL. KeInitializeEvent can be called at any IRQL, not just at PASSIVE_LEVEL. However, you should regard the statements in the DDK as being tantamount to saying that Microsoft might someday impose the documented restriction, which is why I haven't tried to report the true state of affairs.

You can call **KeSetEvent** to place an event into the signalled state:

```
ASSERT(KeGetCurrentIrql() <= DISPATCH_LEVEL);
LONG wassignalled = KeSetEvent(event, boost, wait);
```

As implied by the ASSERT, you must be running at or below DISPATCH_LEVEL to call this function. The **event** argument is a pointer to the event object in question, and **boost** is a value to be added to a waiting thread's priority if setting the event results in satisfying someone's wait. See the sidebar ("That Pesky Third Argument to KeSetEvent") for an explanation of the Boolean **wait** argument, which a WDM driver would almost never want to specify as TRUE. The return value is nonzero if the event was already in the signalled state before the call and 0 if the event was in the not-signalled state.

A multitasking scheduler needs to artificially boost the priority of a thread that waits for I/O operations or synchronization objects in order to avoid starving threads that spend lots of time waiting. This is because a thread that blocks for some reason generally relinquishes its time slice and won't regain the CPU until either it has a relatively higher priority than other eligible threads or other threads that have the same priority finish their time slices. A thread that never blocks, however, gets to complete its time slices. Unless a boost is applied to the thread that repeatedly blocks, therefore, it will spend a lot of time waiting for CPU-bound threads to finish their time slices.

You and I won't always have a good idea of what value to use for a priority boost. A good rule of thumb to follow is to specify IO_NO_INCREMENT unless you have a good reason not to. If setting the event is going to wake up a thread that's dealing with a time-sensitive data flow (such as a sound driver), supply the boost that's appropriate to that kind of device (such as IO_SOUND_INCREMENT). The important thing is to not boost the waiter for a silly reason. For example, if you're trying to handle an IRP_MJ_PNP request synchronously—see Chapter 6—you'll be waiting for lower-level drivers to handle the IRP before you proceed and your completion routine will be calling KeSetEvent. Since Plug and Play requests have no special claim on the processor and occur only infrequently, specify IO_NO_INCREMENT even for a sound card.

THAT PESKY THIRD ARGUMENT TO KESETEVENT

The purpose of the **wait** argument to KeSetEvent is to allow internal code to hand off control from one thread to another very quickly. System components other than device drivers can, for example, create paired event objects that are used by client and server threads to gate their communication. When the server wants to wake up its paired client, it will call KeSetEvent with the **wait** argument set to TRUE and then *immediately* call KeWait*Xxx* to put itself to sleep. The use of **wait** allows these two operations to be done atomically so that no other thread can be awakened in between and possibly wrest control away from the client and the server.

(continued)

---

continued

The DDK has always sort of described what happens internally, but I've found the explanation confusing. I'll try to explain it in a different way so that you can see why you should always say FALSE for this parameter. Internally, the kernel uses a "dispatcher database lock" to guard operations related to thread blocking, waking, and scheduling. KeSetEvent needs to acquire this lock, and so do the KeWait*Xxx* routines. If you say TRUE for this argument, KeSetEvent sets a flag so that KeWait*Xxx* will know you did so, and it returns to you without releasing this lock. When you turn around and (immediately, please—you're running at a higher IRQL than every hardware device and you own a spin lock that's *very* frequently in contention) call KeWait*Xxx*, it needn't acquire the lock all over again. The net effect is that you'll wake up the waiting thread and put yourself to sleep without giving any other thread a chance to start running.

You can see, first of all, that a function which calls KeSetEvent with **wait** set to TRUE has to be in nonpaged memory because it will execute briefly at elevated IRQL. But it's hard to imagine why an ordinary device driver would even need to use this mechanism because it would almost never know better than the kernel which thread ought to be scheduled next. The bottom line: always say FALSE for this parameter. In fact, it's not clear why the parameter has even been exposed to tempt us.

You can determine the current state of an event (at any IRQL) by calling **KeReadStateEvent**:

```
LONG signalled = KeReadStateEvent(event);
```

The return value is nonzero if the event is signalled, 0 if it's not-signalled.

> **NOTE** KeReadStateEvent is not supported in Microsoft Windows 98 even though the other KeReadState*Xxx* functions described here are. The absence of support has to do with how events and other synchronization primitives are implemented in Windows 98.

You can determine the current state of an event and, immediately thereafter, place it in the not-signalled state by calling the **KeResetEvent** function (at or below DISPATCH_LEVEL):

```
ASSERT(KeGetCurrentIrql() <= DISPATCH_LEVEL);
LONG signalled = KeResetEvent(event);
```

If you're not interested in the previous state of the event, you can save a little time by calling **KeClearEvent** instead, as shown at the top of the next page.

```
ASSERT(KeGetCurrentIrql() <= DISPATCH_LEVEL);
KeClearEvent(event);
```

KeClearEvent is faster because it doesn't need to capture the current state of the event before setting it to not-signalled.

Kernel Semaphores

A *kernel semaphore* is an integer counter with associated synchronization semantics. The semaphore is considered signalled when the counter is positive and not-signalled when the counter is 0. The counter cannot take on a negative value. Releasing a semaphore increases the counter, whereas successfully waiting on a semaphore decrements the counter. If the decrement makes the count 0, the semaphore is then considered not-signalled, with the consequence that other KeWait*Xxx* callers who insist on finding it signalled will block. Note that if more threads are waiting for a semaphore than the value of the counter, not all of the waiting threads will be unblocked.

The kernel provides three service functions to control the state of a semaphore object. (See Table 4-3.) You initialize a semaphore by making the following function call at PASSIVE_LEVEL:

```
ASSERT(KeGetCurrentIrql() == PASSIVE_LEVEL);
KeInitializeSemaphore(semaphore, count, limit);
```

In this call, **semaphore** points to a KSEMAPHORE object in nonpaged memory. **Count** is the initial value of the counter, and **limit** is the maximum value that the counter will be allowed to take on, which must be as large as the initial count.

Service Function	Description
KeInitializeSemaphore	Initializes semaphore object
KeReadStateSemaphore	Determines current state of semaphore
KeReleaseSemaphore	Sets semaphore object to the signalled state

Table 4-3. *Service functions for use with kernel semaphore objects.*

If you create a semaphore with a limit of 1, the object is somewhat similar to a mutex in that only one thread at a time will be able to claim it. A kernel mutex has some features that a semaphore lacks, however, to help prevent deadlocks. Accordingly, there's almost no point in creating a semaphore with a limit of 1.

If you create a semaphore with a limit bigger than 1, you have an object that allows multiple threads to access some resource. A familiar theorem in queuing theory dictates that providing a single queue for multiple servers is more fair (that is, results in less variation in waiting times) than providing a separate queue for each of several servers. The average waiting time is the same in both cases, but the variation in waiting times is smaller. (This is why queues in stores are increasingly organized so that customers wait in a single line for the next available clerk.) This kind of semaphore allows you to organize a set of software or hardware servers to take advantage of that theorem.

The owner (or one of the owners) of a semaphore releases its claim to the semaphore by calling **KeReleaseSemaphore**:

```
ASSERT(KeGetCurrentIrql() <= DISPATCH_LEVEL);
LONG wassignalled = KeReleaseSemaphore(semaphore, boost, delta, wait);
```

This operation adds **delta**, which must be positive, to the counter associated with **semaphore**, thereby putting the semaphore into the signalled state and allowing other threads to be released. In most cases, you would specify 1 for this parameter to indicate that one claimant of the semaphore is releasing its claim. The **boost** and **wait** parameters have the same import as the corresponding parameters to KeSetEvent, discussed earlier. The return value is 0 if the previous state of the semaphore was not-signalled and nonzero if the previous state was signalled.

KeReleaseSemaphore doesn't allow you to increase the counter beyond the limit specified when you initialized the semaphore. If you try, it does not adjust the counter at all, and it raises an exception with the code STATUS_SEMAPHORE_ LIMIT_EXCEEDED. Unless someone has a structured exception handler to trap the exception, a bug check will eventuate.

You can also interrogate the current state of a semaphore with this call:

```
ASSERT(KeGetCurrentIrql() <= DISPATCH_LEVEL);
LONG signalled = KeReadStateSemaphore(semaphore);
```

The return value is nonzero if the semaphore is signalled and 0 if the semaphore is not-signalled. You shouldn't assume that the return value is the current value of the counter—it could be any nonzero value if the counter is positive.

Kernel Mutexes

The word *mutex* is a contraction of *mutual exclusion*. A kernel mutex object provides one method (and not necessarily the best one) to serialize access by competing threads to some shared resource. The mutex is signalled if no thread owns it and not-signalled if some thread currently does own it. When a thread gains control of a mutex after calling one of the KeWait*Xxx* routines, the kernel also takes some steps to help avoid possible deadlocks. These are the side effects referred to in the earlier discussion of KeWaitForSingleObject (in the section "Waiting on a Single Dispatcher Object"). The kernel ensures that the thread can't be paged out, and it forestalls all but the delivery of "special" kernel APCs (such as the one that **IoCompleteRequest** uses to complete I/O requests).

It's generally better to use an executive fast mutex rather than a kernel mutex, as I'll explain in more detail later in "Fast Mutex Objects." The main difference between the two is that a kernel mutex can be acquired recursively, whereas an executive fast mutex cannot. That is, the owner of a kernel mutex can make a subsequent call to KeWait*Xxx* specifying the same mutex and have the wait immediately satisfied. A thread that does this must release the mutex an equal number of times before the mutex will be considered free.

The reason you would use a mutex in the first place (instead of relying on elevated IRQL and a spin lock) is that you need to serialize access to an object for a long time or in pagable code. By gating access to a resource through a mutex, you allow other threads to run on the other CPUs of a multiprocessor system, and you also allow your code to cause page faults while still locking out other threads. Table 4-4 lists the service functions you use with mutex objects.

Service Function	Description
KeInitializeMutex	Initializes mutex object
KeReadStateMutex	Determines current state of mutex
KeReleaseMutex	Sets mutex object to the signalled state

Table 4-4. *Service functions for use with kernel mutex objects.*

To create a mutex, you reserve nonpaged memory for a KMUTEX object and make the following initialization call:

```
ASSERT(KeGetCurrentIrql() == PASSIVE_LEVEL);
KeInitializeMutex(mutex, level);
```

where **mutex** is the address of the KMUTEX object, and **level** is a parameter originally intended to help avoid deadlocks when your own code uses more than one mutex. Since the kernel currently ignores the **level** parameter, I'm not going to attempt to describe what it used to mean.

The mutex begins life in the signalled—that is, unowned—state. An immediate call to KeWait*Xxx* would take control of the mutex and put it into the not-signalled state.

You can interrogate the current state of a mutex with this function call:

```
ASSERT(KeGetCurrentIrql() <= DISPATCH_LEVEL);
LONG signalled = KeReadStateMutex(mutex);
```

The return value is 0 if the mutex is currently owned, nonzero if it's currently unowned.

The thread that owns a mutex can release ownership and return the mutex to the signalled state with this function call:

```
ASSERT(KeGetCurrentIrql() <= DISPATCH_LEVEL);
LONG wassignalled = KeReleaseMutex(mutex, wait);
```

The **wait** parameter means the same thing as the corresponding argument to KeSetEvent. The return value is always 0 to indicate that the mutex was previously owned because, if this were not the case, **KeReleaseMutex** would have bugchecked (it being an error for anyone but the owner to release a mutex).

Just for the sake of completeness, I want to mention a macro in the DDK named **KeWaitForMutexObject**. (See WDM.H.) It is defined simply as follows:

```
#define KeWaitForMutexObject KeWaitForSingleObject
```

Using this special name offers no benefit at all. You don't even get the benefit of having the compiler insist that the first argument be a pointer to a KMUTEX instead of any random pointer type.

Kernel Timers

The kernel provides a timer object that functions something like an event that automatically signals itself at a specified absolute time or after a specified interval. It's also possible to create a timer that signals itself repeatedly and to arrange for a DPC callback following the expiration of the timer. Table 4-5 lists the service functions you use with timer objects. With so many different ways of using timers, it will be easiest to describe the use of these functions in several different scenarios.

Service Function	*Description*
KeCancelTimer	Cancels an active timer
KeInitializeTimer	Initializes a one-time notification timer
KeInitializeTimerEx	Initializes a one-time or repetitive notification or synchronization timer
KeReadStateTimer	Determines current state of a timer
KeSetTimer	(Re)specifies expiration time for a notification timer
KeSetTimerEx	(Re)specifies expiration time and other properties of a timer

Table 4-5. *Service functions for use with kernel timer objects.*

Notification Timers Used like Events

In this scenario, we'll create a notification timer object and wait until it expires. First allocate a KTIMER object in nonpaged memory. Then, running at or below DISPATCH_LEVEL, initialize the timer object, as at the top of the next page.

```
PKTIMER timer;        // ← someone gives you this
ASSERT(KeGetCurrentIrql() <= DISPATCH_LEVEL);
KeInitializeTimer(timer);
```

At this point, the timer is in the not-signalled state and isn't counting down—a wait on the timer would never be satisfied. To start the timer counting, call **KeSetTimer** as follows:

```
ASSERT(KeGetCurrentIrql() <= DISPATCH_LEVEL);
LARGE_INTEGER duetime;
BOOLEAN wascounting = KeSetTimer(timer, &duetime, NULL);
```

The **duetime** value is a 64-bit time value expressed in 100-nanosecond units. If the value is positive, it is an absolute time relative to the same January 1, 1601, epoch used for the system timer. If the value is negative, it is an interval relative to the current time. If you specify an absolute time, a subsequent change to the system clock alters the duration of the timeout you experience. That is, the timer doesn't expire until the system clock equals or exceeds whatever absolute value you specify. In contrast, if you specify a relative timeout, the duration of the timeout you experience is unaffected by changes in the system clock. These are the same rules that apply to the timeout parameter to KeWait*Xxx*.

The return value from KeSetTimer, if TRUE, indicates that the timer was already counting down (in which case our call to KeSetTimer would have cancelled it and started the count all over again).

At any time, you can determine the current state of a timer:

```
ASSERT(KeGetCurrentIrql() <= DISPATCH_LEVEL);
BOOLEAN counting = KeReadStateTimer(timer);
```

KeInitializeTimer and KeSetTimer are actually older service functions that have been superseded by newer functions. We could have initialized the timer with this call:

```
ASSERT(KeGetCurrentIqrl() <= DISPATCH_LEVEL);
KeInitializeTimerEx(timer, NotificationTimer);
```

We could also have used the extended version of the set timer function, **KeSetTimerEx**:

```
ASSERT(KeGetCurrentIrql() <= DISPATCH_LEVEL);
LARGE_INTEGER duetime;
BOOLEAN wascounting = KeSetTimerEx(timer, &duetime, 0, NULL);
```

I'll explain a bit further on in this chapter the purpose of extra parameters in these extended versions of the service functions.

Once the timer is counting down, it's still considered to be not-signalled until the specified due time arrives. At that point, the object becomes signalled, and all waiting threads are released. The system guarantees only that the expiration of the timer will be noticed no sooner than the due time you specify. If you specify a due time with a precision finer than the granularity of the system timer (which you can't control), the timeout will be noticed later than the exact instant you specify.

Notification Timers Used with a DPC

In this scenario, we want expiration of the timer to trigger a DPC. You would choose this method of operation if you wanted to be sure that you could service the timeout no matter what priority level your thread had. (Since you can only wait at PASSIVE_LEVEL, regaining control of the CPU after the timer expires is subject to the normal vagaries of thread scheduling. The DPC, however, executes at elevated IRQL and thereby effectively preempts *all* threads.)

We initialize the timer object in the same way. We also have to initialize a KDPC object for which we allocate nonpaged memory. For example:

```
PKDPC dpc; // ← points to KDPC you've allocated
ASSERT(KeGetCurrentIrql() == PASSIVE_LEVEL);
KeInitializeTimer(timer);
KeInitializeDpc(dpc, DpcRoutine, context);
```

You can initialize the timer object by using either KeInitializeTimer or KeInitializeTimerEx, as you please. **DpcRoutine** is the address of a deferred procedure call routine, which must be in nonpaged memory. The **context** parameter is an arbitrary 32-bit value (typed as a PVOID) that will be passed as an argument to the DPC routine. The **dpc** argument is a pointer to a KDPC object for which you provide nonpaged storage. (It might be in your device extension, for example.)

When we want to start the timer counting down, we specify the DPC object as one of the arguments to KeSetTimer or KeSetTimerEx:

```
ASSERT(KeGetCurrentIrql() <= DISPATCH_LEVEL);
LARGE_INTEGER duetime;
BOOLEAN wascounting = KeSetTimer(timer, &duetime, dpc);
```

You could also use the extended form KeSetTimerEx if you wanted to. The only difference between this call and the one we examined in the previous section is that we've specified the DPC object address as an argument. When the timer expires, the system will queue the DPC for execution as soon as conditions permit. This would be at least as soon as you'd be able to wake up from a wait at PASSIVE_LEVEL. Your DPC routine would have the following skeletal appearance:

```
VOID DpcRoutine(PKDPC dpc, PVOID context, PVOID junk1, PVOID junk2)
  {
  ...
  }
```

For what it's worth, even when you supply a DPC argument to KeSetTimer or KeSetTimerEx, you can still call KeWait*Xxx* to wait at PASSIVE_LEVEL if you want.

On a single-CPU system, the DPC would occur before the wait could finish because it executes at higher IRQL.

Synchronization Timers

Like event objects, timer objects come in both notification and synchronization flavors. A notification timer allows any number of waiting threads to proceed once it expires. A synchronization timer, by contrast, allows only a single thread to proceed. Once some thread's wait is satisfied, the timer switches to the not-signalled state. To create a synchronization timer, you must use the extended form of the initialization service function:

```
ASSERT(KeGetCurrentIrql() <= DISPATCH_LEVEL);
KeInitializeTimerEx(timer, SynchronizationTimer);
```

SynchronizationTimer is one of the values of the TIMER_TYPE enumeration. The other value is **NotificationTimer.**

If you use a DPC with a synchronization timer, think of queuing the DPC as being an extra thing that happens when the timer expires. That is, expiration puts the timer into the signalled state *and* queues a DPC. One thread can be released as a result of the timer being signalled.

Periodic Timers

So far, I've discussed only timers that expire exactly once. By using the extended set timer function, you can also request a periodic timeout:

```
ASSERT(KeGetCurrentIrql() <= DISPATCH_LEVEL);
LARGE_INTEGER duetime;
BOOLEAN wascounting = KeSetTimerEx(timer, &duetime, period, dpc);
```

Here, **period** is a periodic timeout, expressed in milliseconds (ms), and **dpc** is an optional pointer to a KDPC object. A timer of this kind expires once at the due time and periodically thereafter. To achieve exactly periodic expiration, specify the same relative due time as the interval. Specifying a zero due time causes the timer to immediately expire, whereupon the periodic behavior takes over. It often makes sense to start a periodic timer in conjunction with a DPC object, by the way, because doing so allows you to be notified without having to repeatedly wait for the timeout.

An Example

One use for kernel timers is to conduct a polling loop in a system thread dedicated to the task of repeatedly checking a device for activity. Not many devices nowadays need to be served by a polling loop, but yours may be one of the few exceptions. I'll discuss this subject in Chapter 9, "Specialized Topics," and the companion disc includes a sample driver (POLLING) that illustrates all of the concepts involved. Part of that sample is the following loop that polls the device at fixed intervals. The logic of the driver is such that the loop can be broken by setting a kill event. Consequently, the driver uses KeWaitForMultipleObjects. The code is actually a bit more complicated than the following fragment, which I've edited to concentrate on the part related to the timer:

```
VOID PollingThreadRoutine(PDEVICE_EXTENSION pdx)
  {
  NTSTATUS status;
  KTIMER timer;
  KeInitializeTimerEx(&timer, SynchronizationTimer);
  PVOID pollevents[] = {
    (PVOID) &pdx->evKill,
    (PVOID) &timer,
    };
  ASSERT(arraysize(pollevents) <= THREAD_WAIT_OBJECTS);

  LARGE_INTEGER duetime = {0};
  #define POLLING_INTERVAL 500
  KeSetTimerEx(&timer, duetime, POLLING_INTERVAL, NULL);
  while (TRUE)
    {
    status = KeWaitForMultipleObjects(arraysize(pollevents),
      pollevents, WaitAny, Executive, KernelMode, FALSE, NULL, NULL);
    if (status == STATUS_WAIT_0)
      break;
    if (<device needs attention>)
      <do something>;
    }
  KeCancelTimer(&timer);
  PsTerminateSystemThread(STATUS_SUCCESS);
  }
```

1. Here we initialize a kernel timer object to act as a synchronization timer. It would have worked just as well to initialize it as a notification timer because only one thread—this one—will ever wait on the timer.

2. We'll need to supply an array of dispatcher object pointers as one of the arguments to KeWaitForMultipleObjects, and this is where we set that up. The first element of the array is the kill event that some other part of the driver might set when it's time for this system thread to exit. The second element is the timer object. The ASSERT statement that follows this array verifies that we have few enough objects in our array such that we can implicitly use the default array of wait blocks in our thread object.

3. The KeSetTimerEx statement starts a periodic timer running. The **duetime** is 0, so the timer goes immediately into the signalled state. It will expire every 500 ms thereafter.

4. Within our polling loop, we wait for the timer to expire or for the kill event to be set. If the wait terminates because of the kill event, we leave the loop, clean up, and exit this system thread. If the wait terminates because the timer has expired, we go on to the next step.

5. This is where our device driver would do something related to our hardware.

Alternatives to Kernel Timers

Rather than using a kernel timer object, you can use two other timing functions that might be more appropriate. First of all, you can call **KeDelayExecutionThread** to wait at PASSIVE_LEVEL for a given interval. This function is obviously less cumbersome than creating, initializing, setting, and awaiting a timer by using separate function calls:

```
ASSERT(KeGetCurrentIrql() == PASSIVE_LEVEL);
LARGE_INTEGER duetime;
NSTATUS status = KeDelayExecutionThread(WaitMode, Alertable, &duetime);
```

Here, **WaitMode**, **Alertable**, and the returned status code have the same meaning as the corresponding parameters to KeWait*Xxx*, and **duetime** is the same kind of timestamp that I discussed previously in connection with kernel timers.

If your requirement is to delay for a very brief period of time (less than 50 microseconds), you can call **KeStallExecutionProcessor** at any IRQL:

```
KeStallExecutionProcessor(nMicroSeconds);
```

The purpose of this delay is to allow your hardware time to prepare for its next operation before your program continues executing. The delay might end up being significantly longer than you request because KeStallExecutionProcessor can be preempted by activities that occur at a higher IRQL than that which the caller is using.

Using Threads for Synchronization

The Process Structure component of the operating system provides a few routines that WDM drivers can use for creating and controlling system threads. I'll be discussing these routines later on in Chapter 9 from the perspective of how you can use these functions to help you manage a device that requires periodic polling. For the sake of thoroughness, I want to mention here that you can use a pointer to a kernel thread object in a call to KeWait*Xxx* to wait for the thread to complete. The thread terminates itself by calling **PsTerminateSystemThread**.

Before you can wait for a thread to terminate, you need to first obtain a pointer to the opaque KTHREAD object that internally represents that thread, which poses a bit of a problem. While running in the context of a thread, you can determine your own KTHREAD easily:

```
ASSERT(KeGetCurrentIrql() <= DISPATCH_LEVEL);
PKTHREAD thread = KeGetCurrentThread();
```

Unfortunately, when you call **PsCreateSystemThread** to create a new thread, you can retrieve only an opaque HANDLE for the thread. To get the KTHREAD pointer, you use an Object Manager service function:

```
HANDLE hthread;
PKTHREAD thread;
PsCreateSystemThread(&hthread, ...);
ObReferenceObjectByHandle(hthread, THREAD_ALL_ACCESS, NULL, KernelMode,
  (PVOID*) &thread, NULL);
ZwClose(hthread);
```

ObReferenceObjectByHandle converts your handle into a pointer to the underlying kernel object. Once you have the pointer, you can discard the handle by calling **ZwClose**. At some point, you need to release your reference to the thread object by making a call to **ObDereferenceObject**:

```
ObDereferenceObject(thread);
```

Thread Alerts and APCs

Internally, the Windows NT kernel uses *thread alerts* as a way of waking threads. It uses an asynchronous procedure call as a way of waking a thread to execute some particular subroutine in that thread's context. The support routines that generate alerts or APCs are not exposed for use by WDM driver writers. But, since the DDK documentation and header files contain a great many references to these concepts, I want to finish this discussion of kernel dispatcher objects by explaining them.

I'll start by describing the "plumbing"—how these two mechanisms work. When someone blocks a thread by calling one of the KeWait*Xxx* routines, they specify by means of a Boolean argument whether the wait is to be "alertable." An alertable wait might finish early—that is, without any of the wait conditions or the timeout being satisfied—because of a thread alert. Thread alerts originate in user mode when someone calls the native API function **NtAlertThread**. The kernel returns the special status value STATUS_ALERTED when a wait terminates early because of an alert.

An APC is a mechanism whereby the operating system can execute a function in the context of a particular thread. The *asynchronous* part of an APC stems from the fact that the system effectively interrupts the target thread to execute an out-of-line subroutine. The action of an APC is somewhat similar to what happens when a hardware interrupt causes a processor to suddenly and, from the point of view of whatever code happens to be running at the time, unpredictably execute an interrupt service routine.

APCs come in three flavors: user-mode, kernel-mode, and special kernel-mode. User-mode code requests a user-mode APC by calling the Win32 API **QueueUserAPC**.

Kernel-mode code requests an APC by calling an undocumented function for which the DDK headers have no prototype. Diligent reverse engineers probably already know the name of this routine and something about how to call it, but it's really just for internal use and I'm not going to say any more about it. The system queues APCs to a specific thread until appropriate execution conditions exist. Appropriate execution conditions depend on the type of APC, as follows:

■ Special kernel APCs execute as soon as possible—that is, as soon as an activity at APC_LEVEL can be scheduled. A special kernel APC can even awaken a blocked thread in many circumstances.

■ Normal kernel APCs execute after all special APCs have been executed but only when the target thread is running and no other kernel-mode APC is executing in this thread.

■ User-mode APCs execute after both flavors of kernel-mode APC for the target thread have been executed but only if the thread has previously been in an alertable wait in user mode. Execution actually occurs the next time the thread is dispatched for execution in user mode.

If the system awakens a thread to deliver an APC, the wait primitive on which the thread was previously blocked returns with one of the special status values STATUS_KERNEL_APC or STATUS_USER_APC.

How APCs Work with I/O Requests

The kernel uses the APC concept for several purposes. We're concerned in this book just with writing device drivers, though, so I'm only going to explain how APCs relate to the process of performing an I/O operation. In one of many possible scenarios, when a user-mode program performs a synchronous **ReadFile** operation on a handle, the Win32 subsystem calls a kernel-mode routine named (as is widely known despite its being undocumented) **NtReadFile**. NtReadFile creates and submits an IRP to the appropriate device driver, which often returns STATUS_PENDING to indicate that it hasn't finished the operation. NtReadFile returns this status code to ReadFile, which thereupon calls **NtWaitForSingleObject** to wait on the file object to which the user-mode handle points. NtWaitForSingleObject, in turn, calls KeWaitForSingleObject to perform a nonalertable, user-mode wait on an event object within the file object.

When the device driver eventually finishes the read operation, it calls IoCompleteRequest, which, in turn, queues a special kernel-mode APC. The APC routine calls KeSetEvent to signal the file object, thereby releasing the application to continue execution. Some sort of APC is required because some of the tasks that need to be performed when an I/O request is completed (such as buffer copying) must occur in the address context of the requesting thread. A kernel-mode APC is required because the thread in question is not in an alertable wait state. A *special* APC is required because the thread is actually ineligible to run at the time we need to deliver the APC. In fact, the APC routine is the mechanism for awakening the thread.

Kernel-mode routines can also call NtReadFile. Drivers should call **ZwReadFile** instead, which uses the same system service interface to reach NtReadFile that user-mode programs use. (Note that NtReadFile is not documented for use by device drivers.) If you obey the injunctions in the DDK documentation when you call ZwReadFile, your call to NtReadFile will look almost like a user-mode call and will be processed in almost the same way, with just two differences. The first, which is quite minor, is that any waiting will be done in kernel mode. The other difference is that if you specified in your call to **ZwCreateFile** that you wanted to do synchronous operations, the I/O Manager will automatically wait for your read to finish. The wait will be alertable or not, depending on the exact option you specify to ZwCreateFile.

How to Specify Alertable and WaitMode Parameters

Now you have enough background to understand the ramifications of the **Alertable** and **WaitMode** parameters in the calls to the various wait primitives. As a general rule, you'll never be writing code that responds synchronously to requests from user mode. You *could* do so for, say, certain I/O control requests. Generally speaking, however, it's better to *pend* any operations that take a long time to finish (by returning STATUS_PENDING from your dispatch routine) and to finish them asynchronously. So, to continue speaking generally, you don't often call a wait primitive in the first place. Thread blocking is appropriate in a device driver in only a few scenarios, which I'll describe in the following sections.

Kernel Threads Sometimes you'll create your own kernel-mode thread—when your device needs to be polled periodically, for example. In this scenario, any waits performed will be in kernel mode because the thread runs exclusively in kernel mode.

Handling Plug and Play Requests I'll show you in Chapter 6 how to handle the I/O requests that the PnP Manager sends your way. Several such requests require *synchronous handling* on your part. In other words, you pass them down the driver stack to lower levels and wait for them to complete. You'll be calling KeWaitForSingleObject to wait in kernel mode because the PnP Manager calls you within the context of a kernel-mode thread. In addition, if you needed to perform subsidiary requests as part of handling a PnP request—for example, to talk to a universal serial bus (USB) device—you'd be waiting in kernel mode.

Handling Other I/O Requests When you're handling other sorts of I/O requests and you know that you're running in the context of a nonarbitrary thread that must get the results of your deliberations before proceeding, it might conceivably be appropriate to block that thread by calling a wait primitive. In such a case, you want to wait in the same processor mode as the entity that called you. Most of the time, you can simply rely on the **RequestorMode** in the IRP you're currently processing. If you somehow gained control by means other than an IRP, you could call **ExGetPreviousMode** to determine the previous processor mode. If you wait in user mode, and if the behavior you want to achieve is that user-mode programs should be able to terminate the wait early by calling QueueUserAPC, you should perform an alertable wait.

The last situation I mentioned—you're waiting in user mode and need to allow user-mode APCs to break in—is the only one I know of in which you'd want to allow alerts when waiting.

The bottom line: perform nonalertable waits unless you know you shouldn't.

OTHER KERNEL-MODE SYNCHRONIZATION PRIMITIVES

The Windows 2000 kernel offers some additional methods for synchronizing execution between threads or for guarding access to shared objects. In this section, I'll discuss the *fast mutex*, which is a mutual exclusion object that offers faster performance than a kernel mutex because it's optimized for the case where no contention is actually occurring. I'll also describe the category of support functions that include the word *Interlocked* in their name somewhere. These functions carry out certain common operations—such as incrementing or decrementing an integer or inserting or removing an entry from a linked list—in an atomic way that prevents multitasking or multiprocessing interference.

Fast Mutex Objects

Compared to kernel mutexes, fast mutexes have the strengths and weaknesses summarized in Table 4-6. On the plus side, a fast mutex is much faster to acquire and release if there's no actual contention for it. On the minus side, you must avoid trying to recursively acquire a fast mutex, and that can mean preventing the delivery of APCs while you own it. Preventing APCs means raising IRQL to APC_LEVEL or above, which effectively negates thread priority and gains you the assurance that your code will execute except while the processor handles a higher-priority interrupt.

Kernel Mutex	*Fast Mutex*
Can be acquired recursively by a single thread (system maintains a claim counter)	Cannot be acquired recursively
Relatively slower	Relatively faster
Owner won't receive any but "special" kernel APCs	Owner won't receive *any* APCs

Table 4-6. *Comparison of kernel and fast mutex objects.* *(continued)*

continued

Kernel Mutex	Fast Mutex
Owner can't be removed from "balance set" (that is, can't be paged out)	No automatic priority boost (if you run at or above APC_LEVEL)
Can be part of a multiple object wait	Cannot be used as an argument to KeWaitForMultipleObjects

Incidentally, the DDK documentation about kernel mutex objects has long said that the kernel gives a priority boost to a thread that claims a mutex. I'm reliably informed that this hasn't actually been true since 1992 (the year, that is, not the Windows 2000 build number).

Table 4-7 summarizes the service functions you use to work with fast mutexes.

Service Function	Description
ExAcquireFastMutex	Acquires ownership of mutex, waiting if necessary
ExAcquireFastMutexUnsafe	Acquires ownership of mutex, waiting if necessary, in circumstance where caller has already disabled receipt of APCs
ExInitializeFastMutex	Initializes mutex object
ExReleaseFastMutex	Releases mutex
ExReleaseFastMutexUnsafe	Releases mutex without reenabling APC delivery
ExTryToAcquireFastMutex	Acquires mutex if possible to do so without waiting

Table 4-7. *Service functions for use with executive fast mutexes.*

To create a fast mutex, you must first allocate a FAST_MUTEX data structure in nonpaged memory. Then you initialize the object by "calling" **ExInitializeFastMutex**, which is really a macro in WDM.H:

```
ASSERT(KeGetCurrentIrql() <= DISPATCH_LEVEL);
ExInitializeFastMutex(FastMutex);
```

where **FastMutex** is the address of your FAST_MUTEX object. The mutex begins life in the unowned state. To acquire ownership later on, call one of these functions:

```
ASSERT(KeGetCurrentIrql() < DISPATCH_LEVEL);
ExAcquireFastMutex(FastMutex);
```

or

```
ASSERT(KeGetCurrentIrql() < DISPATCH_LEVEL);
ExAcquireFastMutexUnsafe(FastMutex);
```

The first of these functions waits for the mutex to become available, assigns ownership to the calling thread, and then raises the current processor IRQL to APC_LEVEL. Raising the IRQL has the effect of blocking delivery of all APCs. The second of these functions doesn't change IRQL. You need to think about potential deadlocks if you use the "unsafe" function to acquire a fast mutex. The situation you must avoid is an APC routine that is running in the same thread context to acquire the same mutex or any other object that can't be recursively locked. Otherwise, you'll run the risk of instantly deadlocking that thread.

If you don't want to wait if the mutex isn't immediately available, use the "try to acquire" function:

```
ASSERT(KeGetCurrentIrql() < DISPATCH_LEVEL);
BOOLEAN acquired = ExTryToAcquireFastMutex(FastMutex);
```

If the return value is TRUE, you now own the mutex. If it's FALSE, someone else owns the mutex and has prevented you from acquiring it.

To release control of a fast mutex and allow some other thread to claim it, call the release function corresponding to the way you acquired the fast mutex:

```
ASSERT(KeGetCurrentIrql() < DISPATCH_LEVEL);
ExReleaseFastMutex(FastMutex);
```

or

```
ASSERT(KeGetCurrentIrql() < DISPATCH_LEVEL);
ExReleaseFastMutexUnsafe(FastMutex);
```

A fast mutex is fast because the acquisition and release steps are optimized for the usual case when there's no contention for the mutex. The critical step in acquiring the mutex is to atomically decrement and test an integer counter that indicates how many threads either own or are waiting for the mutex. If the test indicates that no other thread owns the mutex, no additional work is required. If the test indicates that another thread *does* own the mutex, the current thread blocks on a synchronization event that's part of the FAST_MUTEX object. Releasing the mutex entails atomically incrementing and testing the counter. If the test indicates that no thread is currently waiting, no additional work is required. If another thread is waiting, however, the owner calls KeSetEvent to release one of the waiters.

Interlocked Arithmetic

You can call several service functions in a WDM driver to perform arithmetic in a way that's thread-safe and multiprocessor-safe. See Table 4-8. These routines come in two flavors. The first type of routine has a name beginning with **Interlocked** and performs an atomic operation in such a way that no other thread or CPU can interfere. The other flavor has a name beginning with **ExInterlocked** and uses a spin lock.

Service Function	Description
InterlockedCompareExchange	Compares and conditionally exchanges
InterlockedDecrement	Subtracts one from an integer
InterlockedExchange	Exchanges two values
InterlockedExchangeAdd	Adds two values and returns sum
InterlockedIncrement	Adds one to an integer
ExInterlockedAddLargeInteger	Adds value to 64-bit integer
ExInterlockedAddLargeStatistic	Adds value to ULONG
ExInterlockedAddUlong	Adds value to ULONG and returns initial value
ExInterlockedCompareExchange64	Exchanges two 64-bit values

Table 4-8. *Service functions for interlocked arithmetic.*

The **Interlocked***Xxx* functions can be called at any IRQL; they can also handle pagable data at PASSIVE_LEVEL because they don't require a spin lock. Although the **ExInterlocked***Xxx* routines can be called at any IRQL, they operate on the target data at or above DISPATCH_LEVEL and therefore require a nonpaged argument. The only reason to use an ExInterlocked*Xxx* function is if you have a data variable that you sometimes need to increment or decrement *and* sometimes need to access throughout some series of instructions. You would explicitly claim the spin lock around the multi-instruction accesses and use the ExInterlocked*Xxx* function to perform the simple increments or decrements.

Interlocked*Xxx* Functions

InterlockedIncrement adds one to a long integer in memory and returns the post-increment value to you:

```
LONG result = InterlockedIncrement(pLong);
```

where **pLong** is the address of a variable typed as a LONG (that is, a long integer). Conceptually, the operation of the function is equivalent to the statement **return ++*pLong** in C, but the implementation differs from that simple statement in order to provide thread safety and multiprocessor safety. InterlockedIncrement guarantees that the integer is successfully incremented even if code on other CPUs or in other eligible threads on the same CPU is simultaneously trying to alter the same variable. In the nature of the operation, it cannot guarantee that the value it returns is still the value of the variable even one machine cycle later, because other threads or CPUs will be able to modify the variable as soon as the atomic increment operation completes.

InterlockedDecrement, shown at the top of the following page, is similar to InterlockedIncrement, but it subtracts one from the target variable and returns the postdecrement value, just like the C statement **return --*pLong** but with thread safety and multiprocessor safety.

```
LONG result = InterlockedDecrement(pLong);
```

You call **InterlockedCompareExchange** like this:

```
LONG target;
LONG result = InterlockedCompareExchange(&target, newval, oldval);
```

Here, **target** is a LONG integer used both as input and output to the function, **oldval** is your guess about the current contents of the target, and **newval** is the new value that you want installed into the target if your guess is correct. The function performs an operation similar to that indicated in the following C code, but does so via an atomic operation that's both thread-safe and multiprocessor-safe:

```
LONG CompareExchange(PLONG ptarget, LONG newval, LONG oldval)
  {
  LONG value = *ptarget;
  if (value == oldval)
    *ptarget = newval;
  return value;
  }
```

In other words, the function always returns the previous value of the target variable to you. In addition, if that previous value equals **oldval**, it sets the target equal to the **newval** you specify. The function uses an atomic operation to do the compare and exchange so that the replacement happens only if you're correct in your guess about the previous contents.

You can also call the **InterlockedCompareExchangePointer** function to perform a similar sort of compare and exchange operation with a pointer. This function is either defined as a compiler intrinsic (that is, a function for which the compiler supplies an inline implementation) or a real function call, depending on how wide pointers are on the platform for which you're compiling and on the ability of the compiler to generate inline code. You could use the pointer version of the function, as shown in the following example, to add a structure to the head of a singly-linked list without needing to acquire a spin lock or raise IRQL:

```
typedef struct _SOMESTRUCTURE {
  struct _SOMESTRUCTURE* next;
  ... } SOMESTRUCTURE, *PSOMESTRUCTURE;
...
void InsertElement(PSOMESTRUCTURE p, PSOMESTRUCTURE anchor)
  {
  PSOMESTRUCTURE next, first;
  do
    {
    p->next = first = *anchor;
    next = InterlockedCompareExchangePointer(anchor, p, first);
```

```
   }
 while (next != first);
 }
```

Each time through the loop, we make the assumption that the new element will end up being chained to the current head of the list, the address of which we save in the variable named **first**. Then we call InterlockedCompareExchangePointer to see whether the anchor still points to **first** even these few nanoseconds later. If so, InterlockedCompareExchangePointer will set the anchor to point our new element **p**. The fact that the return value from InterlockedCompareExchangePointer is the same as our assumption causes the loop to terminate. If, for some reason, the anchor no longer points to the same **first** element, we'll discover that fact and repeat the loop.

The last function in this class is **InterlockedExchange**, which simply uses an atomic operation to replace the value of an integer variable and to return the previous value:

```
LONG value;
LONG oldval = InterlockedExchange(&value, newval);
```

As you might have guessed, there's also an **InterlockedExchangePointer** that exchanges a pointer value (64-bit or 32-bit, depending on the platform).

ExInterlocked*Xxx* Functions

Each of the ExInterlocked*Xxx* functions requires that you create and initialize a spin lock before you call it. Note that the operands of these functions must all be in nonpaged memory because the functions operate on the data at elevated IRQL.

ExInterlockedAddLargeInteger adds two 64-bit integers and returns the previous value of the target:

```
LARGE_INTEGER value, increment;
KSPIN_LOCK spinlock;
LARGE_INTEGER prev = ExInterlockedAddLargeInteger(&value,
  increment, &spinlock);
```

Value is the target of the addition and one of the operands. **Increment** is an integer operand that's added to the target. **Spinlock** is a spin lock that you previously initialized. The return value is the target's value before the addition. In other words, the operation of this function is similar to the following function except that it occurs under protection of the spin lock:

```
__int64 AddLargeInteger(__int64* pvalue, __int64 increment)
  {
  __int64 prev = *pvalue;
  *pvalue += increment;
  return prev;
  }
```

Note that the return value is the *preaddition* value, which contrasts with the postincrement return from InterlockedExchange and similar functions. (Also, not all compilers support the __**int64** integer data type, and not all computers can perform a 64-bit addition operation using atomic instructions.)

ExInterlockedAddUlong is analogous to ExInterlockedAddLargeInteger except that it works with 32-bit unsigned integers:

```
ULONG value, increment;
KSPIN_LOCK spinlock;
ULONG prev = ExInterlockedAddUlong(&value, increment, &spinlock);
```

This function likewise returns the preaddition value of the target of the operation.

ExInterlockedAddLargeStatistic is similar to ExInterlockedAddUlong in that it adds a 32-bit value to a 64-bit value. It hadn't been documented in the DDK at press time, so I'll show you its prototype here:

```
VOID ExInterlockedAddLargeStatistic(PLARGE_INTEGER Addend,
  ULONG Increment);
```

This new function is faster than ExInterlockedAddUlong because it doesn't need to return the preincrement value of the **Addend** variable. It therefore doesn't need to employ a spin lock for synchronization. The atomicity provided by this function is, however, only with respect to other callers of the same function. In other words, if you had code on one CPU calling ExInterlockedAddLargeStatistic at the same time as code on another CPU was accessing the Addend variable for either reading or writing, you could get inconsistent results. I can explain why this is so by showing you this paraphrase of the Intel x86 implementation of the function (not the actual source code):

```
mov eax, Addend
mov ecx, Increment
lock add [eax], ecx
lock adc [eax+4], 0
```

This code works correctly for purposes of incrementing the Addend because the lock prefixes guarantee atomicity of each addition operation and because no carries from the low-order 32 bits can ever get lost. The instantaneous value of the 64-bit Addend isn't always consistent, however, because an incrementer might be poised between the ADD and the ADC just at the instant someone makes a copy of the complete 64-bit value. Therefore, even a caller of **ExInterlockedCompareExchange64** on another CPU could obtain an inconsistent value.

Interlocked List Access

The Windows NT executive offers three sets of support functions for dealing with linked lists in a thread-safe and multiprocessor-safe way. These functions support doubly-linked lists, singly-linked lists, and a special kind of singly-linked list called an *S-List*. I discussed noninterlocked doubly-linked and singly-linked lists in the preceding chapter. To close this chapter on synchronization within WDM drivers, I'll explain how to use these interlocked accessing primitives.

If you need the functionality of a FIFO queue, you should use a doubly-linked list. If you need the functionality of a thread-safe and multiprocessor-safe pushdown stack, you should use an S-List. In both cases, to achieve thread safety and multiprocessor safety, you will allocate and initialize a spin lock. The S-List might not actually use the spin lock, however, because the presence of a sequence number might allow the kernel to implement it using just atomic compare-exchange sorts of operations.

The support functions for performing interlocked access to list objects are very similar, so I've organized this section along functional lines. I'll explain how to initialize all three kinds of list. Then I'll explain how to insert an item into all three kinds. After that, I'll explain how to remove items.

Initialization

You can initialize these lists as shown here:

```
LIST_ENTRY DoubleHead;
SINGLE_LIST_ENTRY SingleHead;
SLIST_HEADER SListHead;

InitializeListHead(&DoubleHead);

SingleHead.Next = NULL;

ExInitializeSListHead(&SListHead);
```

Don't forget that you must also allocate and initialize a spin lock for each list. Furthermore, the storage for the list heads and all the items you put into the lists must come from nonpaged memory because the support routines perform their accesses at elevated IRQL. Note that the spin lock isn't used during initialization of the list head because it doesn't make any sense to allow contention for list access before the list has been initialized.

Inserting Items

You can insert items at the head and tail of a doubly-linked list and at the head (only) of a singly-linked list or an S-List:

```
PLIST_ENTRY pdElement, pdPrevHead, pdPrevTail;
PSINGLE_LIST_ENTRY psElement, psPrevHead;
PKSPIN_LOCK spinlock;
```

(continued)

```
pdPrevHead = ExInterlockedInsertHeadList(&DoubleHead, pdElement, spinlock);
pdPrevTail = ExInterlockedInsertTailList(&DoubleHead, pdElement, spinlock);

psPrevHead = ExInterlockedPushEntryList(&SingleHead, psElement, spinlock);

psPrevHead = ExInterlockedPushEntrySList(&SListHead, psElement, spinlock);
```

The return values are the addresses of the elements previously at the head (or tail) of the list in question. Note that the element addresses you use with these functions are the addresses of list entry structures that are usually embedded in larger structures of some kind, and you will need to use the CONTAINING_RECORD macro to recover the address of the surrounding structure.

Removing Items

You can remove items from the head of any of these lists:

```
pdElement = ExInterlockedRemoveHeadList(&DoubleHead, spinlock);

psElement = ExInterlockedPopEntryList(&SingleHead, spinlock);

psElement = ExInterlockedPopEntrySList(&SListHead, spinlock);
```

The return values are NULL if the respective lists are empty. Be sure to test the return value for NULL *before* applying the CONTAINING_RECORD macro to recover a containing structure pointer.

IRQL Restrictions

You can call the S-List functions only while running at or below DISPATCH_LEVEL. The ExInterlocked*Xxx* functions for accessing doubly-linked or singly-linked lists can be called at any IRQL so long as *all* references to the list use an ExInterlocked*Xxx* call. The reason for no IRQL restrictions is that the implementations of these functions disable interrupts, which is tantamount to raising IRQL to the highest possible level. Once interrupts are disabled, these functions then acquire the spin lock you've specified. Since no other code can gain control on the same CPU, and since no code on another CPU can acquire the spin lock, your lists are protected.

> **NOTE** The DDK documentation states this rule in an overly restrictive way for at least some of the ExInterlocked*Xxx* functions. It says that all callers must be running at some single IRQL less than or equal to the DIRQL of your interrupt object. There is, in fact, no requirement that all callers be at the same IRQL, because you can call the functions at *any* IRQL. Likewise, no restriction to <= DIRQL exists either, but there's also no reason for the code you and I write to raise IRQL higher than that.

It's perfectly okay for you to use ExInterlocked*Xxx* calls to access a singly-linked or doubly-linked list (but not an S-List) in some parts of your code and to use the noninterlocked functions (**InsertHeadList** and so on) in other parts of your code if you follow a simple rule. Before using a noninterlocked primitive, acquire the same spin lock that your interlocked calls use. Furthermore, restrict list access to code running at or below DISPATCH_LEVEL. For example:

```
// Access list using noninterlocked calls:

VOID Function1()
  {
  ASSERT(KeGetCurrentIrql() <= DISPATCH_LEVEL);
  KIRQL oldirql;
  KeAcquireSpinLock(spinlock, &oldirql);
  InsertHeadList(...);
  RemoveTailList(...);
  ...
  KeReleaseSpinLock(spinlock, oldirql);
  }

// Access list using interlocked calls:

VOID Function2()
  {
  ASSERT(KeGetCurrentIrql() <= DISPATCH_LEVEL);
  ExInterlockedInsertTailList(..., spinlock);
  }
```

The first function must be running at or below DISPATCH_LEVEL because that's a requirement of calling KeAcquireSpinLock. The reason for the IRQL restriction on the interlocked calls in the second function is as follows: Suppose that **Function1** acquires the spin lock in preparation for performing some list accesses. Acquiring the spin lock raises IRQL to DISPATCH_LEVEL. Now suppose that an interrupt occurs on the same CPU at a higher IRQL and that **Function2** gains control to use one of the ExInterlocked*Xxx* routines. The kernel will now attempt to acquire the same spin lock, and the CPU will deadlock. This problem arises from allowing code running at two different IRQLs to use the same spin lock: Function1 is at DISPATCH_LEVEL, and Function2 is—practically speaking, anyway—at HIGH_LEVEL when it tries to recursively acquire the lock.

Chapter 5

The I/O Request Packet

The operating system uses a data structure known as an I/O request packet, or IRP, to communicate with a kernel-mode device driver. In this chapter, I'll discuss this important data structure and the means by which it's created, sent, processed, and ultimately destroyed. I'll end with a discussion of the relatively complex subject of IRP cancellation. This chapter is rather abstract, I'm afraid, because I haven't yet talked about any of the concepts that surround specific types of IRPs. You might, therefore, want to skim this chapter and refer back to it while you're reading later chapters.

DATA STRUCTURES

Two data structures are crucial to the handling of I/O requests: the I/O request packet itself and the IO_STACK_LOCATION structure. I'll describe both structures in this section.

Structure of an IRP

Figure 5-1 illustrates the IRP data structure, with opaque fields shaded in the usual convention of this book. A brief description of the important fields follows.

MdlAddress (PMDL) is the address of a memory descriptor list (MDL) describing the user-mode buffer associated with this request. The I/O Manager creates this MDL for IRP_MJ_READ and IRP_MJ_WRITE requests if the topmost device object's flags indicate DO_DIRECT_IO. It creates an MDL for the output buffer used with an

IRP_MJ_DEVICE_CONTROL request if the control code indicates METHOD_IN_ DIRECT or METHOD_OUT_DIRECT. The MDL itself describes the user-mode virtual buffer and also contains the physical addresses of locked pages containing that buffer. A driver has to do additional work, which can be quite minimal, to actually access the user-mode buffer.

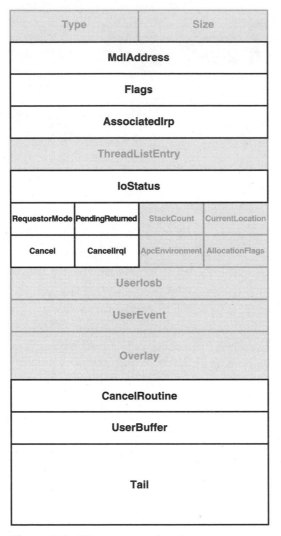

Figure 5-1. *I/O request packet data structure.*

Flags (ULONG) contains flags that a device driver can read but not directly alter. None of these flags are relevant to a Windows Driver Model driver.

AssociatedIrp (union) is a union of three possible pointers. The alternative that a typical WDM driver might want to access is named **AssociatedIrp.SystemBuffer**.

The SystemBuffer pointer holds the address of a data buffer in nonpaged kernel-mode memory. For IRP_MJ_READ and IRP_MJ_WRITE operations, the I/O Manager creates this data buffer if the topmost device object's flags specify DO_BUFFERED_IO. For IRP_MJ_DEVICE_CONTROL operations, the I/O Manager creates this buffer if the I/O control function code indicates that it should. (See Chapter 9, "Specialized Topics.") The I/O Manager copies data sent by user-mode code to the driver into this buffer as part of the process of creating the IRP. Such data includes the data involved in a **WriteFile** call or the so-called input data for a call to **DeviceIoControl**. For read requests, the device driver fills this buffer with data; the I/O Manager later copies the buffer back to the user-mode buffer. For control operations that specify METHOD_BUFFERED, the driver places the so-called output data in this buffer, and the I/O Manager copies it to the user-mode output buffer.

IoStatus (IO_STATUS_BLOCK) is a structure containing two fields that drivers set when they ultimately complete a request. **IoStatus.Status** will receive an NTSTATUS code, while **IoStatus.Information** is a ULONG_PTR that will receive an information value whose exact content depends on the type of IRP and the completion status. A common use of the Information field is to hold the total number of bytes transferred by an operation like IRP_MJ_READ that transfers data. Certain Plug and Play (PnP) requests use this field as a pointer to a structure that you can think of as the answer to a query.

RequestorMode will equal one of the enumeration constants **UserMode** or **KernelMode**, depending on where the original I/O request originated. Drivers sometimes inspect this value to know whether to trust some parameters.

PendingReturned (BOOLEAN) is TRUE if the lowest-level dispatch routine to process this IRP returned STATUS_PENDING. Completion routines reference this field to avoid a potential race condition between completion and dispatch routines.

Cancel (BOOLEAN) is TRUE if **IoCancelIrp** has been called to cancel this request and FALSE if it hasn't (yet) been called. IRP cancellation is a relatively complex topic that I'll discuss fully later on in this chapter (in "Cancelling I/O Requests").

CancelIrql (KIRQL) is the interrupt request level (IRQL) at which the special cancel spin lock was acquired. You reference this field in a cancel routine when you release the spin lock.

CancelRoutine (PDRIVER_CANCEL) is the address of an IRP cancellation routine in your driver. You use **IoSetCancelRoutine** to set this field instead of modifying it directly.

UserBuffer (PVOID) contains the user-mode virtual address of the output buffer for an IRP_MJ_DEVICE_CONTROL request for which the control code specifies METHOD_NEITHER. It also holds the user-mode virtual address of the buffer for read and write requests, but a driver should usually specify one of the device flags DO_BUFFERED_IO or DO_DIRECT_IO and should therefore not usually need to access the field for reads or writes. When handling a METHOD_NEITHER control operation, the driver can create its own MDL using this address.

Tail.Overlay is a structure within a union that contains several members potentially useful to a WDM driver. Refer to Figure 5-2 for a map of the **Tail** union. In the figure, items at the same level as you read left to right are alternatives within a union, while the vertical dimension portrays successive locations within a structure. **Tail.Overlay.DeviceQueueEntry** (KDEVICE_QUEUE_ENTRY) and **Tail.Overlay.-DriverContext** (PVOID[4]) are alternatives within an unnamed union within Tail.Overlay. The I/O Manager uses DeviceQueueEntry as a linking field within the standard queue of requests for a device. At moments when the IRP is not on some queue that uses this field and when you own the IRP, you can use the four pointers in DriverContext in any way you please. **Tail.Overlay.ListEntry** (LIST_ENTRY) is available for you to use as a linking field for IRPs on any private queue you choose to implement.

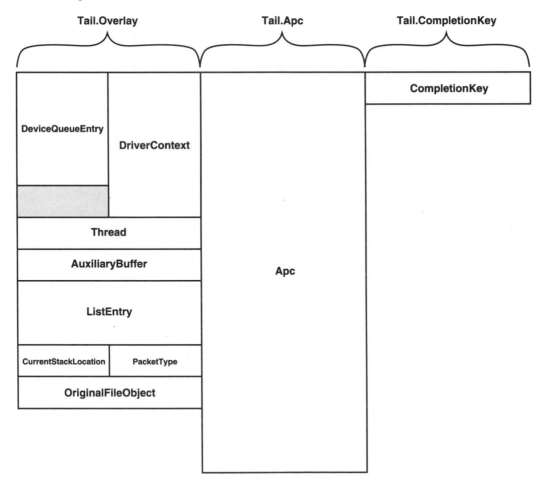

Figure 5-2. *Map of the Tail union in an IRP.*

CurrentLocation (CHAR) and **Tail.Overlay.CurrentStackLocation** (PIO_ STACK_LOCATION) are not documented for use by drivers because support functions like **IoGetCurrentIrpStackLocation** can be used instead. During debugging, however, it might help you to realize that CurrentLocation is the index of the current I/O stack location and CurrentStackLocation is a pointer to it.

The I/O Stack

Whenever any kernel-mode program creates an IRP, it also creates an associated array of IO_STACK_LOCATION structures: one stack location for each of the drivers that will process the IRP and often one more stack location for the use of the originator of the IRP. (See Figure 5-3.) A stack location contains type codes and parameter information for the IRP as well as the address of a completion routine. Refer to Figure 5-4 for an illustration of the stack structure.

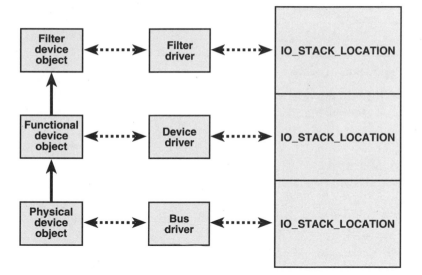

Figure 5-3. *Parallelism between driver and I/O stacks.*

NOTE I'll discuss the mechanics of creating IRPs a bit further on in this chapter. It helps to know right now that the **StackCount** field of a DEVICE_OBJECT indicates how many locations to reserve for an IRP sent to that device's driver.

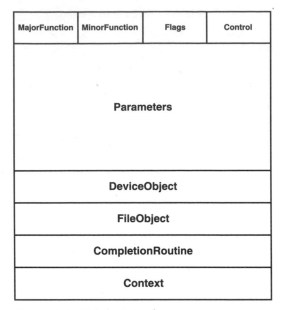

MajorFunction	MinorFunction	Flags	Control
Parameters			
DeviceObject			
FileObject			
CompletionRoutine			
Context			

Figure 5-4. *I/O stack location data structure.*

MajorFunction (UCHAR) is the major function code associated with this IRP. This would be a value like IRP_MJ_READ that corresponds to one of the dispatch function pointers in the MajorFunction table of a driver object. Since this code is in the I/O stack location for a particular driver, it's conceivable that an IRP could start life as an IRP_MJ_READ (for example) and be transformed into something else as it progresses down the stack of drivers. I'll show you examples in Chapter 11, "The Universal Serial Bus," of how a USB driver changes the personality of a read or write request into an internal control operation in order to submit the request to the USB bus driver.

MinorFunction (UCHAR) is a minor function code that further identifies an IRP belonging to a few major function classes. IRP_MJ_PNP requests, for example, are divided into a dozen or so subtypes with minor function codes such as IRP_MN_START_DEVICE, IRP_MN_REMOVE_DEVICE, and so on.

Parameters (union) is a union of substructures, one for each type of request that has specific parameters. The substructures include, for example, **Create** (for IRP_MJ_CREATE requests), **Read** (for IRP_MJ_READ requests), and **StartDevice** (for the IRP_MN_START_DEVICE subtype of IRP_MJ_PNP).

DeviceObject (PDEVICE_OBJECT) is the address of the device object that corresponds to this stack entry. **IoCallDriver** fills in this field.

FileObject (PFILE_OBJECT) is the address of the kernel file object to which the IRP is directed. Drivers often use the FileObject pointer to correlate IRPs in a queue with a request (in the form of an IRP_MJ_CLEANUP) to cancel all queued IRPs in preparation for closing the file object.

CompletionRoutine (PIO_COMPLETION_ROUTINE) is the address of an I/O completion routine installed *by the driver above the one to which this stack location corresponds*. You never set this field directly—instead, you call **IoSetCompletion-Routine**, which knows to reference the stack location below the one that your driver owns. The lowest-level driver in the hierarchy of drivers for a given device never needs a completion routine because it must complete the request. The originator of a request, however, sometimes does need a completion routine but doesn't usually have its own stack location. That's why each level in the hierarchy uses the next lower stack location to hold its own completion routine pointer.

Context (PVOID) is an arbitrary context value that will be passed as an argument to the completion routine. You never set this field directly; it's set automatically from one of the arguments to IoSetCompletionRoutine.

THE "STANDARD MODEL" FOR IRP PROCESSING

Particle physics has its "standard model" for the universe, and so does WDM. Figure 5-5 illustrates a typical flow of ownership for an IRP as it progresses through various stages in its life. Not every type of IRP would go through these steps, and some of the steps might be missing or altered depending on the type of device and the type of IRP. Notwithstanding the possible variability, however, the picture provides a useful starting point for discussion.

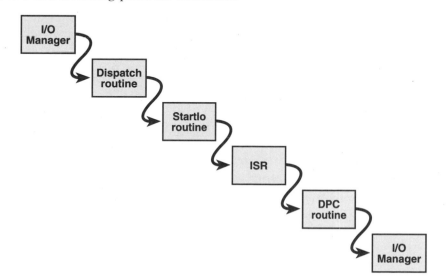

Figure 5-5. *The "standard model" for IRP processing.*

IT'S EVEN MORE COMPLICATED THAN YOU THOUGHT...

The first time you encounter the concepts that make up the standard model for IRP processing, they'll probably seem pretty complicated. Unfortunately, the standard model is also not quite sufficient to handle all the problems that can arise in a regime that includes hot pluggable devices, dynamic resource reconfiguration, and power management. In later chapters, I'll describe another way of queuing and cancelling IRPs that deals with these extra problems. The standard model will seem like a model of clarity when you're done reading about that!

Despite the problems that some devices present, many devices can still employ the standard model (which is, of course, why I'm bothering to explain it here). If your device cannot be removed or reconfigured while the system is running and can reject I/O requests while in a low-power state, you can use the standard model.

Creating an IRP

The IRP begins life when some entity calls an I/O Manager function to create it. In the figure, I used the term *I/O Manager* to describe this entity, as though there were a single system component responsible for creating IRPs. In reality, no such single actor in the population of operating system routines exists, and it would have been more accurate to just say that *something* creates the IRP. Your own driver will be creating IRPs from time to time, for example, and you will occupy the initial ownership box for those particular IRPs.

You can use any of four functions to create a new IRP:

- **IoBuildAsynchronousFsdRequest** builds an IRP on whose completion you don't plan to wait. This function and the next are appropriate for building only certain types of IRP.

- **IoBuildSynchronousFsdRequest** builds an IRP on whose completion you *do* plan to wait.

- **IoBuildDeviceIoControlRequest** builds a synchronous IRP_MJ_DEVICE_CONTROL or IRP_MJ_INTERNAL_DEVICE_CONTROL request.

- **IoAllocateIrp** builds an IRP that is not one of the types supported by the preceding three functions.

The **Fsd** in the first two of these function names stands for *file system driver* (FSD). Although FSDs are the primary users of the functions, any driver is allowed to call them. The DDK also documents a function named **IoMakeAssociatedIrp** for building an IRP that's subordinate to some other IRP. WDM drivers should not call this function. Indeed, completion of associated IRPs doesn't work correctly in Microsoft Windows 98 anyway.

Deciding which of these functions to call and determining what additional initialization you need to perform on an IRP is a rather complicated matter. I'll come back to this subject, therefore, at the end of this chapter.

Forwarding to a Dispatch Routine

After you create an IRP, you call **IoGetNextIrpStackLocation** to obtain a pointer to the first stack location. Then you initialize just that first location. At the very least, you need to fill in the MajorFunction code. Having initialized the stack, you call **IoCallDriver** to send the IRP to a device driver:

```
PDEVICE_OBJECT DeviceObject; // ← something gives you this
PIO_STACK_LOCATION stack = IoGetNextIrpStackLocation(Irp);
stack->MajorFunction = IRP_MJ_Xxx;
<other initialization of "stack">
NTSTATUS status = IoCallDriver(DeviceObject, Irp);
```

The first argument to IoCallDriver is the address of a device object that you've obtained somehow. I'll describe two common ways of getting a device object pointer at the very end of this chapter in "Where Do Device Object Pointers Come From?" For the time being, imagine that these pointers just come to you out of the blue.

The initial stack location pointer in the IRP gets initialized to one *before* the actual first location. Since the I/O stack is an array of IO_STACK_LOCATION structures, you could think of the stack pointer as being initialized to point to the "−1" element, which doesn't exist. (In fact, the stack "grows" from high toward low addresses, but that detail shouldn't obscure the concept I'm trying to describe here.) We therefore ask for the "next" stack location when we want to initialize the first one. IoCallDriver will advance the stack pointer to the 0 entry and extract the major function code that we left there. That's the made-up value IRP_MJ_*Xxx* in this example. Then, IoCallDriver will follow the DriverObject pointer inside the device object to the MajorFunction table belonging to the top-level driver. Recall that the driver's **DriverEntry** function filled that table in with pointers to *dispatch functions* in the driver. IoCallDriver will use the major function code to index the table, and it will then call the function whose address it finds.

You can imagine IoCallDriver as looking something like this (but I hasten to add that this is not a copy of the actual source code):

```
NTSTATUS IoCallDriver(PDEVICE_OBJECT device, PIRP Irp)
  {
  IoSetNextIrpStackLocation(Irp);
```

(continued)

```
    PIO_STACK_LOCATION stack = IoGetCurrentIrpStackLocation(Irp);
    stack->DeviceObject = device;
    ULONG fcn = stack->MajorFunction;
    PDRIVER_OBJECT driver = device->DriverObject;
    return (*driver->MajorFunction[fcn])(device, Irp);
    }
```

Duties of a Dispatch Routine

An archetypal IRP dispatch routine would look similar to this example:

```
NTSTATUS DispatchXxx(PDEVICE_OBJECT device, PIRP Irp)
    {
    PIO_STACK_LOCATION stack = IoGetCurrentIrpStackLocation(Irp);
    PDEVICE_EXTENSION pdx = (PDEVICE_EXTENSION) device->DeviceExtension;
    ...
    return STATUS_Xxx;
    }
```

1. You generally need to access the current stack location to determine parameters or to examine the minor function code.

2. You also generally need to access the device extension you created and initialized during AddDevice.

3. You'll be returning some NTSTATUS code to IoCallDriver, which will propagate the code back to *its* caller.

In this book, I'll be using names of the form **Dispatch*Xxx*** (for example, **DispatchRead**, **DispatchPnp**, and so forth) for the dispatch functions in my sample drivers. Other authors use different conventions for these names. Microsoft recommends, for example, that you use a name like **RandomDispatchRead** for the IRP_MJ_READ dispatch function in a driver named RANDOM.SYS. Conventions like this make it easier to understand debugger traces in some situations, but they also require you to do more typing. Since these names aren't visible outside the name space of your own driver, it's up to you whether you use very specific names as Microsoft recommends or names such as **Fred** that have meaning to you.

Where I used an ellipsis in the prototypical dispatch function above, a dispatch function has to choose between three courses of action. It can complete the request immediately, pass the request down to a lower-level driver in the same driver stack, or queue the request for later processing by other routines in this driver. I'm going to discuss each of these alternatives fully in this chapter, but I'm going to talk about only the queuing possibility now because that's what comes next in the standard model for IRP processing. You see, the largest number of requests that come into a device involves reading or writing data, and you usually need to put these requests into a queue to serialize access to your hardware.

Every device object gets a request queue object "for free," and there's a standard way of using this queue:

```
NTSTATUS DispatchXxx(...)
  {
  ...
  IoMarkIrpPending(Irp);
  IoStartPacket(device, Irp, NULL, NULL);
  return STATUS_PENDING;
  }
```

1. Whenever we return STATUS_PENDING from a dispatch routine (as we're about to do here), we make this call to help the I/O Manager avoid an internal race condition. We must do this *before* we relinquish ownership of the IRP.

2. If our device is currently busy, **IoStartPacket** puts the request onto a queue. If our device is idle, IoStartPacket marks the device as being busy and calls our **StartIo** routine. I'll describe the StartIo routine in the next section. The third argument to IoStartPacket is the address of a ULONG key used for sorting the queue. Disk drivers, for example, might specify a cylinder address here to provide for ordered-seek queuing. If you supply NULL, as here, this request is added to the tail of the queue. The last argument is the address of a cancel routine. I'll discuss cancel routines later in this chapter—they're complicated!

3. We return STATUS_PENDING to tell our caller that we're not done with this IRP yet.

It's very important not to touch the IRP once we call IoStartPacket. By the time that function returns, the IRP may have been completed and the memory it occupies released. The pointer we have might, therefore, now be invalid.

The StartIo Routine

The I/O Manager calls your **StartIo** routine to process one IRP at a time:

```
VOID StartIo(PDEVICE_OBJECT device, PIRP Irp)
  {
  PIO_STACK_LOCATION stack = IoGetCurrentIrpStackLocation(Irp);
  PDEVICE_EXTENSION pdx = (PDEVICE_EXTENSION) device->DeviceExtension;
  ...
  }
```

Your StartIo routine receives control at DISPATCH_LEVEL, meaning that it must not generate any page faults. In addition, the **CurrentIrp** field of the device object and the **Irp** argument will both point to the IRP that's being submitted to you for processing.

Your job in StartIo is to commence the IRP you've been handed. How you do this depends entirely on your device. Often you will need to access hardware registers that are also used by your interrupt service routine (ISR) and, perhaps, by other routines in your driver. In fact, sometimes the easiest way to commence a new operation is to store some state information in your device extension and then fake an interrupt. Since either of these approaches needs to be carried out under protection of the same spin lock that protects your ISR, the correct way to proceed is to call **KeSynchronizeExecution**. For example:

```
VOID StartIo(...)
  {
  ...
  KeSynchronizeExecution(pdx->InterruptObject,
    TransferFirst, (PVOID) pdx);
  }

BOOLEAN TransferFirst(PVOID context)
  {
  PDEVICE_EXTENSION pdx = (PDEVICE_EXTENSION) context;
  ...
  return TRUE;
  }
```

The **TransferFirst** routine shown here is an example of the generic class of *SynchCritSection* routines, so called because they are synchronized with the ISR. I'll discuss the SynchCritSection concept in more detail in Chapter 7, "Reading and Writing Data."

Once StartIo gets the device busy handling the new request, it returns. You'll see the request next when your device interrupts to signal that it's done with whatever transfer you started.

The Interrupt Service Routine

When your device is finished transferring data, it might signal a hardware interrupt. In Chapter 7, I'll show you how to use **IoConnectInterrupt** to "hook" the interrupt. One of the arguments to IoConnectInterrupt is the address of your ISR. When the interrupt occurs, the hardware abstraction layer (HAL) calls your ISR. The ISR runs at the device IRQL (DIRQL) of your particular device and under the protection of a spin lock associated specifically with your ISR. The ISR has the following prototype:

```
BOOLEAN OnInterrupt(PKINTERRUPT InterruptObject, PVOID context)
  {
  ...
  }
```

The first argument of your ISR is the address of the interrupt object created by IoConnectInterrupt, but you're unlikely to use this argument. The second argument is whatever context value you specified in your original call to IoConnectInterrupt; it will probably be the address of your device object or of your device extension, depending on your preference.

I'll discuss the duties of your ISR in detail in Chapter 7 in connection with reading and writing data, the subject to which interrupt handling is most relevant. To carry on with this discussion of the standard model, I need to tell you that one of the likely things for the ISR to do is to schedule a deferred procedure call (DPC). The purpose of the DPC is to let you do things, like calling **IoCompleteRequest**, that can't be done at the rarified DIRQL at which your ISR runs. So, supposing you develop a pointer named **device** to your device object inside the ISR, you'd have a line of code like this one:

```
IoRequestDpc(device, device->CurrentIrp, NULL);
```

You'll next see the IRP in the DPC routine you registered inside AddDevice with your call to **IoInitializeDpcRequest**. The traditional name for that routine is **DpcForIsr** because it's the DPC routine your ISR requests.

Deferred Procedure Call Routine

The **DpcForIsr** routine requested by your ISR receives control at DISPATCH_LEVEL. Generally, its job is to finish up the processing of the IRP that caused the most recent interrupt. Often that job entails calling IoCompleteRequest to complete this IRP and IoStartNextPacket to remove the next IRP from your device queue for forwarding to StartIo.

```
VOID DpcForIsr(PKDPC Dpc PDEVICE_OBJECT device, PIRP Irp, PVOID context)
  {
  ...
  IoStartNextPacket(device, FALSE);
  IoCompleteRequest(Irp, boost);
  }
```

1
2

1. **IoStartNextPacket** removes the next IRP from your queue and sends it to StartIo. The FALSE argument indicates that this IRP can't be cancelled in the normal way. By the time you finish this chapter, you'll know how to handle the more normal case in which you specify TRUE for the second argument.

2. **IoCompleteRequest** completes the IRP you specify as the first argument. The second argument specifies a priority boost for the thread that has been waiting for this IRP. You'll also fill in the IoStatus block within the IRP before calling IoCompleteRequest, as I'll explain later in the section "Completion Mechanics."

The call to IoCompleteRequest is the end of this standard way of handling an I/O request. After that call, the I/O Manager (or whatever created the IRP in the first place) owns the IRP once more. That entity will destroy the IRP and might unblock a thread that has been waiting for the request to complete.

Custom Queues

Some devices operate in such a way that it makes sense to have more than one queue of requests. A common example is a serial port, which can handle independent streams of input and output requests simultaneously. Both IoStartPacket and IoStartNextPacket (and their key-sorting equivalents) work with a queue that you get "for free" as part of the device object. It's relatively easy to create additional queues that work the same way as the standard queue managed by those routines.

To make it easier to discuss things, let's suppose that you need a separate queue to manage IRP_MJ_SPECIAL requests. (There's no such major function code—I made it up just so that we'd have a concrete topic for the discussion.) You would write two helper functions that would do for these special IRPs pretty much the same thing as the StartIo and DpcForIsr routines I mentioned earlier:

■ A StartIo-like function—let's call it **StartIoSpecial**—that starts the next IRP_MJ_SPECIAL request.

■ A DPC function—let's call it **DpcSpecial**—that handles completing an IRP_MJ_SPECIAL request.

You'll also create a KDEVICE_QUEUE object in your device extension. You'd initialize this object during AddDevice:

```
NTSTATUS AddDevice(...)
  {
  ...
  KeInitializeDeviceQueue(&pdx->dqSpecial);
  ...
  }
```

where **dqSpecial** is the name of the KDEVICE_OBJECT we'll use for IRP_MJ_SPECIAL requests. A device queue object is a three-state object. (See Figure 5-6.) These states influence how the support routines for device queues operate:

■ The **idle** state occurs when the device isn't busy handling any requests and the queue is empty. **KeInsertDeviceQueue** and **KeInsertByKeyDeviceQueue** mark the queue busy but empty (the next state) and return FALSE. You shouldn't call **KeRemoveDeviceQueue** or **KeRemoveByKeyDeviceQueue** when the queue is idle.

- The **busy but empty** state occurs when the device is busy but no IRPs are on the queue. KeInsertDeviceQueue and KeInsertByKeyDeviceQueue add an IRP to the end of the queue, put the queue into the busy but not empty state, and return TRUE. KeRemoveDeviceQueue or KeRemoveByKeyDeviceQueue return NULL and put the queue into the idle state.

- The **busy but not empty** state occurs when the device is busy and there's at least one IRP on the queue. KeInsertDeviceQueue and KeInsertByKeyDeviceQueue add an IRP to the end of the queue, leave the queue in this same state, and return TRUE. (This is like what happens in the busy but empty state, except that no state transition occurs.) KeRemoveDeviceQueue or KeRemoveByKeyDeviceQueue remove the first entry from the queue and return its address. In addition, if the queue becomes empty, they put the queue into the busy but empty state.

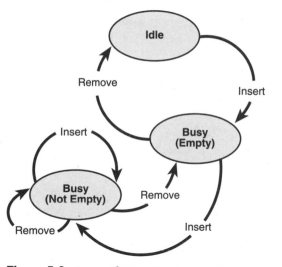

Figure 5-6. *States of a KDEVICE_QUEUE queue.*

We use these support routines and the special device queue in our dispatch and DPC routines, as follows:

```
NTSTATUS DispatchSpecial(PDEVICE_OBJECT fdo, PIRP Irp)
  {
  IoMarkIrpPending(Irp);
  KIRQL oldirql;
  KeRaiseIrql(DISPATCH_LEVEL, &oldirql);
  PDEVICE_EXTENSION pdx = (PDEVICE_EXTENSION) fdo->DeviceExtension;
  if (!KeInsertDeviceQueue(&pdx->dqSpecial,
    &Irp->Tail.Overlay.DeviceQueueEntry))
    StartIoSpecial(fdo, Irp);
```

1 ▷
2 ▷
3 ▷

(continued)

```
      KeLowerIrql(oldirql);
      return STATUS_PENDING;
      }

VOID DpcSpecial(...)
   {
   ...
   PKDEVICE_QUEUE_ENTRY qep = KeRemoveDeviceQueue(&pdx->dqSpecial);
   if (qep)
     StartIoSpecial(fdo, CONTAINING_RECORD(qep, IRP,
       Tail.Overlay.DeviceQueueEntry));
   ...
   }
```

4 ▶

1. As with a "regular" dispatch routine, we mark this IRP as pending because we're going to queue it and return STATUS_PENDING.

2. KeInsertDeviceQueue and our own StartIoSpecial expect to be called at DISPATCH_LEVEL. Hence, we explicitly raise IRQL to that level. We'll use **KeLowerIrql** shortly to lower IRQL back to what it currently is (probably PASSIVE_LEVEL).

3. This call to **KeInsertDeviceQueue** might add the IRP to the queue, in which case the return value will be TRUE and we won't do anything more with the IRP. If the device is currently idle, however, the return value will be FALSE and the IRP will not have been placed on the queue. We therefore call StartIoSpecial directly.

4. This call to **KeRemoveDeviceQueue** from the DPC routine will have one of two results. If the queue is currently empty, the return value will be NULL and we won't do anything more about starting a new request (as there aren't any!). Otherwise, the return value will be the address of the queue linking field within the IRP. We use CONTAINING_RECORD to recover the address of the IRP, which we then pass to StartIoSpecial. Note that this DPC routine is already running at DISPATCH_LEVEL, so we don't need to adjust IRQL before removing an entry from the queue or calling the StartIo routine.

It's no coincidence that my earlier descriptions of StartPacket and StartNextPacket sound so similar to what I've just described. Those functions work with a KDEVICE_QUEUE object named **DeviceQueue** that's one of the opaque fields of a device object, and their logic is the same as your logic when you manage your own device queue.

COMPLETING I/O REQUESTS

Every IRP has an urge toward completion. In the standard processing model, you might complete an IRP in at least two circumstances. The DpcForIsr routine would generally complete the request that's responsible for the most recent interrupt. A dispatch function might also complete an IRP in situations like these:

■ If the request is erroneous in some easily determined way (such as a request to rewind a printer or to eject the keyboard), the dispatch routine should fail the request by completing it with an appropriate status code.

■ If the request calls for information that the dispatch function can easily determine (such as a control request asking for the driver's version number), the dispatch routine should provide the answer and complete the request with a successful status code.

Completion Mechanics

Mechanically, completing an IRP entails filling in the **Status** and **Information** members within the IRP's **IoStatus** block and calling **IoCompleteRequest**. The Status value is one of the codes defined by manifest constants in the DDK header file NTSTATUS.H. Refer to Table 5-1 for an abbreviated list of status codes for common situations. The Information value depends on what type of IRP you're completing and on whether you're succeeding or failing the IRP. Most of the time, when you're failing an IRP (that is, completing it with an error status of some kind), you'll set Information to zero. When you succeed an IRP that involves data transfer, you ordinarily set the Information field equal to the number of bytes transferred.

Status Code	*Description*
STATUS_SUCCESS	Normal completion
STATUS_UNSUCCESSFUL	Request failed, but no other status code describes the reason specifically
STATUS_NOT_IMPLEMENTED	A function hasn't been implemented
STATUS_INVALID_HANDLE	An invalid handle was supplied for an operation
STATUS_INVALID_PARAMETER	A parameter is in error
STATUS_INVALID_DEVICE_REQUEST	The request is invalid for this device
STATUS_END_OF_FILE	End-of-file marker reached
STATUS_DELETE_PENDING	The device is in the process of being removed from the system
STATUS_INSUFFICIENT_RESOURCES	Not enough system resources (often memory) to perform an operation

Table 5-1. *Some commonly used NTSTATUS codes.*

NOTE Always be sure to consult the DDK documentation for the correct setting of IoStatus.Information for the IRP you're dealing with. In some flavors of IRP_MJ_PNP, for example, this field is used as a pointer to a data structure that the PnP Manager is responsible for releasing. If you were to overstore the Information field with zero when failing the request, you would unwittingly cause a resource leak.

Since completing a request is something you do so often, I find it useful to have a helper routine to carry out the mechanics:

```
NTSTATUS CompleteRequest(PIRP Irp, NTSTATUS status, ULONG_PTR Information)
  {
  Irp->IoStatus.Status = status;
  Irp->IoStatus.Information = Information;
  IoCompleteRequest(Irp, IO_NO_INCREMENT);
  return status;
  }
```

I defined this routine in such a way that it returns whatever status value you supply as its second argument. That's because I'm such a lazy typist: the return value allows me to use this helper whenever I want to complete a request and then immediately return a status code. For example:

```
NTSTATUS DispatchControl(PDEVICE_OBJECT device, PIRP Irp)
  {
  PIO_STACK_LOCATION stack = IoGetCurrentIrpStackLocation(Irp);
  ULONG code = stack->Parameters.DeviceIoControl.IoControlCode;
  if (code == IOCTL_TOASTER_BOGUS)
    return CompleteRequest(Irp, STATUS_INVALID_DEVICE_REQUEST, 0);
  ...
  }
```

You might notice that the **Information** argument to the **CompleteRequest** function is typed as a ULONG_PTR. In other words, this value can be either a ULONG or a pointer to something (and therefore potentially 64 bits wide).

When you call IoCompleteRequest, you supply a priority boost value to be applied to whatever thread is currently waiting for this request to complete. You normally choose a boost value that depends on the type of device, as suggested by the manifest constant names listed in Table 5-2. The priority adjustment improves the throughput of threads that frequently wait for I/O operations to complete. Events for which the end user is directly responsible, such as keyboard or mouse operations, result in greater priority boosts in order to give preference to interactive tasks. Consequently, you want to choose the boost value with at least some care. Don't use IO_SOUND_INCREMENT for absolutely every operation a sound card driver finishes, for example—it's not necessary to apply this extraordinary priority increment to a get-driver-version control request.

Manifest Constant	Numeric Priority Boost
IO_NO_INCREMENT	0
IO_CD_ROM_INCREMENT	1
IO_DISK_INCREMENT	1
IO_KEYBOARD_INCREMENT	6
IO_MAILSLOT_INCREMENT	2
IO_MOUSE_INCREMENT	6
IO_NAMED_PIPE_INCREMENT	2
IO_NETWORK_INCREMENT	2
IO_PARALLEL_INCREMENT	1
IO_SERIAL_INCREMENT	2
IO_SOUND_INCREMENT	8
IO_VIDEO_INCREMENT	1

Table 5-2. *Priority boost values for IoCompleteRequest.*

Don't, by the way, complete an IRP with the special status code STATUS_PENDING. Dispatch routines often return STATUS_PENDING as their return value, but you should never set **IoStatus.Status** to this value. Just to make sure, the checked build of IoCompleteRequest generates an ASSERT failure if it sees STATUS_PENDING in the ending status. Another popular value for people to use by mistake is apparently "−1", which doesn't have any meaning as an NTSTATUS code at all. There's a checked-build ASSERT to catch that mistake, too.

Using Completion Routines

You often need to know the results of I/O requests that you pass down to lower levels of the driver hierarchy or that you originate. To find out what happened to a request, you install a *completion routine* by calling **IoSetCompletionRoutine**:

```
IoSetCompletionRoutine(Irp, CompletionRoutine, context,
  InvokeOnSuccess, InvokeOnError, InvokeOnCancel);
```

Irp is the request whose completion you want to know about. **CompletionRoutine** is the address of the completion routine you want called, and **context** is an arbitrary pointer-sized value you want passed as an argument to the completion routine. The **InvokeOn***Xxx* arguments are Boolean values indicating whether you want the completion routine called in three different circumstances:

- **InvokeOnSuccess** means you want the completion routine called when something completes the IRP with a status code that passes the NT_SUCCESS test.

■ **InvokeOnError** means you want the completion routine called when something completes the IRP with a status code that does *not* pass the NT_SUCCESS test.

■ **InvokeOnCancel** means you want the completion routine called when something calls IoCancelIrp before completing the IRP. I worded this quite delicately: IoCancelIrp will set the Cancel flag in the IRP, and that's the condition that gets tested if you specify this argument. A cancelled IRP might end up being completed with STATUS_CANCELLED (which would fail the NT_SUCCESS test) or with any other status at all. If the IRP gets completed with an error and you specified InvokeOnError, InvokeOnError by itself would cause your completion routine to be called. Conversely, if the IRP gets completed without error and you specified Invoke-OnSuccess, InvokeOnSuccess by itself would cause your completion routine to be called. In these cases, InvokeOnCancel would be redundant. But if you left out one or the other (or both) of InvokeOnSuccess or InvokeOnError, the InvokeOnCancel flag would let you see the eventual completion of an IRP whose Cancel flag had been set no matter what status is used for the completion.

At least one of these three flags must be TRUE. Note that IoSetCompletionRoutine is a macro, so you want to avoid arguments that generate side effects. The three flag arguments and the function pointer, in particular, are each referenced twice by the macro.

IoSetCompletionRoutine installs the completion routine address and context argument in the *next* IO_STACK_LOCATION—that is, in the stack location in which the next lower driver will find its parameters. Consequently, the lowest-level driver in a particular stack of drivers does not dare attempt to install a completion routine. Doing so would be pretty futile, of course, because—by definition of what it means to be the lowest-level driver—there's no driver left to pass the request on to.

A completion routine looks like this:

```
NTSTATUS CompletionRoutine(PDEVICE_OBJECT device, PIRP Irp, PVOID context)
  {
  if (Irp->PendingReturned)
    IoMarkIrpPending(Irp);
  ...
  return <some status code>;
  }
```

It receives pointers to the device object and the IRP, and it also receives whatever context value you specified in the call to IoSetCompletionRoutine. Completion routines are usually called at DISPATCH_LEVEL and in an arbitrary thread context, but can be called at PASSIVE_LEVEL or APC_LEVEL. To accommodate the usual case (DISPATCH_LEVEL), completion routines therefore need to be in nonpaged memory and must call only service functions that are callable at DISPATCH_LEVEL. To accommodate the possibility of being called at a lower IRQL, however, a completion routine shouldn't call functions like **KeAcquireSpinLockAtDpcLevel** that assume they're at DISPATCH_LEVEL to start with.

> **NOTE** The device object pointer argument to a completion routine is the value left in the I/O stack location's DeviceObject pointer. IoCallDriver ordinarily sets this value. People sometimes create an IRP with an extra stack location so that they can pass parameters to a completion routine without creating an extra context structure. Such a completion routine gets a NULL device object pointer unless the creator sets the DeviceObject field.

How Completion Routines Get Called

IoCompleteRequest is responsible for calling all of the completion routines that drivers installed in their respective stack locations. The way the process works, as shown in the flowchart in Figure 5-7, is this: Something calls IoCompleteRequest to signal the end of processing for the IRP. IoCompleteRequest then consults the current stack location to see whether the driver *above* the current level installed a completion routine. If not, it moves the stack pointer up one level and repeats the test. This process repeats until a stack location is found that *does* specify a completion routine or until IoCompleteRequest reaches the top of the stack. Then IoCompleteRequest takes steps that eventually result in something releasing the memory occupied by the IRP (among other things).

When IoCompleteRequest finds a stack frame with a completion routine pointer, it calls that routine and examines the return code. If the return code is anything other than STATUS_MORE_PROCESSING_REQUIRED, IoCompleteRequest moves the stack pointer up one level and continues as before. If the return code is STATUS_MORE_PROCESSING_REQUIRED, however, IoCompleteRequest stops dead in its tracks and returns to its caller. The IRP will then be in a sort of limbo state. The driver whose completion routine halted the stack unwinding process is expected to do more work with the IRP.

Within a completion routine, a call to IoGetCurrentIrpStackLocation will retrieve the same stack pointer as was current when something called IoSetCompletionRoutine to install the completion routine pointer. In other words, it returns the stack location above the one which contains the actual pointer to this completion routine. You should not rely in a completion routine on the contents of any lower stack location. To reinforce this rule, IoCompleteRequest zeroes most of the next location just before calling a completion routine.

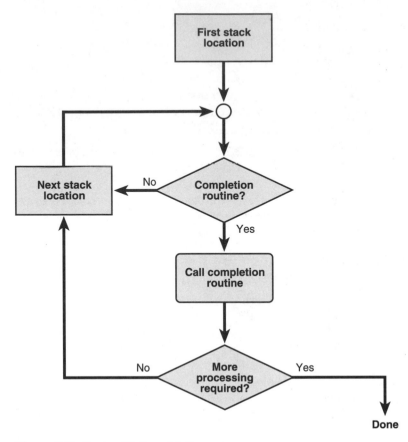

Figure 5-7. *Logic of IoCompleteRequest.*

Why Completion Routines Call IoMarkIrpPending

You may have noticed these two lines at the beginning of the skeleton completion routine I just showed you:

```
if (Irp->PendingReturned)
  IoMarkIrpPending(Irp);
```

This particular piece of boilerplate is required in any completion routine that doesn't return STATUS_MORE_PROCESSING_REQUIRED. If you'd like to know why, read the rest of this section. However, be aware that you should not develop drivers that rely on the information related to how the I/O Manager processes pending IRPs—that process is likely to change in future versions of Windows.

 **Nerd Alert** This explanation is complicated!

To maximize system throughput, the I/O Manager expects drivers to defer the completion of IRPs that take a long time to complete. A driver indicates that completion will be deferred by calling **IoMarkIrpPending** and returning STATUS_PENDING from the dispatch routine. Often, though, the original caller of the I/O Manager wants to wait until the operation finishes before proceeding. The I/O Manager will therefore have logic similar to this (not the actual source code of any particular Microsoft Windows NT function) to deal with the deferred completion:

```
Irp->UserEvent = pEvent; // ← don't do this yourself
status = IoCallDriver(...);
if (status == STATUS_PENDING)
  KeWaitForSingleObject(pEvent, ...);
```

In other words, if IoCallDriver returns STATUS_PENDING, this code will wait on a kernel event. IoCompleteRequest is responsible for setting this event when the IRP finally completes. The address of the event (**UserEvent**) is in one of the opaque fields of the IRP so that IoCompleteRequest can find it. But there's more to the story than that.

To keep things simple for the moment, suppose that there were just one driver involved in processing this request. Its dispatch function does the two things we've discussed: it calls IoMarkIrpPending, and it returns STATUS_PENDING. That status code will be the return value from IoCallDriver as well, so you can see that something is now going to wait on an event. The eventual call to IoCompleteRequest occurs in an arbitrary thread context, so IoCompleteRequest will schedule a *special kernel APC* to execute in the context of the original thread (which is currently blocked). The APC (asynchronous procedure call) routine will set the event, thereby releasing whatever is waiting for the operation to finish. There are reasons we don't need to go into right now for why an APC is used for this purpose instead of a simple call to **KeSetEvent**.

But queuing an APC is relatively expensive. Suppose that, instead of returning STATUS_PENDING, the dispatch routine were to call IoCompleteRequest and return some other status. In this case, the call to IoCompleteRequest is in the same thread context as the caller of IoCallDriver. It's not necessary to queue an APC, therefore. Furthermore, it's not even necessary to call KeSetEvent since the I/O Manager isn't going to be waiting on an event if it doesn't get STATUS_PENDING back from the dispatch routine. If IoCompleteRequest just had a way to know this case were occurring, it could optimize its processing to avoid the APC, couldn't it? That's where IoMarkIrpPending comes in.

What IoMarkIrpPending does—it's a macro in WDM.H, so you can see this for yourself—is set a flag named SL_PENDING_RETURNED in the current stack location. IoCompleteRequest will set the IRP's **PendingReturned** flag equal to whatever value it finds in the topmost stack location. Later on, it inspects this flag to see whether the dispatch routine has returned or will return STATUS_PENDING. If you do your job correctly, it won't matter whether the return from the dispatch routine happens before or after IoCompleteRequest makes this determination. "Doing your job correctly," in this particular case, means calling IoMarkIrpPending before you do anything that might result in the IRP getting completed.

So, anyway, IoCompleteRequest looks at the PendingReturned flag. If it's set, and if the IRP in question is of the kind that normally gets completed asynchronously, IoCompleteRequest simply returns to its caller *without* queuing the APC. It assumes that it's running in the originator's thread context and that some dispatch routine is shortly going to return a nonpending status code to the originator. The originator, in turn, avoids waiting for the event, which is just as well because no one is ever going to signal that event. So far, so good.

Now let's put some additional drivers into the picture. The top-level driver has no clue what will happen below it. It simply passes the request down using code such as the following. (See the next section, "Passing Requests Down to Lower Levels.")

```
IoCopyCurrentIrpStackLocationToNext(Irp);
IoSetCompletionRoutine(Irp, ...);
return IoCallDriver(...);
```

In other words, the top-level driver installs a completion routine, calls IoCallDriver, and then returns whatever status code IoCallDriver happens to return. This process might now repeat additional times as other drivers pass the request down to whatever is really destined to service it. When the request reaches that level, the dispatch routine calls IoMarkIrpPending and returns STATUS_PENDING. The STATUS_PENDING value then percolates all the way back up to the top and out into the originator of the IRP, which will promptly decide to wait for something to signal the event.

But notice that the driver that called IoMarkIrpPending only managed to set SL_PENDING_RETURNED in its own stack location. The drivers above it actually returned STATUS_PENDING, but they didn't call IoMarkIrpPending on their own behalf because they didn't know they'd end up returning STATUS_PENDING as proxies for the guy at the bottom of the stack. Sorting this out is where the boilerplate code in the completion routine comes in, as follows. As IoCompleteRequest walks up the I/O stack, it pauses at each level to set the IRP's PendingReturned flag to the value of the current stack's SL_PENDING_RETURNED flag. If there's no completion routine at this level, it then sets the next higher stack's SL_PENDING_RETURNED if PendingReturned is set and repeats its loop. It doesn't change SL_PENDING_RETURNED if PendingReturned is clear. In this way, SL_PENDING_RETURNED gets propagated from the bottom to the top of the stack, and the IRP's PendingReturned flag ends up TRUE if any of the drivers ever called IoMarkIrpPending.

IoCompleteRequest does *not* automatically propagate SL_PENDING_RETURNED across a completion routine, however. The completion routine must do this itself by testing the IRP's PendingReturned flag (that is, did the driver below me return STATUS_PENDING?) and then calling IoMarkIrpPending. If every completion routine does its job, the SL_PENDING_RETURNED flag makes its way to the top of the stack just as if IoCompleteRequest had done all of its work.

Now that I've explained these intricacies, you can see why it's important for dispatch routines to call IoMarkIrpPending if they're going to explicitly return STATUS_PENDING and why completion routines should conditionally do so. If a completion routine were to break the chain, you'd end up with a thread waiting in vain on an event that's destined never to be signalled. Failing to see PendingReturned, IoCompleteRequest would act as if it were dealing with a same-context completion and therefore would not queue the APC that's supposed to signal the event. The same thing would happen if a dispatch routine were to omit the IoMarkIrpPending call and then return STATUS_PENDING.

On the other hand, it's okay, albeit slightly inefficient, to call IoMarkIrpPending and then complete the IRP synchronously. All that will happen is that IoComplete-Request will queue an APC to signal an event on which no one will ever wait. (Logic is in place to make sure that the event object can't cease to exist before the call to KeSetEvent, too.) This is slower than need be, but it's not harmful.

Do not, by the way, be tempted, in the hope of avoiding the boilerplate call to IoMarkIrpPending inside your completion routine, to code like this:

```
status = IoCallDriver(...);
if (status == STATUS_PENDING)
  IoMarkIrpPending(...);      // ⟵ DON'T DO THIS!
```

The reason this is a bad idea is that you must treat the IRP pointer as poison after you give it away by calling IoCallDriver. Whatever receives the IRP can complete it, allowing something to call **IoFreeIrp**, which will render your pointer invalid long before you regain control from IoCallDriver.

PASSING REQUESTS DOWN TO LOWER LEVELS

The whole goal of the layering of device objects which WDM facilitates is that you want to be able to easily pass IRPs from one layer down to the next. Back in Chapter 2, "Basic Structure of a WDM Driver," I discussed how your AddDevice routine would contribute its portion of the effort required to create a stack of device objects with a statement like this one:

```
pdx->LowerDeviceObject = IoAttachDeviceToDeviceStack(fdo, pdo);
```

where **fdo** is the address of your own device object and **pdo** is the address of the physical device object (PDO) at the bottom of the device stack. **IoAttachDevice-ToDeviceStack** returns to you the address of the device object immediately underneath yours. When you decide to forward an IRP that you received from above, this is the device object you'll specify in the eventual call to IoCallDriver.

When you pass an IRP down, you have the additional responsibility of initializing the IO_STACK_LOCATION that the next driver will use to obtain its parameters. One way of doing this is to perform a physical copy, like this:

```
...
IoCopyCurrentIrpStackLocationToNext(Irp);
status = IoCallDriver(pdx->LowerDeviceObject, Irp);
...
```

IoCopyCurrentIrpStackLocationToNext is a macro in WDM.H that copies all the fields in an IO_STACK_LOCATION—except for the ones that pertain to the I/O completion routines—from the current stack location to the next one. In previous versions of Windows NT, kernel-mode driver writers sometimes copied the entire stack location, which would cause the caller's completion routine to be called *twice*. (Recall that your completion routine pointer goes in the stack location underneath yours.) For an explanation of how this particular trap could bite the unwary developer, see "Secrets of the Universe Revealed! How NT Handles I/O Completion" in *The NT Insider* (May 1997, vol. 4, no. 3). The IoCopyCurrentIrpStackLocationToNext macro, which is new with the WDM, avoids the problem.

Driver writers that don't care what happens to the IRP after they pass it down often use a shortcut to get around actually copying a stack location. In such a situation, they won't be installing a completion routine—I just said they don't care what happens to the IRP. Refer to Figure 5-8 for an illustration of the timing of events in this case.

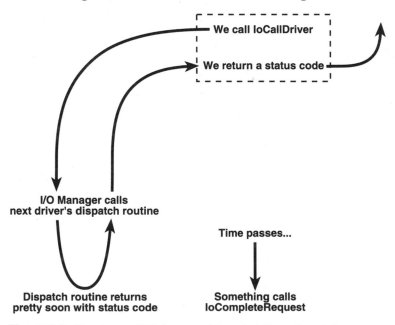

Figure 5-8. *Passing an IRP down and ignoring its ending status.*

There's no reason to spend the machine cycles to copy your stack location to the next location—the one you already have contains the parameters you want the next driver to see as well as whatever completion pointer the driver above you might have specified. You therefore use the following shortcut:

```
NTSTATUS ForwardAndForget(PDEVICE_OBJECT fdo, PIRP Irp)
  {
  PDEVICE_EXTENSION pdx = (PDEVICE_EXTENSION) fdo->DeviceExtension;
  IoSkipCurrentIrpStackLocation(Irp);
  return IoCallDriver(pdx->LowerDeviceObject, Irp);
  }
```

The shortcut is in the function (actually a macro) misleadingly named **IoSkip-CurrentIrpStackLocation**. What this macro does is *retard* the IRP's stack pointer by one position. IoCallDriver will immediately *advance* the stack pointer. The net effect is to not change the stack pointer. When the next driver's dispatch routine calls IoGetCurrentIrpStackLocation, it will retrieve exactly the same IO_STACK_LOCATION pointer that we were working with, and it will thereby process exactly the same request (same major and minor function codes) with the same parameters.

You'll notice that the array of IO_STACK_LOCATIONs contains an entry at the very bottom that won't be used in this scenario. In fact, if drivers underneath us play the same trick, there might be more than one location that won't be used. That's not a problem, though—it just means that something allocated more stack locations than it needed to. It's not a problem that the stack gets unwound a little bit quicker during completion processing, either. IoCompleteRequest doesn't use any absolute indices or pointers when it unwinds the stack. It just starts at whatever the current location is when it gains control and works its way upward calling completion routines. All the completion routines that got installed will get called, and the then-current stack locations will be the ones that their drivers were expecting to work with.

The explanation of why IoSkipCurrentIrpStackLocation works is so tricky that I thought an illustration might help. Figure 5-9 illustrates a situation in which three drivers are in a particular stack: yours (the functional device object [FDO]) and two others (an upper filter device object [FiDO] and the PDO). In the first picture (a), you see the relationship between stack locations, parameters, and completion routines when we do the copy step with IoCopyCurrentIrpStackLocationToNext. In the second picture (b), you see the same relationships when we use the IoSkipCurrent-IrpStackLocation shortcut. In the second picture, the third and last stack location is fallow, but nobody gets confused by that fact.

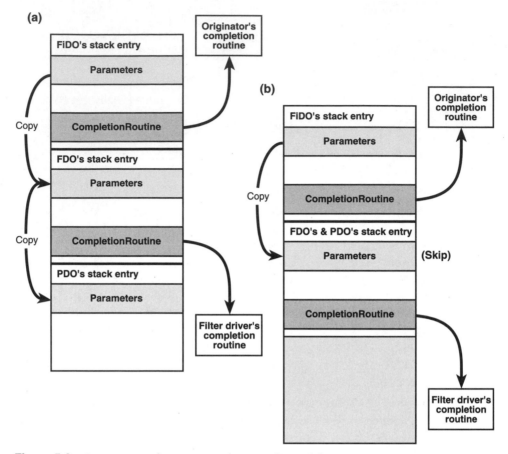

Figure 5-9. *Comparison of copying vs. skipping I/O stack locations.*

CANCELLING I/O REQUESTS

Just as happens with people in real life, programs sometimes change their mind about the I/O requests they've asked you to perform for them. We're not talking about simple fickleness here. Applications might issue requests that will take a long time to complete and then terminate, leaving the request outstanding. Such an occurrence is especially likely in the WDM world, where the insertion of new hardware might require us to stall requests while the Configuration Manager rebalances resources or where you might be told at any moment to power down your device.

To cancel a request in kernel mode, the creator of the IRP calls **IoCancelIrp**. The operating system automatically calls IoCancelIrp for every IRP that belongs to a thread that's terminating with requests still outstanding. A user-mode application can call **CancelIo** to cancel all outstanding asynchronous operations issued by a given thread on a file handle. IoCancelIrp would like to simply complete the IRP it's given with STATUS_CANCELLED, but there's a hitch: it doesn't know where *you* have salted away pointers to the IRP, and it doesn't know for sure whether you're currently processing the IRP. So it relies on a cancel routine you provide to do most of the work of cancelling an IRP.

It turns out that a call to IoCancelIrp is more of a suggestion than a mandate. It would be nice if every IRP that something tried to cancel really got completed with STATUS_CANCELLED. But it's okay if a driver wants to go ahead and finish the IRP normally if that can be done relatively quickly. You should provide a way to cancel I/O requests that might spend significant time waiting in a queue between a dispatch routine and a StartIo routine. How long is significant is a matter for your own sound judgment; my advice is to err on the side of providing for cancellation because it's not that hard to do and makes your driver fit better into the operating system.

 Nerd Alert The explanation of how to put cancellation logic into your driver is unusually intricate, even for kernel-mode programming. You might want to simply cut to the chase and read the code samples without worrying overmuch about how they work.

If It Weren't for Multitasking...

There's an intricate synchronization problem associated with cancelling IRPs. Before I explain the problem and the solution, I want to describe the way cancellation would work in a world where there was no multitasking and no concern with multiprocessor computers. In that Utopia, several pieces of the I/O Manager would fit together with your StartIo routine and with a cancel routine you'd provide, as follows:

■ When you call IoStartPacket, you specify the address of a cancel routine that gets saved in the IRP. When you call IoStartNextPacket (from your DPC routine), you specify TRUE for the Boolean argument that indicates that you're going to use the standard cancellation mechanism. Before IoStartPacket or IoStartNextPacket calls your StartIo routine, it sets the CurrentIrp field of your device object to point to the IRP it's about to send. IoStartNextPacket sets CurrentIrp to NULL if there are no more requests in the queue.

■ One of the first things your StartIo routine does is set the cancel routine pointer in the IRP to NULL.

■ IoCancelIrp unconditionally sets the Cancel flag in the IRP. Then it checks to see whether the IRP specifies a cancel routine. In between the time you call IoStartPacket and the time your StartIo routine gets control, the cancel routine pointer in the IRP will be non-NULL. In this case, IoCancelIrp calls your cancel routine. You remove the IRP from the queue where it currently resides—this is the DeviceQueue member of the device object—and complete the IRP with STATUS_CANCELLED. After StartIo starts processing the IRP, however, the cancel routine pointer will be NULL and IoCancelIrp won't do anything more.

Synchronizing Cancellation

Unfortunately for us as programmers, we write code for a multiprocessing, multitasking environment in which effects can sometimes appear to precede causes. There are at least three race conditions in the logic I just described. Figure 5-10 illustrates these race conditions, and I'll explain them here:

■ Suppose IoCancelIrp gets as far as setting the Cancel flag and then (on another CPU) IoStartNextPacket dequeues the IRP and sends it to StartIo. Since IoCancelIrp will soon send the same IRP to your cancel routine, your StartIo routine shouldn't do anything else with it.

■ It's possible for two actors (your cancel routine and IoStartNextPacket) to both try, more or less simultaneously, to remove the same IRP from the request queue. That obviously won't work.

■ It's possible for StartIo to get past the test for the Cancel flag, the one that you're going to put in because of the first race, and for IoCancelIrp to sneak in to test the cancel routine pointer before StartIo can manage to nullify that pointer. Now you've got a cancel routine that will complete a request that something (probably your DPC routine) will also try to complete. Oops!

The standard way of preventing these races relies on a systemwide spin lock called the cancel spin lock. A thread that wants to cancel an IRP acquires the spin lock once inside IoCancelIrp and releases it inside the driver cancel routine. A thread that wants to start an IRP acquires and releases the spin lock twice: once just before calling StartIo and again inside StartIo. The code in your driver will be as follows:

```
VOID StartIo(PDEVICE_OBJECT fdo, PIRP Irp)
  {
  KIRQL oldirql;
  IoAcquireCancelSpinLock(&oldirql);
  if (Irp != fdo->CurrentIrp || Irp->Cancel)
    {
    IoReleaseCancelSpinLock(oldirql);
    return;
    }
  else
    {
    IoSetCancelRoutine(Irp, NULL);
    IoReleaseCancelSpinLock(oldirql);
    }
  ...
  }
```

```
VOID OnCancel(PDEVICE_OBJECT fdo, PIRP Irp)
  {
  if (fdo->CurrentIrp == Irp)
    {
    IoReleaseCancelSpinLock(Irp->CancelIrql);
    IoStartNextPacket(fdo, TRUE);
    }
  else
    {
    KeRemoveEntryDeviceQueue(&fdo->DeviceQueue,
      &Irp->Tail.Overlay.DeviceQueueEntry);
    IoReleaseCancelSpinLock(Irp->CancelIrql);
    }
  CompleteRequest(Irp, STATUS_CANCELLED, 0);
  }
```

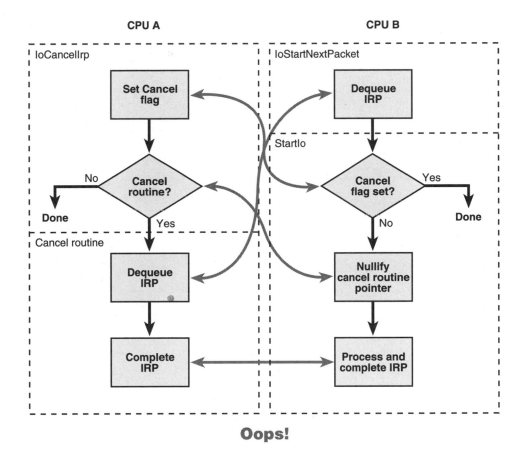

Figure 5-10. *Race conditions during IRP cancellation.*

AVOIDING THE GLOBAL CANCEL SPIN LOCK

Microsoft has identified the global cancel spin lock as a significant bottleneck in multiple CPU systems. You can see why it would be so. Every driver is potentially acquiring and releasing this lock several times for each IRP it processes, and no work can occur on a CPU while it's waiting for the lock. Microsoft Windows 2000 now implements **IoSetCancelRoutine** as an atomic (that is, interlocked) exchange operation, and IoCancelIrp follows a precise sequence that allows some drivers to avoid using the global cancel spin lock altogether. Ervin Peretz's article "The Windows Driver Model Simplifies Management of Device Driver I/O Requests" (*Microsoft Systems Journal,* January 1999), explains a way to support cancellation without using the cancel spin lock. I built on his ideas when I crafted the DEVQUEUE object described in the next chapter, "Plug and Play."

Notwithstanding that it's a bad idea to rely on the global cancel spin lock if you can avoid it, sometimes you can't avoid it. Namely, when you're using the standard model for IRP processing. That's why I'm explaining the whole gory mess in this chapter. Plus, it's good for your character.

Behind the scenes, the system routines that are calling your code will be doing something like the following. (This is not a copy of the actual Windows 2000 source code!)

```
VOID IoStartPacket(PDEVICE_OBJECT device, PIRP Irp,
  PULONG key, PDRIVER_CANCEL cancel)
  {
  KIRQL oldirql;
  IoAcquireCancelSpinLock(&oldirql);
  IoSetCancelRoutine(Irp, cancel);
  device->CurrentIrp = Irp;
  IoReleaseCancelSpinLock(oldirql);
  device->DriverObject->DriverStartIo(device, Irp);
  }

VOID IoStartNextPacket(PDEVICE_OBJECT device, BOOLEAN cancancel)
  {
  KIRQL oldirql;
  if (cancancel)
    IoAcquireCancelSpinLock(&oldirql);
  PKDEVICE_QUEUE_ENTRY p = KeRemoveDeviceQueue(&device->DeviceQueue));
  PIRP Irp = CONTAINING_RECORD(p, IRP, Tail.Overlay.DeviceQueueEntry);
  device->CurrentIrp = Irp;
  if (cancancel)
    IoReleaseCancelSpinLock(oldirql);
```

```
    device->DriverObject->DriverStartIo(device, Irp);
    }

BOOLEAN IoCancelIrp(PIRP Irp)
    {
    IoAcquireCancelSpinLock(&Irp->CancelIrql);
    Irp->Cancel = TRUE;
    PDRIVER_CANCEL cancel = IoSetCancelRoutine(Irp, NULL);
    if (cancel)
        {
        (*cancel)(device, Irp);
        return TRUE;
        }
    IoReleaseCancelSpinLock(&Irp->CancelIrql);
    return FALSE;
    }
```

It should be obvious that the real system routines do more than these sketches suggest. For example, IoStartNextPacket will be testing the return value from the KeRemoveDeviceQueue pointer to see whether it's NULL before just uncritically developing the IRP pointer with CONTAINING_RECORD. I've also left out the **IoStart-NextPacketByKey** routine, a sister routine to IoStartNextPacket that selects a request based on a sorting key.

To prove that this code works, we need to consider three cases. Figure 5-11 on page 207 will help you follow this discussion. We're going to assume that code running on CPU A of a multi-CPU computer wants to cancel a particular IRP and that code running on CPU B wants to start it. Since only two activities are going on with respect to this IRP simultaneously, we don't need to worry about what might happen if there were more than two CPUs.

Case 1: CPU A Gets the Spin Lock First

Suppose that CPU A gets past point 1 by acquiring the spin lock. It sets the Cancel flag and then tests to see whether there's a CancelRoutine for this IRP. The answer is Yes because the code that would nullify the pointer can't run yet without getting past the two acquisitions of the spin lock. So CPU A calls the cancel routine, dequeues the IRP, and then releases the spin lock. CPU B is now able to acquire the spin lock at point 2 and proceeds to remove an IRP from the queue. But this isn't the same IRP—it's whatever IRP was next in the queue. So CPU A will complete the IRP with STATUS_CANCELLED while CPU B goes ahead and initiates the next queued request.

Case 2: CPU B Gets the Spin Lock Just Before CPU A Tries

Now suppose that CPU B manages to get past point 2 and owns the spin lock just before CPU A tries to acquire the lock. CPU B will dequeue the IRP and set the device object's CurrentIrp to point to this IRP. Then it releases the spin lock (briefly) while it calls StartIo. In the meantime, CPU A grabs the spin lock at 1, which will keep CPU B from advancing past 3. CPU A sets the Cancel flag and calls the cancel routine. The cancel routine sees that this is the current IRP, so it releases the spin lock. CPU B is now free to advance past point 3 inside the StartIo routine. It will see that the Cancel flag is set in this IRP, so it will release the lock and just return. At this exact point, the device is idle. CPU A continues executing the cancel routine, however, which calls IoStartNextPacket and then completes the cancelled request.

It's very important not to call IoStartNextPacket while still owning the cancel spin lock because, as you can see by looking at the sketch of that function, it will acquire the lock on its own behalf. If we made the call to IoStartNextPacket while owning the lock, our CPU would deadlock because spin locks can't be recursively acquired.

The code in StartIo also guards against another subtle race condition. You might have wondered why StartIo tests the CurrentIrp field before testing the Cancel flag. (It's part of the C language specification, by the way, that a Boolean operation be evaluated left-to-right with a short circuit when the result is known. If the first part of the **if** test—**Irp != CurrentIrp**—is TRUE, the generated code won't go on to evaluate the second part: **Irp->Cancel**.) Suppose that CPU A manages to *completely finish* completing this IRP before CPU B makes it to point 3. Something on CPU A would call **IoFreeIrp** to release the IRP's storage. CPU B's **Irp** pointer would then become stale, and it would be unsafe to dereference the pointer.

Take another look at the previous code for IoStartNextPacket, and notice that it alters the device object's CurrentIrp pointer under the umbrella of the cancel spin lock. Our cancel routine calls IoStartNextPacket *before* it completes the IRP. Therefore, it's certain that one of the following two situations will occur: either CPU B's StartIo will get the spin lock before CPU A's IoStartNextPacket, in which case the IRP pointer is safe and the Cancel flag will be found set, or CPU B's StartIo will get the spin lock after CPU A's IoStartNextPacket, in which case the **Irp** variable won't be equal to CurrentIrp anymore—IoStartNextPacket changed it—and CPU B won't dereference the pointer.

The close reasoning of the preceding two paragraphs illustrates that, if you don't want to call IoStartNextPacket (or IoStartNextPacketByKey) from the cancel routine, you must be sure to set CurrentIrp to NULL while owning the cancel spin lock.

Whew! No wonder we cut and paste sample code so much!

Case 3: CPU B Gets the Spin Lock Twice

The third and last case to consider is the one in which CPU B manages to get all the way past point 3 and therefore owns the spin lock inside StartIo before CPU A ever tries to acquire the spin lock at point 1. In this case, StartIo will nullify the CancelRoutine pointer in the IRP before releasing the spin lock. CPU A could get as far as setting the Cancel flag in the IRP, but it will never call the cancel routine because the pointer is now NULL. Mind you, CPU B now goes ahead and processes the IRP to completion even though the Cancel flag is set, but this will be okay if it can be done rapidly.

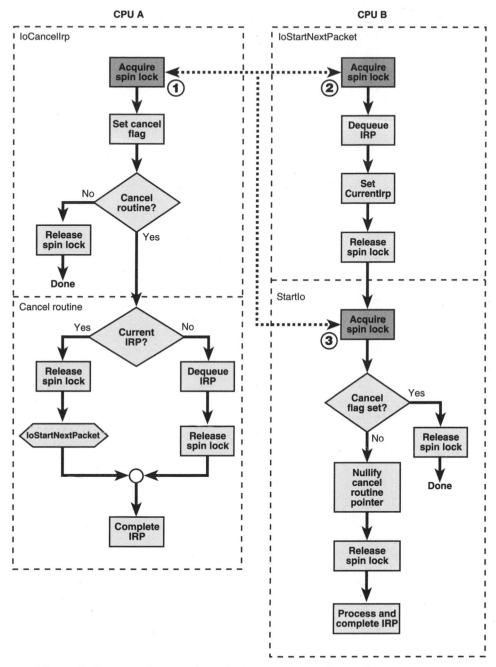

Figure 5-11. *Using the cancel spin lock to guard cancellation logic.*

Closely allied to the subject of IRP cancellation is the I/O request with the major function code IRP_MJ_CLEANUP. To explain how you should process this request, I need to give you a little additional background.

When applications and other drivers want to access your device, they first open a handle to the device. Applications call **CreateFile** to do this; drivers call **ZwCreateFile**. Internally, these functions create a kernel file object and send it to your driver in an IRP_MJ_CREATE request. When whatever opened the handle is done accessing your driver, it will call another function, such as **CloseHandle** or **ZwClose**. Internally, these functions send your driver an IRP_MJ_CLOSE request. Just before sending you the IRP_MJ_CLOSE, however, the I/O Manager sends you an IRP_MJ_CLEANUP so that you can cancel any IRPs that belong to the same file object but which are still sitting in one of your queues. From the perspective of your driver, the one thing all the requests have in common is that the stack location you receive points to the same file object in every instance.

Figure 5-12 illustrates your responsibility when you receive IRP_MJ_CLEANUP.

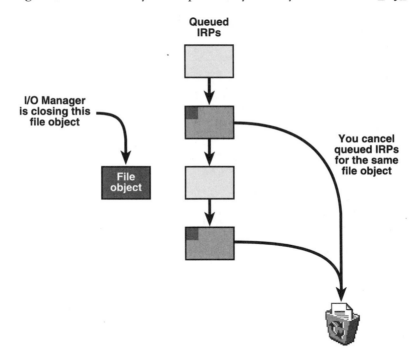

Figure 5-12. *Driver responsibility for IRP_MJ_CLEANUP.*

If you're using the standard model, your dispatch function might look something like this:

```
NTSTATUS DispatchCleanup(PDEVICE_OBJECT fdo, PIRP Irp)
  {
  PDEVICE_EXTENSION pdx = (PDEVICE_EXTENSION) fdo->DeviceExtension;
  PIO_STACK_LOCATION stack = IoGetCurrentIrpStackLocation(Irp);
  PFILE_OBJECT fop = stack->FileObject;
```

```
2       LIST_ENTRY cancellist;
        InitializeListHead(&cancellist);

3       KIRQL oldirql;
        IoAcquireCancelSpinLock(&oldirql);
        KeAcquireSpinLockAtDpcLevel(&fdo->DeviceQueue.Lock);

        PLIST_ENTRY first = &fdo->DeviceQueue.DeviceListHead;
        PLIST_ENTRY next;

4       for (next = first->Flink; next != first; )
          {
          PIRP QueuedIrp = CONTAINING_RECORD(next,
            IRP, Tail.Overlay.ListEntry);
          PIO_STACK_LOCATION QueuedIrpStack =
            IoGetCurrentIrpStackLocation(QueuedIrp);

          PLIST_ENTRY current = next;
          next = next->Flink;

5         if (QueuedIrpStack->FileObject != fop)
            continue;

          IoSetCancelRoutine(QueuedIrp, NULL);
          RemoveEntryList(current);
          InsertTailList(&cancellist, current);
          }

6       KeReleaseSpinLockFromDpcLevel(&fdo->DeviceQueue.Lock);
        IoReleaseCancelSpinLock(oldirql);

7       while (!IsListEmpty(&cancellist))
          {
          next = RemoveHeadList(&cancellist);
          PIRP CancelIrp = CONTAINING_RECORD(next, IRP, Tail.Overlay.ListEntry);
          CompleteRequest(CancelIrp, STATUS_CANCELLED, 0);
          }

8       return CompleteRequest(Irp, STATUS_SUCCESS, 0);
        }
```

1. We're going to look for queued IRPs that belong to the same file object as the one that this IRP_MJ_CLEANUP belongs to. The file object is mentioned in the stack location.

2. Our strategy will be to pull the IRPs we're going to cancel off the main device queue while holding two spin locks. Since there might be more than one IRP, it's convenient to construct another (temporary) list of them, so we initialize a list head here.

3. We need to hold *two* spin locks to safely extract IRPs from our queue. We acquire the global cancel spin lock to prevent interference by IoCancelIrp. We also acquire the spin lock associated with the device queue to prevent interference by **ExInterlocked***Xxx***List** operations on the same queue.

4. This loop allows us to examine each IRP that's on our device queue. We know that no one can be adding or removing IRPs from the queue because we own the spin lock that guards the queue. We can therefore use regular (noninterlocked) list primitives to access the list.

5. When we find an IRP belonging to the same file object, we remove it from the device queue and add it to the temporary **cancellist** queue. We also nullify the cancel routine pointer to render the IRP noncancellable. Notice that we examine the stack for the queued IRP to see which file object the IRP belongs to. It would be a mistake to look at the queued IRP's opaque **Tail.Overlay.OriginalFileObject** field—the I/O Manager uses that field to tell it when to dereference a file object during IRP completion. It can sometimes be NULL, even when the IRP belongs to a particular file object. The stack location, on the other hand, should hold the right file object pointer if whatever created the IRP did its job properly.

6. We release our spin locks at the end of the loop.

7. This loop actually cancels the IRPs we selected during the first loop. At this point, we no longer hold any spin locks, and it will therefore be perfectly okay to call time-consuming and lock-grabbing routines like IoCompleteRequest.

8. This final call to IoCompleteRequest pertains to the IRP_MJ_CLEANUP request itself, which we always succeed.

FILE OBJECTS

Ordinarily, just one driver (the function driver, in fact) in a device stack implements all three of the following requests: IRP_MJ_CREATE, IRP_MJ_CLOSE, and IRP_MJ_CLEANUP. The I/O Manager creates a file object (a regular kernel object) and passes it in the I/O stack to the dispatch routines for all three of these IRPs. Anything that sends an IRP to a device *should* have a pointer to the same file object and *should* insert that pointer into the I/O stack as well. The driver that handles these three IRPs acts as the "owner" of the file object in some sense, in that it's the driver that's entitled to use the **FsContext** and **FsContext2** fields of the object. So, your **DispatchCreate** routine could put something into one of these context fields for use by other dispatch routines and for eventual cleanup by your **DispatchClose** routine.

The real point of the code I just showed you is the first loop, where we remove the IRPs we want to cancel from the device queue. Owning the device queue's spin lock guarantees the integrity of the queue itself. We also need to hold the global cancel spin lock. If we didn't hold it, something could call IoCancelIrp for the same IRP we're removing from the queue, and IoCancelIrp could go on to call our cancel routine. Our cancel routine would block while trying to dequeue the IRP. (Refer to the earlier example of a cancel routine in the "Synchronizing Cancellation" section.) As soon as we release the queue lock, our cancel routine would go on to incorrectly attempt to remove the IRP from the queue and complete it. Both of those steps would be incorrect because we're doing exactly the same two things in this dispatch routine. The solution is to prevent IoCancelIrp from even starting down this road by taking the global spin lock. By the time IoCancelIrp is able to proceed past its own acquisition of the global spin lock, the IRP will appear noncancellable.

You might notice that we acquire the global cancel spin lock first and then the device queue. Acquiring these locks in the other order might lead to a deadlock: our cancel routine and routines in the I/O Manager (such as IoStartPacket) acquire the global lock and then call **Ke*Xxx*DeviceQueue** routines that acquire the queue lock. We don't want there to be a situation in which we acquire the queue lock and then block, waiting for the global lock to be released by something that's waiting for the queue lock.

In an earlier sidebar, "Avoiding the Global Cancel Spin Lock," I mentioned that the global cancel spin lock is a significant system bottleneck. The fact that your IRP_MJ_CLEANUP routine needs to hold that spin lock long enough to examine the entire IRP queue only makes the bottleneck worse. Imagine every driver needing to claim this lock for every call to IoStartPacket, IoStartNextPacket, StartIo, and DispatchCleanup—even when no one is trying to perform the relatively unusual activity of actually cancelling an IRP! Furthermore, as the system becomes more sluggish, IRP queues will tend to build and cleanup dispatch routines will take longer to examine their queues, thereby increasing contention for the global cancel spin lock and slowing the system even further.

Because of the performance bottleneck, you really want to avoid using the global cancel spin lock if you can. Doing so requires you to manage your own IRP queues. How to do *that* will be one of the subjects of the next chapter.

MANAGING YOUR OWN IRPS

Now that I've explained all of the infrastructure for handling IRPs, I can return to the subject of how to create IRPs in your own driver. I already mentioned that there are four different service functions you can call to create an IRP, but I had to defer until now a discussion of how you'd choose among them. The factors that bear on your choice appear at the top of the following page.

- IoBuildAsynchronousFsdRequest and IoBuildSynchronousFsdRequest can be used to build IRPs with only the major function codes listed in Table 5-3.

- IoBuildDeviceIoControlRequest can be used to build IRPs with only one of the major function codes IRP_MJ_DEVICE_CONTROL and IRP_MJ_INTERNAL_DEVICE_CONTROL.

- You need to be sure that something will release the memory occupied by the IRP and by its various hangers-on when something finally calls IoCompleteRequest.

- You might need to plan ahead so that it will be possible for you to cancel the IRP by calling IoCancelIrp.

Major Function Code
IRP_MJ_READ
IRP_MJ_WRITE
IRP_MJ_FLUSH_BUFFERS
IRP_MJ_SHUTDOWN
IRP_MJ_PNP
IRP_MJ_POWER

Table 5-3. *IRP types for IoBuildXxxFsdRequest.*

Using IoBuildSynchronousFsdRequest

The easiest scenario to explain is the one involving **IoBuildSynchronousFsdRequest**. You call this function like this:

```
PIRP Irp = IoBuildSynchronousFsdRequest(MajorFunction, DeviceObject,
  Buffer, Length, StartingOffset, Event, IoStatusBlock);
```

MajorFunction (ULONG) is the major function code for the new IRP. (See Table 5-3.) **DeviceObject** (PDEVICE_OBJECT) is the address of the device object to which you'll initially send the IRP. (See the last section of this chapter, "Where Do Device Object Pointers Come From?" for more information about this parameter.) For read and write requests, you must supply the **Buffer** (PVOID), **Length** (ULONG), and **StartingOffset** (PLARGE_INTEGER) parameters. Buffer is the address of a kernel-mode data buffer, Length is the number of bytes you want to read or write, and StartingOffset is the byte location within the target file where the read or write operation should commence. For the other requests that you can build with this function, these three parameters are ignored. (That's why the function prototype in WDM.H classifies them as "optional," but they're not optional for reads and writes.) The I/O Manager assumes that the buffer address you supply is valid in the current process context. It's up to you to make sure that it is valid.

Event (PKEVENT) is the address of an event object that IoCompleteRequest should set when the operation completes, and **IoStatusBlock** (PIO_STATUS_BLOCK) is the address of a status block in which the ending status and information will be saved. The event object and status block need to be in memory that will persist at least until the operation completes.

If you've created a read or write IRP, you don't need to do anything else before submitting the IRP. If you've created another type of IRP, you'll need to complete the first stack location with additional parameter information; MajorFunction has, however, already been set. You should *not* set the undocumented field Tail.Overlay.OriginalFileObject—doing so will cause a file object to be incorrectly dereferenced on completion. There's probably no reason to set RequestorMode, because it's already been initialized to KernelMode and you've already validated any parameters you're passing in the IRP. (I'm mentioning these two minor points only because I recall reading a published discussion of this service function once upon a time that said you *should* do the two things I just told you not to do.) You can now submit the IRP and wait for it to finish:

```
PIRP Irp = IoBuildSynchronousFsdRequest(...);
NTSTATUS status = IoCallDriver(DeviceObject, Irp);
if (status == STATUS_PENDING)
  KeWaitForSingleObject(Event, Executive, KernelMode, FALSE, NULL);
```

Once the IRP finishes, you can inspect the ending status and information values in your I/O status block.

It's obvious, isn't it, that you must be running at PASSIVE_LEVEL in a nonarbitrary thread context before you wait for the operation to complete?

Cleaning Up

I said earlier that you needed to plan for how the memory occupied by the IRP would get released and that you might have to plan for cancelling an IRP. The first of these two problems is quite easy to solve when you use IoBuildSynchronousFsdRequest to build the IRP: the I/O Manager will release memory for you automatically as part of completing the IRP. In fact, if the request is for a read or write and needs a system buffer or a memory descriptor list—see Chapter 7—the I/O Manager will automatically clean those up, too. The overall convenience of this function is a major reason why you might want to call it.

Although cleanup from a synchonous IRP is easy (because you needn't do anything about it), planning for cancellation is anything but. Read on...

Cancelling a Synchronous IRP

Only two entities in the system are allowed to cancel IRPs. One entity is the I/O Manager code that implements so-called *thread rundown* when a thread terminates while I/O requests are still outstanding. The other entity is the driver that originated the IRP in the first place. But great care is required to avoid an obscure, low-probability problem. Just for the sake of illustration, suppose that you wanted to impose an overall 5-second timeout on an I/O operation. If the time period elapses, you want to cancel the operation. Here is some naive code that, you might suppose, would execute this plan:

```
SomeFunction()
  {
  KEVENT event;
  IoInitializeEvent(&event, ...);
  PIRP Irp = IoBuildSynchronousFsdRequest(...);
  NTSTATUS status = IoCallDriver(DeviceObject, Irp);
  if (status == STATUS_PENDING)
    {
    LARGE_INTEGER timeout;
    timeout.QuadPart = -5 * 10000000;
    if (KeWaitForSingleObject(&event, Executive, KernelMode,
      FALSE, &timeout) == STATUS_TIMEOUT)
      {
      IoCancelIrp(Irp);  // ← don't do this!
      KeWaitForSingleObject(&event, Executive, KernelMode, FALSE, NULL);
      }
    }
  }
```

The second call to **KeWaitForSingleObject** makes sure that the event object doesn't pass out of scope before the I/O Manager is done using it. Whoever owns the IRP is supposed to complete it quickly, so any inordinate delay that might happen at this point is somebody else's bug. (Easy for you and me to say, huh?)

The problem with the preceding code is truly miniscule. Imagine that someone manages to call IoCompleteRequest for this IRP right around the same time we decide to cancel it by calling IoCancelIrp. Maybe the operation finishes shortly after the 5-second timeout terminates the first KeWaitForSingleObject, for example. IoCompleteRequest initiates a process that finishes with a call to IoFreeIrp. If the call to IoFreeIrp were to happen before IoCancelIrp is done mucking about with the IRP, you can see that IoCancelIrp could inadvertently corrupt memory when it touches the CancelIrql, Cancel, and CancelRoutine fields of the IRP. It's also possible, depending on the exact sequence of events, for IoCancelIrp to call a cancel routine, just before someone clears the CancelRoutine pointer in preparation for completing the IRP, and for the cancel routine to be in a race with the completion process.

It's very unlikely that the scenario I just described will happen. But, as James Thurber once said in connection with the chances of being eaten by a tiger on Main Street (one in a million, as I recall), "Once is enough." This kind of bug is almost impossible to find, so you want to prevent it if you can. In current releases of Windows 98 and Windows 2000, a common technique relies on the fact that the call to IoFreeIrp happens in the context of an APC in the thread that originates the IRP. You make sure you're in that same thread, raise IRQL to APC_LEVEL, check whether the IRP has been completed yet, and (if not) call IoCancelIrp. In current systems, you can be sure of blocking the APC and the problematic call to IoFreeIrp. See the USBCAMD sample in the DDK, for example. I've also seen this technique discussed extensively on line and in a technical note on Compuware Numega's Web site.

You should not rely on future releases of Windows always using an APC to perform the cleanup for an IRP. Consequently, you should not rely on boosting IRQL to APC_LEVEL as a way to avoid a race between IoCancelIrp and IoFreeIrp. By "should not" here, I really mean to say that the operating system might conceivably change in some hypothetical future release in such a way that this technique will no longer suffice to guard against the race. Wink, wink, if you get my drift. So, I'll show you another approach.

The key thing we need to accomplish in a solution to the race is to prevent the call to IoFreeIrp from happening until after any possible call to IoCancelIrp. We do this by means of a completion routine that returns STATUS_MORE_PROCESSING_ REQUIRED, as follows:

```
SomeFunction()
  {
  KEVENT event;
  IoInitializeEvent(&event, ...);
  PIRP Irp = IoBuildSynchronousFsdRequest(...);
  IoSetCompletionRoutine(Irp, OnComplete, (PVOID) &event, TRUE, TRUE,
    TRUE);
  NTSTATUS status = IoCallDriver(...);
  if (status == STATUS_PENDING)
    {
    LARGE_INTEGER timeout;
    timeout.QuadPart = -5 * 10000000;
    if (KeWaitForSingleObject(&event, Executive, KernelMode,
      FALSE, &timeout) == STATUS_TIMEOUT)
      {
      IoCancelIrp(Irp);  // ← okay in this context
      KeWaitForSingleObject(&event, Executive, KernelMode, FALSE, NULL);
      }
    }
  }
```

(continued)

```
    KeClearEvent(&event);
    IoCompleteRequest(Irp, IO_NO_INCREMENT);
    KeWaitForSingleObject(&event, Executive, KernelMode, FALSE, NULL);
    }

NTSTATUS OnComplete(PDEVICE_OBJECT junk, PIRP Irp, PVOID pev)
    {
    KeSetEvent((PKEVENT) pev, IO_NO_INCREMENT, FALSE);
    return STATUS_MORE_PROCESSING_REQUIRED;
    }
```

The new code in boldface prevents the race. Suppose IoCallDriver returns STATUS_ PENDING. In a normal case, the operation will complete normally, and some lower- level driver will call IoCompleteRequest. Our completion routine gains control and signals the event on which our mainline is waiting. Since the completion routine returns STATUS_MORE_PROCESSING_REQUIRED, IoCompleteRequest will then stop working on this IRP. We eventually regain control in our **SomeFunction** and notice that our wait terminated normally. The IRP hasn't yet been cleaned up, though, so we need to call IoCompleteRequest *a second time* to trigger the nor- mal cleanup mechanism. We still need to make sure that our event object doesn't pass out of scope too soon, though, so we need to perform a second wait on our event object.

Now suppose we decide we want to cancel the IRP and that Thurber's tiger is loose so we have to worry about the IRP being IoFreeIrp'ed out from under us. Our completion routine will prevent the cleanup mechanism from running by returning STATUS_MORE_PROCESSING_REQUIRED. IoCancelIrp can stomp away to its heart's content on our hapless IRP without causing any harm. The IRP can't be released until the second call to IoCompleteRequest from our mainline, and that can't hap- pen until IoCancelIrp has safely returned.

Using IoAllocateIrp

If you're willing to work a little harder, you can use **IoAllocateIrp** to build an IRP of any type:

```
PIRP Irp = IoAllocateIrp(StackSize, ChargeQuota);
```

where **StackSize** (CCHAR) is the number of I/O stack locations to allocate with the IRP, and **ChargeQuota** (BOOLEAN) indicates whether the process quota should be charged for the memory allocation. Normally, you get the StackSize parameter from the device object to which you're going to send the IRP, and you specify FALSE for the ChargeQuota argument. For example:

```
PDEVICE_OBJECT DeviceObject;
PIRP Irp = IoAllocateIrp(DeviceObject->StackSize, FALSE);
```

When you use IoAllocateIrp, you must install a completion routine, and it must return STATUS_MORE_PROCESSING_REQUIRED. Furthermore, you're responsible for releasing the IRP and any associated objects. If you don't plan to cancel the IRP, your completion routine might look like this:

```
NTSTATUS OnComplete(PDEVICE_OBJECT DeviceObject, PIRP Irp, PVOID Context)
  {
  IoFreeIrp(Irp);
  return STATUS_MORE_PROCESSING_REQUIRED;
  }
```

An IRP created by IoAllocateIrp won't be cancelled automatically if the originating thread terminates.

LOOSE ENDS

I'll close this chapter by describing some other things you need to know that I didn't cover earlier. These include two more ways of building IRPs and a word or two about how to locate a device object to use as a target for IoCallDriver.

Using IoBuildDeviceIoControlRequest

I'll discuss **IoBuildDeviceIoControlRequest** in Chapter 9 when I discuss how to perform I/O control operations. As far as cleanup and cancellation are concerned, IRPs created with this function are like ones created by IoBuildSynchronousFsdRequest.

Using IoBuildAsynchronousFsdRequest

IoBuildAsynchronousFsdRequest is another routine that you can use to build one of the IRPs listed in Table 5-3. The prototype of the function is as follows:

```
PIRP IoBuildAsynchronousFsdRequest(ULONG MajorFunction,
  PDEVICE_OBJECT DeviceObject, PVOID Buffer, ULONG Length,
  PLARGE_INTEGER StartingOffset, PIO_STATUS_BLOCK IoStatusBlock);
```

This prototype differs from that for IoBuildSynchronousFsdRequest in that there's no **Event** argument and the **IoStatusBlock** pointer can be NULL. The DDK goes on to tell you to install a completion routine whose job will be to call IoFreeIrp on this IRP and return STATUS_MORE_PROCESSING_REQUIRED.

I wondered about the different treatment for IRPs built with the two IoBuild-*Xxx*FsdRequest functions, so I dug a little deeper. The code for these two functions is essentially identical. In fact, IoBuildSynchronousFsdRequest calls IoBuildAsynchronous FsdRequest as a subroutine. I'm not telling you anything here that you couldn't find out on your own after five minutes with a kernel debugger. IoBuildSynchronous-FsdRequest's only additional actions are saving your event pointer in the IRP (reasonable, since that's how the I/O Manager can find it to signal it) and putting the IRP on the queue of IRPs for the current thread, which allows the IRP to be cancelled when the thread dies.

I've been able to discern only two situations in which you'd want to call IoBuild-AsynchronousFsdRequest. The first situation is when you find yourself executing in an arbitrary thread context and need to create an IRP. IoBuildAsynchronousFsdRequest is ideal for this purpose, since termination of the current (arbitrary) thread should not result in cancelling the new IRP. The other situation is when you're running at APC_LEVEL in a nonarbitrary thread and need to synchronously—yes, *synchronously*—execute an IRP. IoBuildSynchronousFsdRequest won't work for this purpose because the IRQL blocks the APC that would normally set the event. So you call IoBuildAsynchronousFsdRequest and wait on an event that your completion routine will set. This second case won't come up often, if ever, for a device driver.

In a general case, the completion routine you use with IoBuildAsynchronous-FsdRequest has to do quite a bit more work than just call IoFreeIrp. In fact, you need to duplicate the functionality of the internal routine (**IopCompleteRequest**) that the I/O Manager uses to clean up completed IRPs. You can't just create an IRP with IoBuildAsynchronousFsdRequest and launch it into the void, relying on the I/O Manager to clean up. Since the cleanup requires an APC in the current releases of Windows 98 and Windows 2000, and since it would be incorrect to depend on executing an APC in an arbitrary thread, the I/O Manager doesn't do the cleanup for you. You must do all the cleanup yourself.

If the device object to which you send the IRP has the DO_DIRECT_IO flag set, IoBuildAsynchronousFsdRequest will create an MDL that you must release with code like the following:

```
NTSTATUS CompletionRoutine(...)
  {
  PMDL mdl;
  while ((mdl = Irp->MdlAddress))
    {
    Irp->MdlAddress = mdl->Next;
    IoFreeMdl(mdl);
    }
  ...
  IoFreeIrp(Irp);
```

```
    return STATUS_MORE_PROCESSING_REQUIRED;
    }
```

If the device object to which you send the IRP has the DO_BUFFERED_IO flag set, IoBuildAsynchronousFsdRequest will allocate a system buffer that you need to release. If you're doing an input operation, you also have to copy the input data from the system buffer to your real input buffer—before releasing the memory! If you need to do this copy, you need to be sure that the real buffer is in nonpaged memory because completion routines might run at DISPATCH_LEVEL. You also need to be sure that you've got a kernel address for the buffer, because completion routines run in arbitrary thread context. If these restrictions aren't enough to discourage you from using IoBuildAsynchronousFsdRequest with a DO_BUFFERED_IO device, consider that you must also test the undocumented flag bits IRP_BUFFERED_IO, IRP_INPUT_OPERATION, and IRP_DEALLOCATE_BUFFER to discover what to do in your completion routine. I'm not going to show you the code to do this because I took a solemn pledge to avoid undocumented tricks in this book.

My advice is to use IoBuildAsynchronousFsdRequest only when you know that the device you're sending the IRP to doesn't use DO_BUFFERED_IO.

Where Do Device Object Pointers Come From?

The call to IoCallDriver requires a PDEVICE_OBJECT as its first argument. You might be wondering where you get a pointer to a device object so that you can send an IRP to something.

One of the obvious ways to get a pointer to a device object is by calling **IoAttachDeviceToDeviceStack**, which is something that every WDM driver's AddDevice function does. In all of the sample drivers in this book, you'll see a line of code like this one:

```
pdx->LowerDeviceObject = IoAttachDeviceToDeviceStack(fdo, pdo);
```

We use this device object pointer whenever we want to pass an IRP down the driver stack.

Another common way to locate a device object is to start with an object name that you happen to know about:

```
PUNICODE_STRING DeviceName;   // ← something gives you this
PDEVICE_OBJECT DeviceObject;   // ← an output from this process
PFILE_OBJECT FileObject;        // ← another output
NTSTATUS status = IoGetDeviceObjectPointer(DeviceName,
  <access mask>, &FileObject, &DeviceObject);
```

You get back a pointer to the device object having the name you specify and a pointer to a file object. A file object is the thing a file handle points to. Eventually, you'll need to dereference the file object, as at the top of the next page.

```
ObDereferenceObject(FileObject); // ← DeviceObject now poison!
```

As soon as you dereference the file object, you also release your implicit refer-ence to the device object. If you want to continue using the device object, be sure to reference it first:

```
ObReferenceObject(DeviceObject);
ObDereferenceObject(FileObject); // ← DeviceObject still okay
```

You shouldn't automatically put the preceding two lines of code in your driver, however. In fact, when you send an IRP to a device object whose address you ob-tained by calling **IoGetDeviceObjectPointer**, you should send the address of the file object along:

```
PIRP Irp = IoBuildXxxRequest(...);
PIO_STACK_LOCATION stack = IoGetCurrentIrpStackLocation(Irp);
stack->FileObject = FileObject;
IoCallDriver(DeviceObject, Irp);
```

Here's the explanation for this extra statement. IoGetDeviceObjectPointer inter-nally opens a regular handle to the device object, which causes the driver to receive an IRP_MJ_CREATE request with a pointer to the same file object you'll later be getting as a return value. The driver might create some auxiliary data structure that it asso-ciates with the file object, and it might require access to that structure to handle later IRPs. It will destroy that structure when it processes the IRP_MJ_CLOSE operation that occurs when the last reference to the file object disappears. For this to work right, you need to set the **FileObject** pointer in the first stack location for each IRP you send the driver.

You don't *always* set the file object pointer in a new IRP you create, by the way. If you're the driver that owns the file object by virtue of being the real implementor of IRP_MJ_CREATE, no one below you has any business looking at the file object. In the case I just described, however, the owner of the file object is the driver for the device object you found by calling IoGetDeviceObjectPointer. In that situation, you *must* set the file object pointer.

Chapter 6

Plug and Play

The Plug and Play (PnP) Manager communicates information and requests to device drivers via I/O request packets (IRPs) with a major function code of IRP_MJ_PNP. This type of request is new with Microsoft Windows 2000 and the Windows Driver Model: previous versions of Microsoft Windows NT required device drivers to do most of the work of detecting and configuring their devices. Happily, WDM drivers can let the PnP Manager do that work. To work with the PnP Manager, driver authors will have to understand a few relatively complicated IRPs.

Plug and Play requests play two roles in the WDM. In their first role, these requests instruct the driver when and how to configure or deconfigure itself and the hardware. Table 6-1 lists the roughly two dozen minor functions that a PnP request can designate. Only the bus driver handles the nine minor functions shown with an asterisk; a filter driver or function driver would simply pass these IRPs down the stack. Of the remaining minor functions, three have special importance to a typical filter driver or function driver. The PnP Manager uses IRP_MN_START_DEVICE to inform the function driver what I/O resources it has assigned to the hardware and to instruct the function driver to do any necessary hardware and software setup so that the device can function. IRP_MN_STOP_DEVICE tells the function driver to shut down the device. IRP_MN_REMOVE_DEVICE tells the function driver to shut down the device *and* release the associated device object. I'll discuss these three minor functions in detail in this chapter and the next; along the way, I'll also describe the purpose for the other unstarred minor functions that a filter driver or function driver might need to handle.

IRP Minor Function Code	Description
IRP_MN_START_DEVICE	Configures and initializes device
IRP_MN_QUERY_REMOVE_DEVICE	Can device be removed safely?
IRP_MN_REMOVE_DEVICE	Shuts down and removes device
IRP_MN_CANCEL_REMOVE_DEVICE	Ignores previous QUERY_REMOVE
IRP_MN_STOP_DEVICE	Shuts down device
IRP_MN_QUERY_STOP_DEVICE	Can device be shut down safely?
IRP_MN_CANCEL_STOP_DEVICE	Ignores previous QUERY_STOP
IRP_MN_QUERY_DEVICE_RELATIONS	Gets list of devices which are related in some specified way
IRP_MN_QUERY_INTERFACE	Obtains direct-call function addresses
IRP_MN_QUERY_CAPABILITIES	Determines capabilities of device
IRP_MN_QUERY_RESOURCES*	Determines boot configuration
IRP_MN_QUERY_RESOURCE_REQUIREMENTS*	Determines I/O resource requirements
IRP_MN_QUERY_DEVICE_TEXT*	Obtains description or location string
IRP_MN_FILTER_RESOURCE_REQUIREMENTS	Modifies I/O resource requirements list
IRP_MN_READ_CONFIG*	Reads configuration space
IRP_MN_WRITE_CONFIG*	Writes configuration space
IRP_MN_EJECT*	Ejects the device
IRP_MN_SET_LOCK*	Locks/unlocks device against ejection
IRP_MN_QUERY_ID*	Determines hardware ID of device
IRP_MN_QUERY_PNP_DEVICE_STATE	Determines state of device
IRP_MN_QUERY_BUS_INFORMATION*	Determines parent bus type
IRP_MN_DEVICE_USAGE_NOTIFICATION	Notes creation or deletion of paging, dump, or hibernate file
IRP_MN_SURPRISE_REMOVAL	Notes fact that device has been removed

Table 6-1. *Minor function codes for IRP_MJ_PNP. (* indicates handled only by bus drivers.)*

A second and more complicated purpose of PnP requests is to guide the driver through a series of state transitions, as illustrated in Figure 6-1. WORKING and STOPPED are the two fundamental states of the device. The STOPPED state is the initial state of a device immediately after you create the device object. The WORKING state indicates that the device is fully operational. Two of the intermediate states—PENDINGSTOP and PENDINGREMOVE—arise because of queries that all drivers for a device must process before making the transition from WORKING. SURPRISE-REMOVED occurs after the sudden and unexpected removal of the physical hardware.

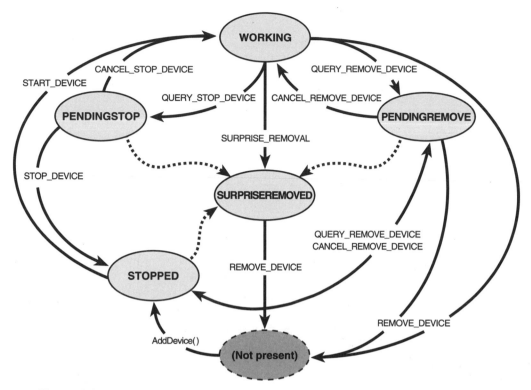

Figure 6-1. *State diagram for a device.*

When I described the standard model for IRP processing in the previous chapter, I indicated that Plug and Play would impose additional requirements on IRP queuing and cancellation. I'll describe a DEVQUEUE object in this chapter that satisfies those requirements and helps you manage the state transitions.

IRP_MJ_PNP DISPATCH FUNCTION

In Chapter 5, "The I/O Request Packet," I explained the mechanics of passing IRPs down the driver stack in two situations: one in which you care about the result and therefore need a completion routine, and the other in which you don't care about the result and therefore don't install a completion routine. Many of the PnP requests fit into the second of these categories—you're receiving the IRP and passing it down, but you don't care what happens to it afterward. To begin with, then, I suggest writing a helper function that you can use to pass a request down in the "don't care" scenario—see the code at the top of the following page.

```
NTSTATUS DefaultPnpHandler(PDEVICE_OBJECT fdo, PIRP Irp)
  {
  IoSkipCurrentIrpStackLocation(Irp);
  PDEVICE_EXTENSION pdx = (PDEVICE_EXTENSION) fdo->DeviceExtension;
  return IoCallDriver(pdx->LowerDeviceObject, Irp);
  }
```

A simplified version of the dispatch function for IRP_MJ_PNP might look like the following:

```
NTSTATUS DispatchPnp(PDEVICE_OBJECT fdo, PIRP Irp)
  {
  PIO_STACK_LOCATION stack = IoGetCurrentIrpStackLocation(Irp);
  ULONG fcn = stack->MinorFunction;

  static NTSTATUS (*fcntab[])(PDEVICE_OBJECT, PIRP) = {
    HandleStartDevice,          // IRP_MN_START_DEVICE
    HandleQueryRemove,          // IRP_MN_QUERY_REMOVE_DEVICE
    <etc.>,
    };

  if (fcn >= arraysize(fcntab))
    return DefaultPnpHandler(fdo, Irp);
  return (*fcntab[fcn])(fdo, Irp);
  }
```

1. All the parameters for the IRP, including the all-important minor function code, are in the stack location. Hence, we obtain a pointer to it by calling **IoGetCurrentIrpStackLocation**.

2. We expect the IRP's minor function code to be one of those listed in Table 6-1.

3. A method of handling the two dozen possible minor function codes is to write a subdispatch function for each one we're going to handle and then to define a table of pointers to those subdispatch functions. Many of the entries in the table will be **DefaultPnpHandler**. Subdispatch functions like **HandleStartDevice** will take pointers to a device object and an IRP as parameters and will return an NTSTATUS code.

4. If we get a minor function code we don't recognize, it's probably because Microsoft defined a new one in a release of the DDK after the DDK with which we built our driver. The right thing to do is to pass the minor function code down the stack by calling the default handler. By the way, **arraysize** is a macro that returns the number of elements in an array. It's defined as **#define arraysize(p) (sizeof(p)/sizeof((p)[0]))**.

5. This is the operative statement in the dispatch routine, with which we index the table of subdispatch functions and call the right one.

USING A FUNCTION POINTER TABLE

Using a table of function pointers to dispatch handlers for minor function codes as I'm showing you in **DispatchPnp** entails some danger. A future version of the operating system might change the meaning of some of the codes. That's not a practical worry except during the beta test phase of a system, though, because a later change would invalidate an unknown number of existing drivers. I like using a table of pointers to subdispatch functions because having separate functions for the minor function codes seems like the right engineering solution to me. If I were designing a C++ class library, for instance, I'd define a base class that used virtual functions for each of the minor function codes.

Most programmers would probably place a **switch** statement in their DispatchPnp routine. You can simply recompile your driver to conform to any reassignment of minor function codes. Recompilation will also highlight—by producing compilation errors!—name changes that might signal functionality shifts. That happened a time or two during the Microsoft Windows 98 and Windows 2000 betas, in fact. Furthermore, an optimizing compiler should be able to use a jump table to produce slightly faster code for a switch statement than for calls to subdispatch functions.

I think the choice between a switch statement and a table of function pointers is mostly a matter of taste, with readability and modularity winning over efficiency in my own evaluation. You can avoid uncertainty during a beta test by placing appropriate assertions into your code. For example, the HandleStartDevice function could assert that **stack->MinorFunction == IRP_MN_START_DEVICE**. If you recompile your driver with each new beta DDK, you'll catch any number reassignments or name changes.

STARTING AND STOPPING YOUR DEVICE

Working with the bus driver, the PnP Manager automatically detects hardware and assigns I/O resources in Windows 2000 and Windows 98. Most modern devices have Plug and Play features that allow system software to detect them automatically and to electronically determine which I/O resources they require. In the case of legacy devices that have no electronic means of identifying themselves to the operating system or of expressing their resource requirements, the registry database contains the information needed for the detection and assignment operations.

> **NOTE** I find it hard to give an abstract definition of the term *I/O resource* that isn't circular (for example, a resource used for I/O), so I'll give a concrete one instead. The WDM encompasses four standard I/O resource types: I/O ports, memory registers, direct memory access (DMA) channels, and interrupt requests.

When the PnP Manager detects hardware, it consults the registry to learn which filter drivers and function drivers will manage the hardware. As I discussed in Chapter 2, "Basic Structure of a WDM Driver," it loads these drivers (if necessary—one or more of them might already be present, having been called into memory on behalf of some other hardware) and calls their **AddDevice** functions. The AddDevice functions, in turn, create device objects and link them into a stack. At this point, the stage is set for the PnP Manager, working with all of the device drivers, to assign I/O resources.

The PnP Manager initially creates a list of resource requirements for each device and allows the drivers to *filter* that list. I'm going to ignore the filtering step for now because not every driver will need to take this step. Given a list of requirements, the PnP Manager can then assign resources so as to harmonize the potentially conflicting requirements of all the hardware present on the system. Figure 6-2 illustrates how the PnP Manager can arbitrate between two different devices that have overlapping requirements for an interrupt request number, for example.

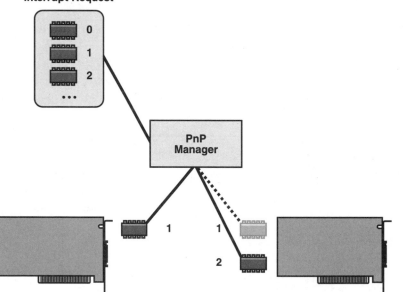

Figure 6-2. *Arbitration of conflicting I/O resource requirements.*

Once the resource assignments are known, the PnP Manager notifies each device by sending it a PnP request with the minor function code IRP_MN_START_DEVICE. Filter drivers are typically not interested in this IRP, so they usually pass the request down the stack by using the DefaultPnpHandler technique I showed you in "IRP_MJ_PNP Dispatch Function." Function drivers, on the other hand, need to do a great deal of work on the IRP to allocate and configure additional software resources and to prepare the device for operation. This work needs to be done, furthermore, at PASSIVE_LEVEL *after* the lower layers in the device hierarchy have processed this IRP.

Forwarding and Awaiting the IRP

To regain control of the IRP_MN_START_DEVICE request after passing it down, the dispatch routine needs to wait for a kernel event that will be signalled by the eventual completion of the IRP in the lower layers. In Chapter 4, "Synchronization," I cautioned you not to block an arbitrary thread. PnP IRPs are sent to you in the context of a system thread that you *are* allowed to block, so that caution is unnecessary. Since forwarding and awaiting an IRP is a potentially useful function in other contexts, I suggest writing a helper routine to perform the mechanics:

```
NTSTATUS ForwardAndWait(PDEVICE_OBJECT fdo, PIRP Irp)
  {
  KEVENT event;
  KeInitializeEvent(&event, NotificationEvent, FALSE);
  IoCopyCurrentIrpStackLocationToNext(Irp);
  IoSetCompletionRoutine(Irp, (PIO_COMPLETION_ROUTINE)
    OnRequestComplete, (PVOID) &event, TRUE, TRUE, TRUE);
  PDEVICE_EXTENSION pdx = (PDEVICE_EXTENSION)
    fdo->DeviceExtension;
  IoCallDriver(pdx->LowerDeviceObject, Irp);
  KeWaitForSingleObject(&event, Executive, KernelMode, FALSE, NULL);
  return Irp->IoStatus.Status;
  }
```

1. We create a kernel event object as an automatic variable. **KeInitialize-Event** must be called at PASSIVE_LEVEL. Luckily, PnP requests are always sent at PASSIVE_LEVEL, so this particular requirement is met. The event object itself must occupy nonpaged memory, too. For most purposes, including this one, you can treat the execution stack as being nonpaged.

2. We must make a copy of the stack parameters for the next driver because we're going to install a completion routine.

3. We specify a completion routine so that we'll know when something underneath us completes this IRP. We might wait for the completion to occur, so we must be sure that our completion routine is called. That's why we specify TRUE for the three flag arguments to indicate that we want **OnRequestComplete** called when the IRP completes normally, completes with an error, or is cancelled. The context argument for the completion routine is the address of our **event** object.

4. **IoCallDriver** calls the next lower driver, which can be a lower filter or the physical device object (PDO) driver itself. The PDO driver will perform some processing and either complete the request immediately or return STATUS_PENDING.

5. No matter what IoCallDriver returns, we call **KeWaitForSingleObject** to wait forever on the kernel event we created earlier. Our completion routine will gain control when the IRP completes to signal this event.

6. Here, we capture the ending status of the IRP and return it to our caller.

Once we call IoCallDriver, we relinquish control of the IRP until something running in some arbitrary thread context calls **IoCompleteRequest** to signal completion of the IRP. IoCompleteRequest will then call our completion routine. Refer to Figure 6-3 for an illustration of the timing involved. The completion routine is particularly simple:

```
NTSTATUS OnRequestComplete(PDEVICE_OBJECT fdo, PIRP Irp, PKEVENT pev)
  {
  KeSetEvent(pev, 0, FALSE);
  return STATUS_MORE_PROCESSING_REQUIRED;
  }
```

1. We set the event on which **ForwardAndWait** can currently be blocked.

2. By returning STATUS_MORE_PROCESSING_REQUIRED, we halt the unwinding process through the I/O stack. None of the completion routines installed by upper filter drivers will be called at the present time, and the I/O Manager will cease its work on this IRP. The situation is just as if IoCompleteRequest has not been called at all—except, of course, that some lower-level completion routines might have been called. At this instant, the IRP is in limbo, but our ForwardAndWait routine will presently retake ownership.

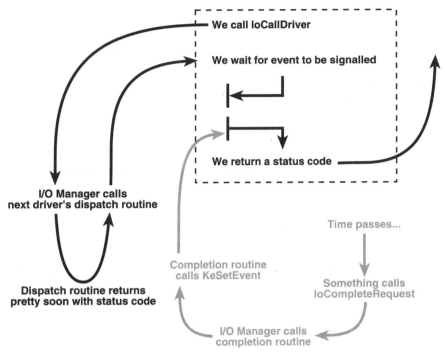

Figure 6-3. *Timing of ForwardAndWait.*

NOTES ON FORWARDANDWAIT

I glossed over two subtleties when I described how ForwardAndWait and OnRequestComplete work together. It's sometimes possible for a thread's kernel stack to be swapped out of physical memory, but only while the thread is blocked in user mode. See David Solomon's *Inside Windows NT, Second Edition* (Microsoft Press, 1998) at page 194 for a state diagram illustrating this possibility. All the calls inside ForwardAndWait that deal with the event object will certainly fulfill the requirement that the **event** object be resident in memory. Since we specified a *kernel mode wait,* our stack can't be swapped out, so **KeSetEvent** will also find the event resident.

Secondly, you might have noticed the absence of the boilerplate code **if (Irp->PendingReturned) IoMarkIrpPending(Irp)** at the beginning of the completion routine. You don't need that statement in a completion routine that will return STATUS_MORE_PROCESSING_REQUIRED. The call can't hurt, of course, and is required in most standard completion routines. That's why all the DDK samples include the code even when it's not strictly necessary.

Extracting Resource Assignments

In the preceding section, I showed you how to use the ForwardAndWait helper routine to send an IRP_MN_START_DEVICE request down the device stack and wait for it to complete. You call ForwardAndWait from a subdispatch routine—reached from the DispatchPnp dispatch routine shown earlier—that has the following skeletal form:

```
NTSTATUS HandleStartDevice(PDEVICE_OBJECT fdo, PIRP Irp)
  {
  Irp->IoStatus.Status = STATUS_SUCCESS;
  NTSTATUS status = ForwardAndWait(fdo, Irp);
  if (!NT_SUCCESS(status))
    return CompleteRequest(Irp, status, Irp->IoStatus.Information);
  PIO_STACK_LOCATION stack = IoGetCurrentIrpStackLocation(Irp);
  status = StartDevice(fdo, <additional args>);
  return CompleteRequest(Irp, status, Irp->IoStatus.Information);
  }
```

1. The bus driver uses the incoming setting of **IoStatus.Status** to determine whether upper-level drivers have handled this IRP. The bus driver makes a similar determination for several other minor functions of IRP_MJ_PNP. We therefore need to initialize the Status field of the IRP to STATUS_SUCCESS before passing it down.

2. **ForwardAndWait** returns a status code. If it denotes some sort of failure in the lower layers, we propagate it back to our own caller. Because our completion routine returned STATUS_MORE_PROCESSING_REQUIRED, we halted the completion process inside IoCompleteRequest. Therefore, we have to complete the request all over again, as shown here.

3. Our configuration information is buried inside the stack parameters. I'll show you where a bit further on.

4. **StartDevice** is a helper routine you write to handle the details of extracting and dealing with configuration information. In my sample drivers, I've placed it in a separate source module named READWRITE.CPP. I'll explain shortly what arguments you would pass to this routine besides the address of the device object.

You might guess (correctly!) that the IRP_MN_START_DEVICE handler has work to do that concerns the transition from the initial STOPPED state to the WORKING state. I can't explain that yet because I need to first explain the ramifications of other Plug and Play requests on state transitions, IRP queuing, and IRP cancellation. So, I'm going to concentrate for a while on the configuration aspects of the PnP requests.

The I/O stack location's **Parameters** union has a substructure named **StartDevice** that contains the configuration information you pass to the StartDevice helper function. See Table 6-2.

Field Name	*Description*
AllocatedResources	Contains raw resource assignments
AllocatedResourcesTranslated	Contains translated resource assignments

Table 6-2. *Fields in the Parameters.StartDevice substructure of an IO_STACK_LOCATION.*

Both **AllocatedResources** and **AllocatedResourcesTranslated** are instances of the same kind of data structure, called a CM_RESOURCE_LIST. This seems like a very complicated data structure if you judge only by its declaration in WDM.H. As used in a start device IRP, however, all that remains of the complication is a great deal of typing. The "lists" will have just one entry, a CM_PARTIAL_RESOURCE_LIST that describes all of the I/O resources assigned to the device. You could use statements like the following to access the two lists:

```
PCM_PARTIAL_RESOURCE_LIST raw, translated;
raw = stack->Parameters.StartDevice
  .AllocatedResources->List[0].PartialResourceList;
translated = stack->Parameters.StartDevice
  .AllocatedResourcesTranslated->List[0].PartialResourceList;
```

The only difference between the last two statements is the reference to either the AllocatedResources or AllocatedResourcesTranslated member of the parameters structure.

The raw and translated resource lists are the logical arguments to send to the StartDevice helper function, by the way:

```
status = StartDevice(fdo, raw, translated);
```

There are two different lists of resources because I/O buses and the CPU can address the same physical hardware in different ways. The raw resources contain numbers that are bus-relative, whereas the translated resources contain numbers that are system-relative. Prior to the WDM, a kernel-mode driver might expect to retrieve raw resource values from the registry, the PCI (Peripheral Component Interconnect) configuration space, or some other source, and to translate them by calling routines such as **HalTranslateBusAddress** or **HalGetInterruptVector**. See, for example, Art Baker's *The Windows NT Device Driver Book: A Guide for Programmers* (Prentice Hall, 1997), at pages 122–62. Both the retrieval and translation steps are done by the PnP Manager now, and all a WDM driver needs to do is access the parameters of a start device IRP as I'm now describing.

What you actually do with the resource descriptions inside your StartDevice function is a subject for the next chapter, "Reading and Writing Data."

IRP_MN_STOP_DEVICE

The stop device request tells you to shut your device down so that the PnP Manager can reassign I/O resources. At the hardware level, shutting down involves pausing or halting current activity and preventing further interrupts. At the software level, it involves releasing the I/O resources you configured at start device time. Within the framework of the dispatch/subdispatch architecture I've been illustrating, you might have a subdispatch function like this one:

```
NTSTATUS HandleStopDevice(PDEVICE_OBJECT fdo, PIRP Irp)
    {
    <complicated stuff>
    StopDevice(fdo, oktouch);
    Irp->IoStatus.Status = STATUS_SUCCESS;
    return DefaultPnpHandler(fdo, Irp);
    }
```

1 ▷
2 ▷
3 ▷

1. Right about here, you need to insert some more or less complicated code that concerns IRP queuing and cancellation. I'll show you the code that belongs in this spot further on in this chapter in "While the Device Is Stopped."

2. In contrast to the start device case, in which we passed the request down and then did device-dependent work, here we do our device-dependent stuff *first* and then pass the request down. The idea is that our hardware will be quiescent by the time the lower layers see this request. I wrote a helper function named **StopDevice** to do the shutdown work. The second argument indicates whether it will be okay for StopDevice to touch the hardware if it needs to. Refer to the sidebar "Touching the Hardware When Stopping the Device" for an explanation of how to set this argument.

3. We always pass PnP requests down the stack. In this case, we don't care what the lower layers do with the request, so we can simply use the DefaultPnpHandler code to perform the mechanics.

The **StopDevice** helper function called in the preceding example is code you write that essentially reverses the configuration steps you took in **StartDevice**. I'll show you that function in the next chapter. One important fact about the function is that you should code it in such a way that it can be called more than once for a single call to StartDevice. It's not always easy for a PnP IRP handler to know whether you've already called StopDevice, but it *is* easy to make StopDevice proof against duplicative calls.

TOUCHING THE HARDWARE WHEN STOPPING THE DEVICE

In the skeleton of **HandleStopDevice**, I used an **oktouch** variable that I didn't show you how to initialize. In the scheme I'm teaching you in this book for writing a driver, the StopDevice function gets a BOOLEAN argument that indicates whether or not it should be safe to address actual I/O operations to the hardware. The idea behind this argument is that you may want to send certain instructions to your device as part of your shutdown protocol, but there might be some reason why you can't. You might want to tell your PCMCIA modem to hang up the phone, for example, but there's no point in trying if the end user has already removed the modem card from the computer.

There's no certain way to know whether your hardware is physically connected to the computer except by trying to access it. Microsoft recommends, however, that if you succeeded in processing a START_DEVICE request, you should go ahead and try to access your hardware when you process STOP_DEVICE and certain other PnP requests. When I discuss how you track PnP state changes later in this chapter, I'll honor this recommendation by setting the oktouch argument TRUE if we believe that the device is currently working and FALSE otherwise.

IRP_MN_REMOVE_DEVICE

Recall that the PnP Manager calls the AddDevice function in your driver to notify you about an instance of the hardware you manage and to give you an opportunity to create a device object. Instead of calling a function to do the complementary operation, however, the PnP Manager sends you a Plug and Play IRP with the minor function code IRP_MN_REMOVE_DEVICE. In response to that, you'll do the same things you did for IRP_MN_STOP_DEVICE to shut down your device, and then you'll delete the device object:

```
NTSTATUS HandleRemoveDevice(PDEVICE_OBJECT fdo, PIRP Irp)
  {
  PDEVICE_EXTENSION pdx = (PDEVICE_EXTENSION) fdo->DeviceExtension;
  <complicated stuff>
  DeregisterAllInterfaces(pdx);
  StopDevice(fdo, oktouch);
  Irp->IoStatus.Status = STATUS_SUCCESS;
  NTSTATUS status = DefaultPnpHandler(fdo, Irp);
  RemoveDevice(fdo);
  return status;
  }
```

This fragment looks very similar to HandleStopDevice, with a couple of additions. **DeregisterAllInterfaces** will disable any device interfaces you registered (probably in AddDevice) and enabled (probably in StartDevice), and it will release the memory occupied by their symbolic link names. **RemoveDevice** will undo all the work you did inside AddDevice. For example:

```
VOID RemoveDevice(PDEVICE_OBJECT fdo)
  {
  PDEVICE_EXTENSION pdx = (PDEVICE_EXTENSION) fdo->DeviceExtension;
  IoDetachDevice(pdx->LowerDeviceObject);
  IoDeleteDevice(fdo);
  }
```

1. This call to **IoDetachDevice** balances the call AddDevice made to **IoAttachDeviceToDeviceStack**.

2. This call to **IoDeleteDevice** balances the call AddDevice made to **IoCreateDevice**. Once this function returns, the device object will no longer exist. If your driver isn't managing any other devices, your driver will shortly be unloaded from memory, too.

You might be troubled by the fact that you call **IoDeleteDevice** at a time when the lower levels of the device hierarchy might still be processing the IRP_MN_REMOVE_DEVICE request. No harm can come from that, however, because the Object Manager maintains a reference count on your device object to prevent it from disappearing while anything has an active pointer to it.

Note, by the way, that you don't get a stop device request followed by a remove device request. The remove device request implies a shutdown, so you do both pieces of work in reply.

IRP_MN_SURPRISE_REMOVAL

Sometimes the end user has the physical ability to remove a device without going through any user interface elements first. If the system detects that such a surprise removal has occurred, it sends the driver a PnP request with the minor function code IRP_MN_SURPRISE_REMOVAL. It will later send an IRP_MN_REMOVE_DEVICE. Unless you previously set the **SurpriseRemovalOK** flag while processing IRP_MN_QUERY_CAPABILITIES (as I'll discuss in Chapter 8, "Power Management"), the system also posts a dialog box to inform the user that it's potentially dangerous to yank hardware out of the computer.

In response to the surprise removal request, a device driver should disable any registered interfaces. This will give applications a chance to close handles to your device if they're on the lookout for the notifications I discuss later in "PnP Notifications." Then the driver should release I/O resources and pass the request down:

```
NTSTATUS HandleSurpriseRemoval(PDEVICE_OBJECT fdo, PIRP Irp)
  {
  PDEVICE_EXTENSION pdx = (PDEVICE_EXTENSION) fdo->DeviceExtension;
  <complicated stuff>
  EnableAllInterfaces(pdx, FALSE);
  StopDevice(fdo, oktouch);
  Irp->IoStatus.Status = STATUS_SUCCESS;
  return DefaultPnpHandler(fdo, Irp);
  }
```

FROM WHENCE IRP_MN_SURPRISE_REMOVAL?

The surprise removal PnP notification doesn't happen as a simple and direct result of the end user yanking the device from the computer. Some bus drivers can know when a device disappears. For example, removing a universal serial bus (USB) device generates an electronic signal that the bus driver notices. For many other buses, however, there isn't any signal to alert the bus driver. The PnP Manager therefore relies on other methods to decide that a device has disappeared.

A function driver can signal the disappearance of its device (if it knows) by calling **IoInvalidateDeviceState** and then returning any of the values PNP_DEVICE_FAILED, PNP_DEVICE_REMOVED, or PNP_DEVICE_DISABLED from the ensuing IRP_MN_QUERY_PNP_DEVICE_STATE. You might want to do this in your own driver if—to give one example of many—your interrupt service routines (ISRs) read all 1-bits from a status port that normally returns a mixture of 1s and 0s. More commonly, a bus driver calls **IoInvalidateDeviceRelations** to trigger a reenumeration and then fails to report the newly missing device. It's worth knowing that when the end user removes a device while the system is hibernating or in another low-power state, the driver receives a series of power management IRPs *before* it receives the IRP_MN_SURPRISE_REMOVAL request.

What these facts mean, practically speaking, is that your driver should be able to cope with errors that might arise from having your device suddenly not present.

MANAGING PNP STATE TRANSITIONS

As I said at the outset of this chapter, WDM drivers need to track their devices through the state transitions diagrammed in Figure 6-1 on page 223. This state tracking also ties in with how you queue and cancel I/O requests. Cancellation in turn implicates the global cancel spin lock, which is a performance bottleneck in a multi-CPU system. The standard model of IRP processing can't solve all these interrelated problems. In this section, therefore, I'll present a new type of object—called a DEVQUEUE—that you can use in your PnP request handlers and in place of the standard model routines **StartPacket** and **StartNextPacket**. DEVQUEUE is my own invention, but it's based on sample drivers, especially PNPPOWER and CANCEL, that used to be in the DDK. See also the discussion of IRP cancellation in Ervin Peretz's "The Windows Driver Model Simplifies Management of Device Driver I/O Requests," (*Microsoft Systems Journal,* January 1999). A portion of the IRP cancellation logic I'm describing also derives from work by Peretz and other Microsoft employees and by Jamie Hanrahan that had not been published at the time I was writing this book.

I described the KDEVICE_QUEUE queue object in the previous chapter as encompassing an idle state, a busy but empty state, and a busy but not empty state. The support routines you use to manipulate a KDEVICE_QUEUE assume that if the device is not currently busy, all you want to do is start any new request running on the device. It's precisely this behavior that we need to overcome to successfully manage PnP states. Figure 6-4 illustrates the states of a DEVQUEUE.

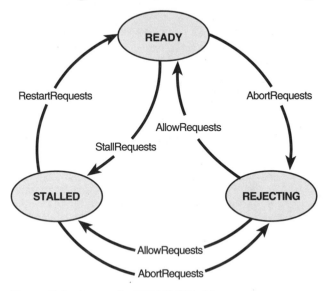

Figure 6-4. *States of a DEVQUEUE object.*

In the READY state, the queue operates much like a KDEVICE_QUEUE, accepting and forwarding requests to your **StartIo** routine in such a way that the device stays busy. In the STALLED state, however, the queue does not forward IRPs to StartIo even when the device is idle. In the REJECTING state, the queue doesn't even accept new IRPs. Figure 6-5 illustrates the flow of IRPs through the queue.

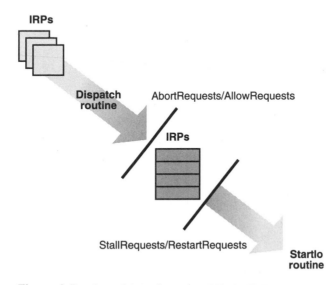

Figure 6-5. *Flow of IRPs through a DEVQUEUE.*

Using DEVQUEUE for IRP Queuing and Cancellation

You define a DEVQUEUE object for each queue of requests you'll manage in the driver. For example, if your device manages reads and writes in a single queue, you'd define one DEVQUEUE:

```
typedef struct _DEVICE_EXTENSION {
  ...
  DEVQUEUE dqReadWrite;
  ...
} DEVICE_EXTENSION, *PDEVICE_EXTENSION;
```

Table 6-3 lists the support functions you can use with a DEVQUEUE.

Support Function	Description
AbortRequests	Aborts current and future requests
AllowRequests	Undoes effect of previous AbortRequests
AreRequestsBeingAborted	Are we currently aborting new requests?
CancelRequest	Generic cancel routine
CheckBusyAndStall	Checks for idle device and stalls requests in one atomic operation
CleanupRequests	Cancels all requests for a given file object in order to service IRP_MJ_CLEANUP
GetCurrentIrp	Determines which IRP is currently being processed by associated StartIo routine
InitializeQueue	Initializes DEVQUEUE object
RestartRequests	Restarts a stalled queue
StallRequests	Stalls the queue
StartNextPacket	Dequeues and starts the next request
StartPacket	Starts or queues a new request
WaitForCurrentIrp	Waits for current IRP to finish

Table 6-3. *DEVQUEUE service routines.*

For the moment, I'll just discuss the support functions that replace functions like **StartPacket** and **StartNextPacket** in the standard IRP processing model. For each queue, you provide a separate StartIo routine. Your DriverEntry routine would not store anything in the **DriverStartIo** pointer field of the driver object. Instead, during AddDevice, you'd initialize your queue object(s) like so:

```
NTSTATUS AddDevice(...)
  {
  ...
  PDEVICE_EXTENSION pdx = ...;
  InitializeQueue(&pdx->dqReadWrite, StartIo);
  ...
  }
```

The dispatch function for an IRP that uses a DEVQUEUE would follow the following pattern:

```
NTSTATUS DispatchWrite(PDEVICE_OBJECT fdo, PIRP Irp)
  {
  <some power management stuff you haven't heard about yet>
  IoMarkIrpPending(Irp);
  StartPacket(&pdx->dqReadWrite, fdo, Irp, OnCancel);
  return STATUS_PENDING;
  }
```

That is, instead of calling **IoStartPacket**, you call the queue's StartPacket function with the address of the queue object, the device object, the IRP, and your cancel routine. At the start of a dispatch routine, you'll also have a small bit of code to handle restoring power after a period of disuse; I'll discuss that code in Chapter 8.

Here's a sketch of the new kind of **StartIo** routine you use with a DEVQUEUE:

```
VOID StartIo(PDEVICE_OBJECT fdo, PIRP Irp)
  {
  <some PnP stuff you haven't heard about yet>
  // start request on device
  }
```

StartIo doesn't worry about IRP cancellation. The cancel routine you use in this scheme is different from a standard one—it simply delegates all work to the DEVQUEUE:

```
VOID OnCancel(PDEVICE_OBJECT fdo, PIRP Irp)
  {
  PDEVICE_EXTENSION pdx = (PDEVICE_EXTENSION) fdo->DeviceExtension;
  CancelRequest(&pdx->dqReadWrite, Irp);
  }
```

CancelRequest will release the global cancel spin lock, which your cancel routine owns when it gets control, and will then cancel the IRP in a thread-safe and multiprocessor-safe way.

The deferred procedure call (DPC) routine you use when the request finishes also looks a little different from the standard-model one I showed you in Chapter 5, as you can see here:

```
VOID DpcForIsr(PKDPC Dpc, PDEVICE_OBJECT device, PIRP junk, PVOID context)
  {
  PIRP Irp = GetCurrentIrp(&pdx->dqReadWrite);
  ...
  StartNextPacket(&pdx->dqReadWrite, device);
  <some PnP stuff you haven't heard about yet>
  CompleteRequest(Irp, ...);
  }
```

Like **IoStartNextPacket**, the **StartNextPacket** function removes the next IRP from the queue and sends it to your (queue-specific) StartIo routine. It also returns the address of the IRP you were processing or NULL to indicate that your device was not processing an IRP. A NULL return value indicates that the IRP was cancelled or aborted for some reason, so it would be incorrect for you to try to complete it. Since you'll obtain the address of the finishing IRP by calling **GetCurrentIrp**, don't use the IRP pointer that comes to you as the third argument to the DPC routine. I named it **junk** to reinforce the point.

The DEVQUEUE also simplifies the handling of an IRP_MJ_CLEANUP. In fact, the code is almost trivial:

```
NTSTATUS DispatchCleanup(PDEVICE_OBJECT fdo, PIRP Irp)
  {
  PDEVICE_EXTENSION pdx = (PDEVICE_EXTENSION) fdo->DeviceExtension;
  PIO_STACK_LOCATION stack = IoGetCurrentIrpStackLocation(Irp);
  CleanupRequests(&pdx->dqReadWrite, stack->FileObject,
    STATUS_CANCELLED);
  return CompleteRequest(Irp, STATUS_SUCCESS, 0);
  }
```

Using DEVQUEUE with PnP Requests

The real point of using a DEVQUEUE instead of a KDEVICE_QUEUE is that a DEVQUEUE makes it easier to manage the transitions between PnP states. In all of my sample drivers, the device extension contains a state variable with the imaginative name **state**. I also define an enumeration named DEVSTATE whose values correspond to the PnP states. When you initialize your device object in AddDevice, you'll call **InitializeQueue** for each of your device queues and also indicate that the device is in the STOPPED state:

```
NTSTATUS AddDevice(...)
  {
  ...
  PDEVICE_EXTENSION pdx = ...;
  InitializeQueue(&pdx->dqRead, StartIoReadWrite);
  pdx->state = STOPPED;
  ...
  }
```

After AddDevice returns, the system sends IRP_MJ_PNP requests to direct you through the various PnP states the device can assume.

Starting the Device

A newly initialized DEVQUEUE is in a STALLED state, such that a call to StartPacket will queue a request even when the device is idle. You'll keep the queue(s) in the STALLED state until you successfully process IRP_MN_START_DEVICE, whereupon you'll execute code like the following:

```
NTSTATUS HandleStartDevice(...)
  {
  status = StartDevice(...);
  if (NT_SUCCESS(status))
    {
    pdx->state = WORKING;
    RestartRequests(&pdx->dqReadWrite, fdo);
    }
  }
```

You record WORKING as the current state of your device, and you call **RestartRequests** for each of your queues to release any IRPs that might have arrived between the time AddDevice ran and the time you received the IRP_MN_START_DEVICE request.

Is It Okay to Stop the Device?

The PnP Manager always asks your permission before sending you an IRP_MN_STOP_DEVICE. The query takes the form of an IRP_MN_QUERY_STOP_DEVICE request that you can succeed or fail as you choose. The query basically means, "Would you be able to immediately stop your device if the system were to send you an IRP_MN_STOP_DEVICE in a few nanoseconds?" You can handle this query in two slightly different ways. Here's the first way, which is appropriate when your device might be busy with an IRP that either finishes quickly or can be easily terminated in the middle:

```
NTSTATUS HandleQueryStop(PDEVICE_OBJECT fdo, PIRP Irp)
  {
  Irp->IoStatus.Status = STATUS_SUCCESS;
  PDEVICE_EXTENSION pdx = (PDEVICE_EXTENSION) fdo->DeviceExtension;
  if (pdx->state != WORKING)
    return DefaultPnpHandler(fdo, Irp);
  if (!OkayToStop(pdx))
    return CompleteRequest(Irp, STATUS_UNSUCCESSFUL, 0);
  StallRequests(&pdx->dqReadWrite);
  WaitForCurrentIrp(&pdx->dqReadWrite);
  pdx->state = PENDINGSTOP;
  return DefaultPnpHandler(fdo, Irp);
  }
```

1. This statement handles a peculiar situation that can arise for a boot device: the PnP Manager might send you a QUERY_STOP when you haven't initialized yet. You want to ignore such a query, which is tantamount to saying "yes."

2. At this point, you perform some sort of investigation to see if it will be okay to revert to the STOPPED state. I'll discuss factors bearing on the investigation immediately below.

3. **StallRequests** puts the DEVQUEUE into the STALLED state so that any new IRP just goes into the queue. **WaitForCurrentIrp** waits until the current request, if there is one, finishes on the device. These two steps make the device quiescent until we know whether the device is really going to stop or not.

4. At this point, we have no reason to demur. We therefore record our state as PENDINGSTOP. Then we pass the request down the stack so that other drivers can have a chance to accept or decline this query.

The other basic way of handling QUERY_STOP is appropriate when your device might be busy with a request that will take a long time and can't be stopped in the middle, such as a tape retension operation that can't be stopped without potentially breaking the tape. In this case, you can use the DEVQUEUE's **CheckBusyAndStall** function. That function returns TRUE if the device is busy, whereupon you'd fail the QUERY_STOP with STATUS_UNSUCCESSFUL. The function returns FALSE if the device is idle, in which case it also stalls the queue. (The operations of checking the state of the device and stalling the queue need to be protected by a spin lock, which is why I wrote this function in the first place.)

You can fail a stop query for many reasons. Disk devices that are used for paging, for example, cannot be stopped. Neither can devices that are used for storing hibernation or crash dump files. (You'll know about these characteristics as a result of an IRP_MN_DEVICE_USAGE_NOTIFICATION request, which I'll discuss later in "Other Configuration Functionality.") Other reasons may also apply to your device.

Even if you succeed the query, one of the drivers underneath you might fail it for some reason. Even if all the drivers succeed the query, the PnP Manager might decide not to shut you down. In any of these cases, you'll receive another PnP request with the minor code IRP_MN_CANCEL_STOP_DEVICE to tell you that your device won't be shut down. You should then clear whatever state you set during the initial query:

```
NTSTATUS HandleCancelStop(PDEVICE_OBJECT fdo, PIRP Irp)
  {
  Irp->IoStatus.Status = STATUS_SUCCESS;
  PDEVICE_EXTENSION pdx = (PDEVICE_EXTENSION) fdo->DeviceExtension;
  if (pdx->state != PENDINGSTOP)
    return DefaultPnpHandler(fdo, Irp);
  NTSTATUS status = ForwardAndWait(fdo, Irp);
  if (NT_SUCCESS(status))
    {
    pdx->state = WORKING;
    RestartRequests(&pdx->dqReadWrite, fdo);
    }
  return CompleteRequest(Irp, status, Irp->IoStatus.Information);
  }
```

We first check to see whether a stop operation is even pending. Some higher-level driver might have vetoed a query that we never saw, so we'd still be in the WORKING state. If we're not in the PENDINGSTOP state, we simply forward the IRP. Otherwise, we send the CANCEL_STOP IRP synchronously to the lower-level drivers. That is, we use our **ForwardAndWait** helper function to send the IRP down the stack and await its completion. We wait for low-level drivers because we're about to resume processing IRPs, and the drivers might have work to do before we send them an IRP. If the lower layers successfully handle this IRP_MN_CANCEL_STOP_DEVICE, we change our **state** variable to indicate that we're back in the WORKING state, and we call **RestartRequests** to unstall the queues we stalled when we succeeded the query.

While the Device Is Stopped

If, on the other hand, all device drivers succeed the query and the PnP Manager decides to go ahead with the shutdown, you'll get an IRP_MN_STOP_DEVICE next. Your subdispatch function would look like this one:

```
NTSTATUS HandleStopDevice(PDEVICE_OBJECT fdo, PIRP Irp)
  {
  Irp->IoStatus.Status = STATUS_SUCCESS;
  PDEVICE_EXTENSION pdx = (PDEVICE_EXTENSION) fdo->DeviceExtension;
  if (pdx->state != PENDINGSTOP);
    {
    <complicated stuff>
    }
  StopDevice(fdo, pdx->state == WORKING);
  pdx->state = STOPPED;
  return DefaultPnpHandler(fdo, Irp);
  }
```

1. We expect the system to send us a QUERY_STOP before it sends us a STOP, so we should already be in the PENDINGSTOP state with all of our queues stalled. There is, however, a bug in Windows 98 such that we can sometimes get a STOP (without a QUERY_STOP) instead of a REMOVE. You need to take some action at this point that causes you to reject any new IRPs, but you mustn't really remove your device object or do the other things you do when you *really* receive a REMOVE request.

2. **StopDevice** is the helper function I've already discussed that deconfigures the device.

3. We now enter thc STOPPED state. We're in almost the same situation as we were when AddDevice was done. That is, all queues are stalled, and the device has no I/O resources. The only difference is that we've left our registered interfaces enabled, which means that applications will not have received removal notifications and will leave their handles open. Applications can also open new handles in this situation. Both aspects are just as they should be, because the stop condition won't last long.

4. As I previously discussed, the last thing we do to handle IRP_MN_STOP_DEVICE is pass the request down to the lower layers of the driver hierarchy.

Is It Okay to Remove the Device?

Just as the PnP Manager asks your permission before shutting your device down with a stop device request, it also might ask your permission before removing your device. This query takes the form of an IRP_MN_QUERY_REMOVE_DEVICE request that you can, once again, succeed or fail as you choose. And, just as with the stop query, the

PnP Manager will use an IRP_MN_CANCEL_REMOVE_DEVICE request if it changes its mind about removing the device.

```
NTSTATUS HandleQueryRemove(PDEVICE_OBJECT fdo, PIRP Irp)
  {
  Irp->IoStatus.Status = STATUS_SUCCESS;
  PDEVICE_EXTENSION pdx = (PDEVICE_EXTENSION) fdo->DeviceExtension;
  if (OkayToRemove(fdo))
    {
    StallRequests(&pdx->dqReadWrite);
    WaitForCurrentIrp(&pdx->dqReadWrite);
    pdx->prevstate = pdx->state;
    pdx->state = PENDINGREMOVE;
    return DefaultPnpHandler(fdo, Irp);
    }
  return CompleteRequest(Irp, STATUS_UNSUCCESSFUL, 0);
  }

NTSTATUS HandleCancelRemove(PDEVICE_OBJECT fdo, PIRP Irp)
  {
  Irp->IoStatus.Status = STATUS_SUCCESS;
  PDEVICE_EXTENSION pdx = (PDEVICE_EXTENSION) fdo->DeviceExtension;
  if (pdx->state != PENDINGREMOVE)
    return DefaultPnpHandler(fdo, Irp);
  NTSTATUS status = ForwardAndWait(fdo, Irp);
  if (NT_SUCCESS(status))
    {
    pdx->state = pdx->prevstate;
    if (pdx->state == WORKING)
      RestartRequests(&pdx->dqReadWrite, fdo);
    }
  return CompleteRequest(Irp, status, Irp->IoStatus.Information);
  }
```

1. This **OkayToRemove** helper function provides the answer to the question, "Is it okay to remove this device?" In general, this answer includes some device-specific ingredients, such as whether the device holds a paging or hibernation file, and so on.

2. Just as I showed you for IRP_MN_QUERY_STOP_DEVICE, you want to stall the request queue and wait for a short period, if necessary, until the current request finishes.

3. If you look at Figure 6-1 on page 223 carefully, you'll notice that it's possible to get a QUERY_REMOVE when you're in either the WORKING or STOPPED state. The right thing to do if the current query is later cancelled is to return to the original state. Hence, I have a **prevstate** variable in the device extension to record the prequery state.

4. We get the CANCEL_REMOVE request when something either above or below us vetoes a QUERY_REMOVE. If we never saw the query, we'll still be in the WORKING state and don't need to do anything with this IRP. Otherwise, we need to forward it to the lower levels before we process it because we want the lower levels to be ready to process the IRPs we're about to release from our queues.

5. Here, we undo the steps we took when we succeeded the QUERY_ REMOVE. We revert to the previous state. If the previous state was WORKING, we stalled the queues when we handled the query and need to unstall them now.

Synchronizing Removal

It turns out that the I/O Manager can send you PnP requests simultaneously with other substantive I/O requests, such as requests that involve reading or writing. It's entirely possible, therefore, for you to receive an IRP_MN_REMOVE_DEVICE at a time when you're still processing another IRP. It's up to you to prevent untoward consequences, and the standard way to do that involves using an IO_REMOVE_LOCK object and several associated kernel-mode support routines.

The basic idea behind the standard scheme for preventing premature removal is that you acquire the remove lock each time you start processing a request and you release the lock when you're done. Before you remove your device object, you make sure that the lock is free. If not, you wait until all references to the lock are released. Figure 6-6 illustrates the process.

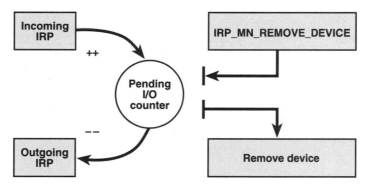

Figure 6-6. *Operation of an IO_REMOVE_LOCK.*

To handle the mechanics of this process, you define a variable in the device extension:

```
struct DEVICE_EXTENSION {
  ...
  IO_REMOVE_LOCK RemoveLock;
  ...
  };
```

You initialize the lock object during **AddDevice**:

```
NTSTATUS AddDevice(PDRIVER_OBJECT DriverObject, PDEVICE_OBJECT pdo)
  {
  ...
  IoInitializeRemoveLock(&pdx->RemoveLock, 0, 0, 256);
  ...
  }
```

The last three parameters to **IoInitializeRemoveLock** are, respectively, a tag value, an expected maximum lifetime for a lock, and a maximum lock count, none of which are used in the free build of the operating system.

These preliminaries set the stage for what you do during the lifetime of the device object. Whenever you receive an I/O request, you call **IoAcquireRemoveLock**. IoAcquireRemoveLock will return STATUS_DELETE_PENDING if a removal operation is underway. Otherwise, it will acquire the lock and return STATUS_SUCCESS. Whenever you finish an I/O operation, you call **IoReleaseRemoveLock**, which will release the lock and might unleash a heretofore pending removal operation. In the context of some purely hypothetical dispatch function that completes the IRP it's handed, the code might look like this:

```
NTSTATUS DispatchSomething(PDEVICE_OBJECT fdo, PIRP Irp)
  {
  PDEVICE_EXTENSION pdx = (PDEVICE_EXTENSION) fdo->DeviceExtension;
  NTSTATUS status = IoAcquireRemoveLock(&pdx->RemoveLock, Irp);
  if (!NT_SUCCESS(status))
    return CompleteRequest(Irp, status, 0);
  ...
  IoReleaseRemoveLock(&pdx->RemoveLock, Irp);
  return CompleteRequest(Irp, <some code>, <info value>);
  }
```

The second argument to IoAcquireRemoveLock and IoReleaseRemoveLock is just a tag value that a checked build of the OS can use to match up acquisition and release calls, by the way.

The calls to acquire and release the remove lock dovetail with additional logic in the PnP dispatch function and the remove device subdispatch function. First, **DispatchPnp** has to obey the rule about locking and unlocking the device, so it will contain the following code that I didn't show you earlier in "IRP_MJ_PNP Dispatch Function":

```
NTSTATUS DispatchPnp(PDEVICE_OBJECT fdo, PIRP Irp)
  {
  PDEVICE_EXTENSION pdx = (PDEVICE_EXTENSION) fdo->DeviceExtension;
  NTSTATUS status = IoAcquireRemoveLock(&pdx->RemoveLock, Irp);
  if (!NT_SUCCESS(status))
    return CompleteRequest(Irp, status, 0);
  ...
```

```
      status = (*fcntab[fcn])(fdo, Irp);
      if (fcn != IRP_MN_REMOVE_DEVICE)
        IoReleaseRemoveLock(&pdx->RemoveLock, Irp);
      return status;
      }
```

In other words, DispatchPnp locks the device, calls the subdispatch routine, and then (usually) unlocks the device afterward. The subdispatch routine for IRP_MN_REMOVE_DEVICE has additional special logic that you also haven't seen yet:

```
NTSTATUS HandleRemoveDevice(PDEVICE_OBJECT fdo, PIRP Irp)
  {
  Irp->IoStatus.Status = STATUS_SUCCESS;
  PDEVICE_EXTENSION pdx = (PDEVICE_EXTENSION) fdo->DeviceExtension;
  AbortRequests(&pdx->dqReadWrite, STATUS_DELETE_PENDING);
  DeregisterAllInterfaces(pdx);
  StopDevice(fdo, pdx->state == WORKING);
  pdx->state = REMOVED;
  NTSTATUS status = DefaultPnpHandler(pdx->LowerDeviceObject, Irp);
  IoReleaseRemoveLockAndWait(&pdx->RemoveLock, Irp);
  RemoveDevice(fdo);
  return status;
  }
```

1. Windows 98 doesn't send the SURPRISE_REMOVAL request, so this REMOVE IRP may be the first indication you have that the device has disappeared. Calling **StopDevice** allows you to release all your I/O resources in case you didn't get an earlier IRP that caused you to release them. Calling **AbortRequests** causes you to complete any queued IRPs and to start rejecting any new IRPs.

2. We pass this request to the lower layers now that we've done our work.

3. The PnP dispatch routine acquired the remove lock. We now call the special function IoReleaseRemoveLockAndWait to release that lock reference and wait until all references to the lock are released. Once the IoReleaseRemoveLockAndWait routine returns, any subsequent call to IoAcquireRemoveLock will elicit a STATUS_DELETE_PENDING status to indicate that device removal is under way.

    NOTE   You'll notice that the IRP_MN_REMOVE_DEVICE handler might block while some IRP finishes. This is certainly okay in Windows 98 and Windows 2000, which were designed with this possibility in mind—the IRP gets sent in the context of a system thread that is allowed to block. Some WDM functionality (a Microsoft developer even called it "embryonic") is present in OEM releases of Microsoft Windows 95, but you can't block a remove device request there. Consequently, if your driver needs to run in Windows 95, you need to discover that fact and avoid blocking. That discovery process is left as an exercise for you.

These are the mechanics of locking and unlocking the device to forestall removing the device while it's still in use. You still need to know when to invoke IoAcquireRemoveLock and IoReleaseRemoveLock to bring that mechanism into play. Basically, an IRP dispatch function that will complete the request quickly should acquire and release the lock.

A dispatch routine that queues an IRP should not acquire the remove lock, however. For a queued IRP, you acquire the lock inside StartIo and release it inside your DPC routine. So, we can expand the earlier skeleton of **StartIo** and **DpcForIsr** as follows:

```
VOID StartIo(PDEVICE_OBJECT fdo, PIRP Irp)
  {
  PDEVICE_EXTENSION pdx =(PDEVICE_EXTENSION) fdo->DeviceExtension;
  NTSTATUS status = IoAcquireRemoveLock(&pdx->RemoveLock, Irp);
  if (!NT_SUCCESS(status))
    {
    CompleteRequest(Irp, status, 0);
    return;
    }

  // start request on device
  }

VOID DpcForIsr(PKDPC Dpc, PDEVICE_OBJECT device, PIRP junk,
  PVOID context)
  {
  PDEVICE_EXTENSION pdx = (PDEVICE_EXTENSION) fdo->DeviceExtension;
  PIRP Irp = GetCurrentIrp(&pdx->dqReadWrite);
  ...
  StartNextPacket(&pdx->dqReadWrite, device);
  IoReleaseRemoveLock(&pdx->RemoveLock, Irp);
  CompleteRequest(Irp, ...);
  }
```

1. We acquire the lock here rather than in the dispatch routine. We don't want the fact that we've got an IRP sitting in our queue to prevent the PnP Manager from shutting us down. It's also better to not have to worry about the remove lock in our cancel routine.

2. **IoAcquireRemoveLock** fails only if a delete operation is pending. Its return value can be either STATUS_SUCCESS or STATUS_DELETE_PENDING. In the failure case, don't call **StartNextPacket**—there's no point in trying to start a new operation when the device is about to disappear. Were we to call StartNextPacket, it would recursively call this routine, which would try to acquire the remove lock and fail, whereupon it would call

StartNextPacket, which would call StartIo, which would...<BSOD due to stack overflow>. You get the idea.

3. This call to **IoReleaseRemoveLock** balances the call inside StartIo.

You should also acquire the remove lock when you successfully process an IRP_MJ_CREATE. In contrast to the other situations we've considered, you don't release the lock before returning from the **DispatchCreate** routine. The balancing call to IoReleaseRemoveLock occurs instead in the dispatch routine for IRP_MJ_CLOSE. In other words, you hold the remove lock for the entire time something has a handle open to your device. Here's a sketch of what I mean:

```
NTSTATUS DispatchCreate(...)
  {
  ...
  IoAcquireRemoveLock(&pdx->RemoveLock, stack->FileObject);
  return CompleteRequest(...);
  }

NTSTATUS DispatchClose(...)
  {
  ...
  IoReleaseRemoveLock(&pdx->RemoveLock, stack->FileObject);
  return CompleteRequest(...);
  }
```

For debugging purposes, the balancing calls to IoAcquireRemoveLock and IoReleaseRemoveLock should use the same value for the second argument. You wouldn't use the IRP pointer as I've done in my other examples because the CREATE and CLOSE requests are different IRPs. The file object will be the same in both requests, though, which is why I used the file object in this example.

If the end user uses the Device Manager to remove a device when some application has an open handle, the operating system declines to remove the device and so informs the user. In that situation, the fact that you've also claimed the remove lock won't influence the course of events because you'll never get the IRP_MN_REMOVE_DEVICE that would cause you to wait for all holders of the lock to release it. If it's possible for the device to be physically removed from the computer without first going through the Device Manager, however, a correctly written application will be looking for a WM_DEVICECHANGE message that signals departure of the device. (See the discussion of user-mode notifications near the end of this chapter in "PnP Notifications".) The application will then close its handles. You should delay IRP_MN_REMOVE_DEVICE until the handles are actually closed, and the locking logic I've just described allows you to do that.

COMPATIBILITY NOTE FOR IO_REMOVE_LOCK

It turns out that the IO_REMOVE_LOCK object and associated service functions are technically not part of the WDM. The declarations your C code needs are actually in WDM.H, and WDM.LIB contains import definitions for the remove-lock functions. But Windows 98 doesn't actually export the functions. A driver that references these functions therefore won't load in Windows 98. This state of affairs is very unfortunate because every WDM driver needs to interlock device removal.

DDK sample programs cope with this incompatibility in one of two ways. Some samples use a custom-built mechanism instead of an IO_REMOVE_LOCK. Others provide functions with names like *Xxx*AcquireRemoveLock, and so on, that mimic the names of the standard remove lock functions.

My sample drivers use a variation on the second of these approaches. By means of **#define** statements, I substitute my own declarations of the IO_REMOVE_LOCK object and support functions for the official ones. Thus, my sample code calls IoAcquireRemoveLock, and so on. In the samples that use GENERIC.SYS, preprocessor trickery actually routes these calls to functions with names like **GenericAcquireRemoveLock** that reside in GENERIC.SYS. In the samples that don't use GENERIC.SYS, the preprocessor trickery routes the calls to functions with names like **AcquireRemoveLock** that are located in a file named REMOVELOCK.CPP.

I could have written my samples in such a way that they would call the standard remove lock functions instead of my own in Windows 2000. To make any of the samples work in Windows 98, I'd have needed to write stub implementations of the remove lock functions and required you to install a stub virtual device driver (VxD) before you could run any of the samples. (See Appendix A, "Coping with Windows 98 Incompatibilities.") I didn't think this was a good way to explain WDM programming.

How DEVQUEUE Works

In contrast to other examples in this book, I'm going to show you the full implementation of the DEVQUEUE object even though the source code is on the companion disc. I'm making an exception in this case because I think an annotated listing of the functions will make it easier for you to understand how to use it.

Initializing a DEVQUEUE

The DEVQUEUE object has this declaration in my DEVQUEUE.H header file:

```
typedef struct _DEVQUEUE {
  LIST_ENTRY head;
  KSPIN_LOCK lock;
  PDRIVER_START StartIo;
  LONG stallcount;
  PIRP CurrentIrp;
  KEVENT evStop;
  NTSTATUS abortstatus;
} DEVQUEUE, *PDEVQUEUE;
```

InitializeQueue initializes one of these objects like this:

```
VOID NTAPI InitializeQueue(PDEVQUEUE pdq, PDRIVER_STARTIO StartIo)
  {
  InitializeListHead(&pdq->head);
  KeInitializeSpinLock(&pdq->lock);
  pdq->StartIo = StartIo;
  pdq->stallcount = 1;
  pdq->CurrentIrp = NULL;
  KeInitializeEvent(&pdq->evStop, NotificationEvent, FALSE);
  pdq->abortstatus = (NTSTATUS) 0;
  }
```

1. We use an ordinary (noninterlocked) doubly-linked list to queue IRPs. We don't need to use an interlocked list because we'll always access it within the protection of our own spin lock.

2. This spin lock guards access to the queue and other fields in the DEVQUEUE structure. It also takes the place of the global cancel spin lock for guarding nearly all of the cancellation process, thereby improving system performance.

3. Each queue has its own associated **StartIo** function that we call automatically in the appropriate places.

4. The stall counter indicates how many times something has requested that IRP delivery to StartIo be stalled. Initializing the counter to 1 means that the IRP_MN_START_DEVICE handler must call RestartRequests to release an IRP.

5. The **CurrentIrp** field records the IRP most recently sent to the StartIo routine. Initializing this field to NULL indicates that the device is initially idle.

6. We use this event to block **WaitForCurrentIrp** when necessary. We'll set this event inside StartNextPacket, which should always be called when the current IRP completes.

7. We reject incoming IRPs in two situations. The first situation is after we irrevocably commit to removing the device, when we must start failing new IRPs with STATUS_DELETE_PENDING. The second situation is during a period of low power, when, depending on the type of device we're managing, we might choose to fail new IRPs with the STATUS_DEVICE_ POWERED_OFF code. The **abortstatus** field records the status code we should use in rejecting IRPs in these situations.

Stalling the Queue

Stalling the IRP queue involves two DEVQUEUE functions:

```
VOID NTAPI StallRequests(PDEVQUEUE pdq)
  {
  InterlockedIncrement(&pdq->stallcount);
  }
```

```
BOOLEAN NTAPI CheckBusyAndStall(PDEVQUEUE pdq)
  {
  KIRQL oldirql;
  KeAcquireSpinLock(&pdq->lock, &oldirql);
  BOOLEAN busy = pdq->CurrentIrp != NULL;
  if (!busy)
    InterlockedIncrement(&pdq->stallcount);
  KeReleaseSpinLock(&pdq->lock, oldirql);
  return busy;
  }
```

1. To stall requests, we just need to set the stall counter to a nonzero value. It's unnecessary to protect the increment with a spin lock because any device that might be racing with us to change the value will also be using an interlocked increment or decrement.

2. Since CheckBusyAndStall needs to operate as an atomic function, we first take the queue's spin lock.

3. **CurrentIrp** being non-NULL is the signal that the device is busy handling one of the requests from this queue.

4. If the device is currently idle, this statement starts stalling the queue, thereby preventing the device from becoming busy later on.

Queuing IRPs

IRPs get added to the queue when a dispatch function calls **StartPacket**:

```
VOID NTAPI StartPacket(PDEVQUEUE pdq, PDEVICE_OBJECT fdo,
  PIRP Irp, PDRIVER_CANCEL cancel)
  {
  KIRQL oldirql;
```

```
                KeAcquireSpinLock(&pdq->lock, &oldirql);
 2  ▷          if (pdq->abortstatus)
                  {
                  KeReleaseSpinLock(&pdq->lock, oldirql);
                  Irp->IoStatus.Status = pdq->abortstatus;
                  IoCompleteRequest(Irp, IO_NO_INCREMENT);
                  }
 3  ▷          else if (pdq->CurrentIrp || pdq->stallcount)
                  {
 4  ▷            IoSetCancelRoutine(Irp, cancel);
                  if (Irp->Cancel && IoSetCancelRoutine(Irp, NULL))
                    {
                    KeReleaseSpinLock(&pdq->lock, oldirql);
                    Irp->IoStatus.Status = STATUS_CANCELLED;
                    IoCompleteRequest(Irp, IO_NO_INCREMENT);
                    }
                  else
                    {
 5  ▷              InsertTailList(&pdq->head, &Irp->Tail.Overlay.ListEntry);
                    KeReleaseSpinLock(&pdq->lock, oldirql);
                    }
 6  ▷          else
                  {
                  pdq->CurrentIrp = Irp;
                  KeReleaseSpinLock(&pdq->lock, DISPATCH_LEVEL);
                  (*pdq->StartIo)(fdo, Irp);
                  KeLowerIrql(oldirql);
                  }
                }
```

1. Acquiring the spin lock allows us to access fields in the DEVQUEUE without interference from the other support routines—principally StartNextPacket—that might be trying to access the same queue.

2. As I described earlier, we sometimes need to reject IRPs on arrival. If **abortstatus** is nonzero, we just complete the request. Our caller will be returning STATUS_PENDING, so it's up to us to do the completion.

3. If the device is currently busy, or if some other part of the driver has stalled this queue, we need to queue the IRP for later processing.

4. We might be in race with an instance of **IoCancelIrp** that is trying to cancel this very IRP. We first install our own cancel routine in the IRP by using **IoSetCancelRoutine**, which performs an (atomic) interlocked exchange. Then we test the **Cancel** flag. If we find the Cancel flag set, our cancel routine might or might not have been called by now, depending on the exact order in which our code and IoCancelIrp executed their program steps. If

our cancel routine *was* called, a second call to IoSetCancelRoutine will return NULL; we can then enqueue the IRP and rely on the cancel routine to immediately dequeue the IRP and complete it. If our cancel routine has not yet been called, it won't be possible for it to ever be called after the second invocation of IoSetCancelRoutine; we will complete the IRP now in this case.

5. This is where we actually queue the IRP. The **Tail.Overlay.ListEntry** field of an IRP was designed for uses like this one.

6. The last case is when the queue is in the READY state and the device is not currently busy. We set the **CurrentIrp** pointer in the DEVQUEUE, release the spin lock, and call the **StartIo** routine at DISPATCH_LEVEL.

I'd like to discuss a pesky nonproblem in the above code. Programs that change CurrentIrp do so while owning our spin lock, so we can be sure there's no ambiguity in our test of CurrentIrp. The stall counter, on the other hand, can be incremented without the spin lock inside **StallRequests**. It should be obvious that the only potential problem occurs when the counter is being incremented from 0 to 1 more or less simultaneously with us, because we behave the same way no matter what nonzero value the counter might have. Consider the potential race with a call to StallRequests that will increment the counter from 0 to 1. If we beat the increment and find the counter 0, we'll go ahead and start a request. That's okay, because the caller of StallRequests is willing to have the device be busy. (If the caller weren't willing, it would have used CheckBusyAndStall instead.) If we find the counter already incremented, we'll queue the IRP, which is also consistent with what the caller of StallRequests intended.

Dequeuing IRPs

The function that dequeues most IRPs is **StartNextPacket**, which is called from a DPC routine:

```
PIRP NTAPI StartNextPacket(PDEVQUEUE pdq, PDEVICE_OBJECT fdo)
  {
  KIRQL oldirql;
  KeAcquireSpinLock(&pdq->lock, &oldirql));
  PIRP CurrentIrp = (PIRP) InterlockedExchangePointer
    (&pdq->CurrentIrp, NULL);
  if (CurrentIrp)
    KeSetEvent(&pdq->evStop, 0, FALSE);
  while (!pdq->stallcount
    && !pdq->abortstatus
    && !IsListEmpty(&pdq->head))
    {
    PLIST_ENTRY next = RemoveHeadList(&pdq->head);
    PIRP Irp = CONTAINING_RECORD(next, IRP, Tail.Overlay.ListEntry);
```

```
6 ▷        if (!IoSetCancelRoutine(Irp, NULL))
             {
             InitializeListHead(&Irp->Tail.Overlay.ListEntry);
             continue;
             }
         pdq->CurrentIrp = Irp;
7 ▷      KeReleaseSpinLockFromDpcLevel(&pdq->lock);
         (*pdq->StartIo)(fdo, Irp);
         KeLowerIrql(oldirql);
         return CurrentIrp;
         }
     KeReleaseSpinLock(&pdq->lock, oldirql);
     return CurrentIrp;
     }
```

1. We first acquire the queue's spin lock so that we can muck about with the internal structure of the object without interference.

2. We'll be returning the address of the current IRP as our return value, and we also want to set the **CurrentIrp** pointer to NULL. Because of the spin lock, we don't need to use an atomic operation to extract and nullify CurrentIrp, but doing so can't hurt either.

3. Some routine might be waiting inside WaitForCurrentIrp for the current request to finish. This call to **KeSetEvent** will satisfy that wait.

4. This series of tests determines whether we can and should dequeue a request. The queue must not be stalled. Neither can we be in the REJECTING state, in which we're rejecting new IRPs. Finally, the queue must contain a request before it makes sense to call **RemoveHeadList**.

5. This code removes the oldest entry in our IRP queue.

6. Nullifying the cancel routine pointer in the IRP will prevent IoCancelIrp from trying to cancel the IRP. It's possible that IoCancelIrp is in the process of trying to cancel this IRP on another CPU at this very moment, in which case we should get NULL as the return value from IoSetCancelRoutine. When CancelRequest gains control, it will need to acquire the queue's spin lock before proceeding further. At that point, it will blindly try to remove this IRP from whatever queue it happens to be on. Calling **InitializeListHead** on the IRP's own chaining field will make it safe for CancelRequest to do this when it eventually gains control of the spin lock and proceeds.

7. This is where we finally pass the newly dequeued IRP to the **StartIo** routine for processing.

The **RestartRequests** function balances a call to StallRequests or CheckBusy-AndStall. It's complicated—very slightly—by the need to send the first IRP to the StartIo routine. Luckily, it can just call StartNextPacket:

```
VOID NTAPI RestartRequests(PDEVQUEUE pdq, PDEVICE_OBJECT fdo)
  {
  if (InterlockedDecrement(&pdq->stallcount) > 0)
    return;
  StartNextPacket(pdq, fdo);
  }
```

Cancelling IRPs

StartPacket registers a cancel routine supplied by its caller, which in turn simply delegates the work to the queue's **CancelRequest** function:

```
VOID NTAPI CancelRequest(PDEVQUEUE pdq, PIRP Irp)
  {
  KIRQL oldirql = Irp->CancelIrql;
  IoReleaseCancelSpinLock(DISPATCH_LEVEL);
  KeAcquireSpinLockAtDpcLevel(&pdq->lock);
  RemoveEntryList(&Irp->Tail.Overlay.ListEntry);
  KeReleaseSpinLock(&pdq->lock, oldirql);
  Irp->IoStatus.Status = STATUS_CANCELLED;
  IoCompleteRequest(Irp, IO_NO_INCREMENT);
  }
```

We're called while we own the global cancel spin lock, which we release almost immediately. After this everything is protected by the queue's spin lock instead. When IoCancelIrp called **IoAcquireCancelSpinLock**, it saved the previous interrupt request level (IRQL) value in the **CancelIrql** field of the IRP, and we need to eventually revert to that same IRQL; hence, we save it in the **oldirql** variable.

> NOTE   The caller of IoCancelIrp is responsible for making sure that the IRP has not already been completed.

IRPs can also be cancelled as a result of an IRP_MJ_CLEANUP, which we'll receive prior to an IRP_MJ_CLOSE. The DEVQUEUE **CleanupRequests** function is almost identical to the standard-model **DispatchCleanup** routine I showed you in the previous chapter. The only substantive difference between the two is that we only need to acquire the queue's spin lock:

```
VOID NTAPI CleanupRequests(PDEVQUEUE pdq, PFILE_OBJECT fop,
  NTSTATUS status)
  {
  LIST_ENTRY cancellist;
  InitializeListhead(&cancellist);
  KIRQL oldirql;
  KeAcquireSpinLock(&pdq->lock, &oldirql);
  PLIST_ENTRY first = &pdq->head;
  PLIST_ENTRY next;
  for (next = first->Flink; next != first; )
    {
    PIRP Irp = CONTAINING_RECORD(next, IRP, Tail.Overlay.ListEntry);
    PIO_STACK_LOCATION stack = IoGetCurrentIrpStackLocation(Irp);
    next = next->Flink;
    if (fop && stack->FileObject != fop)
      continue;
    if (!IoSetCancelRoutine(Irp, NULL))
      continue;
    RemoveEntryList(next);
    InsertTailList(&cancellist, next);
    }
  KeReleaseSpinLock(&pdq->lock, oldirql);
  while (!IsListEmpty(&cancellist))
    {
    next = RemoveHeadList(&cancellist);
    PIRP Irp = CONTAINING_RECORD(next, IRP, Tail.Overlay.ListEntry);
    Irp->IoStatus.Status = status;
    IoCompleteRequest(Irp, IO_NO_INCREMENT);
    }
  }
```

1. Our strategy will be to move the IRPs that need to be cancelled into a private queue under protection of the queue's spin lock. Hence, we initialize the private queue and acquire the spin lock before doing anything else.

2. This loop traverses the entire queue until we return to the list head. Note the absence of a loop increment step—the third clause in the **for** statement. I'll explain why none is desirable in a moment.

3. If we're being called to help out with IRP_MJ_CLEANUP, the **fop** argument is the address of a file object that is about to be closed. We're supposed to isolate the IRPs that pertain to the same file object, which requires us to first find the stack location.

4. If we decide to remove this IRP from the queue, wc won't thereafter have an easy way to find the next IRP in the main queue. We therefore perform the loop increment step here.

5. This especially clever statement is due to Jamie Hanrahan. We need to worry that someone might be trying to cancel the IRP that we're currently looking at during this iteration. They could get only as far as the point where CancelRequest tries to acquire the spin lock. Before getting that far, however, they necessarily had to execute the statement inside IoCancelIrp that nullifies the cancel routine pointer. If we find that pointer NULL when *we* call **IoSetCancelRoutine**, therefore, we can be sure that someone really is trying to cancel this IRP. By simply skipping this IRP during this iteration, we allow the cancel routine to complete it later on.

6. Here's where we take the IRP out of the main queue and put it in the private queue instead.

7. Once we finish moving IRPs into the private queue, we can release our spin lock. Then we go ahead and cancel all the IRPs we moved.

CleanupRequests can be called from elsewhere in the driver, by the way. For example, earlier I showed you a call from the IRP_MN_REMOVE_DEVICE handler, which supplied a NULL file object pointer (in order to select all IRPs) and a status code of STATUS_DELETE_PENDING.

Awaiting the Current IRP

The handler for IRP_MN_STOP_DEVICE might need to wait for the current IRP, if any, to finish by calling **WaitForCurrentIrp**:

```
VOID NTAPI WaitForCurrentIrp(PDEVQUEUE pdq)
  {
  KeClearEvent(&pdq->evStop);
```

```
   ASSERT(pdq->stallcount != 0);
   KIRQL oldirql;
   KeAcquireSpinLock(&pdq->lock, &oldirql);
   BOOLEAN mustwait = pdq->CurrentIrp != NULL;
   KeReleaseSpinLock(&pdq->lock, oldirql);
   if (mustwait)
     KeWaitForSingleObject(&pdq->evStop, Executive, KernelMode,
       FALSE, NULL);
   }
```

1. StartNextPacket signals the **evStop** event each time it's called. We want to be sure that the wait we're about to perform doesn't complete because of a now stale signal, so we clear the event before doing anything else.

2. It doesn't make sense to call this routine without first stalling the queue. Otherwise, StartNextPacket would just start the next packet if there were one, and the device would become busy again.

3. If the device is currently busy, we'll wait on the **evStop** event until something calls StartNextPacket to signal that event. We need to protect our inspection of **CurrentIrp** with the spin lock because, in general, testing a pointer for NULL isn't an atomic event. If the pointer is NULL now, it can't change later because we've assumed that the queue is stalled.

Aborting Requests

Surprise removal of the device demands that we immediately halt every outstanding IRP that might try to touch the hardware. In addition, we want to make sure that all further IRPs get rejected. The **AbortRequests** function helps with these tasks:

```
VOID NTAPI AbortRequests(PDEVQUEUE pdq, NTSTATUS status)
  {
  pdq->abortstatus = status;
  CleanupRequests(pdq, NULL, status);
  }
```

Setting **abortstatus** puts the queue into the REJECTING state so that all future IRPs will be rejected with whatever status value our caller supplied. Calling CleanupRequests at this point—with a NULL file object pointer so that Cleanup-Requests will process the entire queue—empties the queue.

We don't dare try to do anything with the IRP, if any, that's currently active on the hardware. Drivers that don't use the hardware abstraction layer (HAL) to access the hardware—USB drivers, for example, which rely on the hub and host-controller drivers—can count on another driver to fail the current IRP. Drivers that use the HAL might, however, need to worry about hanging the system or, at the very least, leaving an IRP in limbo because the nonexistent hardware can't generate the interrupt that would let the IRP finish. To deal with situations like this, you call **AreRequestsBeingAborted**:

```
NTSTATUS AreRequestsBeingAborted(PDEVQUEUE pdq)
  {
  return pdq->abortstatus;
  }
```

It would be silly, by the way, to use the queue spin lock in this routine. Suppose that we were to capture the instantaneous value of **abortstatus** in a thread-safe and multiprocessor-safe way. The value we return could become obsolete as soon as we release the spin lock.

> **NOTE** If your device might be removed in such a way that an outstanding request simply hangs, you should also have a watchdog timer of some sort running that will let you kill the IRP after some period of time. See the "Watchdog Timers" section in Chapter 9, "Specialized Topics."

Sometimes we need to undo the effect of a previous call to AbortRequest. **AllowRequests** lets us do that:

```
VOID NTAPI AllowRequests(PDEVQUEUE pdq)
  {
  pdq->abortstatus = (NTSTATUS) 0;
  }
```

OTHER CONFIGURATION FUNCTIONALITY

Up to this point I've talked about the important concepts you need to know to write a hardware device driver. To close the chapter, I'll discuss two less important minor function codes—IRP_MN_FILTER_RESOURCE_REQUIREMENTS and IRP_MN_DEVICE_USAGE_NOTIFICATION—that you might need to process in a practical driver. Then I'll discuss how to write a miniature bus driver to support nonstandard controller or multifunction devices. Finally, I'll mention how you can register to receive notifications about PnP events that affect other devices besides your own.

> **NOTE** Other flavors of PnP requests exist that I haven't discussed in this chapter because it's not my purpose to simply reiterate the DDK reference manuals. For example, it's potentially useful to be able to export a direct call interface to other drivers, but you probably don't need to in any garden-variety situation. I'm therefore not going to provide a sample or an explanation of IRP_MN_QUERY_INTERFACE. I'll mention IRP_MN_QUERY_CAPABILITIES in Chapter 8, on power management, to which it's most relevant.

Filtering Resource Requirements

Sometimes the PnP Manager is misinformed about the resource requirements of your driver. This can occur because of hardware and firmware bugs, mistakes in the INF file for a legacy device, or other reasons. The system provides an escape valve in the form of the IRP_MN_FILTER_RESOURCE_REQUIREMENTS request, which affords you a chance to examine and possibly alter the list of resources before the PnP Manager embarks on the arbitration and assignment process that culminates in your receiving a start device IRP.

When you receive a filter request, the **FilterResourceRequirements** substructure of the Parameters union in your stack location points to an IO_RESOURCE_REQUIREMENTS_LIST data structure that lists the resource requirements for your device. In addition, if any of the drivers above you have processed the IRP and modified the resource requirements, the **IoStatus.Information** field of the IRP will point to a second IO_RESOURCE_REQUIREMENTS_LIST, which is the one from which you should work. Your overall strategy will be as follows: If you wish to *add* a resource to the current list of requirements, you do so in your dispatch routine. Then you pass the IRP down the stack synchronously—that is, by using the ForwardAndWait method you use with a start device request. When you regain control, you can *modify* any of the resource descriptions that appear in the list.

Here is a brief and not very useful example that illustrates the mechanics of the filtering process:

```
NTSTATUS HandleFilterResources(PDEVICE_OBJECT fdo, PIRP Irp)
  {
  PDEVICE_EXTENSION pdx = (PDEVICE_EXTENSION) fdo->DeviceExtension;
  PIO_STACK_LOCATION stack = IoGetCurrentIrpStackLocation(Irp);
  PIO_RESOURCE_REQUIREMENTS_LIST original = stack->Parameters
    .FilterResourceRequirements.IoResourceRequirementList;
  PIO_RESOURCE_REQUIREMENTS_LIST filtered =
    (PIO_RESOURCE_REQUIREMENTS_LIST) Irp->IoStatus.Information;
  PIO_RESOURCE_REQUIREMENTS_LIST source =
    filtered ? filtered : original;
  if (source->AlternativeLists != 1)
    return DefaultPnpHandler(fdo, Irp);
  ULONG sizelist = source->ListSize;
  PIO_RESOURCE_REQUIREMENTS_LIST newlist =
    (PIO_RESOURCE_REQUIREMENTS_LIST) ExAllocatePool(PagedPool,
    sizelist + sizeof(IO_RESOURCE_DESCRIPTOR));
  if (!newlist)
    return DefaultPnpHandler(fdo, Irp);
  RtlCopyMemory(newlist, source, sizelist);
  newlist->ListSize += sizeof(IO_RESOURCE_DESCRIPTOR);
```

1

2

3

4

5

(continued)

6 ▷
```
    PIO_RESOURCE_DESCRIPTOR resource =
      &newlist->List[0].Descriptors[newlist->List[0].Count++];
    RtlZeroMemory(resource, sizeof(IO_RESOURCE_DESCRIPTOR));
    resource->Type = CmResourceTypeDevicePrivate;
    resource->ShareDisposition = CmResourceShareDeviceExclusive;
    resource->u.DevicePrivate.Data[0] = 42;
```
7 ▷
```
    Irp->IoStatus.Information = (ULONG_PTR) newlist;
    if (filtered)
      ExFreePool(filtered);
```
8 ▷
```
    NTSTATUS status = ForwardAndWait(fdo, Irp);
    if (NT_SUCCESS(status))
      {
      // stuff
      }
```
9 ▷
```
    Irp->IoStatus.Status = status;
    IoCompleteRequest(Irp, IO_NO_INCREMENT);
    return status;
    }
```

1. The parameters for this request include a list of I/O resource requirements. These would be derived from the device's configuration space, the registry, or wherever the bus driver happens to find them.

2. Higher-level drivers might have already filtered the resources by adding additional ones to the original list. If so, they set the **IoStatus.Information** field to point to the expanded requirements list structure.

3. If there's no filtered list, we will extend the original list. If there's a filtered list, we'll extend that.

4. Theoretically, several alternative lists of requirements could exist, but dealing with that situation is beyond the scope of this simple example.

5. We need to add any resources before we pass the request down the stack. First we allocate a new requirements list and copy the old requirements into it.

6. Taking care to preserve the preexisting order of the descriptors, we add our own resource description. In this example, we're adding a resource that's private to the driver.

7. We store the address of the expanded list of requirements in the IRP's **IoStatus.Information** field, which is where lower-level drivers and the PnP system will be looking for it. If we just extended an already filtered list, we need to release the memory occupied by the old list.

8. We pass the request down using the same **ForwardAndWait** helper function that we used for IRP_MN_START_DEVICE. If we weren't going to modify any resource descriptors on the IRP's way back up the stack, we could just call DefaultPnpHandler here and propagate the returned status.

9. When we complete this IRP, whether we indicate success or failure, we must take care not to modify the Information field of the I/O status block: it might hold a pointer to a resource requirements list that some driver—maybe even ours!—installed on the way down. The PnP Manager will release the memory occupied by that structure when it's no longer needed.

Device Usage Notifications

Disk drivers (and the drivers for disk controllers) in particular sometimes need to know extrinsic facts about how they're being used by the operating system, and the IRP_MN_DEVICE_USAGE_NOTIFICATION request provides a means to gain that knowledge. The I/O stack location for the IRP contains two parameters in the **Parameters.UsageNotification** substructure. See Table 6-4. The **InPath** value (a Boolean) indicates whether the device is in the device path required to support that usage, and the **Type** value indicates one of several possible special usages.

Parameter	*Description*
InPath	TRUE if device is in the path of the Type usage; FALSE if not
Type	Type of usage to which the IRP applies

Table 6-4. *Fields in the Parameters.UsageNotification substructure of an I/O stack location.*

In the subdispatch routine for the notification, you should have a **switch** statement (or other logic) that differentiates among the notifications you know about. In most cases you'll pass the IRP down the stack. Consequently, a skeleton for the subdispatch function is as follows:

```
NTSTATUS HandleUsageNotification(PDEVICE_OBJECT fdo, PIRP Irp)
  {
  PDEVICE_EXTENSION pdx = (PDEVICE_EXTENSION) fdo->DeviceExtension;
  PIO_STACK_LOCATION stack = IoGetCurrentIrpStackLocation(Irp);
  DEVICE_USAGE_NOTIFICATION_TYPE type =
    stack->Parameters.UsageNotification.Type;
  BOOLEAN inpath = stack->Parameters.UsageNotification.InPath;
  switch (type)
    {
  case DeviceUsageTypeHibernation:
    ...
```

(continued)

```
    Irp->IoStatus.Status = STATUS_SUCCESS;
    break;
case DeviceUsageTypeDumpFile:
    ...
    Irp->IoStatus.Status = STATUS_SUCCESS;
    break;
case DeviceUsageTypePaging:
    ...
    Irp->IoStatus.Status = STATUS_SUCCESS;
    break;
default:
    break;
    }
return DefaultPnpHandler(fdo, Irp);
}
```

Set the **Status** field of the IRP to STATUS_SUCCESS for *only* the notifications that you explicitly recognize as a signal to the bus driver that you've processed them. The bus driver will assume that you didn't know about—and therefore didn't process—a notification for which you don't set STATUS_SUCCESS.

You may know that your device can't support a certain kind of usage. Suppose, for example, that some fact that only you know prevents your disk device from being used to store a hibernation file. In such a case, you should fail the IRP if it specifies the InPath value:

```
...
case DeviceUsageTypeHibernation:
    if (inpath)
        return CompleteRequest(Irp, STATUS_UNSUCCESSFUL, 0);
```

In the remainder of this section, I'll briefly describe each of the current usage types.

DeviceUsageTypePaging

The InPath TRUE notification indicates that a paging file will be opened on the device. The InPath FALSE notification indicates that a paging file has been closed. Generally, you should maintain a counter of the number of paging files you've been notified about. While any paging file remains active, you'll fail queries for STOP and REMOVE functions. In addition, when you receive the first paging notification, make sure that your dispatch routines for READ, WRITE, DEVICE_CONTROL, PNP, and POWER requests are locked into memory. (Refer to the information on driver paging in "User and Kernel Mode Address Spaces" in Chapter 3, "Basic Programming Techniques," for more information.) You should also clear the DO_POWER_PAGABLE flag in your device object to force the Power Manager to send you power IRPs at DISPATCH_LEVEL. To be safe, I'd also suggest nullifying any idle-notification registration you might have made. (See Chapter 8 for a discussion of idle detection.)

NOTE In Chapter 8, "Power Management," I'll discuss how to set the DO_POWER_PAGABLE flag in a device object. You need to be sure that you never clear this flag while a device object under yours has the flag set. You would want to clear the flag only in a completion routine, after the lower-level drivers have cleared their own flags. You need a completion routine anyway because you must undo anything you did in your dispatch routine if the IRP fails in the lower layers.

DeviceUsageTypeDumpFile

The InPath TRUE notification indicates that the device has been chosen as the repository for a crash dump file should one be necessary. The InPath FALSE notification cancels that. Maintain a counter of TRUE minus FALSE notifications. While the counter is nonzero:

■ Make sure that your power management code—see Chapter 8—will never take the device out of the D0, or fully on, state.

■ Avoid registering the device for idle detection, and nullify any outstanding registration.

■ Make sure that your driver fails stop and remove queries.

DeviceUsageTypeHibernation

The InPath TRUE notification indicates that the device has been chosen to hold the hibernation state file should one be written. The InPath FALSE notification cancels that. You should maintain a counter of TRUE minus FALSE notifications. Your response to system power IRPs that specify the PowerSystemHibernate state will be different than normal because your device will be used momentarily to record the hibernate file. Elaboration of this particular feature of disk drivers is beyond the scope of this book.

Controller and Multifunction Devices

Two categories of devices don't fit neatly into the PnP framework I've described so far. These categories are *controller* devices, which manage a collection of child devices, and *multifunction* devices, which have several functions on one card. These kinds of devices are similar in that their correct management entails the creation of multiple device objects with independent I/O resources.

It's very easy in Windows 2000 to support PCI, PCMCIA (Personal Computer Memory Card International Association), and USB devices that conform to their respective bus standards for multifunction devices. The PCI bus driver automatically recognizes PCI multifunction cards. For PCMCIA multifunction devices, you can follow the detailed instructions in the DDK for designating MF.SYS as the function driver for your multifunction card; MF.SYS will enumerate the functions on your card and thereby cause the PnP Manager to load individual function drivers. The USB hub driver will normally load separate function drivers for each interface on a one-configuration device.

Except for USB, the original release of Windows 98 lacks the multifunction support that Windows 2000 provides. In Windows 98, to deal with controller or multifunction devices, or to deal with nonstandard devices, you'll need to resort to more heroic means. You'll supply a function driver for your main device and supply separate function drivers for the child devices that connect to the main device. The main device's function driver will act like a miniature bus driver by enumerating the child devices and providing default handling for PnP and power requests. Writing a full-fledged bus driver is a large undertaking, and I don't intend to attempt a description of the process here. I will, however, describe the basic mechanisms you use for enumerating child devices. This information will allow you to write drivers for controller or multifunction devices that don't fit the standard molds provided by Microsoft.

Overall Architecture

In Chapter 2, Figure 2-2 (on page 23) illustrates the topology of device objects when a parent device, such as bus driver, has children. Controller and multifunction devices use a similar topology. The parent device plugs into a standard bus. The driver for the standard bus detects the parent, and the PnP Manager configures it just like any ordinary device—up to a point. After it starts the parent device, the PnP Manager sends a Plug and Play request with the minor function code IRP_MN_QUERY_DEVICE_RELATIONS to learn the so-called bus relations of the parent device. This query occurs for *all* devices, actually, because the PnP Manager doesn't know yet whether the device has children.

In response to the bus relations query, the parent device's function driver locates or creates additional device objects. Each of these objects becomes the PDO at the bottom of the stack for one of the child devices. The PnP Manager will go on to load the function and filter drivers for the child devices, whereupon you end up with a picture like that in Figure 2-2.

The driver for the parent device has to play two roles. In one role, it's the functional device object (FDO) driver for the controller or multifunction device. In the other role, it's the PDO driver for its child devices. In its FDO role, it handles PnP and power requests in the way function drivers normally handle them. In its PDO role, however, it acts as the driver of last resort for PnP and power requests.

Creating Child Device Objects

Somewhere along the way, perhaps at the time it processes IRP_MN_START_DEVICE, the parent driver, in its FDO role, needs to create one or more physical device objects for its children, and it needs to keep track of them for later. The only major complication at this early stage is this: both the FDO and all the PDOs belong to the same driver object, which means that IRPs directed to any of these device objects will come to one set of dispatch routines. The driver needs to handle PnP and power IRPs differently for FDOs and PDOs. Consequently, you need to provide a way for a dispatch function to easily distinguish between an FDO and one of the child PDOs. I dealt with this complication by defining two device extension structures with a common beginning, as follows:

```
// The FDO extension:

typedef struct _DEVICE_EXTENSION {
  ULONG flags;

  ...
  } DEVICE_EXTENSION, *PDEVICE_EXTENSION;

// The PDO extension:

typedef struct _PDO_EXTENSION {
  ULONG flags;

  ...
  } PDO_EXTENSION, *PPDO_EXTENSION;

// The common part:

typedef struct _COMMON_EXTENSION {
  ULONG flags;
  } COMMON_EXTENSION, *PCOMMON_EXTENSION;

#define ISPDO 0x00000001
```

The dispatch routine for IRP_MJ_PNP then looks like this:

```
NTSTATUS DispatchPnp(PDEVICE_OBJECT DeviceObject, PIRP Irp)
  {
  PCOMMON_EXTENSION pcx =
    (PCOMMON_EXTENSION) DeviceObject->DeviceExtension;
  if (pcx->flags & ISPDO)
    return DispatchPnpPdo(DeviceObject, Irp);
  else
    return DispatchPnpFdo(DeviceObject, Irp);
  }
```

MULFUNC, which is available on the companion disc, is a very lame multifunction device: it has just two children, and we always know what they are. I just called them A and B. MULFUNC executes the following code—with more error checking than what I'm showing you here—at IRP_MN_START_DEVICE time to create PDOs for A and B:

```
NTSTATUS StartDevice(PDEVICE_OBJECT fdo, ...)
  {
  PDEVICE_EXTENSION pdx = (PDEVICE_EXTENSION) fdo->DeviceExtension;
  CreateChild(pdx, CHILDTYPEA, &pdx->ChildA);
  CreateChild(pdx, CHILDTYPEB, &pdx->ChildB);
  return STATUS_SUCCESS;
  }
```

```
NTSTATUS CreateChild(PDEVICE_EXTENSION pdx, ULONG flags,
  PDEVICE_OBJECT* ppdo)
  {
  PDEVICE_OBJECT child;
  IoCreateDevice(pdx->DriverObject, sizeof(PDO_EXTENSION),
    NULL, FILE_DEVICE_UNKNOWN, FILE_AUTOGENERATED_DEVICE_NAME,
    FALSE, &child);
  PPDO_EXTENSION px = (PPDO_EXTENSION) child->DeviceExtension;
  px->flags = ISPDO | flags;
  px->DeviceObject = child;
  px->Fdo = pdx->DeviceObject;
  child->Flags &= ~DO_DEVICE_INITIALIZING;
  *ppdo = child;
  return STATUS_SUCCESS;
  }
```

1. CHILDTYPEA and CHILDTYPEB are additional flag bits for the **flags** member that begins the common device extension. If you were writing a true bus driver, you wouldn't create the child PDOs here—you'd enumerate your actual hardware in response to an IRP_MN_QUERY_ DEVICE_RELATIONS and create the PDOs then.

2. We're creating a named device object here, but we're asking the system to automatically generate the name by supplying the FILE_ AUTOGENERATED_DEVICE_NAME flag in the **DeviceCharacteristics** argument slot.

The end result of the creation process is two pointers to device objects (ChildA and ChildB) in the device extension for the parent device's FDO.

Telling the PnP Manager About Our Children

The PnP Manager inquires about the children of every device by sending an IRP_MN_ QUERY_DEVICE_RELATIONS request with a type code of **BusRelations**. Wearing its FDO hat, the parent driver responds to this request with code like the following:

```
NTSTATUS HandleQueryRelations(PDEVICE_OBJECT fdo, PIRP Irp)
  {
  PDEVICE_EXTENSION pdx = ...;
  PIO_STACK_LOCATION stack = ...;
  if (stack->Parameters.QueryDeviceRelations.Type != BusRelations)
    return DefaultPnpHandler(fdo, Irp);
  PDEVICE_RELATIONS newrel = (PDEVICE_RELATIONS)
    ExAllocatePool(PagedPool, sizeof(DEVICE_RELATIONS)
    + sizeof(PDEVICE_OBJECT));
  newrel->Count = 2;
  newrel->Objects[0] = pdx->ChildA;
  newrel->Objects[1] = pdx->ChildB;
  ObReferenceObject(pdx->ChildA);
  ObReferenceObject(pdx->ChildB);
  Irp->IoStatus.Information = (ULONG_PTR) newrel;
  Irp->IoStatus.Status = STATUS_SUCCESS;
  return DefaultPnpHandler(fdo, Irp);
  }
```

1. This IRP can concern several types of relations besides the bus relations we're interested in here. We simply delegate these other queries to the bus driver for the underlying hardware bus.

2. Here, we allocate a structure that will contain two device object pointers. The DEVICE_RELATIONS structure ends in an array with a dimension of 1, so we need only add on the size of an additional pointer when we calculate the amount of memory to allocate.

3. We call **ObReferenceObject** to increment the reference counts associated with each of the device objects we put into the DEVICE_RELATIONS array. The PnP Manager will dereference the objects at an appropriate time.

4. We need to pass this request down to the real bus driver in case it or some lower filter knows additional facts that we didn't know. This IRP uses an unusual protocol for pass-down and completion. You set the **IoStatus** as shown here if you actually handle the IRP; otherwise, you leave the IoStatus alone. Note the use of the **Information** field to contain a pointer to the DEVICE_RELATIONS structure. In other situations we've encountered in this book, the Information field has always held a number.

I glossed over an additional complication in the preceding code fragment that you'll notice in the code sample. An upper filter might have already installed a list of device objects in the IoStatus.Information field of the IRP. We must not lose that list. Rather, we must extend it by adding our own two device object pointers.

The PnP Manager automatically sends a query for bus relations at start time. You can force the query to be sent by calling this service function:

```
IoInvalidateDeviceRelations(pdx->Pdo, BusRelations);
```

You would make this call if you detected the arrival or departure of one of your child devices, for example.

PDO Handling of PnP Requests

Wearing its PDO driver hat, the parent driver must handle Plug and Play IRPs in a way that's very different from how a function driver would handle them. Table 6-5 summarizes the requirements using a shorthand to describe the actions to be taken.

PnP Request	How Handled
IRP_MN_START_DEVICE	Succeed
IRP_MN_QUERY_REMOVE_DEVICE	Succeed
IRP_MN_REMOVE_DEVICE	Succeed
IRP_MN_CANCEL_REMOVE_DEVICE	Succeed
IRP_MN_STOP_DEVICE	Succeed
IRP_MN_QUERY_STOP_DEVICE	Succeed
IRP_MN_CANCEL_STOP_DEVICE	Succeed
IRP_MN_QUERY_DEVICE_RELATIONS	Special processing
IRP_MN_QUERY_INTERFACE	Ignore
IRP_MN_QUERY_CAPABILITIES	Delegate
IRP_MN_QUERY_RESOURCES	Succeed
IRP_MN_QUERY_RESOURCE_REQUIREMENTS	Succeed
IRP_MN_QUERY_DEVICE_TEXT	Succeed
IRP_MN_FILTER_RESOURCE_REQUIREMENTS	Succeed
IRP_MN_READ_CONFIG	Delegate
IRP_MN_WRITE_CONFIG	Delegate
IRP_MN_EJECT	Delegate
IRP_MN_SET_LOCK	Delegate
IRP_MN_QUERY_ID	Special processing
IRP_MN_QUERY_PNP_DEVICE_STATE	Delegate
IRP_MN_QUERY_BUS_INFORMATION	Delegate
IRP_MN_DEVICE_USAGE_NOTIFICATION	Delegate
IRP_MN_SURPRISE_REMOVAL	Succeed
Any other	Ignore

Table 6-5. *PDO driver handling of PnP requests.*

The parent should simply *succeed* many PnP IRPs without doing any particular processing:

```
NTSTATUS SucceedRequest(PDEVICE_OBJECT pdo, PIRP Irp)
  {
  Irp->IoStatus.Status = STATUS_SUCCESS;
  IoCompleteRequest(Irp, IO_NO_INCREMENT);
  return STATUS_SUCCESS;
  }
```

The only remarkable feature of this short subroutine is that it doesn't change the IoStatus.Information field of the IRP. The PnP Manager always initializes this field in some way before launching an IRP. In some cases, the field might be altered by a filter driver or the function driver to point to some data structure or another. It would be incorrect for the PDO driver to alter the field.

The parent driver can *ignore* certain IRPs. Ignoring an IRP is similar to failing it with an error code, except that the driver doesn't change the IRP's status fields:

```
NTSTATUS IgnoreRequest(PDEVICE_OBJECT pdo, PIRP Irp)
  {
  NTSTATUS status = Irp->IoStatus.Status;
  IoCompleteRequest(Irp, IO_NO_INCREMENT);
  return status;
  }
```

A miniature bus driver such as the one I'm discussing can simply *delegate* some PnP requests to the real bus driver that lies underneath the parent device's FDO. Delegation in this case is not quite as simple as just calling IoCallDriver because by the time we receive an IRP as a PDO driver, the I/O stack is generally exhausted. We must therefore create what I call a *repeater IRP* that we can send to the driver stack we occupy as FDO driver:

```
NTSTATUS RepeatRequest(PDEVICE_OBJECT pdo, PIRP Irp)
  {
  PPDO_EXTENSION pdx = (PPDO_EXTENSION) pdo->DeviceExtension;
  PDEVICE_OBJECT fdo = pdx->Fdo;
  PDEVICE_EXTENSION pfx = (PDEVICE_EXTENSION) fdo->DeviceExtension;
  PIO_STACK_LOCATION stack = IoGetCurrentIrpStackLocation(Irp);
```
①
```
  PDEVICE_OBJECT tdo = IoGetAttachedDeviceReference(fdo);
  PIRP subirp = IoAllocateIrp(tdo->StackSize + 1, FALSE);
```
②
```
  PIO_STACK_LOCATION substack = IoGetNextIrpStackLocation(subirp);
  substack->DeviceObject = tdo;
  substack->Parameters.Others.Argument1 = (PVOID) Irp;
```

(continued)

```
3    IoSetNextIrpStackLocation(subirp);
     substack = IoGetNextIrpStackLocation(subirp);
     RtlCopyMemory(substack, stack,
       FIELD_OFFSET(IO_STACK_LOCATION, CompletionRoutine));
     substack->Control = 0;
4    BOOLEAN needsvote = <I'll explain later>;
     IoSetCompletionRoutine(subirp, OnRepeaterComplete, (PVOID) needsvote,
       TRUE, TRUE, TRUE);
5    subirp->IoStatus.Status = STATUS_NOT_SUPPORTED;
     IoMarkIrpPending(Irp);
     IoCallDriver(tdo, subirp);
     return STATUS_PENDING
     }


   NTSTATUS OnRepeaterComplete(PDEVICE_OBJECT tdo, PIRP subirp, PVOID needsvote)
     {
6    ObDereferenceObject(tdo);
     PIO_STACK_LOCATION substack = IoGetCurrentIrpStackLocation(subirp);
7    PIRP Irp = (PIRP) substack->Parameters.Others.Argument1;
8    if (subirp->IoStatus.Status == STATUS_NOT_SUPPORTED)
       {
       if (needsvote)
         Irp->IoStatus.Status = STATUS_UNSUCCESSFUL;
       }
     else
       Irp->IoStatus = subirp->IoStatus;
9    IoFreeIrp(subirp);
10   IoCompleteRequest(Irp, IO_NO_INCREMENT);
11   return STATUS_MORE_PROCESSING_REQUIRED;
     }
```

1. We're going to send the repeater IRP to the topmost filter driver in the stack
    to which our FDO belongs. This service routine returns the address of the
    topmost device object, and it also adds a reference to the object to pre-
    vent the Object Manager from deleting the object for the time being.

2. When we allocate the IRP, we create an extra stack location in which we
    can record some context information for the completion routine we're
    going to install. The **DeviceObject** pointer we place in this extra location
    becomes the first argument to the completion routine.

3. Here, we initialize the first real stack location, which is the one that the
    topmost driver in the FDO stack will receive. Then we install our comple-
    tion routine. This is an instance in which we cannot use the standard
    IoCopyCurrentIrpStackLocationToNext macro to copy a stack location:
    we're dealing with two separate I/O stacks.

4. We need to plan ahead for how we're going to deal with the possibility that the parent device stack doesn't actually handle this repeater IRP. Our later treatment will depend on exactly which minor function of IRP we're repeating in a way I'll describe later on. Mechanically, what we do is calculate a Boolean value—I called it **needsvote**—and pass it as the context argument to our completion routine.

5. You always initialize the status field of a new PnP IRP to hold the special value STATUS_NOT_SUPPORTED. The Driver Verifier will bugcheck if you don't.

6. This statement is how we release our reference to the topmost device object in the FDO stack.

7. We save the address of the original IRP here.

8. This short section sets the completion status for the original IRP. Refer to the following main text for an explanation of what's going on here.

9. We allocated the repeater IRP, so we need to delete it.

10. We can complete the original IRP now that the FDO driver stack has serviced its clone.

11. We must return STATUS_MORE_PROCESSING_REQUIRED because the IRP whose completion we dealt with—the repeater IRP—has now been deleted.

The preceding code deals with a rather complex problem that afflicts the various PnP IRPs that MULFUNC is repeating on the parent device stack. The PnP Manager initializes PnP IRPs to contain STATUS_NOT_SUPPORTED. It can tell whether any driver actually handled one of these IRPs by examining the ending status. If the IRP completes with STATUS_NOT_SUPPORTED, the PnP Manager can deduce that no driver did anything with the IRP. If the IRP completes with any other status, the PnP Manager knows that some driver deliberately either failed or succeeded the IRP but didn't simply ignore it.

A driver like MULFUNC that creates a PnP IRP must follow the same convention by initializing IoStatus.Status to STATUS_NOT_SUPPORTED. As I remarked, the Driver Verifier will bugcheck if you forget to do this. But this initialization gives rise to the following problem: suppose one of the devices in the child stack (that is, above the PDO for the child device) changes IoStatus.Status to another value before passing a particular IRP down to us in our role as PDO driver. We will create a repeater IRP, pre-initialized with STATUS_NOT_SUPPORTED, and pass it down the parent stack (that is, the stack to which we belong in our role as FDO driver). If the repeater IRP completes with STATUS_NOT_SUPPORTED, what status should we use in completing the original IRP? It shouldn't be STATUS_NOT_SUPPORTED, because that would imply that none of the child-stack drivers processed the IRP (but one did, and changed the main IRP's status). That's where the **needsvote** flag comes in.

For some of the IRPs we repeat, we don't care whether a parent driver actually processes the IRP. We say (actually, the Microsoft developers say) that the parent drivers don't need to "vote" on the IRP. If you look carefully at **OnRepeaterComplete**, you'll see that we don't change the main IRP's ending status in this case. For other of the IRPs we repeat, we can't provide a real answer if the parent stack drivers ignore the IRP. For these IRPs, on which the parent must "vote," we fail the main IRP with STATUS_UNSUCCESSFUL. To see which IRPs belong to the "needs vote" class and which IRPs don't, take a look at **RepeatRequest** in the MULFUNC sample (specifically, in PlugPlayPdo.cpp).

If one of the parent drivers actually *does* process the repeater IRP, however, we copy the entire IoStatus field, which includes *both* the Status and Information values, into the main IRP. The Information field might contain the answer to a query, and this copy step is how we pass the answer upwards.

I did one other slightly subtle thing in RepeatRequest, and that is that I marked the IRP pending and returned STATUS_PENDING. Most PnP IRPs complete synchronously so that the call to IoCallDriver will most likely cause immediate completion of the IRP. So why mark the IRP pending and cause the I/O Manager unnecessary pain in the form of needing to schedule an APC as part of completing the main IRP? The reason is that if we don't return STATUS_PENDING from our dispatch function—recall that RepeatRequest is running as a subroutine below the dispatch function for IRP_MJ_PNP—we must return the exact same value that we use when we complete the IRP. Only our completion routine knows which value this will actually be after checking for STATUS_NOT_SUPPORTED and checking the **needsvote** flag.

Handling Device Removal

The PnP Manager is aware of the parent-child relationship between a parent's FDO and its children PDOs. Consequently, when the user removes the parent device, the PnP Manager automatically removes all the children. Oddly enough, though, the parent driver should *not* normally delete a child PDO when it receives an IRP_MN_REMOVE_DEVICE. The PnP Manager expects PDOs to persist until the underlying hardware is gone. A multifunction driver would therefore not delete the children PDOs until it's told to delete the parent FDO. A bus driver, however, would delete a child PDO when it receives IRP_MN_REMOVE_DEVICE after failing to report the device during an enumeration.

MULFUNC deletes the children PDOs when it processes the remove device event for its own FDO.

If you're trying to provide for a controller-type device (as opposed to the non-standard multifunction device I provided an example of), your controller driver needs some additional logic to actually enumerate devices. I've omitted that logic because my sample device's children are always present if the main device is present. And don't forget to restore power to your controller before trying to do the enumeration.

Handling IRP_MN_QUERY_ID

The most important of the PnP requests that a parent driver handles is IRP_MN_QUERY_ID. The PnP Manager issues this request in several forms to determine which device identifiers it will use to locate the INF file for a child device. You respond by returning (in IoStatus.Information) a MULTI_SZ value containing the requisite device identifiers. The MULFUNC device has two children with the (bogus) device identifiers *WCO0604 and *WCO0605—the fourth and fifth drivers for Chapter 6, you see. It handles the query in the following way:

```
NTSTATUS HandleQueryId(PDEVICE_OBJECT pdo, PIRP Irp)
  {
  PPDO_EXTENSION pdx = (PPDO_EXTENSION) pdo->DeviceExtension;
  PIO_STACK_LOCATION stack = IoGetCurrentIrpStackLocation(Irp);
  PWCHAR idstring;
  switch (stack->Parameters.QueryId.IdType)
    {
  case BusQueryInstanceID:
    idstring = L"0000";
    break;
  case BusQueryDeviceID:
    if (pdx->flags & CHILDTYPEA)
      idstring = LDRIVERNAME L"\\*WCO0604";
    else
      idstring = LDRIVERNAME L"\\*WCO0605";
    break;
  case BusQueryHardwareIDs:
    if (pdx->flags & CHILDTYPEA)
      idstring = L"*WCO0604";
    else
      idstring = L"*WCO0605";
    break;
  default:
    return CompleteRequest(Irp, STATUS_NOT_SUPPORTED, 0);
    }
  ULONG nchars = wcslen(idstring);
  ULONG size = (nchars + 2) * sizeof(WCHAR);
  PWCHAR id = (PWCHAR) ExAllocatePool(PagedPool, size);
  wcscpy(id, idstring);
  id[nchars + 1] = 0;
  return CompleteRequest(Irp, STATUS_SUCCESS, (ULONG_PTR) id);
  }
```

1. The *instance* identifier is a single string value that uniquely identifies a device of a particular type on a bus. Using a constant such as "0000" will not work if more than one device of the parent type can appear in the computer.

2. The *device* identifier is a single string of the form "enumerator\type" and basically supplies two components in the name of the hardware registry key. Our ChildA device's hardware key will be in …\Enum\Mulfunc\ *WCO0604\0000, for example.

3. The *hardware* identifiers are strings that uniquely identify a type of device. In this case, I just made up the pseudo-EISA (Extended Industry Standard Architecture) identifiers *WCO0604 and *WCO0605.

> **NOTE** Be sure to use your own name in place of MULFUNC if you construct a device identifier in the manner I showed you here. To emphasize that you shouldn't just copy my sample program's name in a hard-coded constant, I wrote the code to use the manifest constant LDRIVERNAME, which is defined in the DRIVER.H file in the MULFUNC project.

The Windows 98 PnP Manager will tolerate your supplying the same string for a device identifier as you do for a hardware identifier, but the Windows 2000 PnP Manager won't. I learned the hard way to supply a made-up enumerator name in the device ID. Calling **IoGetDeviceProperty** to get the PDO's enumerator name leads to a bug check because the PnP Manager ends up working with a NULL string pointer. Using the parent's enumerator name—ROOT in the case of the MULFUNC sample— leads to the bizarre result that the PnP Manager brings the child devices back after you delete the parent!

Handling IRP_MN_QUERY_DEVICE_RELATIONS

The last PnP request to consider is IRP_MN_QUERY_DEVICE_RELATIONS. Recall that the FDO driver answers this request by providing a list of child PDOs for a bus relations query. Wearing its PDO hat, however, the parent driver need only answer a request for the so-called target device relation by providing the address of the PDO:

```
NTSTATUS HandleQueryRelations(PDEVICE_OBJECT pdo, PIRP Irp)
  {
  PIO_STACK_LOCATION stack = IoGetCurrentIrpStackLocation(Irp);
  NTSTATUS status = Irp->IoStatus.Status;
  if (stack->Parameters.QueryDeviceRelations.Type ==
    TargetDeviceRelation)
    {
    PDEVICE_RELATIONS newrel = (PDEVICE_RELATIONS)
      ExAllocatePool(PagedPool, sizeof(DEVICE_RELATIONS));
    newrel->Count = 1;
    newrel->Objects[0] = pdo;
    ObReferenceObject(pdo);
    status = STATUS_SUCCESS;
    Irp->IoStatus.Information = (ULONG_PTR) newrel;
    }
  Irp->IoStatus.Status = status;
  IoCompleteRequest(Irp, IO_NO_INCREMENT);
  return
```

Handling Child Device Resources

If your device is a controller type, the child devices that plug into it presumably claim their own I/O resources. If you have an automated way to discover the devices' resource requirements, you can return a list of them in response to an IRP_MN_ QUERY_RESOURCE_REQUIREMENTS request. If there is no automated way to discover the resource requirements, the child device's INF file should have a LogConfig section to establish them.

If you're dealing with a multifunction device, chances are that the parent device claims all the I/O resources that the child functions use. If the child functions have separate WDM drivers, you have to devise a way to separate the resources by function and let each function driver know which ones belong to it. This is not simple. The PnP Manager normally tells a function driver about its resource assignments in an IRP_MN_START_DEVICE request. (See the detailed discussion in the next chapter.) There's no normal way for you to force the PnP Manager to use some of *your* resources instead of the ones it assigns, though. Note that responding to a requirements query or a filter request doesn't help because those requests deal with requirements that the PnP Manager will then go on to satisfy using new resources.

Microsoft's MF.SYS driver deals with resource subdivision by using some internal interfaces with the system's resource arbitrators that aren't accessible to us as third-party developers. There are two different ways of subdividing resources: one that works in Windows 2000 and another one that works in Windows 98. Since we can't do what MF.SYS does, we need to find some other way to suballocate resources owned by the parent device. I haven't actually tried to implement either of the two suggestions I'm about to float, but I'm interested in hearing from any reader who carries these ideas further.

If you can control all of the child device function drivers, your parent driver could export a direct-call interface. Child drivers would obtain a pointer to the interface descriptor by sending an IRP_MN_QUERY_INTERFACE request to the parent driver. They would call functions in the parent driver at start device and stop device time to obtain and release resources that the parent actually owns.

If you can't modify the function drivers for your child devices, I believe you could solve the resource subdivision problem by installing a tiny upper filter—see Chapter 9—above each of the child device's FDOs. The only purpose of the filter is to plug in a list of assigned resources to each IRP_MN_START_DEVICE. The filter could communicate via a direct-call interface with the parent driver.

PnP Notifications

Windows 2000 and Windows 98 provide a way to notify both user-mode and kernel-mode components of particular Plug and Play events. Windows 95 has a WM_ DEVICECHANGE message that user-mode programs could process to monitor, and sometimes control, hardware and power changes in the system. The newer operating systems build on WM_DEVICECHANGE to allow user-mode programs to easily detect when some driver enables or disables a registered device interface. Kernel-mode drivers can also register for similar notifications.

> **NOTE** Refer to the documentation for WM_DEVICECHANGE, Register-DeviceNotification, and UnregisterDeviceNotification in the Platform SDK. I'll give you examples of using this message and these APIs, but I won't explain all possible uses of them. Some of the illustrations that follow also assume you're comfortable programming with Microsoft Foundation Classes.

Extensions to WM_DEVICECHANGE

An application with a window can subscribe for WM_DEVICECHANGE messages related to a specific interface GUID (globally unique identifier). Here's an example, drawn from the AUTOLAUNCH sample described in Chapter 12, "Installing Device Drivers," of how to do this:

```
int CAutoLaunch::OnCreate(LPCREATESTRUCT csp)
  {
  DEV_BROADCAST_DEVICEINTERFACE filter = {0};
  filter.dbcc_size = sizeof(filter);
  filter.dbcc_devicetype = DBT_DEVTYP_DEVICEINTERFACE;
  filter.dbcc_classguid = GUID_AUTOLAUNCH_NOTIFY;
  HDEVNOTIFY hNotification = RegisterDeviceNotification(m_hWnd,
    (PVOID) &filter, DEVICE_NOTIFY_WINDOW_HANDLE);
  ...
  }
```

The key statement here is the call to **RegisterDeviceNotification**, which asks the PnP Manager to send our window a WM_DEVICECHANGE message whenever anyone enables or disables a GUID_AUTOLAUNCH_NOTIFY interface. So, suppose a device driver calls **IoRegisterDeviceInterface** with this interface GUID during its AddDevice function. We're asking to be notified when that driver calls **IoSetDeviceInterfaceState** to either enable or disable that registered interface.

> **NOTE** The Platform SDK documentation tells you to call UnregisterDevice-Notification to unregister the notification handle you get back from Register-DeviceNotification. You should certainly do so in Windows 2000, but not in Windows 98. Although Windows 98 supports RegisterDeviceNotification as a way to subscribe for WM_DEVICECHANGE messages pertaining to a specific device interface, UnregisterDeviceNotification seems to destabilize the system. Just calling this function led to a number of random crashes during my own testing. I eventually just stopped calling UnregisterDeviceNotification and nothing bad seemed to happen as a result.

The handler for WM_DEVICECHANGE messages would be something like this:

```
BOOL CAutoLaunch::OnDeviceChange(UINT evtype, DWORD dwData)
  {
  _DEV_BROADCAST_HEADER* dbhdr = (_DEV_BROADCAST_HEADER*) dwData;
  if (!dbhdr || dbhdr->dbcd_devicetype != DBT_DEVTYP_DEVICEINTERFACE)
    return TRUE;
  PDEV_BROADCAST_DEVICEINTERFACE p =
    (PDEV_BROADCAST_DEVICEINTERFACE) dbhdr;
  CString devname = p->dbcc_name;
  if (evtype == DBT_DEVICEARRIVAL)
    <handle arrival>
  else if (evtype == DBT_DEVICEREMOVECOMPLETE)
    <handle removal>
  return TRUE;
  }
```

This handler ignores all messages that don't pertain to device interfaces. The **devname** variable will be the symbolic link name for the device that's arriving or departing. (This is the same name you obtain with **SetupDiGetDeviceInterfaceDetail** and pass to **CreateFile**.) Refer to Chapter 12 for details about how you can use various SetupDi*Xxx* APIs to learn interesting information about the new device.

Knowing When to Close a Device Handle

The PnP Manager won't be able to remove your device object while an application has a handle open. To permit removal to occur, your driver has to somehow induce applications with open handles to close them. A variation on the device interface notification change message considered in the previous section comes to your rescue here.

Once the application has a handle to your device, it should call RegisterDeviceNotification to register for *handle* notifications. (See TESTDLG.CPP in the TEST subdirectory of the PNPEVENT sample on the companion disc.)

```
DEV_BROADCAST_HANDLE filter = {0};
filter.dbch_size = sizeof(filter);
filter.dbch_devicetype = DBT_DEVTYP_HANDLE;
filter.dbch_handle = m_hDevice; // ç the device handle
HDEVNOTIFY hNotify = RegisterDeviceNotification(m_hWnd,
  &filter, DEVICE_NOTIFY_WINDOW_HANDLE);
```

Now the application can be on the lookout for a WM_DEVICECHANGE with an event code (**wParam**) equal to DBT_DEVICEQUERYREMOVE and a **devicetype** of DBT_DEVTYP_HANDLE. That message means that the interface is about to be

disabled, and you should therefore close your handles. You should also unconditionally return TRUE from your message handler.

> **NOTE** According to the Platform SDK documentation, you can return
> BROADCAST_QUERY_DENY in response to a DBT_DEVICEQUERYREMOVE
> message. This special return value supposedly means you don't want the de-
> vice removed or disabled after all. I've encountered wildly different results from
> attempting this in various versions of Windows 98 and Windows 2000. I would
> recommend that you program applications to always succeed this query.

THE PNPEVENT SAMPLE

The PNPEVENT sample driver (or, more properly, the TEST program that's part
of the sample) illustrates how to use WM_DEVICECHANGE for detecting the
arrival and departure of a registered interface and how to know when you must
close a handle to allow a device to be disabled or removed. You can launch
the TEST program either before or after you install the PNPEVENT "device" via
the hardware wizard.

You'll notice a Send Event button in the test program dialog. Clicking that
button causes the driver to signal a custom PnP event. I'll discuss custom events
a bit further on. I've never succeeded in getting a user-mode notification about
a custom event, though, so nothing will appear to happen when you click this
button unless you also happen to be running PNPMON's test program. (See the
PNPMON sample on the companion disc.)

Notifications to Windows 2000 Services

Windows 2000 service programs can also subscribe for PnP notifications. The service
should call **RegisterServiceCtrlHandlerEx** to register an extended control handler
function. Then it can register for service control notifications about device interface
changes. For example, take a look at the following code (and see the AUTOLAUNCH
sample).

```
DEV_BROADCAST_DEVICEINTERFACE filter = {0};
filter.dbcc_size = sizeof(filter);
filter.dbcc_devicetype = DBT_DEVTYPE_DEVICEINTERFACE;
filter.dbcc_classguid = GUID_AUTOLAUNCH_NOTIFY;
m_hNotification = RegisterDeviceNotification(m_hService,
  (PVOID) &filter, DEVICE_NOTIFY_SERVICE_HANDLE);
```

Here, **m_hService** is a service handle provided by the service manager when it starts your service, and DEVICE_NOTIFY_SERVICE_HANDLE indicates that you're registering for service control notifications instead of window messages. After receiving a SERVICE_CONTROL_STOP command, you want to unregister the notification handle:

```
UnregisterDeviceNotification(m_hNotification);
```

When a PnP event involving the interface GUID occurs, the system calls your extended service control handler function:

```
DWORD __stdcall HandlerEx(DWORD ctlcode, DWORD evtype,
  PVOID evdata, PVOID context)
  {
  }
```

where **ctlcode** will equal SERVICE_CONTROL_DEVICEEVENT, **evtype** will equal DBT_DEVICEARRIVAL or one of the other DBT_*Xxx* codes, **evdata** will be the address of a Unicode version of the DEV_BROADCAST_DEVICEINTERFACE structure, and **context** will be whatever context value you specified in your call to the RegisterServiceCtrlHandlerEx function.

Kernel-Mode Notifications

WDM drivers can use **IoRegisterPlugPlayNotification** to subscribe for interface and handle notifications. Here's an exemplary statement from the PNPMON sample driver that registers for notifications about the arrival and departure of an interface GUID designated by an application—PNPMON's TEST.EXE in this case—via an I/O control (IOCTL) operation:

```
status = IoRegisterPlugPlayNotification
  (EventCategoryDeviceInterfaceChange,
  PNPNOTIFY_DEVICE_INTERFACE_INCLUDE_EXISTING_INTERFACES,
  &p->guid, pdx->DriverObject,
  (PDRIVER_NOTIFICATION_CALLBACK_ROUTINE) OnPnpNotify,
  reg, &reg->InterfaceNotificationEntry);
```

The first argument indicates that we want to receive notifications whenever something enables or disables a specific interface GUID. The second argument is a flag indicating that we want to receive callbacks right away for all instances of the interface GUID that are already enabled. This flag allows us to start after some or all of the drivers that export the interface in question and still receive notification callbacks about those interfaces. The third argument is the interface GUID in question. In this case, it comes to us via an IOCTL from an application. The fourth argument is the address of our driver object. The PnP Manager adds a reference to the object so that we can't be unloaded while we have any notification handles outstanding. The fifth argument is the address of a notification callback routine. The sixth argument is a context parameter for the callback routine. In this case, I specified the address of a structure (**reg**) that contains information relative to this registration call. The seventh and final argument gives the address of a variable where the PnP Manager should record a notification handle. We will eventually call **IoUnregisterPlugPlayNotification** with the notification handle.

You need to call IoUnregisterPlugPlayNotification to close the registration handle. Since IoRegisterPlugPlayNotification adds a reference to your driver object, it won't do you any particular good to put this call in your **DriverUnload** routine. DriverUnload won't be called until the reference count drops to 0, which will never happen if DriverUnload itself has the unregistration calls. This problem isn't hard to solve—you just need to pick an appropriate time to unregister, such as when you notice the last interface of a particular type being removed or in response to an IOCTL request from an application.

Given a symbolic link name for an enabled interface, you can also request notifications about changes to the device named by the link. For example:

```
PUNICODE_STRING SymbolicLinkName; // ← input to this process
PDEVICE_OBJECT DeviceObject; // ← an output
PFILE_OBJECT FileObject; // ← another output
IoGetDeviceObjectPointer(&SymbolicLinkName, 0, &FileObject,
  &DeviceObject);
IoRegisterPlugPlayNotification(EventCategoryTargetDeviceChange, 0,
  FileObject, pdx->DriverObject,
  (PDRIVER_NOTIFICATION_CALLBACK_ROUTINE) OnPnpNotify,
  reg, &reg->HandleNotificationEntry);
```

You shouldn't put this code inside your PnP event handler, by the way. **IoGetDeviceObjectPointer** internally performs an open operation for the named device object. A deadlock might occur if the target device were to perform certain kinds of PnP operations. You should instead schedule a work item by calling **IoQueueWorkItem**. Chapter 9 has more information about work items. The PNPMON sample driver illustrates how to use a work item in this particular situation.

The notifications that result from these registration calls take the form of a call to the callback routine you specified:

```
NTSTATUS OnPnpNotify(PPLUGPLAY_NOTIFICATION_HEADER hdr,
  PVOID Context)
  {
  ...
  return STATUS_SUCCESS;
  }
```

The PLUGPLAY_NOTIFICATION_HEADER structure is the common header for several different structures that the PnP Manager uses for notifications:

```
typedef struct _PLUGPLAY_NOTIFICATION_HEADER {
  USHORT Version;
  USHORT Size;
  GUID Event;
  } PLUGPLAY_NOTIFICATION_HEADER,
  *PPLUGPLAY_NOTIFICATION_HEADER;
```

The **Event** GUID indicates what sort of event is being reported to you. See Table 6-6. The DDK header file WDMGUID.H contains the definitions of these GUIDs.

GUID Name	*Purpose of Notification*
GUID_HWPROFILE_QUERY_CHANGE	Okay to change to a new hardware profile?
GUID_HWPROFILE_CHANGE_CANCELLED	Change previously queried about has been cancelled
GUID_HWPROFILE_CHANGE_COMPLETE	Change previously queried about has been accomplished
GUID_DEVICE_INTERFACE_ARRIVAL	A device interface has just been enabled
GUID_DEVICE_INTERFACE_REMOVAL	A device interface has just been disabled
GUID_TARGET_DEVICE_QUERY_REMOVE	Okay to remove a device object?
GUID_TARGET_DEVICE_REMOVE_CANCELLED	Removal previously queried about has been cancelled
GUID_TARGET_DEVICE_REMOVE_COMPLETE	Removal previously queried about has been accomplished

Table 6-6. *PnP notification GUIDs.*

If you receive either of the DEVICE_INTERFACE notifications, you can cast the **hdr** argument to the callback function as a pointer to the following structure:

```
typedef struct _DEVICE_INTERFACE_CHANGE_NOTIFICATION {
  USHORT Version;
  USHORT Size;
  GUID Event;
  GUID InterfaceClassGuid;
  PUNICODE_STRING SymbolicLinkName;
  } DEVICE_INTERFACE_CHANGE_NOTIFICATION,
  *PDEVICE_INTERFACE_CHANGE_NOTIFICATION;
```

In the interface change notification structure, **InterfaceClassGuid** is the interface GUID, and **SymbolicLinkName** is the name of an instance of the interface that's just been enabled or disabled.

If you receive any of the TARGET_DEVICE notifications, you can cast the **hdr** argument as a pointer to this structure instead:

```
typedef struct _TARGET_DEVICE_REMOVAL_NOTIFICATION {
  USHORT Version;
  USHORT Size;
  GUID Event;
  PFILE_OBJECT FileObject;
  } TARGET_DEVICE_REMOVAL_NOTIFICATION,
  *PTARGET_DEVICE_REMOVAL_NOTIFICATION;
```

where **FileObject** is the file object for which you requested notifications.

Finally, if you receive any of the HWPROFILE_CHANGE notifications, **hdr** will really be a pointer to this structure:

```
typedef struct _HWPROFILE_CHANGE_NOTIFICATION {
  USHORT Version;
  USHORT Size;
  GUID Event;
  } HWPROFILE_CHANGE_NOTIFICATION,
  *PHWPROFILE_CHANGE_NOTIFICATION;
```

This doesn't have any more information than the header structure itself—just a different typedef name.

One way to use these notifications is to implement a filter driver for an entire class of device interfaces. (There is a standard way to implement filter drivers, either for a single driver or for a class of devices, based on setting entries in the registry. I'll discuss that subject in Chapter 9. Here, I'm talking about filtering all devices that register a particular interface, for which there's no other mechanism.) In your driver's DriverEntry routine, you'd register for PnP notifications about one or more interface GUIDs. When you receive the arrival notification, you use IoGetDeviceObjectPointer to open a file object and then register for target device notifications about the associated device. You also get a device object pointer from IoGetDeviceObjectPointer, and you can send IRPs to that device by calling IoCallDriver. Be on the lookout for the GUID_TARGET_DEVICE_QUERY_REMOVE notification because you have to dereference the file object before the removal can continue.

THE PNPMON SAMPLE

The PNPMON sample illustrates how to register for and process PnP notifications in kernel mode. To give you something you could run on your computer and actually see working, I designed PNPMON to simply pass notifications back to a user-mode application (named TEST—what else?). This is pretty silly, in that a user-mode application can get these notifications on its own by calling RegisterDeviceNotification.

PNPMON is different from the other driver samples in this book. It's intended to be dynamically loaded as a helper for a user-mode application. The other drivers we look at are intended to manage hardware, real or imagined. The user-mode application uses service manager API calls to load PNPMON, which creates exactly one device object in its DriverEntry routine so that the application can use **DeviceIoControl** to get things done in kernel mode. When the application exits, it closes its handle and calls the service manager to terminate the driver.

PNPMON also includes a Windows 98 VxD that the test application can dynamically load. It's possible to dynamically load a WDM driver in Windows 98 by using an undocumented function (_NtKernLoadDriver, if you care), but there's no way to unload a driver that you've loaded in this way. You don't need to resort to undocumented functions, though, because VxDs can call most of the WDM support routines directly by means of the WDMVXD import library in the Windows 98 DDK. Just about the only extra things you need to do in your VxD project are include WDM.H ahead of the VxD header files and add WDMVXD.CLB to the list of inputs to the linker. So PNPMON.VXD simply registers for PnP notifications as if it were a WDM driver and supports the same IOCTL interface that PNPMON.SYS supports.

Custom Notifications

I'll close this chapter by explaining how a WDM driver can generate custom PnP notifications. To signal a custom PnP event, create an instance of the custom notification structure and call one of **IoReportTargetDeviceChange** or **IoReportTargetDeviceChangeAsynchronous**. The asynchronous flavor returns immediately. The synchronous flavor waits—a long time, in my experience—until the notification has been sent. The notification structure has this declaration:

```
typedef struct _TARGET_DEVICE_CUSTOM_NOTIFICATION {
  USHORT Version;
  USHORT Size;
  GUID Event;
  PFILE_OBJECT FileObject;
  LONG NameBufferOffset;
  UCHAR CustomDataBuffer[1];
  } TARGET_DEVICE_CUSTOM_NOTIFICATION,
  *PTARGET_DEVICE_CUSTOM_NOTIFICATION;
```

Event is the custom GUID you've defined for the notification. **FileObject** is NULL—the PnP Manager will be sending notifications to drivers who opened file objects for the same PDO as you specify in the **IoReport***Xxx* call. **CustomDataBuffer** contains whatever binary data you elect followed by Unicode string data. **NameBufferOffset** is −1 if you don't have any string data; otherwise, it's the length of the binary data that precedes the strings. You can tell how big the total data payload is by subtracting the field offset of CustomDataBuffer from the **Size** value.

Here's how PNPEVENT generates a custom notification when you press the Send Event button in the associated test dialog:

```
struct _RANDOM_NOTIFICATION
  : public _TARGET_DEVICE_CUSTOM_NOTIFICATION {
  WCHAR text[14];
  };
...
_RANDOM_NOTIFICATION notify;
notify.Version = 1;
notify.Size = sizeof(notify);
notify.Event = GUID_PNPEVENT_EVENT;
notify.FileObject = NULL;
notify.NameBufferOffset = FIELD_OFFSET(RANDOM_NOTIFICATION, text)
  - FIELD_OFFSET(RANDOM_NOTIFICATION, CustomDataBuffer);
*(PULONG)(notify.CustomDataBuffer) = 42;
wcscpy(notify.text, L"Hello, world!");
IoReportTargetDeviceChangeAsynchronous(pdx->Pdo, &notify, NULL, NULL);
```

That is, PNPEVENT generates a custom notification whose data payload contains the number **42** followed by the string, **Hello, world!**.

Incidentally, if you want to use the asynchronous reporting API, which I recommend because it returns immediately, you must include NTDDK.H instead of WDM.H and you must link with *both* WDM.LIB and NTOSKRNL.LIB.

The notification shows up in any driver that registered for target device notifications pertaining to a file object for the same PDO. If your notification callback routine gets a notification structure with a nonstandard GUID in the Event field, you can expect that it's somebody's custom notification GUID. You need to understand what the GUID means before you go mucking about in the CustomDataBuffer!

User-mode applications are supposed to be able to receive custom event notifications, too, but I've not been able to get that to work.

WINDOWS 98 COMPATIBILITY NOTES

Windows 98 never sends an IRP_MN_SURPRISE_REMOVAL request. Consequently, a WDM driver needs to treat an unexpected IRP_MN_REMOVE_DEVICE as indicating surprise removal. The code samples I showed you in this chapter accomplish that by calling AbortRequests and StopDevice when they get this IRP out of the blue.

Windows 98 fails calls to the IoReportTargetDeviceChange function with STATUS_NOT_IMPLEMENTED. It doesn't export the symbol IoReportTargetDeviceChangeAsynchronous at all; a driver that calls that function will simply fail to load in Windows 98. Refer to Appendix A for information about how you can stub this and other missing support functions so as to be able to ship a single driver binary.

The architecture of Windows 98 doesn't lend itself at all well to blocking in kernel mode while waiting for user-mode programs to do things. This fact bit me especially hard in connection with one of my USB sample drivers (USBINT). The test program for this sample opens a handle and issues an asynchronous DeviceIoControl call. If you now unplug the device, what's *supposed* to happen is this: the driver receives an IRP_MN_SURPRISE_REMOVAL, whereupon it cancels the outstanding DeviceIoControl. The test program then closes its handle. Meanwhile, back in the driver, the REMOVE_DEVICE handler has blocked on a call to IoReleaseRemoveLockAndWait. When the IRP_MJ_CLOSE arrives, the driver will release the last claim on the remove lock and allow the device removal to proceed. This works just fine in Windows 2000, but it hangs Windows 98 because the test program never gets a chance to run in order to close its handle. (We don't get the SURPRISE_REMOVAL in Windows 98, but we do get a REMOVE_DEVICE that serves the same purpose.) A code path through QUERY_REMOVE does not hang the system, however. Moral: don't acquire the remove lock while a handle is open in Windows 98 if your device can be removed by the user without going through the Device Manager API.

Chapter 7

Reading and Writing Data

All the infrastructure I've described so far in this book leads up to this chapter, where I finally cover how to read and write data from a device. I'll discuss the service functions you call to perform these important operations on a device plugged in to one of the traditional buses, such as PCI (Peripheral Component Interconnect). Since many devices use a hardware interrupt to notify system software about I/O completion or exceptional events, I'll also discuss how to handle an interrupt. Interrupt processing normally requires you to schedule a deferred procedure call (DPC), so I'll describe the DPC mechanism, too. Finally, I'll tell you how to arrange direct memory access (DMA) transfers between your device and main memory.

CONFIGURING YOUR DEVICE

In the previous chapter, I discussed the various IRP_MJ_PNP requests that the Plug and Play (PnP) Manager sends you. IRP_MN_START_DEVICE is the vehicle for giving you information about the I/O resources that have been assigned by the PnP Manager for your use. I showed you how to obtain parallel lists of raw and translated resource descriptions and how to call a **StartDevice** helper function that would have the following prototype:

```
NTSTATUS StartDevice(PDEVICE_OBJECT fdo,
  PCM_PARTIAL_RESOURCE_LIST raw,
  PCM_PARTIAL_RESOURCE_LIST translated)
  {
  ...
  }
```

The time has now come to explain what to do with these resource lists. In summary, you'll extract descriptions of your assigned resources from the translated list and use those descriptions to create additional kernel objects that give you access to your hardware.

The CM_PARTIAL_RESOURCE_LIST structures contain a count and an array of CM_PARTIAL_RESOURCE_DESCRIPTOR structures, as illustrated in Figure 7-1. Each resource descriptor in the array has a **Type** member that indicates what type of resource it describes and some additional members that supply the particulars about some allocated resource. You're not going to be surprised by what you find in this array, by the way: if your device uses an IRQ and a range of I/O ports, you'll get two resource descriptors in the array. One of the descriptors will be for your IRQ, and the other will be for your I/O port range. Unfortunately, you can't predict in advance the order in which these descriptors will happen to appear in the array. Consequently, your StartDevice helper function has to begin with a loop that "flattens" the array by extracting resource values into a collection of local variables. You can later use the local variables to deal with the assigned resources in whatever order you please (which, it goes without saying, can be different from the order in which the PnP Manager chose to present them to you).

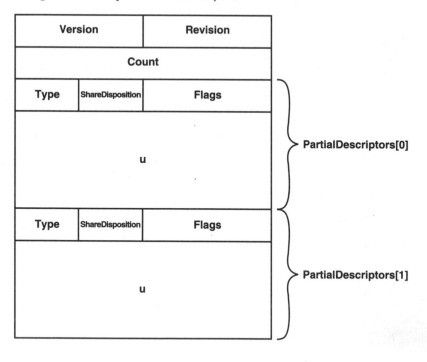

Figure 7-1. *Structure of a partial resource list.*

In sketch, then, your **StartDevice** function looks like this:

```
NTSTATUS StartDevice(PDEVICE_OBJECT fdo,
  PCM_PARTIAL_RESOURCE_LIST raw,
  PCM_PARTIAL_RESOURCE_LIST translated)
  {
  PDEVICE_EXTENSION pdx = (PDEVICE_EXTENSION) fdo->DeviceExtension;
  PCM_PARTIAL_RESOURCE_DESCRIPTOR resource =
    translated->PartialDescriptors;
  ULONG nres = translated->Count;
  <local variable declarations>
  for (ULONG i = 0; i < nres; ++i, ++resource)
    {
    switch (resource->Type)
      {
    case CmResourceTypePort:
      <save port info in local variables>
      break;
    case CmResourceTypeInterrupt:
      <save interrupt info in local variables>
      break;
    case CmResourceTypeMemory:
      <save memory info in local variables>
      break;
    case CmResourceTypeDma:
      <save DMA info in local variables>
      break;
      }
    }
  <use local variables to configure driver & hardware>
  IoSetDeviceInterfaceState(&pdx->ifname, TRUE);
  }
```

1. I'll use the **resource** pointer to point to the current resource descriptor in the variable-length array. By the end of the upcoming loop, it will point past the last valid descriptor.

2. The **Count** member of a resource list indicates how many resource descriptors are in the **PartialDescriptors** array.

3. You should declare appropriate local variables for each of the I/O resources you expect to receive. I'll detail what these would be later on when I discuss how to deal with each of the standard I/O resources.

4. Within the loop over resource descriptors, you use a **switch** statement to save resource description information into the appropriate local variables. In the text, I posited a device that needed just an I/O port range

and an interrupt, and such a device would expect to find resource types **CmResourceTypePort** and **CmResourceTypeInterrupt**. I'm showing the other two standard resource types—**CmResourceTypeMemory** and **CmResourceTypeDma**—for thoroughness.

5. Once outside the loop, the local variables you initialized in the various case labels will hold the resource information you need.

6. If you registered a device interface during AddDevice, this is the time to enable that interface so that applications can find you and open handles to your device.

If you have more than one resource of a particular type, you need to invent a way to tell the resource descriptors apart. To give a concrete (but entirely fictitious) example, suppose that your device uses one 4-KB range of memory for control purposes and a different 16-KB range of memory as a data capture buffer. You expect to receive two CmResourceTypeMemory resources from the PnP Manager. The control memory is the block that's 4 KB long, whereas the data memory is the block that's 16 KB long. If your device's resources have a distinguishing characteristic such as the size difference in the example, you'll be able to tell which resource is which.

When dealing with multiple resources of the same type, don't assume that the resource descriptors will be in the same order that your configuration space lists them in, and don't assume that the same bus driver will always construct resource descriptors in the same order on every platform or every release of the operating system. The first assumption is tantamount to assuming that the bus driver programmer adopted a particular algorithm, while the second is tantamount to assuming that all bus driver programmers think alike and will never change their minds.

I'll explain how to deal with each of the four standard I/O resource types at appropriate places in the remainder of this chapter. Table 7-1 presents an overview of the critical step(s) for each type of resource.

Resource Type	Overview
Port	Possibly maps port range; saves base port address in device extension
Memory	Maps memory range; saves base address in device extension
Dma	Calls IoGetDmaAdapter to create an adapter object
Interrupt	Calls IoConnectInterrupt to create an interrupt object that points to your interrupt service routine (ISR)

Table 7-1. *Overview of processing steps for I/O resources.*

ADDRESSING A DATA BUFFER

When an application initiates a read or write operation, it provides a data buffer by giving the I/O Manager a user-mode virtual address and length. As I said back in Chapter 3, "Basic Programming Techniques," a kernel driver hardly ever accesses memory using a user-mode virtual address because, in general, you can't pin down the thread context with certainty. Microsoft Windows 2000 gives you three ways to access a user-mode data buffer:

■ In the *buffered* method, the I/O Manager creates a system buffer equal in size to the user-mode data buffer. You work with this system buffer. The I/O Manager takes care of copying data between the user-mode buffer and the system buffer.

■ In the *direct* method, the I/O Manager locks the physical pages containing the user-mode buffer and creates an auxiliary data structure called a memory descriptor list (MDL) to describe the locked pages. You work with the MDL.

■ In the *neither* method, the I/O Manager simply passes the user-mode virtual address to you. You work—very carefully!—with the user-mode address.

Figure 7-2 illustrates the first two methods. The last method, of course, is kind of a nonmethod in that the system doesn't do anything to help you reach your data.

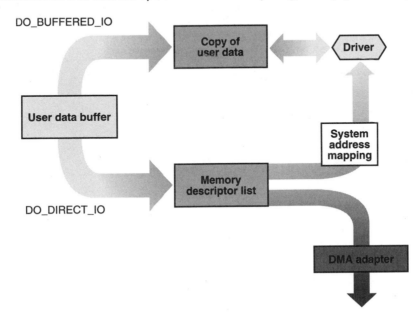

Figure 7-2. *Accessing user-mode data buffers.*

Specifying a Buffering Method

You specify your device's buffering method for reads and writes by setting certain flag bits in your device object shortly after you create it in your **AddDevice** function:

```
NTSTATUS AddDevice(...)
  {
  PDEVICE_OBJECT fdo;
  IoCreateDevice(..., &fdo);
  fdo->Flags |= DO_BUFFERED_IO;
          <or>
  fdo->Flags |= DO_DIRECT_IO;
          <or>
  fdo->Flags |= 0; // i.e., neither direct nor buffered
  }
```

You can't change your mind about the buffering method afterward. Filter drivers might copy this flag setting and will have no way to know if you *do* change your mind and specify a different buffering method.

The Buffered Method

When the I/O Manager creates an IRP_MJ_READ or IRP_MJ_WRITE request, it inspects the direct and buffered flags to decide how to describe the data buffer in the new I/O request packet (IRP). If DO_BUFFERED_IO is set, the I/O Manager allocates nonpaged memory equal in size to the user buffer. It saves the address and length of the buffer in two wildly different places, as shown in boldface in the following code fragment. You can imagine the I/O Manager code being something like this—this is not the actual Microsoft Windows NT source code.

```
PVOID uva;              // ← user-mode virtual buffer address
ULONG length;           // ← length of user-mode buffer

PVOID sva; = ExAllocatePoolWithQuota(NonPagedPoolCacheAligned, length);
if (writing)
  RtlCopyMemory(sva, uva, length);

Irp->AssociatedIrp.SystemBuffer = sva;

PIO_STACK_LOCATION stack = IoGetNextIrpStackLocation(Irp);
if (reading)
  stack->Parameters.Read.Length = length;
else
  stack->Parameters.Write.Length = length;
```

```
<code to send and await IRP>

if (reading)
  RtlCopyMemory(uva, sva, length);

ExFreePool(sva);
```

In other words, the system (copy) buffer address is in the IRP's **Associated-Irp.SystemBuffer** field, and the request length is in the **stack->Parameters** union. This process includes additional details that you and I don't need to know to write drivers. For example, the copy that occurs after a successful read operation actually happens during an asynchronous procedure call (APC) in the original thread context and in a different subroutine than the one that constructs the IRP. The I/O Manager saves the user-mode virtual address (my **uva** variable in the preceding fragment) in the IRP's **UserBuffer** field so that the copy step can find it. Don't count on either of these facts, though—they're subject to change at any time.

The I/O Manager also takes care of releasing the free storage obtained for the system copy buffer when something eventually completes the IRP.

The Direct Method

If you specified DO_DIRECT_IO in the device object, the I/O Manager creates a MDL to describe locked pages containing the user-mode data buffer. The MDL structure has the following declaration:

```
typedef struct _MDL {
  struct _MDL *Next;
  CSHORT Size;
  CSHORT MdlFlags;
  struct _EPROCESS *Process;
  PVOID MappedSystemVa;
  PVOID StartVa;
  ULONG ByteCount;
  ULONG ByteOffset;
} MDL, *PMDL;
```

Figure 7-3 illustrates the role of the MDL. The **StartVa** member gives the virtual address—valid only in the context of the user-mode process that owns the data—of the buffer. **ByteOffset** is the offset of the beginning of the buffer within a page frame, and **ByteCount** is the size of the buffer in bytes. The **Pages** array, which is not formally declared as part of the MDL structure, follows the MDL in memory and contains the numbers of the physical page frames to which the user-mode virtual addresses map.

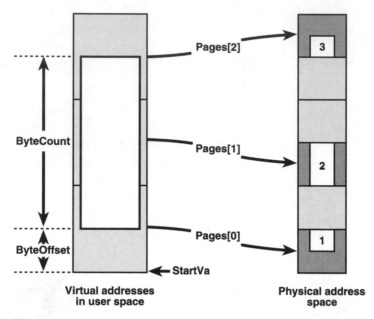

Figure 7-3. *The memory descriptor list structure.*

We never, by the way, access members of an MDL structure directly. We use macros and support functions instead—see Table 7-2.

Macro or Function	*Description*
IoAllocateMdl	Creates an MDL
IoBuildPartialMdl	Builds an MDL for a subset of an existing MDL
IoFreeMdl	Destroys an MDL
MmBuildMdlForNonPagedPool	Modifies an MDL to describe a region of kernel-mode nonpaged memory
MmGetMdlByteCount	Determines byte size of buffer
MmGetMdlByteOffset	Gets buffer offset within first page
MmGetMdlVirtualAddress	Gets virtual address
MmGetPhysicalAddress	Gets physical address corresponding to a virtual address within the MDL-described region

Table 7-2. *Macros and support functions for accessing an MDL.* (continued)

continued

Macro or Function	*Description*
MmGetSystemAddressForMdl	Creates a kernel-mode virtual address that maps to the same locations in memory
MmGetSystemAddressForMdlSafe	Same as MmGetSystemAddressForMdl but preferred in Windows 2000
MmInitializeMdl	(Re)initializes an MDL to describe a given virtual buffer
MmPrepareMdlForReuse	Reinitializes an MDL
MmProbeAndLockPages	Locks pages after verifying address validity
MmSizeOfMdl	Determines how much memory would be needed to create an MDL to describe a given virtual buffer
MmUnlockPages	Unlocks the pages for this MDL

You can imagine the I/O Manager executing code like the following to perform a direct-method read or write:

```
KPROCESSOR_MODE mode;   // ← either KernelMode or UserMode
PMDL mdl = IoAllocateMdl(uva, length, FALSE, TRUE, Irp);
MmProbeAndLockPages(mdl, mode,
  reading ? IoWriteAccess : IoReadAccess);

<code to send and await IRP>

MmUnlockPages(mdl);
ExFreePool(mdl);
```

The I/O Manager first creates an MDL to describe the user buffer. The third argument to **IoAllocateMdl** (FALSE) indicates this is the primary data buffer. The fourth argument (TRUE) indicates that the Memory Manager should charge the process quota. The last argument (**Irp**) specifies the IRP to which this MDL should be attached. Internally, IoAllocateMdl sets **Irp->MdlAddress** to the address of the newly created MDL, which is how you find it and how the I/O Manager eventually finds it so as to clean up.

The key event in this code sequence is the call to **MmProbeAndLockPages**, shown in boldface. This function verifies that the data buffer is valid and can be accessed in the appropriate mode. If we're writing to the device, we must be able to read the buffer. If we're reading from the device, we must be able to write to the buffer. In addition, the function locks the physical pages containing the data buffer and fills in the array of page numbers that follows the MDL proper in memory. In effect, a locked page becomes part of the nonpaged pool until as many callers unlock it as locked it in the first place.

The thing you'll most likely do with an MDL in a direct-method read or write is to pass it as an argument to something else. DMA transfers, for example, require an MDL for the **MapTransfer** step you'll read about later in this chapter in "Performing DMA Transfers." Universal serial bus (USB) reads and writes, to give another example, always work internally with an MDL, so you might as well specify DO_DIRECT_IO and pass the resulting MDLs along to the USB bus driver.

Incidentally, the I/O Manager does save the read or write request length in the stack->Parameters union. It's nonetheless customary for drivers to learn the request length directly from the MDL:

```
ULONG length = MmGetMdlByteCount(mdl);
```

The Neither Method

If you omit both the DO_DIRECT_IO and DO_BUFFERED_IO flags in the device object, you get the neither method by default. The I/O Manager simply gives you a user-mode virtual address and a byte count (as shown in boldface) and leaves the rest to you:

```
Irp->UserBuffer = uva;
PIO_STACK_LOCATION stack = IoGetNextIrpStackLocation(Irp);
if (reading)
  stack->Parameters.Read.Length = length;
else
  stack->Parameters.Write.Length = length;

<code to send and await IRP>
```

PORTS AND REGISTERS

Windows 2000 models driver access to many devices, as depicted in Figure 7-4. Generally, CPUs can have separate memory and I/O address spaces. To access a *memory-mapped* device, the CPU employs a memory-type reference such as a load or a store directed to a virtual address. The CPU translates the virtual address to a physical address by using a set of page tables. To access an *I/O-mapped* device, on the other hand, the CPU invokes some special mechanism such as the x86 IN and OUT instructions.

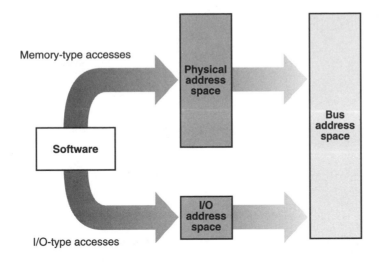

Memory-type accesses

I/O-type accesses

Figure 7-4. *Accessing ports and registers.*

Devices have bus-specific ways of decoding memory and I/O addresses. In the case of the PCI bus, a host bridge maps CPU physical memory addresses and I/O addresses to a bus address space that's directly accessible to devices. Flag bits in the device's configuration space determine whether the bridge maps the device's registers to a memory or an I/O address on CPUs that have both address spaces.

As I've said, some CPUs have separate memory and I/O address spaces. Intel architecture CPUs have both, for example. Other CPUs, such as the Alpha, have just a memory address space. If your device is I/O-mapped, the PnP Manager will give you port resources. If your device is memory-mapped, it will give you memory resources instead.

Rather than have you place reams of conditionally compiled code into your driver for all possible platforms, the Windows NT designers invented the hardware abstraction layer (HAL) to which I've alluded a few times in this book. The HAL provides functions that you use to access port and memory resources. See Table 7-3. As the table indicates, you can READ/WRITE either a single UCHAR/USHORT/ULONG or an array of them from or to a PORT/REGISTER. That makes 24 HAL functions in all that are used for device access. Since a WDM driver doesn't directly rely on the HAL for anything else, you might as well think of these 24 functions as being the entire public interface to the HAL.

Access Width	Functions for Port Access	Functions for Memory Access
8 bits	READ_PORT_UCHAR WRITE_PORT_UCHAR	READ_REGISTER_UCHAR WRITE_REGISTER_UCHAR
16 bits	READ_PORT_USHORT WRITE_PORT_USHORT	READ_REGISTER_USHORT WRITE_REGISTER_USHORT
32 bits	READ_PORT_ULONG WRITE_PORT_ULONG	READ_REGISTER_ULONG WRITE_REGISTER_ULONG
string of 8-bit bytes	READ_PORT_BUFFER_UCHAR WRITE_PORT_BUFFER_UCHAR	READ_REGISTER_BUFFER_UCHAR WRITE_REGISTER_BUFFER_UCHAR
string of 16-bit words	READ_PORT_BUFFER_USHORT WRITE_PORT_BUFFER_USHORT	READ_REGISTER_BUFFER_USHORT WRITE_REGISTER_BUFFER_USHORT
string of 32-bit double words	READ_PORT_BUFFER_ULONG WRITE_PORT_BUFFER_ULONG	READ_REGISTER_BUFFER_ULONG WRITE_REGISTER_BUFFER_ULONG

Table 7-3. *HAL functions for accessing ports and memory registers.*

What goes on inside these access functions is (obviously!) highly dependent on the platform. The Intel x86 version of READ_PORT_CHAR, for example, performs an IN instruction to read one byte from the designated I/O port. The Microsoft Windows 98 implementation goes so far as to overstore the driver's call instruction with an actual IN instruction in some situations. The Alpha version of this routine performs a memory fetch. The Intel x86 version of READ_REGISTER_UCHAR performs a memory fetch also; this function is macro'ed as a direct memory reference on the Alpha. The buffered version of this function (READ_REGISTER_BUFFER_UCHAR), on the other hand, does some extra work in the Intel x86 environment to be sure that all CPU caches get properly flushed when the operation finishes.

The whole point of having the HAL in the first place is so that you don't have to worry about platform differences or about the sometimes arcane requirements for accessing devices in the multitasking, multiprocessor environment of Windows 2000. Your job is quite simple: use a PORT call to access what you think is a port resource, and use a REGISTER call to access what you think is a memory resource.

Port Resources

I/O-mapped devices expose hardware registers that, on some CPU architectures (including Intel x86), are addressed by software using a special I/O address space. On other CPU architectures, no separate I/O address space exists and these registers are addressed using regular memory references. Luckily, you don't need to understand these addressing complexities. If your device requests a port resource, one iteration of your loop over the translated resource descriptors will find a CmResourceTypePort descriptor and you'll save three pieces of information.

```
typedef struct _DEVICE_EXTENSION {
  ...
  PUCHAR portbase;
  ULONG nports;
  BOOLEAN mappedport;
  ...} DEVICE_EXTENSION, *PDEVICE_EXTENSION;

PHYSICAL_ADDRESS portbase;    // base address of range
...
for (ULONG i = 0; i < nres; ++i, ++resource)
  {
  switch (resource->Type)
    {
  case CmResourceTypePort:
    portbase = resource->u.Port.Start;
    pdx->nports = resource->u.Port.Length;
    pdx->mappedport = (resource->Flags & CM_RESOURCE_PORT_IO) == 0;
    break;
    ...
    }
...
if (mappedport)
  {
  pdx->portbase = (PUCHAR) MmMapIoSpace(portbase, nports, MmNonCached);
  if (!pdx->portbase)
    return STATUS_NO_MEMORY;
  }
else
  pdx->portbase = (PUCHAR) portbase.QuadPart;
```

1. The resource descriptor contains a union named **u** that has substructures for each of the standard resource types. **u.Port** has information about a port resource. **u.Port.Start** is the beginning address of a contiguous range of I/O ports, and **u.Port.Length** is the number of ports in the range. The start address is a 64-bit PHYSICAL_ADDRESS value.

2. The **Flags** member of the resource descriptor for a port resource has the CM_RESOURCE_PORT_IO flag set if the CPU architecture has a separate I/O address space to which the given port address belongs.

3. If the CM_RESOURCE_PORT_IO flag was clear, as it will be on an Alpha and perhaps other RISC platforms, you must call **MmMapIoSpace** to obtain a kernel-mode virtual address by which the port can be accessed. The access will really employ a memory reference, but you'll still call the PORT flavor of HAL routines (READ_PORT_UCHAR and so on) from your driver.

4. If the CM_RESOURCE_PORT_IO flag was set, as it will be on an x86 platform, you do not need to map the port address. You'll call the PORT flavor of HAL routines from your driver when you want to access one of your
ports. The HAL routines demand a PUCHAR port address argument, which
is why we cast the base address to that type. The **QuadPart** reference,
by the way, results in your getting a 32-bit or 64-bit pointer, as appropriate to the platform for which you're compiling.

Whether or not the port address needs to be mapped via MmMapIoSpace, you'll
always call the HAL routines that deal with I/O port resources: READ_PORT_UCHAR,
WRITE_PORT_UCHAR, and so on. On a CPU that requires you to map a port address,
the HAL will be making memory references. On a CPU that doesn't require the
mapping, the HAL will be making I/O references; on an x86, this means using one
of the IN and OUT instruction family.

Your **StopDevice** helper routine has a small cleanup task to perform if you
happen to have mapped your port resource:

```
VOID StopDevice(...)
  {
  ...
  if (pdx->portbase && pdx->mappedport)
    MmUnmapIoSpace(pdx->portbase, pdx->nports);
  pdx->portbase = NULL;
  ...
  }
```

Memory Resources

Memory-mapped devices expose registers that software accesses using load and store
instructions. The translated resource value you get from the PnP Manager is a physical address, and you need to reserve virtual addresses to cover the physical memory.
Later on, you'll be calling HAL routines that deal with memory registers, such as
READ_REGISTER_UCHAR, WRITE_REGISTER_UCHAR, and so on. Your extraction
and configuration code would look like this fragment:

```
typedef struct _DEVICE_EXTENSION {
  ...
  PUCHAR membase;
  ULONG nbytes;
  ...} DEVICE_EXTENSION, *PDEVICE_EXTENSION;

PHYSICAL_ADDRESS membase;      // base address of range
...
for (ULONG i = 0; i < nres; ++i, ++resource)
  {
  switch (resource->Type)
```

```
      {
    case CmResourceTypeMemory:
      membase = resource->u.Memory.Start;
      pdx->nbytes = resource->u.Memory.Length;
      break;
    ...
      }
  ...
  pdx->membase = (PUCHAR) MmMapIoSpace(membase, pdx->nbytes,
    MmNonCached);
  if (!pdx->membase)
    return STATUS_NO_MEMORY;
```

1. Within the resource descriptor, **u.Memory** has information about a memory resource. **u.Memory.Start** is the beginning address of a contiguous range of memory locations, and **u.Memory.Length** is the number of bytes in the range. The start address is a 64-bit PHYSICAL_ADDRESS value. It's not an accident that the **u.Port** and **u.Memory** substructures are identical—it's on purpose, and you can rely on it being true if you want to.

2. You must call **MmMapIoSpace** to obtain a kernel-mode virtual address by which the memory range can be accessed.

Your **StopDevice** function unconditionally unmaps your memory resources:

```
VOID StopDevice(...)
  {
  ...
  if (pdx->membase)
    MmUnmapIoSpace(pdx->membase, pdx->nbytes);
  pdx->membase = NULL;
  ...
  }
```

SERVICING AN INTERRUPT

Many devices signal completion of I/O operations by asynchronously interrupting the processor. In this section, I'll discuss how you configure your driver for interrupt handling and how you service interrupts when they occur.

Configuring an Interrupt

You configure an interrupt resource in your StartDevice function by calling **IoConnectInterrupt** using parameters that you can simply extract from a CmResourceType-Interrupt descriptor. Your driver and device need to be entirely ready to work correctly when you call IoConnectInterrupt—you might even have to service an interrupt before the function returns—so you normally make the call near the end of the configuration process. Some devices have a hardware feature that allows you to prevent them from interrupting. If your device has such a feature, disable interrupts before calling IoConnectInterrupt and enable them afterward. The extraction and configuration code for an interrupt would look like this:

```
typedef struct _DEVICE_EXTENSION {
  ...
  PKINTERRUPT InterruptObject;
  ...} DEVICE_EXTENSION, *PDEVICE_EXTENSION;

ULONG vector;              // interrupt vector
KIRQL irql;                // interrupt level
KINTERRUPT_MODE mode;      // latching mode
KAFFINITY affinity;        // processor affinity
BOOLEAN irqshare;          // shared interrupt?
...
for (ULONG i = 0; i < nres; ++i, ++resource)
  {
  switch (resource->Type)
    {
  case CmResourceTypeInterrupt:
    irql = (KIRQL) resource->u.Interrupt.Level;
    vector = resource->u.Interrupt.Vector;
    affinity = resource->u.Interrupt.Affinity;
    mode = (resource->Flags == CM_RESOURCE_INTERRUPT_LATCHED)
      ? Latched : LevelSensitive;
    irqshare = resource->ShareDisposition == CmResourceShareShared;
    break;
  ...
    }
...
status = IoConnectInterrupt(&pdx->InterruptObject,
  (PKSERVICE_ROUTINE) OnInterrupt, (PVOID) pdx, NULL,
  vector, irql, irql, mode, irqshare, affinity, FALSE);
```

1. The **Level** parameter specifies the interrupt request level (IRQL) for this interrupt.

2. The **Vector** parameter specifies the hardware interrupt vector for this interrupt. We don't care what this number is, since we're just going to act as a conduit between the PnP Manager and IoConnectInterrupt. All that matters is that the HAL understand what the number means.

3. **Affinity** is a bit mask that indicates which CPUs will be allowed to handle this interrupt.

4. We need to tell IoConnectInterrupt whether our interrupt is edge-triggered or level-triggered. If the resource **Flags** are CM_RESOURCE_INTERRUPT_ LATCHED, we have an edge-triggered interrupt. Otherwise, we have a level-triggered interrupt.

5. Use this statement to discover whether your interrupt is shared.

In the call to IoConnectInterrupt at the end of this sequence, we will simply regurgitate the values we pulled out of the interrupt resource descriptor. The first argument (**&pdx->InterruptObject**) indicates where to store the result of the con- nection operation—namely, a pointer to a kernel interrupt object that describes your interrupt. The second argument (**OnInterrupt**) is the name of your interrupt service routine; I'll discuss ISRs a bit further on in this chapter. The third argument (**pdx**) is a context value that will be passed as an argument to the ISR each time your device interrupts. I'll have more to say about this context parameter later as well in "Select- ing an Appropriate Context Argument."

The fifth and sixth arguments (**vector** and **irql**) specify the interrupt vector number and interrupt request level, respectively, for the interrupt you're connecting. The eighth argument (**mode**) is either **Latched** or **LevelSensitive** to indicate whether the interrupt is edge-triggered or level-triggered. The ninth argument is TRUE if your interrupt is shared with other devices and FALSE otherwise. The tenth argument (**affinity**) is the processor affinity mask for this interrupt. The eleventh and final argument indicates whether the operating system needs to save the floating-point context when the device interrupts. Since you're not allowed to do floating-point cal- culations in an ISR on an x86 platform, a portable driver would always set this flag to FALSE.

I haven't yet described two other arguments to IoConnectInterrupt. These become important when your device uses more than one interrupt. In such a case, you would create spin locks for your interrupts and initialize them by calling **KeInitializeSpinLock**. You would also calculate the largest IRQL needed by any of your interrupts before connecting any of them. In each call to IoConnectInterrupt, you'd specify the address of the appropriate spin lock for the fourth argument (which is NULL in my example) and you'd specify the maximum IRQL for the seventh argument (which is **irql** in my example). This seventh argument indicates the IRQL used for synchronizing the in- terrupts, which you should make the maximum of all your interrupt IRQLs so that you're troubled by only one of your interrupts at a time.

If, however, your device uses only a single interrupt, you won't need a special spin lock (because the I/O Manager automatically allocates one for you) and the synchronization level for your interrupt will be the same as the interrupt IRQL.

Handling Interrupts

When your device generates an interrupt, the HAL selects a CPU to service the interrupt based on the CPU affinity mask you specified. It raises that CPU's IRQL to the appropriate synchronization level and claims the spin lock associated with your interrupt object. Then it calls your ISR, which would have the following skeletal form:

```
BOOLEAN OnInterrupt(PKINTERRUPT InterruptObject, PVOID Context)
  {
  if (<device not interrupting>)
    return FALSE;
  <handle interrupt>
  return TRUE;
  }
```

Windows NT's interrupt-handling mechanism assumes that hardware interrupts can be shared by many devices. Thus your first job in the ISR is to determine whether your device is interrupting at the present moment. If not, you return FALSE right away so that the HAL can send the interrupt to another device driver. If yes, you clear the interrupt at the device level and return TRUE. Whether the HAL then calls other drivers' ISRs depends on whether the device interrupt is edge-triggered or level-triggered and on other platform details.

Your main job in the ISR is to service your hardware to clear the interrupt. I'll have some general things to say about this job, but the details pretty much depend on how your hardware works. Once you've performed this major task, you return TRUE to indicate to the HAL that you've serviced a device interrupt.

Programming Restrictions in the ISR

ISRs execute at an IRQL higher than DISPATCH_LEVEL. All code and data used in an ISR must therefore be in nonpaged memory. Furthermore, the set of kernel-mode functions that an ISR can call is very limited.

Since an ISR executes at elevated IRQL, it freezes out other activities on its CPU that require the same or a lower IRQL. For best system performance, therefore, your ISR should execute as quickly as possible. Basically, do the minimum amount of work required to service your hardware and return. If there is additional work to do (such as completing an IRP), schedule a DPC to handle that work.

Despite the admonition you usually receive to do the smallest amount of work possible in your ISR, you don't want to carry that idea to an extreme. For example, if you're dealing with a device that interrupts to signal its readiness for the next output byte, go ahead and send the next byte directly from your ISR. It's fundamentally silly to schedule a DPC just to transfer a single byte. Remember that the end user wants you to service your hardware (or else he or she wouldn't have the hardware installed on the computer), and you are entitled to your fair share of system resources to provide that service.

But don't go crazy calculating pi to a thousand decimal places in your ISR, either (unless your device requires you to do something that ridiculous, and it probably doesn't). Good sense should tell you what the right balance of work between an ISR and a DPC routine should be.

Selecting an Appropriate Context Argument

In the call to IoConnectInterrupt, the third argument is an arbitrary context value that eventually shows up as the second argument to your ISR. You want to choose this argument so as to allow your ISR to execute as rapidly as possible; the address of your device object or of your device extension would be a good choice. The device extension is where you'll be storing items—such as your device's base port address—that you'll use in testing whether your device is currently asserting an interrupt. To illustrate, suppose that your device, which is I/O-mapped, has a status port at its base address and that the low-order bit of the status value indicates whether the device is currently trying to interrupt. If you adopt my suggestion, the first few lines of your ISR would read like this:

```
BOOLEAN OnInterrupt(PKINTERRUPT InterruptObject, PDEVICE_EXTENSION pdx)
  {
  UCHAR devstatus = READ_PORT_UCHAR(pdx->portbase);
  if (!(devstatus & 1))
    return FALSE;
  <etc.>
  }
```

The fully optimized code for this function will require only a few instructions to read the status port and test the low-order bit.

If you elect to use the device extension as your context argument, be sure to supply a cast when you call IoConnectInterrupt:

```
IoConnectInterrupt(..., (PKSERVICE_ROUTINE) OnInterrupt, ...);
```

If you omit the cast, the compiler will generate an exceptionally obscure error message because the second argument to your **OnInterrupt** routine (a PDEVICE_EXTENSION) won't match the prototype of the function pointer argument to IoConnect-Interrupt, which demands a PVOID.

Synchronizing Operations with the ISR

As a general rule, the ISR shares data and hardware resources with other parts of the driver. Anytime you hear the word *share,* you should immediately start thinking about synchronization problems. For example, a standard UART (universal asynchronous receiver-transmitter) device has a data port the driver uses for reading and writing data. You'd expect a serial port driver's ISR to access this port from time to time. Changing the baud rate also entails setting a control flag called the *divisor latch,* performing two single-byte write operations to this same data port, and then clearing the divisor latch. If the UART were to interrupt in the middle of changing the baud rate, you can see that a data byte intended to be transmitted could easily end up in the baud-rate divisor register or that a byte intended for the divisor register could end up being transmitted as data.

The system guards the ISR with a spin lock and with a relatively high IRQL—the device IRQL (DIRQL). To simplify the mechanics of obtaining the same spin lock and raising IRQL to the same level as an interrupt, the system provides this service function:

```
BOOLEAN result = KeSynchronizeExecution(InterruptObject,
  SynchRoutine, Context);
```

where **InterruptObject** (PKINTERRUPT) is a pointer to the interrupt object describing the interrupt we're trying to synchronize with, **SynchRoutine** (PKSYNCHRONIZE_ ROUTINE) is the address of a callback function in our driver, and **Context** (PVOID) is an arbitrary context parameter to be sent to the SynchRoutine as an argument. We use the generic term *synch critical section routine* to describe a subroutine that we call by means of **KeSynchronizeExecution**. The synch critical section routine has the following prototype:

```
BOOLEAN SynchRoutine(PVOID Context);
```

That is, it receives a single argument and returns a BOOLEAN result. When it gets control, the current CPU is running at the synchronization IRQL that the original call to IoConnectInterrupt specified, and it owns the spin lock associated with the interrupt. Consequently, interrupts from the device are temporarily blocked out, and the SynchRoutine can freely access data and hardware resources that it shares with the ISR.

KeSynchronizeExecution returns whatever value SynchRoutine returns, by the way. This gives you a way of providing a little bit—actually 8 bits, since BOOLEAN is declared as an unsigned character—of feedback from SynchRoutine to whatever calls KeSynchronizeExecution.

Deferred Procedure Calls

Completely servicing a device interrupt often requires you to perform operations that aren't legal inside an ISR or that are too expensive to carry out at the elevated IRQL of an ISR. To avoid these problems, the designers of Windows NT provided the deferred procedure call mechanism. The DPC is a general-purpose mechanism, but you use it most often in connection with interrupt handling. In the most common scenario, your ISR decides that the current request is complete and requests a DPC . Later on, the kernel calls your DPC routine at DISPATCH_LEVEL. While restrictions on what service routines you can call and on paging still apply, fewer restrictions apply because you're now running at a lower IRQL than inside the ISR. In particular, it's legal to call routines like **IoCompleteRequest** or **IoStartNextPacket** that are logically necessary at the end of an I/O operation.

Every device object gets a DPC object "for free." That is, the DEVICE_OBJECT has a DPC object—named, prosaically enough, **Dpc**—built in. You need to initialize this built-in DPC object shortly after you create your device object:

```
NTSTATUS AddDevice(...)
  {
  PDEVICE_OBJECT fdo;
  IoCreateDevice(..., &fdo);
  IoInitializeDpcRequest(fdo, DpcForIsr);
  ...
  }
```

IoInitializeDpcRequest is a macro in WDM.H that initializes the device object's built-in DPC object. The second argument is the address of the DPC procedure that I'll show you presently.

With your initialized DPC object in place, your ISR can request a DPC by using the following macro:

```
BOOLEAN OnInterrupt(...)
  {
  ...
  IoRequestDpc(pdx->DeviceObject, NULL, NULL);
  ...
  }
```

This call to **IoRequestDpc** places your device object's DPC object in a systemwide queue, as illustrated in Figure 7-5.

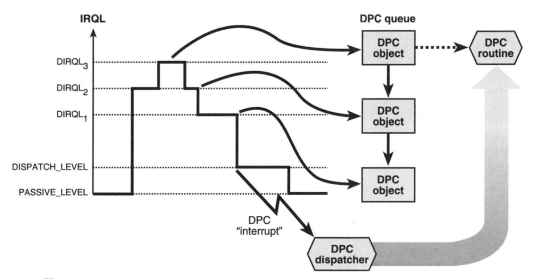

Figure 7-5. *Processing DPC requests.*

The two NULL parameters are context values that don't really have a good use in this particular situation. Later on, when no other activity is occurring at DISPATCH_LEVEL, the kernel removes your DPC object from the queue and calls your DPC routine, which has the following prototype:

```
VOID DpcForIsr(PKDPC Dpc, PDEVICE_OBJECT fdo, PIRP junk, PVOID Context)
  {
  }
```

What you do inside the DPC routine depends in great measure on how your device works. A likely task would be to complete the current IRP and release the next IRP from the queue. If you use the "standard model" for IRP queuing, the code would be as follows:

```
VOID DpcForIsr(...)
  {
  PIRP Irp = fdo->CurrentIrp;
  IoStartNextPacket(fdo, TRUE);
  IoCompleteRequest(Irp, <boost value>);
  }
```

The TRUE argument to **IoStartNextPacket** indicates that the next IRP is cancellable—meaning that the original call to **IoStartPacket** specified a cancel routine—and causes IoStartNextPacket to acquire and release the global cancel spin lock around its access to the device queue and **CurrentIrp**.

In this code fragment, we rely on the fact that the I/O Manager sets the device object's CurrentIrp field to point to the IRP it sends to our **StartIo** routine. The IRP we want to complete is the one that's the CurrentIrp when we commence the DPC routine. It's customary to call IoStartNextPacket before **IoCompleteRequest** so that we can get our device busy with a new request before we start the potentially long process of completing the current IRP.

If you use the DEVQUEUE object presented in the previous chapter for IRP queuing, the code would be similar:

```
VOID DpcForIsr(...)
  {
  PDEVICE_EXTENSION pdx = ...;
  PIRP Irp = GetCurrentIrp(&pdx->dqRead);
  StartNextPacket(&pdx->dqRead, fdo);
  IoCompleteRequest(Irp, <boost value>);
  }
```

DPC Scheduling

I've glossed over two fairly important details and a minor one about DPCs until now. The first important detail is implicit in the fact that you have a DPC *object* that gets put onto a queue by IoRequestDpc. If your device generates an additional interrupt before the DPC routine actually runs, and if your ISR requests another DPC, the kernel will simply ignore the second request. In other words, your DPC object will be on the queue one time no matter how many DPCs are requested by successive invocations of your ISR, and the kernel will call your callback routine only one time. During that one invocation, your DPC routine needs to accomplish all the work related to all the interrupts that have occurred since the last DPC.

As soon as the DPC dispatcher dequeues your DPC object, it's possible for something to queue it again, even while your DPC routine executes. This won't cause you any grief if the object happens to be queued on the same CPU both times. The second important detail about DPC processing, therefore, has to do with CPU affinity. Normally, the kernel queues a DPC object for handling on the same processor that requests the DPC—for example, the processor that just handled an interrupt and called IoRequestDpc. As soon as the DPC dispatcher dequeues the DPC object and calls your callback routine on one CPU, it's theoretically possible for your device to interrupt on a *different* CPU, which might end up requesting a DPC that could execute simultaneously on that different CPU. Whether simultaneous execution of your DPC routine poses a problem or not depends, obviously, on the details of your coding.

You can avoid the potential problems that might come from having your DPC routine simultaneously active on multiple CPUs in several ways. One way, which isn't the best, is to designate a particular CPU for running your DPC by calling **KeSetTargetProcessorDpc**. Also, you could theoretically restrict the CPU affinity of your interrupt when you first connect it; if you never queue the DPC except from your ISR, you'll never be executing the DPC on any different CPU. The real reason you're able to specify the CPU affinity of a DPC or an interrupt, however, is to improve performance by allowing the code and data accessed during your DPC or ISR routines to remain in a cache.

You can also use a spin lock or other synchronization primitive to prevent interference between two instances of your DPC routine. Be careful of using a spin lock here: you often need to coordinate the hypothetical multiple instances of your DPC routine with your ISR, and an ISR runs at too high an IRQL to use an ordinary spin lock. An interlocked list—that is, one you manipulate by using support functions in the same family as **ExInterlockedInsertHeadList**—might help you, since (so long as you never explicitly acquire the same spin lock that you use to guard the list) you can use the list at any IRQL. Interlocked forms of the bitwise OR and AND operators also might help by allowing you to manage a bit mask (such as a mask indicating recent interrupt conditions) that controls what your DPC routine is supposed to accomplish; you can cobble these functions together with the help of **InterlockedCompareExchange**.

Most simply, you can just make sure that your device won't interrupt in between the time you request a DPC and the time your DPC routine finishes its work. ("Yo, hardware guys, stop flooding me with interrupts!")

The third DPC detail, which I consider less crucial than the two I've just explained, concerns the *importance* of the DPC. By calling **KeSetImportanceDpc**, you can designate one of three importance levels for your DPC:

- **MediumImportance** is the default and indicates that the DPC should be queued after all currently queued DPCs. If the DPC is queued to another processor, that other processor won't necessarily be interrupted right away to service the DPC. If it's queued to the current processor, the kernel will request a DPC interrupt as soon as possible to begin servicing DPCs.

- **HighImportance** causes the DPC to be queued first. If two or more high importance DPCs get requested at about the same time, the last one queued gets serviced first.

- **LowImportance** causes the DPC to be queued last. In addition, the kernel won't necessarily request a DPC interrupt for whatever processor is destined to service the DPC.

The net effect of a DPC's importance level is to influence, but not necessarily control, how soon the DPC occurs. Even a DPC that has low importance might trigger a DPC interrupt on another CPU if that other CPU reaches some threshold for queued DPCs or if DPCs haven't been getting processed fast enough on it. If your device is capable of interrupting again before your DPC routine runs, changing your DPC to low importance will increase the likelihood that you'll have multiple work items to perform. If your DPC has an affinity for some CPU other than the one that requests the DPC, choosing high importance for your DPC will increase the likelihood that your ISR will still be active when your DPC routine begins to run. But neither of these possibilities is a certainty; conversely, altering or not altering your importance can't prevent either of them from happening.

Custom DPC Objects

You can create other DPC objects besides the one named **Dpc** in a device object. Simply reserve storage—in your device extension or some other persistent place that isn't paged—for a KDPC object, and initialize it:

```
typedef struct _DEVICE_EXTENSION {
  ...
  KDPC CustomDpc;
  ... };
```

```
KeInitializeDpc(&pdx->CustomDpc, (PKDEFERRED_ROUTINE) DpcRoutine, fdo);
```

In the call to **KeInitializeDpc**, the second argument is the address of a DPC routine in nonpaged memory, and the third argument is an arbitrary context parameter that will be sent to the DPC routine as its second argument.

To request a deferred call to a custom DPC routine, call **KeInsertQueueDpc**:

```
BOOLEAN inserted = KeInsertQueueDpc(&pdx->CustomDpc, arg1, arg2);
```

Here, **arg1** and **arg2** are arbitrary context pointers that will be passed to the custom DPC routine. The return value is FALSE if the DPC object was already in a processor queue and TRUE otherwise.

Also, you can also remove a DPC object from a processor queue by calling **KeRemoveQueueDpc**.

A Simple Interrupt-Driven Device

I wrote the PCI42 sample driver (available on the companion disc) to illustrate how to write the various different driver routines that a typical interrupt-driven, non-DMA device might use. The method used to handle such a device is often called programmed I/O (PIO) because program intervention is required to transfer each unit of data.

PCI42 is a dumbed-down driver for the S5933 PCI chip set from Applied Micro Circuits Corporation (AMCC). The S5933 acts as a matchmaker between the PCI bus and an add-on device that implements the actual function of a device. The S5933 is very flexible. In particular, you can program nonvolatile RAM so as to initialize the PCI configuration space for your device in any desired way. PCI42 uses the S5933 in its factory default state, however.

To grossly oversimplify matters, a WDM driver communicates with the add-on device connected to an S5933 either by doing DMA (which I'll discuss in the next major section of this chapter) or by sending and receiving data through a set of mailbox registers. PCI42 will be using one byte in one of the mailbox registers to transfer data one byte at a time.

The AMCC development kit for the S5933 (part number S5933DK1) includes two breadboard cards and an ISA (Industry Standard Architecture) interface card that connects to the S5933 development board via a ribbon cable. The ISA card allows you to access the S5933 from the add-on device side in order to provide software simulation of the add-on function. One component of the PCI42 sample is a driver (S5933DK1.SYS) for the ISA card that exports an interface for use by test programs.

Hardware people will snicker at the simplicity of the way PCI42 manages the device. The advantage of using such a trivial example is that you'll be able to see each step in the process of handling an I/O operation unfold at human speed. So chortle right back if your social dynamics allow it.

Initializing PCI42

The **StartDevice** function in PCI42 handles a port resource and an interrupt resource. The port resource describes a collection of sixteen 32-bit operation registers in I/O space, and the interrupt resource describes the host manifestation of the device's INTA# interrupt capability. At the end of StartDevice, we have the following device-specific code:

```
NTSTATUS StartDevice(...)
  {
  ...
```

(continued)

```
ResetDevice(pdx);
status = IoConnectInterrupt(...);
KeSynchronizeExecution(pdx->InterruptObject,
  (PKSYNCHRONIZE_ROUTINE) SetupDevice, pdx);
return STATUS_SUCCESS;
}
```

That is, we invoke a helper routine (**ResetDevice**) to reset the hardware. One of the tasks for ResetDevice is to prevent the device from generating any interrupts, insofar as that's possible. Then we call **IoConnectInterrupt** to connect the device interrupt to our ISR. Even before IoConnectInterrupt returns, it's possible for our device to generate an interrupt, so everything about our driver and the hardware has to be ready to go beforehand. After connecting the interrupt, we invoke another helper routine named **SetupDevice** to program the device to act the way we want it to. We must synchronize this step with our ISR because it uses the same hardware registers as our ISR would use, and we don't want any possibility of sending the device inconsistent instructions. The SetupDevice call is the last step in PCI42's StartDevice because—contrary to what I told you in Chapter 2, "Basic Structure of a WDM Driver"—PCI42 hasn't registered any device interfaces and therefore has none to enable at this point.

ResetDevice is highly device-specific and reads as follows:

```
VOID ResetDevice(PDEVICE_EXTENSION pdx)
  {
  PAGED_CODE();
```

1
```
  WRITE_PORT_ULONG((PULONG) (pdx->portbase + MCSR), MCSR_RESET);

  LARGE_INTEGER timeout;
  timeout.QuadPart = -10 * 10000; // i.e., 10 milliseconds
```

2
```
  KeDelayExecutionThread(KernelMode, FALSE, &timeout);
  WRITE_PORT_ULONG((PULONG) (pdx->portbase + MCSR), 0);
```

3
```
  WRITE_PORT_ULONG((PULONG) (pdx->portbase + INTCSR),
    INTCSR_INTERRUPT_MASK);
  }
```

1. The S5933 has a master control/status register (MCSR) that controls bus-mastering DMA transfers and other actions. Asserting four of these bits resets different features of the device. I defined the constant **MCSR_RESET** to be a mask containing all four of these reset flags. This and other manifest constants for S5933 features are in the S5933.H file that's part of the PCI42 project.

2. Three of the reset flags pertain to features internal to the S5933 and take effect immediately. Setting the fourth flag to 1 asserts a reset signal for the add-on function. To deassert the add-on reset, you have to explicitly reset

this flag to 0. In general, you want to give the hardware a little bit of time to recognize a reset pulse. **KeDelayExecutionThread**, which I discussed in Chapter 4, "Synchronization," puts this thread to sleep for about 10 milliseconds. You can raise or lower this constant if your hardware has different requirements, but don't forget that the timeout will never be less than the granularity of the system clock. Since we're blocking our thread, we need to be running at PASSIVE_LEVEL in a nonarbitrary thread context. Those conditions are met because our ultimate caller is the PnP Manager, which has sent us an IRP_MN_START_DEVICE in the full expectation that we'd be blocking the system thread we happen to be in.

3. The last step in resetting the device is to clear any pending interrupts. The S5933 has six interrupt flags in an interrupt control/status register (INTCSR). Writing 1 bits in these six positions clears all pending interrupts. (If we write back a mask value that has a 0 bit in one of the interrupt flag positions, the state of that interrupt is not affected. This kind of flag bit is called *read/write-clear* or just R/WC.) Other bits in the INTCSR enable interrupts of various kinds. By writing 0 bits in those locations, we're disabling the device to the maximum extent possible.

Our **SetupDevice** function is quite simple:

```
VOID SetupDevice(PDEVICE_EXTENSION pdx)
  {
  WRITE_PORT_ULONG((PULONG) (pdx->portbase + INTCSR),
    INTCSR_IMBI_ENABLE
    | (INTCSR_MB1 << INTCSR_IMBI_REG_SELECT_SHIFT)
    | (INTCSR_BYTE0 << INTCSR_IMBI_BYTE_SELECT_SHIFT)
    );
  }
```

This function reprograms the INTCSR to specify that we want an interrupt to occur when there's a change to byte 0 of inbound mailbox register 1. We could have specified other interrupt conditions for this chip, including the emptying of a particular byte of a specified outbound mailbox register, the completion of a read DMA transfer, and the completion of a write DMA transfer.

Starting a Read Operation

PCI42's **StartIo** routine follows the pattern we've already studied:

```
VOID StartIo(IN PDEVICE_OBJECT fdo, IN PIRP Irp)
  {
  PDEVICE_EXTENSION pdx = (PDEVICE_EXTENSION) fdo->DeviceExtension;
  PIO_STACK_LOCATION stack = IoGetCurrentIrpStackLocation(Irp);
  NTSTATUS status = IoAcquireRemoveLock(&pdx->RemoveLock, Irp);
  if (!NT_SUCCESS(status))
    {
```

(continued)

```
        CompleteRequest(Irp, status, 0);
        return;
        }

    if (!stack->Parameters.Read.Length)
        {
        StartNextPacket(&pdx->dqReadWrite, fdo);
        CompleteRequest(Irp, STATUS_SUCCESS, 0);
        return;
        }
```

1 ▷
```
    pdx->buffer = (PUCHAR) Irp->AssociatedIrp.SystemBuffer;
    pdx->nbytes = stack->Parameters.Read.Length;
    pdx->numxfer = 0;
```

2 ▷
```
    KeSynchronizeExecution(pdx->InterruptObject,
        (PKSYNCHRONIZE_ROUTINE) TransferFirst, pdx);
    }
```

1. Here, we save parameters in the device extension to describe the ongoing progress of the input operation we're about to undertake. PCI42 uses the DO_BUFFERED_IO method, which isn't typical but helps make this driver simple enough to be used as an example.

2. Since our interrupt is connected, our device can interrupt at any time. The ISR will want to transfer data bytes when interrupts happen, but we want to be sure that the ISR is never confused about which data buffer to use or about the number of bytes we're trying to read. To restrain our ISR's eagerness, we put a flag in the device extension named **activerequest** that's ordinarily FALSE. Now is the time to set that flag to TRUE. As usual when dealing with a shared resource, we need to synchronize the setting of the flag with the code in the ISR that tests it, and we therefore need to invoke a SynchCritSection routine as I previously discussed. It might also happen that a data byte is already available, in which case the first interrupt will never happen. **TransferFirst** is a helper routine that checks for this eventuality and reads the first byte. The add-on function has ways of knowing that we emptied the mailbox, so it will presumably send the next byte in due course. Here's TransferFirst:

```
VOID TransferFirst(PDEVICE_EXTENSION pdx)
    {
    pdx->activerequest = TRUE;
    ULONG mbef = READ_PORT_ULONG((PULONG) (pdx->portbase + MBEF));
    if (!(mbef & MBEF_IN1_0))
        return;

    *pdx->buffer = READ_PORT_UCHAR(pdx->portbase + IMB1);
    ++pdx->buffer;
```

```
  ++pdx->numxfer;
  if (--pdx->nbytes == 0)
    {
    pdx->activerequest = FALSE;
    IoRequestDpc(pdx->DeviceObject, NULL, NULL);
    }
  }
```

The S5933 has a mailbox empty/full register (MBEF) whose bits indicate the current status of each byte of each mailbox register. Here, we check whether the register byte we're using for input (inbound mailbox register 1, byte 0) is presently unread. If so, we read it. That might exhaust the transfer count. We already have a subroutine (**DpcForIsr**) that knows what to do with a complete request, so we request a DPC if this first byte turns out to satisfy the request. (Recall that we're executing at DIRQL under protection of an interrupt spin lock because we've been invoked as a SynchCritSection routine, so we can't just complete the IRP right now.)

Handling the Interrupt

In normal operation with PCI42, the S5933 interrupts when a new data byte arrives in mailbox 1. The following ISR then gains control:

```
BOOLEAN OnInterrupt(PKINTERRUPT InterruptObject, PDEVICE_EXTENSION pdx)
  {
  ULONG intcsr = READ_PORT_ULONG((PULONG) (pdx->portbase + INTCSR));
  if (!(intcsr & INTCSR_INTERRUPT_PENDING))
    return FALSE;

  BOOLEAN dpc = FALSE;

  PIRP Irp = GetCurrentIrp(&pdx->dqReadWrite);

  if (!Irp
    || AreRequestsBeingAborted(&pdx->dqReadWrite)
    || Irp->Cancel)
    {
    pdx->nbytes = 0;
    dpc = Irp != NULL;
    }

  while (intcsr & INTCSR_INTERRUPT_PENDING)
    {
    if (intcsr & INTCSR_IMBI)
      {
      if (pdx->nbytes && pdx->activerequest)
        {
        *pdx->buffer = READ_PORT_UCHAR(pdx->portbase + IMB1);
        ++pdx->buffer;
```

(continued)

```
        ++pdx->numxfer;
        if (!--pdx->nbytes)
          dpc = TRUE;
        }
      }
```

6 ▷
```
      WRITE_PORT_ULONG((PULONG) (pdx->portbase + INTCSR), intcsr);
```

7 ▷
```
      intcsr = READ_PORT_ULONG((PULONG) (pdx->portbase + INTCSR));
      }
```

8 ▷
```
  if (dpc)
    {
  pdx->activerequest = FALSE;
  IoRequestDpc(pdx->DeviceObject, NULL, NULL);
    }
```

```
  return TRUE;
  }
```

1. Our first task is to discover whether our own device is trying to interrupt now. We read the S5933's INTCSR and test a bit (INTCSR_INTERRUPT_ PENDING) that summarizes all pending causes of interrupts. If this bit is clear, we return immediately. The reason I chose to use the device extension pointer as the context argument to this routine—back when I called IoConnectInterrupt—should now be clear: we need immediate access to this structure to get the base port address.

2. When we use a DEVQUEUE, we rely on the queue object to keep track of the current IRP. This interrupt might be one that we don't expect because we're not currently servicing any IRP. In that case, we still have to clear the interrupt but shouldn't do anything else.

3. It's also possible that a Plug and Play or power event has occurred that will cause any new IRPs to be rejected by the dispatch routine. The DEVQUEUE's **AreRequestsBeingAborted** function tells us that fact so that we can abort the current request right now. Aborting an active request is a reasonable thing to do with a device such as this that proceeds byte by byte. Similarly it's a good idea to check whether the IRP has been cancelled if it will take a long time to finish the IRP. If your device interrupts only when it's done with a long transfer, you could leave this test out of your ISR.

4. We're now embarking on a loop that will terminate when all of our device's current interrupts have been cleared. At the end of the loop, we'll reread the INTCSR to determine whether any more interrupt conditions have arisen. If so, we'll repeat the loop. We're not being greedy with CPU time

here—we want to avoid letting interrupts cascade into the system because servicing an interrupt is by itself relatively expensive.

5. If the S5933 has interrupted because of a mailbox event, we'll read a new data byte from the mailbox into the I/O buffer for the current IRP. If you were to look in the MBEF register immediately after the read, you'd see that the bit corresponding to inbound mailbox register 1, byte 0, gets cleared by the read. Note that we needn't test the MBEF to determine whether our byte has actually changed because we programmed the device to interrupt only upon a change to that single byte.

6. Writing the INTCSR with its previous contents has the effect of clearing the six R/WC interrupt bits, not changing a few read-only bits, and preserving the original setting of all read/write control bits.

7. Here, we read the INTCSR to determine whether additional interrupt conditions have arisen. If so, we'll repeat this loop to service them.

8. As we progressed through the preceding code, we set the BOOLEAN **dpc** variable to TRUE if a DPC is now appropriate to complete the current IRP.

The DPC routine for PCI42 is as follows:

```
VOID DpcForIsr(PKDPC Dpc, PDEVICE_OBJECT fdo, PIRP junk, PVOID Context)
  {
  PDEVICE_EXTENSION pdx = (PDEVICE_EXTENSION) fdo->DeviceExtension;
  NTSTATUS status = STATUS_SUCCESS;
  PIRP Irp = GetCurrentIrp(&pdx->dqReadWrite);
  ULONG info = pdx->numxfer;
  StartNextPacket(&pdx->dqReadWrite, fdo);
  CompleteRequest(Irp, status, info);
  }
```

Testing PCI42

If you want to examine PCI42 in operation, you need to do several things. First obtain and install an S5933DK1 development board, including the ISA add-in interface card. Use the Add Hardware wizard to install the S5933DK1.SYS driver and the PCI42.SYS driver. (I found that Windows 98 initially identified the development board as a nonworking sound card and that I had to remove it in the Device Manager before I could install PCI42 as its driver. Windows 2000 handled the board normally, but I did encounter an annoying setup freeze when trying to upgrade from one release candidate to another during the beta phase.)

Then run *both* the ADDONSIM and TEST programs, which are in the PCI42 directory tree on the companion disc. ADDONSIM writes a data value to the mailbox via the ISA interface. TEST reads a data byte from PCI42. Determining the value of the data byte is left as an exercise for you.

DIRECT MEMORY ACCESS

Windows 2000 supports direct memory access transfers based on the abstract model of a computer depicted in Figure 7-6. In this model, the computer is considered to have a collection of *map registers* that translate between physical CPU address and bus addresses. Each map register holds the address of one physical page frame. Hardware accesses memory for reading or writing by means of a "logical," or bus-specific, address. The map registers play the same role as page table entries for software by allowing hardware to use different numeric values for their addresses than the CPU understands.

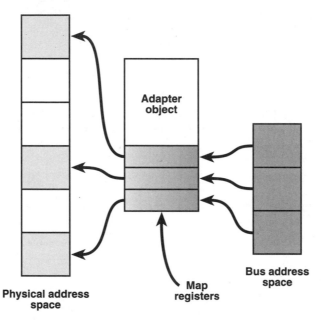

Figure 7-6. *Abstract computer model for DMA transfers.*

Some CPUs, such as the Alpha, have actual hardware map registers. One of the steps in initializing a DMA transfer—specifically, the MapTransfer step I'll discuss presently—reserves some of these registers for your use. Other CPUs, such as the Intel x86, do not have map registers, but you write your driver as if they did. The MapTransfer step on such a computer might end up reserving use of physical memory buffers that belong to the system, in which case the DMA operation will proceed using the reserved buffer. Obviously, something has to copy data to or from the DMA buffer before or after the transfer. In certain cases—for example, when dealing with a bus-master device that has scatter/gather capability—the MapTransfer phase might do all of nothing on an architecture without map registers.

The Windows 2000 kernel uses a data structure known as an *adapter object* to describe the DMA characteristics of a device and to control access to potentially shared resources, such as system DMA channels and map registers. You get a pointer to an adapter object by calling **IoGetDmaAdapter** during your StartDevice processing. The adapter object has a pointer to a structure named **DmaOperations** that, in turn, contains pointers to all the other functions you need to call. See Table 7-4. These functions take the place of global functions (such as **IoAllocateAdapter**, **IoMapTransfer**, and the like) that you would have used in previous versions of Windows NT. In fact, the global names are now macros that invoke the DmaOperations functions.

DmaOperations Function Pointer	*Description*
PutDmaAdapter	Destroys adapter object
AllocateCommonBuffer	Allocates a common buffer
FreeCommonBuffer	Releases a common buffer
AllocateAdapterChannel	Reserves adapter and map registers
FlushAdapterBuffers	Flushes intermediate data buffers after transfer
FreeAdapterChannel	Releases adapter object and map registers
FreeMapRegisters	Releases map registers only
MapTransfer	Programs one stage of a transfer
GetDmaAlignment	Gets address alignment required for adapter
ReadDmaCounter	Determines residual count
GetScatterGatherList	Reserves adapter and construct scatter/gather list
PutScatterGatherList	Releases scatter/gather list

Table 7-4. *DmaOperations function pointers for DMA helper routines.*

Transfer Strategies

How you perform a DMA transfer depends on several factors:

■ If your device has bus-mastering capability, it has the necessary electronics to access main memory if you tell it a few basic facts, such as where to start, how many units of data to transfer, whether you're performing an input or an output operation, and so on. You'll consult with your hardware designers to sort out these details, or else you'll be working from a specification that tells you what to do at the hardware level.

■ A device with scatter/gather capability can transfer large blocks of data to or from discontiguous areas of physical memory. Using scatter/gather is advantageous for software because it eliminates the need to acquire large blocks of contiguous page frames. Pages can simply be locked wherever they're found in physical memory, and the device can be told where they are.

■ If your device is not a bus master, you'll be using the system DMA controller on the motherboard of the computer. This style of DMA is sometimes called *slave DMA*. The system DMA controller associated with the ISA bus has some limitations on what physical memory it can access and how large a transfer it can perform without reprogramming. The controller for an EISA bus lacks these limits. You won't have to know—at least, not in Windows 2000—which type of bus your hardware plugs in to because the operating system is able to take account of these different restrictions automatically.

■ Ordinarily, DMA operations involve programming hardware map registers or copying data either before or after the operation. If your device needs to read or write data continuously, you don't want to do either of these steps for each I/O request—they might slow down processing too much to be acceptable in your particular situation. You can, therefore, allocate what's known as a *common buffer* that your driver and your device can both simultaneously access at any time.

Notwithstanding the fact that many details will be different depending on how these four factors interplay, the steps you perform will have many common features. Figure 7-7 illustrates the overall operation of a transfer. You start the transfer in your StartIo routine by requesting ownership of your adapter object. Ownership has meaning only if you're sharing a system DMA channel with other devices, but the Windows 2000 DMA model demands that you perform this step anyway. When the I/O Manager is able to grant you ownership, it allocates some map registers for your temporary use and calls back to an *adapter control* routine you provide. In your adapter control routine, you perform a *transfer mapping* step to arrange the first (maybe the only) stage of the transfer. Multiple stages can be necessary if sufficient map registers aren't available; your device must be capable of handling any delay that might occur between stages.

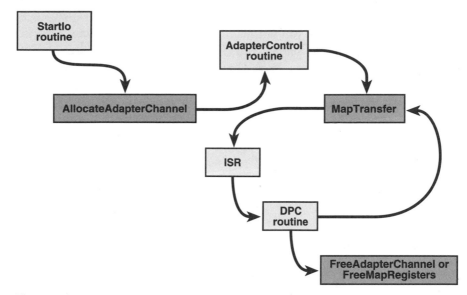

Figure 7-7. *Flow of ownership during DMA.*

Once your adapter control routine has initialized the map registers for the first stage, you signal your device to begin operation. Your device will instigate an interrupt when this initial transfer completes, whereupon you'll schedule a DPC. The DPC routine will initiate another staged transfer, if necessary, or else it will complete the request.

Somewhere along the way, you'll release the map registers and the adapter object. The timing of these two events is one of the details that differs based on the factors I summarized earlier in this section.

Performing DMA Transfers

Now I'll go into detail about the mechanics of what's often called a *packet-based* DMA transfer, wherein you transfer a discrete amount of data by using the data buffer that accompanies an I/O request packet. Let's start simply and suppose that you face what will be a very common case nowadays: your device is a PCI bus master but does not have scatter/gather capability.

To start with, when you create your device object, you'd ordinarily indicate that you want to use the direct method of data buffering by setting the DO_DIRECT_IO flag. You'd choose the direct method because you'll eventually be passing the address of a memory descriptor list as one of the arguments to the MapTransfer function you'll be calling. This choice poses a bit of a problem with regard to buffer alignment, though. Unless the application uses the FILE_FLAG_NO_BUFFERING flag in its call to **CreateFile**, the I/O Manager won't enforce the device object's **Alignment-Requirement** on user-mode data buffers. (It doesn't enforce the requirement for a kernel-mode caller at all except in the checked build.) If your device or the HAL requires DMA buffers to begin on some particular boundary, therefore, you might end up copying a small portion of the user data to a correctly aligned internal buffer to meet the alignment requirement—either that or fail any request that has a mis-aligned buffer.

In your StartDevice function, you create an adapter object by using code like the following:

```
INTERFACE_TYPE bustype;
ULONG junk;
IoGetDeviceProperty(pdx->Pdo, DevicePropertyLegacyBusType,
  sizeof(bustype), &bustype, &junk);

DEVICE_DESCRIPTION dd;
RtlZeroMemory(&dd, sizeof(dd));
dd.Version = DEVICE_DESCRIPTION_VERSION;
dd.Master = TRUE;
dd.InterfaceType = bustype;
dd.MaximumLength = MAXTRANSFER;
dd.Dma32BitAddresses = TRUE;

pdx->AdapterObject = IoGetDmaAdapter(pdx->Pdo, &dd, &pdx->nMapRegisters);
```

The last statement in this code fragment is the important one. **IoGetDmaAdapter** will communicate with the bus driver or the HAL to create an adapter object, whose address it returns to you. The first parameter (**pdx->Pdo**) identifies the physical device object (PDO) for your device. The second parameter points to a DEVICE_DESCRIPTION structure that you initialize to describe the DMA characteristics of your device. The last parameter indicates where the system should store the maximum number of map registers you'll ever be allowed to attempt to reserve during a single transfer. You'll notice that I reserved two fields in the device extension (**AdapterObject** and **nMapRegisters**) to receive the two outputs from this function.

In your **StopDevice** function, you destroy the adapter object with this call:

```
VOID StopDevice(...)
  {
  ...
  if (pdx->AdapterObject)
    (*pdx->AdapterObject->DmaOperations->PutDmaAdapter)
      (pdx->AdapterObject);
  pdx->AdapterObject = NULL;
  ...
  }
```

You won't expect to receive an official DMA resource when your device is a bus master. That is, your resource extraction loop won't need a CmResourceTypeDma case label. The PnP Manager doesn't assign you a DMA resource because your hardware itself contains all the necessary electronics for performing DMA transfers, so nothing additional needs to be assigned to you.

Previous versions of Windows NT relied on a service function named **HalGet-Adapter** to acquire the DMA adapter object. That function still exists for compatibility, but new WDM drivers should call IoGetDmaAdapter instead. The difference between the two is that IoGetDmaAdapter first issues an IRP_MN_QUERY_INTERFACE Plug and Play IRP to determine whether the physical device object supports the GUID_BUS_INTERFACE_STANDARD direct call interface. If so, IoGetDmaAdapter uses that interface to allocate the adapter object. If not, it simply calls HalGetAdapter.

Table 7-5 summarizes the fields in the DEVICE_DESCRIPTION structure you pass to IoGetDmaAdapter. The only fields that are relevant for a bus-master device are those shown in the preceding StartDevice code fragment. The HAL might or might not need to know whether your device recognizes 32-bit or 64-bit addresses—the Intel x86 HAL uses this flag only when you allocate a common buffer, for example—but you should indicate that capability anyway to retain portability. By zeroing the entire structure, we set **ScatterGather** to FALSE. Since we won't be using a system DMA channel, none of **DmaChannel**, **DmaPort**, **DmaWidth**, **DemandMode**, **AutoInitialize**, **IgnoreCount**, and **DmaSpeed** will be examined by the routine that creates our adapter object.

Field Name	*Description*	*Relevant To Device*
Version	Version number of structure—initialize to DEVICE_DESCRIPTION_VERSION	All
Master	Bus-master device—set based on your knowledge of device	All
ScatterGather	Device supports scatter/gather list—set based on your knowledge of device	All
DemandMode	Use system DMA controller's demand mode—set based on your knowledge of device	Slave
AutoInitialize	Use system DMA controller's autoinitialize mode—set based on your knowledge of device	Slave
Dma32BitAddresses	Can use 32-bit physical addresses	Common buffer

Table 7-5. *Device description structure used with IoGetDmaAdapter.* *(continued)*

continued

Field Name	Description	Relevant To Device
IgnoreCount	Controller doesn't maintain an accurate transfer count—set based on your knowledge of device	Slave
Reserved1	Reserved—must be FALSE	
Dma64BitAddresses	Can use 64-bit physical addresses	Common buffer
DoNotUse2	Reserved—must be 0	
DmaChannel	DMA channel number—initialize from Channel attribute of resource descriptor	Slave
InterfaceType	Bus type—use result of IoGetDeviceProperty call to get DevicePropertyLegacyBusType	All
DmaWidth	Width of transfers—set based on your knowledge of device to Width8Bits, Width16Bits, or Width32Bits	Slave
DmaSpeed	Speed of transfers—set based on your knowledge of device to Compatible, TypeA, TypeB, TypeC, or TypeF	Slave
MaximumLength	Maximum length of a single transfer—set based on your knowledge of device (and round up to a multiple of PAGE_SIZE)	All
DmaPort	Microchannel-type bus port number—initialize from Port attribute of resource descriptor	Slave

To initiate an I/O operation, your StartIo routine first has to reserve the adapter object by calling the object's **AllocateAdapterChannel** routine. One of the arguments to AllocateAdapterChannel is the address of an adapter control routine that the I/O Manager will call when the reservation has been accomplished. Here's an example of code you would use to prepare and execute the call to AllocateAdapterChannel:

```
typedef struct _DEVICE_EXTENSION {
  ...
  PADAPTER_OBJECT AdapterObject; // device's adapter object
  ULONG nMapRegisters; // max # map registers
  ULONG nMapRegistersAllocated; // # allocated for this xfer
  ULONG numxfer;      // # bytes transferred so far
  ULONG xfer;         // # bytes to transfer during this stage
  ULONG nbytes;       // # bytes remaining to transfer
```

```
       PVOID vaddr;         // virtual address for current stage
       PVOID regbase;       // map register base for this stage
       ...
       } DEVICE_EXTENSION, *PDEVICE_EXTENSION;

VOID StartIo(PDEVICE_OBJECT fdo, PIRP Irp)
  {
  PDEVICE_EXTENSION pdx = (PDEVICE_EXTENSION) fdo->DeviceExtension;
  NTSTATUS status = IoAcquireRemoveLock(&pdx->RemoveLock, Irp);
  if (!NT_SUCCESS(status))
    {
    CompleteRequest(Irp, status, 0);
    return;
    }

  PMDL mdl = Irp->MdlAddress;
  pdx->numxfer = 0;
  pdx->xfer = pdx->nbytes = MmGetMdlByteCount(mdl);
  pdx->vaddr = MmGetMdlVirtualAddress(mdl);

  ULONG nregs = ADDRESS_AND_SIZE_TO_SPAN_PAGES(pdx->vaddr,
    pdx->nbytes);
  if (nregs > pdx->nMapRegisters)
    {
    nregs = pdx->nMapRegisters;
    pdx->xfer = nregs * PAGE_SIZE - MmGetMdlByteOffset(mdl);
    }
  pdx->nMapRegistersAllocated = nregs;

  status = (*pdx->AdapterObject->DmaOperations
    ->AllocateAdapterChannel)(pdx->AdapterObject, fdo, nregs,
    (PDRIVER_CONTROL) AdapterControl, pdx);
  if (!NT_SUCCESS(status))
    {
    IoReleaseRemoveLock(&pdx->RemoveLock, Irp);
    CompleteRequest(Irp, status, 0);
    StartNextPacket(&pdx->dqReadWrite, fdo);
    }
  }
```

1. Your device extension needs several fields related to DMA transfers. The comments indicate the uses for these fields.

2. This is the appropriate time to claim the remove lock to forestall PnP removal events during the pendency of the I/O operation. The balancing call to **IoReleaseRemoveLock** occurs in the DPC routine that ultimately completes this request.

3. These few statements initialize fields in the device extension for the first stage of the transfer.

4. Here, we calculate how many map registers we'll ask the system to reserve for our use during this transfer. We begin by calculating the number required for the whole transfer. The ADDRESS_AND_SIZE_TO_SPAN_PAGES macro takes into account that the buffer might span a page boundary. The number we end up with might, however, exceed the maximum allowed us by the original call to IoGetDmaAdapter. In that case, we need to perform the transfer in multiple stages. We therefore scale back the first stage so as to use only the allowable number of map registers. We also need to remember how many map registers we're allocating (in the **nMapRegistersAllocated** field of the device extension) so that we can release exactly the right number later on.

5. In this call to **AllocateAdapterChannel**, we specify the address of the adapter object, the address of our own device object, the calculated number of map registers, and the address of our adapter control procedure. The last argument (**pdx**) is a context parameter for the adapter control procedure.

In general, several devices can share a single adapter object. Adapter object sharing happens in real life only when you rely on the system DMA controller; bus-master devices own dedicated adapter objects. But, since you don't need to know how the system decides when to create adapter objects, you shouldn't make any assumptions about it. In general, then, the adapter object might be busy when you call AllocateAdapterChannel, and your request might therefore be put into a queue until the adapter object becomes available. Also, all DMA devices on the computer share a set of map registers. Further delay can ensue until the requested number of registers becomes available. Both of these delays occur inside AllocateAdapterChannel, which calls your adapter control procedure when the adapter object and all the map registers you asked for are available.

Even though a PCI bus-mastering device owns its own adapter object, if the device doesn't have scatter/gather capability, it requires the use of map registers. On CPUs like Alpha that have map registers, AllocateAdapterChannel will reserve them for your use. On CPUs like Intel that don't have map registers, AllocateAdapterChannel will reserve use of a software surrogate, such as a contiguous area of physical memory.

WHAT GETS QUEUED IN ALLOCATEADAPTERCHANNEL?

The object that AllocateAdapterChannel puts into queues to wait for the adapter object or the necessary number of map registers is your device object. Some device architectures allow you to perform more than one DMA transfer simultaneously. Since you can put only one device object into an adapter object queue at a time (without crashing the system, that is), you need to create dummy device objects to take advantage of that multiple-DMA capability.

As I've been discussing, AllocateAdapterChannel eventually calls your adapter control routine (at DISPATCH_LEVEL, just like your StartIo routine does). You have two tasks to accomplish. First, you should call the adapter object's MapTransfer routine to prepare the map registers and other system resources for the first stage of your I/O operation. In the case of a bus-mastering device, MapTransfer will return a logical address that represents the starting point for the first stage. This logical address might be the same as a CPU physical memory address, and it might not be. All you need to know about it is that it's the right address to program into your hardware. MapTransfer might also trim the length of your request to fit the map registers it's using, which is why you need to supply the address of the variable that contains the current stage length as an argument.

Your second task is to perform whatever device-dependent steps are required to inform your device of the physical address and to start the operation on your hardware:

```
IO_ALLOCATION_ACTION AdapterControl(PDEVICE_OBJECT fdo,
  PIRP junk, PVOID regbase, PDEVICE_EXTENSION pdx)
  {
  PIRP Irp = GetCurrentIrp(&pdx->dqReadWrite);
  PMDL mdl = Irp->MdlAddress;
  PIO_STACK_LOCATION stack = IoGetCurrentIrpStackLocation(Irp);
  BOOLEAN isread = stack->MajorFunction == IRP_MJ_READ;
  pdx->regbase = regbase;
  KeFlushIoBuffers(mdl, isread, TRUE);
  PHYSICAL_ADDRESS address =
    (*pdx->AdapterObject->DmaOperations->MapTransfer)
    (pdx->AdapterObject, mdl, regbase, pdx->vaddr, &pdx->xfer,
    !isread);
  ...
  return DeallocateObjectKeepRegisters;
  }
```

The numbered markers 1–7 point to lines in the code above.

1. The second argument—which I named **junk**—to **AdapterControl** is whatever was in the CurrentIrp field of the device object when you called AllocateAdapterChannel. When you use a DEVQUEUE for IRP queuing, you need to ask the DEVQUEUE object what IRP is current. If you use the standard model, wherein IoStartPacket and IoStartNextPacket manage the queue, **junk** would be the right IRP. In that case, I'd have named it **Irp** instead.

2. There are few differences between code to handle input and output operations using DMA, so it's often convenient to handle both operations in a single subroutine. This line of code examines the major function code for the IRP to decide whether a read or write is occurring.

3. The **regbase** argument to this function is an opaque handle that identifies the set of map registers that have been reserved for your use during

this operation. You'll need this value later, so you should save it in your device extension.

4. **KeFlushIoBuffers** makes sure that the contents of all processor memory caches for the memory buffer you're using are flushed to memory. The third argument (TRUE) indicates that you're flushing the cache in preparation for a DMA operation. The CPU architecture might require this step because, in general, DMA operations proceed directly to or from memory without necessarily involving the caches.

5. The **MapTransfer** routine programs the DMA hardware for one stage of a transfer and returns the physical address where the transfer should start. Notice that you supply the address of an MDL as the second argument to this function. Since you need an MDL at this point, you would ordinarily have opted for the DO_DIRECT_IO buffering method when you first created your device object, and the I/O Manager would therefore have automatically created the MDL for you. You also pass along the map register base address (**regbase**). You indicate which portion of the MDL is involved in this stage of the operation by supplying a virtual address (**pdx->vaddr**) and a byte count (**pdx->xfer**). MapTransfer will use the virtual address argument to calculate an offset into the buffer area, from which it can determine the physical page numbers containing your data.

6. This is the point at which you program your hardware in the device-specific way that is required. You might, for example, use one of the WRITE_*Xxx* HAL routines to send the physical address and byte count values to registers on your card, and you might thereafter strobe some command register to begin transferring data.

7. We return the constant **DeallocateObjectKeepRegisters** to indicate that we're done using the adapter object but are still using the map registers. In this particular example (PCI bus master), there will never be any contention for the adapter object in the first place, so it hardly matters that we've released the adapter object. In other bus-mastering situations, though, we might be sharing a DMA controller with other devices. Releasing the adapter object allows those other devices to begin transfers by using a disjoint set of map registers from the ones we're still using.

An interrupt usually occurs shortly after you start the transfer, and the interrupt service routine usually requests a DPC to deal with completion of the first stage of the transfer. Your DPC routine would look something like this:

```
VOID DpcForIsr(PKDPC Dpc, PDEVICE_OBJECT fdo, PIRP junk, PVOID Context)
  {
  PDEVICE_EXTENSION pdx = (PDEVICE_EXTENSION) fdo->DeviceExtension;
```

```
1    PIRP Irp = GetCurrentIrp(&pdx->dqReadWrite);
     PMDL mdl = Irp->MdlAddress;
     BOOLEAN isread = IoGetCurrentIrpStackLocation(Irp)
       ->MajorFunction == IRP_MJ_READ;
2    (*pdx->AdapterObject->DmaOperations->FlushAdapterBuffers)
       (pdx->AdapterObject, mdl, pdx->regbase, pdx->vaddr,
       pdx->xfer, !isread);
3    pdx->nbytes -= pdx->xfer;
     pdx->numxfer += pdx->xfer;
     NTSTATUS status = STATUS_SUCCESS;
4    ...
     if (pdx->nbytes && NT_SUCCESS(status))
       {
5    pdx->vaddr = (PVOID) ((PUCHAR) pdx->vaddr + pdx->xfer);
     pdx->xfer = pdx->nbytes;
6    ULONG nregs = ADDRESS_AND_SIZE_TO_SPAN_PAGES(pdx->vaddr,
       pdx->nbytes);
     if (nregs > pdx->nMapRegistersAllocated)
       {
     nregs = pdx->nMapRegistersAllocated;
     pdx->xfer = nregs * PAGE_SIZE;
       }
     PHYSICAL_ADDRESS address =
       (*pdx->AdapterObject->DmaOperations->MapTransfer)
       (pdx->AdapterObject, mdl, pdx->regbase, pdx->vaddr,
       pdx->xfer, !isread);
     ...
       }
     else
       {
     ULONG numxfer = pdx->numxfer;
7    (*pdx->AdapterObject->DmaOperations->FreeMapRegisters)
       (pdx->AdapterObject, pdx->regbase,
       pdx->nMapRegistersAllocated);
8    IoReleaseRemoveLock(&pdx->RemoveLock, Irp);
     StartNextPacket(&pdx->dqReadWrite, fdo);
     CompleteRequest(Irp, status, numxfer);
       }
     }
```

1. When you use a DEVQUEUE for IRP queuing, you rely on the queue object to keep track of the current IRP.

2. The **FlushAdapterBuffers** routine handles the situation in which the transfer required use of intermediate buffers owned by the system. If you've done an input operation that spanned a page boundary, the input data is now sitting in an intermediate buffer and needs to be copied to the user-mode buffer.

3. Here, we update the residual and cumulative data counts after the transfer stage that just completed.

4. At this point, you determine whether the current stage of the transfer completed successfully or with an error. You might, for example, read a status port or inspect the results of a similar operation performed by your interrupt routine. In this example, I set the **status** variable to STATUS_ SUCCESS with the expectation that you'd change it if you discovered an error here.

5. If the transfer hasn't finished yet, you need to program another stage. The first step in this process is to calculate the virtual address of the next portion of the user-mode buffer. Bear in mind that this calculation is merely working with a number—we're not actually trying to access memory by using this virtual address. Accessing the memory would be a bad idea, of course, because we're currently executing in an arbitrary thread context.

6. The next few statements are almost identical to the ones we performed in the first stage for StartIo and AdapterControl. The end result will be a logical address that can be programmed into your device. It might or might not correspond to a physical address as understood by the CPU. One slight wrinkle is that we're constrained to use only as many map registers as were allocated by the adapter control routine; StartIo saved that number in the **nMapRegistersAllocated** field of the device extension.

7. If the entire transfer is now complete, we need to release the map registers we've been using.

8. The remaining few statements in the DPC routine handle the mechanics of completing the IRP that got us here in the first place. We release the remove lock to balance the acquisition that we did inside StartIo.

Transfers Using Scatter/Gather Lists

If your hardware has scatter/gather support, the system has a much easier time doing DMA transfers to and from your device. The scatter/gather capability permits the device to perform a transfer involving pages that aren't contiguous in physical memory.

Your StartDevice routine creates its adapter object in just about the same way I've already discussed, except (of course) that you'll set the **ScatterGather** flag to TRUE.

The traditional method—that is, the method you would have used in previous versions of Windows NT—to program a DMA transfer involving scatter/gather functionality is practically identical to the packet-based example considered in the previous section, "Performing DMA Transfers." The only difference is that instead of making one call to MapTransfer for each stage of the transfer, you need to make multiple calls. Each call gives you the information you need for a single element in a *scatter/gather list* that contains a physical address and length. When you're done with the loop, you can send the scatter/gather list to your device by using some device-specific method, and you can then initiate the transfer.

I'm going to make some assumptions about the framework into which you'll fit the construction of a scatter/gather list. First, I'll assume that you've defined a manifest constant named **MAXSG** that represents the maximum number of scatter/gather list elements your device can handle. To make life as simple as possible, I'm also going to assume that you can just use the SCATTER_GATHER_LIST structure defined in WDM.H to construct the list:

```
typedef struct _SCATTER_GATHER_ELEMENT {
  PHYSICAL_ADDRESS Address;
  ULONG Length;
  ULONG_PTR Reserved;
  } SCATTER_GATHER_ELEMENT, *PSCATTER_GATHER_ELEMENT;

typedef struct _SCATTER_GATHER_LIST {
  ULONG NumberOfElements;
  ULONG_PTR Reserved;
  SCATTER_GATHER_ELEMENT Elements[];
  } SCATTER_GATHER_LIST, *PSCATTER_GATHER_LIST;
```

Finally, I'm going to suppose that you can simply allocate a maximum-sized scatter/gather list in your AddDevice function and leave it lying around for use whenever you need it:

```
pdx->sglist = (PSCATTER_GATHER_LIST)
  ExAllocatePool(NonPagedPool, sizeof(SCATTER_GATHER_LIST) +
  MAXSG * sizeof(SCATTER_GATHER_ELEMENT));
```

With this infrastructure in place, your **AdapterControl** procedure would look like this:

```
IO_ALLOCATION_ACTION AdapterControl(PDEVICE_OBJECT fdo,
  PIRP junk, PVOID regbase, PDEVICE_EXTENSION pdx)
  {
  PIRP Irp = GetCurrentIrp(&pdx->dqReadWrite);
  PMDL mdl = Irp->MdlAddress;
  BOOLEAN isread = IoGetCurrentIrpStackLocation(Irp)
    ->MajorFunction == IRP_MJ_READ;
  pdx->regbase = regbase;
  KeFlushIoBuffers(mdl, isread, TRUE);
  PSCATTER_GATHER_LIST sglist = pdx->sglist;

  ULONG xfer = pdx->xfer;
  PVOID vaddr = pdx->vaddr;
  pdx->xfer = 0;
  ULONG isg = 0;
```

1 ▷

2 ▷

(continued)

```
3      while (xfer && isg < MAXSG)
        {
       ULONG elen = xfer;
4      sglist->Elements[isg].Address =
         (*pdx->AdapterObject->DmaOperations->MapTransfer)
         (pdx->AdapterObject, mdl, regbase, pdx->vaddr,
         &elen, !isread);
       sglist->Elements[isg].Length = elen;
5      xfer -= elen;
       pdx->xfer += elen;
       vaddr = (PVOID) ((PUCHAR) vaddr + elen);
6      ++isg;
        }
     sglist->NumberOfElements = isg;
7    ...
8    return DeallocateObjectKeepRegisters;
     }
```

1. See the earlier discussion (in "Performing DMA Transfers") of how to get a pointer to the correct IRP in an adapter control procedure.

2. We previously (in StartIo) calculated **pdx->xfer** based on the allowable number of map registers. We're going to try to transfer that much data now, but the allowable number of scatter/gather elements might further limit the amount we can transfer during this stage. During the following loop, **xfer** will be the number of bytes that we haven't yet mapped and we'll recalculate **pdx->xfer** as we go.

3. Here's the loop I promised you where we call MapTransfer to construct scatter/gather elements. We'll continue the loop until we've mapped the entire stage of this transfer or until we run out of scatter/gather elements, whichever happens first.

4. When we call **MapTransfer** for a scatter/gather device, it will modify the length argument (**elen**) to indicate how much of the MDL starting at the given virtual address (**vaddr**) is physically contiguous and can therefore be mapped by a single scatter/gather list element. It will also return the physical address of the beginning of the contiguous region.

5. Here's where we update the variables that describe the current stage of the transfer. When we leave the loop, **xfer** will be down to 0 (or else we'll have run out of scatter/gather elements), **pdx->xfer** will be up to the total of all the elements we were able to map, and **vaddr** will be up to the byte after the last one we mapped. We don't update the **pdx->vaddr** field in the device extension—we're doing that in our DPC routine. Just another one of those pesky details....

6. Here's where we increment the scatter/gather element index to reflect the fact that we've just used one up.

7. At this point, we have **isg** scatter/gather elements that we should program into our device in whatever hardware-dependent way is appropriate. Then we should start the device working on the request.

8. Returning **DeallocateObjectKeepRegisters** is appropriate for a bus-mastering device. You can theoretically have a nonmaster device with scatter/gather capability, and it would return **KeepObject** instead.

Your device now performs its DMA transfer and, presumably, interrupts to signal completion. Your ISR requests a DPC, and your DPC routine initiates the next stage in the operation. The DPC routine would perform a MapTransfer loop like the one I just showed you as part of that initiation process. I'll leave the details of that code as an exercise for you.

Using GetScatterGatherList

Windows 2000 provides a shortcut to avoid the relatively cumbersome loop of calls to MapTransfer in the common case in which you can accomplish the entire transfer by using either no map registers or no more than the maximum number of map registers returned by IoGetDmaAdapter. The shortcut, which is illustrated in the SCATGATH sample on the companion disc, involves calling the **GetScatterGatherList** routine instead of AllocateAdapterChannel. Your **StartIo** routine looks like this:

```
VOID StartIo(PDEVICE_OBJECT fdo, PIRP Irp)
  {
  PDEVICE_EXTENSION pdx = (PDEVICE_EXTENSION) fdo->DeviceExtension;
  PIO_STACK_LOCATION stack = IoGetCurrentIrpStackLocation(Irp);
  NTSTATUS status = IoAcquireRemoveLock(&pdx->RemoveLock, Irp);
  if (!NT_SUCCESS(status))
    {
    CompleteRequest(Irp, status, 0);
    return;
    }
  PMDL mdl = Irp->MdlAddress;
  ULONG nbytes = MmGetMdlByteCount(mdl);
  PVOID vaddr = MmGetMdlVirtualAddress(mdl);
  BOOLEAN isread = stack->MajorFunction == IRP_MJ_READ;
  pdx->numxfer = 0;
  pdx->nbytes = nbytes;
  status = (*pdx->AdapterObject->DmaOperations->GetScatterGatherList)
    (pdx->AdapterObject, fdo, mdl, vaddr, nbytes,
    (PDRIVER_LIST_CONTROL) DmaExecutionRoutine, pdx, !isread);
```

(continued)

```
if (!NT_SUCCESS(status))
  {
  IoReleaseRemoveLock(&pdx->RemoveLock, Irp);
  CompleteRequest(Irp, status, 0);
  StartNextPacket(&pdx->dqReadWrite, fdo);
  }
}
```

The call to GetScatterGatherList, shown in bold in the previous code fragment, is the main difference between this StartIo routine and the one we looked at in the preceding section. GetScatterGatherList waits, if necessary, until you can be granted use of the adapter object and all the map registers you need. Then it builds a SCATTER_GATHER_LIST structure and passes it to the **DmaExecutionRoutine**. You can then program your device by using the physical addresses in the scatter/gather elements and initiate the transfer:

```
VOID DmaExecutionRoutine(PDEVICE_OBJECT fdo, PIRP junk,
  PSCATTER_GATHER_LIST sglist, PDEVICE_EXTENSION pdx)
  {
  PIRP Irp = GetCurrentIrp(&pdx->dqReadWrite);
  pdx->sglist = sglist;
  ...
  }
```

1. You'll need the address of the scatter/gather list in the DPC routine, which will release it by calling **PutScatterGatherList**.

2. At this point, program your device to do a read or write using the address and length pairs in the scatter/gather list. If the list has more elements than your device can handle at one time, you'll need to perform the whole transfer in stages. If you can program a stage fairly quickly, I'd recommend adding logic to your interrupt service routine to initiate the additional stages. If you think about it, your DmaExecutionRoutine is probably going to be synchronizing with your ISR anyway to start the first stage, so this extra logic is probably not large. I programmed the SCATGATH sample with this idea in mind.

When the transfer finishes, call the adapter object's PutScatterGatherList to release the list and the adapter:

```
VOID DpcForIsr(PKDPC Dpc, PDEVICE_OBJECT fdo, PIRP junk, PVOID Context)
  {
  ...
  (*pdx->AdapterObject->DmaOperations->PutScatterGatherList)
    (pdx->AdapterObject, pdx->sglist, !isread);
  ...
  }
```

To decide whether you can use GetScatterGatherList, you need to be able to predict whether you'll meet the preconditions for its use. On an Intel 32-bit platform, scatter/gather devices on a PCI or EISA bus can be sure of not needing any map registers. Even on an ISA bus, you'll be allowed to request up to 16 map register surrogates (eight if you're also a bus-mastering device) unless physical memory is so tight that the I/O system can't allocate its intermediate I/O buffers. In that case, you wouldn't be able to do DMA using the traditional method either, so there'd be no point in worrying about it.

If you can't predict with certainty at the time you code your driver that you'll be able to use GetScatterGatherList, my advice is to just fall back on the traditional loop of MapTransfer calls. You'll need to put that code in place anyway to deal with cases in which GetScatterGatherList won't work, and having two pieces of logic in your driver is just unnecessary complication.

Transfers Using the System Controller

If your device is not a bus master, DMA capability requires that it use the system DMA controller. As I've said, people often use the phrase *slave DMA*, which emphasizes that such a device is not master of its own DMA fate. The system DMA controllers have several characteristics that affect the internal details of how DMA transfers proceed:

- There are a limited number of DMA *channels* that all slave devices must share. AllocateAdapterChannel has real meaning in a sharing situation, since only one device can be using a particular channel at a time.

- You can expect to find a CmResourceTypeDma resource in the list of I/O resources delivered to you by the PnP Manager.

- Your hardware is wired, either physically or logically, to the particular channel it uses. If you can configure the DMA channel connection, you'll need to send the appropriate commands at StartDevice time.

- The system DMA controllers for an ISA bus computer are able to access data buffers in only the first 16 megabytes of physical memory. Four channels for transferring data 8 bits at a time and three channels for transferring data 16 bits at a time exist. The controller for 8-bit channels doesn't correctly handle a buffer that crosses a 64-KB boundary; the controller for 16-bit channels doesn't correctly handle a buffer that crosses a 128-KB boundary.

Notwithstanding these factors, your driver code will be very similar to the bus-mastering code we've just discussed. Your StartDevice routine just works a little harder to set up its call to IoGetDmaAdapter, and your AdapterControl and DPC routines apportion the steps of releasing the adapter object and map registers differently.

In StartDevice, you have a little bit of additional code to determine which DMA channel the PnP Manager has assigned for you, and you also need to initialize more of the fields of the DEVICE_DESCRIPTION structure for IoGetDmaAdapter:

```
NTSTATUS StartDevice(...)
  {
  ULONG dmachannel;    // system DMA channel #
  ULONG dmaport;       // MCA bus port number
  ...
  for (ULONG i = 0; i < nres; ++i, ++resource)
    {
    switch (resource->Type)
      {
      case CmResourceTypeDma:
        dmachannel = resource->u.Dma.Channel;
        dmaport = resource->u.Dma.Port;
        break;
      }
    }
  ...
  INTERFACE_TYPE bustype;
  IoGetDeviceProperty(...);

  DEVICE_DESCRIPTION dd;
  RtlZeroMemory(&dd, sizeof(dd));
  dd.Version = DEVICE_DESCRIPTION_VERSION;
  dd.InterfaceType = bustype;
  dd.MaximumLength = MAXTRANSFER;

  dd.DmaChannel = dmachannel;
  dd.DmaPort = dmaport;
  dd.DemandMode = ??;
  dd.AutoInitialize = ??;
  dd.IgnoreCount = ??;
  dd.DmaWidth = ??;
  dd.DmaSpeed = ??;

  pdx->AdapterObject = IoGetDmaAdapter(...);
  }
```

1. The I/O resource list will have a DMA resource, from which you need to extract the channel and port numbers. The channel number identifies one of the DMA channels supported by a system DMA controller. The port number is relevant only on a Micro Channel Architecture (MCA)–bus machine.

2. Refer to the previous discussion of how to determine the bus type (in "Performing DMA Transfers").

3. Beginning here, you have to initialize several fields of the DEVICE_
DESCRIPTION structure based on your knowledge of your device. See
Table 7-5 on pages 325–26.

Everything about your adapter control and DPC procedures will be identical to
the code we looked at earlier for handling a bus-mastering device without scatter/
gather capability, except for two small details. First, **AdapterControl** returns a
different value:

```
IO_ALLOCATION_ACTION AdapterControl(...)
  {
  ...
  return KeepObject;
  }
```

The return value **KeepObject** indicates that we want to retain control over the map
registers *and* the DMA channel we're using. Second, since we didn't release the
adapter object when AdapterControl returned, we have to do so in the DPC routine
by calling **FreeAdapterChannel** instead of **FreeMapRegisters**:

```
VOID DpcForIsr(...)
  {
  ...
  (*pdx->AdapterObject->DmaOperations->FreeAdapterChannel)
    (pdx->AdapterObject);
  ...
  }
```

By the way, you don't need to remember how many map registers you were
assigned—I previously showed you an nMapRegistersAllocated variable in the device
extension to be used for this purpose—since you won't be calling FreeMapRegisters.

Using a Common Buffer

As I mentioned in "Transfer Strategies," you might want to allocate a common buffer
for your device to use in performing DMA transfers. A common buffer is an area of
nonpaged, physically contiguous memory. Your driver uses a fixed virtual address
to access the buffer. Your device uses a fixed logical address to access the same buffer.

You can use the common buffer area in several ways. You can support a device that continuously transfers data to or from memory by using the system DMA
controller's autoinitialize mode. In this mode of operation, completion of one transfer triggers the controller to immediately reinitialize for another transfer.

Another use for a common buffer area is as a means to avoid extra data copying. The MapTransfer routine often copies the data you supply into auxiliary buffers
owned by the I/O Manager and used for DMA. If you're stuck with doing slave DMA

on an ISA bus, it's especially likely that MapTransfer will copy data to conform to the 16-MB address and buffer alignment requirements of the ISA DMA controller. But if you have a common buffer, you'll avoid the copy steps.

Allocating a Common Buffer

You'd normally allocate your common buffer at StartDevice time after creating your adapter object:

```
typedef struct _DEVICE_EXTENSION {
  ...
  PVOID vaCommonBuffer;
  PHYSICAL_ADDRESS paCommonBuffer;
  ...
  } DEVICE_EXTENSION, *PDEVICE_EXTENSION;

dd.Dma32BitAddresses = ??;
dd.Dma64BitAddresses = ??;
pdx->AdapterObject = IoGetDmaAdapter(...);
pdx->vaCommonBuffer =
  (*pdx->AdapterObject->DmaOperations->AllocateCommonBuffer)
  (pdx->AdapterObject, <length>, &pdx->paCommonBuffer, FALSE);
```

Prior to calling IoGetDmaAdapter, you set the **Dma32BitAddresses** and **Dma64Bit-Addresses** flags in the DEVICE_DESCRIPTION structure to state the truth about your device's addressing capabilities. That is, if your device can address a buffer using any 32-bit physical address, set Dma32BitAddresses to TRUE. If it can address a buffer using any 64-bit physical address, set Dma64BitAddresses to TRUE.

In the call to **AllocateCommonBuffer**, the second argument is the byte length of the buffer you want to allocate. The fourth argument is a BOOLEAN value that indicates whether you want the allocated memory to be capable of entry into the CPU cache (TRUE) or not (FALSE).

AllocateCommonBuffer returns a virtual address. This address is the one you use within your driver to access the allocated buffer area. AllocateCommonBuffer also sets the PHYSICAL_ADDRESS pointed to by the third argument to be the logical address used by your device for its own buffer access.

> **NOTE** The DDK carefully uses the term *logical address* to refer to the address value returned by MapTransfer and the address value returned by the third argument of AllocateCommonBuffer. On many CPU architectures, a logical address will be a physical memory address that the CPU understands. On other architectures, it might be an address that only the I/O bus understands. Perhaps *bus address* would have been a better term.

Slave DMA with a Common Buffer

If you're going to be performing slave DMA, you must create an MDL to describe the virtual addresses you receive. The actual purpose of the MDL is to occupy an argument slot in an eventual call to MapTransfer. MapTransfer won't end up doing any copying, but it requires the MDL to discover that it doesn't need to do any copying! You'd normally create the MDL in your StartDevice function just after allocating the common buffer:

```
pdx->vaCommonBuffer = ...;
pdx->mdlCommonBuffer = IoAllocateMdl(pdx->vaCommonBuffer,
  <length>, FALSE, FALSE, NULL);
MmBuildMdlForNonPagedPool(pdx->mdlCommonBuffer);
```

To perform an output operation, first make sure by some means (such as an explicit memory copy) that the common buffer contains the data you want to send to the device. The other DMA logic in your driver will be essentially the same as I showed you earlier (in "Performing DMA Transfers"). You'll call AllocateAdapterChannel. It will call your adapter control routine, which will call KeFlushIoBuffers—if you allocated a cacheable buffer—and then call MapTransfer. Your DPC routine will call FlushAdapterBuffers and FreeAdapterChannel. In all of these calls, you'll specify the common buffer's MDL instead of the one that accompanied the read or write IRP you're processing. Some of the service routines you call won't do as much work when you have a common buffer as when you don't, but you must call them anyway. At the end of an input operation, you might need to copy data out of your common buffer to some other place.

To fulfill a request to read or write more data than fits in your common buffer, you might need to periodically refill or empty the buffer. The adapter object's **ReadDmaCounter** function allows you to determine the progress of the ongoing transfer to help you decide what to do.

Bus-Master DMA with a Common Buffer

If your device is a bus master, allocating a common buffer allows you to dispense with calling AllocateAdapterChannel, MapTransfer, and FreeMapRegisters. You don't need to call those routines because AllocateCommonBuffer also reserves the map registers, if any, needed for your device to access the buffer. Each bus-master device has an adapter object that isn't shared with other devices and for which you therefore need never wait. Since you have a virtual address you can use to access the buffer at any time, and since your device's bus-mastering capability allows it to access the buffer by using the physical address you've received back from AllocateCommonBuffer, no additional work is required.

Cautions About Using Common Buffers

A few cautions are in order with respect to common buffer allocation and usage. Physically contiguous memory is scarce in a running system—so scarce that you might not be able to allocate the buffer you want unless you stake your claim quite early in the life of a new session. The Memory Manager makes a limited effort to shuffle memory pages around to satisfy your request, and that process can delay the return from AllocateCommonBuffer for a period of time. But the effort might fail, and you must be sure to handle the failure case. Not only does a common buffer tie up potentially scarce physical pages, but it can also tie up map registers that could otherwise be used by other devices. For both these reasons, you should use a common-buffer strategy advisedly.

Another caution about common buffers arises from the fact that the Memory Manager necessarily gives you one or more full pages of memory. Allocating a common buffer that's just a few bytes long is wasteful and should be avoided. On the other hand, it's also wasteful to allocate several pages of memory that don't actually need to be physically contiguous. As the DDK suggests, therefore, it's better to make several requests for smaller blocks if the blocks don't have to be contiguous.

Releasing a Common Buffer

You would ordinarily release the memory occupied by your common buffer in your StopDevice routine just before you destroy the adapter object:

```
(*pdx->AdapterObject->DmaOperations->FreeCommonBuffer)
  (pdx->AdapterObject, <length>, pdx->paCommonBuffer,
  pdx->vaCommonBuffer, FALSE);
```

The second parameter to **FreeCommonBuffer** is the same length value you used when you allocated the buffer. The last parameter indicates whether the memory is cacheable, and it should be the same as the last argument you used in the call to AllocateCommonBuffer.

A Simple Bus-Master Device

The PKTDMA sample driver on the companion disc illustrates how to perform bus-master DMA operations without scatter/gather support using the AMCC S5933 PCI matchmaker chip. I've already discussed details of how this driver initializes the device in StartDevice and how it initiates a DMA transfer in StartIo. I've also discussed nearly all of what happens in this driver's AdapterControl and DpcForIsr routines. I indicated earlier that these routines would have some device-dependent code for starting an operation on the device; I wrote a helper function named **StartTransfer** for that purpose:

```
VOID StartTransfer(PDEVICE_EXTENSION pdx, PHYSICAL_ADDRESS address,
  BOOLEAN isread)
  {
  ULONG mcsr = READ_PORT_ULONG((PULONG)(pdx->portbase + MCSR);
  ULONG intcsr = READ_PORT_ULONG((PULONG)(pdx->portbase + INTCSR);
  if (isread)
    {
    mcsr |= MCSR_WRITE_NEED4 | MCSR_WRITE_ENABLE;
    intcsr |= INTCSR_WTCI_ENABLE;
```

```
    WRITE_PORT_ULONG((PULONG)(pdx->portbase + MWTC), pdx->xfer);
    WRITE_PORT_ULONG((PULONG)(pdx->portbase + MWAR), address.LowPart);
    }
  else
    {
    mcsr |= MCSR_READ_NEED4 | MCSR_READ_ENABLE;
    intcsr |= INTCSR_RTCI_ENABLE;
    WRITE_PORT_ULONG((PULONG)(pdx->portbase | MRTC), pdx->xfer);
    WRITE_PORT_ULONG((PULONG)(pdx->portbase + MRAR), address.LowPart);
    }
  WRITE_PORT_ULONG((PULONG)(pdx->portbase + INTCSR), intcsr);
  WRITE_PORT_ULONG((PULONG)(pdx->portbase + MCSR), mcsr);
  }
```

This routine sets up the S5933 operations registers for a DMA transfer and then starts the transfer running. The steps in the process are:

1. Program the address (**M*x*AR**) and transfer count (**M*x*TC**) registers appropriate to the direction of data flow. AMCC chose to use the term *read* to describe an operation in which data moves from memory to the device. Therefore, when we're implementing an IRP_MJ_WRITE, we program a read operation at the chip level. The address we use is the logical address returned by MapTransfer.

2. Enable an interrupt when the transfer count reaches 0 by writing to the **INTCSR**.

3. Start the transfer by setting one of the transfer-enable bits in the **MCSR**.

It's not obvious from this fragment of code, but the S5933 is actually capable of doing a DMA read and a DMA write at the same time. I wrote PKTDMA in such a way that only one operation (either a read or a write) can be occurring. To generalize the driver to allow both kinds of operation to occur simultaneously, you would need to (a) implement separate queues for read and write IRPs, and (b) create *two* device objects and *two* adapter objects—one pair for reading and the other for writing—so as to avoid the embarrassment of trying to queue the same object twice inside AllocateAdapterChannel. I thought putting that additional complication into the sample would end up confusing you. (I know I'm being pretty optimistic about my expository skills to imply that I haven't *already* confused you, but it could have been worse.)

Handling Interrupts in PKTDMA

PCI42 included an interrupt routine that did a small bit of work to move some data. PKTDMA's interrupt routine is a little simpler:

```
BOOLEAN OnInterrupt(PKINTERRUPT InterruptObject, PDEVICE_EXTENSION pdx)
  {
  ULONG intcsr = READ_PORT_ULONG((PULONG) (pdx->portbase + INTCSR));
  if (!(intcsr & INTCSR_INTERRUPT_PENDING))
    return FALSE;
```

(continued)

```
    ULONG mcsr = READ_PORT_ULONG((PULONG) (pdx->portbase + MCSR));
1   WRITE_PORT_ULONG((PULONG) (pdx->portbase + MCSR),
      mcsr & ~(MCSR_WRITE_ENABLE | MCSR_READ_ENABLE));

2   intcsr &= ~(INTCSR_WTCI_ENABLE | INTCSR_WTCI_ENABLE);

    BOOLEAN dpc = GetCurrentIrp(&pdx->dqReadWrite) != NULL;

    while (intcsr & INTCSR_INTERRUPT_PENDING)
      {
3     InterlockedOr(&pdx->intcsr, intcsr);
      WRITE_PORT_ULONG((PULONG) (pdx->portbase + INTCSR), intcsr);
      intcsr = READ_PORT_ULONG((PULONG) (pdx->portbase + INTCSR));
      }

    if (dpc)
      IoRequestDpc(pdx->DeviceObject, NULL, NULL);

    return TRUE;
    }
```

I'll only discuss the ways in which this ISR differs from the one in PCI42:

1. The S5933 will keep trying to transfer data—subject to the count register, that is—so long as the enable bits are set in the **MCSR**. This statement clears both bits. If your driver were handling simultaneous reads and writes, you'd determine which kind of operation had just finished by testing the interrupt flags in the **INTCSR** and then disable just the transfer in that direction.

2. We'll shortly write back to the **INTCSR** to clear the interrupt. This statement ensures that we'll also *disable* the transfer-count-0 interrupts so that they can't occur anymore. Once again, a driver that handles simultaneous reads and writes would disable only the interrupt that just occurred.

3. **InterlockedOr** is a helper routine I wrote so that I wouldn't have to worry about racing with DpcForIsr in accumulating interrupt flags.

Testing PKTDMA

You can test PKTDMA if you have an S5933DK1 development board. If you ran the PCI42 test, you already installed the S5933DK1.SYS driver to handle the ISA add-on interface card. If not, you'll need to install that driver for this test. Then install PKTDMA.SYS as the driver for the S5933 development board itself. You can then run the TEST.EXE test program that's in the PKTDMA\TEST\DEBUG directory. TEST will perform a write for 8192 bytes to PKTDMA. It will also issue a **DeviceIoControl** to S5933DK1 to read the data back from the add-on side, and it will verify that it read the right values.

Chapter 8

Power
Management

Technophobes may take solace in the fact that they retain ultimate control over their electronic servants so long as they control the power switch. Power is, of course, the sine qua non of computing, but personal computers haven't done an especially good job of managing it until quite recently.

More effective power management is important for at least three reasons. First, as a matter of sound ecology, using less power helps to minimize the impact of computing on the environment. Not only do computers require power, but so do the air-conditioning systems for the rooms where the computers reside. A second reason better power management is needed is familiar to many travelers: battery technology simply hasn't kept pace with the demand for mobile computing of all kinds. And, finally, greater consumer acceptance of PCs as home appliances depends on improving power management. Current machines have noisy fans and squealing disk drives when they're on, and they take a long time to start up from the power-off state. Decreasing the power-up latency and eliminating unnecessary noise—which also means minimizing power consumption so that less cooling is required—will be necessary before PCs can comfortably occupy consumer niches.

In this chapter, I'll discuss the role WDM drivers play in power management in the Microsoft Windows 2000 and Microsoft Windows 98 operating systems. The first major section of the chapter, "The WDM Power Model," presents an overview of the concepts you need to know about. The second section, "Managing Power Transitions," is the meat of the chapter: I'll describe there the very complicated tasks a typical function driver carries out. I'll finish the chapter with a discussion of some ancillary responsibilities a WDM function driver has with respect to power management.

THE WDM POWER MODEL

In Windows 2000 and Windows 98, the operating system takes over most of the job of managing power. This makes sense because only the operating system really knows what's going on, of course. A system BIOS charged with power management, for example, can't tell the difference between an application's use of the screen and a screen saver's. But the operating system can tell the difference and thus can determine whether it's okay to turn off the display.

As the global *power policy owner* for the computer, the operating system supports user interface elements that give the end user ultimate control over power decisions. These elements include the control panel, commands in the Start menu, and APIs for controlling device wake-up features. The Power Manager component of the kernel implements the operating system's power policies by sending I/O request packets (IRPs) to devices. WDM drivers have the primarily passive role of responding to these IRPs, although you'll probably find this passivity to incorporate a lot of active motion when I show you how much code is involved.

The Roles of WDM Drivers

One of the drivers for a device acts as the power policy owner for the device. Since the function driver most often fills this role, I'll continue discussing power management as though that were invariably the case. Just bear in mind that your device might have unique requirements that mandate giving the responsibilities of policy owner to some filter driver or to the bus driver instead.

The function driver receives IRPs (system IRPs) from the Power Manager that pertain to changes in the overall power state of the system. Acting as policy owner for the device, it translates these instructions into device terms and originates new IRPs (device IRPs). When responding to the device IRPs, the function driver worries about the details that pertain to the device. Devices might carry onboard *context information* that you don't want to lose during a period of low power. Keyboard drivers, for example, might hold the state of locking keys (such as CAPS-LOCK, NUM-

LOCK, and SCROLL-LOCK), LEDs, and so on. The function driver is responsible for saving and restoring that context. Some devices have a *wake-up feature* that allows them to wake up a sleeping system when external events occur; the function driver works together with the end user to make sure that the wake-up feature is available when needed. Many function drivers manage queues of substantive IRPs—that is, IRPs that read or write data to the device, and they need to stall or release those queues as power wanes and waxes.

The bus driver at the bottom of the device stack is responsible for controlling the flow of current to your device and for performing whatever electronic steps are necessary to arm or disarm your device's wake-up feature.

A filter driver normally acts as a simple conduit for power requests, passing them down to lower-level drivers by using the special protocol I'll describe a bit further on.

Device Power and System Power States

The Windows Driver Model uses the same terms to describe power states as does the Advanced Configuration and Power Interface (ACPI) specification. (See *http://www.teleport.com/~acpi/spec.htm.*) Devices can assume the four states illustrated in Figure 8-1. In the D0 state, the device is fully functional. In the D3 state, the device is using no (or very minimal) power and is therefore not functioning (or is functioning at a very low level). The intermediate D1 and D2 states denote two different somnolent states for the device. As a device moves from D0 to D3, it consumes less and less power. In addition, it remembers less and less *context* information about its current state. Consequently, the *latency* period needed for the device's transition back to D0 increases.

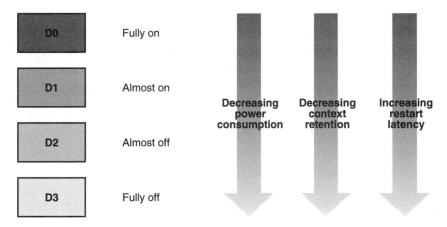

Figure 8-1. *ACPI device power states.*

Microsoft has formulated class-specific requirements for different types of devices. I found these requirements on line at *http://www.microsoft.com/hwdev/specs/PMref/*. The specifications mandate, for example, that every device support at least the D0 and D3 states. Input devices (keyboards, mice, and so on) should also support the D1 state. Modem devices, on the other hand, should additionally support D2. These differences in specifications for device classes stem from likely usage scenarios and industry practice.

The operating system doesn't deal directly with the power states of devices—that's exclusively the province of device drivers. Rather, the system controls power by using a set of system power states that are analogous to the ACPI device states. See Figure 8-2. The Working state is the full-power, fully functional state of the computer. Programs are able to execute only when the system is in the Working state.

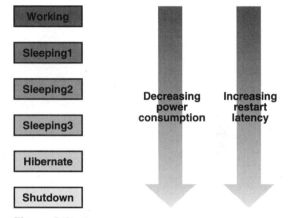

Figure 8-2. *System power states.*

The other system power states correspond to reduced power configurations in which no instructions execute. The Shutdown state is the power-off state. (Discussing the Shutdown state seems like discussing an unanswerable question such as "What's inside a black hole?" Like the event horizon surrounding a black hole, though, the *transition* to Shutdown is something you'll need to know about as your device spirals in.) The Hibernate state is a variant of Shutdown in which the entire state of the computer is recorded on disk so that a live session can be restarted when power comes back. The three sleeping states between Hibernate and Working encompass gradations in power consumption.

Power State Transitions

The system initializes in the Working state. This almost goes without saying, because the computer is, by definition, in the Working state whenever it's executing instructions. Most devices start out in the D0 state, although the policy owner for the device might put it into a lower power state when it's not actually in use. After the system is up and running, then, it reaches a steady state in which the system power level is Working and devices are in various states depending on activity and capability.

End user actions and external events cause subsequent transitions between power states. A common transition scenario arises when the user uses the Shut Down command on the Start menu to put the machine into standby. In response, the Power Manager first asks each driver whether the prospective loss of power will be okay by sending an IRP_MJ_POWER request with the minor function code IRP_MN_QUERY_POWER. If all drivers acquiesce, the Power Manager sends a second power IRP with the minor function code IRP_MN_SET_POWER. Drivers put their devices into lower power states in response to this second IRP. If any driver vetoes the query, the Power Manager still sends an IRP_MN_SET_POWER request, but it usually specifies the *current* power level instead of the one originally proposed.

The system doesn't always send IRP_MN_QUERY_POWER requests, by the way. Some events (such as the end user unplugging the computer or the battery expiring) must be accepted without demur, and the operating system won't issue a query when they occur. But when a query is issued, and when a driver accepts the proposed state change by passing the request along, the driver undertakes that it won't start any operation that might interfere with the expected set-power request. A tape driver, for example, would make sure that it's not currently retensioning a tape—the interruption of which might break the tape—before succeeding a query for a low-power state. In addition, the driver would reject any subsequent retension command until (and unless) a countervailing set-power request arrives to signal abandonment of the state change.

Handling IRP_MJ_POWER Requests

The Power Manager communicates with drivers by means of an IRP_MJ_POWER I/O request packet. Four minor function codes are currently possible. See Table 8-1.

Minor Function Code	Description
IRP_MN_QUERY_POWER	Determine if prospective change in power state can safely occur
IRP_MN_SET_POWER	Instructs driver to change power state
IRP_MN_WAIT_WAKE	Instructs bus driver to arm wake-up feature; provides way for function driver to know when wake-up signal occurs
IRP_MN_POWER_SEQUENCE	Provides optimization for context saving and restoring

Table 8-1. *Minor function codes for IRP_MJ_POWER.*

The **Power** substructure in the IO_STACK_LOCATION's **Parameters** union has four parameters that describe the request, of which only two will be of interest to most WDM drivers. See Table 8-2.

Field Name	Description
SystemContext	A context value used internally by the Power Manager
Type	DevicePowerState or SystemPowerState (values of POWER_STATE_TYPE enumeration)
State	Power state—either a DEVICE_POWER_STATE enumeration value or a SYSTEM_POWER_STATE enumeration value
ShutdownType	A code indicating the reason for a transition to PowerSystemShutdown

Table 8-2. *Fields in the Parameters.Power substructure of an IO_STACK_LOCATION.*

All drivers—both filter drivers and the function driver—generally pass every power request down the stack to the driver underneath them. The only exceptions are an IRP_MN_QUERY_POWER request that the driver wants to fail and an IRP that arrives while the device is being deleted.

Special rules govern how you pass power requests down to lower-level drivers. Refer to Figure 8-3 for an overview of the process in the three possible variations you might use. First, before releasing control of a power IRP, you must call **PoStartNextPowerIrp**. You do so even if you are completing the IRP with an error status. The reason for this call is that the Power Manager maintains its own queue of power requests and must be told when it will be okay to dequeue and send the next request to your device. In addition to calling PoStartNextPowerIrp, you must call the special routine **PoCallDriver** (instead of **IoCallDriver**) to send the request to the next driver.

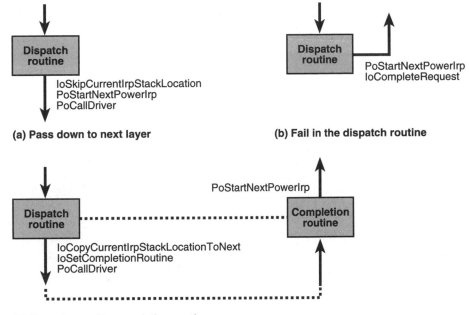

(a) Pass down to next layer   (b) Fail in the dispatch routine

(c) Pass down with completion routine

Figure 8-3. *Handling IRP_MJ_POWER requests.*

NOTE Not only does the Power Manager maintain a queue of power IRPs for each device, but it maintains *two* such queues. One queue is for system power IRPs (that is, IRP_MN_SET_POWER requests that specify a system power state). The other queue is for device power IRPs (that is, IRP_MN_SET_POWER requests that specify a device power state). One IRP of each kind can be simultaneously active. Your driver might also be handling a Plug and Play (PnP) request and any number of substantive IRPs at the same time, too, by the way.

The following function illustrates the mechanical aspects of passing a power request down the stack:

```
NTSTATUS DefaultPowerHandler(IN PDEVICE_OBJECT fdo, IN PIRP Irp)
    {
    PoStartNextPowerIrp(Irp);
    IoSkipCurrentIrpStackLocation(Irp);
    PDEVICE_EXTENSION pdx = (PDEVICE_EXTENSION) fdo->DeviceExtension;
    return PoCallDriver(pdx->LowerDeviceObject, Irp);
    }
```

1 ▶
2 ▶
3 ▶

1. **PoStartNextPowerIrp** tells the Power Manager that it can dequeue and send the next power IRP. You must make this call for every power IRP you receive at a time when you own the IRP. In other words, the call must occur either in your dispatch routine before you send the request to PoCallDriver or in a completion routine.

2. We use **IoSkipCurrentIrpStackLocation** to retard the IRP's stack pointer by one position in anticipation that PoCallDriver will immediately advance it. This is the same technique I've already discussed for passing a request down and ignoring what happens to it afterwards.

3. You use **PoCallDriver** to forward power requests. Microsoft implemented this function to forestall the minimal, but nonetheless measurable, impact on performance that might result from adding conditional logic to IoCallDriver to handle power management.

The function driver takes the two steps of passing the IRP down and performing its device-specific action in a neatly nested order, as shown in Figure 8-4: When *removing* power—that is, when changing to a lower power state—it performs the device-dependent step first and then passes the request down. When *adding* power—when changing to a higher power state—it passes the request down and performs the device-dependent step in a completion routine. This neat nesting of operations guarantees that the pathway leading to the hardware has power while the driver manipulates the hardware.

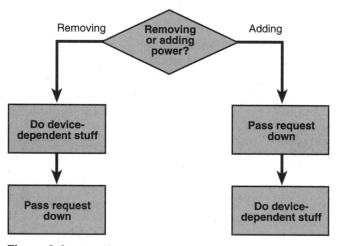

Figure 8-4. *Handling system power requests.*

Power IRPs come to you in the context of a system thread that you must not block. You can't block the thread for any of several reasons. If your device has the INRUSH characteristic, or if you've cleared the DO_POWER_PAGABLE flag in your device object, the Power Manager will send you IRPs at DISPATCH_LEVEL. You remember, of course, that you can't block a thread while executing at DISPATCH_LEVEL. Even if you've set DO_POWER_PAGABLE, however, so that you get power IRPs at PASSIVE_LEVEL, you can cause a deadlock by requesting a device power IRP while servicing a system IRP and then blocking: the Power Manager might not send you the device IRP until your system IRP dispatch routine returns, so you'll wait forever.

The function driver normally needs to perform several steps that require time to finish as part of handling some power requests. The DDK points out that you can *delay* the completion of power IRPs by periods that the end user won't find perceptible under the circumstances, but being able to delay doesn't mean being able to block. The requirement that you can't block while these operations finish means lavish use of completion routines to make the steps asynchronous.

Implicit in the notion that IRP_MN_QUERY_POWER poses a question for you to answer "Yes" or "No" is the fact that you can fail an IRP with that minor function code. Failing the IRP is how you say "No." You don't have any such freedom with IRP_MN_SET_POWER requests, however: you must carry out the instructions they convey.

MANAGING POWER TRANSITIONS

Performing power management tasks correctly requires very accurate coding, and there are many complicating factors. For example, your device might have the ability to wake up the system from a sleeping state. Deciding whether to succeed or fail a query, and deciding which device power state corresponds to a given new system power state, depends on whether your wake-up feature is currently armed. You may have powered down your own device because of inactivity, and you need to provide for restoring power when a substantive IRP comes along. Maybe your device is an "inrush" device that needs a large spike of current to power on, in which case the Power Manager treats you specially. And so on.

When I thought about solving all the problems of handling query-power and set-power operations in a traditional way—that is, with normal-looking dispatch and completion routines—I was daunted by the sheer number of different subroutines that would be required and that would end up doing fairly similar things. I therefore decided to build my power support around a finite state machine that could easily deal with the asynchronous nature of the activities.

I'll explain this finite state machine as it appears in GENERIC.SYS, which is a support driver that most of the code samples on the companion disc use. Appendix B, "Using GENERIC.SYS," explains the client interface to GENERIC.SYS in complete detail. GENERIC.SYS amounts to a kernel-mode DLL containing helper functions for WDM drivers. You could think of it as a generic class driver with broad applicability. Client drivers, including most of my own sample drivers, delegate handling of power IRPs to GENERIC.SYS by calling **GenericDispatchPower**. GENERIC.SYS also implements the DEVQUEUE object I discussed in Chapter 6, "Plug and Play."

Overview of the Finite State Machine

I wrote a function named **HandlePowerEvent** to implement the finite state machine that manages power IRPs. I call this function with two arguments:

```
NTSTATUS HandlePowerEvent(PPOWCONTEXT ctx, enum POWEVENT event);
```

The first argument is a context structure that contains a state variable, among other things:

```
typedef struct _POWCONTEXT {
  LONG id;
  LONG eventcount;
  PGENERIC_EXTENSION pdx;
  PIRP irp;
  enum POWSTATE state;
  NTSTATUS status;
  PKEVENT pev;
  DEVICE_POWER_STATE devstate;
  UCHAR MinorFunction;
  BOOLEAN UnstallQueue;
} POWCONTEXT, *PPOWCONTEXT;
```

The **id** and **eventcount** fields are for debugging. If you compile POWER.CPP in the GENERIC project with the preprocessor macro VERBOSETRACE defined as a nonzero value, the POWTRACE macro will produce volumes of trace messages. I used this feature to debug the finite state machine. The prebuilt version of

GENERIC.SYS on the companion disc was built without VERBOSETRACE to cut down on the sheer number of trace messages you'd be confronted with when you began to try out my samples.

The **pdx** member points to GENERIC's portion of the device extension for a given device. There are just a couple of members in the device extension that are important for power management, and I'll mention them later in "Initial Handling for a New IRP." The **irp** member points to the power IRP that the finite state machine is currently working on; **state** is the state variable for the machine. The **status** member is the ending status of an IRP. In some situations, we want to wait while HandlePowerEvent originates and completes a device power IRP; we use the event pointed to by **pev** to await completion in those situations. The **devstate** member holds the device power state we want to use in a device IRP, and **MinorFunction** holds the minor function code (IRP_MN_QUERY_POWER or IRP_MN_SET_POWER) we want to use in that IRP. Finally, **UnstallQueue** indicates whether we want the state machine to unstall the substantive IRP queue when it finishes handling the current power IRP.

The second argument to HandlePowerEvent is an event code that indicates why we're calling the function. There are just these few event codes:

- **NewIrp** indicates that we are submitting a new power IRP to the finite state machine for processing. The context structure's **irp** member points to the IRP in question.

- **MainIrpComplete** indicates that an IRP is complete.

- **AsyncNotify** indicates that some other asynchronous activity has occurred.

HandlePowerEvent uses the value of the state variable and the event code to determine an action to take. See Table 8-3. (In the table, by the way, an empty cell denotes an impossible situation that leads to an ASSERT failure in the checked build of GENERIC.SYS.) An action corresponds to a series of program steps that advance the power IRP along its processing path.

State	Event		
	NewIrp	**MainIrpComplete**	**AsyncNotify**
InitialState	TriageNewIrp		
SysPowerUpPending		SysPowerUpComplete	
SubPowerUpPending			SubPowerUpComplete
SubPowerDownPending			SubPowerDownComplete
SysPowerDownPending		SysPowerDownComplete	
DevPowerUpPending		DevPowerUpComplete	
DevPowerDownPending		CompleteMainIrp	
ContextSavePending			ContextSaveComplete
ContextRestorePending			ContextRestoreComplete
DevQueryUpPending		DevQueryUpComplete	
DevQueryDownPending		DevQueryDownComplete	
QueueStallPending			QueueStallComplete
FinalState			

Table 8-3. *Table giving initial action for each event and state.*

Since many of the events require multiple actions in some situations, I coded **HandlePowerEvent** in what may seem at first like a peculiar way, as follows:

```
NTSTATUS HandlePowerEvent(...)
  {
  NTSTATUS status;
  POWACTION action = ...;
  while (TRUE)
    {
    switch (action)
      {
      case <someaction>:
        action = <someotheraction>;
        continue;
```

```
      case <anotheraction>:
        break;
        }
      break;
      }
    return status;
    }
```

That is, the function amounts to a **switch** on the **action** code imbedded within an infinite loop. An action case that performs a **continue** statement repeats the loop; this is how I string together a series of actions during one call to the function. An action case that performs a **break** from the **switch** reaches another **break** statement that exits from the loop, whereupon the function returns.

I adopted this coding style for the state machine because I really took to heart the structured programming precepts I learned in my youth. I wanted there to be just one return statement in this whole function to make it easier to prove that the function worked correctly. To aid in the proof, I developed a couple of rules for myself that I could test either by inspection or with ASSERT statements at the end of the function. Here are the rules:

■ Every code path eventually leads to a **break** statement and, hence, to a **return** from the function. Somewhere along the path, someone has to change the **status** variable (I initialize it to −1 and then test to be sure it got changed) and the **state** variable (I test to be sure it got changed).

■ Any **continue** statement should be preceded by a change in the **action** variable.

■ Any case that might generate a recursive call to HandlePowerEvent—for example, by calling PoCallDriver, which might cause a completion event to be signalled before it returns—must immediately **break** from the loop without touching the context structure or the IRP.

Initial Handling for a New IRP

When we receive a new query-power or set-power IRP, we create a context structure to drive the finite state machine and call HandlePowerEvent:

```
NTSTATUS GenericDispatchPower(PGENERIC_EXTENSION pdx, PIRP Irp)
    {
    NTSTATUS status = IoAcquireRemoveLock(pdx->RemoveLock, Irp);
```

(continued)

```
     if (!NT_SUCCESS(status))
       return CompleteRequest(Irp, status);
     PIO_STACK_LOCATION stack = IoGetCurrentIrpStackLocation(Irp);
     ULONG fcn = stack->MinorFunction;
     if (fcn == IRP_MN_SET_POWER || fcn == IRP_MN_QUERY_POWER)
       {
       PPOWCONTEXT ctx = (PPOWCONTEXT) ExAllocatePool(NonPagedPool,
         sizeof(POWCONTEXT));
       RtlZeroMemory(ctx, sizeof(POWCONTEXT));
       ctx->pdx = pdx;
       ctx->irp = Irp;
       status = HandlePowerEvent(ctx, NewIrp);
       }
     IoReleaseRemoveLock(pdx->RemoveLock, Irp);
     return status;
     }
```

1. The client driver provides a remove lock that both it and GENERIC use to guard against premature removal of the device object. The actual code in GENERIC is a little more complicated than I'm showing you here, in that the remove lock isn't required. The actual code therefore tests the **RemoveLock** pointer for NULL before using it. There are other unimportant respects, including error checking, in which GENERIC differs from the simplified version I'm showing throughout this chapter.

2. For set and query operations, we allocate nonpaged memory for the context structure and initialize it. The **state** variable gets initialized to **InitialState**, which is numerically equal to 0, by the call to **RtlZeroMemory**.

The initial state of the finite state machine is InitialState. When we call HandlePowerEvent for the NewIrp event, the first action taken will be the following, which I named **TriageNewIrp**:

```
case TriageNewIrp:
  {
  status = STATUS_PENDING;
  IoMarkIrpPending(Irp);
  IoAcquireRemoveLock(pdx->RemoveLock, Irp);
  if (stack->Parameters.Power.Type == SystemPowerState)
    {        // system IRP
    if (stack->Parameters.Power.State.SystemState < pdx->syspower)
      {
      action = ForwardMainIrp;
```

```
                    ctx->state = SysPowerUpPending;
                    }
                else
                    {
                    action = SelectDState;
                    ctx->state = SubPowerDownPending;
                    }
                }           // system IRP
            else
                {           // device IRP
                ctx->state = QueueStallPending;
                if (!pdx->StalledForPower)
                    {
                    ctx->UnstallQueue = TRUE;
                    pdx->StalledForPower = TRUE;
                    NTSTATUS qstatus = StallRequestsAndNotify(pdx->dqReadWrite,
                        GenericSaveRestoreComplete, ctx);
                    if (qstatus == STATUS_PENDING)
                        break;
                    }
                action = QueueStallComplete;
                }           // device IRP
            continue;
            }
```

1. We always pend the power IRPs that come to us. In nearly every case, we need to delay completing the IRP until after some asynchronous activity occurs.

2. We acquire the remove lock an extra time beyond the acquisition that occurs in the dispatch routine. We'll release this instance of the lock when we finally complete the IRP.

3. If the power state in the IRP is numerically less than the **syspower** value we carry around in the device extension, the IRP relates to a higher system power state.

4. This statement illustrates how **HandlePowerEvent** can perform more than one action during a single invocation. Later on we'll execute a **continue** statement that repeats the infinite loop. The **action** value will be different, however, which will cause us to execute a different piece of code.

5. This statement illustrates how action cases can alter the state of the finite state machine. To simplify the conditional compilation I used for debugging print statements, the actual code in GENERIC uses a macro named SETSTATE to perform this assignment, by the way.

6. We're about to call a function (**StallRequestsAndNotify**) that might cause recursion into this function. We're not allowed to touch the context structure afterwards, so we set this flag now. The flag means that **CompleteMainIrp** should call **RestartRequests** to unstall the queue.

7. This statement illustrates how an action case can cause **HandlePowerEvent** to return. This **break** statement exits from the **switch** on **action**. Immediately after the **switch** statement is another **break**, which exits from the **while** loop in which the **switch** is embedded.

Basically, TriageNewIrp is distinguishing between system power IRPs (that is, IRPs whose **Type** is **SystemPowerState**) that increase the power level, system power IRPs that leave the power level alone or reduce it, and device power IRPs (that is, IRPs whose **Type** is **DevicePowerState**), regardless of whether they raise or lower the power level. The state machine doesn't distinguish at this stage between QUERY_POWER and SET_POWER requests, so they end up being treated very similarly up to a point.

For us to know whether power is rising or falling, our device extension needs two variables for keeping track of system power and device power states:

```
typedef struct _GENERIC_EXTENSION {
  ...
  DEVICE_POWER_STATE devpower; // current dev power state
  SYSTEM_POWER_STATE syspower; // current sys power state
  } GENERIC_EXTENSION, *PGENERIC_EXTENSION;
```

We initialize these values to **PowerDeviceD0** and **PowerSystemWorking**, respectively, when the client driver first registers with GENERIC.SYS.

You can guess from context that the device extension also has a BOOLEAN member named **StalledForPower**. This flag, when set, indicates that the substantive IRP queue is presently stalled for purposes of power management. Incidentally, you'll notice (if you've got the right sort of nasty and suspicious mind to be doing device driver programming, that is) that I'm not explicitly synchronizing access to the power state fields or this flag. No additional synchronization is required beyond the serialization that the Power Manager already imposes.

I'll discuss the three initial categories of IRPs separately now.

System Power IRPs That Increase Power

If a system power IRP implies an increase in the system power level, you'll forward it immediately to the next lower driver. In your completion routine for the system power IRP, you'll request the corresponding device power IRP and return STATUS_MORE_PROCESSING_REQUIRED to temporarily halt the completion process. In a completion routine for the device power IRP, you'll finish the completion processing for the system power IRP. Figure 8-5 diagrams the flow of the IRP through all of the drivers. Figure 8-6 is a state diagram that shows how our finite state machine handles the IRP.

System power IRP

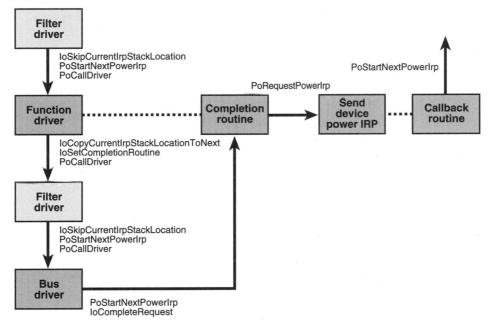

Figure 8-5. *IRP flow when increasing system power.*

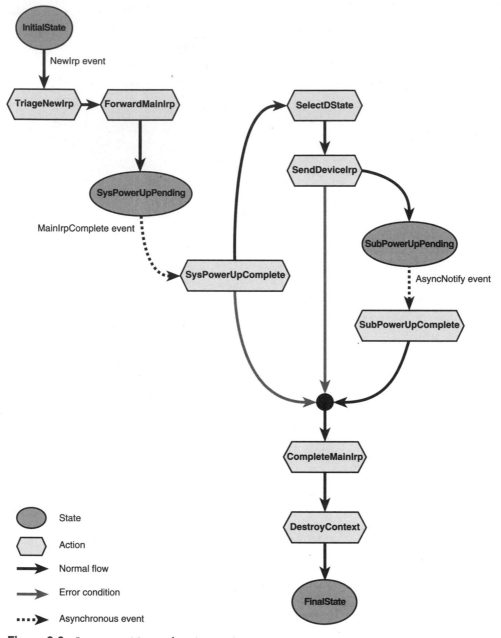

Figure 8-6. *State transitions when increasing system power.*

In terms of how the code works, I showed you earlier that TriageNewIrp puts the machine into the **SysPowerUpPending** state and requests the **ForwardMainIrp** action, which is as follows:

```
case ForwardMainIrp:
  {
  IoCopyCurrentIrpStackLocationToNext(Irp);
  IoSetCompletionRoutine(Irp, (PIO_COMPLETION_ROUTINE)
    MainCompletionRoutine, (PVOID) ctx, TRUE, TRUE, TRUE);
  PoCallDriver(pdx->LowerDeviceObject, Irp);
  break;
  }
```

HandlePowerEvent will now return STATUS_PENDING, as mandated by the code we already saw in TriageNewIrp. This return value percolates back out through GenericDispatchPower and, presumably, the client driver's IRP_MJ_POWER dispatch function.

Our next contact with this IRP is when the bus driver completes it. Our own **MainCompletionRoutine** gets control as part of the completion process, saves the IRP's ending status in the context structure's **status** field, and invokes the finite state machine:

```
NTSTATUS MainCompletionRoutine(PDEVICE_OBJECT junk, PIRP Irp,
  PPOWCONTEXT ctx)
  {
  ctx->status = Irp->IoStatus.Status;
  return HandlePowerEvent(ctx, MainIrpComplete);
  }
```

Our initial action will be **SysPowerUpComplete**:

```
case SysPowerUpComplete:
  {
  if (!NT_SUCCESS(ctx->status))
    action = CompleteMainIrp;
  else
    {
    if (stack->MinorFunction == IRP_MN_SET_POWER)
      pdx->syspower = stack->Parameters.Power.State.SystemState;
    action = SelectDState;
    ctx->state = SubPowerUpPending;
    status = STATUS_MORE_PROCESSING_REQUIRED;
    }
  continue;
  }
```

1. If the IRP failed in the lower levels of the driver hierarchy, we're going to let it complete without doing any more work on this power event. I'll explain in the next section, "Dealing with Failure," what **CompleteMainIrp** does.

2. This is where we record the new system power state. We use the **syspower** value when we check to see whether a new system IRP is raising or lowering power.

3. We've been called from **MainCompletionRoutine** and now want to interrupt completion of the system IRP while we process the device IRP we're about to originate. Hence, we'll cause MainCompletionRoutine to return STATUS_MORE_PROCESSING_REQUIRED.

Dealing with Failure

If the IRP failed, you can see that we'll do the **CompleteMainIrp** action next:

```
case CompleteMainIrp:
  {
  PoStartNextPowerIrp(Irp);
  if (event == MainIrpComplete)
    status = ctx->status;
  else
    {
    Irp->IoStatus.Status = ctx->status;
    IoCompleteRequest(Irp, IO_NO_INCREMENT);
    }
  IoReleaseRemoveLock(pdx->RemoveLock, Irp);
  if (ctx->UnstallQueue)
    {
    pdx->StalledForPower = FALSE;
    RestartRequests(pdx->dqReadWrite, pdx->DeviceObject);
    }
  action = DestroyContext;
  continue;
  }
```

Line markers in left margin: 1, 2 (at PoStartNextPowerIrp and if statement), 3 (at else), 4, 5 (at IoReleaseRemoveLock and if (ctx->UnstallQueue))

1. Here's the call to **PoStartNextPowerIrp** that we must make for each power IRP while we still own it.

2. If we were entered to handle a **MainIrpComplete** event, our caller must have been **MainCompletionRoutine**, and the first action routine will have set **status** equal to STATUS_MORE_PROCESSING_REQUIRED to short-circuit the completion process. Since we've decided we want to complete this IRP after all—that's why we're at **CompleteMainIrp**—the right thing to do is to return a different status code and allow the completion process to take its normal course.

3. If we were entered for any other event, we need to explicitly complete the IRP.

4. This **IoReleaseRemoveLock** call balances the call to **IoAcquireRemoveLock** that we did during TriageNewIrp.

5. I'll explain what this block of code is all about when I talk about device IRPs later in this chapter.

When handling a system power IRP that increases power, the machine enters CompleteMainIrp after a MainIrpComplete event. CompleteMainIrp will therefore arrange to return the error status we originally fetched (inside MainCompletionRoutine) from the IRP. That will permit the completion process to continue. There are other code paths we haven't studied yet in which CompleteMainIrp calls **IoCompleteRequest** instead. CompleteMainIrp finishes by requesting yet another action:

```
case DestroyContext:
  {
  if (ctx->pev)
    KeSetEvent(ctx->pev, IO_NO_INCREMENT, FALSE);
  else
    ExFreePool(ctx);
  break;
  }
```

1. This branch is taken when **SendDeviceSetPower** calls the state machine engine to create and wait for a device IRP.

2. This branch is taken when **GenericDispatchPower** calls the state machine engine to process an IRP.

DestroyContext is, of course, the last action the finite state machine ever performs.

Mapping the System State to a Device State

The other possible path out of SysPowerUpComplete generates a device power IRP with a power state that corresponds to the system power state. We perform the mapping of system to device states in the **SelectDState** action:

```
case SelectDState:
  {
  SYSTEM_POWER_STATE sysstate =
    stack->Parameters.Power.State.SystemState;
  if (sysstate == PowerSystemWorking)
    ctx->devstate = PowerDeviceD0;
  else
    {
    DEVICE_POWER_STATE maxstate =
      pdx->devcaps.DeviceState[sysstate];
    DEVICE_POWER_STATE minstate = pdx->WakeupEnabled ?
      pdx->devcaps.DeviceWake : PowerDeviceD3;
    ctx->devstate = minstate > maxstate ? minstate : maxsstate;
    }
  ctx->MinorFunction = stack->MinorFunction;
  action = SendDeviceIrp;
  continue;
  }
```

By the way, the Power Manager never transitions directly from one low system power state to another: it always moves via PowerSystemWorking. That's why I coded SelectDState to choose one mapping for PowerSystemWorking and a different mapping for all other system power states.

In general, we always want to put our device into the lowest power state that's consistent with current device activity, with our own wake-up feature (if any), with device capabilities, and with the impending state of the system. These factors can interplay in a relatively complex way. To explain them fully, I need to digress briefly and talk about a Plug and Play IRP that I avoided discussing in Chapter 6: IRP_MN_QUERY_CAPABILITIES.

The PnP Manager sends a capabilities query shortly after starting your device and perhaps at other times. The parameter for the request is a DEVICE_CAPABILITIES structure that contains several fields relevant to power management. Since this is the only time in this book I'm going to discuss this structure, I'm showing you the entire declaration:

```
typedef struct _DEVICE_CAPABILITIES {
    USHORT Size;
    USHORT Version;
    ULONG DeviceD1:1;
    ULONG DeviceD2:1;
    ULONG LockSupported:1;
    ULONG EjectSupported:1;
    ULONG Removable:1;
    ULONG DockDevice:1;
    ULONG UniqueID:1;
    ULONG SilentInstall:1;
    ULONG RawDeviceOK:1;
    ULONG SurpriseRemovalOK:1;
    ULONG WakeFromD0:1;
    ULONG WakeFromD1:1;
    ULONG WakeFromD2:1;
    ULONG WakeFromD3:1;
    ULONG HardwareDisabled:1;
    ULONG NonDynamic:1;
    ULONG Reserved:16;

    ULONG Address;
    ULONG UINumber;

    DEVICE_POWER_STATE DeviceState[PowerSystemMaximum];
    SYSTEM_POWER_STATE SystemWake;
    DEVICE_POWER_STATE DeviceWake;
    ULONG D1Latency;
    ULONG D2Latency;
    ULONG D3Latency;
} DEVICE_CAPABILITIES, *PDEVICE_CAPABILITIES;
```

Table 8-4 describes the fields in this structure that relate to power management.

Field	Description
DeviceState	Array of highest device states possible for each system state
SystemWake	Lowest system power state from which the device can generate a wake-up signal for the system—PowerSystem-Unspecified indicates that device can't wake up the system
DeviceWake	Lowest power state from which the device can generate a wake-up signal—PowerDeviceUnspecified indicates that device can't generate a wake-up signal
D1Latency	Approximate worst-case time (in 100-microsecond units) required for device to switch from D1 to D0 states
D2Latency	Approximate worst-case time (in 100-microsecond units) required for device to switch from D2 to D0 states
D3Latency	Approximate worst-case time (in 100-microsecond units) required for device to switch from D3 to D0 states
WakeFromD0	Flag indicating whether device's system wake-up feature is operative when the device is in the indicated state
WakeFromD1	Same as above
WakeFromD2	Same as above
WakeFromD3	Same as above

Table 8-4. *Power-management fields in DEVICE_CAPABILITIES structure.*

You normally handle the query capabilities IRP synchronously by passing it down and waiting for the lower layers to complete it. After the pass-down, you'll make any desired changes to the capabilities recorded by the bus driver. Your subdispatch routine would look like this one:

```
NTSTATUS HandleQueryCapabilities(IN PDEVICE_OBJECT fdo,
  IN PIRP Irp)
  {
  PIO_STACK_LOCATION stack = IoGetCurrentIrpStackLocation(Irp);
  PDEVICE_EXTENSION pdx = (PDEVICE_EXTENSION) fdo->DeviceExtension;
  PDEVICE_CAPABILITIES pdc = stack->
    Parameters.DeviceCapabilities.Capabilities;
  if (pdc->Version < 1)
    return DefaultPnpHandler(fdo, Irp);
  NTSTATUS status = ForwardAndWait(fdo, Irp);
  if (NT_SUCCESS(status))
    {
    stack = IoGetCurrentIrpStackLocation(Irp);
```

1 ▷

```
     pdc = stack->Parameters.DeviceCapabilities.Capabilities;
     <stuff>
     pdx->devcaps = *pdc;
     }
   return CompleteRequest(Irp, status);
   }
```

2
3

1. The device capabilities structure has a version number member, which is currently always equal to 1. The structure is designed to always be upward compatible, so you'll be able to work with the version defined in the DDK that you build your driver with *and* with any later incarnation of the structure. If, however, you're confronted with a structure that's older than you're able to work with, you should just ignore this IRP by passing it along.

2. Here's where you can override any capabilities that were set by the bus driver.

3. It's a good idea to make a copy of the capabilities structure. I already described how you'll use the **DeviceState** map when you receive a system power IRP. You might have occasion to consult other fields in the structure, too.

Don't bother altering the characteristics structure before you pass this IRP down: the bus driver will completely reinitialize it. When you regain control, you can modify **SystemWake** and **DeviceWake** to specify a higher power state than the bus driver thought was appropriate. You can't specify a lower power state for the wake-up fields, and you can't override the bus driver's decision that your device is incapable of waking the system. If your device is ACPI-compliant, the ACPI filter will set the **LockSupported**, **EjectSupported**, and **Removable** flags automatically based on the ACPI Source Language (ASL) description of the device—you won't need to worry about these capabilities.

You might want to set the **SurpriseRemovalOK** flag at point "2" in the capabilities handler. Setting the flag suppresses the dialog box that Windows 2000 normally presents when it detects the sudden and unexpected removal of a device. It's normally okay for the end user to remove a universal serial bus (USB) or 1394 device without first telling the system, and the function driver should set this flag to avoid annoying the user.

To return to our discussion of SelectDState, suppose we're dealing with a set-power request that will take the computer from Working to Sleeping1; we'll therefore execute the second branch of the **if** statement in SelectDState. Let's suppose that the bus driver knows that our device can be in any of the states D0, D1, D2, or D3 when the system is in Sleeping1. When it answered the PnP capabilities query it would therefore have filled in **DeviceState [PowerSystemSleeping1]** in the device capabilities structure with the value PowerDeviceD0 because D0 is the *highest* power state our device can occupy for this system state. We'll initially record PowerDeviceD0, then, as the value of **maxstate**.

Our device might also have a wake-up feature. I'll say more about wake-up later on. If so, the bus driver will have set the DeviceWake member of the capabilities structure equal to the *lowest* power state from which wake-up can occur. Let's suppose that value is **PowerDeviceD1**. If our wake-up feature happens to be enabled right now, we'll set **minstate** to PowerDeviceD1.

If we don't have a wake-up feature, however, or if we have one and it's not currently enabled, we're free to choose any device power state lower than the **maxstate** value we derived from the device capabilities structure. We could blindly choose D3, but that wouldn't be right for every type of device because generally speaking it takes longer to resume from D3 to D0 than from D2 or D1. The choice you make in this case therefore depends on factors for which I can't give you cut-and-dried guidance. If your device is capable of the D2 state, for example, you might decide to enter D2 for any of the system sleeping states and reserve D3 for the hibernate and shutdown states.

It seems reasonable to leave your device in a low power state when the system resumes from a sleeping state. The DDK suggests you do this, and so does good sense. There are two situations in which you would need to restore your device to D0 when the system goes to Working. The first situation is when your device has the INRUSH characteristic. In this case, the Power Manager won't send power IRPs to any other INRUSH device until you've powered on your device. The second situation is when you've got substantive IRPs queued and waiting to run once power is back. Notwithstanding what a good idea it seems to be to just leave your device in a low power state, you'll notice that the code fragment I just showed you for SelectDState unconditionally picks the D0 state. In my testing, Windows 2000 seemed to hang coming out of standby if I didn't do that. Maybe there's a mistake in my code or in the operating system. Stay tuned to my errata page for more information about this.

Requesting a Device Power IRP

In Chapter 5, "The I/O Request Packet," I discussed support functions such as **IoAllocateIrp** that you can use to build IRPs. You don't use those functions when you want to create power IRPs, though. (Actually, you *would* use one of those functions for an IRP_MN_POWER_SEQUENCE request, but not for the other IRP_MJ_POWER requests.) Instead, you use **PoRequestPowerIrp**, as shown here in the code for the

SendDeviceIrp action we'd perform after SelectDState:

```
case SendDeviceIrp:
  {
  if (win98 && ctx->devstate == pdx->devpower)
    {
    ctx->status = STATUS_SUCCESS;
    action = actiontable[ctx->state][AsyncNotify];
    continue;
    }
  POWER_STATE powstate;
  powstate.DeviceState = ctx->devstate;
  NTSTATUS postatus = PoRequestPowerIrp(pdx->Pdo,
    ctx->MinorFunction, powstate, (PREQUEST_POWER_COMPLETE)
    PoCompletionRoutine, ctx, NULL);
  if (NT_SUCCESS(postatus))
    break;
  action = CompleteMainIrp;
  ctx->status = postatus;
  continue;
  }
```

1. Refer to "Windows 98 Compatibility Notes" at the end of this chapter for an explanation of what this section of code is all about.

2. The first argument to **PoRequestPowerIrp** is the address of the physical device object (PDO) for our device. Note that the IRP we're requesting will actually get sent to the topmost filter device object (FiDO) anyway. The second argument is the minor function code for the IRP we want to send. This will either be IRP_MN_QUERY_POWER or IRP_MN_SET_POWER in our case. The third argument is a POWER_STATE that should contain a device power state value when we're requesting a query or set operation. The fourth and fifth arguments are, respectively, the address of a callback routine for when the IRP finishes and a context parameter for that function. The last argument is an optional address of a PIRP variable to receive the address of the IRP that PoRequestPowerIrp creates.

3. **PoRequestPowerIrp** normally returns STATUS_PENDING after creating and launching the power IRP you've requested. This, and any success code, in fact, mean that our callback function will eventually be called. It will generate another call to **HandlePowerEvent**, so we're done with this invocation of the engine.

4. If **PoRequestPowerIrp** fails, it never created the IRP and our callback function will never be called. We therefore want to fail the system IRP with whatever status code we've gotten.

In the system power-up scenario I'm currently discussing, our state machine will be in the **SubPowerUpPending** state when we get to SendDeviceIrp. The status variable will be STATUS_MORE_PROCESSING_REQUIRED, which is the right value for MainCompletionRoutine to return if we're going to wait for the device IRP to finish. Normally, then, when we break from SendDeviceIrp, we'll interrupt the completion processing for the system power IRP for the time being.

I'll discuss what happens to the device IRP we request via PoRequestPowerIrp later on.

Finishing the System IRP

Eventually, the device IRP that SendDeviceIrp requests will finish, whereupon the Power Manager will call the **PoCompletionRoutine** callback routine. It in turn calls Handle-PowerEvent with the event code **AsyncNotify**. Our first action in the SubPower-UpPending state will be **SubPowerUpComplete**:

```
case SubPowerUpComplete:
  {
  if (status == -1)
    status = STATUS_SUCCESS;
  action = CompleteMainIrp;
  continue;
  }
```

The only job performed by this action routine is to alter the **status** variable. The reason we do that is that we have an ASSERT statement at the end of HandlePowerEvent to make sure someone changes **status**. In this exact scenario, it doesn't matter what status value we return because PoCompletionRoutine is a void function. But you don't want to trigger an ASSERT and a BSOD unless something is really wrong.

The next action after SubPowerUpComplete is CompleteMainIrp, which leads to DestroyContext. You've already seen what those action routines do.

System Power IRPs That Decrease Power

If the system power IRP implies no change or a reduction in the system power level, you'll request a device power IRP with the same minor function code (set or query) and a device power state that corresponds to the system state. When the device power IRP completes, you'll forward the system power IRP to the next lower driver. You'll need a completion routine for the system power IRP so that you can make the requisite call to PoStartNextPowerIrp and so that you can perform some additional cleanup. See Figure 8-7 for an illustration of how the IRPs flow through the system in this case.

System power IRP

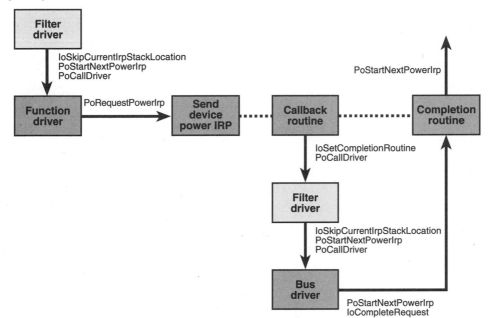

Figure 8-7. *IRP flow when decreasing system power.*

Figure 8-8 diagrams how our finite state machine handles this type of IRP. TriageNewIrp puts the state machine into the **SubPowerDownPending** state and jumps to the SelectDState action. You already saw that SelectDState selects a device power state and leads to a SendDeviceIrp action to request a device power IRP. In the system power-down scenario, we'll be specifying a lower power state in this device IRP.

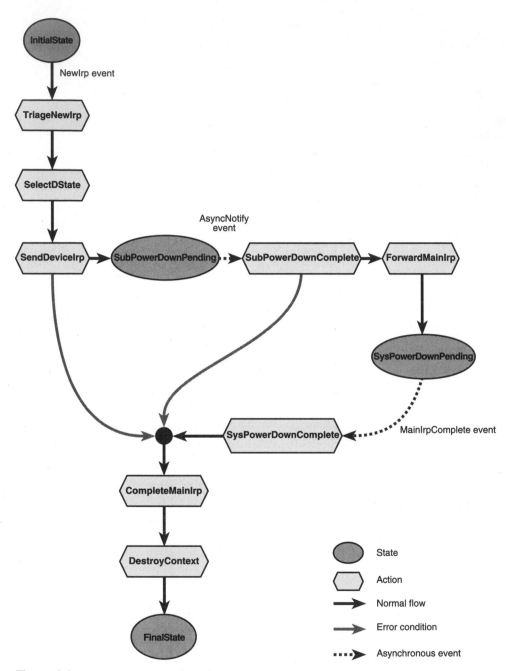

Figure 8-8. *State transitions when decreasing system power.*

When the device IRP finishes, we execute **SubPowerDownComplete**:

```
case SubPowerDownComplete:
  {
  if (status == -1)
    status = STATUS_SUCCESS;
  if (NT_SUCCESS(ctx->status))
    {
    ctx->state = SysPowerDownPending;
    action = ForwardMainIrp;
    }
  else
    action = CompleteMainIrp;
  continue;
  }
```

As you can see, if the device IRP fails, we fail the system IRP too. If the device IRP succeeds, we enter the **SysPowerDownPending** state and exit via ForwardMainIrp. When the system IRP finishes, and MainCompletionRoutine runs, we'll execute **SysPowerDownComplete**:

```
case SysPowerDownComplete:
  {
  if (stack->MinorFunction == IRP_MN_SET_POWER)
    pdx->syspower = stack->Parameters.Power.State.SystemState;
  action = CompleteMainIrp;
  continue;
  }
```

The only purpose of this action is to record the new system power state in our device extension and then to exit via CompleteMainIrp and DestroyContext.

Device Power IRPs

All we actually do with system power IRPs is act as a conduit for them and request a device IRP either as the system IRP travels down the driver stack or as it travels back up. We have more work to do with device power IRPs, however.

To begin with, we don't want our device occupied by any substantive I/O operations while a change in the device power state is under way. As early as we can in a sequence that leads to powering down our device, therefore, we wait for any outstanding operation to finish, and we stop processing new operations. Since we're not allowed to block the system thread in which we receive power IRPs, an asynchronous mechanism is required. Once the current IRP finishes, we'll continue processing the device IRP.

If the device power IRP implies an increase in the device power level, we'll forward it to the next lower driver. Refer to Figure 8-9 for an illustration of how the IRP flows through the system. The bus driver will process a device set-power IRP by, for example, using whatever bus-specific mechanism is appropriate to turn on the flow of electrons to your device, and it will complete the IRP. Your completion routine will initiate whatever operations are required to restore context information to the device, and it will return STATUS_MORE_PROCESSING_REQUIRED to interrupt the completion process for the device IRP. When the context restore operation finishes, you'll resume processing substantive IRPs and finish completing the device IRP.

Device power IRP

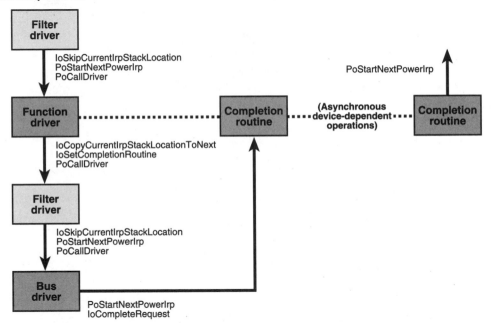

Figure 8-9. *IRP flow when increasing device power.*

If the device power IRP implies no change or a reduction in the device power level, you perform any device-specific processing (asynchronously, as we've discussed) and then forward the device IRP to the next lower driver. See Figure 8-10. The "device-specific processing" for a set operation includes saving device context information, if any, in memory so that you can restore it later. There probably isn't any device-specific processing for a query operation beyond deciding whether to succeed or fail the query. The bus driver completes the request. In the case of a query operation, you can expect the bus driver to complete the request with STATUS_SUCCESS to indicate acquiescence in the proposed power change. In the case of a set operation, you can expect the bus driver to take whatever bus-dependent steps are required to put your device into the specified device power state. Your completion routine cleans up by calling PoStartNextPowerIrp, among other things.

Device power IRP

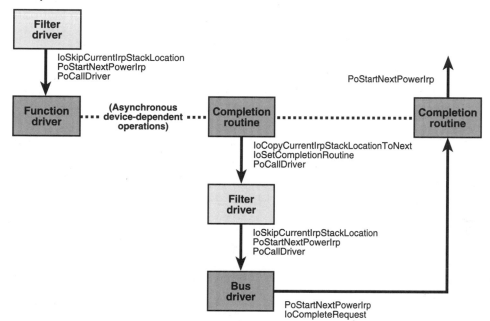

Figure 8-10. *IRP flow when decreasing device power.*

I invented **StallRequestsAndNotify** for use in TriageNewIrp. (It's so new that Chapter 6, where all the other DEVQUEUE functions are described, was already beyond my reach when I created it.) The first step it performs is to stall the request queue. If the device is currently busy, it records a callback routine address—in this case, **GenericSaveRestoreComplete**, which I'm overloading for purposes of receiving a notification—and returns STATUS_PENDING. TriageNewIrp will then exit in the **QueueStallPending** state.

If the device isn't busy, StallRequestsAndNotify returns STATUS_SUCCESS without arranging any callback; the device can't become busy now because the queue is stalled. TriageNewIrp will then go directly to the **QueueStallComplete** action.

We reach the QueueStallComplete routine either directly from TriageNewIrp (when the device is idle or if the queue was previously stalled for some other power-related reason) or when the client driver calls **StartNextPacket** to indicate that it's finished processing the current IRP. StartNextPacket calls the notification routine we gave to StallRequestsAndNotify, and that routine signals an AsyncNotify event to the state machine. QueueStallComplete now separates the device IRP into one of four categories, as follows:

```
case QueueStallComplete:
  {
  if (stack->MinorFunction == IRP_MN_SET_POWER)
    {
    if (stack->Parameters.Power.State.DeviceState < pdx->devpower)
      {
      action = ForwardMainIrp;
      SETSTATE(DevPowerUpPending);
      }
    else
      action = SaveContext;
    }
  else
    {
    if (stack->Parameters.Power.State.DeviceState < pdx->devpower)
      {
      action = ForwardMainIrp;
      SETSTATE(DevQueryUpPending);
      }
    else
      action = DevQueryDown;
    }
  continue;
  }
```

The upshot of QueueStallComplete is that we perform the next action indicated in Table 8-5 for the type of IRP we're dealing with.

Minor Function	*More or Less Power?*	*Next Action*
IRP_MN_QUERY_POWER	More power	ForwardMainIrp
	Less or same power	DevQueryDown
IRP_MN_SET_POWER	More power	ForwardMainIrp
	Less or same power	SaveContext

Table 8-5. *Next action for device IRPs.*

Setting a Higher Device Power State

Figure 8-11 diagrams the state transitions that occur for an IRP_MN_SET_POWER that specifies a higher device power state than that which is current.

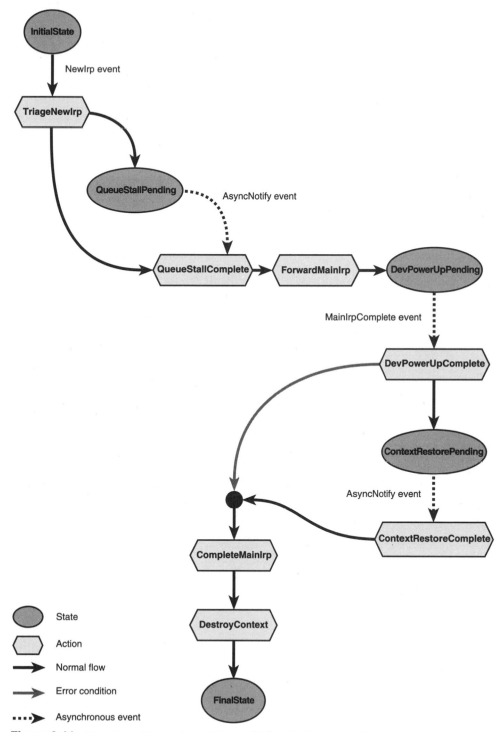

Figure 8-11. *State transitions when setting a higher device power state.*

ForwardMainIrp will install a completion routine and send the IRP down the driver stack. When MainCompletionRoutine eventually gains control, it signals a **MainIrpComplete** event. We will be in the **DevPowerUpPending** state, so we'll execute the **DevPowerUpComplete** action:

```
case DevPowerUpComplete:
  {
  if (!NT_SUCCESS(ctx->status) || stack->MinorFunction !=
    IRP_MN_SET_POWER)
    {
    action = CompleteMainIrp;
    continue;
    }
  status = STATUS_MORE_PROCESSING_REQUIRED;
  DEVICE_POWER_STATE oldpower = pdx->devpower;
  pdx->devpower = stack->Parameters.Power.State.DeviceState;
  if (pdx->RestoreContext)
    {
    ctx->state = ContextRestorePending;
    (*pdx->RestoreDeviceContext)(pdx->DeviceObject, oldpower,
      pdx->devpower, ctx);
    break;
    }
  action = ContextRestoreComplete;
  continue;
  }
```

The main task we need to accomplish is restoring any device context that was lost during the previous power-down transition. Since we're not allowed to block our thread, we initiate whatever operations are required and return STATUS_MORE_ PROCESSING_REQUIRED to interrupt the completion of the device IRP. When the restore operations finish, the client driver calls GenericSaveRestoreComplete, which signals an AsyncNotify event. We'll be in the **ContextRestorePending** state at that point, so we'll perform the **ContextRestoreComplete** action:

```
case ContextRestoreComplete:
  {
  if (event == AsyncNotify)
    status = STATUS_SUCCESS;
  action = CompleteMainIrp;
  if (!NT_SUCCESS(ctx->status) || pdx->devpower != PowerDeviceD0)
    continue;
  ctx->UnstallQueue = TRUE;
  continue;
  }
```

The main result of this action routine is that we unstall the queue of substantive IRPs at the conclusion of an IRP_MN_SET_POWER to the D0 state. We exit via CompleteMainIrp and DestroyContext.

Querying for a Higher Device Power State

You shouldn't expect to receive an IRP_MN_QUERY_POWER that refers to a higher power state than your device is already in, but you shouldn't crash the system if you happen to receive one. The following code shows what GENERIC does when such a query completes in the lower level drivers. (Refer to Figure 8-12 for a state diagram.)

```
case DevQueryUpComplete:
  {
  if (NT_SUCCESS(ctx->status) && pdx->QueryPower)
    if (!(*pdx->QueryPower)(pdx->DeviceObject, pdx->devpower,
      stack->Parameters.Power.State.DeviceState))
      ctx->status = STATUS_UNSUCCESSFUL;
  action = CompleteMainIrp;
  continue;
  }
```

That is, GENERIC allows the client driver to accept or veto the query by calling its **QueryPower** function, and then it exits via CompleteMainIrp and DestroyContext.

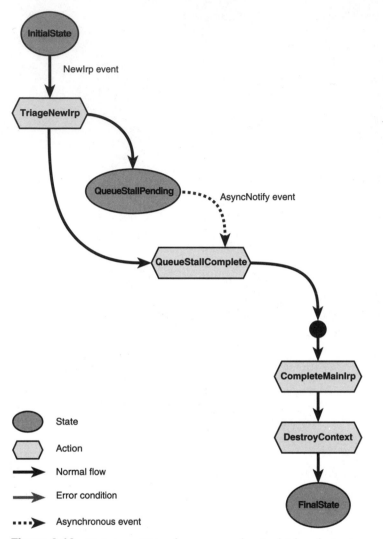

Figure 8-12. *State transitions for a query about a higher device power state.*

Setting a Lower Device Power State

If the IRP is an IRP_MN_SET_POWER for the same or a lower device power state than current, the finite state machine goes through the state transitions diagrammed in Figure 8-13.

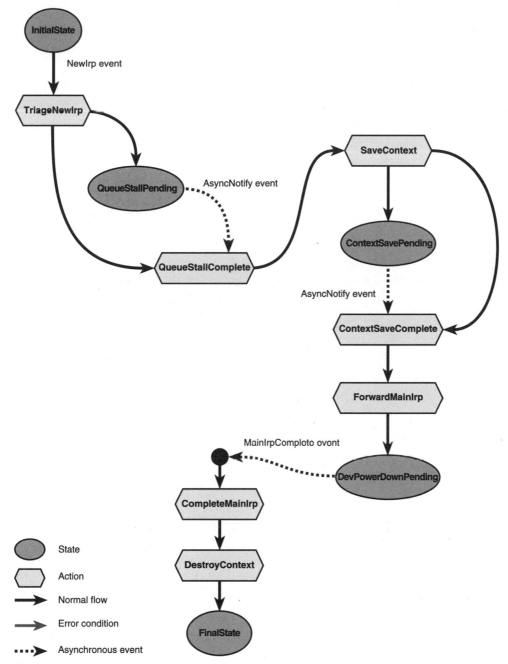

Figure 8-13. *State transitions when setting a lower device power state.*

The legend for the figure:
- State
- Action
- Normal flow
- Error condition
- Asynchronous event

SaveContext will initiate an asynchronous process to save any device context that will be lost when the device loses power:

```
case SaveContext:
  {
  DEVICE_POWER_STATE devpower =
    stack->Parameters.Power.State.DeviceState;
  if (pdx->SaveDeviceContext && devpower > pdx->devpower)
    {
    ctx->state = ContextSavePending;
    (*pdx->SaveDeviceContext)(pdx->DeviceObject, pdx->devpower,
      devpower, ctx);
    break;
    }
  action = ContextSaveComplete;
  }
```

When the save operations finish, the client driver calls GenericSaveRestore-Complete, which signals an AsyncNotify event. We'll be in the **ContextSavePending** state at that point, so we'll perform the **ContextSaveComplete** action:

```
case ContextSaveComplete:
  {
1 if (event == AsyncNotify)
    status = STATUS_SUCCESS;
  ctx->state = DevPowerDownPending;
  action = ForwardMainIrp;
  DEVICE_POWER_STATE devpower =
    stack->Parameters.Power.State.DeviceState;
2 if (devpower <= pdx->devpower)
    continue;
3 pdx->devpower = devpower;
4 if (devpower > PowerDeviceD0)
    ctx->UnstallQueue = FALSE;
  continue;
  }
```

1. We'll come directly here from **GenericSaveRestoreComplete**, and we need to change status to prevent an ASSERT failure (but not for any other reason).

2. If we didn't actually change power, there's no more work to do here.

3. This is where we record the new device power state when we're powering down.

4. If the device is now in a low-power or no-power state, we want to leave the substantive IRP queue stalled.

The next action, ForwardMainIrp, sends the device IRP down the driver stack. The bus driver will turn the physical flow of current off and complete the IRP. We'll see it next when MainCompletionRoutine signals a MainIrpComplete event, which takes us directly to CompleteMainIrp and thence to DestroyContext.

Querying for a Lower Device Power State

An IRP_MN_QUERY_POWER that specifies the same or a lower device power state than current is the basic vehicle by which a function driver gets to vote on changes in power levels. Although the DDK doesn't specifically say you should create one of these requests when you handle a system query, it's a good idea to do so. You have to handle device queries anyway and might as well put all the query logic in one place. Figure 8-14 shows how our state machine will handle such a query.

The **DevQueryDown** action follows QueueStallComplete for this kind of IRP:

```
case DevQueryDown:
  {
  DEVICE_POWER_STATE devpower =
    stack->Parameters.Power.State.DeviceState;
  if (devpower > pdx->devpower
    && pdx->QueryPower
    && !(*pdx->QueryPower)(pdx->DeviceObject,
    pdx->devpower, devpower))
    {
    ctx->status = STATUS_UNSUCCESSFUL;
    action = DevQueryDownComplete;
    continue;
    }
  ctx->state = DevQueryDownPending);
  action = ForwardMainIrp;
  continue;
  }
```

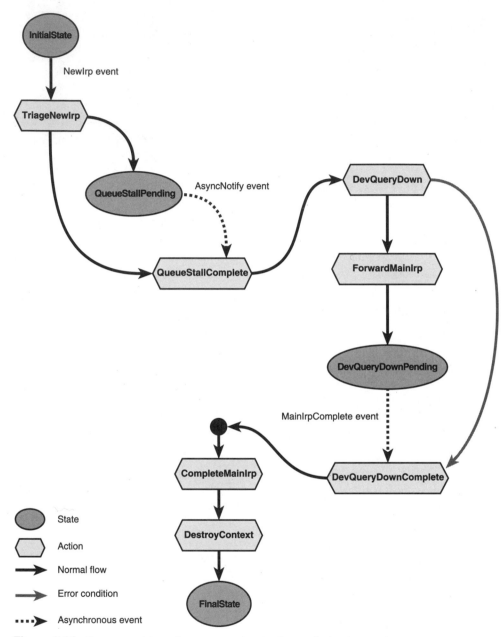

Figure 8-14. *State transitions for a query about a lower device power state.*

GENERIC basically lets the client driver decide whether the query should succeed. If the client driver says "Yes," we enter the **DevQueryDownPending** state and exit via ForwardMainIrp to send the query down the driver stack. Completion of the IRP sends us to the **DevQueryDownComplete** action:

```
case DevQueryDownComplete:
  {
  if (NT_SUCCESS(ctx >status))
    ctx->UnstallQueue = FALSE;
  action = CompleteMainIrp;
  continue;
  }
```

The basic action we take is to leave the substantive IRP queue stalled if the query succeeds. (CompleteMainIrp will unstall the queue if it sees the **UnstallQueue** flag set in the context structure. Clearing the flag causes this step to be skipped.) Recall that we first stalled the queue when we received the query. We'll leave it stalled until someone eventually sends us a set-power IRP to put the device into D0.

ADDITIONAL POWER MANAGEMENT DETAILS

In this section, I'll describe some additional details about power management, including flags you might need to set in your device object, controlling your device's wake-up feature, arranging for power-down requests after your device has been idle for a predetermined time, and optimizing context restore operations.

Flags to Set in AddDevice

Three flag bits in a device object—see Table 8-6—control various aspects of power management. After you call **IoCreateDevice** in your **AddDevice** function, all three of these bits will be set to 0, and you can set one or more of them depending on circumstances.

Flag	*Brief Description*
DO_POWER_PAGABLE	Driver's IRP_MJ_POWER dispatch routine must run at PASSIVE_LEVEL
DO_POWER_INRUSH	Powering on this device requires a large amount of current
DO_POWER_NOOP	Device doesn't participate in power management

Table 8-6. *Power-management flags in DEVICE_OBJECT.*

Set the DO_POWER_PAGABLE flag if your dispatch function for IRP_MJ_POWER requests must run at PASSIVE_LEVEL. The flag has the name it does because, as you know, paging is allowed at PASSIVE_LEVEL only. If you leave this flag set to 0, the Power Manager is free to send you power requests at DISPATCH_LEVEL. In fact, it always will do so in the current release of Windows 2000.

Set the DO_POWER_INRUSH flag if your device draws so much current when powering up that other devices should not be allowed to power up simultaneously. The problem solved by this flag is familiar to people who've experienced multiple simultaneous spikes of electricity demand at the end of a power outage—having all your appliances trying to cycle on at the same time can blow the main breaker. The Power Manager guarantees that only one inrush device at a time will be powered up. Furthermore, it sends power requests to inrush devices at DISPATCH_LEVEL, which implies that you may not also set the DO_POWER_PAGABLE flag.

The system's ACPI filter driver will set the INRUSH flag in the PDO automatically if the ASL description of the device so indicates. All that's required for the system to properly serialize inrush power is that some device object in the stack have the INRUSH flag set, so you won't need to set the flag in your own device object too. If the system can't automatically determine that you require inrush treatment, however, you would need to set the flag yourself.

Set the DO_POWER_NOOP flag if your driver isn't managing hardware and needn't participate in power management. When PoCallDriver sees this flag set in a device object, it simply completes the IRP with STATUS_SUCCESS without even calling the corresponding driver's dispatch routine.

The settings of the PAGABLE and INRUSH flags need to be consistent in all the device objects for a particular device. If the PDO has the PAGABLE flag set, every device object should also have PAGABLE set. Otherwise, a bug check with the code DRIVER_POWER_STATE_FAILURE may occur. (It's legal for a PAGABLE device to be layered on top of a non-PAGABLE device, just not the other way around.) If a device object has the INRUSH flag set, neither it nor any lower device objects should be PAGABLE, or else an INTERNAL_POWER_ERROR bug check will occur. If you're writing a disk driver, don't forget that you may change back and forth from time to time between pagable and nonpagable status in response to device usage PnP notifications about paging files.

Device Wake-Up Features

Some devices have a hardware wake-up feature, which allows them to wake up a sleeping computer when an external event occurs. See Figure 8-15. The power switch on the current crop of PCs is such a device. So are many modems and network cards, which are able to listen for incoming calls and packets, respectively.

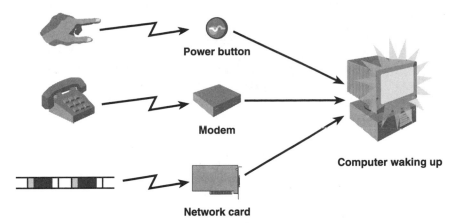

Figure 8-15. *Examples of devices that wake the system.*

If your device has a wake-up feature, your function driver has additional power management responsibilities beyond the ones we've already discussed. The first additional responsibility is to handle the IRP_MN_WAIT_WAKE flavor of IRP_MJ_ POWER. Most devices don't need to do any processing in their dispatch functions for WAIT_WAKE requests beyond installing a standard I/O completion routine and passing the IRP down the driver stack. The bus drivers for the USB and Peripheral Component Interconnect (PCI) bus, for example, implement the bus specifications for arming, disarming, and detecting wake-up. More explicitly, if your device doesn't have additional features related to device wake-up beyond the ones prescribed by the relevant bus specification, you don't need any special processing.

You want to fail IRP_MN_QUERY_POWER requests that specify a power state incompatible with your wake-up feature. If the query is for a system state, compare the proposed new state with the SystemWake field in the device capabilities structure, which gives the lowest system state from which your device can wake up the system. If the query is for a device state, compare the proposed new state with the DeviceWake field, which gives the lowest device state from which your device can issue the wake-up signal. If the result of the comparison shows that the proposed power state is too low, fail the query with STATUS_INVALID_DEVICE_STATE. Otherwise, process the query in the way I've already discussed.

You need to *originate* an IRP_MN_WAIT_WAKE at appropriate times. To do this, call PoRequestPowerIrp as illustrated by this code fragment:

```
typedef struct _DEVICE_EXTENSION {
  PIRP WaitWakeIrp;
  };

NTSTATUS SomeFunction(...)
  {
  ...
```

(continued)

```
POWER_STATE junk;
junk.SystemState = pdx->devcaps.SystemWake;
status = PoRequestPowerIrp(pdx->Pdo, IRP_MN_WAIT_WAKE,
  junk, (PREQUEST_POWER_COMPLETE) WaitWakeCallback,
  pdx, &pdx->WaitWakeIrp);
...
}
```

The last extra responsibility related to wake-up is to cancel the WAIT_WAKE IRP when it's no longer needed using code like this:

```
PIRP Irp = (PIRP) InterlockedExchangePointer(&pdx->WaitWakeIrp, NULL);
if (Irp)
  IoCancelIrp(Irp);
```

For most devices, you need to perform three tasks when the WAIT_WAKE completes. You should nullify the member of the device extension structure that points to the active WAIT_WAKE IRP. That will prevent some other part of your driver from thinking that the WAIT_WAKE is still active. You should initiate a device set-power IRP to restore power to your device. Some devices might need to perform some sort of device-specific operation to disarm the device's wake-up feature at this point, too. Finally, you might want to automatically reissue a WAIT_WAKE so that your device's wake-up feature remains armed for the future. The first of these tasks—nullifying the WAIT_WAKE IRP pointer—ought to be done in a standard I/O completion routine that your dispatch routine installs. The other two tasks—repowering your device and requesting a new WAIT_WAKE IRP—should be done in the callback routine (**WaitWakeCallback** in my fragment) that you specify in your call to PoRequestPowerIrp.

> **NOTE** It looks to me as though it's very difficult to be 100 percent sure that you're calling **IoCancelIrp** for your WAIT_WAKE request with a valid pointer. You could decide to cancel the IRP a nanosecond before your I/O completion routine nullifies your cached pointer to the IRP. The completion process could run its course, ending with a call to IoFreeIrp from inside the Power Manager as soon as your callback routine returns. Thereafter, IoCancelIrp or the bus driver's cancel routine could try to work with the now-invalid IRP. This is the same "tiger on Main Street" problem that I discussed in Chapter 5. Between us, I and one of the Microsoft developers who reviewed this code came up with an elegant solution that's unfortunately too big to fit in the margin. Please refer to the GENERIC sample on the companion disc.

When to Launch WAIT_WAKE

In the preceding section, I showed you how to launch a WAIT_WAKE IRP, how to cancel one, and what to do when one completes. You should be wondering *when* you should launch this IRP in the first place.

The first part of the answer to "when?" is that you need a way to know whether the end user wants your device's wake-up feature to be armed. Your driver should arm the wake-up feature unless the end user says not to. The end user will interact with some sort of user interface element (such as a control panel applet similar to POWCPL.DLL) to indicate whether your wake-up feature should be armed when the system powers down. The user interface element communicates in turn with your driver, either by using a private IOCTL interface or by setting a WMI control. You then remember the arm/disarm setting. At some point in the evolution of Windows 2000, user-mode programs will perhaps be able to use the so far unimplemented **RequestDeviceWakeup** and **CancelDeviceWakeupRequest** APIs to trigger WMI calls to your driver.

The second part of the answer concerns when you invoke PoRequestPowerIrp to request the WAIT_WAKE. The DDK indicates that you *may* request a WAIT_WAKE at any time when your device is in the D0 state and a device power transition is not in progress. Good times are when you're told by the end user to enable your wake-up feature and when you process a system power query that will reduce the device power state.

You should disable wake-up (and cancel an outstanding WAIT_WAKE) whenever you're told to do so by the end user and also when you process an IRP_MN_STOP_DEVICE request.

Idle Detection

As a general matter, the end user would prefer that your device not draw any power if it isn't being used. You can register with the Power Manager to be sent a low-power device IRP when your device remains idle for a specified period. The mechanics of the idle detection scheme involve two service functions: **PoRegisterDeviceForIdle-Detection** and **PoSetDeviceBusy**.

To register for idle detection, make this service function call:

```
pdx->idlecount = PoRegisterDeviceForIdleDetection(pdx->Pdo,
  ulConservationTimeout, ulPerformanceTimeout, PowerDeviceD3);
```

The first argument to PoRegisterDeviceForIdleDetection is the address of the PDO for your device. The second and third arguments specify timeout periods measured in seconds. The conservation period will apply when the system is trying to conserve power, such as when running on battery power. The performance period will apply when the system is trying to maximize performance, such as when running on AC power. The fourth argument specifies the device power state into which you want your device to be forced if it's idle for longer than whichever of the timeout periods applies.

Indicating That You're Not Idle

The return value from PoRegisterDeviceForIdleDetection is the address of a long integer that the system uses as a counter. Every second, the Power Manager increments that integer. If it reaches the appropriate timeout value, the Power Manager sends you a device set-power IRP indicating the power state you registered. At various places in your driver, you'll reset this counter to 0 to restart the idle detection period:

```
if (pdx->idlecount)
  PoSetDeviceBusy(pdx->idlecount);
```

PoSetDeviceBusy is a macro in the WDM.H header file that uncritically dereferences its pointer argument to store a 0. It turns out that PoRegisterDeviceForIdle-Detection can return a NULL pointer, so you should check for NULL before calling PoSetDeviceBusy.

Now that I've described what PoSetDeviceBusy does, you can see that its name is slightly misleading. It doesn't tell the Power Manager that your device is "busy," in which case you'd expect to have to make another call later to indicate that your device is no longer "busy." Rather, it indicates that, at the particular instant you use the macro, your device is not idle. I'm not making this point as a mere semantic quibble. If your device is busy with some sort of active request, you'll want to have logic that forestalls idle detection. So, you might want to call PoSetDeviceBusy from many places in your driver: from various dispatch routines, from your **StartIo** routine, and so on. Basically, you want to make sure that the detection period is longer than the longest time that can elapse between the calls to PoSetDeviceBusy that you make during the normal processing of a request.

> NOTE **PoRegisterSystemState** allows you to prevent the Power Manager from changing the system power state, but you can't use it to forestall idle timeouts. Besides, it isn't implemented in Windows 98, so calling it is contraindicated for drivers that need to be portable between Windows 2000 and Windows 98.

Choosing Idle Timeouts

Picking the idle timeout values isn't necessarily simple. Certain kinds of devices can specify −1 to indicate the standard power policy timeout for their class of device. At the time of this writing, only FILE_DEVICE_DISK and FILE_DEVICE_MASS_STORAGE devices are in this category. While you'll probably want to have default values for the timeout constants, their values should ultimately be under end user control. Underlying the method by which a user gives you these values is a tale of considerable complexity.

Unless your device is one for which the system designers planned a generic idle detection scheme, you'll need to provide a user-mode component that allows the end user to specify timeout values. To fit in best with the rest of the operating system, that piece should be a property page extension to the Power control panel applet. That is, you should provide a user-mode DLL that implements the **IShellPropSheetExt** and **IShellExtInit** COM interfaces. This DLL would fit the general description of a shell extension DLL, which is the topic you would research if you wanted to learn all the ins and outs of writing this particular piece of user interface software.

Learning about COM in general and shell extension DLLs in particular seems to me like a case of the tail wagging the dog insofar as driver programming goes. So the WDMIDLE sample on the companion disc includes a shell extension DLL (POWCPL.DLL) that you can copy and adapt. If you install this sample, you'll start noticing a new property page in the Power Options property sheet. See Figure 8-16. POWCPL.DLL uses the user-mode functions we discussed in Chapter 2, "Basic Structure of a WDM Driver," to enumerate all the devices that have registered a GUID_WDMIDLE interface, and it presents their "friendly" names in a list box. It uses a private I/O control (IOCTL) scheme—see Chapter 9, "Specialized Topics"— to query and alter the idle timeout constants used by WDMIDLE.SYS. Using IOCTLs for this purpose gives you a workable scheme for both Windows 2000 and Windows 98. Another possible method uses the COM interfaces that are part of WMI. (See Chapter 10, "Windows Management Instrumentation.") This method is a great deal more cumbersome and doesn't work in the original release of Windows 98, which is why I didn't code POWCPL.DLL to use it.

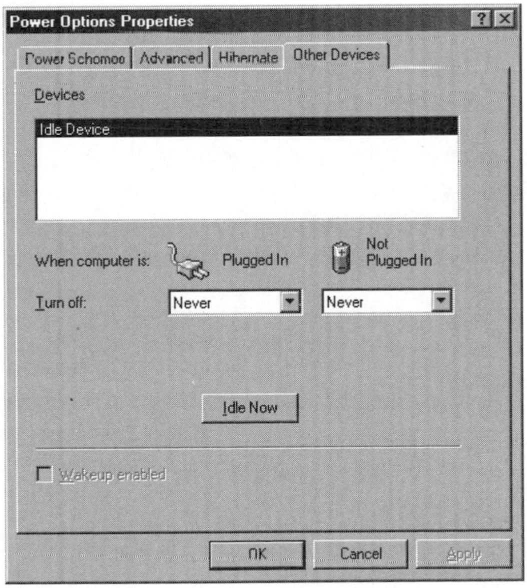

Figure 8-16. *The property page for idle devices.*

On the driver side of the user interface is a handler for IRP_MJ_DEVICE_
CONTROL to answer queries and honor requests to alter power management settings.
The end user expects that settings, once specified, will remain in effect in subsequent
sessions. The driver therefore needs to record the current values of the constants in
the registry by using the functions I discussed in Chapter 3, "Basic Programming Techniques." Furthermore, at **StartDevice** time, the driver needs to read those persistent
settings from the registry to initialize the driver according to the user's expectations.

All of these details, though important to delivering a polished product, are rather
tangential to the issues of power management that I'm discussing in this chapter, so
I won't discuss the code here.

Waking Up from an Idle State

If you implement idle detection, you'll also have to provide a way to restore power
to your device at some later time—no one else will do it for you. I wrote a function
named **SendDeviceSetPower** to deal with this detail. You would have code like this
in the dispatch function for an IRP that needs power:

```
NTSTATUS DispatchWrite(IN PDEVICE_OBJECT fdo, IN PIRP Irp)
  {
  PDEVICE_EXTENSION pdx =
    (PDEVICE_EXTENSION) fdo->DeviceExtension;
  if (pdx->idlecount)
    PoSetDeviceBusy(pdx->idlecount);

  if (pdx->powerstate > PowerDeviceD0)
    {
    NTSTATUS status = SendDeviceSetPower(fdo, PowerDeviceD0, FALSE);
    if (!NT_SUCCESS(status))
      return CompleteRequest(Irp, status, 0);
    }

  IoMarkIrpPending(Irp);
  StartPacket(&pdx->dqReadWrite, fdo, Irp, OnCancel);
  return STATUS_PENDING;
  }
```

1. This is the dispatch routine for IRP_MJ_WRITE requests in some driver.
   At the beginning of the routine is one of the places you should call
   PoSetDeviceBusy to reset the idle countdown that's occurring once each
   second.

2. You might have powered down your device after a period of inactivity, or you might simply have left it off when the system resumed from standby. Whatever the reason, no one else in the system will realize that your device needs power right now, and so you have to initiate the power-on sequence.

3. If the device set-power request should fail for some reason, you should fail the write request.

4. The rest of this dispatch routine is the same as I've discussed in earlier chapters. We mark the IRP pending, put it into the queue of write requests, and return STATUS_PENDING to tell our caller that we didn't finish the IRP in our dispatch routine.

In general, we get read and write requests in an arbitrary thread context, so we should not block that thread. When we power ourselves back on, therefore, we return without waiting for the power-up operation to finish. The DEVQUEUE takes care of starting the request when power is finally back.

The SendDeviceSetPower helper routine calls PoRequestPowerIrp directly. The resulting device IRP gets handled in the same way as we've already discussed.

Using Sequence Numbers to Optimize State Changes

You might want to use an optimization technique in connection with removing and restoring power to your device. Two background facts will help you make sense of the optimization technique. First, the bus driver doesn't always power down a device even when it receives a device set-power IRP. This particular bit of intransigence arises because of the way computers are wired together. There might be one or more power channels, and there might be any random collection of devices wired to any given channel. These devices are said to share a *power relation*. A particular device can't be powered down unless all the other devices on the same power channel are powered down as well. So, to use the macabre example that I sometimes give my seminar students, suppose the modem *you* want to power down happens to share a power channel with your computer's heart-lung machine—the system can't power down your modem until the bypass operation is over.

The second background fact is that some devices require a great deal of time to change power. To return to the previous example, suppose that your modem were such a device. At some point, you received and passed along a device set-power request to put your modem to sleep. Unbeknownst to you, however, the bus driver didn't actually power down the modem. When the time comes to restore power, you could save some time if you knew that your modem hadn't lost power. That's where this particular optimization comes into play.

At the time you remove power, you can create and send a power request with the minor function code IRP_MN_POWER_SEQUENCE to the drivers underneath yours. Even though this IRP is technically an IRP_MJ_POWER, you use IoAllocateIrp instead of PoRequestPowerIrp to create it. You still use PoStartNextPowerIrp and PoCallDriver when you handle it, though. The request completes after the bus driver stores three sequence numbers in an array you provide. The sequence numbers indicate how many times your device has been put into the D1, D2, and D3 states. When you're later called upon to restore power, you create and send another IRP_MN_ POWER_SEQUENCE request to obtain a new set of sequence numbers. If the new set is the same as the set you captured at power-down time, you know that no state change has occurred and that you can bypass whatever expensive process would be required to restore power.

Since IRP_MN_POWER_SEQUENCE simply optimizes a process that will work without the optimization, you needn't use it. Furthermore, the bus driver needn't support it, and you shouldn't treat failure of a power-sequence request as indicative of any sort of error. The GENERIC sample on disc actually includes code to use the optimization, but I didn't want to further complicate the textual discussion of the state machine by showing it here.

WINDOWS 98 COMPATIBILITY NOTES

Windows 98 incompletely implements many power management features. Consequently, the Windows 98 environment will forgive your mistakes more readily than Windows 2000 will, facilitating the initial development of a driver. But, since Windows 98 tolerates mistakes that Windows 2000 won't tolerate, you must be sure to test all of your driver's power functionality under Windows 2000.

The Importance of DO_POWER_PAGABLE

The DO_POWER_PAGABLE flag has additional and unexpected significance in Windows 98. Unless every device object, including the PDO and all filter devices, in your particular stack has this flag set, the I/O Manager tells the Windows 98 Configuration Manager that the device only supports the D0 power state and is incapable of waking the system. Thus, an additional consequence of not setting the DO_POWER_PAGABLE flag is that any idle notification request you make by calling PoRegisterDeviceForIdleDetection is effectively ignored—that is, you'll never receive a power IRP as a result of being idle too long. Another consequence is that your device's wake-up feature, if any, won't be used.

Requesting Device Power IRPs

Windows 98 appears to have a bug whereby PoRequestPowerIrp can appear to succeed—that is, it returns STATUS_PENDING—without actually causing you to receive a device set-power IRP. The problem arises when you ask for a set-power IRP that specifies the same device state that your device is already in—the Windows 98 Configuration Manager "knows" that there's no news to report by sending a configuration event to the configuration function that NTKERN operates on your behalf. Mind you, if you're waiting for a device IRP to complete, your device will simply stop responding at this point.

I used an obvious workaround to overcome this problem: if we're running under Windows 98 and detect that we're about to request a device power IRP for the same power state as the device already occupies, I simply pretend that the device IRP succeeded. In terms of the state transitions that HandlePowerEvent goes through, I jump from SendDeviceIrp directly to whatever action (SubPowerUpComplete or SubPowerDownComplete) is appropriate.

PoCallDriver

PoCallDriver just calls IoCallDriver in Windows 98. Consequently, it would be easy for you to make the mistake of using IoCallDriver to forward power IRPs. There is, however, an even worse problem in Windows 98.

The Windows 2000 version of PoCallDriver makes sure that it sends power IRPs to DO_POWER_PAGABLE drivers at PASSIVE_LEVEL and to INRUSH or nonpaged drivers at DISPATCH_LEVEL. I took advantage of that fact in GENERIC to forward power IRPs in situations where HandlePowerEvent is called at DISPATCH_LEVEL from an I/O completion routine. The Windows 98 version, since it's just IoCallDriver under a different name, doesn't switch IRQL. As it happens, *all* power IRPs in Windows 98 should be sent at PASSIVE_LEVEL. So I wrote a helper routine named SafePoCallDriver for use in GENERIC that queues an executive work item—refer to Chapter 9—to send the IRP at PASSIVE_LEVEL.

Other Differences

You should know about a few other differences between the way Windows 98 and Windows 2000 handle power management features. I'll describe them briefly and indicate how they might affect the development of your drivers.

When you call PoRegisterDeviceForIdleDetection, you must supply the address of the PDO rather than your own device object. That's because, internally, the system needs to find the address of the DEVNODE that the Windows 98 Configuration Manager works with, and that's accessible only from the PDO. You can also use the PDO as the argument in Windows 2000, so you might as well write your code that way in the first place.

The **PoSetPowerState** support routine is a no-operation in Windows 98. Furthermore, although it's documented as returning the previous device or system power state, the Windows 98 version returns whatever state argument you happen to supply. This is the *new* state rather than the old state—or maybe just a random number that occupies an uninitialized variable that you happened to use as an argument to the function: no one checks.

PoStartNextPowerIrp is a no-operation in Windows 98, so it would be easy for you to forget to call it if you do your development in Windows 98.

As best I can tell, the PO_POWER_NOOP flag in a device object doesn't do anything in Windows 98. Accordingly, there's no point in setting it in the hope of avoiding the need to handle power IRPs.

The service routines having to do with device power relations (**PoRegisterDeviceNotify** and **PoCancelDeviceNotify**) are not defined in Windows 98. As far as I can tell, Windows 98 also doesn't issue a PowerRelations query to gather the information needed to support the callbacks in the first place. The service routines **PoRegisterSystemState**, **PoSetSystemState**, and **PoUnregisterSystemState** are also not implemented in Windows 98. To load a driver in Windows 98 that calls these or other undefined service functions, you'll need to supply a virtual device driver with stubs, as I'll describe in Appendix A, "Coping with Windows 98 Incompatibilities."

Chapter 9

Specialized Topics

In the preceding eight chapters, I've described most of the features of a full-blown WDM driver suitable for any random sort of hardware device. But you should understand a few more general-purpose techniques, and I'll describe them in this chapter. In the chapter's first section, I'll explain how to create a filter driver that sits above or below the function driver and modifies the standard behavior evoked by the function driver. Then I'll describe how to log errors for eventual viewing by a system administrator. After that, I'll discuss the very important subject of how you use I/O control (IOCTL) operations to allow an application to control your hardware or features of your driver. That discussion includes an explanation of how a WDM driver can alert an application to "interesting" events. I'll wrap up the chapter with instructions about how to create your own system threads, how to queue work items for execution within the context of existing system threads, and how to set up watchdog timers for unresponsive devices.

FILTER DRIVERS

The Windows Driver Model assumes that a hardware device can have several drivers that each contribute in some way to the successful management of the device. The WDM accomplishes the layering of drivers by means of a stack of device objects. I discussed this concept in Chapter 2, "Basic Structure of a WDM Driver." Up until now, I've been talking exclusively about the *function driver* that manages the main functionality of a device. In this section, I'll describe how you write a *filter driver* that resides above or below the function driver and modifies the behavior of the device in some way by filtering the I/O request packets (IRPs) that flow through it.

A filter driver that's above the function driver is called an *upper filter driver;* a filter driver that's below the function driver (but still above the bus driver) is called a *lower filter driver.* The mechanics of building either type of filter are exactly the same, even though the drivers themselves serve different purposes. In fact, you build a filter driver just as you build any other WDM driver—with a **DriverEntry** routine, an **AddDevice** routine, a bunch of dispatch functions, and so on.

The intended purpose of an upper filter driver is to facilitate supporting a device that behaves in most respects like a generic device of its class but that has some additional functionality. You can rely, perhaps, on a generic function driver to support the generic behavior. To deal with the extra functionality, you write an upper filter driver to intervene in the flow of I/O requests. To give a silly example, suppose there existed a standard class of toaster device for which someone had written a standard driver. And suppose that your particular toaster had an Advanced Waffle Eject feature that caused your toaster to pop toasted waffles two feet into the air. Controlling this AWEsome feature would be a natural job for an upper filter driver. See Figure 9-1.

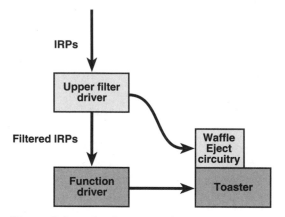

Figure 9-1. *Role of an upper filter driver.*

Another use for upper filter drivers is to compensate for bugs in the hardware or in the function driver. If you're going to deploy a filter driver for this purpose, Microsoft implores you to version-stamp the driver and, insofar as it's under your control, to change the version number of whatever component you're compensating for when the bug someday gets fixed. Otherwise, it will be harder for Microsoft to install automatic updates.

Lower filter drivers can't intervene in the normal operation of a device with which the function driver communicates directly. That's because the function driver will implement most substantive requests by making hardware abstraction layer (HAL) calls that directly access the hardware. The filter driver, of course, sees only those IRPs that something above chooses to pass down to it, and it never knows about the HAL calls.

A lower filter driver might find employment in the stack of drivers for a USB (universal serial bus) device, however. For such devices, the function driver uses internal control IRPs as containers for USB request blocks (URBs). A lower filter driver could monitor and modify these IRPs, perhaps. See Figure 9-2.

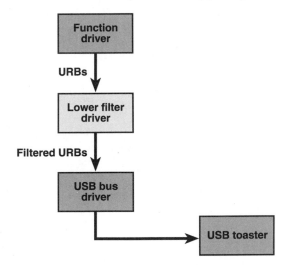

Figure 9-2. *Role of a lower filter driver.*

Another possible use for a lower filter driver, suggested by one of my seminar students, is to help you write a bus-independent driver. Imagine a device packaged as a PCI (Peripheral Component Interconnect) expansion card, a PCMCIA (Personal Computer Memory Card International Association) card, a USB device, and so on. You could write a function driver that is totally independent of the bus architecture, except that it wouldn't be able to talk to the device. You'd also write several lower filter drivers, one for each possible bus architecture, as illustrated in Figure 9-3. You'd install the appropriate one of these for a particular instance of the hardware. When your function driver needed to talk to the hardware, it would send an IRP (perhaps an IRP_MJ_INTERNAL_DEVICE_CONTROL) down to the filter.

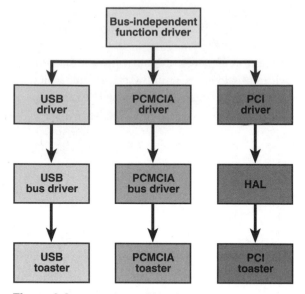

Figure 9-3. *Using lower filter drivers to achieve bus independence.*

DriverEntry Routine

The **DriverEntry** routine for a filter driver is very similar to that for a function driver. The major difference is that a filter driver must install dispatch routines for every type of IRP, not just for the types of IRP it expects to handle:

```
extern "C" NTSTATUS DriverEntry(PDRIVER_OBJECT DriverObject,
  PUNICODE_STRING RegistryPath)
  {
  DriverObject->DriverUnload = DriverUnload;
  DriverObject->DriverExtension->AddDevice = AddDevice;
  for (int i = 0; i < arraysize(DriverObject->MajorFunction); ++i)
    DriverObject->MajorFunction[i] = DispatchAny;
  DriverObject->MajorFunction[IRP_MJ_POWER] = DispatchPower;
  DriverObject->MajorFunction[IRP_MJ_PNP] = DispatchPnp;
  return STATUS_SUCCESS;
  }
```

A filter driver has a **DriverUnload** and an AddDevice function just as any other driver does. I filled the major function table with the address of a routine named **DispatchAny** that would pass any random request down the stack. I specified specific dispatch routines for power and Plug and Play (PnP) requests.

The reason that a filter driver has to handle every conceivable type of IRP has to do with the order in which driver AddDevice functions get called *vis-à-vis* DriverEntry. In general, a filter driver has to support all the same IRP types that the driver immediately underneath it supports. If a filter were to leave a particular

MajorFunction table entry in its default state, IRPs of that type would get failed with STATUS_INVALID_DEVICE_REQUEST. (The I/O Manager includes a default dispatch function that simply completes a request with this status. The driver object initially comes to you with all the MajorFunction table entries pointing to that default routine.) But you won't know until AddDevice time which device object(s) are underneath you. You could investigate the dispatch table for each lower device driver inside AddDevice and plug in the needed dispatch pointers in your own MajorFunction table, but remember that you might be in multiple device stacks, so you might get multiple AddDevice calls. It's easier to just declare support for all IRPs at DriverEntry time.

AddDevice Routine

Filter drivers have **AddDevice** functions that get called for each appropriate piece of hardware. You'll be calling **IoCreateDevice** to create an unnamed device object and **IoAttachDeviceToDeviceStack** to plug in to the driver stack. In addition, you'll need to copy a few settings from the device object underneath you:

```
NTSTATUS AddDevice(PDRIVER_OBJECT DriverObject, PDEVICE_OBJECT pdo)
  {
  PDEVICE_OBJECT fido;
  NTSTATUS status = IoCreateDevice(DriverObject,
    sizeof(DEVICE_EXTENSION), NULL, FILE_DEVICE_UNKNOWN,
    0, FALSE, &fido);
  if (!NT_SUCCESS(status))
    return status;
  PDEVICE_EXTENSION pdx = (PDEVICE_EXTENSION) fido->DeviceExtension;
  __try
    {
    pdx->DeviceObject = fido;
    pdx->Pdo = pdo;
    PDEVICE_OBJECT fdo = IoAttachDeviceToDeviceStack(fido, pdo);
    pdx->LowerDeviceObject = fdo;
    fido->Flags |= fdo->Flags &
      (DO_DIRECT_IO | DO_BUFFERED_IO | DO_POWER_PAGABLE
      | DO_POWER_INRUSH);
    fido->DeviceType = fdo->DeviceType;
    fido->Characteristics = fdo->Characteristics;
    fido->Flags &= ~DO_DEVICE_INITIALIZING;
    }
  __finally
    {
    if (!NT_SUCCESS(status))
      IoDeleteDevice(fido);
    }
  return status;
  }
```

The part that's different from a function driver is shown in boldface. Basically, we're propagating a few flag bits, the **DeviceType** value, and the **Characteristics** value from the device object next beneath us. We need to make these copies because the I/O Manager bases some of its decisions on what it sees in the topmost device object. In particular, whether a read or write IRP gets a memory descriptor list (MDL) or a system copy buffer depends on what the top object's DO_DIRECT_IO and DO_BUFFERED_IO flags are. We don't need to copy the **SectorSize** or **Alignment- Requirement** members of the lower device object—IoAttachDeviceToDeviceStack will do that automatically.

> **NOTE** The reason I told you that you have to declare your choice of buffered versus direct I/O in AddDevice and that you can't change you mind afterward should now be clear: a filter driver might copy your settings at AddDevice time and won't have any way to know about a later change.

There's ordinarily no need for a filter device object (FiDO) to have its own name. If the function driver names its device object and creates a symbolic link, or if the function driver registers a device interface for its device object, an application will be able to open a handle for the device. Every IRP sent to the device gets sent first to the topmost FiDO driver, whether or not that FiDO has its own name.

Do not use the FILE_DEVICE_SECURE_OPEN characteristics flag when you create a FiDO object. The PnP Manager propagates this flag, and a few others, up and down the device object stack. It's not your decision whether to enforce security checking on file opens—it's the function driver's and maybe the bus driver's.

Dispatch Routines

You write a filter driver in the first place because you want to modify the behavior of a device in some way. Therefore, you'll have dispatch functions that do *something* with some of the IRPs that come your way. But you'll be passing most of the IRPs down the stack, and you pretty much know how to do this already:

```
NTSTATUS DispatchAny(PDEVICE_OBJECT fido, PIRP Irp)
  {
  PDEVICE_EXTENSION pdx = (PDEVICE_EXTENSION) fido->DeviceExtension;
  NTSTATUS status = IoAcquireRemoveLock(&pdx->RemoveLock, Irp);
  if (!NT_SUCCESS(status))
    return CompleteRequest(Irp, status, 0);
  IoSkipCurrentIrpStackLocation(Irp);
  status = IoCallDriver(pdx->LowerDeviceObject, Irp);
  IoReleaseRemoveLock(&pdx->RemoveLock, Irp);
  return status;
  }

NTSTATUS DispatchPnp(PDEVICE_OBJECT fido, PIRP Irp)
  {
  PDEVICE_EXTENSION pdx = (PDEVICE_EXTENSION) fido->DeviceExtension;
  NTSTATUS status = IoAcquireRemoveLock(&pdx->RemoveLock, Irp);
```

```
  if (!NT_SUCCESS(status))
    return CompleteRequest(Irp, status, 0);
  PIO_STACK_LOCATION stack = IoGetCurrentIrpStackLocation(Irp);
  ULONG fcn = stack->MinorFunction;
  IoSkipCurrentIrpStackLocation(Irp);
  status = IoCallDriver(pdx->LowerDeviceObject, Irp);
  if (fcn == IRP_MN_REMOVE_DEVICE)
    {
    IoReleaseRemoveLockAndWait(&pdx->RemoveLock, Irp);
    IoDetachDevice(pdx->LowerDeviceObject);
    IoDeleteDevice(fido);
    }
  else
    IoReleaseRemoveLock(&pdx->RemoveLock, Irp);
  return status;
  }

NTSTATUS DispatchPower(PDEVICE_OBJECT fido, PIRP Irp)
  {
  PoStartNextPowerIrp(Irp);
  PDEVICE_EXTENSION pdx = (PDEVICE_EXTENSION) fido->DeviceExtension;
  NTSTATUS status = IoAcquireRemoveLock(&pdx->RemoveLock, Irp);
  if (!NT_SUCCESS(status))
    return CompleteRequest(Irp, status, 0);
  IoSkipCurrentIrpStackLocation(Irp);
  status = PoCallDriver(pdx->LowerDeviceObject, Irp);
  IoReleaseRemoveLock(&pdx->RemoveLock, Irp);
  return status;
  }
```

It's necessary, by the way, to acquire and release the remove lock for a filter driver's device object, as shown in these examples. The initial call to **IoAcquire-RemoveLock** checks whether a device removal is currently pending for the FiDO. If so, the dispatch function fails the IRP immediately with STATUS_DELETE_PENDING, the only nonsuccess value that IoAcquireRemoveLock ever returns. While the filter owns its remove lock in one dispatch function, another thread that might be trying to process an IRP_MN_REMOVE_DEVICE inside **DispatchPnp** will block inside **IoReleaseRemoveLockAndWait**. What's thereby prevented is the call to **IoDetachDevice**, which might allow the lower device object to disappear. Our own device object is protected from deletion by a reference that was obtained by the caller before sending us this IRP—by using **IoGetAttachedDeviceReference**, for example.

Except for IRP_MJ_PNP, all dispatch functions in a filter driver need to be in nonpaged memory, and none should assume they're being called at PASSIVE_LEVEL. Here are two real-world examples of why this might matter. First, a lower filter for a USB device will be receiving and passing along IRP_MJ_INTERNAL_DEVICE_CONTROL requests that contain URBs. (See Chapter 11, "The Universal Serial Bus.")

Some of these IRPs arrive at PASSIVE_LEVEL. Others might arrive at DISPATCH_LEVEL because they're coming from an I/O completion routine. The second example involves a disk driver, which might start out handling power requests at PASSIVE_LEVEL because it's set the DO_POWER_PAGABLE flag. The disk driver might subsequently learn that its device is being used to hold a paging file or some other special file, whereupon it will lock down its power handler and clear the DO_POWER_PAGABLE flag. All of a sudden, any filter driver in the same stack will start getting power requests at DISPATCH_LEVEL.

> **NOTE** You should follow this guideline when you program a filter driver: *First, do no harm.* In other words, don't cause drivers above or below you to fail because you perturbed anything at all in their environment or in the flow of IRPs.

LOGGING ERRORS

In the discussions of error handling up until now, I've been concerned only with detecting (and propagating) status codes and with doing various things in the checked build to help debug problems that show up as errors. Even in the free build of a driver, however, some errors are serious enough that we want to be sure the system administrator knows about them. For example, maybe a disk driver discovers that the disk's physical surface has an unusually large number of bad sectors. Or maybe a driver is encountering unexpectedly frequent data errors or some sort of difficulty configuring or starting the device.

To deal with these types of situations, a driver can write an entry to the system error log. The Event Viewer applet—one of the administrative tools on a Microsoft Windows 2000 system—can later display this entry so that an administrator can learn about the problem. See Figure 9-4 for an illustration of the Event Viewer. Another way to indicate sudden errors is by signaling a Windows Management Instrumentation (WMI) event. I'll discuss event logging in this section; WMI is the subject of Chapter 10, "Windows Management Instrumentation."

Production of an administrative report from the error log involves the steps diagrammed in Figure 9-5. A driver uses the kernel-mode service function **IoWriteErrorLogEntry** to send an *error log packet* data structure to the event logger service. The packet contains a numeric code instead of message text. As time permits, the event logger writes packets to a logging file on disk. Later, the Event Viewer combines the packets in the log file with message text drawn from a collection of *message files* to produce the report. The message files are ordinary 32-bit DLLs containing text appropriate to all possible logged events in the local language.

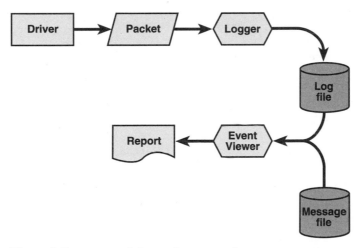

Figure 9-4. *The Windows 2000 Event Viewer.*

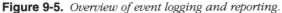

Figure 9-5. *Overview of event logging and reporting.*

Your job as a driver author is to create appropriate error log packets when noteworthy events occur. As a practical matter, you'll probably also be the person who has to build the message file in at least one natural language. I'll describe both aspects of error logging in the next two sections.

Creating an Error Log Packet

To log an error, a driver creates an IO_ERROR_LOG_PACKET data structure and sends it to the kernel-mode logger. The packet is a variable-length structure—see Figure 9-6—with a fixed-size header containing general information about the event you're logging. **ErrorCode** indicates what event you're logging; it correlates with the message text file I'll describe shortly. After the fixed header comes an array of doublewords called **DumpData**, which contains **DumpDataSize** bytes of data that the Event Viewer will display in hexadecimal notation when asked for detailed information about this event. The size is in bytes even though the array is declared as consisting of 32-bit integers. After the DumpData, the packet can contain zero or more null-terminated Unicode strings that will end up being substituted into the formatted message text by the Event Viewer. The string area begins **StringOffset** bytes from the start of the packet and contains **NumberOfStrings** strings.

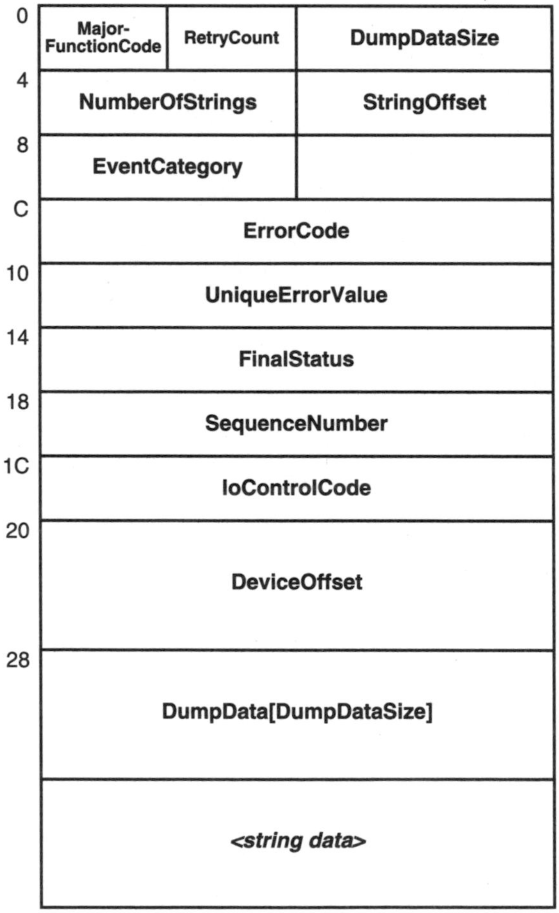

Figure 9-6. *The IO_ERROR_LOG_PACKET structure.*

You don't have to fill in any of the fixed-header members besides the ones I just mentioned. But they add, perhaps, diagnostic utility to the log entries, which might help you track down problems.

Since the logging packet is of variable length, your first job is to determine how much memory is needed for the packet you want to create. Add the size of the fixed header to the number of bytes of DumpData to the number of bytes occupied by the substitution strings (including their null terminators). For example, the following code fragment, taken from the EVENTLOG sample on the companion disc, allocates an error log packet big enough to hold 4 bytes of dump data plus a single string:

```
VOID LogEvent(NTSTATUS code, PDEVICE_OBJECT fdo)
  {
  PWSTR myname = L"EventLog";
  ULONG packetlen = (wcslen(myname) + 1) * sizeof(WCHAR)
    + sizeof(IO_ERROR_LOG_PACKET) + 4;
  if (packetlen > ERROR_LOG_MAXIMUM_SIZE)
    return;
  PIO_ERROR_LOG_PACKET p = (PIO_ERROR_LOG_PACKET)
    IoAllocateErrorLogEntry(fdo, (UCHAR) packetlen);
  if (!p)
    return;
  ...
  }
```

One trap for the unwary in this sequence is that error log packets have a maximum length of 152 bytes, the value of ERROR_LOG_MAXIMUM_SIZE. Furthermore, the size argument to **IoAllocateErrorLogEntry** is a UCHAR, which is only 8 bits wide. It would be very easy to ask for a packet that was, say, 400 bytes long and be embarrassed when only 144 bytes get allocated. (400 is 0x190; 144 is 0x90, which is what you'd get after the truncation to 8 bits.)

Notice that the first argument to IoAllocateErrorLogEntry is the address of a device object. The name, if any, of that device object will appear in eventual log entries in place of the %1 substitution escape, which I will discuss more in the next section.

This code fragment also illustrates the action you should take in response to a problem allocating a log entry: *none*. It's not considered an error if you can't log some other error, so you don't want to fail any IRP, generate a bug check, or do anything else that will cause your processing to terminate. In fact, you'll notice that this **LogEvent** helper function is VOID because no programmer should be concerned enough about whether it succeeds or fails to have put a check into his or her code.

After successfully allocating the log packet, your next job is to initialize the structure and hand off control of it to the logger. For example:

```
...
memset(p, 0, sizeof(IO_ERROR_LOG_PACKET));
p->ErrorCode = code;

p->DumpDataSize = 4;
p->DumpData[0] = <whatever>;

p->StringOffset = sizeof(IO_ERROR_LOG_PACKET) + p->DumpDataSize;
p->NumberOfStrings = 1;
wcscpy((PWSTR) ((PUCHAR) p + p->StringOffset), myname);

IoWriteErrorLogEntry(p);
}
```

When logging a device error, you'd fill in more of the fields in the header than just the error code. For information about these other fields, consult the IoAllocate-ErrorLogEntry function in the DDK documentation.

Creating a Message File

The Event Viewer uses the ErrorCode in an error packet to locate the text of an appropriate message in one of the message files associated with your driver. A message file is just a DLL with a message resource containing text in one or more natural languages. Since a WDM driver uses the same executable file format as a DLL, the message file for your private messages could just be your driver file itself. I'll give you an introduction here to building a message file. You can find additional information on MSDN and in James D. Murray's *Windows NT Event Logging* (O'Reilly & Associates, 1998) at pages 125–57.

Figure 9-7 illustrates the process by which you attach message text to your driver. You begin by creating a message source file with the file extension MC. Your build script uses the message compiler (MC.EXE) to translate the messages. One of the outputs of the message compiler is a header file containing symbolic constants for your messages; you include that file in your driver, and the constants end up being the ErrorCode values for the events you log. The other outputs from the message compiler are a set of intermediate files containing message text in one or more natural languages and a resource script file (.RC) that lists those intermediate files. Your build script goes on to compile the resource file and to specify the translated resources as input to the linkage editor. At the end of the build, your driver contains the message resources required to support the Event Viewer.

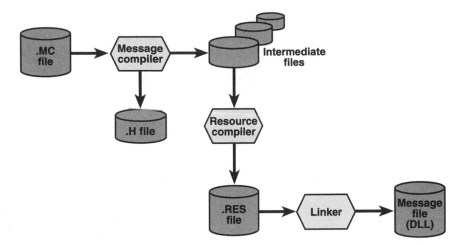

Figure 9-7. *Creating a message file.*

The following is an example of a simple message source file. (This is part of the EVENTLOG sample program.)

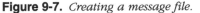

1
```
MessageIdTypedef = NTSTATUS
```

2
```
SeverityNames = (
  Success        = 0x0:STATUS_SEVERITY_SUCCESS
  Informational  = 0x1:STATUS_SEVERITY_INFORMATIONAL
  Warning        = 0x2:STATUS_SEVERITY_WARNING
  Error          = 0x3:STATUS_SEVERITY_ERROR
  )
```

3
```
FacilityNames = (
  System    = 0x0
  Eventlog  = 0x2A:FACILITY_EVENTLOG_ERROR_CODE
  )
```

4
```
LanguageNames = (
  English  = 0x0409:msg00001
  German   = 0x0407:msg00002
  French   = 0x040C:msg00003
  )
```

5
```
MessageId = 0x0001
Facility = Eventlog
Severity = Informational
SymbolicName = EVENTLOG_MSG_TEST
```

(continued)

```
6    Language = English
     %2 said, "Hello, world!"
     .
     Language = German
     %2 hat gesagt, «Wir sind nicht mehr im Kansas!»
     .
     Language = French
     %2 a dit, «Mon chien a mangé mon devoir!»
     .
```

1. The **MessageIdTypedef** statement allows you to specify a symbol that will appear as a cast operator in the definition of each of the message identifier constants generated by this message file. For example, later we'll define a message with the symbolic name EVENTLOG_MSG_TEST. The presence of the MessageIdTypedef statement causes the header file generated by the message compiler to define this symbol as **((NTSTATUS)0x602A0001L)**.

2. The **SeverityNames** statement allows you to define your own names for the four possible severity codes. The names on the left side of the equal signs (Success, Informational, and so on) appear in the definition of messages elsewhere in this very file. The symbol after the colon ends up being defined—in the header output file—as equal to the number before the colon. For example, **#define STATUS_SEVERITY_SUCCESS 0x0**.

3. The **FacilityNames** statement allows you to define your own names for the facility codes that will be included in the message identifier definitions. Here, we've said we'll use the name **Eventlog** in Facility statements later. The message compiler generates the statement **#define FACILITY_ EVENTLOG_ERROR_CODE 0x2A** as a result of the third line of the FacilityNames statement.

4. The **LanguageNames** statement allows you to define your own names for the languages into which you've translated your messages. Here, we've said we'll use the name English elsewhere in the file when we mean to specify LANGID 0x0409, which is Standard English in the normal Microsoft Windows NT scheme of languages. The name after the colon is the name of the intermediate binary file that receives the compiled messages for this particular language.

5. Each individual message definition contains some header statements followed by the text of the message in each of the languages supported by this message source file. The **MessageId** statement can specify an

absolute number, as in this example, or it can specify a delta from the last message (such as **MessageId = +1**). You specify the facility code and severity by using names defined at the start of the message source file. You also specify, with the **SymbolicName** statement, a symbolic name for this message. The message compiler will define this symbol in the header file it generates.

6. For each language you specified in the LanguageNames statement, you have a message text definition like this one. It begins with a **Language** statement that uses one of the language names you defined. Text for the message follows. Each message text definition ends with a line containing just a period. (With respect to the German and French nontranslations of the phrase "Hello, world!" it will help you to know that at the time I wrote this chapter I was in the process of studying the *passé composé* in my French class and a revival of *The Wizard of Oz* was underway in theaters.)

Within the message texts, you can indicate by means of a percent sign followed by an integer the places where you want string substitution to occur. **%1** refers to the name of the device object that generated the message. That name is an implicit parameter when you create an error log entry; you don't have to specify it directly. **%2**, **%3**, and so on, correspond to the first, second, and so on, Unicode strings you append to the log entry. In the example we've been following, **%2** will be replaced by **EventLog** because we put that string into our error packet.

This way of indicating substitution is especially useful in that you're free to put strings into the text in whatever order is appropriate for the language you're dealing with. So, if your message text read "The %1 %2 fox jumped over the %3 dog" in English, it might read "Der %3 Hund wurde vom %1 %2 Fuchs übergesprungen" in German. (This is a silly example, of course. If the driver supplied "quick", "brown", and "lazy" for the substitution strings, they'd appear in English in all displayed versions of the message. But I think you get the point I'm trying to make about word order.)

The Event Viewer can't find your message file without a little bit of help in the form of some registry entries. A key named EventLog resides in the services branch of the Windows NT registry—that is, the collection of subkeys below HKLM\System\CurrentControlSet\Services. Each driver or other service that logs events has its own subkey below that. Each service-specific subkey has values named **EventMessageFile** and **TypesSupported**. The EventMessageFile value is a REG_SZ or REG_EXPAND_SZ type that names all of the message files that the Event Viewer might need to access to format the messages your driver generates. This value would have a data string like "%SystemRoot%\System32\iologmsg.dll; %SystemRoot%\System32\Drivers\EventLog.sys". IOLOGMSG.DLL contains the text of all the standard NTSTATUS.H codes, by the way. Consult the sidebar below for some tantalizing hints about how to automatically set these registry entries when you install your driver. The TypesSupported value should just be a REG_DWORD type equalling "7" to indicate that your driver can generate all possible events—that is, errors, warnings, and informational messages. (The fact that you even need to specify this value seems like a historical artifact of some kind.)

A PRACTICAL NOTE ABOUT MESSAGE FILES

Two practical facts about putting message resources into your driver are difficult to discover: how precisely you make your build script compile your messages, and how you convince the system's hardware installer to put the necessary entries into the registry so the Event Viewer will find your messages. Art Baker's *The Windows NT Device Driver Book: A Guide for Programmers* (Prentice Hall, 1997) alludes to a solution to the first problem on page 308. The DDK's discussion of INF files explains how to solve the second problem with syntax in an **AddService** statement.

Like the other sample programs in this book, the EVENTLOG sample is based on a Microsoft Visual C++ 6.0 project file. I modified the project definition to include a custom build step for EVENTLOG.MC and to include the resulting .RC file in the build. If you open the project settings, you'll see what I mean.

Later in this book (in Chapter 12, "Installing Device Drivers"), I'll discuss the general topic of how you use an INF file to install drivers. To see how you specify your message file in an INF file, take a look at DEVICE.INF in the EVENTLOG project directory and, specifically, at its AddService statement. You'll see that the AddService line points to an **EventLogLogging** section that, in turn, uses the **AddReg** statement to point to an **EventLogAddReg** section. The latter section adds EventMessageFile and TypesSupported values to the service-specific subkey of the event logger service.

I/O CONTROL OPERATIONS

If you look at the various types of requests that come to a device, most of them involve reading or writing data. On occasion, however, an application needs to perform an IOCTL operation on a device. An application uses the standard Microsoft Win32 API function **DeviceIoControl** to perform such an operation. On the driver side, an application's call to DeviceIoControl turns into an IRP with the major function code IRP_MJ_DEVICE_CONTROL.

The DeviceIoControl API

The user-mode DeviceIoControl API has the following prototype:

```
result = DeviceIoControl(Handle, Code, InputData, InputLength,
  OutputData, OutputLength, &Feedback, &Overlapped);
```

Handle (HANDLE) is an open handle open to the device. You obtain this handle by calling **CreateFile** in the following manner:

```
Handle = CreateFile("\\\\.\\IOCTL", GENERIC_READ | GENERIC_WRITE,
  0, NULL, OPEN_EXISTING, flags, NULL);
if (Handle == INVALID_HANDLE_VALUE)
  <error>
...
CloseHandle(Handle);
```

The **flags** argument to CreateFile is either FILE_FLAG_OVERLAPPED or zero to indicate whether or not you'll be performing asynchronous operations with this file handle. While you have the handle open, you can make calls to **ReadFile**, **WriteFile**, or **DeviceIoControl**. When you're done accessing the device, you should explicitly close the handle by calling **CloseHandle**. Bear in mind, though, that the operating system automatically closes any handles that are left open when your process terminates.

The **Code** (DWORD) argument to DeviceIoControl is a control code that indicates what control operation you want to perform. I'll discuss how you define these codes a bit further on (in "Defining I/O Control Codes"). The **InputData** (PVOID) and **InputLength** (DWORD) arguments describe a data area that you are sending *to* the device driver. (That is, this data is input from the perspective of the driver.) The **OutputData** (PVOID) and **OutputLength** (DWORD) arguments describe a data area that the driver can completely or partially fill with information that it wants to send back to you. (That is, this data is output from the perspective of the driver.) The driver will update the **Feedback** variable (a DWORD) to indicate how many bytes of output data it gave you back. Figure 9-8 illustrates the relationship of these buffers with the application and driver. The **Overlapped** (OVERLAPPED) structure is used to help control an asynchronous operation, which is the subject of the next section. If you specified FILE_FLAG_OVERLAPPED in the call to CreateFile, you must specify the OVERLAPPED structure pointer. If you didn't specify FILE_FLAG_OVERLAPPED, you might as well supply NULL for this last argument because the system is going to ignore it anyway.

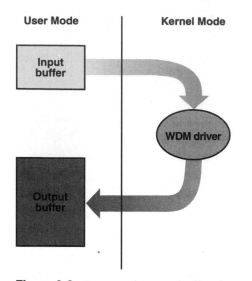

Figure 9-8. *Input and output buffers for DeviceIoControl.*

Whether a particular control operation requires an input buffer or an output buffer depends on the function being performed. For example, an IOCTL that retrieves the driver's version number would probably require an output buffer only. An IOCTL that merely notifies the driver of some fact pertaining to the application would probably require only an input buffer. You can imagine still other operations that would require either both or neither of the input and output buffers—it all depends on what the control operation does.

The return value from DeviceIoControl is a Boolean value that indicates success (if TRUE) or failure (if FALSE). In a failure situation, the application can call **GetLastError** to find out why the call failed.

Synchronous and Asynchronous Calls to DeviceIoControl

When you make a synchronous call to DeviceIoControl, the calling thread blocks until the control operation completes. For example:

```
HANDLE Handle = CreateFile("\\\\.\\IOCTL", ..., 0, NULL);
DWORD version, junk;
if (DeviceIoControl(Handle, IOCTL_GET_VERSION_BUFFERED,
  NULL, 0, &version, sizeof(version), &junk, NULL))
  printf("IOCTL.SYS version %d.%2d\n", HIWORD(version),
    LOWORD(version));
else
  printf("Error %d in IOCTL_GET_VERSION_BUFFERED call\n",
    GetLastError());
```

Here, we open the device handle without the FILE_FLAG_OVERLAPPED flag. Our subsequent call to DeviceIoControl therefore doesn't return until the driver supplies the answer we're asking for.

When you make an asynchronous call to DeviceIoControl, the calling thread does not block immediately. Instead, it continues processing until it reaches the point where it requires the result of the control operation. At that point, it calls some API that will block the thread until the driver completes the operation. For example:

```
HANDLE Handle = CreateFile("\\\\.\\IOCTL", ...,
  FILE_FLAG_OVERLAPPED, NULL);
DWORD version, junk;
OVERLAPPED Overlapped;

Overlapped.hEvent = CreateEvent(NULL, TRUE, FALSE, NULL);
DWORD code;

if (DeviceIoControl(Handle, ..., &Overlapped))
  code = 0;
else
  code = GetLastError();

<continue processing>

if (code == ERROR_IO_PENDING)
  {
  if (GetOverlappedResult(Handle, &Overlapped, &junk, TRUE))
    code = 0;
  else
    code = GetLastError();
  }
CloseHandle(Overlapped.hEvent);
if (code != 0)
  <error>
```

Two major differences exist between this asynchronous example and the earlier synchronous example. First, we specify the FILE_FLAG_OVERLAPPED flag in the call to CreateFile. Second, the call to DeviceIoControl specifies the address of an OVERLAPPED structure, within which we've initialized the **hEvent** event handle to describe a manual reset event. (For more information about events and thread synchronization in general, see Jeffrey Richter's *Programming Applications for Microsoft Windows, Fourth Edition* [Microsoft Press, 1999].)

The asynchronous call to DeviceIoControl will have one of three results. First, it might return TRUE, meaning that the device driver's dispatch routine was able to complete the request right away. Second, it might return FALSE, and GetLastError might retrieve the special error code ERROR_IO_PENDING. This result indicates that the driver's dispatch routine returned STATUS_PENDING and will complete the control operation later. Note that ERROR_IO_PENDING isn't really an error—it's one of the two ways in which the system indicates that everything is proceeding normally. The third possible result from the asynchronous call to DeviceIoControl is a FALSE return value coupled with a GetLastError value other than ERROR_IO_PENDING. Such a result would be a real error.

At the point at which the application needs the result of the control operation, it calls one of the Win32 synchronization primitives, such as **GetOverlappedResult**, **WaitForSingleObject**, or the like. GetOverlappedResult, the synchronization primitive I use in this example, is especially convenient because it also retrieves the bytes-transferred feedback value and sets the GetLastError result to indicate the result of the I/O operation. Although you could call WaitForSingleObject or a related API—passing the **Overlapped.hEvent** event handle as an argument—you wouldn't be able to learn the results of the DeviceIoControl operation; you'd just learn that the operation had finished.

Defining I/O Control Codes

The **Code** argument to DeviceIoControl is a 32-bit numeric constant that you define using the CTL_CODE preprocessor macro that's part of both the DDK and the Platform SDK. Figure 9-9 illustrates the way in which the operating system partitions one of these 32-bit codes into subfields.

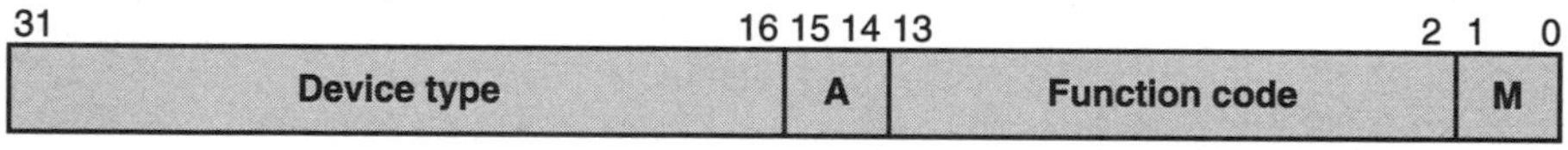

31	16	15 14 13	2	1 0
Device type		A	Function code	M

Figure 9-9. *Fields in an I/O control code.*

The fields have the following interpretation:

- The device type (16 bits, first argument to CTL_CODE) is supposed to indicate what type of device implements this control operation. I'm unaware of any "IOCTL police" inside either Microsoft Windows 98 or Microsoft Windows 2000, however, and I believe that the content of the field is actually pretty arbitrary. It is customary, though, to use the same value (for example, FILE_DEVICE_UNKNOWN) that you use in the driver when you call IoCreateDevice.

- The access code (2 bits, fourth argument to CTL_CODE) indicates the access rights an application needs to its device handle to issue this control operation.

- The function code (12 bits, second argument to CTL_CODE) indicates precisely which control operation this code describes. Microsoft reserves the first half of the range of this field—that is, values 0 through 2047. You and I therefore assign values in the range 2048 through 4095. I'm pretty sure I'll never feel cramped by being able to define only 2048 IOCTLs for one of my devices.

- The buffering method (2 bits, third argument to CTL_CODE) indicates how the I/O Manager is to handle the input and output buffers supplied by the application. I'll have a great deal to say about this field in the next section when I describe how to implement IRP_MJ_DEVICE_CONTROL in a driver.

I want to clarify one point of possible confusion. When you create your driver, you're free to design a series of IOCTL operations that applications can use in talking to your driver. Although some other driver author might craft a set of IOCTL operations that uses exactly the same numeric values for control codes, the system will never be confused by the overlap because IOCTL codes are interpreted by only the driver to which they're addressed. Mind you, if you opened a handle to a device belonging to that hypothetical other driver and then tried to send what you thought was one of your own IOCTLs to it, confusion would definitely ensue.

Mechanically, your life and the life of application programmers who need to call your driver will be easier if you place all of your IOCTL definitions in a dedicated header file. In the samples on the companion disc, the projects each have a header named IOCTLS.H that contains these definitions. For example:

```
#ifndef CTL_CODE
  #pragma message ("CTL_CODE undefined. Include winioctl.h or wdm.h")
#endif

#define IOCTL_GET_VERSION_BUFFERED \
  CTL_CODE(FILE_DEVICE_UNKNOWN, 0x800, METHOD_BUFFERED, FILE_ANY_ACCESS)
#define IOCTL_GET_VERSION_DIRECT \
  CTL_CODE(FILE_DEVICE_UNKNOWN, 0x801, METHOD_OUT_DIRECT, FILE_ANY_ACCESS)
#define IOCTL_GET_VERSION_NEITHER \
  CTL_CODE(FILE_DEVICE_UNKNOWN, 0x802, METHOD_NEITHER, FILE_ANY_ACCESS)
```

The reason for the message #pragma, by the way, is that I'm forever forgetting to include the header file (WINIOCTL.H) that defines CTL_CODE for user-mode programs, and I also tend to forget the name. Better a message that will tell me what I'm doing wrong than a few minutes grep'ing through the include directory, I always say.

Handling IRP_MJ_DEVICE_CONTROL

Each user-mode call to DeviceIoControl causes the I/O Manager to create an IRP with the major function code IRP_MJ_DEVICE_CONTROL and to send that IRP to the driver dispatch routine at the top of the stack for the addressed device. The top stack location contains the parameters listed in Table 9-1. Filter drivers might interpret some private codes themselves but will—if correctly coded, that is—pass all others down the stack. A dispatch function that understands how to handle the IOCTL will reside somewhere in the driver stack—most likely in the function driver, in fact.

Parameters.DeviceIoControl field	Description
OutputBufferLength	Length of the output buffer—sixth argument to DeviceIoControl
InputBufferLength	Length of the input buffer—fourth argument to DeviceIoControl
IoControlCode	Control code—second argument to DeviceIoControl
Type3InputBuffer	User-mode virtual address of input buffer for METHOD_NEITHER

Table 9-1. *Stack location parameters for IRP_MJ_DEVICE_CONTROL.*

A skeletal dispatch function for control operations looks like this:

```
#pragma PAGEDCODE

NTSTATUS DispatchControl(PDEVICE_OBJECT fdo, PIRP Irp)
  {
  PAGED_CODE();
  PDEVICE_EXTENSION pdx = (PDEVICE_EXTENSION) fdo->DeviceExtension;
  NTSTATUS status = IoAcquireRemoveLock(&pdx->RemoveLock, Irp);
  if (!NT_SUCCESS(status))
    return CompleteRequest(Irp, status, 0);
  ULONG info = 0;

  PIO_STACK_LOCATION stack = IoGetCurrentIrpStackLocation(Irp);
  ULONG cbin = stack->Parameters.DeviceIoControl.InputBufferLength;
  ULONG cbout = stack->Parameters.DeviceIoControl.OutputBufferLength;
  ULONG code = stack->Parameters.DeviceIoControl.IoControlCode;

  switch (code)
    {

    ...
```

5 ►

```
default:
  status = STATUS_INVALID_DEVICE_REQUEST;
  break;

}

IoReleaseRemoveLock(&pdx->RemoveLock, Irp);
return CompleteRequest(Irp, status, info);
}
```

1. You can be sure of being called at PASSIVE_LEVEL, so there's no particular reason for a simple dispatch function to be anywhere but paged memory.

2. Like other dispatch functions, this one needs to claim the remove lock while it does its work. That prevents the device object from disappearing out from underneath us because of a PnP event.

3. The next few statements extract the function code and buffer sizes from the parameters union in the I/O stack. You often need these values no matter which specific IOCTL you're processing, so I find it easier to always include these statements in the function.

4. This is where you get to exercise your own creativity by inserting **case** labels for the various IOCTL operations you support.

5. It's a good idea to return a meaningful status code if you're given an IOCTL operation you don't understand.

The way you handle each IOCTL depends on two factors. The first, and most important, of these is the actual purpose of the IOCTL in your scheme of things. (Duh.) The second factor, which is critically important to the mechanics of your code, is the method you selected for buffering user-mode data.

In Chapter 7, "Reading and Writing Data," I discussed how you work with a user-mode program sending you a buffer load of data for output to your device or filling a buffer with input from your device. As I indicated there, when it comes to read and write requests, you have to make up your mind at AddDevice time whether you're going to use the so-called buffered method or direct method (or neither of them) for accessing user-mode buffers in all read and write requests. Control requests also utilize one of these addressing methods, but they work a little differently. Rather than specify a global addressing method via device-object flags, you specify the addressing method for each IOCTL by means of the two low-order bits of the function code. Consequently, you can have some IOCTLs that use the buffered method, some that use a direct method, and some that use neither method. Moreover, the methods you pick for IOCTLs don't affect in any way how you address buffers for read and write IRPs.

You choose one or the other buffering method based on several factors. Most IOCTL operations transfer much less than a page worth of data in either direction and therefore use the METHOD_BUFFERED method. Operations that will transfer more than a page of data should use one of the direct methods. The names of the direct methods seem to oppose common sense: you use METHOD_IN_DIRECT if the application is sending data to the driver and METHOD_OUT_DIRECT if it's the other way around. If you know that you'll get control in the same thread context as the application—usually true for IOCTL operations because no filter driver above you should be pending these and calling you later in an arbitrary thread context—you could use METHOD_NEITHER and decide on the fly how to access user-mode data.

METHOD_BUFFERED

With METHOD_BUFFERED, the I/O Manager creates a kernel-mode copy buffer big enough for the larger of the user-mode input and output buffers. When your dispatch routine gets control, the user-mode input data is sitting in the copy buffer. Before completing the IRP, you fill the copy buffer with the output data you want to send back to the application. When you complete the IRP, you set the **IoStatus.Information** field equal to the number of output bytes you put into the copy buffer. The I/O Manager then copies that many bytes of data back to user mode and sets the feedback variable equal to that same count. Figure 9-10 illustrates these copy operations.

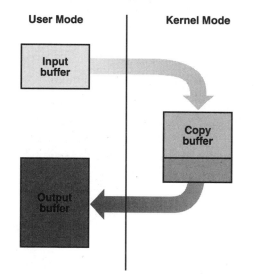

Figure 9-10. *Buffer management with METHOD_BUFFERED.*

Inside the driver, you access both buffers at the same address—namely, the **AssociatedIrp.SystemBuffer** pointer in the IRP. Once again, this is a kernel-mode virtual address that points to a copy of the input data. It obviously behooves you to finish processing the input data before you overwrite this buffer with output data. (I hardly need to tell you—it's the kind of mistake you'll make only once.)

Here's a simple example, drawn from the IOCTL sample program, of the code-specific handling for a METHOD_BUFFERED operation:

```
case IOCTL_GET_VERSION_BUFFERED:
  {
  if (cbout < sizeof(ULONG))
    {
    status = STATUS_INVALID_BUFFER_SIZE;
    break;
    }
  PULONG pversion = (PULONG) Irp->AssociatedIrp.SystemBuffer;
  *pversion = 0x0004000A;
  info = sizeof(ULONG);
  break;
  }
```

We first verify that we've been given an output buffer at least long enough to hold the doubleword we're going to store there. Then we use the SystemBuffer pointer to address the system copy buffer, into which we store the result of this simple operation. The **info** local variable ends up as the IoStatus.Information field when the surrounding dispatch routine completes this IRP. The I/O Manager copies that much data from the system copy buffer back to the user-mode buffer.

A SECURITY HOLE?

I always get a slight nervous feeling when I think about the importance of the buffering and access-control flags in an IOCTL function code. Suppose some malicious application were to submit an IOCTL that used flag values other than the ones I intended. Would that cause a driver to crash or do something else it shouldn't? Well, usually not.

Most of the time, you code the dispatch function for IOCTL requests with a **switch** statement. The case labels reference numeric constants that must match exactly with all 32 bits of whatever code the application supplies. So, if an application were to change any of the bits in an IOCTL code, none of the case labels in the driver would match and some (presumably benign) default action would occur.

The DIRECT Buffering Methods

Both METHOD_IN_DIRECT and METHOD_OUT_DIRECT are handled the same way in the driver. They differ only in the access rights required for the user-mode buffer. METHOD_IN_DIRECT needs read access; METHOD_OUT_DIRECT needs read and write access. With both of these methods, the I/O Manager provides a kernel-mode copy buffer (at AssociatedIrp.SystemBuffer) for the input data and an MDL for the output data buffer. Refer to Chapter 7 for all the gory details about MDLs and to Figure 9-11 for an illustration of this method of managing the buffers.

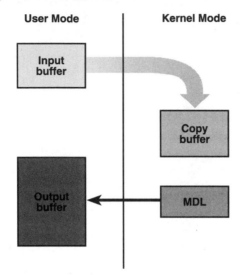

Figure 9-11. *Buffer management with METHOD_XXX_DIRECT.*

Here's an example of a simple handler for a METHOD_*XXX*_DIRECT request:

```
case IOCTL_GET_VERSION_DIRECT:
  {
  if (cbout < sizeof(ULONG))
    {
    status = STATUS_INVALID_BUFFER_SIZE;
    break;
    }
  PULONG pversion = (PULONG)
    MmGetSystemAddressForMdl(Irp->MdlAddress);
  *pversion = 0x0004000B;
  info = sizeof(ULONG);
  break;
  }
```

The only substantive difference between this example and the previous one is the bold line. (I also altered the reported version number so that I could easily know I was invoking the correct IOCTL from the test program.) With either DIRECT-method request, we use the MDL pointed to by the **MdlAddress** field of the IRP to access the user-mode output buffer. You can do direct memory access (DMA) using this address. In this example, I just called **MmGetSystemAddressForMdl** to get a kernel-mode alias address pointing to the physical memory described by the MDL.

METHOD_NEITHER

With METHOD_NEITHER, the I/O Manager doesn't try to translate the user-mode virtual addresses in any way. You get (in the **Type3InputBuffer** parameter in the stack location) the user-mode virtual address of the input buffer, and you get (in the **UserBuffer** field of the IRP) the user mode virtual address of the output buffer. Neither address is of any use unless you know you're running in the same process context as the user-mode caller. If you *do* know you're in the right process context, you can just directly dereference the pointers:

```
case IOCTL_GET_VERSION_NEITHER:
  {
  if (cbout < sizeof(ULONG))
    {
    status = STATUS_INVALID_BUFFER_SIZE;
    break;
    }
  PULONG pversion = (PULONG) Irp->UserBuffer;
  if (Irp->RequestorMode != KernelMode)
    {
    __try
      {
      ProbeForWrite(pversion, sizeof(ULONG), 1);
      *pversion = 0x0004000A;
      }
    __except(EXCEPTION_EXECUTE_HANDLER)
      {
      status = GetExceptionCode();
      break;
      }
    }
  else
    *pversion = 0x0004000A;
  info = sizeof(ULONG);
  break;
  }
```

As shown in the previous code in boldface, the only real glitch here is that you want to make sure that it's OK to write into any buffer you get from an untrusted source. Refer to Chapter 3 ("Basic Programming Techniques") if you're rusty about structured exceptions. **ProbeForWrite** is a standard kernel-mode service routine for testing whether a given user-mode virtual address can be written. The second argument indicates the length of the data area you want to probe, and the third argument indicates the alignment you require for the data area. In this example, we want to be sure that we can access four bytes for writing, but we're willing to tolerate single-byte alignment for the data area itself. What ProbeForWrite (and its companion function **ProbeForRead**) actually tests is whether the given address range has the correct alignment and occupies the user-mode portion of the address space—it doesn't actually try to write to (or read from) the memory in question.

Conventional wisdom holds that you should never access user-mode memory directly in the way I just showed you for fear that some other thread in the same process might call **VirtualFree** to release memory in between the time of the **ProbeFor**_Xxx_ call and the time you make the access. According to this conventional wisdom, you should therefore always create an MDL and call MmGetSystemAddressForMdl to obtain a safe virtual address. In fact, however, it's perfectly safe to directly access the user-mode pointer if three things are true: First, you must be running in the process context to which the buffer belongs. Second, you must have done a ProbeFor_Xxx_. Finally, you must perform the access within a structured exception frame. If any portion of the buffer happens to belong to non-existent pages at the time of the access, the memory manager will raise an exception instead of immediately bug-checking. Your exception handler will backstop the exception and prevent the system from crashing.

Internal I/O Control Operations

The system uses IRP_MJ_DEVICE_CONTROL to implement a DeviceIoControl call from user mode. Drivers sometimes need to talk to each other too, and they use the related IRP_MJ_INTERNAL_DEVICE_CONTROL to do so. A typical code sequence is as follows:

```
ASSERT(KeGetCurrentIrql() == PASSIVE_LEVEL);
KEVENT event;
KeInitializeEvent(&event, NotificationEvent, FALSE);
IO_STATUS_BLOCK iostatus;
PIRP Irp = IoBuildDeviceIoControlRequest(IoControlCode,
  DeviceObject, pInBuffer, cbInBuffer, pOutBuffer, cbOutBuffer,
  TRUE, &event, &iostatus);
if (IoCallDriver(DeviceObject, Irp) == STATUS_PENDING)
  KeWaitForSingleObject(&event, Executive, KernelMode, FALSE, NULL);
```

Being at PASSIVE_LEVEL is a requirement for calling **KeInitializeEvent** and **IoBuildDeviceIoControlRequest** as well as for blocking on the event object as shown here.

The **IoControlCode** argument to IoBuildDeviceIoControlRequest is a control code expressing the operation you want the target device driver to perform. This code is the same kind of code as you use with regular control operations. **DeviceObject** is a pointer to the DEVICE_OBJECT whose driver will perform the indicated operation. The input and output buffer parameters serve the same purpose as their counterparts in a user-mode DeviceIoControl call. The seventh argument, which I specified as TRUE in this fragment, indicates that you're building an internal control operation. (You could say FALSE here to create an IRP_MJ_DEVICE_CONTROL instead.) I'll describe the purpose of the **event** and **iostatus** arguments in a bit.

IoBuildDeviceIoControlRequest builds an IRP and initializes the first stack location to describe the operation code and buffers you specify. It returns the IRP pointer to you so that you can do any additional initialization that might be required. In Chapter 11, for example, I'll show you how to use an internal control request to submit a URB to the USB bus driver. Part of that process involves setting a stack parameter field to point to the URB. You then call **IoCallDriver** to send the IRP to the target device. Whatever the return value, you wait on the **event** object you specified as the eighth argument to IoBuildDeviceIoControlRequest. The I/O Manager will set the event when the IRP finishes, and it will also fill in your **iostatus** structure with the ending status and information values. Finally, it will call **IoFreeIrp** to release the IRP. Consequently, you don't want to access the IRP pointer at all after you call IoCallDriver.

Since internal control operations require cooperation between two drivers, fewer rules about sending them exist than you'd guess from what I've just described. You don't have to use IoBuildDeviceIoControlRequest to create one of them, for example: you could just call **IoAllocateIrp** and perform your own initialization. Provided that the target driver isn't expecting to handle internal control operations solely at PASSIVE_LEVEL, you could also send one of these IRPs at DISPATCH_LEVEL, say from inside an I/O completion or deferred procedure call (DPC) routine. (Of course, you couldn't use IoBuildDeviceIoControlRequest in such a case, and you couldn't wait for the IRP to finish. But you could *send* it because IoAllocateIrp and IoCallDriver can run at DISPATCH_LEVEL or below.) You don't even have to use the I/O stack parameter fields exactly like you would for a regular IOCTL. In fact, calls to the USB bus driver use the field that would ordinarily be the output buffer length to hold the URB pointer. So, if you're designing an internal control protocol for two of your own drivers, just think of IRP_MJ_INTERNAL_DEVICE_CONTROL as being an envelope for whatever kind of message you want to send.

It's not a good idea to use the same dispatch routine for internal and external control operations, by the way, at least not without checking the major function code of the IRP. Here's an example of why not. Suppose that your driver has an external control interface that allows an application to query the version number of your driver *and* an internal control interface that allows a trusted kernel-mode caller to determine some vital secret that you don't want to share with user-mode programs. Then suppose that you use one routine to handle both interfaces, as in this example:

```
NTSTATUS DriverEntry(...)
  {
  DriverObject->MajorFunction[IRP_MJ_DEVICE_CONTROL] =
    DispatchControl;
  DriverObject->MajorFunction[IRP_MJ_INTERNAL_DEVICE_CONTROL] =
    DispatchControl;
  ...
  }

NTSTATUS DispatchControl(...)
  {
  ...
  switch (code)
    {
```

(continued)

```
case IOCTL_GET_VERSION:
  ...
case IOCTL_INTERNAL_GET_SECRET:
  ...           // ← exposed for user-mode calls
  }
}
```

If an application is able to somehow determine the numeric value of IOCTL_ INTERNAL_GET_SECRET, it can issue a regular DeviceIoControl call and bypass the intended security on that function.

Notifying Applications of Interesting Events

One extremely important use of IOCTL operations is to give a WDM driver a way to notify an application that an interesting event has occurred. To motivate this discussion, suppose you had an application that needed to work closely with your driver in such a way that whenever a certain kind of hardware event occurred your driver would alert the application so that it could take some sort of user-visible action. For example, a button press on a medical instrument might trigger an application to begin collecting and displaying data. Whereas Windows provides a couple of ways for a driver to signal an application in this kind of situation—namely, asynchronous procedure calls or posted window messages—those methods don't work in Windows 2000 because the operating system lacks the necessary infrastructure to make them work. A method that does work, though, is having the application issue an IOCTL operation that the driver completes when the interesting event, whatever it might be, occurs. Implementing this scheme requires excruciating care on the driver side, so I'll explain the mechanics in detail.

The central idea in this section is that when the application wants to receive event notifications from the driver, it calls DeviceIoControl:

```
HANDLE hDevice = CreateFile("\\\\.\\<driver-name>", ...);
BOOL okay = DeviceIoControl(hDevice, IOCTL_WAIT_NOTIFY,
  ...);
```

(IOCTL_WAIT_NOTIFY, by the way, is the control code I used in the NOTIFY sample on the companion disc.)

The driver will pend this IOCTL and complete it later. If other considerations didn't intrude, the code in the driver might be as simple as this:

```
NTSTATUS DispatchControl(...)
  {
  ...
  switch (code)
    {
  case IOCTL_WAIT_NOTIFY:
    pdx->NotifyIrp = Irp;
```

```
    IoMarkIrpPending(Irp);
    return STATUS_PENDING;
    ...
    }
}

VOID OnInterestingEvent(...)
    {
    ...
    CompleteRequest(pdx->NotifyIrp, STATUS_SUCCESS, 0);
    }
```

APPLICATION NOTIFICATION BY USING EVENTS

Sometimes all you need to do in a driver is notify an application that an event has occurred, without passing any explanatory data to the application. A standard technique for doing so involves an ordinary Win32 event that the driver signals. To use this method, the application first calls **CreateEvent** or **OpenEvent** to open a handle to an event object, which it then passes to the driver via DeviceIoControl. The driver can convert the user-mode handle to an object pointer by making this call:

```
PKEVENT pEvent;
status = ObReferenceObjectByHandle(hEvent, EVENT_MODIFY_STATE,
  *ExEventObjectType, Irp->RequestorMode, (PVOID*) &pEvent, NULL);
```

Note that the IOCTL must be handled at PASSIVE_LEVEL and in the context of the process that owns the **hEvent** handle.

At this point, the driver has a pointer to a KEVENT object, which it can use as an argument to **KeSetEvent** at an auspicious moment. The driver also owns a reference to the event object, and it must call **ObDereferenceObject** at some point. The right time to dereference the object depends on the exact way the application and the driver fit together. A good guideline might be to dereference the event as part of handling the IRP_MJ_CLOSE for the handle used in the IRP_MJ_DEVICE_CONTROL that supplied the event handle in the first place. The EVWAIT driver sample on the companion disc illustrates this particular method.

The kernel service routines **IoCreateNotificationEvent** and **IoCreate-SynchronizationEvent** create event objects that can also be shared by user-mode programs. They are unavailable in Windows 98 and, therefore, unavailable to true WDM drivers.

The "other considerations" I just so conveniently tucked under the rug are, of course, all important in crafting a working driver. The originator of the IRP might decide to cancel it. The application might call **CancelIo**, or termination of the application thread might cause a kernel-mode component to call **IoCancelIrp**. In either case, we must provide a cancel routine so that the IRP gets completed. If power is removed from our device, or if our device is suddenly removed from the computer, we need to abort any outstanding IOCTL requests. In general, any number of IOCTLs might need to be aborted. Consequently, we'll need a linked list of them. Since multiple threads might be trying to access this linked list, we'll also need a spin lock so that we can access the list safely.

Working with an Asynchronous IOCTL

To simplify my own life, I wrote a set of helper routines for managing asynchronous IOCTLs. The two most important of these routines are named **CacheControlRequest** and **UncacheControlRequest**. They assume that you're willing to accept only one asynchronous IOCTL having a particular control code per device object and that you can, therefore, reserve a pointer cell in the device extension to point to the IRP that's currently outstanding. In NOTIFY, I call this pointer cell **NotifyIrp**. You accept the asynchronous IRP this way:

```
IoAcquireRemoveLock(...);
switch (code)
  {
case IOCTL_WAIT_NOTIFY:
  if (<parameters invalid in some way>)
    status = STATUS_INVALID_PARAMETER;
  else
    status = CacheControlRequest(pdx, Irp, &pdx->NotifyIrp);
  break;
  }

IoReleaseRemoveLock(...);
return status == STATUS_PENDING ? status :
  CompleteRequest(Irp, status, info);
```

The important statement here is the call to CacheControlRequest, which registers this IRP in such a way that we'll be able to cancel it later, if necessary. It also records the address of this IRP in the NotifyIrp member of our device extension. We expect it to return STATUS_PENDING, in which case we avoid completing the IRP and simply return STATUS_PENDING to our caller.

NOTE You could easily generalize the scheme I'm describing to permit an application to have an IRP of each type outstanding for each open handle. Instead of putting the current IRP pointers in your device extension, put them instead into a structure that you associate with the FILE_OBJECT that corresponds to the handle. You'll get a pointer to this FILE_OBJECT in the I/O stack location for IRP_MJ_CREATE, IRP_MJ_CLOSE, and, in fact, all other IRPs generated for the file handle. You can use either the **FsContext** or **FsContext2** field of the file object for any purpose you choose.

Later, when whatever event the application is waiting for occurs, we execute code like this:

```
PIRP nfyirp = UncacheControlRequest(pdx, &pdx->NotifyIrp);
if (nfyirp)
  {
  <do something>
  CompleteRequest(nfyirp, STATUS_SUCCESS, <info value>);
  }
```

This logic retrieves the address of the pending IOCTL_WAIT_NOTIFY request, does something to provide data back to the application, and then completes the pending I/O request packet.

How the Helper Routines Work

I hid a wealth of complications inside the CacheControlRequest and UncacheControlRequest functions. These two functions provide a thread-safe and multiprocessor-safe mechanism for keeping track of asynchronous IOCTL requests. They use a variation on the techniques we've discussed elsewhere in the book for safely queuing and dequeuing IRPs at times when someone else might be flitting about trying to cancel the IRP. There's a little bit of extra code to show you, though (refer to CONTROL.CPP in the NOTIFY sample on the companion disc):

```
typedef struct _DEVICE_EXTENSION {
  KSPIN_LOCK IoctlListLock;
  LIST_ENTRY PendingIoctlList;
  } DEVICE_EXTENSION, *PDEVICE_EXTENSION;

NTSTATUS CacheControlRequest(PDEVICE_EXTENSION pdx, PIRP Irp,
  PIRP* pIrp)
```

(continued)

```
       {
       KIRQL oldirql;
1 ▷    KeAcquireSpinLock(&pdx->IoctlListLock, &oldirql);
       NTSTATUS status;
2 ▷    if (*pIrp)
         status = STATUS_UNSUCCESSFUL;
3 ▷    else if (pdx->IoctlAbortStatus)
         status = pdx->IoctlAbortStatus;
       else
         {
4 ▷      IoSetCancelRoutine(Irp, OnCancelPendingIoctl);
         if (Irp->Cancel && IoSetCancelRoutine(Irp, NULL))
           status = STATUS_CANCELLED;
         else
            {
5 ▷        IoMarkIrpPending(Irp);
           status = STATUS_PENDING;
6 ▷        PIO_STACK_LOCATION stack = IoGetCurrentIrpStackLocation(Irp);
           stack->Parameters.Others.Argument1 = (PVOID) *pIrp;
           IoSetCompletionRoutine(Irp, (PIO_COMPLETION_ROUTINE)
             OnCompletePendingIoctl, (PVOID) pdx, TRUE, TRUE, TRUE);
           PFILE_OBJECT fop = stack->FileObject;
7 ▷        IoSetNextIrpStackLocation(Irp);
           stack = IoGetCurrentIrpStackLocation(Irp);
           stack->DeviceObject = pdx->DeviceObject;
           stack->FileObject = fop;

           *pIrp = Irp;
           InsertTailList(&pdx->PendingIoctlList,
             &Irp->Tail.Overlay.ListEntry);
           }
         }
       KeReleaseSpinLock(&pdx->IoctlListLock, oldirql);
       return status;
       }

   VOID OnCancelPendingIoctl(PDEVICE_OBJECT fdo, PIRP Irp)
     {
     KIRQL oldirql = Irp->CancelIrql;
     IoReleaseCancelSpinLock(DISPATCH_LEVEL);
     PDEVICE_EXTENSION pdx = (PDEVICE_EXTENSION) fdo->DeviceExtension;
     KeAcquireSpinLockAtDpcLevel(&pdx->IoctlListLock);
     RemoveEntryList(&Irp->Tail.Overlay.ListEntry);
     KeReleaseSpinLock(&pdx->IoctlListLock, oldirql);
     Irp->IoStatus.Status = STATUS_CANCELLED;
     IoCompleteRequest(Irp, IO_NO_INCREMENT);
     }
```

```
NTSTATUS OnCompletePendingIoctl(PDEVICE_OBJECT junk, PIRP Irp,
  PDEVICE_EXTENSION pdx)
  {
  KIRQL oldirql;
  KeAcquireSpinLock(&pdx->IoctlListLock, &oldirql);
  PIO_STACK_LOCATION stack = IoGetCurrentIrpStackLocation(Irp);
  PIRP* pIrp = (PIRP*) stack->Parameters.Others.Argument1;
  if (*pIrp == Irp)
    *pIrp = NULL;
  KeReleaseSpinLock(&pdx->IoctlListLock, oldirql);
  return STATUS_SUCCESS;
  }

PIRP UncacheControlRequest(PDEVICE_EXTENSION pdx, PIRP* pIrp)
  {
  KIRQL oldirql;
  KeAcquireSpinLock(&pdx->IoctlListLock, &oldirql);
  PIRP Irp = (PIRP) InterlockedExchangePointer(pIrp, NULL);
  if (Irp)
    {
    if (IoSetCancelRoutine(Irp, NULL))
      {
      RemoveEntryList(&Irp->Tail.Overlay.ListEntry);
      }
    else
      Irp = NULL;
    }
  KeReleaseSpinLock(&pdx->IoctlListLock, oldirql);
  return Irp;
  }
```

(margin markers: 8, 9, 10)

1. We use a spin lock to guard the list of pending IOCTLs and also to guard all of the pointer cells that are reserved to point to the current instance of each different type of asynchronous IOCTL request.

2. This is where we enforce the rule—it's more of a design decision, really—that only one IRP of each type can be outstanding at one time.

3. This **if** statement accommodates the fact that we may need to start failing incoming IRPs at some point because of PnP or power events.

4. Since we'll pend this IRP for what might be a long time, we need to have a cancel routine for it. I've discussed cancel logic so many times in this book that I feel sure you'd rather not read about it once more.

5. Here, we've decided to go ahead and cache this IRP so that we can complete it later. Since we're going to end up returning STATUS_PENDING from our **DispatchControl** function, we need to call **IoMarkIrpPending**.

6. We need to have a way to NULL out the cache pointer cell when we cancel the IRP. It's very difficult to get context parameters into a cancel routine, so I decided to set up an I/O completion routine instead. I use the **Parameters.Others.Argument1** slot in the stack to record the cache pointer address.

7. In order for the completion routine we've just installed to get called, we must advance the I/O stack pointer by calling **IoSetNextIrpStack-Location**. In this particular driver, we know there must be at least one more stack location for us to use because our AddDevice function would have failed if there hadn't been a driver object underneath ours. The device and file object pointers that later routines need come from the then-current stack location, so we must initialize them as well.

8. This statement is the point of installing a completion routine. If the IRP gets cancelled, we'll eventually gain control to nullify the cache pointer.

9. In the normal course of events, this statement uncaches an IRP.

10. Now that we've uncached our IRP, we don't want it to be cancelled any more. If **IoSetCancelRoutine** returns NULL, however, we know that this IRP is currently in the process of being cancelled. We return a NULL IRP pointer in that case.

NOTIFY also has an IRP_MJ_CLEANUP handler for pending IOCTLs that looks just about the same as the cleanup handlers I've discussed for read and write operations. Finally, it includes an **AbortPendingIoctls** helper function for use at power-down or surprise removal time, as follows:

```
VOID AbortPendingIoctls(PDEVICE_EXTENSION pdx, NTSTATUS status)
  {
  InterlockedExchange(&pdx->IoctlAbortStatus, status);
  CleanupControlRequests(pdx, status, NULL);
  }
```

CleanupControlRequests is the handler for IRP_MJ_CLEANUP. I wrote it in such a way that it cancels *all* outstanding IRPs if the third argument—normally a file object pointer—is NULL.

NOTIFY is a bit too simple to serve as a complete model for a real-world driver. Here are some additional considerations for you to mull over in your own design process:

■ A driver might have several types of events that trigger notifications. You could decide to deal with these by using a single IOCTL code, in which case you'd indicate the type of event by some sort of output data, or by using multiple IOCTL codes.

■ You might want to allow multiple threads to register for events. If that's the case, you certainly can't have a single IRP pointer in the device extension—you need a way of keeping track of all the IRPs that relate to a particular type of event. If you use only a single type of IOCTL for all notifications, one way to keep track is to rely on the PendingIoctlList I've already discussed. Then, when an event occurs, you execute a loop in which you call **ExInterlockedRemoveHeadList** and **IoCompleteRequest** to empty the pending list. (I avoided this complexity in NOTIFY by fiat—I decided I'd run only one instance of the test program at a time.)

■ Your IOCTL dispatch routine might be in a race with the activity that generates events. For example, in the USBINT sample I'll discuss in Chapter 11, we have a potential race between the IOCTL dispatch routine and the pseudointerrupt routine that services an interrupt endpoint on a USB device. To avoid losing events or taking inconsistent actions, you need a spin lock. Refer to the USBINT sample on the companion disc for an illustration of how to use the spin lock appropriately. (Synchronization wasn't an issue in NOTIFY because by the time a human being is able to perform the keystroke that unleashes the event signal, the notification request is almost certainly pending. If not, the signal request gets an error.)

MORE ABOUT THE NOTIFY SAMPLE

NOTIFY consists of a WDM device driver (in the SYS subdirectory) and a Win32 console-mode test program (in the TEST subdirectory). You can install the driver via the Add New Hardware wizard or the FASTINST utility. Then you can launch the test program. It will spawn a separate thread to issue the IOCTL_WAIT_NOTIFICATION I/O control request. Then it prompts you to execute a keystroke or to press Ctrl+Break to end the test. If you type a key, the test program performs an IOCTL_GENERATE_EVENT, passing the scan code of your keystroke as input data. The driver then completes the pending notification IRP after storing this scan code as output data. Alternatively, if you hit Ctrl+Break at the point at which TEST is prompting you for a keystroke, this will eventually cause the I/O Manager to cancel the outstanding notification IRP.

SYSTEM THREADS

In all the device drivers considered so far in the book, we haven't been overly concerned about the thread context in which our driver subroutines have executed. Much of the time, our subroutines run in an arbitrary thread context, which means we can't block and can't directly access user-mode virtual memory. Some devices are very difficult to program when faced with the first of these constraints.

Some devices are best handled by *polling*. A device that can't asynchronously interrupt the CPU, for example, needs to be interrogated from time to time to check its state. In other cases, the natural way to program the device might be to perform an operation in steps with waits in between. A floppy disk driver, for example, goes through a series of steps to perform an operation. In general, the driver has to command the drive to spin up to speed, wait for the spin-up to occur, commence the transfer, wait a short while, and then spin the drive back down. You could design a driver that operates as a finite state machine to allow a callback function to properly sequence operations. It would be much easier, though, if you could just insert event and timer waits at the appropriate spots of a straight-line program.

Dealing with situations that require you to periodically interrogate a device is easy with the help of a *system thread* belonging to the driver. A system thread is a thread that operates within the overall umbrella of a process belonging to the operating system as a whole. I'll be talking exclusively about system threads that execute solely in kernel mode. In the next section, I'll describe the mechanism by which you create and destroy your own system threads. Then I'll give an example of how to use a system thread to manage a polled input device.

Creating and Terminating System Threads

To launch a system thread, you call **PsCreateSystemThread**. One of the arguments to this service function is the address of a *thread procedure* that acts as the main program for the new thread. When the thread procedure is going to terminate the thread, it calls **PsTerminateSystemThread**, which does not return. Generally speaking, you need to provide a way for a PnP event to tell the thread to terminate and to wait for the termination to occur. Combining all these factors, you'll end up with code that performs the functions of these three subroutines:

```
typedef struct _DEVICE_EXTENSION {
  ...
  KEVENT evKill;
  PKTHREAD thread;
  };

NTSTATUS StartThread(PDEVICE_EXTENSION pdx)
  {
  NTSTATUS status;
```

```
        HANDLE hthread;
①      KeInitializeEvent(&pdx->evKill, NotificationEvent, FALSE);
②      status = PsCreateSystemThread(&hthread, THREAD_ALL_ACCESS,
          NULL, NULL, NULL, (PKSTART_ROUTINE) ThreadProc, pdx);
        if (!NT_SUCCESS(status))
          return status;
③      ObReferenceObjectByHandle(hthread, THREAD_ALL_ACCESS, NULL,
          KernelMode, (PVOID*) &pdx->thread, NULL);
④      ZwClose(hthread);
        return STATUS_SUCCESS;
        }

    VOID StopThread(PDEVICE_EXTENSION pdx)
        {
⑤      KeSetEvent(&pdx->evKill, 0, FALSE);
⑥      KeWaitForSingleObject(pdx->thread, Executive, KernelMode, FALSE, NULL);
⑦      ObDereferenceObject(pdx->thread);
        }

    VOID ThreadProc(PDEVICE_EXTENSION pdx)
        {
        ...
⑧      KeWaitForXxx(<at least pdx->evKill>);
        ...
⑨      PsTerminateSystemThread(STATUS_SUCCESS);
        }
```

1. Declare a KEVENT named **evKill** in the device extension to provide a way for a PnP event to signal the thread to terminate. This is the appropriate time to initialize the event.

2. This statement launches the new thread. The return value for a successful call is a thread handle that appears at the location pointed to by the first argument. The second argument specifies the access rights you require to the thread; THREAD_ALL_ACCESS is the appropriate value to supply here. The next three arguments pertain to threads that are part of user-mode processes and should be NULL when a WDM driver calls this function. The next-to-last argument (**ThreadProc**) designates the main program for the thread. The last argument (**pdx**) is a context argument that will be the one and only argument to the thread procedure.

3. To wait for the thread to terminate, you need the address of the underlying KTHREAD object instead of the handle you get back from PsCreate-SystemThread. This call to **ObReferenceObjectByHandle** gives you that address.

4. We don't actually need the handle once we have the address of the KTHREAD, so we call **ZwClose** to close that handle.

5. A routine such as **StopDevice**—which performs the device-specific part of IRP_MN_STOP_DEVICE in my scheme of driver modularization—can call **StopThread** to halt the system thread. The first step is to set the **evKill** event.

6. This call illustrates how to wait for the thread to finish. A kernel thread object is one of the dispatcher objects on which you can wait. It assumes the signalled state when the thread finally finishes. In Windows 2000, you always perform this wait to avoid the embarrassment of having your driver's image unmapped while one of your system threads executes the last few instructions of its shutdown processing. That is, don't just wait for a special "kill acknowledgment" event that the thread sets just before it exits—the thread has to execute PsTerminateSystemThread before your driver can safely unload. *Refer also to an important Windows 98 compatibility note ("Waiting for System Threads to Finish") at the end of this chapter.*

7. This call to **ObDereferenceObject** balances the call to ObReference-ObjectByHandle that we made when we created the thread in the first place. It's necessary to allow the Object Manager to release the memory used by the KTHREAD object that formerly described our thread.

8. The thread procedure will contain miscellaneous logic that depends on the exact goal you're trying to accomplish. If you block while waiting for some external event, you should call **KeWaitForMultipleObjects** and specify the **evKill** event as one of the objects.

9. When you detect that evKill has been signalled, you call the **PsTerminate-SystemThread** function, which terminates the thread. Consequently, it doesn't return. Note that you can't terminate a system thread except by calling this function in the context of the thread itself.

Using a System Thread for Device Polling

If you had to write a driver for a device that can't interrupt the CPU to demand service, a system thread devoted to polling the device may be the way to go. I'll show you one way to use a system thread for this purpose. This example is based on a hypothetical device with two input ports. One port acts as a control port; it delivers a 0 byte when no input data is ready and a 1 byte when input data is ready. The other port delivers a single byte of data and resets the control port.

In the sample I'll show you, we spawn the system thread when we process the IRP_MN_START_DEVICE request. We terminate the thread when we receive a Plug and Play request such as IRP_MN_STOP_DEVICE or IRP_MN_REMOVE_DEVICE that requires us to release our I/O resources. The thread spends most of its time blocked. When the **StartIo** routine begins to process an IRP_MJ_READ request, it sets an event that the polling thread has been waiting for. The polling thread then enters a loop to service the request. In the loop, the polling thread first blocks for a fixed polling interval. After the interval expires, the thread reads the control port. If the control port is 1, the thread reads a data byte. The thread then repeats the loop until the request is satisfied, whereupon it goes back to sleep until StartIo receives another request.

The thread routine in the POLLING sample is as follows:

```
VOID PollingThreadRoutine(PDEVICE_EXTENSION pdx)
  {
  NTSTATUS status;
  KTIMER timer;
  KeInitializeTimerEx(&timer, SynchronizationTimer);

  PVOID mainevents[] = {
    (PVOID) &pdx->evKill,
    (PVOID) &pdx->evRequest,
    };

  PVOID pollevents[] = {
    (PVOID) &pdx->evKill,
    (PVOID) &timer,
    };

  ASSERT(arraysize(mainevents) <= THREAD_WAIT_OBJECTS);
  ASSERT(arraysize(pollevents) <= THREAD_WAIT_OBJECTS);

  BOOLEAN kill = FALSE;

  while (!kill)
    {    // until told to quit
    status = KeWaitForMultipleObjects(arraysize(mainevents),
      mainevents, WaitAny, Executive, KernelMode, FALSE,
      NULL, NULL);
    if (!NT_SUCCESS(status) || status == STATUS_WAIT_0)
      break;
    ULONG numxfer = 0;
    LARGE_INTEGER duetime = {0};
    #define POLLING_INTERVAL 500
```

(continued)

```
5   KeSetTimerEx(&timer, duetime, POLLING_INTERVAL, NULL);

    PIRP Irp = GetCurrentIrp(&pdx->dqReadWrite);

6   while (TRUE)
      {   // read next byte
7     if (Irp->Cancel)
        {
        status = STATUS_CANCELLED;
        break;
        }
      status = AreRequestsBeingAborted(&pdx->dqReadWrite);
      if (!status)
        break;
8     status = KeWaitForMultipleObjects(arraysize(pollevents),
        pollevents, WaitAny, Executive, KernelMode, FALSE,
        NULL, NULL);
      if (!NT_SUCCESS(status))
        {
        kill = TRUE;
        break;
        {
      if (status == STATUS_WAIT_0)
        {
        status = STATUS_DELETE_PENDING;
        kill = TRUE;
        break;
        }
9     if (pdx->nbytes)
        {
        if (READ_PORT_UCHAR(pdx->portbase) == 1)
          {
          *pdx->buffer++ = READ_PORT_UCHAR(pdx->portbase + 1);
          --pdx->nbytes;
          ++numxfer;
          }
        }
      if (!pdx->nbytes)
        break;
      }   // read next byte
    KeCancelTimer(&timer);
    StartNextPacket(&pdx->dqReadWrite, pdx->DeviceObject);
    if (Irp)
      {
      IoReleaseRemoveLock(&pdx->RemoveLock, Irp);
```

```
       CompleteRequest(Irp, STATUS_SUCCESS, numxfer);
      }
   }    // until told to quit

 PsTerminateSystemThread(STATUS_SUCCESS);
 }
```

1. We'll be using this kernel timer later to control the frequency with which we poll the device.

2. We'll call **KeWaitForMultipleObjects** twice in this function to block the polling thread until something of note happens. These two arrays provide the addresses of the dispatcher objects on which we'll wait. The **ASSERT** statements verify that we're waiting for few enough events such that we can use the array of wait blocks that's built in to the thread object.

3. This loop terminates when an error occurs or when **evKill** becomes signalled. We'll then terminate the entire polling thread.

4. This wait terminates when either **evKill** or **evRequest** becomes signalled. Our StartIo routine will signal evRequest to indicate that an IRP exists for us to service.

5. The call to **KeSetTimerEx** starts our timer counting. This is a repetitive timer that expires once based on the due time and periodically thereafter. We're specifying a 0 due time, which will cause us to poll the device immediately. The POLLING_INTERVAL is measured in milliseconds.

6. This inner loop terminates when either the kill event becomes signalled or we're done with the current IRP.

7. While we're going about our business in this loop, the current IRP might get cancelled, or we might receive a PnP or power IRP that requires us to abort this IRP.

8. In this call to **KeWaitForMultipleObjects**, we take advantage of the fact that a kernel timer acts like an event object. The call finishes when either **evKill** is signalled (meaning we should terminate the polling thread altogether) or the timer expires (meaning we should execute another poll).

9. This is the actual polling step in this driver. We read the control port, whose address is the base port address given to us by the PnP Manager. If the value indicates that data is available, we read the data port.

The StartIo routine that works with this polling routine first sets the **buffer** and **nbytes** fields in the device extension; you saw the polling routine use them to sequence through an input request. Then it sets the **evRequest** event to wake up the polling thread.

You can organize a polling driver in other ways besides the one I just showed you. For example, you could spawn a new polling thread each time an arriving request finds the device idle. The thread services requests until the device becomes idle, whereupon it terminates. This strategy would be better than the one I illustrated if long periods elapse between spurts of activity on the device, because the polling thread wouldn't be occupying virtual memory during the long intervals of quiescence. If, however, your device is more or less continuously busy, the first strategy might be better because it avoids repeating the overhead of starting and stopping the polling thread.

EXERCISING THE POLLING SAMPLE

You can test the POLLING sample driver on Windows 98 only. Follow the directions on the companion disc for launching the DEVTEST simulator for the fake hardware that POLLING manages. Then launch the user-mode TEST program to perform a read operation.

EXECUTIVE WORK ITEMS

From time to time, you might wish that you could temporarily *lower* the processor's interrupt request level (IRQL) to carry out some task or another that must be done at PASSIVE_LEVEL. Lowering IRQL is, of course, a definite no-no. So long as you're running at or below DISPATCH_LEVEL, however, you can queue an *executive work item* to request a callback into your driver later. The callback occurs at PASSIVE_LEVEL in the context of a worker thread owned by the operating system. Using a work item can save you the trouble of creating your own thread that you only occasionally wake up.

I'll describe a simple way of using an executive work item. First declare a structure that starts with an unnamed instance of the WORK_QUEUE_ITEM structure. Here's an example drawn from the WORKITEM sample on the companion disc:

```
struct _RANDOM_JUNK {
  struct _WORK_QUEUE_ITEM;
  <other stuff>
  } RANDOM_JUNK, *PRANDOM_JUNK;
```

DECLARING THE WORK-ITEM STRUCTURE

The ability to have an unnamed union or structure that's a member of a bigger structure is a Microsoft extension to the C/C++ language. In the example shown in the text, you can directly reference members of the standard WORK_QUEUE_ITEM without needing to supply an intermediate level of name qualification.

If you're able to use C++ syntax—as I'm doing in the sample programs—there's a better way to declare a structure like the one I showed you in the text:

```
struct _RANDOM_JUNK : public _WORK_QUEUE_ITEM {
  <other stuff>
  };
typedef _RANDOM_JUNK RANDOM_JUNK, *PRANDOM_JUNK;
```

This syntax says that _RANDOM_JUNK is derived from _WORK_QUEUE_ITEM, meaning that it inherits all of the same members as the base structure. You're probably familiar with the concept of deriving C++ classes from other classes, but you can derive structures as well. Using this method of declaration, you can still directly reference WORK_QUEUE_ITEM fields without extra name qualification, but you won't be relying on a Microsoft language extension to do so.

When you're ready, allocate an instance of this structure from the heap and initialize it:

```
PRANDOM_JUNK item = (PRANDOM_JUNK) ExAllocatePool(PagedPool,
  sizeof(RANDOM_JUNK);
ExInitializeWorkItem(item, (PWORKER_THREAD_ROUTINE) Callback,
  (PVOID) item);
<additional initialization>
```

In the call to **ExInitializeWorkItem**, the first argument (**item**) is the address of the WORK_QUEUE_ITEM embedded in your structure. ExInitializeWorkItem is actually a macro that simply references WORK_QUEUE_ITEM fields using this pointer; I didn't need to supply a cast here because I declared the WORK_QUEUE_ITEM as an unnamed structure member. The second argument (**Callback**) is the address of a callback routine elsewhere in your driver. The third and final argument is a context parameter that will eventually be used as the single argument to the callback routine. I used the **item** pointer here for reasons that will become apparent when I show you the callback routine. ExInitializeWorkItem merely initializes that part of your structure (that is, WORK_QUEUE_ITEM) that the system knows about. After calling ExInitializeWorkItem, you need to do any initialization of your own data members that might be required.

At this point, you're ready to ask the system to put your work item into a queue, which can be done using the **ExQueueWorkItem** function:

```
ExQueueWorkItem(item, QueueIdentifier);
```

QueueIdentifier can be either of these two values:

- **DelayedWorkQueue** indicates that you want your work item executed in the context of a system worker thread that executes at variable priority—that is, not at a real-time priority level.

- **CriticalWorkQueue** indicates that you want your work item executed in the context of a system worker thread that executes at a real-time priority.

You choose the delayed or the critical work queue depending on the urgency of the task you're trying to perform. Putting your item into the critical work queue will give it priority over all noncritical work in the system at the possible cost of reducing the CPU time available for other critical work. In any case, the activities you perform in your callback can always be preempted by activities that run at an elevated IRQL.

After you queue the work item, the operating system will call you back in the context of a system worker thread having the characteristics you specified as the second argument to ExQueueWorkItem. You'll be at IRQL PASSIVE_LEVEL. What you do inside the callback routine is pretty much up to you except for one requirement: you must release or otherwise reclaim the memory occupied by the work queue item. Here's a skeleton for a work-item callback routine:

```
VOID Callback(PRANDOM_JUNK item)
  {
  PAGED_CODE();
  ...
  ExFreePool(item);
  }
```

This callback receives a single argument (**item**), which is the context parameter you supplied earlier in the call to ExInitializeWorkItem. This fragment also shows the call to **ExFreePool** that balances the allocation we did earlier. Since you must release the work item memory if you allocated it from the heap in the first place, it's often convenient to pass the work queue item address itself as the context parameter. That's what I did here, in fact, because the work queue item occupies the first several bytes of the RANDOM_JUNK structure.

I have one more important point to make about work items. You can't remove a work item from the system queue. If, however, you were to honor a PnP request to remove your device, it's possible (though pretty unlikely) for your driver to be removed from memory while a work item is still pending. The remove lock mechanism I described in Chapter 6, "Plug and Play," gives you a perfect way to prevent this from happening, as follows:

- Before you queue a work item, use **IoAcquireRemoveLock** to establish a claim that will prevent your driver from being unloaded.

- At the end of the work-item callback routine, call **IoReleaseRemoveLock** to release that claim. To do this, you'll need to have access to your device extension inside the callback routine. Chances are you'll need the device extension pointer for other reasons, anyway. So, you'll probably want to put a device extension or device object pointer inside the RANDOM_JUNK structure (to which you'll probably also give a better name!).

In addition, your callback routine needs to take whatever steps are necessary to avoid accessing hardware that's been surprise-removed or depowered, and so on.

IoAllocateWorkItem, IoQueueWorkItem, and IoFreeItem

Windows 2000 provides a new set of functions—**IoAllocateWorkItem**, **IoQueueWorkItem**, and **IoFreeItem**—that Microsoft recommends you use instead of the executive support functions I just described. The new functions surround calls to the executive-level functions with code that claims a reference to a device object you specify. That reference prevents *your* device object from disappearing, but it doesn't hold off the processing of IRP_MN_REMOVE_DEVICE requests. So long as you understand that you must prevent the disappearance of your driver and any resources that your work-item callback will access until after the callback executes, there's no compelling reason to use the new functions.

ABOUT THE WORKITEM SAMPLE

The WORKITEM sample driver on the companion disc illustrates the bare mechanics of using an executive work item. It's basically a reprise of the NOTIFY sample that works like this: The test application issues a DeviceIoControl with a code of IOCTL_SUBMIT_ITEM. The driver treats this as an asynchronous IOCTL by using the techniques I described earlier in this chapter. It also queues a work item before returning from the DEVICE_CONTROL dispatch function. When the work item callback occurs, the driver then completes the IOCTL_SUBMIT_ITEM.

WATCHDOG TIMERS

Some devices won't notify you when something goes wrong—they simply don't respond when you talk to them. Each device object has an associated IO_TIMER object that you can use to avoid indefinitely waiting for an operation to finish. While the timer is running, the I/O Manager will call a timer callback routine once a second. Within the timer callback routine, you can take steps to terminate any outstanding operations that should have finished but didn't.

You initialize the timer object at AddDevice time:

```
NTSTATUS AddDevice(...)
  {
  ...
  IoInitializeTimer(fdo, (PIO_TIMER_ROUTINE) OnTimer, pdx);
  ...
  }
```

where **fdo** is the address of your device object, **OnTimer** is the timer callback routine, and **pdx** is a context argument for the I/O Manager's calls to OnTimer.

You start the timer counting by calling **IoStartTimer**, and you stop it from counting by calling **IoStopTimer**. In between, your OnTimer routine is called once a second.

The PIOFAKE sample on the companion disc illustrates one way of using the IO_TIMER as a watchdog. I put a **timer** member into the device extension for this fake device:

```
typedef struct _DEVICE_EXTENSION {
  ...
  LONG timer;
  ...
  } DEVICE_EXTENSION, *PDEVICE_EXTENSION;
```

When I process an IRP_MJ_CREATE after a period with no handles open to the device, I start the timer counting. When I process the IRP_MJ_CLOSE that closes the last handle, I stop the timer:

```
NTSTATUS DispatchCreate(...)
  {
  ...
  if (InterlockedIncrement(&pdx->handles == 1)
    {
    pdx->timer = -1;
    IoStartTimer(fdo);
    }
  ...
  }
```

```
NTSTATUS DispatchClose(...)
  {
  ...
  if (InterlockedDecrement(&pdx->handles) == 0)
    IoStopTimer(fdo);
  ...
  }
```

The **timer** cell begins life with the value −1. I set it to 10 (meaning 10 seconds) in the StartIo routine and again after each interrupt. Thus, I allow 10 seconds for the device to digest an output byte and to generate an interrupt that indicates readiness for the next byte. (See the sidebar "More About PIOFAKE" for an explanation of the way this nonexistent device works.) The work to be done by the OnTimer routine at each 1-second tick of the timer needs to be synchronized with the interrupt service routine (ISR). Consequently, I use **KeSynchronizeExecution** to call a helper routine (**CheckTimer**) at device IRQL (DIRQL) under protection of the interrupt spin lock. The timer-tick routines dovetail with the ISR and DPC routines as shown in this excerpt:

```
VOID OnTimer(PDEVICE_OBJECT fdo, PDEVICE_EXTENSION pdx)
  {
  KeSynchronizeExecution(pdx->InterruptObject,
    (PKSYNCHRONIZE_ROUTINE) CheckTimer, pdx);
  }

VOID CheckTimer(PDEVICE_EXTENSION pdx)
  {
  if (pdx->timer <= 0 || --pdx->timer > 0)
    return;
  PIRP Irp = GetCurrentIrp(&pdx->dqReadWrite);
  if (!Irp)
    return;
  Irp->IoStatus.Status = STATUS_IO_TIMEOUT;
  Irp->IoStatus.Information = 0;
  IoRequestDpc(pdx->DeviceObject, Irp, NULL);
  }

BOOLEAN OnInterrupt(...)
  {
  ...
  if (pdx->timer <= 0)
    return TRUE;
  if (!pdx->nbytes)
    {
    Irp->IoStatus.Status = STATUS_SUCCESS;
    Irp->IoStatus.Information = pdx->numxfer;
```

1 ► (line marker for `if (pdx->timer <= 0 || --pdx->timer > 0)`)
2 ► (line marker for `PIRP Irp = GetCurrentIrp(&pdx->dqReadWrite);`)
3 ► (line marker for `Irp->IoStatus.Status = STATUS_IO_TIMEOUT;`)
4 ► (line marker for `if (pdx->timer <= 0)`)

(continued)

```
        pdx->timer = -1;
        IoRequestDpc(pdx->DeviceObject, Irp, NULL);
        }
      ...
    pdx->timer = 10;
    }

VOID DpcForIsr(...)
  {
  ...
  PIRP Irp = StartNextPacket(&pdx->dqReadWrite, fdo);
  IoCompleteRequest(Irp, IO_NO_INCREMENT);
  ...
  }
```

5 (marker)

6 (marker)

1. A timer value of −1 means that no request is currently pending. A value of 0 means that the current request has timed out. In either case, we don't want or need to do any more work in this routine. The second part of the **if** expression decrements the timer. If it hasn't counted down to 0 yet, we return without doing anything else.

2. This driver uses a DEVQUEUE, so we call the DEVQUEUE routine **GetCurrentIrp** to get the address of the request we're currently processing. If this value is NULL, the device is currently idle.

3. At this point, we've decided we want to terminate the current request because nothing has happened for 10 seconds. We request a DPC after filling in the IRP status fields. This particular status code (STATUS_IO_TIMEOUT) turns into a Win32 error code (ERROR_SEM_TIMEOUT) for which the standard error text ("The semaphore timeout period has expired") doesn't really indicate what's gone wrong. If the application that has requested this operation is under your control, you should provide a more meaningful explanation.

4. If the timer equals 0, the current request has timed out. The **CheckTimer** routine requested a DPC, so we don't need or want to do any more work in the ISR besides dismissing the interrupt. By setting **timer** to −1, we prevent the next invocation of CheckTimer from requesting another DPC for this same request.

5. We allow 10 seconds between interrupts.

6. Whatever requested this DPC also filled in the IRP's status fields. We therefore need to call only **IoCompleteRequest**.

MORE ABOUT PIOFAKE

The PIOFAKE sample driver works with a nonexistent device that follows a programmed I/O (PIO) model. The device has a single output port to which you can write ASCII characters. After it digests a data byte, it generates an interrupt on its IRQ line.

   If you install PIOFAKE in Windows 2000 and run the associated TEST program, nothing will happen for 10 seconds. Then PIOFAKE will time out because it hasn't seen an interrupt, whereupon the test application will report a timeout error.

   In Windows 98, you can use the DEVTEST device simulator to exercise the PIO part of this sample driver. Refer to the instructions in PIOFAKE.HTM for additional information.

WINDOWS 98 COMPATIBILITY NOTES

There are some minor differences between Windows 98 and Windows 2000 insofar as the material discussed in this chapter goes.

Error Logging

Windows 98 doesn't implement an error-logging file or an Event Viewer. When you call **IoWriteErrorLogEntry** in Windows 98, all that happens is that several lines of data appear on your debugging terminal. I find the formatting of this information unaesthetic, so I prefer to simply not use the error-logging facility under Windows 98. Refer to Appendix A, "Coping with Windows 98 Incompatibilities," for suggestions about how to determine whether you're running Windows 98 or Windows 2000.

I/O Controls and Windows 98 Virtual Device Drivers

A Win32 application can use DeviceIoControl to communicate with a Windows 98 virtual device driver (VxD) as well as a WDM driver. Three subtle and minor differences exist between IOCTLs for WDM drivers and IOCTLs for VxDs. The most important difference has to do with the meaning of the device handle you obtain from CreateFile. When working with a WDM driver, the handle is for a specific *device,* whereas you get a handle for the *driver* when you're talking to a VxD. In practice, a VxD might need to implement a pseudohandle mechanism (embedded within the IOCTL data flow) to allow applications to refer to specific instances of the hardware managed by the VxD.

   Another difference between VxD and WDM control operations concerns the assignment of numeric control codes. As I discussed earlier, you define a control code for a WDM driver by using the CTL_CODE macro, and you can't define more than

2048 codes. For a VxD, all 32-bit values except 0 and −1 are available. If you want to write an application that can work with either a VxD or a WDM driver, use CTL_CODE to define your control codes, since a VxD will be able to work with the resulting numeric values.

The last difference is a pretty minor one: the second-to-last argument to DeviceIoControl—a PDWORD pointing to a feedback variable—is required when you call a WDM driver but not when you call a VxD. In other words, if you're calling a WDM driver, you must supply a non-NULL value pointing to a DWORD. If you're calling a VxD, however, you can specify NULL if you're not interested in knowing how many data bytes are going into your output buffer. It shouldn't hurt to supply the feedback variable when you call a VxD, though. Furthermore, the fact that this pointer can be NULL is something that a VxD writer might easily overlook, and you might provoke a bug if your application takes advantage of the freedom to say NULL.

Caution About Pending IOCTL Operations

If an application uses the pending IOCTL technique to wait for your driver to tell it about hardware events, the application necessarily has a handle open while it's running. If your device can be removed from the computer by surprise, you need to fail the pending IOCTL(s) to encourage the application to close its handles. In Windows 2000, you could delay handling the eventual IRP_MN_REMOVE_DEVICE request until all handles get closed. You don't dare delay in Windows 98, however, because of the deadlock possibility I described at the end of Chapter 6. If you look at my sample drivers, and at NOTIFY in particular, you'll see that they do not acquire the remove lock when they process IRP_MJ_CREATE. That means that they will allow themselves to be unloaded even though handles are open. Luckily, Windows 98 is able to deal with the aftermath without further incident.

Waiting for System Threads to Finish

Windows 98 doesn't support the use of a pointer to a thread object (a PKTHREAD) as an argument to **KeWaitForSingleObject** or **KeWaitForMultipleObjects**. Those support functions simply pass their object pointer arguments through to VWIN32.VXD without any sort of validity checking, and VWIN32 crashes because the thread objects don't have the structure members needed to support synchronization use.

If you need to wait for a kernel-mode thread to complete in Windows 98, therefore, you'll need to have the thread signal an event just before it calls **PsTerminate-SystemThread**. It's possible that signalling this event will cause the terminating thread to lose control to a thread waiting for the same event. The terminating thread would then still be alive technically, but I don't think anything awful can happen as a result in Windows 98. In Windows 2000, however, you could easily find the driver unloaded out from under the terminating thread; be sure to wait on the thread object itself in Windows 2000.

Chapter 10

Windows
Management
Instrumentation

Microsoft Windows 2000 supports a facility named Windows Management Instrumentation (WMI) as a way to manage the computer system. WMI is Microsoft's implementation of a broader industry standard called Web-Based Enterprise Management (WBEM). The goal of WMI is to provide a model for system management and the description of management data in an enterprise network that's as independent as possible from a specific API set or data object model. Such independence facilitates the development of general mechanisms for creating, transporting, and displaying data and for exercising control over individual system components.

WDM drivers fit into WMI in three ways. See Figure 10-1. First, WMI responds to requests for data that (usually) convey information about performance. Second, controller applications of various kinds can use the facilities of WMI to control generic features of conforming devices. Finally, WMI provides an event-signalling mechanism that allows drivers to notify interested applications of important events. I'll discuss all three of these aspects of driver programming in this chapter. To help you understand the test programs that accompany the driver samples for this chapter, I'm also going to describe how the user-mode side of WMI works.

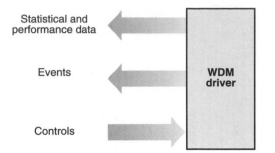

Statistical and
performance data

Events

Controls

WDM
driver

Figure 10-1. *The role of a WDM driver in WMI.*

THE WMI AND WBEM NAMES

The Common Information Model (CIM) is a specification for Web-based enter-prise management supported by the Distributed Management Task Force (DMTF), formerly named the Desktop Management Task Force. Microsoft named its implementation of the Common Information Model "WBEM," which was essen-tially "CIM for Windows." The kernel-mode portion of CIM for Windows was called "WMI." In order to get CIM more widely adopted, DMTF started a mar-keting initiative and used WBEM as the name of CIM. Microsoft then renamed its implementation of WBEM to WMI and renamed WMI (the kernel-mode por-tion) to "WMI extensions for WDM." That being said, WMI is compliant with the CIM and WBEM specification.

I'm afraid my usage of the various different terms in this chapter won't go very far to resolve the confusion you might feel at this point. I'd suggest that you think "WMI" whenever you see "CIM" or "WBEM" in this book and any documentation Microsoft provides. You'll probably then at least be thinking about the same concept that I and Microsoft are trying to write about—until something with a name like "Windows Basic Extensions for Mortals" or "Com-pletely Integrated Mouse" comes along, that is. Then you're on your own.

WMI CONCEPTS

Figure 10-2 diagrams the overall architecture of WMI. In the WMI model, the world is divided into *consumers* and *providers* of data and events. Consumers consume, and providers provide, blocks of data that are *instances* of abstract *classes*. The concept involved here is no different from that of a class in the C++ language. Just like C++

classes, WMI classes have data members and *methods* that implement *behaviors* for objects. What goes inside a data block isn't specified by WMI—that depends on who's producing and for what purpose. When it comes to device drivers, though, the content of a WMI data block is most likely going to be statistical in nature. Consumers of driver data, therefore, are often performance monitors of one kind or another.

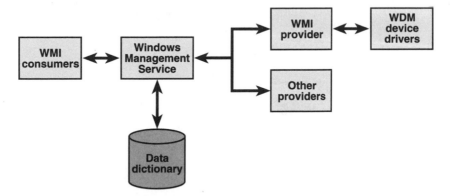

Figure 10-2. *The world of WMI.*

WMI allows for multiple *namespaces,* each of which contains classes belonging to one or more user-mode providers. Providers register with the Windows Management Service by using COM interfaces that are documented in the Platform SDK. When Windows 2000 ships, the operating system (including all device drivers) will support a namespace called **root\cimv2**, which stands for Version 2 of the Common Information Model. At the time of this writing, the structure of the CIMV2 namespace was rather fluid, with the consequence that Microsoft has temporarily decided to use another namespace, **root\wmi**, for device driver classes.

A WDM driver can act as a provider of instances of a WMI class. The description of all the classes a driver can provide data for is known as the driver's *schema*. You define a schema by using a language named the *Managed Object Format,* or MOF. The system maintains a data dictionary known as the *repository* that contains the definitions of all known schemas. Assuming you do all the right things in your driver, the system will automatically put your schema into the repository when it initializes your driver.

A Sample Schema

Later in this chapter, I'll show you a sample named WMI42.SYS, which is available on the companion disc. This sample has the following MOF schema:

1 ▶
```
[Dynamic, Provider("WMIProv"),
 WMI,
 Description("Wmi42 Sample Schema"),
 guid("A0F95FD4-A587-11d2-BB3A-00C04FA330A6"),
 locale("MS\\0x409")]
```

2 ▶
```
class Wmi42
{
    [key, read]
     string InstanceName;

    [read] boolean Active;

    [WmiDataId(1),
     Description("The Answer to the Ultimate Question")
     ]
    uint32 TheAnswer;
};
```

I don't propose to describe all the details of the MOF syntax; that information is available as part of the Platform SDK and WMI SDK (*http://msdn.microsoft.com/developer/sdk/*) documentation. You can either construct your MOF by hand, as I did for this simple example, or use a tool named WBEM CIM Studio that comes with the Platform SDK and WMI SDK. Here, however, is a brief explanation of the contents of this MOF file:

1. The provider named **WMIProv** is the system component that knows how to instantiate this class. It understands, for example, how to call into kernel mode and send an I/O request packet (IRP) to an appropriate driver. It can find the right driver by means of the globally unique identifier (GUID) that appears near the beginning of the file.

2. This schema declares a class named **WMI42**, which coincidentally has the same name as our driver. Instances of the class have *properties* named **InstanceName**, **Active**, and **TheAnswer**.

As developers, we would run the MOF compiler on this schema definition to produce a binary file that eventually ends up as a resource in our driver executable file. (*Resource* in this sense is the same concept that application developers have in mind when they build dialog box templates, string tables, and other things that are part of their project's resource script.) Part of the process of initializing our driver is telling the WMI provider where the resource is so that it can read the schema and augment the repository.

We should also run a utility named WMIMOFCK.EXE, which is available in the DDK, after compiling our schema. This utility performs additional checks to make sure that the schema is compatible with WMI.

MOF FILES AND BETA RELEASES

WMI was under active development during much of the Windows 2000 beta-testing period, and not all of the plumbing was complete. Depending on which release of Windows 2000 you're using, you might need to run the MOF compiler an extra time before you'll be able to run the sample programs described in this chapter. During the extra run, you'll manually update the WMI repository so that various COM interfaces can access your driver's schema. Use the following command-line syntax to place your schema into the WMI namespace:

```
mofcomp -N:root\wmi <name>
```

Thereafter, you'll be able to use development tools like WBEMTEST.EXE to test your driver, and the console-mode test programs that accompany the samples will also work. (MOFTEST.EXE and WBEMTEST.EXE are included in the %windir%\system32\wbem directory for Windows 2000 and the %windir%\system\wbem directory for Microsoft Windows 98. In Windows 98, you will need to install WMI. See "Windows 98 Compatibility Notes" at the end of this chapter for some additional information.)

WDM DRIVERS AND WMI

The kernel-mode support for WMI is based primarily on IRPs with the major code IRP_MJ_SYSTEM_CONTROL. You must register your desire to receive these IRPs by making the following call:

```
IoWMIRegistrationControl(fdo, WMI_ACTION_REGISTER);
```

The appropriate time to make the registration call is in the **AddDevice** routine at a point when it would be safe for the system to send the driver a system control IRP. In due course, the system will send you an IRP_MJ_SYSTEM_CONTROL request to obtain detailed registration information about your device. You'll balance the registration call with another call at **RemoveDevice** time:

```
IoWMIRegistrationControl(fdo, WMI_ACTION_DEREGISTER);
```

If any WMI requests are outstanding at the time you make the deregistration call, **IoWMIRegistrationControl** waits until they complete. It's therefore necessary to make sure that your driver is still capable of responding to IRPs when you deregister. You can fail new IRPs with STATUS_DELETE_PENDING, but you have to respond.

Before explaining how to service the registration request, I'll describe how you handle system control IRPs in general. An IRP_MJ_SYSTEM_CONTROL request can have any of the minor function codes listed in Table 10-1.

Minor Function Code	Description
IRP_MN_QUERY_ALL_DATA	Get all instances of every item in a data block
IRP_MN_QUERY_SINGLE_INSTANCE	Get every item in a single instance of a data block
IRP_MN_CHANGE_SINGLE_INSTANCE	Replace every item in a single instance of a data block
IRP_MN_CHANGE_SINGLE_ITEM	Change one item in a data block
IRP_MN_ENABLE_EVENTS	Enable event generation
IRP_MN_DISABLE_EVENTS	Disable event generation
IRP_MN_ENABLE_COLLECTION	Start collecting "expensive" statistics
IRP_MN_DISABLE_COLLECTION	Stop collecting "expensive" statistics
IRP_MN_REGINFO	Get detailed registration information
IRP_MN_EXECUTE_METHOD	Execute a method function

Table 10-1. *Minor function codes for IRP_MJ_SYSTEM_CONTROL.*

The **Parameters** union in the stack location includes a **WMI** substructure with parameters for the system control request:

```
struct {
  ULONG_PTR ProviderId;
  PVOID DataPath;
  ULONG BufferSize;
  PVOID Buffer;
  } WMI;
```

ProviderId is a pointer to the device object to which the request is directed. **Buffer** is the address of an input/output area where the first several bytes are mapped by the WNODE_HEADER structure. **BufferSize** gives the size of the buffer area. Your dispatch function will extract some information from this buffer and will also return results in the same memory area. For all the minor functions except IRP_MN_REGINFO, **DataPath** is the address of a 128-bit GUID that identifies a class of data block. The DataPath field is either WMIREGISTER or WMIUPDATE (0 or 1, respectively) for an IRP_MN_REGINFO request, depending on whether you're being told to provide initial registration information or just to update the information you supplied earlier.

When you design your driver, you must choose between two ways of handling system control IRPs. One method is relying on the facilities of the WMILIB support "driver." WMILIB is really a kernel-mode DLL that exports services you can call from your driver to handle some of the annoying mechanics of IRP processing. The other method is simply handling the IRPs yourself. If you use WMILIB, you'll end up writing less code but you won't be able to use every last feature of WMI to its fullest— you'll be limited to the subset supported by WMILIB. Furthermore, your driver won't run under the original retail release of Microsoft Windows 98 because WMILIB wasn't available then. *Before you let the lack of WMILIB in original Windows 98 ruin your day, consult the compatibility notes at the end of this chapter.*

WMILIB suffices for most drivers, so I'm going to limit my discussion to using WMILIB. The DDK documentation describes how to handle system control IRPs yourself if you absolutely have to.

Delegating IRPs to WMILIB

In your dispatch routine for system control IRPs, you delegate most of the work to WMILIB with code like the following:

```
WMIGUIDREGINFO guidlist[] = {
  {&GUID_WMI42_SCHEMA, 1, WMIREG_FLAG_INSTANCE_PDO},
  };
```

(continued)

```
WMILIB_CONTEXT libinfo = {
  arraysize(guidlist),
  guidlist,
  QueryRegInfo,
  QueryDataBlock,
  SetDataBlock,
  SetDataItem,
  ExecuteMethod,
  FunctionControl,
  };

NTSTATUS DispatchWmi(IN PDEVICE_OBJECT fdo, IN PIRP Irp)
  {
  PDEVICE_EXTENSION pdx = (PDEVICE_EXTENSION) fdo->DeviceExtension;
  NTSTATUS status = IoAcquireRemoveLock(&pdx->RemoveLock, Irp);
  if (!NT_SUCCESS(status))
    return CompleteRequest(Irp, status, 0);

  SYSCTL_IRP_DISPOSITION disposition;
  status = WmiSystemControl(&libinfo, fdo, Irp, &disposition);

  switch (disposition)
    {

  case IrpProcessed:
    break;

  case IrpNotCompleted:
    IoCompleteRequest(Irp, IO_NO_INCREMENT);
    break;

  default:
  case IrpNotWmi:
  case IrpForward:
    IoSkipCurrentIrpStackLocation(Irp);
    status = IoCallDriver(pdx->LowerDeviceObject, Irp);
    break;
    }

  IoReleaseRemoveLock(&pdx->RemoveLock, Irp);
  return status;
  }
```

1. The WMILIB_CONTEXT structure declared at file scope describes the class GUIDs your driver supports and lists several callback functions that WMILIB uses to handle WMI requests in the appropriate device-dependent and driver-dependent way.

2. As with other dispatch routines, we acquire and release the remove lock while handling this IRP. The problem we prevent is having the device object underneath us disappear because of a Plug and Play (PnP) event. Our own device object cannot disappear because our call to IoWMIRegistrationControl acquired a reference to it.

3. This statement calls WMILIB to handle the IRP. We pass the address of our WMILIB_CONTEXT structure. It's customary to use a static context structure, by the way, because the information in it is unlikely to change from one IRP to the next. **WmiSystemControl** returns two pieces of information: an NTSTATUS code and a SYSCTL_IRP_DISPOSITION value.

4. Depending on the disposition code, we might have additional work to perform on this IRP. If the code is **IrpProcessed**, the IRP has already been completed and we need do nothing more with it. This case would be the normal one for minor functions other than IRP_MN_REGINFO.

5. If the disposition code is **IrpNotCompleted**, completing the IRP is our responsibility. This case would be the normal one for IRP_MN_REGINFO. WMILIB has already filled in the **IoStatus** block of the IRP, so we need only call **IoCompleteRequest**.

6. The **default** and **IrpNotWmi** cases shouldn't arise in Windows 2000. We'd get to the default label if we weren't handling all possible disposition codes; we'd get to the IrpNotWmi case label if we sent an IRP to WMILIB that didn't have one of the minor function codes that specifies WMI functionality.

7. The **IrpForward** case occurs for system control IRPs that are intended for some other driver. Recall that the ProviderId parameter indicates the driver that is supposed to handle this IRP. WmiSystemControl compares that value to the device object pointer we supply as the second function argument. If they're not the same, it returns IrpForward so that we'll send the IRP down the stack to the next driver.

The way a WMI consumer matches up to your driver in your driver's role as a WMI provider is based on the GUID(s) you supply in the context structure. When a consumer wants to retrieve data, it (indirectly) accesses the data dictionary in the WMI repository to translate a symbolic object name into a GUID. The GUID is part of the MOF syntax I showed you earlier. You specify the same GUID in your context structure, and WMILIB takes care of the matching.

WMILIB will call routines in our driver to perform device-dependent or driver-dependent processing. Most of the time, the callback routines will perform the requested operation synchronously. However, except in the case of IRP_MN_REGINFO, we can defer processing by returning STATUS_PENDING and completing the request later. If a callback routine will pend the operation, it should call **IoAcquireRemoveLock** an extra time. Whoever completes the request should make the balancing call to **IoReleaseRemoveLock**.

The QueryRegInfo Callback

The first system control IRP we'll receive after making our registration call has the minor function code IRP_MN_REGINFO. When we pass this IRP to WmiSystemControl, it turns around and calls the **QueryRegInfo** function—it finds the function's address in our WMILIB_CONTEXT structure. Here's how WMI42.SYS handles this callback:

```
NTSTATUS QueryRegInfo(PDEVICE_OBJECT fdo, PULONG flags,
  PUNICODE_STRING instname, PUNICODE_STRING* regpath,
  PUNICODE_STRING resname, PDEVICE_OBJECT* pdo)
  {
  PDEVICE_EXTENSION pdx = (PDEVICE_EXTENSION) fdo->DeviceExtension;
  *flags = WMIREG_FLAG_INSTANCE_PDO;
  *regpath = &servkey;
  RtlInitUnicodeString(resname, L"MofResource");
  *pdo = pdx->Pdo;
  return STATUS_SUCCESS;
  }
```

We set **regpath** to the address of a UNICODE_STRING structure that contains the name of the service registry key describing our driver. This key is the one below …\System\CurrentControlSet\Services. Our **DriverEntry** routine received the name of this key as an argument and saved it in the global variable **servkey**. We set **resname** to the name we chose to give our schema in our resource script. Here's the resource file for WMI42.SYS so that you can see where this name comes from:

```
#include <windows.h>

LANGUAGE LANG_ENGLISH, SUBLANG_NEUTRAL
MofResource MOFDATA wmi42.bmf
```

WMI42.BMF is where our build script puts the compiled MOF file. You can name this resource anything you want to, but **MofResource** is traditional (in a tradition stretching back to, uh, last Tuesday). All that matters about the name is that you specify the *same* name when you service the QueryRegInfo call.

How we set the remaining values depends on how our driver wants to handle instance naming. I'll come back to the subject of instance naming later in the chapter (in "Instance Naming"). The simplest choice, and the one Microsoft strongly recommends, is the one I adopted in WMI42.SYS: have the system automatically generate names that are *static* based on the name the bus driver gave to the physical device object (PDO). When we make this choice of naming method, we do the following tasks in QueryRegInfo:

- Set the WMIREG_FLAG_INSTANCE_PDO flag in the GUID list that's part of the context structure. Setting the flag in the GUID list means that the instance names for data blocks of the associated WMI class will use the PDO name.

- Set the WMIREG_FLAG_INSTANCE_PDO flag in the **flags** value we're returning to WMILIB. Setting the flag here tells WMILIB that at least one of our objects uses PDO naming.

- Set the **pdo** value we're returning to WMILIB. In my sample drivers, my device extension has a field named **Pdo** that I set at AddDevice time to make it available at times like this.

Apart from making your life easier, basing your instance names on the PDO allows viewer applications to automatically determine your device's friendly name and other properties without you doing anything more in your driver.

When you return a successful status from QueryRegInfo, WMILIB goes on to create a complicated structure called a WMIREGINFO that includes your GUID list, your registry key, your resource name, and information about your instance names. It returns to your dispatch function, which then completes the IRP and returns. Figure 10-3 diagrams this process.

The QueryDataBlock Callback

The information you provide in your answer to the initial registration query allows the system to route relevant data operations to you. User-mode code can use various COM interfaces to get and set data values at several levels of aggregation. Table 10-2 summarizes the four possibilities.

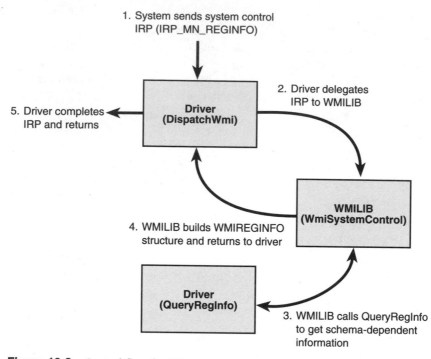

Figure 10-3. *Control flow for IRP_MN_REGINFO.*

IRP Minor Function	WMILIB Callback	Description
IRP_MN_QUERY_ALL_DATA	QueryDataBlock	Get all items of all instances
IRP_MN_QUERY_SINGLE_INSTANCE	QueryDataBlock	Get all items of one instance
IRP_MN_CHANGE_SINGLE_INSTANCE	SetDataBlock	Set all items of one instance
IRP_MN_CHANGE_SINGLE_ITEM	SetDataItem	Set one item in one instance

Table 10-2. *Forms of data queries.*

When someone wants to learn the value(s) of the data you're keeping, they send you a system control IRP with one of the minor function codes IRP_MN_QUERY_ALL_DATA or IRP_MN_QUERY_SINGLE_INSTANCE. If you're using WMILIB, you'll delegate the IRP to WmiSystemControl, which will then call your **QueryDataBlock** callback routine. You'll provide the requested data, call another WMILIB routine named **WmiCompleteRequest** to complete the IRP, and then return to WMILIB to unwind the process. In this situation, WmiSystemControl will return the **IrpProcessed** disposition code because you've already completed the IRP. Refer to Figure 10-4 for a diagram of the overall control flow.

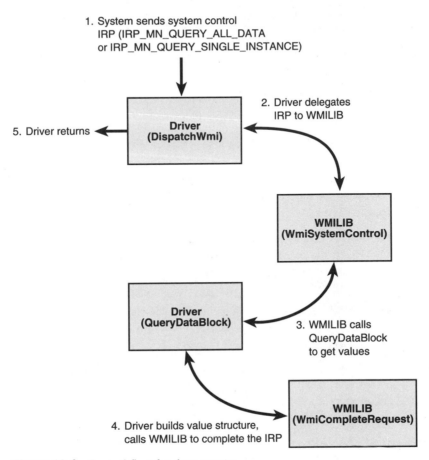

Figure 10-4. *Control flow for data queries.*

Your QueryDataBlock callback can end up being a relatively complex function if your driver is maintaining multiple instances of a data block that varies in size from one instance to the next. I'll discuss the complications later in "Dealing with Multiple Instances." The WMI42 sample shows how to handle a simpler case in which your driver maintains only one instance of the WMI class:

```
NTSTATUS QueryDataBlock(PDEVICE_OBJECT fdo, PIRP Irp,
  ULONG guidindex, ULONG instindex, ULONG instcount,
  PULONG instlength, ULONG bufsize, PUCHAR buffer)
  {
  if (!instlength || bufsize < sizeof(ULONG))
    return WmiCompleteRequest(fdo, Irp, STATUS_BUFFER_TOO_SMALL,
      sizeof(ULONG), IO_NO_INCREMENT);

  PDEVICE_EXTENSION pdx = (PDEVICE_EXTENSION) fdo->DeviceExtension;
```

(continued)

2 ▶
```
        PULONG pvalue = (PULONG) buffer;
        *pvalue = pdx->TheAnswer;
        instlength[0] = sizeof(ULONG);
```

3 ▶
```
        return WmiCompleteRequest(fdo, Irp, STATUS_SUCCESS, sizeof(ULONG),
          IO_NO_INCREMENT);
        }
```

1. We're obliged to make this check to verify that the buffer area is large enough to accommodate the data and data length values we're going to put there. The first part of the test—is there an **instlength** array?—is boilerplate. The second part of the test—is the buffer big enough for a ULONG?—is where we verify that all of our data values will fit. In this simple driver, we're providing only a single ULONG value.

2. The **buffer** parameter points to a memory area where we can put our data. The **instlength** parameter points to an array where we're supposed to place the length of each data instance we're returning. Here, we install the single ULONG data value our schema calls for—the value of the **TheAnswer** property—and its length. Figuring out what TheAnswer actually is numerically is left as an exercise for the reader.

3. The WMILIB specification requires us to complete the IRP by calling the **WmiCompleteRequest** helper routine. The fourth argument indicates how much of the buffer area we used for data values. By now, the other arguments should be self-explanatory.

You'll notice that I didn't discuss the purpose of the **guidindex**, **instindex**, and **instcount** arguments to QueryDataBlock. I'll come back to those a bit further on in "Dealing with Multiple Instances" when I discuss some of the more complicated features of WMI. In WMI42.SYS, you should expect these values to be 0, 0, and 1, respectively.

The SetDataBlock Callback

The system might ask you to change an entire instance of one of your classes by sending you an IRP_MN_CHANGE_SINGLE_INSTANCE request. WmiSystemControl processes this IRP by calling your **SetDataBlock** callback routine. A simple version of this routine might look like this:

1 ▶
```
NTSTATUS SetDataBlock(PDEVICE_OBJECT fdo, PIRP Irp, ULONG guidindex,
  ULONG instindex, ULONG bufsize, PUCHAR buffer)
  {
  PDEVICE_EXTENSION pdx = (PDEVICE_EXTENSION) fdo->DeviceExtension;
  if (bufsize == sizeof(ULONG)
    {
    pdx->TheAnswer = *(PULONG) buffer;
    status = STATUS_SUCCESS;
```

```
    info = sizeof(ULONG);
    }
else
    status = STATUS_INFO_LENGTH_MISMATCH, info = 0;
return WmiCompleteRequest(fdo, Irp, status, info, IO_NO_INCREMENT);
}
```

1. The system should already know—based on the MOF declaration—how big an instance of each class is and should give us a buffer that's exactly the right size. If it doesn't, we'll end up failing this IRP. Otherwise, we'll copy a new value for the data block into the place where we keep our copy of that value.

2. We're responsible for completing the IRP by calling **WmiComplete-Request**.

The SetDataItem Callback

Sometimes consumers want to change just one field in one of the WMI objects we support. Each field has an identifying number that appears in the **WmiDataId** property of the field's MOF declaration. (The **Active** and **InstanceName** properties are not changeable and don't have identifiers. Furthermore, they're implemented by the system and don't even appear in the data blocks we work with.) To change the one field, the consumer references the field's ID. We then receive an IRP_MN_CHANGE_SINGLE_ITEM request, which WmiSystemControl processes by calling our **SetDataItem** callback routine:

```
NTSTATUS SetDataItem(PDEVICE_OBJECT fdo, PIRP Irp, ULONG guidindex,
  ULONG instindex, ULONG id, ULONG bufsize, PUCHAR buffer)
  {
  PDEVICE_EXTENSION pdx = (PDEVICE_EXTENSION) fdo->DeviceExtension;
  NTSTATUS status;
  ULONG info;

  if (bufsize == sizeof(ULONG))
    {
    pdx->TheAnswer = *(PULONG) buffer;
    status = STATUS_SUCCESS;
    info = sizeof(ULONG);
    }
  else
    status = STATUS_INFO_LENGTH_MISMATCH, info = 0;

  return WmiCompleteRequest(fdo, Irp, status, info, IO_NO_INCREMENT);
  }
```

In my WMI42.SYS sample, you'll notice that this SetDataItem routine is identical to SetDataBlock because my class has only a single item.

NOTE   The WMI system code that generates calls to the SetDataItem routine was apparently not complete in the beta version of Windows 2000 with which I tested my sample drivers. The only way I was able to invoke this routine was by using an internal Microsoft testing tool, and I always ended up with an item ID of 0 instead of the 1 that's declared in the MOF schema. I don't know whether there was a bug in this internal tool, in the operating system, or in my own understanding of how this was supposed to work. I advise that you fail calls to this routine with STATUS_WMI_NOT_SUPPORTED until you're sure the item ID means what you think it should.

Advanced Features

The preceding discussion covers much of what you need to know to provide meaningful performance information for metering applications. Use your imagination here: instead of providing just a single statistic (TheAnswer), you could accumulate and return any number of performance measures that are relevant to your specific device. You can support, however, some additional WMI features for more specialized purposes. I'll discuss these features now.

Dealing with Multiple Instances

WMI allows you to create multiple instances of a particular class data block for a single device object. You might want to provide multiple instances if your device is a controller or some other device into which other devices plug; each instance might represent data about one of the child devices. Mechanically, you specify the number of instances of a class in the WMIGUIDREGINFO structure for the GUID associated with the class. If WMI42 had three different instances of its standard data block, for example, it would have used the following GUID list in its WMILIB_CONTEXT structure:

```
WMIGUIDREGINFO guidlist[] = {
  {&GUID_WMI42_SCHEMA, 3, WMIREG_FLAG_INSTANCE_PDO},
  };
```

The only difference between this GUID list and the one I showed you earlier is the instance count here is 3 instead of 1. This list declares that there will be three instances of the WMI42 data block, each with its own value for the three properties (that is, InstanceName, Active, and TheAnswer) that belong in that block.

If the number of instances changes over time, you can call IoWmiRegistrationControl with the action code WMIREG_ACTION_UPDATE_GUID to cause the system to send you another registration request, which you'll process using an updated copy of your WMILIB_CONTEXT structure. If you're going to be changing your registration information, you should probably allocate the WMILIB_CONTEXT structure and GUID list from the free pool rather than use static variables, by the way.

If user-mode code were to enumerate all instances of GUID_WMI42_SCHEMA, it would find three instances. This result might present a confusing picture to user-mode code, though. It's impossible to tell a priori that the three instances disclosed by the enumeration belong to a single device, as opposed to a situation in which three WMI42 devices each expose a single instance of the same class. To allow WMI clients to sort out the difference between the two situations, your schema should include a property (such as a device name or the like) that can function as a key.

Once you allow for the possibility of multiple instances, several of your WMILIB callbacks will require changes from the simple examples I showed you earlier. In particular:

■ QueryDataBlock should be able to return the data block for a single instance or for any number of instances beginning at a specific index.

■ SetDataBlock should interpret its instance number argument to decide which instance to change.

■ SetDataItem should likewise interpret its instance number argument to locate the instance within which the affected data item will be found.

Figure 10-5 illustrates how your QueryDataBlock function uses the output buffer when it's asked to provide more than one instance of a data block. Imagine that you were asked to provide data for two instances beginning at instance number 2. You'll copy the data values, which I've shown as being of different sizes, into the data buffer. You start each instance on an 8-byte boundary. You indicate the total number of bytes you consume when you complete the query, and you indicate the lengths of each individual instance by filling in the **instlength** array, as shown in the figure.

Instance Naming

Each instance of a WMI class has a unique name. Consumers that know the name of an instance can perform queries and invoke method routines. Consumers that don't know the names of the instance(s) you provide can learn them by enumerating the class. In any case, you're responsible for generating the names that consumers use or discover.

I showed you the simplest way—from the driver's perspective, that is—of naming instances of a custom data block, which is to request that WMI automatically generate a static, unique name based on the name of the PDO for your device. If your PDO has the name **Root*WCO0A01\\0000**, for example, a PDO-based name for a single instance of some data block would be **Root*WCO0A01\\0000_0**. The _0 at the end is what makes this name unique. The name is static in that it persists until you deregister or update your registration information.

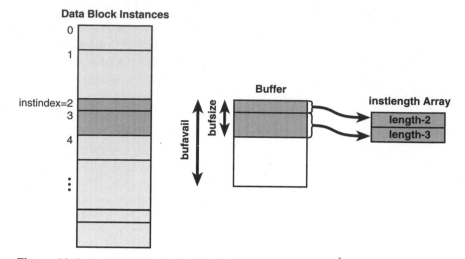

Figure 10-5. *Getting multiple data block instances.*

Basing instance names on the PDO name is obviously convenient because all you need to do in the driver is set the WMIREG_FLAG_INSTANCE_PDO flag in each WMIGUIDREGINFO structure and in the **flags** variable that WMILIB passes to your QueryRegInfo callback routine. The author of a consumer application can't know what this name will be, however, because the name will vary depending on how your device was installed. To make the instance names slightly more predictable, you can elect to use a constant *base name* for object instances instead. You indicate this choice by *omitting* the WMIREG_FLAG_INSTANCE_PDO flag from your WMIGUIDREGINFO structures and by responding in the following way to the registration query:

```
NTSTATUS QueryRegInfo(PDEVICE_OBJECT fdo, PULONG flags,
  PUNICODE_STRING instname, PUNICODE_STRING* regpath,
  PUNICODE_STRING resname, PDEVICE_OBJECT* pdo)
  {
  *flags = WMIREG_FLAG_INSTANCE_BASENAME;
  *regpath = &servkey;
  RtlInitUnicodeString(resname, L"MofResource");
  static WCHAR basename[] = L"WMIEXTRA";
  instname->Buffer = (PWCHAR) ExAllocatePool(PagedPool,
    sizeof(basename));
  if (!instname->Buffer)
    return STATUS_INSUFFICIENT_RESOURCES;
  instname->MaximumLength = sizeof(basename);
  instname->Length = sizeof(basename) - 2;
  RtlCopyMemory(instname->Buffer, basename, sizeof(basename));
  }
```

The parts of this function that differ from the previous example of QueryRegInfo are in boldface. In the WMIEXTRA sample, only one instance of each data block exists, and each receives the instance name **WMIEXTRA** with no additional decoration.

If you elect to use a base name, try to avoid generic names such as Toaster because of the confusion that can ensue. The purpose of this feature is to let you use specific names like AcmeWaffleToaster.

In some circumstances, static instance names won't suit your needs. If you maintain a population of data blocks that changes frequently, using static names means that you have to request a registration update each time the population changes. The update is relatively expensive, and you should avoid requesting one often. You can assign *dynamic* instance names to the instances of your data blocks instead of static names. The instance names then become part of the queries and replies that you deal with in your driver. Unfortunately, WMILIB doesn't support the use of dynamic instance names. To use this feature, therefore, you'll have to fully implement support for the IRP_MJ_SYSTEM_CONTROL requests that WMILIB would otherwise interpret for you. Describing how to handle these IRPs yourself is beyond the scope of this book, but the DDK documentation contains detailed information about how to go about it.

Dealing with Multiple Classes

WMI42 deals with only one class of data block. If you want to support more than one class, you need to have a bigger array of GUID information structures, as WMIEXTRA does:

```
WMIGUIDREGINFO guidlist[] = {
  {&GUID_WMIEXTRA_EVENT, 1,
    WMIREG_FLAG_INSTANCE_PDO | WMIREG_FLAG_EVENT_ONLY_GUID},
  {&GUID_WMIEXTRA_EXPENSIVE, 1,
    WMIREG_FLAG_EXPENSIVE | WMIREG_FLAG_INSTANCE_PDO},
  {&GUID_WMIEXTRA_METHOD, 1,
    WMIREG_FLAG_INSTANCE_PDO},
  };
```

Before calling one of your callback routines, WMILIB looks up the GUID accompanying the IRP in your list. If the GUID isn't in the list, WMILIB fails the IRP. If it's in the list, WMILIB calls your callback routine with the **guidindex** parameter set equal to the index of the GUID in your list. By inspecting this parameter, you can tell which data block you're being asked to work with.

You can use the special flag WMIREG_FLAG_REMOVE_GUID in a GUID information structure. The purpose of this flag is to remove a particular GUID from the list of supported GUIDs during a registration update. Using this flag also prevents WMILIB from calling you to perform an operation on a GUID that you're trying to remove.

Expensive Statistics

It can sometimes be burdensome to collect all of the statistics that are potentially useful to an end user or administrator. For example, it would be possible for a disk driver (or, more likely, a filter driver sitting in the same stack as a disk driver) to collect histogram data showing how often I/O requests reference a particular sector of the disk. This data would be useful to a disk-defragmenting program because it would allow the most frequently accessed sectors to be placed in the middle of a disk for optimal seek time. You wouldn't want to routinely collect this data, though, because of the amount of memory needed for the collection. That memory would have to be nonpaged, too, because of the possibility that a particular I/O request would be for page swapping.

WMI allows you to declare a particular data block as being *expensive* so that you don't need to collect it except on demand, as shown in this excerpt from the WMIEXTRA sample program:

```
WMIGUIDREGINFO guidlist[] = {
  ...
  {&GUID_WMIEXTRA_EXPENSIVE, 1,
    WMIREG_FLAG_EXPENSIVE},
  ...
};
```

The WMIREG_FLAG_EXPENSIVE flag indicates that the data block identified by GUID_WMIEXTRA_EXPENSIVE has this expensive characteristic.

When an application expresses interest in retrieving values from an expensive data block, WMI sends you a system control IRP with the minor function code IRP_MN_ENABLE_COLLECTION. When no applications are interested in an expensive data block anymore, WMI sends you another IRP with the minor function code IRP_MN_DISABLE_COLLECTION. If you delegate these IRPs to WMILIB, it will turn around and call your **FunctionControl** callback routine to either enable or disable collection of the values in the data block:

```
NTSTATUS FunctionControl(PDEVICE_OBJECT fdo, PIRP Irp,
  ULONG guidindex, WMIENABLEDISABLECONTROL fcn, BOOLEAN enable)
  {
  ...
  return WmiCompleteRequest(fdo, Irp, STATUS_SUCCESS, 0,
    IO_NO_INCREMENT);
  }
```

In these arguments, **guidindex** is the index of the GUID for the expensive data block in your list of GUIDs, **fcn** will equal the enumeration value **WmiDataBlockControl** to indicate that collection of an expensive statistic is being either enabled or disabled, and **enable** will be TRUE or FALSE to indicate whether you should or should not collect the statistic, respectively. As shown in this fragment, you call WmiComplete-Request prior to returning from this function.

An application "expresses interest" in a data block, by the way, by retrieving an **IWbemClassObject** interface pointer bound to a particular instance of your data block's WMI class. Notwithstanding the fact that an application has to discover an instance of the class, no instance index appears in the call to your FunctionControl callback. The instruction to collect or not collect the expensive statistic therefore applies to all instances of your class.

WMI Events

WMI provides a way for providers to notify consumers of interesting or alarming events. A device driver might use this facility to alert a user to some facet of device operation that requires user intervention. For example, a disk driver might notice that an unusually large number of bad sectors have accumulated on a disk. Logging such an event as described in Chapter 9, "Specialized Topics," is one way to inform the human world of this fact, but an administrator has to actively look at the event log to see the entry. If someone were to write an event-monitoring applet, however, and if you were to fire a WMI event when you noticed the degradation, the event could be brought immediately to the user's attention.

WMI events are just regular WMI classes used in a special way. In MOF syntax, you must derive the data block from the abstract **WMIEvent** class, as illustrated in this excerpt from WMIEXTRA's MOF file:

```
[Dynamic, Provider("WMIProv"),
 WMI,
 Description("Event Info from WMIExtra"),
 guid("c4b678f6-b6e9-11d2-bb87-00c04fa330a6"),
 locale("MS\\0x409")]

class wmiextra_event : WMIEvent
{
    [key, read]
     string InstanceName;

    [read] boolean Active;

    [WmiDataId(1), read] uint32 EventInfo;

};
```

Although events can be normal data blocks, you might not want to allow applications to read and write them separately. If not, use the EVENT_ONLY flag in your declaration of the GUID:

```
WMIGUIDREGINFO guidlist[] = {
  ...
  {&GUID_WMIEXTRA_EVENT, 1,
    WMIREG_FLAG_INSTANCE_PDO | WMIREG_FLAG_EVENT_ONLY_GUID},
  ...
  };
```

When an application expresses interest in knowing about a particular event, WMI sends your driver a system control IRP with the minor function code IRP_MN_ENABLE_EVENTS. When no application is interested in an event anymore, WMI sends you another IRP with the minor function code IRP_MN_DISABLE_EVENTS. If you delegate these IRPs to WMILIB, you'll receive a call in your FunctionControl callback to specify the GUID index in your list of GUIDs, a **fcn** code of WmiEventControl, and a Boolean **enable** flag.

To fire an event, construct an instance of the event class in nonpaged memory and call **WmiFireEvent**. For example:

```
PULONG junk = (PULONG) ExAllocatePool(NonPagedPool, sizeof(ULONG));
*junk = 42;
WmiFireEvent(fdo, (LPGUID) &GUID_WMIEXTRA_EVENT, 0, sizeof(ULONG), junk);
```

The WMI subsystem will release the memory that's occupied by the event object in due course.

WMI Method Routines

In addition to defining mechanisms for transferring data and signalling events, WMI prescribes a way for consumers to invoke *method routines* implemented by providers. WMIEXTRA defines the following class that includes a method routine:

```
[Dynamic, Provider("WMIProv"),
 WMI,
 Description("WMIExtra class with method"),
 guid("cd7ec27d-b6e9-11d2-bb87-00c04fa330a6"),
 locale("MS\\0x409")]

class wmiextra_method
{
    [key, read]
     string InstanceName;

    [read] boolean Active;

    [Implemented, WmiMethodId(1)] uint32
     AnswerMethod([in,out] uint32 TheAnswer);

};
```

This declaration indicates that **AnswerMethod** accepts an input/output argument named **TheAnswer** (a 32-bit unsigned integer) and returns a 32-bit unsigned integer as its result.

When you delegate system control IRPs to WMILIB, a method routine call manifests itself in a call to your **ExecuteMethod** callback routine:

```
NTSTATUS ExecuteMethod(PDEVICE_OBJECT fdo, PIRP Irp,
  ULONG guidindex, ULONG instindex, ULONG id,
  ULONG cbInbuf, ULONG cbOutbuf, PUCHAR buffer)
  {
  NSTATUS status = STATUS_SUCCESS;
  ULONG bufused = 0;
  ...
  return WmiCompleteRequest(fdo, Irp, status, bufused,
    IO_NO_INCREMENT);
  }
```

The **buffer** area contains an image of the input class, whose length is **cbInbuf**. Your job is to perform the method and overstore the buffer area with an image of the output class. You complete the request with the byte size (**bufused**) of the output class. In the WMIEXTRA case, I put the following code in place of the ellipsis. (I've omitted the error checking.)

```
switch (guidindex)
  {
case 2:
  bufused = sizeof(ULONG);
  (*(PULONG) buffer)++;
  break;
default:
  status = STATUS_WMI_GUID_NOT_FOUND;
  break;
  }
```

This particular method routine simply adds 1 to its input argument.

Some of the details surrounding method routine calls were still ambiguous when I was writing this chapter. Here are some issues for you to think about:

■ There is no way for a driver to return a value from a method call. You can return only an output argument class instance.

■ You specify the input and output arguments in your schema as though you were describing a function. The system translates the argument descriptions into two WMI classes: one for the input arguments and another for the output arguments. It's easy enough for a user-mode consumer to learn the contents of these classes, but you have to guess the memory layout of the corresponding structures when you program your driver. I guessed correctly that a single 32-bit unsigned integer argument would occupy a ULONG location in the input/output buffer, but no great intellectual effort was involved in this simple case.

■ Simply enumerating an instance of a class like **wmiextra_method** triggers a request for the data block. You must succeed the data query even if the class that contains the method routine has no data members. In such a case, you can just complete the query with a 0 data length.

Standard Data Blocks

Microsoft has defined some standardized data blocks for various types of devices. If your device belongs to a class for which standardized data blocks are defined, you should support those blocks in your driver. Consult WMICORE.MOF in the DDK to see the class definitions, and see Table 10-3.

Device Type	Standard Class	Description
Keyboard	MSKeyboard_PortInformation	Configuration and performance information
Mouse	MSMouse_PortInformation	Configuration and performance information
Disk	MSDiskDriver_Geometry	Format information
	MSDiskDriver_Performance	Performance information
Storage	MSStorageDriver_FailurePredictStatus	Determine whether drive is predicting a failure
	MSStorageDriver_FailurePredictData	Failure prediction data
	MSStorageDriver_FailurePredictEvent	Event fired when failure is predicted
	MSStorageDriver_FailurePredictFunction	Methods related to failure prediction
Serial	MSSerial_PortName	Name of port
	MSSerial_CommInfo	Communication parameters
	MSSerial_HardwareConfiguration	I/O resource information
	MSSerial_PerformanceInformation	Performance information
	MSSerial_CommProperties	Communication parameters
Parallel	MSParallel_AllocFreeCounts	Counts of allocation and free operations
	MSParallel_DeviceBytesTransferred	Transfer counts

Table 10-3. *Standard data blocks.*

To implement your support for a standard data block, include the corresponding GUID in the list you report back from the registration query. Implement supporting code for getting and putting data, enabling and disabling events, and so on, using the techniques I've already discussed. Don't include definitions of the standard data blocks in your own schema; those class definitions are already in the repository, and you don't want to override them.

In many cases, by the way, a Microsoft class driver will be providing the actual WMI support for these standard classes—you might not have any work to do.

Standard Controls

Windows 2000 will someday employ WMI as a method of sending certain common commands to drivers. In particular, management applications will be able to send commands related to power management by means of WMI. At the present time, only two such commands are defined. See Table 10-4.

WMI Class (WMICORE.MOF)	*GUID Name (WDMGUID.H)*	*Purpose*
MSPower_DeviceEnable	GUID_POWER_DEVICE_ ENABLE	Should device dynamically power on and off while the system is working?
MSPower_DeviceWakeEnable	GUID_POWER_DEVICE_ WAKE_ENABLE	Should device arm its wake-up feature?

Table 10-4. *Standard WMI commands.*

If you refer to WMICORE.MOF, you'll see that the **DeviceEnable** and **DeviceWakeEnable** classes include only a Boolean member named **Enable** that a WMI client can either read or write. To support these two classes in your driver, include the two GUIDs in the list of GUIDs you pass to WMILIB and use code to get and set instances of this class. The code to handle these details is so similar to WMI42 that I won't show it to you here.

If you trace back through the beta releases of Windows 2000, it looks like Microsoft originally planned to implement another WMI class (probably with the name MSPower_DeviceTimeouts) that would query and set the two timeout values you use when you register with the Power Manager for idle detection. That plan appears to have fallen by the wayside. The GUID definition (GUID_POWER_DEVICE_ TIMEOUTS) still appears in WDMGUID.H, though.

USER-MODE APPLICATIONS AND WMI

User-mode support for WMI relies on the facilities of COM. To summarize a very complicated situation, the Windows Management Service acts as the clearinghouse for information flowing between consumers and providers by implementing several COM interfaces. Providers register their existence with Windows Management via certain interfaces. Consumers indirectly communicate with providers via interfaces.

All of these interfaces are documented in the Platform SDK, so I'm going to illustrate only the important method routines a consumer uses. I'll start, though, by explaining the basic mechanics of using COM for those readers who have little or no experience with COM.

Just Enough COM

As I said, this section is for readers who don't know the basics of using COM interfaces. I spent years deliberately avoiding COM because its unique terminology made me think it was too intricate to understand. I won't say that COM aficionados want it that way, but I will say that I was once roundly criticized for presenting the following simplified overview to a conference audience.

You'll encounter three crucial terms when you hear about COM. In COM, an *object* is a software entity that implements the *methods* belonging to an *interface*. (People in my generation will be imagining Bill Cosby saying, "R-i-g-h-t! What's an interface?" just about now.) The key element you deal with when acting as a COM client is a pointer to an interface, which you can dereference to invoke the method routines. You get an interface pointer either because someone gives it to you or because you call an API that returns it to you. From the perspective of a client program, some mysterious "them" takes care of creating and destroying objects.

What's an Interface?

Now let's go through these three concepts more slowly, starting with the last one. An interface is nothing more than a C++ class that has a bunch of virtual member functions but no data members and no nonvirtual member functions. You can implement or use a COM interface in many languages, not just C++. But because C++ gives us a common ground for understanding the concept, I'll forge ahead as if C++ were the only language you'd ever use. Here's the declaration of a simple interface as it might look before being translated into the language of COM:

```
class IUnknown
{
public:
  virtual long __stdcall QueryInterface(const GUID& riid,
    void** ppvObject);
  virtual unsigned long __stdcall AddRef();
  virtual unsigned long __stdcall Release();
};
```

Instances of **IUnknown** (objects in COM) implement three public, virtual functions (methods) named **QueryInterface**, **AddRef**, and **Release**. AddRef and Release are part of the mechanism by which COM makes sure that objects persist long enough for clients to make use of them. QueryInterface is how client programs obtain pointers to additional interfaces that an object supports.

In the Interface Definition Language (IDL) of COM, this interface description would look like this:

```
interface IUnknown
{
  HRESULT QueryInterface(REFIID riid, void** ppvObject);
  ULONG AddRef();
  ULONG Release();
};
```

Apart from the syntactic differences, I think it's obvious how the IDL description of this interface relates to a C++ class declaration. An IDL compiler can be used that translates an interface declaration like this into syntax understandable by C and C++ compilers. Some programming languages understand the IDL syntax without a translation, even.

Just like C++ classes, interfaces can be derived from other interfaces. In COM, one doesn't declare interfaces with more than one base class. In addition, every COM interface derives ultimately from IUnknown—meaning that every COM object supports the QueryInterface, AddRef, and Release methods. Here's an example from the WMI world that we'll be using later on:

```
interface IWbemLocator : IUnknown
{
  HRESULT ConnectServer(BSTR strNetworkResource,
    BSTR strUser, BSTR strPassword, BSTR strLocale,
    long lSecurityFlags, BSTR strAuthority,
    IWbemContext* pCtx, IWbemServices** ppNameSpace);
};
```

So, an object that implements **IWBemLocator** has *four* method routines: QueryInterface, AddRef, Release, and **ConnectServer**.

Creating and Destroying Objects

Getting an interface pointer that you can use to talk to an object is possible in many ways. Calling **CoCreateInstance** is a common way:

```
IWbemLocator* locator;
HRESULT hr = CoCreateInstance(CLSID_WbemLocator, NULL,
  CLSCTX_INPROC_SERVER, IID_IWbemLocator, (PVOID*) &locator);
```

CoCreateInstance consults the registry to locate a server that can instantiate a **CLSID_WbemLocator** class of object. CLSID_WbemLocator is a 128-bit GUID of the same kind I mentioned in Chapter 2 ("Basic Structure of a WDM Driver") in connection with registered device interfaces. It's called a *class identifier* because it identifies a kind, or class, of COM object. The HKEY_CLASSES_ROOT branch of the registry contains a key named **CLSID**, the subkeys of which are the ASCII representations of all the class identifiers that COM knows anything about. In the example we're considering, CLSID_WbemLocator would be conventionally represented as {4590f811-1d3a-11d0-891f-00aa004b2e24}, and the CLSID key includes a subkey named exactly that in the registry. A subkey named **InProcServer32** designates a DLL (named WBEMPROX.DLL, a part of the WMI core) as the server that implements this class of object.

Having located the class key in the registry, CoCreateInstance loads the designated server into your address space and uses magic we don't need to discuss here to instantiate a WbemLocator object and develop a pointer to the IWbemLocator interface that the object supports. (**IID_IWbemLocator** is another GUID declared in WBEMCLI.H, which you'll #include in your consumer project files.)

Following a successful call to CoCreateInstance, you'll have an interface pointer that you can use like any pointer to a C++ class to call the method functions associated with the interface. Somewhere in the world (maybe not even on the same computer) a concrete object exists that implements those method functions. The object occupies storage and the executable program whose instructions comprise the implementation also occupies storage. At some point in time, presumably, you'll be done using your interface pointer and will be prepared to destroy the object and, maybe, unload the program. The question is, when? That's where AddRef and Release come in.

Each COM object has a reference count. Whenever someone obtains a pointer to an interface on the object, the program that implements the object increments the reference count. So, CoCreateInstance will always return a referenced interface pointer, and you can be sure that the pointer will remain valid for the time being. You can increase the reference count on an object explicitly by calling AddRef. When you're done using an interface pointer, you call the Release method. The implementation of Release decrements the reference count. If the count drops to 0, the implementation deletes the object. When a server doesn't own any more objects, it can be unloaded.

Your job as a COM client is simply to release your reference to an interface when you no longer need the underlying object. The following stylized coding sequence is pretty typical:

```
IWbemLocator* locator;
HRESULT hr = CoCreateInstance(...);
if (SUCCEEDED(hr))
  {
  ...
  locator->Release();
  }
```

Accessing WMI Information

When you want to access WMI facilities in user mode, you need to first establish a connection to a particular namespace. Within the context of the namespace, you can then find instances of WMI classes. You can query and set the data blocks associated with class instances, invoke their method routines, and monitor the events that they generate.

Connecting to a Namespace

When you connect to a WMI namespace, you obtain a pointer to an **IWbemServices** interface that Windows Management implements. The following code—based on the TEST program in the WMI42 sample—shows how to do this:

1
```
HRESULT hr = CoInitializeEx(NULL, 0);
if (!SUCCEEDED(hr))
   return;
```
2
```
hr = CoInitializeSecurity(NULL, -1, NULL, NULL,
   RPC_C_AUTHN_LEVEL_NONE, RPC_C_IMP_LEVEL_IMPERSONATE,
   NULL, 0, 0);
if (!SUCCEEDED(hr))
   {
   CoUninitialize();
   return;
   }

IWbemLocator* locator;
```
3
```
hr = CoCreateInstance(CLSID_WbemLocator, NULL,
   CLSCTX_INPROC_SERVER, IID_IWbemLocator, (PVOID*) &locator);
if (SUCCEEDED(hr))
   {
   IWbemServices* services;
   BSTR pnamespace = SysAllocString(L"root\\CIMV2");
```
4
```
   hr = locator->ConnectServer(pnamespace, NULL, NULL, 0, 0
      &services);
   SysFreeString(pnamespace);
   if (SUCCEEDED(hr))
      {
```
5
```
      IClientSecurity* security;
      hr = services->QueryInterface(IID_IClientSecurity,
         (PVOID*) &security);
      if (SUCCEEDED(hr))
         {
```

(continued)

```
        security->SetBlanket(services, RPC_C_AUTHN_WINNT,
          RPC_C_AUTHZ_NONE, NULL, RPC_C_AUTHN_LEVEL_CONNECT,
          RPC_C_IMP_LEVEL_IMPERSONATE, NULL, EOAC_NONE);
        security->Release();
        }
    // use the services interface
    services->Release();
    }
  locator->Release();
  }
CoUninitialize();
```

1. Every program that uses COM calls CoInitialize or **CoInitializeEx** to initialize the COM library and calls **CoUninitialize** to close the COM library.

2. Never mind why you need to do this.

3. Here's where we instantiate a WbemLocator object and get a pointer to its **IWbemLocator** interface. If this call succeeds, we'll eventually release our reference to the interface.

4. We use the **IWbemLocator** interface to connect to the CIMV2 namespace. (In beta releases, this should be the WMI namespace.) One of the quirks of using the **ConnectServer** method is that you must make a copy of the Unicode name of the namespace by calling **SysAllocString**.

5. *Really* never mind! I spent a couple of days figuring out that a call to **IClientSecurity::SetBlanket** was needed here, because at the time I was writing this chapter the SDK documentation hadn't caught up to the implementation. (@#$!)

6. This is the point at which you can use the **IWbemServices** interface pointer to locate WMI class instances and access other WMI services.

Enumerating Class Instances

Using an IWbemServices interface, you can enumerate all the instances of a particular WMI class. WMI42's test program, for example, enumerates all the WMI42 class instances with the following code:

```
IEnumWbemClassObject* enumerator = NULL;
BSTR bs = SysAllocString(L"WMI42");
HRESULT hr = services->CreateInstanceEnum(bs,
  WBEM_FLAG_SHALLOW | WBEM_FLAG_RETURN_IMMEDIATELY |
  WBEM_FLAG_FORWARD_ONLY, NULL, &enumerator);
SysFreeString(bs);
if (SUCCEEDED(hr))
  {
```

```
while (TRUE)
  {
  ULONG junk;
  IWbemClassObject* cop = NULL;
  hr = Enumerator->Next(INFINITE, 1, &cop, &junk);
  if (hr == WBEM_S_FALSE)
    break;
  if (!SUCCEEDED(hr))
    break;
  // Use IWbemClassObject interface
  cop->Release();
  }
enumerator->Release();
}
```

1. **IWbemServices::CreateInstanceEnum** will create an enumerator for all instances of a named WMI class. This interface has two quirks that I discovered the hard way. First, the class name must be passed in a separately allocated BSTR. Also, you must initialize the target interface pointer to NULL even though it's supposedly only an output argument—a crash ensues if the pointer is invalid to start with.

2. The instance enumerator's **Next** method delivers pointers to successive instances of the class in the form of an **IWbemClassObject** interface pointer. The Next method returns WBEM_S_FALSE when there are no more instances of the class. Initializing the supposed output argument to NULL is required to avoid a crash with this interface, too.

Getting and Setting Item Values

The **IWbemClassObject** interface is the key that unlocks the WMI functionality of your driver. With a pointer to this interface, you can easily get or set the values of items in a data block:

```
IWbemClassObject* cop;
VARIANT answer;
BSTR propname = SysAllocString(L"TheAnswer");
cop->Get(propname, 0, &answer, NULL, NULL);
VariantClear(&answer);

answer.vt = VT_I4;
answer.lVal = 6 * 9; // should be done in base 13!
cop->Put(propname, 0, &answer, 0);
VariantClear(&answer);

SysFreeString(propname);
```

In these fragments, we use a system string to name the property (that is, the item within our schema) we want to get or put, and we use an OLE VARIANT structure (which can hold any type of data) as the data value. Calling the **Get** method on this interface results in our driver getting a QUERY_ALL_DATA or QUERY_SINGLE_INSTANCE. Calling the **Put** method results in a CHANGE_SINGLE_INSTANCE or CHANGE_SINGLE_ITEM. You can observe for yourself what happens by loading the WMI42 sample driver and invoking the test program a time or two. You shouldn't try to predict exactly which type of IRP will be used to support a Get or Put call because the WMI provider is free to package data requests to drivers in any convenient way.

Receiving Event Notifications

To receive notifications that WMI events have occurred, an application has to register interest in specific events. To register interest, you must formulate a query in the so-called WMI Query Language (WQL). WQL is a great deal like the Structured Query Language (SQL) one uses in the world of relational databases. For example, to sign up to receive WMIEXTRA_EVENT notifications, you could submit the following query:

```
IWbemServices* services;
BSTR query = SysAllocString(L"select * from WMIEXTRA_EVENT");
BSTR language = SysAllocString(L"WQL");
IEnumWbemClassObject* enumerator = NULL;
HRESULT hr = services->ExecNotificationQuery(language, query,
  WBEM_FLAG_FORWARD_ONLY | WBEM_FLAG_RETURN_IMMEDIATELY,
  NULL, &enumerator);
SysFreeString(language);
SysFreeString(query);
if (SUCCEEDED(hr))
  {
  ...
  enumerator->Release();
  }
```

The flag arguments to **ExecNotificationQuery** must be specified exactly as shown, by the way.

Once you have the enumeration interface, you can call its **Next** method to poll for events. For example:

```
IWbemClassObject* cop = NULL;
DWORD junk;
hr = enumerator->Next(1000, 1, &cop, &junk);
```

In this call, we specify that we will wait up to 1000 milliseconds to obtain one event. If an event is already pending or fires within this timeout period, Next will return us a (referenced) IWbemClassObject pointer. Recall from the previous discussion of how a driver fires an event that the event is represented by an instance of a WMI class. We can therefore call the object's Get method to interrogate properties of the event.

In a real-world application, you should use **ExecNotificationQueryAsync** instead of ExecNotificationQuery. The asynchronous form of the query allows you to provide an **IWbemObjectSink** interface that WMI can call when events occur. Please refer to the Platform SDK for additional information.

Calling Method Routines

Invoking a method routine requires just a few deceptively simple statements, as shown in the following excerpt from WMIEXTRA's test program:

```
IWbemServices* services; // ← developed as shown earlier
IWbemClassObject* result = NULL;
BSTR pmethod = SysAllocString(L"AnswerMethod");
BSTR objpath;              // ← more about this later
IWbemClassObject* inarg; // ← ditto

HRESULT hr = services->ExecMethod(objpath, pmethod, 0, NULL,
  inarg, &result, NULL);
...
result->Release();
SysFreeString(pmethod);
<more cleanup>
```

Calling **ExecMethod** invokes the method routine. You supply values for the input arguments in the **inarg** object. The result of the call appears as the **result** object.

Invoking a method in this way would be almost trivial if it weren't for two complicating factors. First, you have to come up with the full pathname (that is, the **objpath** argument to ExecMethod) to the object you want to address. And you must construct and initialize a WMI object to contain the input arguments (if any) for the method call. I found the first of these tasks to be a gigantic pain in the neck, as shown by the following snippet from WMIEXTRA's test program:

```
IWbemServices* services;  // ← someone gives me this
BSTR pclass = SysAllocString(L"wmiextra_method");
BSTR objpath = NULL;
HRESULT hr;

IEnumWbemClassObject* enumerator = NULL;
hr = services->CreateInstanceEnum(pclass, <etc.>);
if (SUCCEEDED(hr))
  {
  IWbemClassObject* instance = NULL;
  ULONG junk;
  hr = enumerator->Next(INFINITE, 1, &instance, &junk);
  if (SUCCEEDED(hr))
    {
```

(continued)

```
    VARIANT instname;
    BSTR propname = SysAllocString(L"InstanceName");
    hr = instance->Get(propname, 0, &instname, NULL, NULL);
    SysFreeString(propname);
    if (SUCCEEDED(hr))
      {
      WCHAR fullpath[256];
      WCHAR escapedname[256];
      <code to double backslashes in instname>
      swprintf(fullpath, L"%ws.InstanceName=\"%s\"",
        pclass, escapedname);
      objpath = SysAllocString(fullpath);
      VariantClear(&instname);
      }
    instance->Release();
    }
  enumerator->Release();
  }
```

Ugh. Especially the part (which I omitted here in the text) that goes through the instance name and changes each backslash to two backslashes. In my opinion, there should be a method on the IWbemClassObject interface that you can call to get the full pathname of an object. Such a method would prevent our needing to discover the algorithm that some other system component has used to construct the instance name. But, as I frequently find to be the case, no one asked me for my opinion.

The Platform SDK documentation describes how to build the input arguments (that is, the **inarg** argument to ExecMethod). Here's how I did it for WMIEXTRA:

```
IWbemClassObject* cop = NULL; // ← the class, not an instance
hr = services->GetObject(pclass, 0, NULL, &cop, NULL);
if (SUCCEEDED(hr))
  {
  IWbemClassObject* iop = NULL; // ← another class
  hr = cop->GetMethod(pmethod, 0, &iop, NULL);
  if (SUCCEEDED(hr))
    {
    IWbemClassObject* inarg = NULL; // ← an instance of iop
    hr = iop->SpawnInstance(0, &inarg);
    if (SUCCEEDED(hr))
      {
      BSTR argname = SysAllocString(L"TheAnswer");
      VARIANT argval;
      argval.vt = VT_I4;
      argval.lVal = 41;
      hr = inarg->Put(argname, 0, &argval, 0);
```

```
    SysFreeString(argname);

    <the actual call to ExecMethod>

    inarg->Release();
    }
  iop->Release();
  }
cop->Release();
}
```

This code uses the data dictionary to obtain a description of the input argument class (the **iop** variable). It then creates and initializes an instance of the input argument class (the **inarg** variable) for use as an argument to the method routine.

I didn't check, but I assume that MFC provides a streamlined way to do all of this.

WINDOWS 98 COMPATIBILITY NOTES

Since a well-crafted driver should support WMI, and since WMILIB isn't available in the original Windows 98, you might need to provide a virtual device driver (VxD) stub for the WMILIB functions so that your driver will load. Consult Appendix A, "Coping with Windows 98 Incompatibilities," for more information about writing a VxD stub. (The WDMSTUB VxD discussed in the appendix doesn't include the WMILIB functions, but the appendix describes how you might invent them.)

A number of bugs afflicted the WMI support in the original retail release of Windows 98. The updates to Windows 98 (Second Edition and Service Pack 1) fixed these bugs. (Or some of them, anyway. I have a laptop that runs Windows 2000 and WMI just fine, but WMI won't initialize under Windows 98 Second Edition on this computer.) Even so, the standard setup procedure doesn't install WMI by default. To install it yourself, open Add/Remove Programs in the Control Panel, select the Windows Setup tab, and request installation of Web-Based Enterprise Mgmt within the Internet Tools category.

Chapter 11

The Universal Serial Bus

End user convenience is the keynote of the universal serial bus (USB). The Plug and Play (PnP) concept has simplified the process of installing certain types of hardware on existing PCs. However, configuration issues continue to plague end users with respect to legacy devices such as serial and parallel ports, keyboards, and mice. The USB specification also identifies port availability as one of the factors limiting proliferation of low-speed to medium-speed peripherals, including modems, answering machines, scanners, and personal digital assistants. USB helps solve these problems by providing a uniform method of connecting a potentially large number of self-identifying low-to-medium-speed devices—that is, devices that require less than a 1.5-megabyte-per-second data rate and that can electronically identify themselves to system software—through a single PC port.

Although this book concerns software, some of the electrical and mechanical aspects of USB are important to software developers. From the end user's point of view, USB's main feature is the use by every device of an identical 4-conductor wire with a standardized plug that fits into a socket on the back of the PC or on a hub device plugged into the PC. Furthermore, you can attach or remove USB devices at will without explicitly opening or closing the applications that use them and without worrying about electrical damage.

This chapter covers two broad topics. In the first part of the chapter, I'll describe the programming architecture of USB. This architecture encompasses several ideas, including a hierarchical method for attaching devices to a computer, a generic scheme for power management, and a standard for self-identification that relies on a hierarchy of descriptors on board the hardware. The USB architecture also employs a scheme for subdividing fixed-duration *frames* into *packets* that convey data to and from devices. Finally, USB allows for four different ways of transporting data between the host computer and *endpoints* on devices. One method, named *isochronous,* permits a fixed amount of data to be moved without error correction every millisecond (ms). The other methods, named *control, bulk,* and *interrupt,* allow relatively small amounts of data (64 bytes or less) to be moved with error correction.

In the second part of this chapter, I'll describe the additional features of a Windows Driver Model driver for a USB device over and above the features you already know about. Rather than communicate directly with hardware by using hardware abstraction layer (HAL) function calls, a USB driver relies heavily on the bus driver (USBD.SYS). To send a request to its device, the driver creates a *USB request block* (URB), which it submits to the bus driver. Configuring a USB device, for example, requires the driver to submit several URBs for reading descriptors and sending commands. USBD.SYS in turn schedules requests onto the bus according to demand and available bandwidth.

The ultimate source for information about USB is the official specification, which was at revision level 1.1 when this book went to press. The specification and various other documents produced by the USB committee and its working groups were available on line at *http://www.usb.org/developers/*. Don Anderson's *Universal Serial Bus System Architecture* (Addison-Wesley, 1997) recapitulates much of the specification in useful form.

NOTE ON SAMPLE PROGRAMS

Anchor Chips, Incorporated (*http://www.anchorchips.com*), kindly provided me one of their EZ-USB development kits. The Anchor Chips USB chip set revolves around a modified 8051 microprocessor and additional core logic to perform some of the low-level protocol functions mandated by the USB specification. The development board also contains additional external memory, a UART and serial connector, a set of push buttons, and an LED readout to facilitate development and debugging of 8051 firmware using Anchor Chips' software framework. One of the key features of the Anchor Chips chip set is that you can download firmware over the USB connection easily. For a programmer like me with a phobia for hardware in general and EEPROM programming in particular, that feature is a godsend.

(continued)

---

continued

The USB sample drivers on the companion disc illustrate the simplest possible USB devices and stand alone as examples of how to perform various tasks. If you happen to have an Anchor Chips development kit, however, you can also try out these samples with real firmware. Each sample contains a WDM driver in a SYS subdirectory, a Microsoft Win32 test program in a TEST subdirectory, and a firmware program in an EZUSB directory. You can follow the directions in the HTM files included with each sample to build these components or to simply install the prebuilt versions that are on the disc.

A word of caution is in order here. Anchor Chips provides a reduced-function version of 8051 development tools authored by Keil Elektronik GmbH. You'll need an unlimited version of those tools (which you must license separately from Keil) to develop real firmware and even to build some of my samples. You might also need some perseverance to get past the rather dated interface offered by these 16-bit programming tools. But, by the time you read this, Keil will have introduced new, considerably improved 32-bit tools for the 8051 called uVision2.

PROGRAMMING ARCHITECTURE

The authors of the USB specification anticipated that programmers would need to understand how to write host and device software without necessarily needing or wanting to understand the electrical characteristics of the bus. Chapter 5, "USB Data Flow Model," and Chapter 9, "USB Device Framework," of the specification describe the features most useful to driver authors. In this section, I'll summarize those chapters.

Device Hierarchy

Figure 11-1 illustrates the topology of a simple USB setup. A host controller unit connects to the system bus like other I/O devices might. The operating system communicates with the host controller by means of I/O ports or memory registers, and it receives event notifications from the host controller through an ordinary interrupt signal. The host controller in turn connects to a tree of USB devices. One kind of device, called a *hub,* serves as a connection point for other devices. Hubs can be daisy-chained together to a maximum depth defined by the USB specification. Other kinds of devices, such as cameras, mice, keyboards, and so on, plug into hubs. For the sake of precision, USB uses the term *function* to describe a device that isn't a hub.

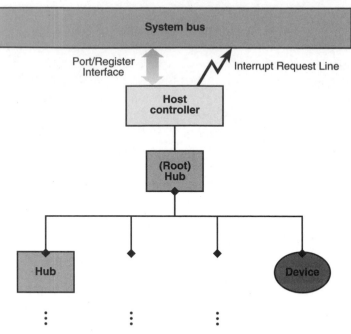

Figure 11-1. *Hierarchy of USB devices.*

High-Speed and Low-Speed Devices

The USB specification provides for high-speed and low-speed devices. A low-speed device communicates at 1.5 megabits per second, whereas a high-speed device communicates eight times faster, at 12 megabits per second. A hub can tell the difference between high-speed and low-speed devices by electrical means. Communication normally occurs on the bus at the high speed, and hubs normally don't send data to low-speed devices. The operating system prefaces any message destined for a low-speed device with a special *preamble* packet that causes the hubs to temporarily enable the low-speed devices.

Power

The USB cable carries power as well as data signals. Each hub can supply electrical power to the devices attached to it and, in the case of subsidiary hubs, to downstream devices as well. USB imposes limits on how much power a bus-powered device can consume. These limits vary depending on whether the device is plugged in to a powered hub, how far the device is from the nearest powered hub, and so on. In addition, USB allows devices to operate in a low-power state and consume very little power—just enough to support wake-up and configuration signalling. Instead of relying on bus power, you can build independently powered hubs and devices.

USB devices are able to wake up the system from a low-power state. When the system goes to low power, the operating system places the USB in the low-power state as well. A device possessing an enabled remote wake-up feature can later signal upstream to wake up upstream hubs, the USB host controller, and eventually the entire system.

USB device designers should be aware of some limitations on wake-up signalling. First, remote system wake-up works only on a computer with an Advanced Configuration and Power Interface (ACPI) enabled BIOS. Older systems support either Advanced Power Management (APM) or no power management standard at all. Another limitation has to do with driver notification. WDM provides a method—the IRP_MN_WAIT_WAKE flavor of a power I/O request packet (IRP)—to notify a driver when its device wakes up the system. No notification occurs, however, if a device comes out of its low-power state when the system is already in the working state.

What's in a Device?

In general, each USB device can have one or more *configurations* that govern how it behaves. See Figure 11-2. A common reason to use more than one configuration relates to operating system support. You might, for example, have a simple configuration that the system BIOS uses and a more complex configuration that your Windows driver uses.

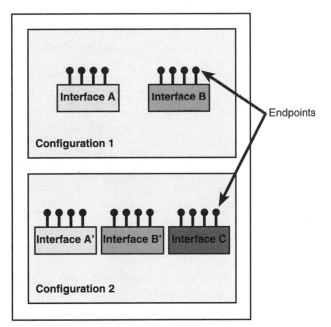

Figure 11-2. *Device configurations, interfaces, and endpoints.*

Each configuration of a device embodies one or more *interfaces* that prescribe how software should access the hardware. This concept of an interface is similar to the concept I discussed in Chapter 2 ("Basic Structure of a WDM Driver") in connection with naming devices. That is, devices that support the same interface are essentially interchangeable in terms of software because they respond to the same commands in the same specified way. Also, interfaces frequently have *alternate settings* that correspond to different bandwidth requirements.

A device interface exposes one or more *endpoints,* each of which serves as a terminus for a communications pipe. Figure 11-3 diagrams a layered communication model that illustrates the role of a pipe and an endpoint. At the lowest level, the USB wire connects the host bus controller to the bus interface on a device. At the second level, a *control pipe* connects system software to a logical device. At the third and highest level, a bundle of pipes connects client software with the collection of interfaces that constitutes the device's function. Information actually flows vertically up and down both sides of the diagram, but it's useful to think of the pipes as carrying information horizontally between the corresponding layers.

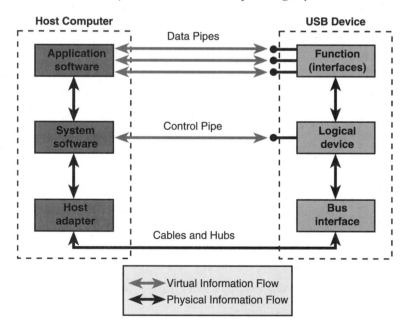

Figure 11-3. *Layered model for USB communication.*

A set of drivers provided by Microsoft occupies the lower edge of the system software box in the figure. These drivers include a host controller driver (OPENHCI.SYS or UHCD.SYS), a hub driver (USBHUB.SYS), and a class driver used by the controller driver (USBD.SYS). For convenience, I'll lump all of these drivers together under the name *USBD* because that's the component our drivers primarily interact with. Collectively, they manage the hardware connection and the mechanics of communicating over the various pipes. WDM drivers, such as the ones you and I might write, occupy the upper edge of the system software box. Broadly speaking, the job of a WDM driver is to translate requests from client software into transactions that USBD can carry out. Client software deals with the actual functionality of the device. For example, an image-rendering application might occupy the client software slot opposite a still-image function such as that of a digital camera.

Information Flow

USB defines four methods of transferring data, as summarized in Table 11-1. The methods differ in the amount of data that can be moved in a single transaction—see the next section for an explanation of the term *transaction*—in whether any particular periodicity or latency can be guaranteed, and in whether errors will be automatically corrected. Each method corresponds to a particular type of endpoint. In fact, endpoints of a given type (that is, control, bulk, interrupt, or isochronous) always communicate with the host by using the corresponding transfer type.

Transfer Type	Description	Lossless?	Size(s)	Latency Guarantee?
Control	Used to send and receive structured information of a control nature	Yes	≤ 8, 16, 32, or 64 bytes	Best effort
Bulk	Used to send or receive small blocks of unstructured data	Yes	≤ 8, 16, 32, or 64 bytes	No
Interrupt	Like a bulk pipe, but includes a maximum latency	Yes	≤ 64 bytes	Polled at guaranteed minimum rate
Isochronous	Used to send or receive large blocks of unstructured data with guaranteed periodicity	No	≤ 1023 bytes	Fixed portion of every 1-ms frame

Table 11-1. *Data transfer types.*

Endpoints have several attributes in addition to their type. One endpoint attribute is the maximum amount of data that the endpoint can provide or consume in a single transaction. Control and bulk endpoints must specify one of a few discrete values, whereas interrupt and isochronous endpoints can specify any value less than or equal to an overall maximum. In general, any single transfer can involve less than the maximum amount of data that the endpoint is capable of handling. Another attribute of an endpoint is its direction, described as either *input* (information moves from the device to the host) or *output* (information moves from the host to the device). Finally, each endpoint has a number that functions along with the input/output direction indicator as the address of the endpoint.

USB uses a *polling* protocol in which the host requests the device to carry out some function on a more or less regular basis. When a device needs to send data to the host, the host must somehow note this and issue a request to the device to send the data. In particular, USB devices don't interrupt the host computer in the traditional sense. In place of an asynchronous interrupt, USB provides interrupt endpoints that the host polls periodically.

Information Packaging

When a client program sends or receives data over a USB pipe, it first calls a Win32 API that ultimately causes the function driver (that's us) to receive an IRP. The driver's job is to direct the client request into a pipe ending at the appropriate endpoint on the device. It submits the requests to the bus driver, which breaks the requests into *transactions*. The bus driver schedules the transactions for presentation to the hardware. Information flows on the bus in *frames* that occur once every millisecond. The bus driver must correlate the duration of all outstanding transactions so as to fit them into frames. Figure 11-4 illustrates the result of this process.

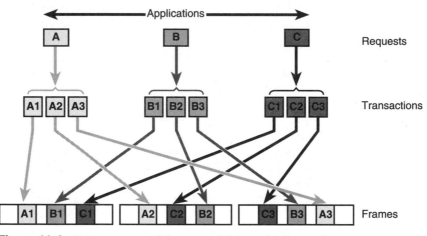

Figure 11-4. *Transaction and frame model for information flow.*

In USB, a transaction has one or more *phases*. A phase is a token, data, or handshake packet. Depending on the type, a transaction consists of a *token phase,* an optional *data phase,* and an optional *handshake phase,* as shown in Figure 11-5. During the token phase, the host transmits a packet of data to all currently config-ured devices. The token packet includes a device address and (often) an endpoint number. Only the addressed device will process the transaction; devices neither read nor write data on the bus for the duration of transactions addressed to other devices. During the data phase, data is placed on the bus. For output transactions, the host puts data on the bus and the addressed device consumes it. For input transactions, the roles are reversed and the device places data onto the bus for consumption by the host. During the handshake phase, either the device or the host places a packet onto the bus that provides status information. When a device provides the hand-shake packet, it can send an ACK packet to indicate successful receipt of information, a NAK packet to indicate that it's busy and didn't attempt to receive information, or a STALL packet to indicate that the transaction was correctly received but logically invalid in some way. When the host provides the handshake, it can send only an ACK packet.

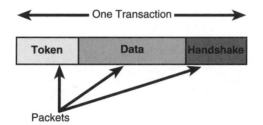

Figure 11-5. *Phases of a bus transaction.*

You'll notice that there's no handshake packet that means, "I found a transmission error in this transaction." Whoever is waiting for an acknowledgment is expected to realize that lack of acknowledgment implies an error and to retry the transaction. The USB designers believe that errors will be infrequent, by the way, which means that any occasional delay because of retries won't have a big effect on throughput.

MORE ABOUT DEVICE ADDRESSING

The previous text says that *all* configured devices receive the electrical signals associated with every transaction. This is almost true, but a true renaissance programmer should know two more details. When a USB device first comes on line, it responds to a default address (which happens to be numerically zero, but you don't need to know that). Certain electrical signalling occurs to alert the host bus driver that a new device has arrived on the scene, whereupon the bus driver assigns a device address and sends a control transaction to tell "device number zero" what its real address is. From then on, the device answers only to the real address.

(continued)

continued

The other detail concerns low-speed devices. The electronics of a low-speed device might misinterpret data arriving eight times faster than it expects. Furthermore, the cable connecting a low-speed device to the hub is not shielded and might generate undesirable electromagnetic interference if driven at high speed. Consequently, low-speed devices are not connected most of the time. That is, a hub keeps low-speed devices electrically isolated while high-speed transactions are occurring. When the host wants to communicate with a low-speed device, it sends a special *preamble packet* to switch the bus to low-speed operation for the duration of a single packet that begins shortly after the preamble. Thus, low-speed devices get an opportunity to see only low-speed transactions, but high-speed devices see all transactions.

States of an Endpoint

In general, an endpoint can be in any of the states illustrated in Figure 11-6. In the Idle state, the endpoint is ready to process a new transaction initiated by the host. In the Busy state, the endpoint is busy processing a transaction and can't handle a new one. If the host tries to initiate a transaction to a busy endpoint (other than a control endpoint, as described in the next section), the device will respond with a NAK handshake packet to cause the host to retry later. Errors that the device detects in its own functionality (not including transmission errors) cause the device to send a STALL handshake packet for its current transaction and to enter the Stalled state. Control endpoints automatically unstall when they get a new transaction, but the host must send a clear feature control request to any other kind of endpoint before addressing another request to a stalled endpoint.

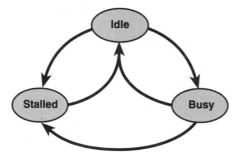

Figure 11-6. *States of an endpoint.*

Control Transfers

A *control transfer* conveys control information to or from a control endpoint on a device. For example, one part of the overall process by which the operating system configures a USB device is performing input control transfers to read various *descriptor* structures kept onboard the device. Another part of the configuration process involves an output control transfer to establish one of the many possible configurations as current and to enable one or more interfaces. Control transfers are lossless in that the bus driver retries erroneous transfers up to three times before giving up and reporting an error status to upstream software. As indicated in Table 11-1, control endpoints must specify a maximum data transfer length of 8, 16, 32, or 64 bytes. An individual transaction can involve less data than the indicated maximum but not more.

Control transactions are a high priority in USB. A device isn't allowed to claim business as an excuse to avoid handling a control transaction. Moreover, the bus driver reserves up to 10 percent of each frame time for control transactions. Assuming a light enough load, therefore, the host can be sure of completing a control transaction within one millisecond. A heavier load, however, might force a pending control transaction into a later frame, with the result that higher latencies are possible.

Every device has at least one control endpoint numbered 0 that responds to input and output control transactions. Strictly speaking, endpoints belong to configurations, but endpoint 0 is an exception in that it terminates the default control pipe for a device. Endpoint 0 is active even before the device receives its configuration and no matter what other endpoints (if any) are available. A device need not have additional control endpoints besides endpoint 0 (although the USB specification allows for the possibility) because endpoint 0 can service most control requests perfectly well. If you define a vendor-specific request that can't complete within the frame, however, you should create an additional control endpoint to forestall having your onboard handler preempted by a new transaction.

Each control transaction includes a SETUP token, which can be followed by an optional data phase in which additional data moves to or from the device and a handshake phase in which the device responds with an ACK packet, a STALL packet, or not at all. See Figure 11-7. Devices are required to accept control transfers at all times and can therefore not respond with NAK to indicate a busy endpoint. Sending an invalid request to a control endpoint elicits a STALL response, but the device automatically clears the stall condition when it receives the next SETUP packet. This special case of stalling is called *protocol stall* in the USB specification—see Section 8.5.2.4.

The SETUP token that prefaces a control transfer consists of eight data bytes, as illustrated in Figure 11-8. In this and other data layout figures, I'm showing data bytes in the order in which they're transmitted over the USB wire, but I'm showing bits within individual bytes starting with the high-order bit. Bits are transmitted over the wire starting with the least-significant bit, but host software and device firmware typically work with data after the bits have been reversed. Intel computers and the USB bus protocols employ the little-endian data representation in which the least-significant byte of a multibyte data item occupies the lowest address. The 8051 microprocessor used in several USB chip sets, including the Anchor Chips chip set, is actually a big-endian computer. Firmware must therefore take care to reverse data bytes appropriately.

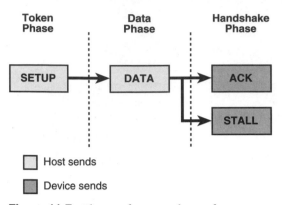

Host sends

Device sends

Figure 11-7. *Phases of a control transfer.*

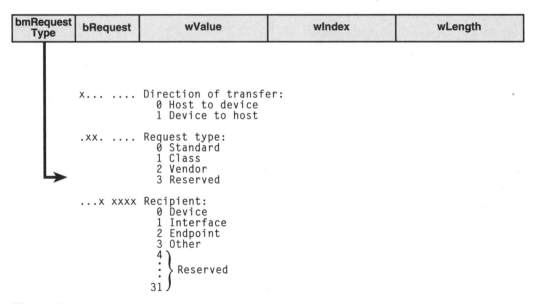

Figure 11-8. *Contents of a SETUP token.*

Notice in the figure that the first byte of a SETUP token indicates the direction of information flow, a request type, and the type of entity that is the target of the control transfer. The request types are *standard* (defined as part of the USB specification), *class* (defined by the USB working group responsible for a given class of device), and *vendor* (defined by the maker of the device). Control requests can be addressed to the device as a whole, to a specified interface, to a specified endpoint, or to some other vendor-specific entity on the device. The second byte of the SETUP token indicates which request of the type indicated in the first byte is being made. Table 11-2 lists the standard requests that are currently defined. For information about class-specific requests, consult the appropriate device class specification. (See the first URL I gave you at the beginning of this chapter for information on how to find these specifications.) Device manufacturers are free to define their own vendor-specific request codes. For example, Anchor Chips uses the request code A0h to download firmware from the host.

NOTE Note that control requests that affect the state of some particular endpoint are sent to a *control endpoint* and not to the endpoint whose state is affected.

Request Code	Symbolic Name	Description	Possible Recipients
0	GET_STATUS	Gets status information	Any
1	CLEAR_FEATURE	Clears a two-state feature	Any
2		(Reserved)	
3	SET_FEATURE	Sets a two-state feature	Any
4		(Reserved)	
5	SET_ADDRESS	Sets device address	Device
6	GET_DESCRIPTOR	Gets device, configuration, or string descriptor	Device
7	SET_DESCRIPTOR	Sets a descriptor (optional)	Device
8	GET_CONFIGURATION	Gets current configuration index	Device
9	SET_CONFIGURATION	Sets new current configuration	Device
10	GET_INTERFACE	Gets current alternate setting index	Interface
11	SET_INTERFACE	Enables alternate setting	Interface
12	SYNCH_FRAME	Reports synchronization frame number	(Isochronous) Endpoint

Table 11-2. *Standard device requests.*

The remainder of the SETUP packet contains a **value** code whose meaning depends on which request is being made, an **index** value with similarly mutable meaning, and a **length** field that indicates how many bytes of data are to be transferred during the data phase of the control transaction. The index field contains the endpoint or interface number when a control request addresses an endpoint or interface. A 0 value for the data length implies that this particular transaction has no data phase.

I'm not going to exhaustively describe all of the details of the various standard control requests; you should consult Section 9.4 of the USB specification for full information. I do want to briefly discuss the concept of a device *feature,* however. USB envisages that any of the addressable entities belonging to a device can have features that can be represented by the state of a single bit. Two such features are standardized for all devices.

The DEVICE_REMOTE_WAKEUP feature—a feature belonging to the device as a whole—indicates whether or not the device should use its ability (if any) to remotely wake up the computer when external events occur. Host software (specifically, the bus driver) enables or disables this feature by addressing a SET_FEATURE or CLEAR_FEATURE command, respectively, to the device and specifying a value code of 1 to designate the wake-up feature. The DDK uses the symbolic name USB_FEATURE_REMOTE_WAKEUP for this feature code.

The ENDPOINT_HALT feature—a feature belonging to an endpoint—indicates whether or not the endpoint is in the *functional stall* state. Host software can force an endpoint to stall by sending the endpoint a SET_FEATURE command with a value code of 0 to designate ENDPOINT_HALT. The firmware that manages the endpoint might independently decide to stall, too. Host software (once again, the bus driver) clears the stall condition by sending a CLEAR_FEATURE command with a value code of 0. The DDK uses the symbolic name USB_FEATURE_ENDPOINT_STALL for this feature code.

The USB specification does not prescribe ranges of device or endpoint feature codes for vendor use. To avoid possible standardization issues later, you should avoid defining device-level or endpoint-level features. Instead, define your own vendor-type control transactions. Notwithstanding this advice, later in this chapter I'll show you a sample driver (FEATURE) that controls the 7-segment LED display on the Anchor Chips development board. For purposes of that sample, I defined an interface-level feature numbered 42. (USB currently defines a few interface-level features for power management, so you would not want to emulate my example except for learning about how features work.)

Bulk Transfers

A *bulk transfer* conveys up to 64 bytes of data to or from a bulk endpoint. Like control transfers, bulk transfers are lossless. Unlike control transfers, bulk transfers don't have any particular guaranteed latency. If the host has room left over in a frame after accommodating other bandwidth reservations, it will schedule pending bulk transfers.

Figure 11-9 illustrates the phases that make up a bulk transfer. The transfer begins with either an IN or an OUT token that addresses the device and endpoint. In the case of an output transaction, a data phase follows in which data moves from the host to the device and then a handshake phase in which the device provides status feedback. If the endpoint is busy and unable to accept new data, it generates a NAK packet during the handshake phase—the host will retry the output transaction later.

If the endpoint is stalled, it generates a STALL packet during the handshake phase—the host must later clear the halt condition before retrying the transmission. If the endpoint receives and processes the data correctly, it generates an ACK packet in the handshake phase. The only remaining case is the one in which the endpoint doesn't correctly receive the data for some reason and simply doesn't generate a handshake—the host will detect the absence of any acknowledgment and automatically retry up to three times.

Following the IN token that introduces an input bulk transfer, the device performs one of two operations. If it can, it sends data to the host, whereupon the host either generates an ACK handshake packet to indicate error-free receipt of the data or stays mute to indicate some sort of error. If the host detects an error, the absence of an ACK to the device causes the data to remain available—the host will retry the input operation later on. If the endpoint is busy or halted, however, the device generates a NAK or STALL handshake instead of sending data. The NAK indicates that the host should retry the input operation later, and the STALL requires the host to eventually send a clear feature command to reset the halt condition.

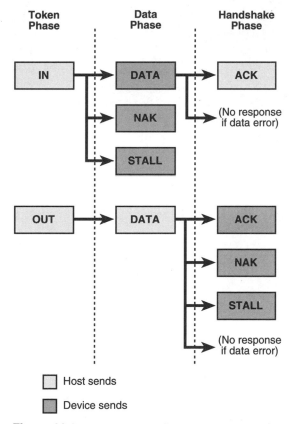

Figure 11-9. *Phases of a bulk or interrupt transfer.*

Interrupt Transfers

An *interrupt transfer* is practically identical to a bulk transfer insofar as the operation of the bus and the device are concerned. It moves up to 64 bytes of data losslessly to or from an interrupt endpoint. The only difference between interrupt and bulk transfers has to do with latency. An interrupt endpoint specifies a polling interval in the range 1–255 milliseconds. The host reserves sufficient bandwidth to make sure of performing an IN or OUT transaction directed toward the endpoint at least as frequently as the polling interval.

> **NOTE** Note that USB devices don't generate asynchronous interrupts: they always respond to a poll. You might need to know that the Microsoft host controller drivers effectively round the polling interval specified in an interrupt endpoint descriptor down to a power of 2 no greater than 32. For example, an endpoint that specifies a polling interval of 31 milliseconds will actually be polled every 16 milliseconds. A specified polling interval between 32 and 255 milliseconds results in an actual polling interval of 32 milliseconds.

Isochronous Transfers

An *isochronous transfer* moves up to 1023 data bytes to or from an isochronous endpoint during every bus frame. Because of the guaranteed periodicity of isochronous transfers, they are ideal for time-sensitive data such as audio signals. The guarantee of periodicity comes at a price, however: isochronous transfers that fail because of data corruption don't get retried automatically. The USB designers assumed that isochronous data streams can tolerate occasional small losses.

An isochronous transaction consists of an IN or OUT token followed by a data phase in which data moves to or from the host. No handshake phase occurs because no errors are retried. See Figure 11-10.

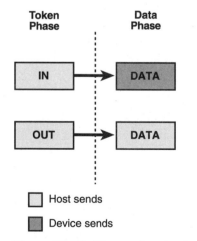

Figure 11-10. *Phases of an isochronous transfer.*

The host reserves up to 90 percent of the bus bandwidth for isochronous and interrupt transfers. In fact, system software needs to reserve bandwidth in advance to make sure that all active devices can be accommodated.

Descriptors

USB devices maintain onboard data structures known as *descriptors* to allow for self-identification to host software. Table 11-3 lists the different descriptor types. Each descriptor begins with a two-byte header containing the byte count of the entire descriptor (including the header) and a type code. As a matter of fact, if you ignore the special case of a string descriptor—concerning which, see "String Descriptors" a bit further on—the length of a descriptor is implied by its type because all descriptors of a given type have the same length. The explicit length is nonetheless present in the header to provide for future extensibility. Additional, type-specific data follows the fixed header.

In the remainder of this section, I'll describe the layout of each type of descriptor by using the data structures defined in the DDK (specifically, in USB100.H). The official rendition of this information is in Section 9.6 of the USB specification.

Descriptor Type	*Description*
Device	Describes an entire device
Configuration	Describes one of the configurations of a device
Interface	Describes one of the interfaces that's part of a configuration
Endpoint	Describes one of the endpoints belonging to an interface
String	Contains a human-readable Unicode string describing the device, a configuration, an interface, or an endpoint
Configuration power	Describes power-management capabilities of a device configuration
Interface power	Describes power-management capabilities of a device function

Table 11-3. *Descriptor types.*

Device Descriptors

Each device has a single device descriptor that identifies the device to host software. The host uses a GET_DESCRIPTOR control transaction directed to endpoint 0 to read this descriptor. The device descriptor has the following definition in the DDK:

```
typedef struct _USB_DEVICE_DESCRIPTOR {
  UCHAR bLength;
  UCHAR bDescriptorType;
  USHORT bcdUSB;
  UCHAR bDeviceClass;
  UCHAR bDeviceSubClass;
  UCHAR bDeviceProtocol;
  UCHAR bMaxPacketSize0;
  USHORT idVendor;
```

(continued)

```
    USHORT idProduct;
    USHORT bcdDevice;
    UCHAR iManufacturer;
    UCHAR iProduct;
    UCHAR iSerialNumber;
    UCHAR bNumConfigurations;
} USB_DEVICE_DESCRIPTOR, *PUSB_DEVICE_DESCRIPTOR;
```

The **bLength** field in a device descriptor will equal 18, and the **bDescriptor-Type** field will equal 1 to indicate that it's a device descriptor. The **bcdUSB** field contains a version code (in binary-coded decimal) indicating the version of the USB specification to which this descriptor conforms. Current devices use the value 0x0100 or 0x0110 here to indicate conformance with the 1.0 or 1.1 specifications, respectively.

The values **bDeviceClass**, **bDeviceSubClass**, and **bDeviceProtocol** identify the type of device. Possible device class codes are defined by the USB specification and at the time of this writing include the codes listed in Table 11-4. Individual device class working groups within the USB committee define subclass and protocol codes for each device class. For example, the audio class has subclass codes for control, streaming, and MIDI streaming interfaces. And the mass storage class defines protocol codes for various methods of using endpoints for data transfer.

You can specify a class for an entire device or at the interface level, but in practice the device class, subclass, and protocol codes are often in an interface descriptor rather than in the device descriptor. (The device descriptor contains 0 for these codes in such cases.) USB also provides an escape valve for unusual types of devices in the form of the device class code 255. A vendor can use this type code to designate a nonstandard device for which the subclass and protocol codes provide the vendor-specific description. For example, a device built around the Anchor Chips chip set comes on line with a device descriptor having class, subclass, and protocol codes all equal to 255 to indicate an Anchor Chips default device. That device is primarily capable of accepting a vendor-specific control request to download firmware that will change the personality of the device to something else having its own (new) set of descriptors.

The **bMaxPacketSize0** field of the device descriptor gives the maximum size of a data packet for a control transfer over endpoint 0. There isn't a separate endpoint descriptor for this endpoint (which every device has to implement), so this field is the only place where the number can be presented. Since this field is at offset 7 within the descriptor, the host can always read enough of the descriptor to retrieve this value even if endpoint 0 is capable only of the minimum size transfer (eight bytes). Once the host knows how big endpoint 0 transfers can be, it can structure subsequent requests appropriately.

The **idVendor** and **idProduct** fields specify a vendor code and a vendor-specific product identifier for the device. **bcdDevice** specifies a release number (such as 0x0100 for version 1.0) for the device. These three fields determine which driver the host software will load when it detects the device. The USB organization assigns vendor codes, and each vendor assigns its own product codes.

Symbolic Name	Class Code	Description
USB_DEVICE_CLASS_RESERVED	0	Indicates that class codes are in the interface descriptors
USB_DEVICE_CLASS_AUDIO	1	Devices used to manipulate analog or digital audio, voice, and other sound-related data (but not including transport mechanisms)
USB_DEVICE_CLASS_COMMUNICATIONS	2	Telecommunications devices such as modems, telephones, answering machines, and so on
USB_DEVICE_CLASS_HUMAN_INTERFACE	3	Human interface devices such as keyboards, mice, and so on
USB_DEVICE_CLASS_MONITOR	4	Display monitors
USB_DEVICE_CLASS_PHYSICAL_INTERFACE	5	HID devices involving real-time physical feedback, such as force-feedback joysticks
USB_DEVICE_CLASS_POWER	6	HID devices that perform power management, such as batteries, chargers, and so on
USB_DEVICE_CLASS_PRINTER	7	Printers
USB_DEVICE_CLASS_STORAGE	8	Mass storage devices, such as disk and CD-ROM
USB_DEVICE_CLASS_HUB	9	USB hubs
USB_DEVICE_CLASS_VENDOR_SPECIFIC	255	Vendor-defined device class

Table 11-4. *USB device class codes.*

DEVICE VERSION NUMBERING

Microsoft strongly encourages vendors to increment the device version number for each revision of hardware or firmware to facilitate downstream software updates. Often, a vendor releases a new version of hardware along with a revised driver. Also, hardware updates sometimes invalidate software patches or filter drivers that were present so as to address earlier hardware bugs. An automatic update mechanism might therefore have trouble updating a system if it can't determine which revision of the hardware it's working with.

The **iManufacturer**, **iProduct**, and **iSerialNumber** fields identify string descriptors that provide a human-readable description of the manufacturer, the product, and the unit serial number. These strings are optional, and a 0 value in one of these fields indicates the absence of the descriptor. If you put a serial number on a device, Microsoft recommends that you make it unique for each physical device.

Lastly, the **bNumConfigurations** field indicates how many configurations the device is capable of. Microsoft drivers work only with the first configuration (number 1, that is) of a device. I'll explain later, in "Configuration," what you might do for a device that has multiple configurations.

Configuration Descriptors

Each device has one or more configuration descriptors that describe the various configurations of which the device is capable. System software reads a configuration descriptor by performing a GET_DESCRIPTOR control transaction addressed to endpoint 0. The DDK defines the configuration descriptor structure as follows:

```
typedef struct _USB_CONFIGURATION_DESCRIPTOR {
  UCHAR bLength;
  UCHAR bDescriptorType;
  USHORT wTotalLength;
  UCHAR bNumInterfaces;
  UCHAR bConfigurationValue;
  UCHAR iConfiguration;
  UCHAR bmAttributes;
  UCHAR MaxPower;
} USB_CONFIGURATION_DESCRIPTOR, *PUSB_CONFIGURATION_DESCRIPTOR;
```

The **bLength** and **bDescriptorType** fields will be 9 and 2, respectively, to indicate a configuration descriptor nine bytes in length. The **wTotalLength** field contains the total length of this configuration descriptor plus the interface and endpoint descriptors that are part of the configuration. In general, the host performs one GET_DESCRIPTOR request to retrieve the nine-byte configuration descriptor proper and then *another* GET_DESCRIPTOR request specifying this total length. The second request, therefore, transfers the *grand unified* descriptor. (It's impossible to retrieve interface and endpoint descriptors except as part of a configuration descriptor.)

The **bNumInterfaces** field indicates how many interfaces are part of the configuration. The count includes just the interfaces themselves, not each alternate setting of an interface. The purpose of this field is to allow for multifunction devices such as keyboards that have embedded locator (mouse and the like) functionality.

The **bConfigurationValue** field is an index that identifies the configuration. You use this value in a SET_CONFIGURATION control request to select the configuration. The first configuration descriptor for a device has a 1 here. (Selecting configuration 0 puts the device in an unconfigured state in which only endpoint 0 is active.)

The **iConfiguration** field is an optional string descriptor index pointing to a Unicode description of the configuration. Zero indicates the absence of a string description.

The **bmAttributes** byte contains a bit mask describing power and perhaps other characteristics of this configuration. See Table 11-5. The unmentioned bits are reserved for future standardization. A configuration supporting remote wake-up would have the remote wake-up attribute set. The high-order two bits interact with the **MaxPower** field of the configuration descriptor to describe the power characteristics of the configuration. Basically, every configuration sets the high-order bit (which used to mean the device was powered from the bus) and also sets MaxPower to the maximum number of two milliamp power units that it will draw from the bus. A configuration that uses some local power will also set the self-powered attribute bit.

Bit mask	Symbolic Name	Description
80h	USB_CONFIG_BUS_POWERED	Obsolete—should always be set to 1
40h	USB_CONFIG_SELF_POWERED	Configuration is self-powered
20h	USB_CONFIG_REMOTE_WAKEUP	Configuration has a remote wake-up feature

Table 11-5. *Configuration attribute bits.*

Interface Descriptors

Each configuration has one or more interface descriptors that describe the interface(s) that provide device functionality. System software can fetch an interface descriptor only as part of a GET_DESCRIPTOR control request that retrieves the entire configuration descriptor of which the interface descriptor is a part. The DDK defines the interface descriptor structure as follows:

```
typedef struct _USB_INTERFACE_DESCRIPTOR {
  UCHAR bLength;
  UCHAR bDescriptorType;
  UCHAR bInterfaceNumber;
  UCHAR bAlternateSetting;
  UCHAR bNumEndpoints;
  UCHAR bInterfaceClass;
  UCHAR bInterfaceSubClass;
  UCHAR bInterfaceProtocol;
  UCHAR iInterface;
} USB_INTERFACE_DESCRIPTOR, *PUSB_INTERFACE_DESCRIPTOR;
```

The **bLength** and **bDescriptorType** fields will be 9 and 4, respectively, to indicate an interface descriptor nine bytes in length. **bInterfaceNumber** and

bAlternateSetting are index values that can be used in a SET_INTERFACE control transaction to specify activation of the interface. These numbers are essentially arbitrary, but it's customary to number the interfaces within a configuration starting with zero and to number the alternate settings of each interface starting with zero, too.

The **bNumEndpoints** field indicates how many endpoints—other than 0, which is assumed to always be present—are part of the interface.

The **bInterfaceClass**, **bInterfaceSubClass**, and **bInterfaceProtocol** fields describe the functionality provided by the interface. A nonzero class code should be one of the device class codes I discussed earlier, in which case the subclass and protocol codes would have the same meaning as well. Zero values in these fields are not allowed at the present time—zero is reserved for future standardization.

Finally, **iInterface** is the index of a string descriptor containing a Unicode description of the interface. Zero indicates that no string is present.

Endpoint Descriptors

Each interface has zero or more endpoint descriptors that describe the endpoint(s) that handle transactions with the host. System software can fetch an endpoint descriptor only as part of a GET_DESCRIPTOR control request that retrieves the entire configuration descriptor of which the endpoint descriptor is a part. The DDK defines the endpoint descriptor structure as follows:

```
typedef struct _USB_ENDPOINT_DESCRIPTOR {
  UCHAR bLength;
  UCHAR bDescriptorType;
  UCHAR bEndpointAddress;
  UCHAR bmAttributes;
  USHORT wMaxPacketSize;
  UCHAR bInterval;
} USB_ENDPOINT_DESCRIPTOR, *PUSB_ENDPOINT_DESCRIPTOR;
```

The **bLength** and **bDescriptorType** fields will be 7 and 5, respectively, to indicate an endpoint descriptor of length seven bytes. **bEndpointAddress** encodes the directionality and number of the endpoint, as illustrated in Figure 11-11. For example, an address value of 0x82 denotes an IN endpoint numbered 2, and an address of 0x02 denotes an OUT endpoint that's also numbered 2. Except for endpoint 0, you can have two different endpoints that share the same number but perform transfers in the opposite direction.

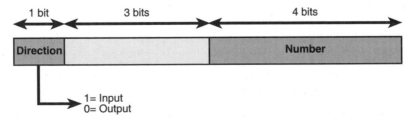

Figure 11-11. *Bit assignments within an endpoint descriptor's address field.*

The low-order two bits of **bmAttributes** indicate the type of the endpoint. See Table 11-6. The remaining bits are reserved for future standardization and should currently be set to 0.

Symbolic Name	Value	Endpoint Type
USB_ENDPOINT_TYPE_CONTROL	0	Control endpoint
USB_ENDPOINT_TYPE_ISOCHRONOUS	1	Isochronous endpoint
USB_ENDPOINT_TYPE_BULK	2	Bulk transfer endpoint
USB_ENDPOINT_TYPE_INTERRUPT	3	Interrupt endpoint

Table 11-6. *Type codes for endpoints.*

The **wMaxPacketSize** value indicates the largest amount of data the endpoint can transfer during one transaction. Table 11-1 (on page 493) lists the possible values for this field for each type of endpoint. (Even though Table 11-1 explicitly concerns transfer types, note that endpoint types map one to one with transfer types.) For example, a control or bulk endpoint would specify one of the values 8, 16, 32, or 64. An interrupt endpoint would specify a value in the range 0–64, inclusive. An isochronous endpoint would specify a number less than 1024.

Interrupt and isochronous endpoint descriptors also specify a polling interval measure in milliseconds in the **bInterval** field. This number indicates how often the host should poll the endpoint for a possible data transfer. For an interrupt endpoint, it can range from 1 to 255 and represents the maximum period between polls. An isochronous endpoint should specify 1 because it's polled during every frame—once per millisecond, in other words.

String Descriptors

A device, configuration, or endpoint descriptor contains optional string indices that identify human-readable strings. The strings themselves are stored on the device in Unicode in the form of USB string descriptors. System software can read a string descriptor by addressing a GET_DESCRIPTOR control request to endpoint 0. The DDK declares the string descriptor structure as follows:

```
typedef struct _USB_STRING_DESCRIPTOR {
  UCHAR bLength;
  UCHAR bDescriptorType;
  WCHAR bString[1];
} USB_STRING_DESCRIPTOR, *PUSB_STRING_DESCRIPTOR;
```

The **bLength** value is variable, depending on how long the string data is. The **bDescriptorType** field will be 3 to indicate that this is a string descriptor. The **bString** data contains the string data itself. Any null terminator would be included in the descriptor length.

USB devices can support strings in multiple languages. String number 0 is an array of supported language identifiers rather than a character string. (A string index of 0 used in another descriptor denotes the absence of a string reference. Thus, index number 0 is available for this special use.) The language identifiers are of the same LANGID type that Win32 programs use. For example, 0x0409 is the code for American English. The USB specification doesn't prescribe what happens if you ask a device to return a string descriptor for a language that the device doesn't advertise supporting, so you should read the string-zero array before issuing requests for string descriptors. Consult Section 9.6.5 of the USB specification for more information about language identifiers.

Other Descriptors

USB is an evolving specification, and I can present only a snapshot of its evolution at the time of writing. A USB working group recently finalized a specification for interface-level power management, for example. You can read about it at the USB Web site, and the DDK header file USB100.H contains definitions for it. Time doesn't permit us (me and the publisher, that is) to explore the ramifications of this new facility. Luckily, it would appear that WDM driver writers don't need to know about them—interpreting Interface Feature descriptors is the province of the hub driver rather than a WDM function or filter driver.

WORKING WITH THE BUS DRIVER

In contrast to drivers for devices that attach to traditional PC buses such as PCI (Peripheral Component Interconnect), a USB device driver never talks directly to its hardware. Instead, it creates an instance of the data structure known as the USB request block that it then submits to the bus driver.

Think of USBD.SYS as the entity to which you submit URBs. The call to USBD takes the form of an IRP with the major function code IRP_MJ_INTERNAL_ DEVICE_CONTROL. USBD in turn schedules bus time in some frame or another to carry out the operation encoded in the URB.

In this section, I'll describe the mechanics of working with USBD to carry out the typical operations a USB function driver performs. I'll first describe how to build and submit a URB. Then I'll discuss the mechanics of configuring and reconfiguring your device. Finally, I'll outline how your driver can manage each of the four types of communication pipes.

Initiating Requests

To create a URB, you allocate memory for the URB structure and invoke an initialization routine to fill in the appropriate fields for the type of request you're about to send. Suppose, for example, that you were beginning to configure your device in response to an IRP_MN_START_DEVICE request. One of your first tasks might be to read the device descriptor. You might use the following snippet of code to accomplish this task:

```
USB_DEVICE_DESCRIPTOR dd;
URB urb;
UsbBuildGetDescriptorRequest(&urb,
  sizeof(_URB_CONTROL_DESCRIPTOR_REQUEST),
  USB_DEVICE_DESCRIPTOR_TYPE, 0, 0, &dd, NULL,
  sizeof(dd), NULL);
```

We first declare a local variable (named **urb**) to hold a **URB** data structure. The URB is declared (in USBDI.H) as a union of several substructures, one for each of the requests you might want to make of a USB device. We're going to be using the **UrbControlDescriptorRequest** substructure of the URB union, which is declared as an instance of **struct _URB_CONTROL_DESCRIPTOR_REQUEST**. Using an automatic variable like this is fine if you know the stack has enough room to hold the largest possible URB and if you'll await completion of the URB before allowing the variable to pass out of scope.

You can, of course, dynamically allocate the memory for a URB from the heap if you want:

```
PURB urb = (PURB) ExAllocatePool(NonPagedPool,
  sizeof(_URB_CONTROL_DESCRIPTOR_REQUEST));
if (!urb)
  return STATUS_INSUFFICIENT_RESOURCES;
UsbBuildGetDescriptorRequest(urb, ...);
...
ExFreePool(urb);
```

UsbBuildGetDescriptorRequest is documented like a normal service routine, but it's actually a macro (declared in USBDLIB.H) that generates inline statements to initialize the fields of the get descriptor request substructure. The DDK headers define one of these macros for most types of URBs you might want to build. See Table 11-7. As is true of preprocessor macros in general, you should avoid using expressions that have side effects in the arguments to this macro.

Helper Macro	Type of Transaction
UsbBuildInterruptOrBulkTransferRequest	Input or output to an interrupt or bulk endpoint
UsbBuildGetDescriptorRequest	GET_DESCRIPTOR control request for endpoint 0
UsbBuildGetStatusRequest	GET_STATUS request for a device, an interface, or an endpoint

Table 11-7. *Helper macros for building URBs.* *(continued)*

continued

Helper Macro	Type of Transaction
UsbBuildFeatureRequest	SET_FEATURE or CLEAR_FEATURE request for a device, an interface, or an endpoint
UsbBuildSelectConfigurationRequest	SET_CONFIGURATION
UsbBuildSelectInterfaceRequest	SET_INTERFACE
UsbBuildVendorRequest	Any vendor-defined control request

In the previous code fragment, we specify that we want to retrieve the device descriptor information into a local variable (**dd**) whose address and length we supply. URBs that involve data transfer allow you to specify a nonpaged data buffer in either of two ways. You can specify the virtual address and length of the buffer, as I did in the fragment. Alternatively, you can supply a memory descriptor list (MDL) for which you've already done the probe-and-lock step by calling **MmProbeAndLockPages**.

MORE ABOUT URBs

Internally, the bus driver always uses an MDL to describe data buffers. If you specify a buffer address, USBD creates the MDL itself. If you happen to already have an MDL, it would be counterproductive to call **MmGetSystemAddressForMdl** and pass the resulting virtual address to USBD: USBD will turn around and create *another* MDL to describe the same buffer!

The URB also has a chaining field named **Urblink** that USBD uses internally to submit a series of URBs all at once to the host controller driver. The various macro functions for initializing URBs also have an argument in which you could theoretically supply a value for this linking field. You and I should *always* supply NULL because the concept of linked URBs hasn't been fully implemented—trying to link data transfer URBs will lead to system crashes, in fact.

Sending a URB

Having created a URB, you need to create and send an internal I/O control (IOCTL) request to the USBD driver, which is sitting somewhere lower in the driver hierarchy for your device. In many cases, you'll want to wait for the device's answer and you'll use a helper routine like this one:

```
NTSTATUS SendAwaitUrb(PDEVICE_OBJECT fdo, PURB urb)
  {
  PDEVICE_EXTENSION pdx = (PDEVICE_EXTENSION) fdo->DeviceExtension;
```

```
KEVENT event;
KeInitializeEvent(&event, NotificationEvent, FALSE);
IO_STATUS_BLOCK iostatus;
PIRP Irp = IoBuildDeviceIoControlRequest
  (IOCTL_INTERNAL_USB_SUBMIT_URB, pdx->LowerDeviceObject,
  NULL, 0, NULL, 0, TRUE, &event, &iostatus);
PIO_STACK_LOCATION stack = IoGetNextIrpStackLocation(Irp);
stack->Parameters.Others.Argument1 = (PVOID) urb;
NTSTATUS status = IoCallDriver(pdx->LowerDeviceObject, Irp);
if (status  == STATUS_PENDING)
  {
  KeWaitForSingleObject(&event, Executive, KernelMode, FALSE, NULL);
  status = iostatus.Status;
  }
return status;
}
```

1. We're going to wait for the URB to complete, so we need to create a kernel event object on which to wait. This technique is very similar to the one I used in the **ForwardAndWait** helper routine in Chapter 6, "Plug and Play."

2. The easiest way to build the internal IOCTL IRP we need is to call **IoBuild-DeviceIoControlRequest**, which does it for us. The first argument (**IOCTL_INTERNAL_USB_SUBMIT_URB**) specifies the I/O control code of the control request and indicates to USBD that we're submitting a URB. The second argument (**pdx->LowerDeviceObject**) specifies the device object that will initially receive the request; IoBuildDeviceIoControlRequest uses this pointer to decide how many stack locations to reserve when it builds the IRP. The next four parameters, which are NULL or 0 in this example, describe input and output buffers that we don't need when we're submitting a URB. The seventh parameter is TRUE to indicate that we're creating an IRP_MJ_INTERNAL_DEVICE_CONTROL request instead of an IRP_MJ_DEVICE_CONTROL request. The last two parameters designate the event on which we'll await completion of the URB and an IO_STATUS_BLOCK that will receive the ending status from the operation.

3. The address of the URB we're submitting goes in the **Argument1** field of the **Parameters.Others** substructure within the top stack location. This field occupies the same offset in the stack location as the **OutputBuffer-Length** parameter for a normal IOCTL request.

4. We send the request to the next driver in the usual way—by calling **IoCall-Driver**. USBD will now process the request to completion, whereupon the I/O Manager will delete the IRP and signal our event. Since we haven't provided our own completion routine, we can't be certain that the I/O Manager will signal our event in all possible completion cases. Hence, we wait for the event only if the return value from the lower level dispatch outine is STATUS_PENDING.

> **NOTE** It bears emphasizing that drivers package URBs into normal IRPs with the major function code IRP_MJ_INTERNAL_DEVICE_CONTROL. To provide for an upper filter driver to send its own URBs, every driver for a USB device should have a dispatch function that passes this IRP down to the next layer.

Status Returns from URBs

When you submit a URB to the USB bus driver, you eventually receive back an NTSTATUS code that describes the result of the operation. Internally, the bus driver uses another set of status codes with the typedef name USBD_STATUS. These codes are not NTSTATUS codes.

When USBD completes a URB, it sets the URB's **UrbHeader.Status** field to one of these USBD_STATUS values. You can examine this value in your driver to glean more information about how your URB fared. The **URB_STATUS** macro in the DDK simplifies accessing:

```
NTSTATUS status = SendAwaitUrb(fdo, &urb);
USBD_STATUS ustatus = URB_STATUS(&urb);
...
```

There's no particular protocol for preserving this status and passing it back to an application, however. You're pretty much free to do what you will with it.

Configuration

The USB bus driver automatically detects attachment of a new USB device. It then reads the device descriptor structure to determine what sort of device has suddenly appeared. The vendor and product identifier fields of the descriptor, together with other descriptors, determine which driver needs to be loaded.

The Configuration Manager calls the driver's **AddDevice** function in the normal way. AddDevice does all the tasks you've already heard about: it creates a device object, links the device object into the driver hierarchy, and so on. The Configuration Manager eventually sends the driver an IRP_MN_START_DEVICE Plug and Play request. Back in Chapter 6, I showed you how to handle that request by calling a helper function named **StartDevice** with arguments describing the translated and untranslated resource assignments for the device. One piece of good news is that you needn't worry about I/O resources at all in a USB driver, because you have none. So you could write a StartDevice helper function with the following skeletal form:

```
NTSTATUS StartDevice(PDEVICE_OBJECT fdo)
  {
  PDEVICE_EXTENSION pdx = (PDEVICE_EXTENSION) fdo->DeviceExtension;
  <configure device>
  return STATUS_SUCCESS;
  }
```

I glibly said *configure device* where you'll write rather a lot of code to configure the hardware. But, as I said, you needn't concern yourself with I/O ports, interrupts, direct memory access (DMA) adapter objects, or any of the other resource-oriented elements I described in Chapter 7.

WHERE'S THE DRIVER?

I'll discuss the mechanics of installing WDM drivers in Chapter 12, "Installing Device Drivers." It will help to understand some of those details right now, however. Let's suppose that your device has a vendor ID of 0x0547 and a product ID of 0x102A. I've borrowed the vendor ID belonging to Anchor Chips (with their permission) for purposes of this illustration. I'm using the product ID for the USB42 sample (the Answer Device) that you'll find on the companion disc.

USB describes many methods for the operating system to locate a device driver (or set of drivers) based on the device, configuration, and interface descriptors on a device. See *Universal Serial Bus Common Class Specification* (Rev. 1.0, December 16, 1997), Section 3.10. My samples all rely on the second highest priority method, whereby the vendor and product identifiers alone determine the driver.

Confronted with a device having the vendor and product identifiers I just mentioned, the Configuration Manager will look for a registry entry that contains information about a device named **USB\VID_0547&PID_102A**. If no such entry exists in the registry, the Configuration Manager will trigger the new hardware wizard to locate an INF file describing such a device. The wizard might prompt the end user for a disk, or it might find the INF file already present on the computer. The wizard will then install the driver and populate the registry. Once the Configuration Manager locates the registry entries, it can dynamically load the driver. That's where we come in.

The executive overview of what you need to accomplish in StartDevice is as follows. First you'll select a configuration for the device. If your device is like most devices, it has just one configuration. Refer to the sidebar "Multifunction Devices" for advice about what to do if your device has more than one configuration. Once you select the configuration, you choose one or more of the interfaces that are part of that configuration. It's not uncommon for a device to support multiple interfaces, by the way. Having chosen a configuration and a set of interfaces, you send a select configuration URB to the bus driver. The bus driver in turn issues commands to the device to enable the configuration and interfaces. The bus driver creates *pipes* that allow you to communicate with the endpoints in the selected interfaces and provides handles by which you can access the pipes. It also creates handles for the configuration and the interfaces. You extract the handles from the completed URB and save them for future use. That accomplished, you're done with the configuration process.

MULTIFUNCTION DEVICES

If your device has one configuration and multiple interfaces, the Microsoft bus driver will handle it automatically as a *composite,* or multifunction, device. You supply function drivers for each of the interfaces on the device by using INF files that specify the interface class and subclass instead of a vendor and product ID. The bus driver creates a physical device object (PDO) for each interface, whereupon the PnP Manager loads the separate function drivers you've provided. When one of these function drivers reads a configuration descriptor, the bus driver provides an edited version of the descriptor that describes just one interface.

If your device has more than one configuration, however, the bus driver doesn't perform the magic that allows you to just furnish separate function drivers. Your driver needs to decide which configuration to select and needs to manage all of the interfaces in the configuration you choose. You will also need to deal with all of the interfaces on your device if your INF file uses the vendor and product ID method for specifying a device identifier.

Refer to Chapter 12 for more information about the possible forms of device identifier in an INF file.

Reading a Configuration Descriptor

It's best to think of a fixed-size configuration descriptor as the header for a variable-length structure that describes a configuration, all its interfaces, and all the interfaces' endpoints. See Figure 11-12.

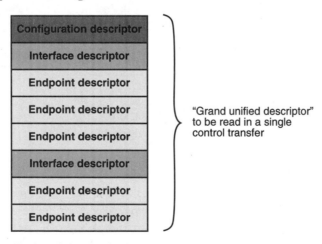

Figure 11-12. *Structure of a configuration descriptor.*

You must read the entire variable-length structure into a contiguous area of memory because the hardware won't allow you to directly access the interface and endpoint descriptors. Unfortunately, you don't initially know how long the combined structure is. The following fragment of code shows how you can use two URBs to read a configuration descriptor:

```
ULONG iconfig = 1;
URB urb;
USB_CONFIGURATION_DESCRIPTOR tcd;
UsbBuildGetDescriptorRequest(&urb,
  sizeof(_URB_CONTROL_DESCRIPTOR_REQUEST),
  USB_CONFIGURATION_DESCRIPTOR_TYPE,
  iconfig, 0, &tcd, NULL, sizeof(tcd), NULL);
SendAwaitUrb(fdo, &urb);
ULONG size = tcd.wTotalLength;
PUSB_CONFIGURATION_DESCRIPTOR pcd =
  (PUSB_CONFIGURATION_DESCRIPTOR) ExAllocatePool(
  NonPagedPool, size);
UsbBuildGetDescriptorRequest(&urb,
  sizeof(_URB_CONTROL_DESCRIPTOR_REQUEST),
  USB_CONFIGURATION_DESCRIPTOR_TYPE,
  iconfig, 0, pcd, NULL, size, NULL);
SendAwaitUrb(fdo, &urb);
...
ExFreePool(pcd);
```

In this fragment, we issue one URB to read a configuration descriptor—I specified configuration number 1, which is the first one—into a temporary descriptor area named **tcd**. This descriptor contains the length (**wTotalLength**) of the combined structure that includes configuration, interface, and endpoint descriptors. We allocate that much memory and issue a second URB to read the entire descriptor. At the end of the process, the **pcd** variable points to the whole shebang. (Don't leave out the error checking as I just did—see the code samples on the companion disc for examples of how to handle the many errors that might arise in this short sequence.)

If your device has a single configuration, go ahead to the next step using the descriptor set you've just read. Otherwise, you'll need to enumerate the configurations (that is, step the **iconfig** variable from 1 to the **bNumConfigurations** value in the device descriptor) and apply some sort of algorithm to pick between them.

Selecting the Configuration

You eventually have to select a configuration by sending a series of control commands to the device to set the configuration and enable the desired interfaces. We'll be using a function named **USBD_CreateConfigurationRequestEx** to create the URB for this series of commands. One of its arguments is an array of pointers to descriptors for the interfaces you intend to enable. Your next step in configuration after settling on the configuration you want to use, therefore, is to prepare this array.

READING A STRING DESCRIPTOR

For reporting or other purposes, you might want to retrieve some of the string descriptors that your device might provide. In the USB42 sample, for example, the device contains English-language descriptors for the vendor, product, and serial number as well as for the single configuration and interface supported by the device. I wrote the following helper function for reading string descriptors:

```
NTSTATUS GetStringDescriptor(PDEVICE_OBJECT fdo, UCHAR istring,
  PUNICODE_STRING s)
  {
  NTSTATUS status;
  PDEVICE_EXTENSION pdx = (PDEVICE_EXTENSION) fdo->DeviceExtension;
  URB urb;

  UCHAR data[256];

  if (!pdx->langid)
    {
    UsbBuildGetDescriptorRequest(&urb,
      sizeof(_URB_CONTROL_DESCRIPTOR_REQUEST),
      USB_STRING_DESCRIPTOR_TYPE,
      0, 0, data, NULL, sizeof(data), NULL);
    status = SendAwaitUrb(fdo, &urb);
    if (!NT_SUCCESS(status))
      return status;
    pdx->langid = *(LANGID*)(data + 2);
    }

  UsbBuildGetDescriptorRequest(&urb,
    sizeof(_URB_CONTROL_DESCRIPTOR_REQUEST),
    USB_STRING_DESCRIPTOR_TYPE,
    istring, pdx->langid, data, NULL, sizeof(data), NULL);
  status = SendAwaitUrb(fdo, &urb);
  if (!NT_SUCCESS(status))
    return status;

  ULONG nchars = (data[0] - 2) / 2;
  PWSTR p = (PWSTR) ExAllocatePool(PagedPool, data[0]);
  if (!p)
    return STATUS_INSUFFICIENT_RESOURCES;
  memcpy(p, data + 2, nchars*2);
  p[nchars] = 0;
```

(continued)

continued

```
  s->Length = (USHORT) (2 * nchars);
  s->MaximumLength = (USHORT) ((2 * nchars) + 2);
  s->Buffer = p;

  return STATUS_SUCCESS;
  }
```

The new and interesting part of this function—given that you already know a lot about kernel-mode programming if you've been reading this book sequentially—is the initialization of the URB to fetch a string descriptor. In addition to supplying the index of the string we want to get, we also supply a standard LANGID language identifier. This is the same kind of language identifier that you use in a Win32 application. As I mentioned earlier, devices can provide strings in multiple languages, and string descriptor 0 contains a list of the supported language identifiers. To make sure to always ask for a supported language, I read string 0 the first time this routine executes and arbitrarily choose the first language as the one to ask for. In the actual sample drivers, the identifier will always be 0x0409, which identifies American English. USBD.SYS passes this language identifier along with the string index as a parameter for the get descriptor request it sends to the device. The device itself is responsible for deciding which string to return.

The output from my **GetStringDescriptor** function is a UNICODE_STRING that you use in the normal way. You would eventually call **RtlFreeUnicodeString** to release the string buffer.

I used GetStringDescriptor in the USB42 sample to generate extra debugging output about the device. For example, StartDevice contains code similar to this fragment:

```
UNICODE_STRING sd;
if (pcd->iConfiguration
  && NT_SUCCESS(GetStringDescriptor(fdo,
  pcd->iConfiguration, &sd)))
  {
  KdPrint(("USB42 - Selecting configuration named %ws\n",
    sd.Buffer));
  RtlFreeUnicodeString(&sd);
  }
```

I actually used a macro so that I wouldn't have to type this same code a bunch of times, but you get the idea.

Recall that when we read the configuration descriptor, we also read all of its interface descriptors into adjacent memory. This memory therefore contains a series of descriptors: a configuration descriptor, an interface descriptor followed by all of its endpoints, another interface descriptor followed by all of *its* endpoints, and so on. One way of choosing interfaces is to parse through this collection of descriptors and remember the addresses of the interface descriptors you're interested in. The bus driver provides a routine named **USBD_ParseConfigurationDescriptorEx** to simplify that task:

```
PUSB_INTERFACE_DESCRIPTOR pid;
pid = USBD_ParseConfigurationDescriptorEx(pcd, StartPosition,
  InterfaceNumber, AlternateSetting, InterfaceClass,
  InterfaceSubclass, InterfaceProtocol);
```

In this function, **pcd** is the address of the grand unified configuration descriptor. **StartPosition** is either the address of the configuration descriptor (the first time you make this call) or the address of a descriptor at which you want to begin searching. The remaining parameters specify criteria for a descriptor search. The value −1 indicates that you don't want the corresponding criterion to be employed in the search. You can look for the next interface descriptor that has zero or more of these attributes:

- The given **InterfaceNumber**
- The given **AlternateSetting** index
- The given **InterfaceClass** index
- The given **InterfaceSubclass** index
- The given **InterfaceProtocol** index

When USBD_ParseConfigurationDescriptorEx returns an interface descriptor to you, you save it as the **InterfaceDescriptor** member of an element in an array of USBD_INTERFACE_LIST_ENTRY structures, and then you advance past the interface descriptor so that you can parse the next one. The array of interface list entries will be one of the parameters to the eventual call to USBD_CreateConfigurationRequestEx, so I need to say a little more about it. Each entry in the array is an instance of the following structure:

```
typedef struct _USBD_INTERFACE_LIST_ENTRY {
    PUSB_INTERFACE_DESCRIPTOR InterfaceDescriptor;
    PUSBD_INTERFACE_INFORMATION Interface;
} USBD_INTERFACE_LIST_ENTRY, *PUSBD_INTERFACE_LIST_ENTRY;
```

When you initialize an entry in the array, you set the **InterfaceDescriptor** member equal to the address of an interface descriptor that you want to enable and you set the **Interface** member to NULL. You define one entry for each interface, and then you add an additional entry whose InterfaceDescriptor is NULL to mark the end. For example, in my USB42 sample, I know in advance that only one interface exists, so I use the following code to create the interface list:

```
PUSB_INTERFACE_DESCRIPTOR pid =
  USBD_ParseConfigurationDescriptorEx(pcd, pcd, -1, -1, -1, -1, -1);
USBD_INTERFACE_LIST_ENTRY interfaces[2] = {
  {pid, NULL},
  {NULL, NULL},
  };
```

That is, I parse the configuration descriptor to locate the first (and only) interface descriptor. Then I define a 2-element array to describe that one interface.

If you need to enable more than one interface because you're providing your own multifunction device support, you'll repeat the parsing call in a loop. For example:

```
ULONG size = (pcd->bNumInterfaces + 1) *
  sizeof(USBD_INTERFACE_LIST_ENTRY);
PUSBD_INTERFACE_LIST_ENTRY interfaces =
  (PUSBD_INTERFACE_LIST_ENTRY) ExAllocatePool(NonPagedPool, size);
RtlZeroMemory(interfaces, size);
ULONG i = 0;
PUSB_INTERFACE_DESCRIPTOR pid = (PUSB_INTERFACE_DESCRIPTOR) pcd;
while ((pid = USBD_ParseConfigurationDescriptorEx(pcd, pid, ...)))
  interfaces[i++].InterfaceDescriptor = pid++;
```

1. We first allocate memory to hold as many interface list entries as there are interfaces in this configuration, plus one. We zero the entire array. Wherever we leave off in filling the array during the subsequent loop, the next entry will be NULL to mark the end of the array.

2. The parsing call includes whatever criteria are relevant to your device. In the first iteration of the loop, **pid** points to the configuration descriptor. In later iterations, it points just past the interface descriptor returned by the preceding call.

3. Here, we initialize the pointer to an interface descriptor. The postincrement of **i** causes the next iteration to initialize the next element in the array. The postincrement of **pid** advances past the current interface descriptor so that the next iteration parses the next interface. (If you call **USBD_ ParseConfigurationDescriptorEx** with the second argument pointing to an interface descriptor that meets your criteria, you'll get back a pointer to that same descriptor. If you don't advance past that descriptor before making the next call, you're doomed to repeat the loop forever.)

The next step in the configuration process is to create a URB that we'll submit—soon, I promise—to configure the device:

```
PURB selurb = USBD_CreateConfigurationRequestEx(pcd, interfaces);
```

In addition to creating a URB (to which **selurb** points at this moment), USBD_CreateConfigurationRequestEx also initializes the **Interface** members of your USBD_INTERFACE_LIST entries to point to USBD_INTERFACE_INFORMATION structures. These information structures are physically located in the same memory block as the URB and will, therefore, be released back to the heap when you eventually call **ExFreePool** to return the URB. An interface information structure has the following declaration:

```
typedef struct _USBD_INTERFACE_INFORMATION {
  USHORT Length;
  UCHAR InterfaceNumber;
  UCHAR AlternateSetting;
  UCHAR Class;
  UCHAR SubClass;
  UCHAR Protocol;
  UCHAR Reserved;
  USBD_INTERFACE_HANDLE InterfaceHandle;
  ULONG NumberOfPipes;
  USBD_PIPE_INFORMATION Pipes[1];
  } USBD_INTERFACE_INFORMATION, *PUSBD_INTERFACE_INFORMATION;
```

The array of pipe information structures is what we're really interested in at this point, since the other fields of the structure will be filled in by USBD when we submit this URB. Each of them looks like this:

```
typedef struct _USBD_PIPE_INFORMATION {
  USHORT MaximumPacketSize;
  UCHAR EndpointAddress;
  UCHAR Interval;
  USBD_PIPE_TYPE PipeType;
  USBD_PIPE_HANDLE PipeHandle;
  ULONG MaximumTransferSize;
  ULONG PipeFlags;
  } USBD_PIPE_INFORMATION, *PUSBD_PIPE_INFORMATION;
```

So, we have an array of USBD_INTERFACE_LIST entries, each of which points to a USBD_INTERFACE_INFORMATION structure that contains an array of USBD_PIPE_INFORMATION structures. Our immediate task is to fill in the **Maximum-TransferSize** member of each of those pipe information structures if we don't want to accept the default value chosen by USBD. The default value is USBD_DEFAULT_MAXIMUM_TRANSFER_SIZE, which was equal to PAGE_SIZE in the DDK I was using at the time I wrote this book. The value we specify isn't directly related either to the maximum transfer size for the endpoint (which governs how many bytes can be moved in a single bus transaction) or to the amount of data the endpoint can absorb in a series of transactions (which is determined by the amount of memory available on the device). Instead, it represents the largest amount of data we will attempt to move with a single URB. This can be less than the largest amount of data that an application might send to the device or receive from the device, in which case our driver must be prepared to break application requests into pieces no bigger than this maximum size. I'll discuss how that task can be accomplished later in "Managing Bulk Transfer Pipes."

The reason that we have to supply a maximum transfer size is rooted in the scheduling algorithm that the host controller drivers use to divide URB requests into transactions within bus frames. If we send a large amount of data, it's possible for our data to hog a frame to the exclusion of other devices. We therefore want to moderate our demands on the bus by specifying a reasonable maximum size for the URBs that we'll send at once.

The code needed to initialize the pipe information structures is something like this:

```
for (ULONG ii = 0; ii < <number of interfaces>; ++ii)
  {
  PUSBD_INTERFACE_INFORMATION pii = interfaces[ii].Interface;
  for (ULONG ip = 0; ip < pii->NumberOfPipes; ++ip)
    pii->Pipes[ip].MaximumTransferSize = <some constant>;
  }
```

NOTE The USBD_CreateConfigurationRequestEx function initializes the MaximumTransferSize member of each pipe information structure to USBD_DEFAULT_MAXIMUM_TRANSFER_SIZE and the PipeFlags member to 0. Bear this in mind when you look at older driver samples and when you write your own driver.

Once you've initialized the pipe information structures, you're finally ready to submit the configuration URB:

```
SendAwaitUrb(fdo, selurb);
```

Finding the Handles

Successful completion of the select configuration URB leaves behind various handle values that you should record for later use:

- The **UrbSelectConfiguration.ConfigurationHandle** member of the URB is a handle for the configuration.

- The **InterfaceHandle** member of each USBD_INTERFACE_INFORMATION structure contains a handle for the interface.

■ Each of the USBD_PIPE_INFORMATION structures has a **PipeHandle** for the pipe ending in the corresponding endpoint.

For example, the USB42 sample records two handle values (in the device extension):

```
typedef struct _DEVICE_EXTENSION {
  ...
  USBD_CONFIGURATION_HANDLE hconfig;
  USBD_PIPE_HANDLE hpipe;
  } DEVICE_EXTENSION, *PDEVICE_EXTENSION;

pdx->hconfig = selurb->UrbSelectConfiguration.ConfigurationHandle;
pdx->hpipe = interfaces[0].Interface->Pipes[0].PipeHandle;
ExFreePool(selurb);
```

At this point in the program, the select configuration URB is no longer needed and can be discarded.

Shutting Down the Device

When your driver receives an IRP_MN_STOP_DEVICE request, you should place the device into its unconfigured state by creating and submitting a select configuration request with a NULL configuration pointer:

```
URB urb;
UsbBuildSelectConfigurationRequest(&urb,
  sizeof(_URB_SELECT_CONFIGURATION), NULL);
SendAwaitUrb(fdo, &urb);
```

Managing Bulk Transfer Pipes

The companion disc has two sample programs that illustrate bulk transfers. The first and simplest is named USB42. It has an input bulk endpoint that delivers back the constant value 42 each time you read it. (I call this the Answer device because the number 42 is Douglas Adams's answer to the Ultimate Question of Life, the Universe and Everything in *The Hitchhiker's Guide to the Galaxy*. Most readers probably already knew that, actually, given our common affinity for science fiction.) The code to do the reading is as follows:

```
URB urb;
UsbBuildInterruptOrBulkTransferRequest(&urb,
  sizeof(_URB_BULK_OR_INTERRUPT_TRANSFER),
  pdx->hpipe, Irp->AssociatedIrp.SystemBuffer, NULL, cbout,
  USBD_TRANSFER_DIRECTION_IN | USBD_SHORT_TRANSFER_OK, NULL);
status = SendAwaitUrb(fdo, &urb);
```

This code runs in the context of the handler for a **DeviceIoControl** call that uses the buffered method for data access, so the **SystemBuffer** field of the IRP points to the place to which data should be delivered. The **cbout** variable is the size of the data buffer we're trying to fill.

There's not much to explain about this request. You indicate with a flag whether you're reading (USBD_TRANSFER_DIRECTION_IN) or writing (no such flag) the endpoint. You can optionally indicate with another flag bit (USBD_SHORT_TRANSFER_OK) whether you're willing to tolerate having the device provide or consume less data than the maximum for the endpoint. The pipe handle is something you capture at IRP_MN_START_DEVICE time in the manner already illustrated.

The LOOPBACK sample is considerably more complicated than USB42. The device it manages has two bulk transfer endpoints, one for input and another for output. You can feed up to 16,384 bytes into the output pipe, and you can retrieve what you put in from the input pipe. The driver itself uses standard IRP_MJ_READ and IRP_MJ_WRITE requests for data movement. Handling read and write requests is so similar that the dispatch routines simply delegate these requests to a helper function named **ReadWrite**:

```
NTSTATUS DispatchRead(PDEVICE_OBJECT fdo, PIRP Irp)
  {
  return ReadWrite(fdo, Irp, TRUE);
  }

NTSTATUS DispatchWrite(PDEVICE_OBJECT fdo, PIRP Irp)
  {
  return ReadWrite(fdo, Irp, FALSE);
  }

NTSTATUS ReadWrite(PDEVICE_OBJECT fdo, PIRP Irp, BOOLEAN read)
  {
  PDEVICE_EXTENSION pdx = (PDEVICE_EXTENSION) fdo->DeviceExtension;
  NTSTATUS status = IoAcquireRemoveLock(&pdx->RemoveLock, Irp);
  if (!NT_SUCCESS(status))
    return CompleteRequest(Irp, status, 0);
  ...
  IoMarkIrpPending(Irp);
  IoSetCompletionRoutine(Irp, (PIO_COMPLETION_ROUTINE)
    OnReadWriteComplete, ...);
  IoCallDriver(...);
  return STATUS_PENDING;
  }
```

In summary, ReadWrite acquires the remove lock, creates a URB to do a bulk transfer, installs a completion routine, and submits the URB to the bus driver. The function deals with the two complications that make this sample more informative than USB42: the I/O operation might result in an error, and the request might need to be broken up to be handled in stages.

LOOPBACK's overall strategy for submitting requests to the bus driver is to change the personality of the read or write IRP into an IRP_MJ_INTERNAL_DEVICE_CONTROL containing a URB and send this altered IRP down the stack. To us and every driver above us, the IRP looks like an IRP_MJ_READ or IRP_MJ_WRITE because one of those two values will be in the **MajorFunction** field of the corresponding stack location. To the drivers below us, however, the IRP looks like an internal control request. The completion routine will resubmit this same IRP to perform the second and subsequent stages of a large transfer. Both features of this strategy are perfectly legal but will probably seem novel if you're seeing them for the first time. Without the error checking that's in the real LOOPBACK sample, here's ReadWrite and its associated completion routine in all their glory:

```
struct _RWCONTEXT : public _URB
   {
   ULONG_PTR va;
   ULONG length;
   PMDL mdl;
   ULONG numxfer;
   };

NTSTATUS ReadWrite(PDEVICE_OBJECT fdo, PIRP Irp, BOOLEAN read)
   {
   PDEVICE_EXTENSION pdx = (PDEVICE_EXTENSION) fdo->DeviceExtension;
   NTSTATUS status = IoAcquireRemoveLock(&pdx->RemoveLock, Irp);
   if (!NT_SUCCESS(status))
      return CompleteRequest(Irp, status, 0);
   USBD_PIPE_HANDLE hpipe = read ? pdx->hinpipe : pdx->houtpipe;

   LONG haderr;
   if (read)
      haderr = InterlockedExchange(&pdx->inerror, 0);
   else
      haderr = InterlockedExchange(&pdx->outerror, 0);
   if (haderr && !NT_SUCCESS(ResetPipe(fdo, hpipe)))
      ResetDevice(fdo);

   PRWCONTEXT ctx = (PRWCONTEXT) ExAllocatePool(NonPagedPool,
      sizeof(RWCONTEXT));
```

```
        RtlZeroMemory(ctx, sizeof(RWCONTEXT));

5       ULONG length = Irp->MdlAddress
          ? MmGetMdlByteCount(Irp->MdlAddress) : 0;
        if (!length)
          {
          IoReleaseRemoveLock(&pdx->RemoveLock, Irp);
          return CompleteRequest(Irp, STATUS_SUCCESS, 0);
          }
        ULONG_PTR va = (ULONG_PTR) MmGetMdlVirtualAddress(Irp->MdlAddress);

        ULONG urbflags = (read ? USBD_TRANSFER_DIRECTION_IN
                                : USBD_TRANSFER_DIRECTION_OUT);

6       ULONG seglen = length;
        if (seglen > MAXTRANSFER)
          seglen = (ULONG_PTR) PAGE_ALIGN(va) + PAGE_SIZE - va;

7       PMDL mdl = IoAllocateMdl((PVOID) va, PAGE_SIZE, FALSE, FALSE, NULL);
        IoBuildPartialMdl(Irp->MdlAddress, mdl, (PVOID) va, seglen);

8       UsbBuildInterruptOrBulkTransferRequest(ctx,
            sizeof(_URB_BULK_OR_INTERRUPT_TRANSFER),
            hpipe, NULL, mdl, seglen, urbflags, NULL);

        ctx->va = va + seglen;
        ctx->length = length - seglen;
        ctx->mdl = mdl;
        ctx->numxfer = 0;

        PIO_STACK_LOCATION stack = IoGetNextIrpStackLocation(Irp);
        stack->MajorFunction = IRP_MJ_INTERNAL_DEVICE_CONTROL;
        stack->Parameters.Others.Argument1 = (PVOID) (PURB) ctx;
        stack->Parameters.DeviceIoControl.IoControlCode =
          IOCTL_INTERNAL_USB_SUBMIT_URB;

        IoSetCompletionRoutine(Irp, (PIO_COMPLETION_ROUTINE)
          OnReadWriteComplete, (PVOID) ctx, TRUE, TRUE, TRUE);

        IoMarkIrpPending(Irp);
        status = IoCallDriver(pdx->LowerDeviceObject, Irp);
        return STATUS_PENDING;
        }

    NTSTATUS OnReadWriteComplete(PDEVICE_OBJECT fdo, PIRP Irp, PRWCONTEXT ctx)
      {
```

(continued)

```
      PDEVICE_EXTENSION pdx = (PDEVICE_EXTENSION) fdo->DeviceExtension;
      BOOLEAN read =
        (ctx->UrbBulkOrInterruptTransfer.TransferFlags &
        USBD_TRANSFER_DIRECTION_IN) != 0;
      ctx->numxfer +=
        ctx->UrbBulkOrInterruptTransfer.TransferBufferLength;

      NTSTATUS status = Irp->IoStatus.Status;
```
9
```
      if (NT_SUCCESS(status) && ctx->length)
        {
```
10
```
        ULONG seglen = ctx->length;
        if (seglen > MAXTRANSFER)
          seglen = (ULONG_PTR) PAGE_ALIGN(ctx->va) +
            PAGE_SIZE - ctx->va;

        IoBuildPartialMdl(Irp->MdlAddress, ctx->mdl,
          (PVOID) ctx->va, seglen);
```
11
```
        ctx->UrbBulkOrInterruptTransfer.TransferBufferLength = seglen;

        PIO_STACK_LOCATION stack = IoGetNextIrpStackLocation(Irp);
        stack->MajorFunction = IRP_MJ_INTERNAL_DEVICE_CONTROL;
        stack->Parameters.Others.Argument1 = (PVOID) (PURB) ctx;
        stack->Parameters.DeviceIoControl.IoControlCode =
          IOCTL_INTERNAL_USB_SUBMIT_URB;
        IoSetCompletionRoutine(Irp, (PIO_COMPLETION_ROUTINE)
          OnReadWriteComplete, (PVOID) ctx, TRUE, TRUE, TRUE);

        ctx->va += seglen;
        ctx->length -= seglen;
```
12
```
        IoCallDriver(pdx->LowerDeviceObject, Irp);
        return STATUS_MORE_PROCESSING_REQUIRED;
        }
```
13
```
      if (NT_SUCCESS(status))
        Irp->IoStatus.Information = ctx->numxfer;
      else
        {
        if (read)
          InterlockedIncrement(&pdx->inerror);
        else
          InterlockedIncrement(&pdx->outerror);
        }
```

```
ExFreePool(ctx->mdl);
ExFreePool(ctx);
IoReleaseRemoveLock(&pdx->RemoveLock, Irp);

return status;
}
```

1. ReadWrite needs to create a URB that it will share with **OnReadWrite-Complete**, and it needs to provide some additional context information to keep track of the ongoing progress of the operation. This RWCONTEXT structure encompasses both purposes. (Deriving one structure from another as shown here is a C++ stratagem for declaring a structure that begins with the members of the base structure.) In addition to the URB, this structure includes **va**, the virtual address of the current portion of the user-mode buffer; **length**, the residual count for this operation; **mdl**, a partial memory descriptor list describing the current segment of the transfer; and **numxfer**, the cumulative number of bytes transferred.

2. We acquire the remove lock here. The balancing call to **IoRelease-RemoveLock** occurs in the completion routine.

3. This is one of a few places where ReadWrite needs to distinguish between read and write requests. Here, we're obtaining the handle of the pipe through which we'll move data.

4. Either the input or the output pipe might have had an error the last time we tried to use it, in which case either **inerror** or **outerror** will be set in the device extension. Before launching a new operation, we try to reset the pipe that had the error. If that doesn't work, we reset the entire device. I'll explain the **ResetPipe** and **ResetDevice** helper functions in the next section.

5. This driver declared itself as using the DO_DIRECT_IO buffering method at AddDevice time, so the IRP has a pointer to a memory descriptor list describing the (locked) pages containing the user-mode buffer. It's customary to obtain the transfer length from the MDL, as shown here, rather than from the stack location.

6. We'll be performing the operation in blocks no bigger than a page. The choice of PAGE_SIZE as a maximum transfer size was a design choice, and you might pick a different value as previously described. To gain whatever benefits might flow from processing a page-aligned buffer, I also decided to make the first transfer short, if necessary, so that later transfers would be page-aligned.

7. We'll be using a partial memory descriptor list for each segment of the transfer. We need an MDL that has the capacity to describe the largest number of pages we'll transfer in a single segment. This number is either one or two, depending on the alignment of the buffer. After allocating the MDL, we call **IoBuildPartialMdl** to map the initial segment.

8. We're ready at this point to build and submit a URB for the first segment of the read or write. The key task here is our initialization of the next driver's stack entry to describe an internal control operation instead of a read or write. The main advantage of doing this is that we don't need extra, fairly involved logic to handle cancellation of a subsidiary IRP when the main read/write IRP gets cancelled.

9. When one stage in the transfer completes successfully, the bus driver calls **IoCompleteRequest** and our completion routine gains control. If the request isn't finished yet, we'll resubmit the URB with a new buffer address and length. Otherwise, we'll allow the completion process to run its course. Don't forget that the IRP we're dealing with originally came to us with a major function code of IRP_MJ_READ or IRP_MJ_WRITE.

10. Here we set up the partial MDL for the next segment of the transfer. The user-mode virtual address is pretty useless per se because this completion routine executes in an arbitrary thread context. **IoBuildPartialMdl** is mapping a subset of a master MDL that's already been probed and locked, however. Since it merely copies physical page numbers from the master MDL, it doesn't depend on executing in any particular memory context.

11. Here we set up the URB and I/O stack for the next stage. The only field in the URB that requires change is the byte count. The URB's MDL pointer, flags, and so on, are as ReadWrite left them. (The MDL itself changed, but its location in memory didn't.) We need to completely reinitialize the next stack location, however, because IoCompleteRequest set most of it to 0.

12. We reissue this IRP to the bus driver and return the status code STATUS_MORE_PROCESSING_REQUIRED to halt the completion process inside IoCompleteRequest. When this new stage finishes, this completion routine will regain control.

13. Beginning here we handle the final completion of the read/write request. We set the **IoStatus.Information** field to be the total number of bytes we've successfully transferred and clean up the memory we allocated in ReadWrite. We also release the remove lock to balance the acquisition that ReadWrite did.

You might notice that the completion routine in this sample doesn't contain the standard boilerplate code to conditionally call **IoMarkIrpPending**. That's not necessary in this case because we made that call in ReadWrite.

You'll also notice that when the completion routine calls **IoCallDriver** to resubmit the URB, it then *unconditionally* returns STATUS_MORE_PROCESSING_ REQUIRED. There's an important but subtle reason for this behavior. If the bus driver accepts the new URB normally, it will return STATUS_PENDING to us. (This is just how USBD works—it's not a general characteristic of bus drivers.) In this case, we certainly should return STATUS_MORE_PROCESSING_REQUIRED because we want **IoCompleteRequest** to stop processing the IRP for the time being. The bus driver will complete it again later. If the bus driver were to fail the new submission, however, or if it were for some reason to complete it in the dispatch routine, it will have called IoCompleteRequest before returning. *We've already processed that completion event in a recursive call!* We shouldn't, therefore, do anything more with this IRP or allow the initial invocation of IoCompleteRequest to do anything with it either. Returning STATUS_MORE_PROCESSING_REQUIRED is always the right thing to do here.

Error Recovery

I can't say much of a general nature about recovering from errors in USB operations. When you send or receive data to a bulk transfer endpoint, the bus and bus driver take care of retrying garbled transmissions. Consequently, if your URB appears to complete successfully, you can be confident that the data you intended to transfer has in fact been transferred correctly. When an error occurs, however, your driver needs to attempt some sort of recovery. The first line of defense is generally to unstall the endpoint with which you've been trying to communicate so that you can try again. Here's a helper routine named **ResetPipe** that will do that:

```
NTSTATUS ResetPipe(PDEVICE_OBJECT fdo, USBD_PIPE_HANDLE hpipe)
  {
  URB urb;
  urb.UrbHeader.Length = (USHORT) sizeof(_URB_PIPE_REQUEST);
  urb.UrbHeader.Function = URB_FUNCTION_RESET_PIPE;
  urb.UrbPipeRequest.PipeHandle = hpipe;

  NTSTATUS status = SendAwaitUrb(fdo, &urb);
  return status;
  }
```

As you can see, all that's required is to submit a URB with the RESET_PIPE function code. Since this helper routine indirectly waits for the URB to complete, you must be running at PASSIVE_LEVEL to call it. What this URB does, in USB terms, is clear the ENDPOINT_HALT feature. If the endpoint was stalled, it then becomes ready for the next transaction.

If you're unable to reset the pipe, you can then try to reset the entire device by using this **ResetDevice** function:

```
VOID ResetDevice(PDEVICE_OBJECT fdo)
  {
  PDEVICE_EXTENSION pdx = (PDEVICE_EXTENSION) fdo->DeviceExtension;

  KEVENT event;
  KeInitializeEvent(&event, NotificationEvent, FALSE);
  IO_STATUS_BLOCK iostatus;

  PIRP Irp = IoBuildDeviceIoControlRequest
    (IOCTL_INTERNAL_USB_RESET_PORT, pdx->LowerDeviceObject,
    NULL, 0, NULL, 0, TRUE, &event, &iostatus);
  if (!Irp)
    return;

  NTSTATUS status = (IoCallDriver(pdx->LowerDeviceObject, Irp);
  if (status == STATUS_PENDING)
    KeWaitForSingleObject(&event, Executive, KernelMode,
      FALSE, NULL);
  }
```

The port-reset command causes the hub driver to reinitialize the device while preserving the existing configuration. This process might fail somewhere along the way, in which case the command will complete with an error status. If the device turns out to be missing, for example, the hub driver fails the request with STATUS_ UNSUCCESSFUL.

Managing Interrupt Pipes

From the device side of the bus, an interrupt pipe is practically identical to a bulk transfer pipe. The only important difference from that perspective is that the host will be polling an interrupt endpoint with some guaranteed frequency. The device will respond with NAK except at instants when it will present an interrupt to the host. To report an interrupt event, the device ACKs the host after providing whatever morsel of data is supposed to accompany the interrupt.

From the driver's perspective, managing an interrupt pipe is quite a bit more complicated than managing a bulk pipe. When the driver needs to read or write data to a bulk pipe, it just creates an appropriate URB and sends it to the bus driver. But for an interrupt pipe to serve its intended purpose of notifying the host of interesting hardware events, the driver basically needs to keep a read request outstanding at all times. I don't recommend using a system-polling thread in this case because power management greatly complicates the management of the separate thread. The best way to keep a read request active is to use the same idea I showed you in LOOPBACK, where we have a completion routine that keeps recycling a URB.

The USBINT sample illustrates how to manage an interrupt pipe with a URB that's always active. I wrote a few helper routines to assist in the job. I won't describe all of these functions in detail; please refer to the READWRITE.CPP file with the USBINT sample on the companion disc.

CreateInterruptUrb   CreateInterruptUrb creates the URB and an associated IRP. The device extension has fields named **PollingUrb** and **PollingIrp** that point to these two structures. We call this function during our processing of IRP_MN_START_ DEVICE.

DeleteInterruptUrb   DeleteInterruptUrb is the counterpart of CreateInterruptUrb. Whenever we're shutting the device down, we call this function to release the IRP and URB memory blocks.

StartInterruptUrb   StartInterruptUrb launches a URB to poll the device's interrupt endpoint. We call this function whenever we activate the device, which we do when we open the first handle after a period in which no handles were open. (We also power the device on at the same time. We can't have a URB outstanding when the device is powered down, but we want one outstanding when the device is powered up in order to service an application.)

OnInterrupt   OnInterrupt is a standard I/O completion routine that functions as an interrupt routine for the device. It looks like this:

```
NTSTATUS OnInterrupt(PDEVICE_OBJECT junk, PIRP Irp,
  PDEVICE_EXTENSION pdx)
  {
  if (NT_SUCCESS(Irp->IoStatus.Status))
    {
    KdPrint(("USBINT - Interrupt!\n"));
    StartInterruptUrb(pdx->DeviceObject);
    }

  return STATUS_MORE_PROCESSING_REQUIRED;
  }
```

1. This is where you would do whatever interrupt processing is required by your device. In the USBINT sample, there's code at this point to increment a count of pending interrupts or complete a pending IOCTL that an application is using as a means of knowing when interrupts occur.

2. Here, we initiate another poll for an interrupt using the same URB.

3. We return STATUS_MORE_PROCESSING_REQUIRED because we don't want IoCompleteRequest to do anything else with the IRP.

MORE ABOUT THE USBINT SAMPLE

The USBINT sample on the companion disc illustrates how to manage a device with an interrupt pipe. The device firmware (in the EZUSB subdirectory) defines a device with a single input interrupt endpoint. Each time you press and release the F1 button on the Anchor Chips development board, the firmware increments the integer being displayed in the 7-segment LED and arms the endpoint to deliver four bytes of data on the next IN transaction. The driver (in the SYS subdirectory) continuously tries to read the endpoint. The test program (in the TEST subdirectory) issues DeviceIoControl calls to count and display the interrupts that occur. Terminate the test program with Ctrl+Break. The number displayed by the device should match the low-order digit displayed by the test program.

Control Requests

If you refer back to Table 11-2 on page 499, you'll notice that there are 11 standard types of control requests. You and I will never explicitly issue SET_ADDRESS requests. The bus driver does that when a new device initially comes on line; by the time we ever get control in a WDM driver, the bus driver has assigned an address to the device and read the device descriptor to learn that *we're* the device driver. I've already discussed how to create the URBs that cause the bus driver to send control requests for getting descriptors or for setting a configuration or interface in the "Initiating Requests" and "Configuration" sections. In this section, I'll fill in the blanks related to the remaining kinds of control transactions.

Controlling Features

If we want to set or clear a feature of a device, an interface, or an endpoint, we submit a feature URB. For example, the following code (which appears in the FEATURE sample driver on the companion disc) sets a vendor-defined interface feature:

```
URB urb;
UsbBuildFeatureRequest(&urb,
  URB_FUNCTION_SET_FEATURE_TO_INTERFACE,
  FEATURE_LED_DISPLAY, 1, NULL);
status = SendAwaitUrb(fdo, &urb);
```

The second argument to **UsbBuildFeatureRequest** indicates whether we want to set or clear a feature belonging to the device, an interface, an endpoint, or another vendor-specific entity on the device. This parameter takes eight possible values, and you could guess without me telling you that they're formed according to the following formula:

```
URB_FUNCTION_ [SET | CLEAR] _FEATURE_TO_
   [DEVICE | INTERFACE | ENDPOINT | OTHER]
```

The third argument to UsbBuildFeatureRequest identifies the feature in question. In the FEATURE sample, I invented a feature called FEATURE_LED_DISPLAY. The fourth argument identifies a particular entity of whatever type is being addressed. In this example, I wanted to address interface 1, so I coded 1.

USB defines two standard features that you might be tempted to control yourself using a feature URB: the remote wake-up feature and the endpoint stall feature. You don't, however, need to set or clear these features yourself because the bus driver does so automatically. When you issue an IRP_MN_WAIT_WAKE request—see Chapter 8, "Power Management"—the bus driver ensures that the device's configuration allows for remote wake-up, and it also automatically enables the remote wake-up feature for the device. The bus driver issues a clear feature request to unstall a device when you issue a RESET_PIPE URB.

ABOUT THE FEATURE SAMPLE

The FEATURE sample on the companion disc illustrates how to set or clear a feature. The device firmware (in the EZUSB subdirectory) defines a device with no endpoints. The device supports an interface-level feature numbered 42, which is the FEATURE_LED_DISPLAY referenced symbolically in the driver. When the feature is set, the Anchor Chips development board's 7-segment LED display becomes illuminated and shows how many times the feature has been set since the device was attached (modulo 10). When the feature is clear, the LED display shows only the decimal point.

The FEATURE device driver (in the SYS subdirectory) contains code to set and clear the feature and to exercise a few other control commands in response to IOCTL requests. Refer to CONTROL.CPP to see this code, which isn't much more complicated than the code fragments displayed in the text.

The test program (in the TEST subdirectory) is a Win32 console application that performs a DeviceIoControl to set the custom feature; issues additional DeviceIoControl calls to obtain status masks, the configuration number, and the alternate setting for the single interface; waits five seconds; and then performs another DeviceIoControl to clear the feature. Each time you run the test, you should see the development board's display light up for five seconds, showing successively larger decimal integers.

Determining Status

If you want to obtain the current status of the device, an interface, or an endpoint, you formulate a get status URB. For example:

```
URB urb;
USHORT epstatus;
UsbBuildGetStatusRequest(&urb, URB_FUNCTION_GET_STATUS_FROM_ENDPOINT,
  <index>, &epstatus, NULL, NULL);
SendAwaitUrb(fdo, &urb);
```

You can use four different URB functions in a get status request, and they allow you to retrieve the current status mask for the device as a whole, for a specified interface, for a specified endpoint, or for a vendor-specific entity. See Table 11-8.

The status mask for a device indicates whether the device is self-powered and whether or not its remote wake-up feature is enabled. See Figure 11-13. The mask for an endpoint indicates whether or not the endpoint is currently stalled. See Figure 11-14. USB now defines interface-level status bits related to power management. Refer to the "USB Feature Specification: Interface Power Management" document on line at the USB Web site, which at press time was available at *http://www.usb.org/ developers/devclass.html*. USB should never prescribe vendor-specific status bits since they're, by definition, up to vendors to specify.

Operation Code	*Retrieve Status From...*
URB_FUNCTION_GET_STATUS_FROM_DEVICE	Device as a whole
URB_FUNCTION_GET_STATUS_FROM_INTERFACE	Specified interface
URB_FUNCTION_GET_STATUS_FROM_ENDPOINT	Specified endpoint
URB_FUNCTION_GET_STATUS_FROM_OTHER	Vendor-specific object

Table 11-8. *URB function codes used for getting status.*

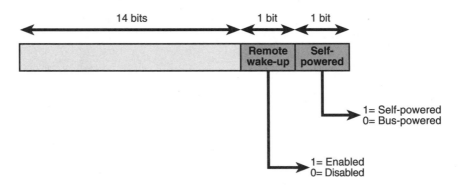

Figure 11-13. *Bits in device status.*

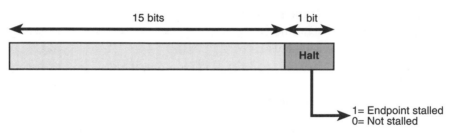

Figure 11-14. *Bits in endpoint status.*

Managing Isochronous Pipes

The purpose of an isochronous pipe is to allow the host and the device to exchange time-critical data with guaranteed regularity. The bus driver will devote up to 90 percent of the bus bandwidth to isochronous and interrupt transfers. What this means is that every 1-ms frame will include reserved time slots long enough to accommodate maximum-sized transfers to or from each of the isochronous and interrupt endpoints that are currently active. Figure 11-15 illustrates this concept for three different devices. Devices A and B each have an isochronous endpoint, for which a fixed and relatively large amount of time is reserved in every frame. Device C has an interrupt endpoint whose polling frequency is once every two frames; it has a reservation for a small portion of every second frame. During frames that don't include a poll of Device C's interrupt endpoint, additional bandwidth would be available, perhaps for bulk transfers or other purposes.

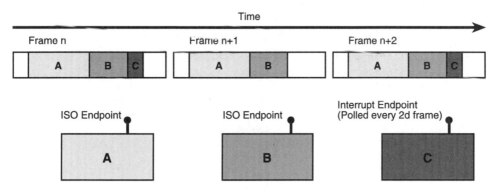

Figure 11-15. *Allocation of bandwidth to isochronous and interrupt endpoints.*

Reserving Bandwidth

The bus driver reserves bandwidth for you when you enable an interface by examining the endpoint descriptors that are part of the interface. Reserving bandwidth is just like buying a theater ticket, though: you don't get a refund if you don't use the space. Consequently, it's important to enable an interface that contains an isochronous endpoint only when you'll be using the bandwidth you thereby reserve, and it's important that the endpoint's declared maximum transfer size be approximately the amount you intend to use. Normally, a device with isochronous capability has a default interface that doesn't have any isochronous or interrupt endpoints. When you know you're about to access that capability, you enable an *alternate setting* of the same interface that *does* have the isochronous or interrupt endpoints.

An example will clarify the mechanics of reserving bandwidth. The USBISO sample on the companion disc has an interface with a default and an alternate setting. The default setting has no endpoints. The alternate setting has an isochronous endpoint with a maximum transfer size of 256 bytes. See Figure 11-16.

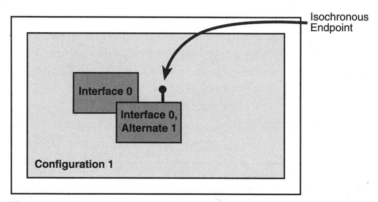

Figure 11-16. *Descriptor structure for the USBISO device.*

At StartDevice time, we select a configuration based on the default interface. Since the default interface doesn't have an isochronous or interrupt endpoint in it, we don't reserve any bandwidth just yet. When someone opens a handle to the device, however, we invoke the following **SelectAlternateInterface** helper function to switch to the alternate setting for our interface. (Again, I've omitted the error checking.)

```
NTSTATUS SelectAlternateInterface(PDEVICE_OBJECT fdo)
  {
  PDEVICE_EXTENSION pdx = (PDEVICE_EXTENSION) fdo->DeviceExtension;
  PUSB_INTERFACE_DESCRIPTOR pid =
    USBD_ParseConfigurationDescriptorEx(pdx->pcd, pdx->pcd,
      0, 1, -1, -1, -1);
  ULONG npipes = pid->bNumEndpoints;
  ULONG size = GET_SELECT_INTERFACE_REQUEST_SIZE(npipes);
  PURB urb = (PURB) ExAllocatePool(NonPagedPool, size);
  RtlZeroMemory(urb, size);
```

```
UsbBuildSelectInterfaceRequest(urb, size, pdx->hconfig, 0, 1);
urb->UrbSelectInterface.Interface.Length =
   GET_USBD_INTERFACE_SIZE(npipes);
urb->UrbSelectInterface.Interface.Pipes[0].MaximumTransferSize =
   PAGE_SIZE;
NTSTATUS status = SendAwaitUrb(fdo, &urb);
if (NT_SUCCESS(status))
   {
   pdx->hinpipe =
      urb.UrbSelectInterface.Interface.Pipes[0].PipeHandle;
   status = STATUS_SUCCESS;
   }
ExFreePool(urb);
return status;
}
```

1. Before we can allocate space for the URB, we need to know how many pipe descriptors it will contain. The most common way to find this number is to go back to the grand unified configuration descriptor and find the descriptor for interface 0, alternate setting 1. That descriptor contains a count of endpoints, which is the same as the number of pipes that we're about to open.

2. GET_SELECT_INTERFACE_REQUEST_SIZE calculates the number of bytes needed to hold a select interface request that will open the specified number of pipes. We can then allocate memory for the URB and initialize it to 0. The real code sample on the companion disc checks to make sure that the call to **ExAllocatePool** succeeded, by the way.

3. Here, we build a URB to select alternate setting 1 (the last argument) of interface number 0 (the next-to-last argument).

4. We must do these two additional initialization steps to finish setting up the URB. Failing to set the interface information structure's length earns you a STATUS_BUFFER_TOO_SMALL failure right away. Failing to set the **MaximumTransferSize** fields of the pipe descriptors earns you a STATUS_INVALID_PARAMETER when you try to read or write the pipe.

5. When we submit this URB, USBD automatically closes the current setting of this interface, including all of its endpoints. Then USBD tells the device to enable the alternate setting, and it creates pipe descriptors for the endpoints that are part of the alternate setting. If opening the new interface fails for some reason, USBD reopens the previous interface, and all your previous interface and pipe handles remain valid.

6. My **SendAwaitUrb** helper function simply returns an error if it's unable to select the one-and-only alternate setting for this interface. I'll have a bit more to say about how you should handle errors after this numbered list.

7. In addition to selecting the new interface at the device level, USBD also creates an array of pipe descriptors from which we can extract handles for later use.

The select interface call might fail because not enough free bandwidth exists to accommodate our endpoint. We would find out about the failure by examining the URB status:

```
if (URB_STATUS(&urb) == USBD_STATUS_NO_BANDWIDTH)
   ...
```

Dealing with lack of bandwidth poses a bit of a problem. The operating system doesn't currently provide a convenient way for competing drivers to negotiate a fair allocation. Neither does it provide for any sort of notification that some other driver has failed to acquire needed bandwidth so that we might give up some of ours. In this state of affairs, therefore, you have two basic choices. One choice is to provide multiple alternate interface settings, each of which has a different maximum transfer size for its isochronous endpoint(s). When you detect an allocation failure, you can try to select progressively less-demanding settings until you finally succeed.

A savvy end user who's able to launch the Windows 2000 Device Manager applet can display a property page for the USB host controller—see Figure 11-17—that displays information about the current allocation of bandwidth. Double-clicking one of the devices listed in the page brings up the property display for the device in question. A well-crafted page could perhaps communicate with the associated device driver in order to scale back its demand for bandwidth. This whole area seems ripe for a more automatic Microsoft-driven solution, though.

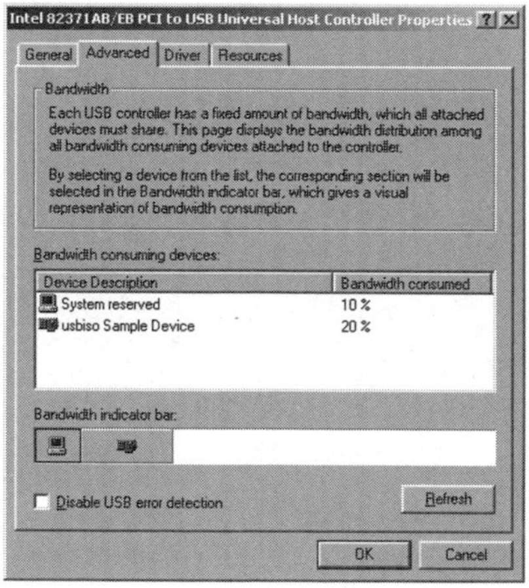

Figure 11-17. *A property page for the USB host controller.*

Your other choice for handling lack of bandwidth is to allow an IRP to fail in such a way that an application can alert the end user to the problem. Perhaps the end user can unplug something so that your device can be accommodated. This is the option I chose in the USBISO sample except I didn't bother to put code into the test application that would respond to a bandwidth allocation failure—TEST.EXE will just fail. To adopt this option, you need to know how the failure shows up back in user mode. If the URB fails with USBD_STATUS_NO_BANDWIDTH, the NTSTATUS code you get back from the internal control IRP is STATUS_DEVICE_DATA_ERROR, which isn't very specific. An application call to **GetLastError** would retrieve ERROR_CRC as the error code. There's no easy way for an application to discover that the real cause of the error is a lack of bandwidth, unfortunately. If you're interested in diving down this particular rat hole to reach a conclusion, read the sidebar.

HOW AN APPLICATION DISCOVERS YOU'RE OUT OF BANDWIDTH

Suppose you do what USBISO does and try to select the high-bandwidth alternate interface when you receive an IRP_MJ_CREATE. Further suppose you complete the IRP with the status code you get back when there's not enough bandwidth—namely, STATUS_DEVICE_DATA_ERROR. Your application caller will eventually see ERROR_CRC, as I said in the main text. What now? The application can't send you an IOCTL to find out the real cause of the error because it doesn't have a handle to your device. You failed the IRP_MJ_CREATE, remember? So maybe you need to have a way for people to open handles to your device that doesn't try to reserve bandwidth. Then you need some other way for an application to ask for bandwidth, perhaps by means of an IOCTL operation. Or perhaps your application just interprets ERROR_CRC from a call to **CreateFile** as meaning there's no bandwidth. Actual data errors are pretty unlikely, after all, so that interpretation would be correct much of the time.

But the best solution would be a specific NTSTATUS code and matching Win32 error code that means "no bandwidth." Keep your eyes on NTSTATUS.H and WINERROR.H for future developments.

USBISO performs the converse operation of selecting the original default interface when it receives the IRP_MJ_CLOSE for the last remaining open handle. That operation entails issuing another select interface URB, but with the value 0 for the alternate interface index.

Initiating a Series of Isochronous Transfers

You can use an isochronous pipe either to read or write data in discrete chunks or to provide or consume data in a continuous stream. Data streaming is probably the most frequent occupation for an isochronous pipe, actually. But, in addition to understanding the mechanics of working with the USB bus driver, you must understand and solve additional problems related to data buffering, rate matching, and so on, if you want to operate a streaming pipe. The *kernel-streaming* component of the operating system deals with all these additional problems. Unfortunately, we didn't have time to include a chapter on kernel streaming in this book. I'm therefore going to show you only how to program a discrete transfer over an isochronous pipe.

To read from or write to an isochronous pipe, you'll of course use a URB with the appropriate function code. But there are a few wrinkles that you haven't seen yet associated with creating and submitting the isochronous URB. First, you must be aware of how the device will break up a transfer into *packets*. In general, the device is free to accept or deliver any amount of data less than the endpoint's declared maximum. (Any leftover bandwidth on the bus simply won't be used.) The packet size the device will use doesn't have any other necessary relation with the endpoint maximum, with the maximum amount of data you said you'd transfer in a URB, or with the amount of data the device and application can exchange in a series of transactions. The firmware for the USBISO device, for example, works with 16-byte packets even though the isochronous endpoint in question can handle up to 256 bytes per frame according to its descriptor. You must have a priori knowledge of how big these packets will be before you construct a URB because the URB must include an array of descriptors for each packet that will be exchanged and each of these descriptors must indicate how big the packet will be.

In an impractical simple situation, you could allocate an isochronous URB in the following way:

```
ULONG length = MmGetMdlByteCount(Irp->MdlAddress);
ULONG packsize = 16; // a constant in USBISO
ULONG npackets = (length + packsize - 1) / packsize;
ASSERT(npackets <= 255);
ULONG size = GET_ISO_URB_SIZE(npackets);
PURB urb = (PURB) ExAllocatePool(NonPagedPool, size);
RtlZeroMemory(urb, size);
```

The key step in this fragment is the use of the **GET_ISO_URB_SIZE** macro to calculate the total size needed for an isochronous URB to transfer a given number of data packets. A single URB can accommodate a maximum of 255 isochronous packets, by the way, which is why I put the ASSERT statement into this code. Limiting the application to just 255 packets is not practical, as I said, so we will do something more complex in the real USBISO sample driver. For the time being, though, I just want to describe the mechanics of building a single URB for an isochronous (ISO) transfer.

There being no **UsbBuild***Xxx***Request** macro for building an isochronous URB, we go on to initialize the new URB by hand:

```
urb->UrbIsochronousTransfer.Hdr.Length = (USHORT) size;
urb->UrbIsochronousTransfer.Hdr.Function =
  URB_FUNCTION_ISOCH_TRANSFER;
urb->UrbIsochronousTransfer.PipeHandle = pdx->hinpipe;
urb->UrbIsochronousTransfer.TransferFlags =
  USBD_TRANSFER_DIRECTION_IN | USBD_SHORT_TRANSFER_OK |
  USBD_START_ISO_TRANSFER_ASAP;
urb->UrbIsochronousTransfer.TransferBufferLength = length;
urb->UrbIsochronousTransfer.TransferBufferMDL =
  Irp->MdlAddress;
urb->UrbIsochronousTransfer.NumberOfPackets = npackets;

for (ULONG i = 0; i < npackets; ++i, length -= packsize)
  {
  urb->UrbIsochronousTransfer.IsoPacket[i].Offset = i * packsize;
  }
```

The array of packet descriptors collectively describes the entire data buffer that we'll read in to or write out from. This buffer has to be contiguous in virtual memory, which basically means that you need a single MDL to describe it. It would be pretty hard to violate this rule. Reinforcing the idea of contiguity, each packet descriptor contains just the offset and length for a portion of the entire buffer and not an actual pointer. The host controller driver is responsible for setting the length; you're responsible for setting the offset.

The second wrinkle with starting an isochronous transfer involves timing. USB uniquely identifies each 1-ms frame with an ever-increasing number. It's sometimes important that a transfer begin in a specific frame. USBD allows you to indicate this fact by explicitly setting the **StartFrame** field of the URB. I'll discuss how and why you might need to be explicit about the starting frame number in the next section. USBISO doesn't depend on timing, however. It therefore sets the USBD_START_ISO_TRANSFER_ASAP flag to indicate that the transfer should be started as soon as possible.

The final wrinkle in isochronous processing has to do with how the transfer ends. The URB itself will succeed overall even though one or more packets had data errors. The URB has a field named **ErrorCount** that indicates how many packets encountered errors. If this ends up nonzero, you could loop through the packet descriptors to examine their individual status fields.

Achieving Acceptable Performance

To achieve acceptable performance for an isochronous transfer that requires more than one URB, you need to program your driver in a more complex way than any of the samples I've shown you so far. As soon as one URB finishes, you want the bus driver to immediately start processing the next one. Interposing a completion routine (as in the LOOPBACK sample) won't be fast enough. The least complex strategy to keep data moving is the one employed by the USBISO sample: create a set of subsidiary IRP/URB pairs and submit them all at once.

> **NOTE** The need to create multiple IRPs, and the consequent enormous complication of cancellation logic, arises because you can currently submit only one URB with an IRP. If it were possible to use the UrbLink field to chain a series of URBs from a single IRP, you wouldn't need all the complication I'm about to describe.

The basic idea behind USBISO's read/write logic is to have the completion routine for subsidiary IRPs complete the main read/write IRP when the last subsidiary IRP finishes. To make this idea work, I declared the following special-purpose context structure:

```
typedef struct _RWCONTEXT {
  PDEVICE_EXTENSION pdx;
  PIRP mainirp;
  NTSTATUS status;
  ULONG numxfer;
  ULONG numirps;
  LONG numpending;
  LONG refcnt;
  struct {
    PIRP irp;
    PURB urb;
    PMDL mdl;
    } sub[1];
  } RWCONTEXT, *PRWCONTEXT;
```

The dispatch routine for IRP_MJ_READ—USBISO doesn't handle IRP_MJ_WRITE requests—calculates the number of subsidiary IRPs required for the complete transfer and allocates one of these context structures, as follows:

```
ULONG packsize = 16;
ULONG segsize = USBD_DEFAULT_MAXIMUM_TRANSFER_SIZE;
if (segsize / packsize > 255)
  segsize = 255 * packsize;
ULONG numirps = (length + segsize - 1);
```

```
ULONG ctxsize = sizeof(RWCONTEXT) +
  (numirps - 1) * sizeof(((PRWCONTEXT) 0)->sub);
PRWCONTEXT ctx = (PRWCONTEXT) ExAllocatePool(NonPagedPool, ctxsize);
RtlZeroMemory(ctx, ctxsize);
ctx->numirps = ctx->numpending = numirps;
ctx->pdx = pdx;
ctx->mainirp = Irp;
ctx->refcnt = 2;
Irp->Tail.Overlay.DriverContext[0] = (PVOID) ctx;
```

I'll explain the purpose of the last two statements in this sequence when I discuss USBISO's cancellation logic. We now perform a loop to construct **numirps** IRP_MJ_INTERNAL_DEVICE_CONTROL requests. At each iteration of the loop, we call **IoAllocateIrp** to create an IRP with one more stack location than is required by the device object immediately under us. We also allocate a URB to control one stage of the transfer and a partial MDL to describe the current stage's portion of the main I/O buffer. We record the address of the IRP, the URB, and the partial MDL in an element of the RWCONTEXT structure's **sub** array. We initialize the URB in the same way as I showed you earlier. Then we initialize the subsidiary IRP's first *two* I/O stack locations, as follows:

```
IoSetNextIrpStackLocation(subirp);
PIO_STACK_LOCATION stack = IoGetCurrentIrpStackLocation(subirp);
stack->DeviceObject = fdo;
stack->Parameters.Others.Argument1 = (PVOID) urb;
stack->Parameters.Others.Argument2 = (PVOID) mdl;

stack = IoGetNextIrpStackLocation(subirp);
stack->MajorFunction = IRP_MJ_INTERNAL_DEVICE_CONTROL;
stack->Parameters.Others.Argument1 = (PVOID) urb;
stack->Parameters.DeviceIoControl.IoControlCode =
  IOCTL_INTERNAL_USB_SUBMIT_URB;

IoSetCompletionRoutine(subirp, (PIO_COMPLETION_ROUTINE)
  OnStageComplete, (PVOID) ctx, TRUE, TRUE, TRUE);
```

The first stack location is for use by the **OnStageComplete** completion routine we install. The second is for use by the lower-level driver.

Once we've built all the IRPs and URBs, it's time to submit them to the bus driver. Before we do so, however, it's prudent to check whether the main IRP has been cancelled, and it's necessary to install a completion routine for the main IRP. The logic at the end of the dispatch routine looks like the code on the following page.

```
IoSetCancelRoutine(Irp, OnCancelReadWrite);
if (Irp->Cancel)
  {
  status = STATUS_CANCELLED;
  if (IoSetCancelRoutine(Irp, NULL))
    --ctx->refcnt;
  }
else
  status = STATUS_SUCCESS;

IoSetCompletionRoutine(Irp, (PIO_COMPLETION_ROUTINE) OnReadWriteComplete,
  (PVOID) ctx, TRUE, TRUE, TRUE);
IoMarkIrpPending(Irp);
IoSetNextIrpStackLocation(Irp);

if (!NT_SUCCESS(status))
  {
  for (i = 0; i < numirps; ++i)
    {
    if (ctx->sub[i].urb)
      ExFreePool(ctx->sub[i].urb);
    if (ctx->sub[i].mdl)
      IoFreeMdl(ctx->sub[i].mdl);
    }
  CompleteRequest(Irp, status, 0);
  return STATUS_PENDING;
  }

for (i = 0; i < numirps; ++i)
  IoCallDriver(pdx->LowerDeviceObject, ctx->sub[i].irp);

return STATUS_PENDING;
```

Handling Cancellation of the Main IRP

To explain the two completion routines that I'm using in this example—that is, **OnReadWriteComplete** for the main IRP and **OnStageComplete** for each subsidiary IRP—I need to explain how USBISO handles cancellation of the main IRP. Cancellation is a concern because we've submitted a potentially large number of subsidiary IRPs that might take some time to finish. We can't complete the main IRP until all of the subsidiary IRPs complete. We should, therefore, provide a way to cancel the main IRP and all outstanding subsidiary IRPs.

I'm sure you recall from Chapter 5, "The I/O Request Packet," that IRP cancellation implicates a number of knotty synchronization issues. If anything, the situation in this driver is worse than usual.

USBISO's cancellation logic is complicated by the fact that we can't control the timing of calls to the subsidiary IRP's completion routine—those IRPs are owned by the bus driver once we submit them. Suppose you wrote the following cancel routine:

```
VOID OnCancelReadWrite(PDEVICE_OBJECT fdo, PIRP Irp)
  {
  IoReleaseCancelSpinLock(Irp->CancelIrql);
  PRWCONTEXT ctx = (PRWCONTEXT)
    Irp->Tail.Overlay.DriverContext[0];
  for (ULONG i = 0; i < ctx->numirps; ++i)
    IoCancelIrp(ctx->sub[i].irp);
  <additional steps>
  }
```

1. We saved the address of the RWCONTEXT structure in the **DriverContext** area of the IRP precisely so that we could retrieve it here. DriverContext is ours to use so long as we own the IRP. Since we returned STATUS_ PENDING from the dispatch routine, we never relinquished ownership.

2. Here, we cancel all the subsidiary IRPs. If a subsidiary IRP has already completed or is currently active on the device, the corresponding call to **IoCancelIrp** won't do anything. If a subsidiary IRP is still in the host controller driver's queue, the host controller driver's cancel routine will run and complete the subsidiary IRP. In all three cases, therefore, we can be sure that all subsidiary IRPs will be completed sometime soon.

This version of **OnCancelReadWrite** is *almost* complete, by the way, but it needs an additional step that I'll show you after I've explained the synchronization problem we need to solve. I can illustrate the problem by showing the completion routines we'll use with two naive mistakes built in. Here's the completion routine for one stage of the total transfer:

```
NTSTATUS OnStageComplete(PDEVICE_OBJECT fdo, PIRP subirp,
  PRWCONTEXT ctx)
  {
  PIO_STACK_LOCATION stack = IoGetCurrentIrpStackLocation(Irp);
  PIRP mainirp = ctx->mainirp;
  PURB urb = (PURB) stack->Parameters.Others.Argument1;
```

(continued)

```
    if (NT_SUCCESS(Irp->IoStatus.Status))
2     ctx->numxfer += urb->UrbIsochronousTransfer
        .TransferBufferLength;
    else
3     ctx->status = Irp->IoStatus.Status;
4   ExFreePool(urb);
    IoFreeMdl((PMDL) stack->Parameters.Others.Argument2);
5   IoFreeIrp(subirp);   // ← don't do this
6   if (InterlockedDecrement(&ctx->numpending) == 0)
      {
      IoSetCancelRoutine(mainirp, NULL); // ← also needs some work
      mainirp->IoStatus.Status = ctx->status;
      IoCompleteRequest(mainirp, IO_NO_INCREMENT);
      }
    return STATUS_MORE_PROCESSING_REQUIRED;
    }
```

1. This stack location is the extra one that the dispatch routine allocated. We need the address of the URB for this stage, and the stack was the most convenient place to save that address.

2. When a stage completes normally, we update the cumulative transfer count for the main IRP here. The final value of **numxfer** will end up in the main IRP's **IoStatus.Information** field.

3. We initialized **status** to STATUS_SUCCESS by zeroing the entire context structure. If any stage completes with an error, this statement will record the error status. The final value will end up in the main IRP's **IoStatus.Status** field.

4. We no longer need the URB or the partial MDL for this stage, so we release the memory they occupied here.

5. This call to **IoFreeIrp** is the naive part of this completion routine, as I'll explain shortly.

6. When the last stage completes, we'll also complete the main IRP. Once we've submitted the subsidiary IRPs, this is the only place where we complete the main IRP, so we can be sure that the main IRP pointer is valid.

Here's the naive version of the completion routine for the main IRP:

```
NTSTATUS OnReadWriteComplete(PDEVICE_OBJECT fdo, PIRP Irp,
  PRWCONTEXT ctx)
  {
  PDEVICE_EXTENSION pdx = (PDEVICE_EXTENSION) ctx->pdx;
```

```
1    if (Irp->Cancel)
       Irp->IoStatus.Status = STATUS_CANCELLED;
     else if (NT_SUCCESS(Irp->IoStatus.Status))
       Irp->IoStatus.Information = ctx->numxfer;

2    ExFreePool(ctx);     // ← don't do this

3    IoReleaseRemoveLock(&pdx->RemoveLock, Irp);
4    return STATUS_SUCCESS;
     }
```

1. If someone tried to cancel the main IRP, this statement will set the corresponding ending status.

2. Releasing the context structure's memory is a problem, as I'll explain.

3. This call to **IoReleaseRemoveLock** balances the acquisition we did in the dispatch function.

4. If we return any value at all besides STATUS_MORE_PROCESSING_ REQUIRED, IoCompleteRequest will continue its work without altering the completion status of the IRP.

I've been building up to a big and dramatic exposé of a synchronization problem associated with IRP cancellation, and here it finally is: suppose our cancel routine gets called after one or more of the calls to **IoFreeIrp** has already happened inside OnStageComplete? You can see that we might call **IoCancelIrp** with an invalid pointer in such a case. Or, suppose that the cancel routine gets called more or less simultaneously with OnReadWriteComplete. In that case, we might have the cancel routine accessing the context structure after it gets deleted.

You might attempt to solve these problems with various subterfuges. Could OnStageComplete nullify the appropriate subsidiary IRP pointer in the context structure, and could **OnCancelReadWrite** check before calling IoCancelIrp? (Yes, but there's still no way to guarantee that the call to IoFreeIrp doesn't squeeze in between whatever test OnCancelReadWrite makes and the moment when IoCancelIrp is finally done modifying the cancel-related fields of the IRP.) Could you protect the various cleanup steps with a spin lock? (That's a horrible idea, because you'd be holding the spin lock across calls to time-consuming functions.) Could you take advantage of knowing that the current release of Windows 2000 always cleans up completed IRPs in an APC routine? (No, for the reasons I discussed back in Chapter 5.)

I struggled long and hard with this problem before inspiration finally struck. Why not, I finally realized, protect the context structure and subsidiary IRP pointers with a reference count so that *both* the cancel routine and the main completion routines could share responsibility for cleaning them up? That's what I ended up doing. I put a reference count field (**refcnt**) into the context structure and initialized it to the value 2. One reference is for the cancel routine; the other is for the main completion routine. I wrote the following helper function to release the memory objects that are the source of the problem:

```
BOOLEAN DestroyContextStructure(PRWCONTEXT ctx)
  {
  if (InterlockedDecrement(&ctx->refcnt) > 0)
    return FALSE;
  for (ULONG i = 0; i < ctx->numirps; ++i)
    if (ctx->sub[i].irp)
      IoFreeIrp(ctx->sub[i].irp);
  ExFreePool(ctx);
  return TRUE;
  }
```

I call this routine at the end of the cancel routine:

```
VOID OnCancelReadWrite(PDEVICE_OBJECT fdo, PIRP Irp)
  {
  IoReleaseCancelSpinLock(Irp->CancelIrql);
  PRWCONTEXT ctx = (PRWCONTEXT)
    Irp->Tail.Overlay.DriverContext[0];
  for (ULONG i = 0; i < ctx->numirps; ++i)
    IoCancelIrp(ctx->sub[i].irp);
  PDEVICE_EXTENSION pdx = ctx->pdx;
  if (DestroyContextStructure(ctx))
    {
    CompleteRequest(Irp, STATUS_CANCELLED, 0);
    IoReleaseRemoveLock(&pdx->RemoveLock, Irp);
    }
  }
```

I omitted the call to IoFreeIrp in the stage completion routine and added one more line of code to decrement the reference count once it's certain that the cancel routine hasn't been, and can no longer, be called:

```
NTSTATUS OnStageComplete(PDEVICE_OBJECT fdo, PIRP subirp,
  PRWCONTEXT ctx)
  {
  PIO_STACK_LOCATION stack = IoGetCurrentIrpStackLocation(Irp);
  PIRP mainirp = ctx->mainirp;
  PURB urb = (PURB) stack->Parameters.Others.Argument1;
```

```
    if (NT_SUCCESS(Irp->IoStatus.Status))
      ctx->numxfer += urb->UrbIsochronousTransfer.TransferBufferLength;
    else
      ctx->status = Irp->IoStatus.Status;
    ExFreePool(urb);
    IoFreeMdl((PMDL) stack->Parameters.Others.Argument2);
    if (InterlockedDecrement(&ctx->numpending) == 0)
      {
      if (IoSetCancelRoutine(mainirp, NULL))
        InterlockedDecrement(&ctx->refcnt);
      mainirp->IoStatus.Status = ctx->status;
      IoCompleteRequest(mainirp, IO_NO_INCREMENT);
      }
    return STATUS_MORE_PROCESSING_REQUIRED;
    }
```

Recall that **IoSetCancelRoutine** returns the previous value of the cancel pointer. If that's NULL, the cancel routine has already been called and will call **DestroyContext-Structure**. If that's not NULL, however, it will no longer be possible for the cancel routine to ever be called, and we must use up the cancel routine's claim on the context structure.

I also replaced the unconditional call to ExFreePool in the main completion routine with a call to DestroyContextStructure:

```
NTSTATUS OnReadWriteComplete(PDEVICE_OBJECT fdo, PIRP Irp,
  PRWCONTEXT ctx)
  {
  PDEVICE_EXTENSION pdx = (PDEVICE_EXTENSION) ctx->pdx;
  if (Irp->Cancel)
  · Irp->IoStatus.Status = STATUS_CANCELLED;
  else if (NT_SUCCESS(Irp->IoStatus.Status))
    Irp->IoStatus.Information = ctx->numxfer;

  if (DestroyContextStructure(ctx))
    {
    IoReleaseRemoveLock(&pdx->RemoveLock, Irp);
    return STATUS_SUCCESS;
    }
  else
    return STATUS_MORE_PROCESSING_REQUIRED;
  }
```

Here's how this extra logic works. If the cancel routine ever gets called, it will run through the context structure calling IoCancelIrp for each of the subsidiary IRPs. Even if all of them have already completed, these calls will still be safe because we won't have called IoFreeIrp yet. The reference to the context structure will also be safe because we won't have called ExFreePool yet. The cancel routine finishes up by calling DestroyContextStructure, which will decrement the reference counter. If the main completion routine hasn't run yet, DestroyContextStructure will return FALSE, whereupon the cancel routine will return. The context structure still exists at this point, which is good because the main completion routine will reference it soon. The completion routine's eventual call to DestroyContextStructure will release the subsidiary IRPs and the context structure itself. The completion routine will then give up the remove lock that we acquired in the dispatch routine and return STATUS_SUCCESS in order to allow the main IRP to finish completing.

Suppose that calls to the cancel and main completion routines happen in the other order. In that case, OnReadWriteComplete's call to DestroyContextStructure will simply decrement the reference count and return FALSE, whereupon OnReadWrite-Complete will return STATUS_MORE_PROCESSING_REQUIRED. The context structure still exists. We can also be sure that we still own the IRP and the DriverContext field from which the cancel routine will fetch the context pointer. The cancel routine's call to DestroyContextStructure will, however, reduce the reference count to 0, release the memory, and return TRUE. The cancel routine will then release the remove lock and call IoCompleteRequest for the main IRP. That adds up to *two* calls to IoCompleteRequest for the same IRP. You know that you're not allowed to complete the same IRP twice, but the prohibition is not against calling IoCompleteRequest twice per se. If the first invocation of IoCompleteRequest results in calling a completion routine that returns STATUS_MORE_PROCESSING_REQUIRED, a subsequent, duplicate call is perfectly okay.

The only remaining case in this analysis is when the cancel routine never gets called at all. This is, of course, the *normal* case because IRPs don't usually get cancelled. We discover this fact when we call IoSetCancelRoutine in preparation for completing the main IRP. If IoSetCancelRoutine returns a non-NULL value, we know that IoCancelIrp has not yet been called for the main IRP. (Had it been, the cancel pointer would *already* be NULL, and IoSetCancelRoutine would have returned NULL.) Furthermore, we know that our own cancel routine can now never be called and will therefore not have a chance to reduce the reference count. Consequently, we reduce the reference count by hand so that OnReadWriteComplete's call to DestroyContextStructure will release the memory.

WHERE'S THE SYNCHRONIZATION?

You'll notice that I didn't use a spin lock to guard the code I just showed you earlier for testing for cancellation inside the dispatch routine. Synchronization between that code and some hypothetical caller of IoCancelIrp is implicit in the facts that IoSetCancelRoutine is an interlocked exchange operation and that IoCancelIrp sets the Cancel flag before calling IoSetCancelRoutine. Refer to the discussion in Chapter 5 for a sketch of how IoCancelIrp works.

Our dispatch routine's first call to IoSetCancelRoutine might occur after IoCancelIrp sets the Cancel flag but before IoCancelIrp does its own call to IoSetCancelRoutine. Our dispatch routine will see that the Cancel flag is set and make a second call to IoSetCancelRoutine. If this second call happens to precede IoCancelIrp's call to IoSetCancelRoutine, the cancel routine will not be called. We will also decrement the reference count on the context structure so that it gets released on the first call to DestroyContextStructure.

If our dispatch routine's second call to IoSetCancelRoutine follows IoCancelIrp's, we will not decrement the reference count. One or the other of the cancel routine or the completion routine will end up releasing the context structure.

If our dispatch routine tests the Cancel flag before IoCancelIrp sets it, or if IoCancelIrp has never even been called for this IRP, we'll go ahead and start the subsidiary IRPs. If IoCancelIrp was called in the distant past before we installed a cancel routine, it will have simply set the Cancel flag and returned. What happens after that is just the same as when our dispatch routine nullifies the cancel pointer before IoCancelIrp calls IoSetCancelRoutine.

So, you see, you don't always need a spin lock to give you multiprocessor safety: sometimes an atomic interlocked operation will do the trick by itself.

ASSOCIATED IRPS?

At first blush, **IoMakeAssociatedIrp** looks like an alternative way to create the subsidiary IRPs that USBISO needs. The idea behind IoMakeAssociatedIrp is that you could create a number of *associated* IRPs to fulfill a *master* IRP. When the last associated IRP completes, the I/O Manager automatically creates the master IRP.

Unfortunately, associated IRPs are not a good way to solve any of the problems that USBISO grapples with. Most important, WDM drivers aren't supposed to use IoMakeAssociatedIrp. Indeed, the completion logic for associated IRPs is incorrect in Windows 98—it doesn't call any completion routines for the master IRP when the last associated IRP finishes. Even in Windows 2000, however, the I/O Manager won't cancel associated IRPs when the master IRP is cancelled. Furthermore, the call to IoFreeIrp for an associated IRP occurs inside IoCompleteRequest, in whatever thread context happens to be current. This fact makes it harder to safely cancel the associated IRPs.

Streaming Isochronous Transfers

In the preceding section, I described a technique for performing a single long transfer over an isochronous pipe. You might need to arrange to transmit a continuous stream of data instead. I'll provide a quick sketch here of how you might do that.

In a streaming driver, you need to provide one or more data buffers that you can continuously transfer to or from the device without missing any frames. You also need to allocate at least two IRP/URB pairs that you use for the transfers. In this situation, the ability to chain URBs wouldn't help you even if it worked: you need to know when each URB finishes, and the only way to find out is when the associated IRP's completion routine gets called.

You initially submit all the IRPs to the bus driver. When one IRP completes, you immediately (in a completion routine) recycle it. The idea is to always have a URB queued in the host controller driver ready to run as soon as the current URB finishes. You might need to tune the size or number of data buffers and the number of IRP/URB pairs to avoid buffer overruns caused by temporary failures of your consumer or provider to keep up with the device.

Synchronizing Isochronous Transfers

Synchronicity is an important attribute of many types of isochronous data streams. To give a simple example, suppose you have two speakers and a microphone attached to a computer. You want the audio data rendered by the speakers to be synchronized with the data coming from the microphone in the sense that audible sound keeps up with the microphone input. You also want the sound coming out of one speaker to be synchronized with the other speaker.

Achieving acceptable synchronicity can be hard for several reasons. Section 5.10 of the USB specification describes these reasons and the hardware bases for their resolution in detail. I'm only going to summarize the challenges so that I can point you to the support USBD provides for drivers.

The sources and sinks of data might have different sample sizes and rates. A microphone, for example, might generate 8,000 one-byte samples every second, and a speaker might consume 44,100 32-bit samples every second. (This is the same example carried through Section 5.10 of the USB specification.) Some hardware or software agent must employ a scaling and interpolation process to match the source and sink.

Devices have inherent internal delays, too. A data source might need time to capture and encode data before sending it to the host, and a data sink might need time to decode and render data. In the simple example I gave of a single source with two similar sinks, these delays wouldn't be important. But imagine a situation in which multiple input devices, each with its own delay characteristics, were trying to capture different aspects of the same series of external events. (For example, a collection of microphones and MIDI devices.) Some agent needs to understand the delays that were introduced by the various source devices so as to "line up" the data streams received by the host. Some agent also needs to understand the delays that the sink devices will introduce so as to cause the actual output signals to reach the external environment at the right times. Since USB requires device delays to be measured in frame units, a driver deals with delay by explicitly setting the StartFrame member of the isochronous transfer URBs it generates. To set this field, you perform a calculation starting either with the frame number during which some input data arrived—which you can retrieve from the completed URB's StartFrame member—or with the current frame number.

Finally, devices must provide some way to synchronize their internal clocks with the rest of the system. Synchronization is required in the first place because clocks can *drift* over time (that is, they can become progressively less synchronized because of slight differences in oscillator frequency) or they can *jitter* (that is, their rate can vary up and down because of thermal or other fluctuations). USB identifies three alternative methods for an endpoint to synchronize its clock: asynchronous, synchronous, and adaptive.

An asynchronous endpoint can't synchronize its operation with any external source. A source endpoint implicitly informs the host of its data rate by the amount of data it provides. A sink endpoint would need to have access to an auxiliary synchronization endpoint, such as an interrupt endpoint, to report back its progress in consuming data.

A synchronous endpoint ties its operation to the 1-kHz frame rate of the bus. It does so either by slaving its own clock to the start-of-frame (SOF) packet that begins every frame or by forcing the bus frame rate to match its own clock. USB allows any one device to be the *frame master* and to alter the duration of frames to be more or less than the standard one millisecond. On the driver side, you issue a URB with the function code URB_FUNCTION_TAKE_FRAME_LENGTH_CONTROL to become the frame master, and you issue another URB with the function code URB_FUNCTION_ RELEASE_FRAME_LENGTH_CONTROL to relinquish your status as frame master. While you are the master, you can issue URBs with the function codes URB_ FUNCTION_GET_FRAME_LENGTH and URB_FUNCTION_SET_FRAME_LENGTH to get and set the frame length, respectively.

An adaptive source endpoint has some way (a control pipe, for example) of receiving feedback from a data sink that allows it to generate samples that are already matched to the sink. An adaptive sink endpoint simply adapts to the rate information that's implicit in the data stream it receives.

Chapter 12

Installing Device Drivers

Early in the device driver development process, it is important to devote some thought to how an end user will install your driver and install the hardware it serves. Microsoft Windows 2000 and Microsoft Windows 98 use a text file with the file extension INF to control most of the activities associated with installing drivers. You provide the INF file. It either goes on a diskette or on a disc that you package with the hardware, or else Microsoft puts it on the Windows 2000 installation disc. In the INF file, you tell the operating system which file(s) to copy onto the end user's hard disk, which registry entries to add or modify, and so on.

In this chapter, I'll discuss several aspects of installing your driver. I'll lead you through the important parts of a simple INF file to help you tie together the DDK documentation about INF file syntax. I'll explain in detail the format of device identifiers used for various types of devices—this information is hard to come by right now, as it happens. I'll discuss how to initialize property values in a device's hardware registry key and how to access those properties later from drivers and applications. Since I had to define a custom device class for all the sample "devices" used in this book, I thought it would help you to see how I did that. To round out this chapter (and, in fact, the entire book), I'll discuss a method you can use to cause an application to start automatically when the PnP Manager starts one of your devices.

THE INF FILE

An INF file contains a collection of *sections* introduced by a section name in brackets. Most sections contain a series of directives of the form "keyword = value". The INF file begins with a **Version** section that identifies the type of device described by entries in the file:

```
[Version]
Signature=$CHICAGO$
Class=Sample
ClassGuid={894A7460-A033-11d2-821E-444553540000}
```

Signature can be one of the three magic values **$Chicago$**, **$Windows NT$** (with one space), or **$Windows 95$** (also with one space). **Class** identifies the class of device. Table 12-1 lists the predefined classes that Windows 2000 already supports. **ClassGuid** uniquely identifies the device class. The DDK header file DEVGUID.H defines the globally unique identifiers (GUIDs) for standard device classes, and the DDK documentation entry for the Version section documents them as well.

In a production INF file, you will also need to have **DriverVer** and **CatalogFile** statements in the **Version** section. You should also have a comment (that is, any line that starts with a semicolon) containing the word "copyright" to satisfy the CHKINF utility I'll describe in the section "Tools for INF Files" later in this chapter. The operating systems will accept INF files that lack these details, but Microsoft won't certify your driver package without them. Refer to the DDK documentation for more details about the required INF syntax.

I find it useful to think of the bulk of an INF file as the linear description of a tree structure. Each section is a node in the tree, and each directive is a pointer to another section. Figure 12-1 illustrates the concept.

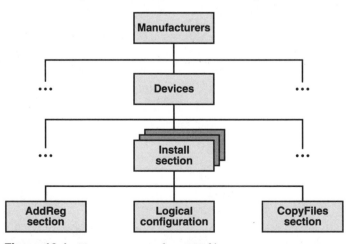

Figure 12-1. *Tree structure of an INF file.*

INF Class Name	Description
1394	IEEE 1394 host bus controllers (but not peripherals)
Battery	Battery devices
CDROM	CD-ROM drives, including SCSI and IDE
DiskDrive	Hard disk drives
Display	Video adapters
FDC	Floppy disk controllers
FloppyDisk	Floppy disk drives
HDC	Hard disk controllers
HIDClass	Human input devices
Image	Still-image capture devices, including cameras and scanners
Infrared	NDIS miniport drivers for Serial-IR and Fast-IR ports
Keyboard	Keyboards
MediumChanger	SCSI media changer devices
Media	Multimedia devices, including audio, DVD, joysticks, and full-motion video capture devices
Modem	Modems
Monitor	Display monitors
Mouse	Mouse and other pointing devices
MTD	Memory technology driver for memory devices
Multifunction	Combination devices
MultiportSerial	Intelligent multiport serial cards
Net	Network adapter cards
NetClient	Network file system and print providers (client side)
NetService	Server-side support for network file systems
NetTrans	Network protocol drivers
PCMCIA	PCMCIA and CardBus host controllers (but not peripherals)
Ports	Serial and parallel ports
Printer	Printers
SCSIAdapter	SCSI and RAID controllers, host bus adapter miniports, and disk array controllers
SmartCardReader	Smart card readers
System	System devices
TapeDrive	Tape drives
USB	USB host controllers and hubs (but not peripherals)
Volume	Logical storage volume drivers

Table 12-1. *Device classes for INF files.*

At the apex of the tree is a **Manufacturer** section that lists all the companies with hardware described in the file. For example:

```
[manufacturer]
"Walter Oney Software"=DeviceList
"Finest Organization On Earth Yet"=FOOEY

[DeviceList]
...

[FOOEY]
...
```

Each individual manufacturer's *model* section (DeviceList and FOOEY in the example) describes one or more devices:

```
[DeviceList]
Description=InstallSectionName,DeviceId
...
```

where **Description** is a human-readable description of the device and **DeviceId** identifies a hardware device. The **InstallSectionName** parameter identifies (or points to, in my tree metaphor) another section of the INF file that contains instructions for installing the software for a particular device. An example of an entry for a single type of device might be this (drawn from the PKTDMA sample in Chapter 7, "Reading and Writing Data"):

```
[DeviceList]
"AMCC S5933 Development Board (DMA)"=DriverInstall,PCI\VEN_10E8&DEV_4750
```

The information in the Manufacturer section and in the model section(s) for individual manufacturers comes into play when the system needs to install a driver for a piece of hardware. A Plug and Play (PnP) device announces its presence and identity electronically. A bus driver detects it automatically and constructs a device identifier using onboard data. The system then attempts to locate preinstalled INF files that describe that particular device. INF files reside in the INF subdirectory of the Windows directory. If the system can't find a suitable INF file, it asks the end user to specify one.

A legacy device can't announce its own presence or identity. The end user therefore launches the add hardware wizard to install a legacy device and helps the wizard locate the right INF file. Key steps in this process include specifying the type of device being installed and the name of the manufacturer. See Figure 12-2.

The hardware wizard constructs dialogs such as Figure 12-2 by enumerating all the INF files for a particular type of device, all of the statements in their Manufacturer sections, and all of the model statements for each of the manufacturers. You can guess that the manufacturer names that appear in the left pane of the dialog come from the left sides of Manufacturer statements and that the device types that appear in the right pane come from the left sides of model statements.

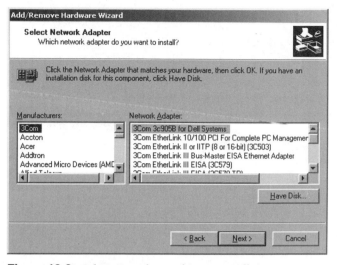

Figure 12-2. *Selecting a device during installation.*

MORE ABOUT HARDWARE WIZARD DIALOGS

Once the wizard is past the stage of looking for PnP devices, it builds a list of device classes and uses various **SetupDi***Xxx* routines from SETUPAPI.DLL to retrieve icons and descriptions. The information that SETUPAPI uses to implement these routines ultimately comes from the registry, where it was placed by entries in **ClassInstall32** sections. Not every device class will be represented in the list—the wizard will suppress information about classes that have the **NoInstallClass** attribute.

After the end user selects a device class, the wizard calls SETUPAPI functions to construct lists of manufacturers and devices as described in the text. Devices mentioned in **ExcludeFromSelect** statements will be absent from these lists.

Install Sections

An *install section* contains the actual instructions that the installer needs to install software for a device. We've been considering the PKTDMA sample. For that device, the DeviceList model section specifies the name DriverInstall. I find it useful to think of this name as identifying an *array* of sections, one for each Windows platform. The "zero" element in this array has the base name of the section (DriverInstall). You can have platform-specific array elements whose names start with the base name and contain one of the suffixes listed in Table 12-2. The device installer looks for the install section having the most specialized suffix. Suppose, for example, that you have install sections with no suffix, with the **.NT** suffix, and with the **.NTx86** suffix. If you're installing into Windows 2000 on an Intel x86 platform, the installer will use the .NTx86 section. If you're installing into Windows 2000 on a non-Intel platform, it would use the .NT section. If you're installing into Windows 98, it would use the section without a suffix.

Platform	*Install Section Suffix*
Any platform including Windows 98	[none]
Any Windows 2000 platform	.NT
Windows 2000 on Intel x86	.NTx86

Table 12-2. *Install section suffixes for each platform.*

Because of the search rules I just outlined, all of the INF files for my sample drivers have the no-suffix and .NT-suffix install sections. That makes the INF files work fine on any Intel platform. (As you probably know by now, Microsoft and Compaq dropped support for the current 32-bit version of Windows 2000 on the Alpha platform just as this book was going to press. We therefore made no provision for testing my samples on the Alpha.)

Further along in this chapter, I'll be discussing other INF sections whose names begin with the name of the install section. If you have multiple install sections in your "array," these other sections have to include the platform-dependent suffix in their names, too. For example, I'll be discussing a Services section that you use to install a description of the driver into the registry. You would form the name of this section by taking the base name of the install section (for example, DriverInstall) plus the platform suffix (for example, NT) and adding the word Services, ending up with [DriverInstall.NT.Services].

A typical Windows 2000 install section would contain a **CopyFiles** directive and nothing else:

```
[DriverInstall.nt]
CopyFiles=DriverCopyFiles
```

This CopyFiles directive indicates that we want the installer to use the information in another INF section for copying files onto the end user hard disk. For the PKTDMA sample, the other section is named DriverCopyFiles:

```
[DriverCopyFiles]
pktdma.sys,,,2
```

This section directs the installer to copy PKTDMA.SYS to the end user's hard disk.

The statements in a CopyFiles section have this general form:

```
Destination,Source,Temporary,Flags
```

Destination is the name (without any directory name) of the file as it will eventually exist on the end user system. **Source** is the name of the file as it exists on the distribution media, if that name is different from the Destination name; otherwise, it's just blank as in the example. In Windows 98, if you might be installing a file that will be in use at the time of installation, you specify a temporary name in the **Temporary** parameter. Windows 98 will rename the temporary file to the Destination name on the next reboot. It's not necessary to use this parameter for Windows 2000 installs because the system automatically generates temporary names.

The **Flags** parameter contains a bit mask that governs whether the system will decompress a file and how the system deals with situations in which a file by the same name already exists. The interpretation of the flags depends in part on whether the INF and driver are part of a package that Microsoft has digitally signed after certification. Table 12-3 on the following page is a list of all these flag bits. The italicized flags in the table are ignored in a digitally signed package. I used a double line to delimit groups of mutually exclusive flags. Thus, in an unsigned package, you could specify one or the other of the NOSKIP or WARN_IF_SKIP flags, but not both.

The file name by itself is not sufficient to tell the installer what it needs to know to copy a file. It also needs to know which directory you want the file copied to. In addition, if you have multiple diskettes in the installation set, it needs to know which diskette contains the source file. These pieces of information come from other sections of the INF file, as suggested by Figure 12-3. In the PKTDMA example, these sections are as follows:

```
[DestinationDirs]
DefaultDestDir=10,System32\Drivers

[SourceDisksFiles]
pktdma.sys=1

[SourceDisksNames]
1="WDM Book Companion Disc",disk1
```

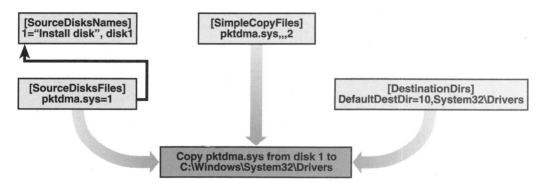

Figure 12-3. *Source and destination information for file copies.*

Symbolic Name	Numeric Value	Description
COPYFLG_REPLACEONLY	0x00000400	Copy only if destination file already exists
COPYFLG_NODECOMP	0x00000800	Don't decompress file
COPYFLG_FORCE_FILE_IN_USE	0x00000008	Always copy under temporary name and rename on next boot
COPYFLG_NO_OVERWRITE	0x00000010	Don't overwrite an existing file (other flags can't be used with this flag)
COPYFLG_REPLACE_BOOT_FILE	0x00001000	Replace boot file needed by the loader, which will prompt user to reboot
COPYFLG_NOPRUNE	0x00002000	Copy this file even if Setup thinks it's already present
COPYFLG_NOVERSIONCHECK	0x00000004	Overwrite a file even if it's a newer version than the source file
COPYFLG_NO_VERSION_DIALOG	0x00000020	Don't present the dialog that allows the user to decide whether to overwrite a newer file
COPYFLG_OVERWRITE_OLDER_ONLY	0x00000040	Only overwrite an older version of the file
COPYFLG_NOSKIP	0x00000002	Don't allow the user to skip this file
COPYFLG_WARN_IF_SKIP	0x00000001	Allow the user to skip this file and provide a warning

Table 12-3. *Flags in a CopyFile section directive.*

The **SourceDisksFiles** section indicates that the installer can find PKTDMA.SYS on disk number 1 of the set. The **SourceDisksNames** section indicates that disk number 1 has a human-readable label of "WDM Book Companion Disc" and contains a file named "disk1" that the installer can look for to verify that the correct diskette is in the drive. Note that these section names have an interior "s" that's very easy to miss.

The **DestinationDirs** section specifies the target directories for copy operations. **DefaultDestDir** is the target directory to use for any file whose target directory isn't otherwise specified. You use a numeric code to specify the target directory because the end user might choose to install Windows 2000 to a directory with a nonstandard name. Please refer to the DDK documentation entry for the DestinationDirs section for a complete list of the codes—only a few of them are in common use, as follows:

- Directory 10 is the Windows directory (for example, "\Windows" or "\Winnt").

- Directory 11 is the System directory (for example, "\Windows\System" or "\Winnt\System32").

- Directory 12 is the Drivers directory on a Windows 2000 system (for example, "\Winnt\System32\Drivers"). Unfortunately, this number has a different meaning on a Windows 98 system (for example, "\Windows\System\Iosubsys").

WDM drivers reside in the Drivers directory. If your CopyFiles section applies only to a Windows 2000 installation, you can just specify directory number 12. If you want to share a CopyFiles section between Windows 98 and Windows 2000 installs, however, I recommend that you specify "10,System32\Drivers" instead because it identifies the Drivers directory in both cases.

Defining the Driver Service

The INF syntax I've described so far is sufficient for your driver file(s) to be copied onto the end user's hard disk. You must also arrange for the PnP Manager to know which files to load. A **.Services** section accomplishes that goal, as in this example:

```
[DriverInstall.NT.Services]
AddService=PKTDMA,2,DriverService

[DriverService]
ServiceType=1
StartType=3
ErrorControl=1
ServiceBinary=%10%\system32\drivers\pktdma.sys
```

The 2 in the **AddService** directive indicates that the PKTDMA service will be the function driver for the device. You form the name of this section by appending the word "Services" to the name of the install section to which it applies.

The end result of these directives will be a key in the HKEY_LOCAL_MACHINE\System\CurrentControlSet\Services branch of the registry named PKTDMA (the first parameter in the AddService directive). It will define the service entry for the driver as a kernel-mode driver (**ServiceType** equal to 1) that should be demand-loaded by the PnP Manager (**StartType** equal to 3). Errors that occur during loading should be logged but should not by themselves prevent the system from starting (**ErrorControl** equal to 1). The executable image can be found in \Winnt\System32\Drivers\pktdma.sys (the value of **ServiceBinary**). By the way, when you look in the registry, you'll see that the name of the executable file is stored under the name **ImagePath** rather than ServiceBinary.

It's a good idea to make the name of the service (PKTDMA in this example) the same as the filename (PKTDMA.SYS in this example) of your driver binary file. Not only does this make it obvious which service name corresponds to which driver, but it also avoids a problem that can arise when two different service keys point to the same driver: any device that uses the same driver as a then-started device but under a different service name can't itself start.

Device Identifiers

For true Plug and Play devices, the device identifier that appears in a manufacturer's model section of an INF is very important. Plug and Play devices are those that can electronically announce their presence and identity. A bus enumerator can find these devices automatically, and it can read some sort of onboard information to find out what kind each device is. Universal serial bus (USB) devices, for example, include vendor and product identification codes in their device descriptors, and the configuration space of Peripheral Component Interconnect (PCI) devices includes vendor and product codes.

When an enumerator detects a device, it constructs a list of device identification strings. One entry in the list is a complete identification of the device. This entry will end up naming the hardware key in the registry. Additional entries in the list are "compatible" identifiers. The PnP Manager uses all of the identifiers in the list when it tries to match a device to an INF file. Enumerators place more specific identifiers ahead of less specific identifiers so that vendors can supply specific drivers that will be found in preference to more general drivers. The algorithm for constructing the strings depends on the enumerator, as follows:

PCI Devices

The full device identifier has the form

```
PCI\VEN_vvvv&DEV_dddd&SUBSYS_ssssssss&REV_rr
```

where **vvvv** is the vendor identifier that the PCI Special Interest Group assigned to the manufacturer of the card, **dddd** is the device identifier that the manufacturer assigned to the card, **ssssssss** is the subsystem id (often zero) reported by the card, and **rr** is the revision number.

For example, the display adapter on my current laptop computer (based on the Chips and Technologies 65550 chip) has this identifier:

```
PCI\VEN_102C&DEV_00E0&SUBSYS_00000000&REV_04
```

A device can also match an INF model with any of these identifiers:

```
PCI\VEN_vvvv&DEV_dddd&SUBSYS_ssssssss
PCI\VEN_vvvv&DEV_dddd&REV_rr
PCI\VEN_vvvv&DEV_dddd
PCI\VEN_vvvv&DEV_dddd&REV_rr&CC_ccss
PCI\VEN_vvvv&DEV_dddd&CC_ccsspp
PCI\VEN_vvvv&DEV_dddd&CC_ccss
```

```
PCI\VEN_vvvv&CC_ccsspp
PCI\VEN_vvvv&CC_ccss
PCI\VEN_vvvv
PCI\CC_ccsspp
PCI\CC_ccss
```

in which **cc** is the base class code from the configuration space, **ss** is the subclass code, and **pp** is the programming interface. For example, the following additional identifiers for my laptop's display adapter would have matched the information in an INF file:

```
PCI\VEN_102C&DEV_00E0&SUBSYS_00000000
PCI\VEN_102C&DEV_00E0&REV_04
PCI\VEN_102C&DEV_00E0
PCI\VEN_102C&DEV_00E0&REV_04&CC_0300
PCI\VEN_102C&DEV_00E0&CC_030000
PCI\VEN_102C&DEV_00E0&CC_0300
PCI\VEN_102C&CC_030000
PCI\VEN_102C&CC_0300
PCI\VEN_102C
PCI\CC_030000
PCI\CC_0300
```

The INF that the system actually used for driver installation was the third one, which includes just the vendor and device identifiers.

PCMCIA Devices

The device identifier for a simple device has the form

```
PCMCIA\Manufacturer-Product-Crc
```

For example, the device identifier for the 3Com network card on my current laptop computer is

```
PCMCIA\MEGAHERTZ-CC10BT/2-BF05
```

For an individual function on a multifunction device, the identifier has the form

```
PCMCIA\Manufacturer-Product-DEVdddd-Crc
```

where **Manufacturer** is the name of the manufacturer and **Product** is the name of the product. The PCMCIA enumerator retrieves these strings directly from tuples on the card. **Crc** is the 4-digit hexadecimal CRC checksum for the card. The child function number (**dddd** in the template) is a decimal number without leading zeros.

If the card doesn't have a manufacturer name, the identifier will have one of these three forms:

```
PCMCIA\UNKNOWN_MANUFACTURER-Crc
PCMCIA\UNKNOWN_MANUFACTURER-DEVdddd-Crc
PCMCIA\MTD-0002
```

(The last of these three alternatives is for a flash memory card with no manufacturer identifier on the card.)

In addition to the device identifier just described, an INF file's model section can also contain an identifier composed by replacing the 4-digit hexadecimal CRC with a string containing the 4-digit hexadecimal manufacturer code, a hyphen, and the 4-digit hexadecimal manufacturer information code (both from onboard tuples). For example:

```
PCMCIA\MEGAHERTZ-CC10BT/2-0128-0103
```

SCSI Devices

The complete device identifier is

```
SCSI\ttttvvvvvvvvpppppppppppppppprrrr
```

where **tttt** is a device type code, **vvvvvvvv** is an 8-character vendor identifier, **pppppppppppppppp** is a 16-character product identifier, and **rrrr** is a 4-character revision level value. The device type code is the only one of the identifier components that doesn't have a fixed length. The bus driver determines this portion of the device identifier by indexing an internal string table with the device type code from the device's inquiry data, as shown in Table 12-4. The remaining components are just the strings that appear in the device's inquiry data but with special characters (including space, comma, and any nonprinting graphic) replaced with an underscore.

SCSI Type Code	Device Type	Generic Type
DIRECT_ACCESS_DEVICE (0)	Disk	GenDisk
SEQUENTIAL_ACCESS_DEVICE (1)	Sequential	
PRINTER_DEVICE (2)	Printer	GenPrinter
PROCESSOR_DEVICE (3)	Processor	
WRITE_ONCE_READ_MULTIPLE_DEVICE (4)	Worm	GenWorm
READ_ONLY_DIRECT_ACCESS_DEVICE (5)	CdRom	GenCdRom
SCANNER_DEVICE (6)	Scanner	GenScanner
OPTICAL_DEVICE (7)	Optical	GenOptical
MEDIUM_CHANGER (8)	Changer	ScsiChanger
COMMUNICATION_DEVICE (9)	Net	ScsiNet
	Other	ScsiOther

Table 12-4. *Type names for SCSI devices.*

For example, a disk drive on one of my workstations has this identifier:

```
SCSI\DiskSEAGATE_ST39102LW_____0004
```

The bus driver also creates these additional identifiers:

```
SCSI\ttttvvvvvvvvpppppppppppppppppp
SCSI\ttttvvvvvvvv
SCSI\vvvvvvvvpppppppppppppppppppr
vvvvvvvvpppppppppppppppppppr
gggg
```

In the third and fourth of these additional identifiers, **r** represents just the first character of the revision identifier. In the last identifier, **gggg** is the generic type code from Table 12-4.

To carry forward the example of my disk drive, the bus driver generated these additional device identifiers:

```
SCSI\DiskSEAGATE_ST39102LW_____
SCSI\DiskSEAGATE_
SCSI\DiskSEAGATE_ST39102LW_____0
SEAGATE_ST39102LW_____0
GenDisk
```

The last of these (**GenDisk**) is the one that appeared as the device identifier in the INF file that the PnP Manager actually used to install a driver for this disk. In fact, the generic identifier is *usually* the one that's in the INF file because SCSI drivers tend to be generic.

IDE Devices

IDE devices receive device identifiers that are very similar to SCSI identifiers:

```
IDE\ttttvpvprrrrrrrr
IDE\vpvprrrrrrrr
IDE\ttttvpvp
vpvprrrrrrrr
gggg
```

Here, **tttt** is a device type name (same as SCSI); **vpvp** is a string containing the vendor name, an underscore, the vendor's product name, and enough underscores to bring the total to 40 characters; **rrrrrrrr** is an 8-character revision number; and **gggg** is a generic type name (almost the same as SCSI type names in Table 12-4). For IDE changer devices, the generic type name is **GenChanger** instead of **ScsiChanger**; other IDE generic names are the same as SCSI.

For example, here are the device identifiers generated for an IDE hard drive on one of my desktop systems:

```
IDE\DiskMaxtor_91000D8_____SASX1B18
IDE\Maxtor_91000D8_____SASX1B18
IDE\DiskMaxtor_91000D8_____
Maxtor_91000D8_____SASX1B18
GenDisk
```

ISAPNP Devices

The ISAPNP enumerator constructs two hardware identifiers:

```
ISAPNP\id
*altid
```

where **id** and **altid** are EISA-style identifiers for the device—three letters to identify the manufacturer and 4 hexadecimal digits to identify the particular device. If the device in question is one function of a multifunction card, the first identifier in the list takes this form:

```
ISAPNP\id_DEVnnnn
```

where **nnnn** is the decimal index (with leading zeros) of the function.

For example, the codec function of the Crystal Semiconductor audio card on one of my desktop machines has these two hardware identifiers:

```
ISAPNP\CSC6835_DEV0000
*CSC0000
```

The second of these identifiers is the one that matched the actual INF file.

USB Devices

The complete device identifier is

```
USB\VID_vvvv&PID_dddd&REV_rrrr
```

where **vvvv** is the 4-digit hexadecimal vendor code assigned by the USB committee to the vendor, **dddd** is the 4-digit hexadecimal product code assigned to the device by the vendor, and **rrrr** is the revision code. All three of these values appear in the device descriptor or interface descriptor for the device.

An INF model section can also specify these alternatives:

```
USB\VID_vvvv&PID_dddd
USB\CLASS_cc&SUBCLASS_ss&PROT_pp
USB\CLASS_cc&SUBCLASS_ss
USB\CLASS_cc
USB\COMPOSITE
```

where **cc** is the class code from the device or interface descriptor, **ss** is the subclass code, and **pp** is the protocol code. These values are in 2-digit hexadecimal format.

1394 Devices

The 1394 bus driver constructs these identifiers for a device:

```
1394\VendorName&ModelName
1394\UnitSpecId&UnitSwVersion
```

where **VendorName** is the name of the hardware vendor, **ModelName** identifies the device, **UnitSpecId** identifies the software specification authority, and **UnitSw-Version** identifies the software specification. The information used to construct these identifiers comes from the device's configuration ROM.

If a device has vendor and model name strings, the 1394 bus driver uses the first identifier as the hardware ID and the second identifier as the one and only compatible ID. If a device lacks a vendor or model name string, the bus driver uses the second identifier as the hardware ID.

Since I don't have a 1394 bus on any of my computers, I relied on fellow driver writer Jeff Kellam to provide me with two examples. The first example is for a Sony camera, for which the device identifier is

```
1394\SONY&CCM-DS250_1.08
```

The second example is for the 1394 bus itself operating in diagnostic mode; this device identifier is

```
1394\031887&040892
```

Identifiers for Generic Devices

The PnP Manager also works with device identifiers for generic devices that can appear on many different buses. These identifiers are of the form

```
*PNPdddd
```

where **dddd** is a 4-digit hexadecimal type identifier. At press time, the official list of these identifiers was at *http://www.microsoft.com/hwdev/download/respec/devids.txt*.

The Hardware Registry Key

The hardware registry key records information about a particular hardware instance your driver manages. Each enumerator of devices has its own registry key below HKEY_LOCAL_MACHINE\System\CurrentControlSet\Enum. When the enumerator finds a device with a particular identifier, it creates a key for the identifier and a subkey for each instance of the same device. For example, the PKTDMA device has the identifier PCI\VEN_10E8&DEV_4750. The first instance of this device in your system might have a hardware key named like this:

```
\Registry\Machine\System\CurrentControlSet\Enum\
  PCI\VEN_10E8&DEV_4750\BUS_00&DEV_04&FUNC_00
```

Standard Properties

The PnP Manager stores certain standard information about the device in the hardware key. You can retrieve this information in a WDM driver by calling **IoGetDevice-Property** with one of the property codes listed in Table 12-5.

Property Name	Value Name	Source	Description
DevicePropertyDeviceDescription	DeviceDesc	First parameter in model statement	Description of device
DevicePropertyHardwareId	HardwareID	Third parameter in model statement	Identifies device
DevicePropertyCompatibleIDs	CompatibleIDs	Created by bus driver during detection	Device types that can be considered to match
DevicePropertyClassName	Class	Class parameter in Version section of INF	Name of device class
DevicePropertyClassGuid	ClassGUID	ClassGuid para-meter in Version section of INF	Unique identifier of device class
DevicePropertyDriverKeyName	Driver	Created automati-cally as part of in-stallation process	Name of service (software) key that specifies driver
DevicePropertyManufacturer	Mfg	Manufacturer in whose model section device was found	Name of hardware manufacturer
DevicePropertyFriendlyName	FriendlyName	Explicit AddReg in INF file, or class installer	"Friendly" name suit-able for presentation to the user

Table 12-5. *Standard device properties in the hardware key.*

For example, to retrieve the description of a device, use the following code. (See the **AddDevice** function in the DEVPROP sample.)

```
WCHAR name[256];
ULONG junk;
status = IoGetDeviceProperty(pdo,
  DevicePropertyDeviceDescription, sizeof(name), name, &junk);
KdPrint((DRIVERNAME
  " - AddDevice has succeeded for '%ws' device\n", name));
```

Notice from Table 12-5 that the PnP Manager and bus driver together manage to create all of the standard device properties automatically except for the friendly name. You can supply a friendly name by an explicit statement in your INF file if you want:

```
[DriverInstall.NT.hw]
AddReg=DriverHwAddReg

[DriverHwAddReg]
HKR,,FriendlyName,,"Packet DMA Demonstration Device"
```

Mind you, *every* device of this particular type that is installed on a particular machine will end up with the same friendly name if you adopt this approach. The end user will obviously be confused if more than one device has the same friendly name. If you anticipate that there might be duplicate friendly names, you should provide a co-installer DLL to compute unique names.

User-mode applications can retrieve the standard device properties with **SetupDiGetDeviceRegistryProperty**. Use the following method within the context of an enumeration of registered interfaces using the setup APIs:

```
HDEVINFO info = SetupDiGetClassDevs(...);
SP_DEVINFO_DATA did = {sizeof(SP_DEVINFO_DATA)};
SetupDiGetDeviceInterfaceDetail(info, ..., &did);
TCHAR fname[256];
SetupDiGetDeviceRegistryProperty(info, &did,
  SPDRP_FRIENDLYNAME, NULL, (PBYTE) fname,
  sizeof(fname), NULL);
```

Refer to the DDK documentation of SetupDiGetDeviceRegistryProperty for a list of the SPDRP_*XXX* values you can specify to retrieve the various properties.

As you can see, you must supply a device information set handle (an HDEVINFO) and an SP_DEVINFO_DATA structure as arguments to SetupDiGetDeviceRegistry-Property. That's easy to do if you're in the middle of a loop enumerating instances of a device interface. But suppose all you have is the symbolic name of the device? You can use the following trick, which I found to be pretty obscure when one of the Microsoft developers showed it to me, to construct these two crucial parameters:

```
LPCTSTR devname;   // ⬅ someone gives you this
HDEVINFO info = SetupDiCreateDeviceInfoList(NULL, NULL);
SP_DEVICE_INTERFACE_DATA ifdata = {sizeof(SP_DEVICE_INTERFACE_DATA)};
SetupDiOpenDeviceInterface(info, devname, 0, &ifdata);
SP_DEVINFO_DATA did = {sizeof(SP_DEVINFO_DATA)};
SetupDiGetDeviceInterfaceDetail(info, &ifdata, NULL, 0, NULL, &did);
```

You can go on to call routines such as SetupDiGetDeviceRegistryProperty in the normal way at this point.

> **NOTE** In Windows 98 and Windows NT version 4, application programs used the CFGMGR32 set of APIs to obtain information about devices and to interact with the PnP Manager. These APIs continue to be supported for purposes of compatibility in Windows 98 and Windows 2000, but Microsoft discourages their use in new code. For that reason, I'm not even showing you examples of calling them. You might be tempted—as I initially was—to use them because they seem to be better documented. If you know where to look for the documentation, that is. Have patience: Microsoft will get around to documenting the SetupDi*Xxx* functions in enough detail for us mortals to use them effectively.

Nonstandard Properties

The PnP Manager creates a subkey of the hardware key named **Device Parameters**. This subkey contains nonstandard properties of the device. You can initialize nonstandard properties in a hardware add registry section in your INF:

```
[DriverInstall.nt.hw]
AddReg=DriverHwAddReg

[DriverHwAddReg]
HKR,,SampleInfo,,"%wdmbook%\chap7\pktdma\pktdma.htm"
```

WDM drivers can easily open a handle to the device parameter key by calling **IoOpenDeviceRegistryKey**. Applications can access the key by using **SetupDiOpenDevRegKey**.

Tools for INF Files

If you look in the TOOLS subdirectory of the Windows 2000 DDK, you'll find two useful utilities for working with INF files. GENINF will help you build a new INF file, and CHKINF will help you validate an INF file. At the time I'm writing this, I'm using the RC1 release of the DDK, in which GENINF is still pretty rudimentary. By the time you read this, GENINF will either have grown to a robust tool with a completely different user interface than it now has, or else it will have been dropped from the kit. Either way, I can't give you any useful information about how to use it.

CHKINF is actually a BAT file that runs a PERL script to examine and validate an INF file. You'll obviously need a PERL implementation to use this tool. I got a copy from *http://www.perl.com*.

You can run CHKINF most easily from a command prompt. For example:

```
E:\Ntddk\tools\chkinf>chkinf C:\wdmbook\chap12\devprop\sys\device.inf
```

CHKINF generates HTML output files in an HTM subdirectory. Figure 12-4 shows the output I received when checking DEVICE.INF for DEVPROP sample.

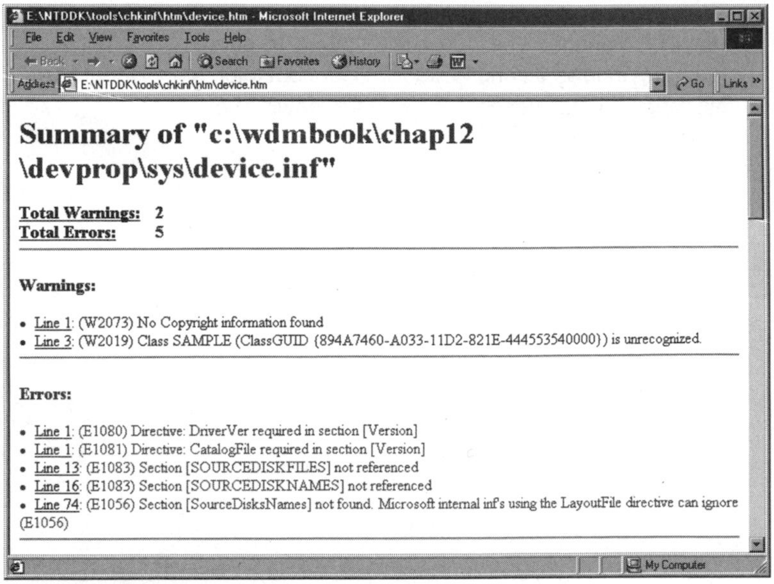

Figure 12-4. *Example of CHKINF output.*

In Windows 2000, the device installer logs various information about the operations it performs in a disk file named SETUPAPI.LOG in the Windows NT directory. You can control the verbosity of the log and the name of the log file by manually changing entries in the registry key named HKEY_LOCAL_MACHINE\Software\Microsoft\Windows\CurrentVersion\Setup. Please consult the DDK documentation for detailed information about these settings.

DEFINING A DEVICE CLASS

Let's suppose you have a device that doesn't fit into one of the device classes Microsoft has already defined. When you're initially testing your device and your driver, you can get away with using the **Unknown** class in your INF file. Production devices are not supposed to be in the Unknown class, however. You should instead place your custom device into a new device class that you define in the INF file. I'll explain how to create a custom class in this section.

The INF example I showed you earlier relied on a custom device class:

```
[Version]
Signature=$CHICAGO$
Class=Sample
ClassGuid={894A7460-A033-11d2-821E-444553540000}
```

In fact, all of the samples in this book use the Sample class.

When you want to define a new class of device, you only need to do one task: run GUIDGEN to create a unique GUID for the class. You can add polish to the user interface for your device class by doing some additional tasks, such as writing a property page provider for use with the Device Manager and putting some special entries into the registry key your class uses. You can also provide filter drivers and parameter overrides that will be used for every device of your class. You control each of these additional features by statements in your INF file. For example:

```
[ClassInstall32]
AddReg=SamclassAddReg
CopyFiles=SamclassCopyFiles

[SamclassAddReg]
HKR,,,,"WDM Book Sample"
...

[SamclassCopyFiles]
...
```

The illustrated registry entry turns into the "friendly name" for the device class in the Device Manager and in the list of device types displayed by the add hardware wizard. I'll explain some of the additional registry entries you might want to add to the class key in the following sections.

> **NOTE** None of my INF files has a **ClassInstall32** section. None is needed because the setup program for the sample disc puts the necessary class information directly into the registry. If you define your own device class as part of a production driver package, however, you will need this section. Note also that Microsoft discourages installing a new class without using an INF.

A Property Page Provider

Way back in Chapter 1, "Introduction"—in Figure 1-6 on page 13, to be precise—I showed you a screen shot of the property page I invented for use with the Sample device class. The SAMCLASS sample on the companion disc is the source code for the property page provider that produced that page, and I'm now going to explain how it works.

A property page provider for a device class is a 32-bit DLL with the following contents:

- An exported entry point for each class for which the DLL supplies property pages

- Dialog resources for each property page

- A dialog procedure for each property page

In general, a single DLL can provide property pages for several device classes. Microsoft supplies some DLLs with the operating system that do this, for example. SAMCLASS, however, provides only a single page for a single class of device. Its only exported entry point is the following function:

```
extern "C" BOOL CALLBACK EnumPropPages
  (PSP_PROPSHEETPAGE_REQUEST p,
  LPFNADDPROPSHEETPAGE AddPage, LPARAM lParam)
  {
  PROPSHEETPAGE page;
  HPROPSHEETPAGE hpage;
  memset(&page, 0, sizeof(page));
  page.dwSize = sizeof(PROPSHEETPAGE);
  page.hInstance = hInst;
  page.pszTemplate = MAKEINTRESOURCE(IDD_SAMPAGE);
  page.pfnDlgProc = PageDlgProc;
  <some more stuff>
  hpage = CreatePropertySheetPage(&page);
  if (!hpage)
    return TRUE;
  if (!(*AddPage)(hpage, lParam))
    DestroyPropertySheetPage(hpage);
  return TRUE;
  }
```

When the Device Manager is about to construct the property sheet for a device, it consults the class registry key to see if there's a property page provider. You can designate a provider with a line like the following in your INF file:

```
[SamclassAddReg]
HKR,,EnumPropPages32,,"samclass.dll,EnumPropPages"
```

The Device Manager loads the DLL you specify (SAMCLASS.DLL) and calls the designated entry point (**EnumPropPages**). If the function returns TRUE, the Device Manager will display the property page; otherwise, it won't. The function can add zero or more pages by calling the **AddPage** function as shown in the preceding example.

Inside the SP_PROPSHEETPAGE_REQUEST structure your enumeration function receives as an argument, you'll find two very useful pieces of information: a handle to a device information set, and the address of an SP_DEVINFO_DATA structure that pertains to the device you're concerned with. These data items (but not, unfortunately, the SP_PROPSHEETPAGE_REQUEST structure that contains them) remain valid for as long as the property page is visible, and it would be useful for you to be able to access them inside the dialog procedure you write for your property page. Windows SDK Programming 101 (well, maybe 102, because this is a little obscure) taught you how to do this. First create an auxiliary structure whose address you pass to **CreatePropertySheetPage** as the **lParam** member of the PROPSHEETPAGE structure:

```
struct SETUPSTUFF {
  HDEVINFO info;
  PSP_DEVINFO_DATA did;
  };

BOOL EnumPropPages(...)
  {
  PROPSHEETPAGE page;
  ...
  SETUPSTUFF* stuff = new SETUPSTUFF;
  stuff->info = p->DeviceInfoSet;
  stuff->did = p->DeviceInfoData;
  page.lParam = (LPARAM) stuff;

  page.pfnCallback = PageCallbackProc;
  page.dwFlags = PSP_USECALLBACK;
  ...
  }

UINT CALLBACK PageCallbackProc(HWND junk, UINT msg, LPPROPSHEETPAGE p)
  {
  if (msg == PSPCB_RELEASE && p->lParam)
    delete (SETUPSTUFF*) p->lParam;
  return TRUE;
  }
```

The WM_INITDIALOG message that Windows sends to your dialog procedure gets an lParam value that's a pointer to the same PROPSHEETPAGE structure, so you can retrieve the **stuff** pointer there. You can then use **SetWindowLong** and **GetWindowLong** to save any desired information in the DWL_USER slot associated with the dialog object. In SAMCLASS, I chose to determine the name of a readme file that would describe the sample driver. I'll show you the code for doing that in a couple of paragraphs.

You also need to provide a way to delete the SETUPSTUFF structure when it's no longer needed. The easiest way, which works whether or not you ever get a WM_INITDIALOG message—you won't if there's an error constructing your property page—is to use a property page callback function as shown in the preceding fragment.

You can do all sorts of things in a custom property page. For the sample class, I wanted to provide a button that would bring up an explanation for each sample device. To keep things as general as possible, I decided to put a **SampleInfo** value naming the explanation file in the device's hardware registry key. To invoke a viewer for the explanation file, it suffices to call **ShellExecute**, which will interpret the file extension and locate an appropriate viewer application. For my book samples, the explanation files are HTML files, so the viewer in question will be your Web browser.

Most of the work in SAMCLASS occurs in the WM_INITDIALOG handler. (Error checking is again omitted.)

```
case WM_INITDIALOG:
  {
  SETUPSTUFF* stuff = (SETUPSTUFF*) ((LPPROPSHEETPAGE) lParam)->lParam;
  BOOL okay = FALSE;
  TCHAR name[256];
  SetupDiGetDeviceRegistryProperty(stuff->info, stuff->did,
    SPDRP_FRIENDLYNAME, NULL, (PBYTE) name, sizeof(name), NULL);
  SetDlgItemText(hdlg, IDC_SAMNAME, name);

  HKEY hkey = SetupDiOpenDevRegKey(stuff->info, stuff->did,
    DICS_FLAG_GLOBAL, 0, DIREG_DEV, KEY_READ);
  DWORD length = sizeof(name);
  RegQueryValueEx(hkey, "SampleInfo", NULL, NULL,
    (LPBYTE) name, &length);
  LPSTR infofile;
  DoEnvironmentSubst(name, sizeof(name));
  infofile = (LPSTR) GlobalAlloc(GMEM_FIXED, strlen(name)+1);
  strcpy(infofile, name);
  SetWindowLong(hdlg, DWL_USER, (LONG) infofile);
  RegCloseKey(hkey);
  break;
  }
```

1. Here, we determine the **FriendlyName** for the device and put it into a static text control. The actual code sample receives the device description if there's no friendly name.

2. The next few statements determine the **SampleInfo** filename from the hardware key's parameter subkey.

3. The strings I put in the registry are of the form %wdmbook%\chap12\ devprop\devprop.htm, in which %wdmbook% indicates substitution by the value of the WDMBOOK environment variable. The call to **Do-EnvironmentSubst**, a standard Win32 API, expands the environment variable.

4. I need to remember the name of the SampleInfo file somewhere, and **SetWindowLong** provides a convenient way to do that.

When the end user—that would be you in this particular situation, I think— presses the More Information button on the property page, the dialog procedure receives a WM_COMMAND message, which it processes as on the next page.

```
case WM_COMMAND:
  switch (LOWORD(wParam))
    {
  case IDB_MOREINFO:
    {
    LPSTR infofile = (LPSTR) GetWindowLong(hdlg, DWL_USER);
    ShellExecute(hdlg, NULL, infofile, NULL, NULL, SW_SHOWNORMAL);
    return TRUE;
    }
    }
  break;
```

ShellExecute will launch the application associated with the SampleInfo file—namely, your Web browser—whereupon you can view the file and find all sorts of interesting information.

Other Class-Specific Information

In the preceding section, I showed you how an **EnumPropPages32** registry entry controls the display of property pages for devices belonging to your custom class. Here are some other registry entries that you can use to tailor features of the class:

- **Installer32** designates a DLL that performs installation functions for devices belonging to the class. Writing a class installer is a huge undertaking, not least because the DDK documentation hasn't caught up to the software in this area. I didn't attempt to write a class installer for the Sample class.

- **Class** is the class name as it should be spelled in INF file **Class=** statements.

- **Icon** designates an icon to use in user interface displays about the class. This value is a string containing a decimal integer. A positive value designates an icon in the Installer32 DLL; documentation says that the system will find the icon in your EnumPropPages32 DLL if you don't have a class installer, but I didn't find that to be the case. A negative number designates an icon (whose index is the absolute value) in SETUPAPI.DLL. If you don't specify an icon, the system uses a nondescript gray diamond. I decided to use the value −5 for the Sample class, which designates an icon that looks vaguely like a PCI card. In fact, the system uses the same icon for network cards, but I liked this choice better than the others.

- **NoInstallClass**, if present and not equal to 0, indicates that some enumerator will automatically detect any device belonging to this class. If the class has this attribute, the hardware wizard won't include this class in the list of device classes it presents to the end user.

- **SilentInstall**, if present and not equal to 0, causes the PnP manager to install devices of this class without presenting any dialogs to the end user.

- **UpperFilters** and **LowerFilters** specify service names for filter drivers. The PnP Manager loads these filters for *every* device belonging to the class. (You specify filter drivers that apply to just one device in the device's hardware key.)

- **NoDisplayClass**, if present and not equal to 0, suppresses devices of this class from the Device Manager display.

A class key may also specify **DeviceCharacteristics**, **DeviceType**, and/or **Security** properties that contain overriding values for certain device attributes. I discussed these values in Chapter 2, "Basic Structure of a WDM Driver," in the section "The Role of the Registry." The PnP Manager applies these overrides when it creates a physical device object (PDO). I'm guessing here, but I suspect that someday a system administrator will somehow be able to examine and change these properties.

LAUNCHING AN APPLICATION

You can enhance the end user experience of your hardware by providing an application that starts whenever one of your devices exists. Microsoft provides a special-purpose mechanism for still-image cameras but hasn't provided a general-purpose mechanism that other devices can use. I'll describe just such a mechanism, named AutoLaunch, in this section.

The AutoLaunch Service

Windows 98 and Windows 2000 both provide for notifications to applications when hardware events occur. Microsoft Windows 95 introduced the WM_DEVICECHANGE message. As originally conceived for Windows 95, the system broadcasts this message in user mode to all top-level windows for each of several possible device events.

Building on WM_DEVICECHANGE, Windows 2000 generates notifications to interested service applications whenever a device driver enables or disables a registered device interface. I wrote an AutoLaunch service to take advantage of these notifications. The service subscribes for notifications about a special interface GUID by calling a new user-mode API named **RegisterDeviceNotification**:

```
#include <dbt.h>

DEV_BROADCAST_DEVICEINTERFACE filter = {0};
filter.dbcc_size = sizeof(filter);
filter.dbcc_devicetype = DBT_DEVTYP_DEVICEINTERFACE;
filter.dbcc_classguid = GUID_AUTOLAUNCH_NOTIFY;
```

(continued)

```
HDEVNOTIFY hNotification = RegisterDeviceNotification(hService,
  (PVOID) &filter, DEVICE_NOTIFY_SERVICE_HANDLE);
```

To receive the interface notifications, the service must initialize by calling **RegisterServiceCtrlHandlerEx** instead of **RegisterServiceCtrlHandler** in its **ServiceMain** function:

```
hService = RegisterServiceCtrlHandlerEx(<svcname>,
  HandlerEx, <context>);
```

When you call RegisterServiceCtrlHandlerEx, you specify a **HandlerEx** event handler function that receives three more parameters than a standard service **Handler** function:

```
DWORD __stdcall HandlerEx(DWORD ctlcode, DWORD evtype,
  PVOID evdata, PVOID context)
  {
  }
```

In the situation we're concerned with here, **ctlcode** will equal SERVICE_CONTROL_DEVICEEVENT, **evtype** will equal DBT_DEVICEARRIVAL, and **evdata** will be the address of a device interface broadcast structure. The **context** parameter will be whatever value you specified as the third argument to RegisterServiceCtrlHandlerEx.

The device interface broadcast structure looks like this:

```
struct _DEV_BROADCAST_DEVICEINTERFACE_W {
  DWORD dbcc_size;
  DWORD dbcc_devicetype;
  DWORD dbcc_reserved;
  GUID dbcc_classguid;
  WCHAR dbcc_name[1];
  };
```

The **dbcc_devicetype** value will be DBT_DEVTYP_DEVICEINTERFACE. The **dbcc_classguid** will be the 128-bit interface GUID that some device driver enabled or disabled, and the **dbcc_name** will be the symbolic link name you can use to open a handle to the device. This particular structure comes in both ANSI and Unicode versions. The service notification always uses the Unicode version, even if your service happens to have been built, as AutoLaunch is, using ANSI.

Triggering AutoLaunch

To trigger a device interface arrival notification to AutoLaunch, a driver simply has to register and enable an interface by using the AutoLaunch GUID:

```
typedef struct _DEVICE_EXTENSION {
  ...
  UNICODE_STRING AutoLaunchInterfaceName;
  } DEVICE_EXTENSION, *PDEVICE_EXTENSION;
```

```
NTSTATUS AddDevice(...)
  {
  ...
  IoRegisterDeviceInterface(pdo, &GUID_AUTOLAUNCH_NOTIFY,
    NULL, &pdx->AutoLaunchInterfaceName);
  ...
  }

NTSTATUS StartDevice(PDEVICE_OBJECT fdo, ...)
  {
  ...
  IoSetDeviceInterfaceState(&pdx->AutoLaunchInterfaceName, TRUE);
  ...
  }
```

I discussed device interfaces in Chapter 2 as a method of giving a name to a device so that an application could find the device and open a handle to it. A single device can register as many interfaces as make sense. In this particular situation, you would register an AutoLaunch interface *in addition to* any interfaces that you might support. The only purpose of the AutoLaunch interface is to generate the notification for which the service is waiting.

When your driver enables its GUID_AUTOLAUNCH_NOTIFY interface, the system sends the AutoLaunch service a device arrival notification, which the service processes in this function:

```
DWORD CAutoLaunch::HandleDeviceChange(DWORD evtype,
  _DEV_BROADCAST_HEADER* dbhdr)
  {
  if (!dbhdr
    || evtype != DBT_DEVICEARRIVAL
    || dbhdr->dbcd_devicetype != DBT_DEVTYP_DEVICEINTERFACE)
    return 0;
  PDEV_BROADCAST_DEVICEINTERFACE_W p =
    (PDEV_BROADCAST_DEVICEINTERFACE_W) dbhdr;
  CString devname = p->dbcc_name;
  HDEVINFO info = SetupDiCreateDeviceInfoList(NULL, NULL);
  SP_DEVICE_INTERFACE_DATA ifdata =
    {sizeof(SP_DEVICE_INTERFACE_DATA)};
  SP_DEVINFO_DATA devdata = {sizeof(SP_DEVINFO_DATA)};
  SetupDiOpenDeviceInterface(info, devname, 0, &ifdata);
  SetupDiGetDeviceInterfaceDetail(info, &ifdata, NULL, 0, NULL,
    &devdata);
  OnNewDevice(devname, info, &devdata);
  SetupDiDestroyDeviceInfoList(info);
  return 0;
  }
```

1. There are other notifications besides the ones we're interested in. Some of them are queries. Returning 0 is how we indicate success or acquiescence to some query we don't specifically process. In fact, the real AUTOLAUNCH sample on the disc handles the DBT_DEVICEREMOVE-COMPLETE notification too so that it can keep track of which arrival notifications it's already processed and avoid duplication during system startup. I left that detail out here to avoid clutter.

2. I built the AutoLaunch sample without UNICODE. This statement therefore converts the UNICODE linkname in the notification structure to ANSI.

My **OnNewDevice** function is going to spawn a new process to perform whatever command line it finds in the registry. It was most convenient to use the device's *hardware key* as a repository for the command line. The code to do this is as follows:

```
void CAutoLaunch::OnNewDevice(const CString& devname,
  HDEVINFO info, PSP_DEVINFO_DATA devdata)
  {
  HKEY hkey = SetupDiOpenDevRegKey(info, devdata, DICS_FLAG_GLOBAL,
    0, DIREG_DEV, KEY_READ);

  DWORD junk;
  TCHAR buffer[_MAX_PATH];
  DWORD size = sizeof(buffer);
  CString Command;
  RegQueryValueEx(hkey, "AutoLaunch", NULL, &junk,
    (LPBYTE) buffer, &size);
  Command = buffer;

  CString FriendlyName;
  SetupDiGetDeviceRegistryProperty(info, devdata,
    SPDRP_FRIENDLYNAME, NULL, (PBYTE) buffer, sizeof(buffer), NULL);
  FriendlyName.Format(_T("\"%s\""), buffer);

  RegCloseKey(hkey);

  ExpandEnvironmentStrings(Command, buffer, arraysize(buffer));
  CString name;
  name.Format(_T("\"%s\""), (LPCTSTR) devname);
  Command.Format(buffer, (LPCTSTR) name, (LPCTSTR) FriendlyName);

  STARTUPINFO si = {sizeof(STARTUPINFO)};
  si.lpDesktop = "WinSta0\\Default";
  si.wShowWindow = SW_SHOW;
```

```
    PROCESS_INFORMATION pi;
7   CreateProcess(NULL, (LPTSTR) (LPCTSTR) Command, NULL, NULL,
      FALSE, 0, NULL, NULL, &si, &pi);
8   CloseHandle(pi.hProcess);
    CloseHandle(pi.hThread);
    }
```

1. This statement opens the **Device Parameters** subkey of the device's hardware registry key.

2. The INF file put an **AutoLaunch** value in the registry. We read that value here.

3. Here we fetch the **FriendlyName** of the device for use as a command line argument. There might be blanks in the name, so we want to put quotes around it before submitting the command.

4. I wanted to allow the command line template in the registry to include environment variables surrounded by **%** characters. This statement expands the environment strings.

5. I also wanted the command line template to use a **%s** escape to indicate where the device name and friendly name belong. This statement produces a command line with the substitution taken care of.

6. We're about to call CreateProcess to execute the command. Unless we're careful, the command will use the same hidden desktop as our own service process, which is not going to be very useful to the end user! So we create a STARTUPINFO structure that specifies the interactive session desktop.

7. Here's where we actually launch the application whose name we found in the registry. **CreateProcess** returns right away; the application lives on until someone closes it.

8. CreateProcess also gives us handles to the process and its initial thread. We need to close those handles, or else the process and thread will never go away.

Chickens and Eggs

The process I just described works great in a steady-state situation, where the AutoLaunch service is already up and running on a computer when a device comes along and tries to launch a special application. Two other situations need to be dealt with, though.

First, devices that are already plugged in when the system is bootstrapped will manage to register their GUID_AUTOLAUNCH_NOTIFY interfaces before the service manager starts up the AutoLaunch service. Yet, you still (presumably) want the AutoLaunch applications to start too.

AutoLaunch deals with this startup issue by enumerating all instances of the interface when it first starts:

```
VOID CAutoLaunch::EnumerateExistingDevices(const GUID* guid)
  {
  HDEVINFO info = SetupDiGetClassDevs(guid, NULL, NULL,
    DIGCF_PRESENT | DIGCF_INTERFACEDEVICE);
  SP_INTERFACE_DEVICE_DATA ifdata;
  ifdata.cbSize = sizeof(ifdata);
  DWORD devindex;
  for (devindex = 0;
    SetupDiEnumDeviceInterfaces(info, NULL, guid, devindex, &ifdata);
    ++devindex)
    {
    DWORD needed;
    SetupDiGetDeviceInterfaceDetail(info, &ifdata, NULL, 0,
      &needed, NULL);
    PSP_INTERFACE_DEVICE_DETAIL_DATA detail =
      (PSP_INTERFACE_DEVICE_DETAIL_DATA) malloc(needed);
    detail->cbSize = sizeof(SP_INTERFACE_DEVICE_DETAIL_DATA);
    SP_DEVINFO_DATA devdata = {sizeof(SP_DEVINFO_DATA)};
    SetupDiGetDeviceInterfaceDetail(info, &ifdata, detail,
      needed, NULL, &devdata);
    CString devname = detail->DevicePath;
    free((PVOID) detail);
    OnNewDevice(devname, guid);
    }
  }
```

The only interesting lines of code in this whole function are the ones in bold face, where we obtain the necessary SP_DEVINFO_DATA structure and symbolic link name. We then call **OnNewDevice** (the function you've already seen) to deal with this pre-existing device.

Getting the Service Running

The second startup situation you have to deal with is when your device is being installed for the first time onto a machine that's never seen the AutoLaunch service before. Your INF file needs to define the AutoLaunch service and copy the service binary file onto the end user computer. It can add a registry entry to the so-called **RunOnce** key to trigger the service. For example:

```
[DestinationDirs]
AutoLaunchCopyFiles=10
[etc.]
```

```
[DriverInstall.NT]
CopyFiles=DriverCopyFiles,AutoLaunchCopyFiles
AddReg=DriverAddReg.NT

[DriverAddReg.NT]
HKLM,%RUNONCEKEYNAME%,AutoLaunchStart,,\
  "rundll32 StartService,StartService AutoLaunch"

[DriverInstall.NT.Services]
AddService=AutoLaunch,,AutoLaunchService
[etc.]

[AutoLaunchCopyFiles]
AutoLaunch.exe,,,0x60
StartService.exe,,,0x60

[AutoLaunchService]
ServiceType=16
StartType=2
DisplayName="AutoLaunch Service"
ErrorControl=1
ServiceBinary=%10%\AutoLaunch.exe

[Strings]
RUNONCEKEYNAME="Software\Microsoft\Windows\CurrentVersion\RunOnce"
```

Refer to the DEVICE.INF in the SYS subdirectory of the AUTOLAUNCH sample for the full picture.

After the installation of your device finishes, the system executes any commands that are within the RunOnce registry key. The command we put there starts the AutoLaunch service if it's not already running. Note that STARTSERVICE.DLL is a tiny DLL I wrote that starts a service without displaying any user interface or popping up a dialog box. You'll want to use RUNDLL32 as the command verb in the RunOnce value so that it will work correctly with a remote install of your driver package.

> **NOTE** Microsoft Knowledge Base article Q173039 suggests that the immediate-processing behavior of entries in the RunOnce key is essentially a side effect of a call to RUNDLL32. One of the Microsoft developers responsible for the device installer has assured me that the RunOnce values are always processed at the conclusion of installing a new device, regardless of what this article says.

WINDOWS 98 COMPATIBILITY NOTES

Windows 98 uses completely different technology for installing and maintaining devices than Windows 2000. In this section, I'll describe some of the ways this might affect you.

Property Page Providers

A property page provider for a new device class must be a 16-bit DLL. Look at SAMCLS16 on the companion disc if you want to see an example, and don't discard your 16-bit compiler just yet!

Registry Usage

Windows 98 uses a software registry key to locate device drivers. To initialize this key, your Windows 98 install section should have an **AddReg** directive similar to this example:

```
[DriverInstall]
AddReg=DriverAddReg
<other install directives>

[DriverAddReg]
HKR,,DevLoader,,*ntkern
HKR,,NTMPDriver,,pktdma.sys
```

That is, you designate NTKERN.VXD as the device loader for your device, and you designate your WDM driver as the **NTMPDriver** for which NTKERN looks. In addition, you omit a **.Services** section because Windows 98 doesn't use it.

In contrast to Windows 2000, Windows 98 puts standard and nonstandard device properties in the hardware key instead of separating the nonstandard properties into a **Device Parameters** subkey. This turns out to be lucky, since you can't use **IoGetDeviceProperty** to retrieve standard properties in Windows 98. (See the next section for the reason.)

Getting Device Properties

Windows 98 (including Windows 98 Second Edition) incorrectly implements IoGetDeviceProperty for the standard properties in a device's hardware key. To retrieve these properties in a WDM driver, you should use **IoOpenDeviceRegistryKey** and interrogate the property by name. The DEVPROP sample illustrates how to do this for the standard device description property.

Application Launching

Windows 98 doesn't have a service manager, so you can't run AutoLaunch as a service. The next best thing is an executable named in the registry's **Run** keyword. Part of the AutoLaunch package is an ALNCH98.EXE applet that can be executed in this way. It provides a tray icon that you can use if you want it to halt.

Appendix A

Coping with Windows 98 Incompatibilities

I closed many of the chapters in this book with a series of Microsoft Windows 98 compatibility notes. While Microsoft originally planned that you'd be able to ship a single driver binary file for both Windows 98 and Microsoft Windows 2000, the sad fact is that so lofty a goal might prove elusive in practice. Not surprisingly, Windows 2000 continued to evolve long after Windows 98 was up and running on millions of PCs, and it supports several kernel-mode service functions that Windows 98 does not. If a WDM driver calls one of these functions, Windows 98 simply won't load the driver because it can't resolve the reference to the symbol. In this appendix, I'll describe a static virtual device driver (VxD)—the WDMSTUB sample on the companion disc—that resolves a few of these symbols. Once you have the ability to load a driver that calls functions that Windows 98 doesn't normally support, you might find that you need a way to determine at run time whether you're running under Windows 98 or Windows 2000; I'll also describe a heuristic that you can use to make this determination.

DEFINING STUBS FOR KERNEL-MODE ROUTINES

The stub technique used in WDMSTUB.VXD relies on the same basic trick that Microsoft crafted to port several hundred kernel-mode support functions from Microsoft Windows NT to Windows 98—that is, extending the symbol tables that the run-time loader uses when it resolves import references. To extend the symbol tables, you first define three data tables that will persist in memory:

- A name table that gives the names of the functions you're defining

- An address table that gives the addresses of the functions

- An ordinal table that correlates the name and address tables

Here are some of the table entries from WDMSTUB:

```
static char* names[] = {
  "PoRegisterSystemState",
  ...
  "ExSystemTimeToLocalTime",
  ...
  };

static WORD ordinals[] = {
  0,
  ...,
  6,
  ...
  };

static PFN addresses[] = {
  (PFN) PoRegisterSystemState,
  ...
  (PFN) ExSystemTimeToLocalTime,
  ...
  };
```

The purpose of the ordinal table is to provide the index within **addresses** of the entry for a given **names** entry. That is, the function named by **names[i]** is **address[ordinals[i]]**.

If it weren't for a version compatibility problem I'll describe in a moment, you could call **_PELDR_AddExportTable** as follows:

```
HPEEXPORTTABLE hExportTable = 0;

extern "C" BOOL OnDeviceInit(DWORD dwRefData)
  {
  _PELDR_AddExportTable(&hExportTable,
    "ntoskrnl.exe",
    arraysize(addresses), // ← don't do it this way!
    arraysize(names), 0,
    (PVOID*) names,
    ordinals, addresses, NULL);
  return TRUE;
  }
```

The call to _PELDR_AddExportTable extends the table of symbols that the loader uses when it tries to resolve import references from NTOSKRNL.EXE, which is of course the Windows 2000 kernel. NTKERN.VXD, the main support module for WDM drivers in Windows 98, initializes this table with the addresses of the several hundred functions it supports. WDMSTUB.VXD is a static VxD with an initialization order later than NTKERN and earlier than the Windows 98 Configuration Manager. Consequently, WDMSTUB's export definitions will be in place by the time the system loads any WDM drivers. In effect, then, WDMSTUB is an extension to NTKERN.

Version Compatibility

The version compatibility problem to which I alluded earlier is this: Windows 98 supports a particular subset of the Windows 2000 functions used by WDM drivers. Windows 98, Second Edition, supports a larger subset. The next version of Windows, code-named Millennium, will support a still larger subset (maybe even a superset, given that it will be released after Windows 2000). You would not want your stub VxD to duplicate one of the functions that the OS supports. What WDMSTUB actually does during initialization, therefore, is dynamically construct the tables that it passes to _PELDR_AddExportTable:

```
HPEEXPORTTABLE hExportTable = 0;

extern "C" BOOL OnDeviceInit(DWORD dwRefData)
  {
  char** stubnames = (char**) _HeapAllocate(sizeof(names), HEAPZEROINIT);
  PFN* stubaddresses = (PFN*) _HeapAllocate(sizeof(addresses),
    HEAPZEROINIT);
  WORD* ordinals = (WORD*) _HeapAllocate(arraysize(names) * sizeof(WORD),
    HEAPZEROINIT);
  int i, istub;
  for (i = 0, istub = 0; i < arraysize(names); ++i)
    {
    if (_PELDR_GetProcAddress((HPEMODULE) "ntoskrnl.exe", names[i], NULL)
      == 0)
      {
      stubnames[istub] = names[i];
      ordinals[istub] = istub;
      stubaddresses[istub] = addresses[i];
      ++istub;
      }
    }
  _PELDR_AddExportTable(&hExportTable, "ntoskrnl.exe", istub,
    istub, 0, (PVOID*) stubnames, ordinals, stubaddresses, NULL);
  return TRUE;
  }
```

The line appearing in bold face is the crucial step here—it makes sure that we don't inadvertently replace a function that already exists in NTKERN or another system VxD.

There's one annoying glitch in the version compatibility solution I just outlined. Windows 98, Second Edition, exports just three of the four support functions for managing the IO_REMOVE_LOCK object. The missing function is **IoRemoveLockAndWaitEx**, if you care. My WDMSTUB.VXD driver compensates for this omission by stubbing either all or none of the remove lock functions based on whether or not this function is missing.

Stub Functions

The main purpose of WDMSTUB.VXD is to resolve symbols that your driver might reference but not actually call. For some functions, such as **PoRegisterSystemState**, WDMSTUB.VXD simply contains a stub that will return an error indication if it is ever called:

```
PVOID PoRegisterSystemState(PVOID hstate, ULONG flags)
  {
  ASSERT(KeGetCurrentIrql() < DISPATCH_LEVEL);
  return NULL;
  }
```

BUILDING WDMSTUB

To get WDMSTUB to build correctly, I needed to incorporate a couple of nonstandard features. Each stub function must use the **__stdcall** calling convention, whereas VxDs normally use **__cdecl**.

I wanted to call **KeGetCurrentIrql** and maybe other WDM service functions from the stub VxD. A standard way to do this is to include WDM.H or NTDDK.H before all of the VxD header files and link with the WDMVXD.LIB import library. WDMVXD.LIB assumes that the functions you're trying to import are declared with the **__declspec(dllimport)** directive, which is normally true when you include either WDM.H or NTDDK.H. This is because they're all declared using a preprocessor macro named NTKERNALAPI, which normally gets #defined as __declspec(dllimport). Unfortunately, if you try to *define* a function that's marked as dllimport, the compiler assumes you meant to *export* the function. A VxD's first export must be the device description block (DDB) that defines the driver, though, and not some random exported stub function. I guessed that specifying ordinal number 1 for the DDB in my module definition file would force the DDB to be the first export, but I was mistaken. At the end of this rather sad story, I ended up with a VxD that wouldn't load.

To get past all of these problems with import vs. export declarations, I had to coerce NTDDK.H not to define NTKERNELAPI in the normal way. (See STDVXD.H in the WDMSTUB project.) That leaves the module with unresolved references to symbols like **_KeGetCurrentIrql@0** because of the limited vocabulary of WDMVXD.LIB. In the particular case of KeGetCurrentIrql, one can issue a standard **VxDCall** to a service named **ObsoleteKeGetCurrentIrql** and reach the right function in the Windows 98 kernel. Alternatively, one could define a function (with a name like MyGetCurrentIrql) that calls KeGetCurrentIrql and place it in a source module that you compile with the normal setting for NTKERNELAPI.

Sometimes, though, you don't need to write a stub that fails the function call—you can actually implement the function, as in this example:

```
VOID ExLocalTimeToSystemTime(PLARGE_INTEGER localtime,
  PLARGE_INTEGER systime)
  {
  systime->QuadPart = localtime->QuadPart + GetZoneBias();
  }
```

where **GetZoneBias** is a helper routine that determines the time zone *bias*—that is, the number of units by which local time differs from Greenwich mean time—by interrogating the **ActiveTimeBias** value in the **TimeZoneInformation** registry key.

Table A-1 lists the kernel-mode support functions that WDMSTUB.VXD exports.

Support Function	*Remarks*
ExLocalTimeToSystemTime	Implemented
ExSystemTimeToLocalTime	Implemented
IoAcquireRemoveLockEx	Implemented
IoAllocateWorkItem	Implemented
IoFreeWorkItem	Implemented
IoInitializeRemoveLockEx	Implemented
IoQueueWorkItem	Implemented
IoReleaseRemoveLockEx	Implemented
IoReleaseRemoveLockAndWaitEx	Implemented
IoCreateNotificationEvent	Stub—always fails
IoCreateSynchronizationEvent	Stub—always fails
IoReportTargetDeviceChangeAsynchronous	Stub—always fails
KdDebuggerEnabled	Implemented
KeEnterCriticalRegion	Implemented
KeLeaveCriticalRegion	Implemented
KeNumberProcessors	Always returns 1
KeSetTargetProcessorDpc	Implemented
PoCancelDeviceNotify	Stub—always fails
PoRegisterDeviceNotify	Stub—always fails
PoRegisterSystemState	Stub—always fails
PoSetSystemState	Stub—always fails
PoUnregisterSystemState	Stub—always fails
PsGetVersion	Implemented
RtlInt64ToUnicodeString	Stub—always fails
RtlUlongByteSwap	Implemented
RtlUlonglongByteSwap	Implemented
RtlUshortByteSwap	Implemented

Table A-1. *Functions exported by WDMSTUB.VXD.*

DETERMINING THE OPERATING SYSTEM VERSION

Once you've managed to get your device driver loaded—a feat that might require, as I've just discussed, arranging to define Windows 98 stubs for certain support routines—you may need to base run-time decisions on which version of the operating system happens to be in charge of the computer. You might want, for example, to call functions that aren't, strictly speaking, part of the WDM. **IoReportTargetDeviceChangeAsynchronous**, which I used in the PNPEVENT sample, is such a function.

It's very easy for an application to learn the operation system platform by calling **GetVersionEx**. The closest equivalent function in kernel mode is **IoIsWdmVersionAvailable**:

```
BOOLEAN IoIsWdmVersionAvailable(MajorVersion, MinorVersion);
```

Windows 2000 supports WDM version 1.10, which corresponds to the WDM_ MAJORVERSION (1) and WDM_MINORVERSION (10) constants in the file WDM.H. Windows 98 (including Windows 98, Second Edition) supports WDM version 1.0 only. You can use this difference in support level to tell which platform you happen to be running on.

OTHER HEURISTICS FOR OPERATING SYSTEM VERSION

I used to rely on different heuristics for determining the operating system version until experience and changes in the operating system made them obsolete. In the original retail release of Windows 98, for example, the **DriverExtension** of your driver object had a **ServiceKeyName** with zero length when the system invoked your **DriverEntry** in a normal way. Windows 2000, on the other hand, supplies a nonempty string for this parameter. So do later editions of Windows 98, which makes this heuristic useful only for detecting the original Windows 98.

Vireo Software used to suggest using the presence of a registry key named \Registry\Machine\SAM as an indicator for Windows 2000. This test isn't reliable for drivers that load during Windows 2000 startup, though, so you shouldn't rely on this test either. The company currently recommends a test based on the facts that the registry key HKLM\System\CurrentControlSet\Control\Class will exist in Windows 2000 but not Windows 98 and that the key HKLM\System\CurrentControlSet\Services\Class will exist in Windows 98 but not Windows 2000.

Appendix B

Using GENERIC.SYS

This appendix explains the public interface to the GENERIC.SYS support library that most of the sample drivers in this book use. I need to explain a few things about GENERIC first.

I built GENERIC for the simple reason that I kept needing to change the Plug and Play (PnP) and power support for my sample drivers while I was writing this book. I'll probably have to change that support after this book is published, too. Rather than try to change over 20 sample drivers each time I learned some new fact about PnP and power management, I decided to build GENERIC and let it handle all the IRP_MJ_PNP and IRP_MJ_POWER requests that came my way.

I kept WDMWIZ.AWX (the subject of the next appendix) and GENERIC in synchrony. That is, if you build a driver using WDMWIZ, you'll end with the same functionality whether or not you elect to use GENERIC. If you decide to use GENERIC, your driver will call GENERIC to handle some of the more complicated things that WDM drivers do. If you decide not to use it, your driver will include all that code.

I designed GENERIC to be redistributed as part of WDM driver packages, but only under a royalty-free license agreement that will protect end users from inconsistency. Please consult the sample program license agreement for more details about this.

Finally, I used Microsoft's AUTODUCK tool to automatically generate documentation for the functions GENERIC exports. AUTODUCK takes specially formatted comments in source code and turns them into documentation. If you remember to update the comments, you can keep your documentation up-to-date fairly painlessly. You'll find the documentation in the GENERIC directory on the companion disc under the name GENERIC.RTF. I could lie and tell you we put it there for your convenience or so that I could change it up until the last minute—which I did!—but the truth is that we printed the covers before we knew exactly how many pages were in the book, and there turned out to be too many. So much for any illusions you may have treasured about the intellectual purity of the publishing process.

Using WDMWIZ.AWX

This appendix describes how to use the WDMWIZ.AWX custom wizard to build a driver project for use with Microsoft Visual C++ version 6.0. I built this wizard because I wanted an easy and reproducible way to generate the sample drivers for this book. I've included it on the companion disc because I knew you'd want an easy way to generate drivers as you read through the book.

The WDMBOOK.HTM file on the companion disc tells you how to install this wizard on your system. Once you've installed it, you'll find a WDM Driver Wizard item on the Projects tab of the New dialog box that Visual C++ presents when you create a new project.

WDMWIZ.AWX is not a product and never will be. I would like to know about situations in which it generates incorrect code, but I'm not planning to make any changes to the admittedly clunky user interface. Furthermore, you're on your own as far as quality assurance for your finished driver goes.

BASIC DRIVER INFORMATION

The initial page (shown in Figure C-1) asks you for basic information about the driver you want to build.

For Type Of Driver, you can specify these choices:

- **Generic Function Driver**   Builds a function driver for a generic device. (Note that use of the word *generic* here is unfortunate because it has nothing to do with GENERIC.SYS.)
- **Generic Filter Driver**   Builds a filter driver with default handling for all types of IRP.
- **USB Function Driver**   Builds a function driver for a USB device.
- **Empty Driver Project**   Builds a project with no files but with options set up for building a WDM driver.

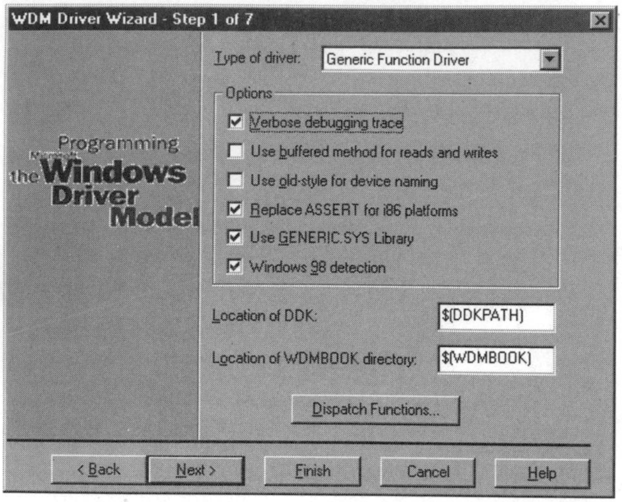

Figure C-1. *Page for entering basic driver information.*

You can select the following options:

- **Verbose Debugging Trace** If you check this option, the driver project files will include many **KdPrint** macro calls to trace important operations in the driver.

- **Use Buffered Method For Reads And Writes** Set this option if you want to use the DO_BUFFERED_IO method for read and write operations. Clear this option if you want to use DO_DIRECT_IO instead.

- **Use Old-Style For Device Naming** Set this option to generate named device objects. Clear this option to generate a driver that uses a device interface instead. The second choice (device interface) is the one Microsoft prefers for WDM drivers.

- **Replace ASSERT For i86 Platforms** The DDK's **ASSERT** macro calls a kernel-mode support routine (**RtlAssert**) that's a no-operation in the free build of Microsoft Windows 2000. The checked build of your driver will therefore not stop in the free build of the operating system. Set this option to redefine ASSERT so that the checked build of your driver halts even in the free build of the operating system.

- **Use GENERIC.SYS Library** Set this option to make use of the standardized driver code in GENERIC.SYS. Clear this option to put all that standardized code in your own driver.

- **Windows 98 Detection** Set this option to include a run-time check for whether your driver is running under Windows 98 or Windows 2000. Clear this option to omit the check.

You can also specify the base pathname where you've installed the Windows 2000 DDK and the samples for this book. The default values—$(DDKPATH) and $(WDMBOOK)—rely on the environment variables that the sample setup program creates.

Finally you can click the Dispatch Functions button to specify the types of IRP your driver will handle, as Figure C-2 shows. The dialog box embodies some design decisions that you can't override. Your driver will include support for IRP_MJ_PNP and IRP_MJ_POWER. If you specify handling for IRP_MJ_CREATE, you'll get support for IRP_MJ_CLOSE. If you specify handling for IRP_MJ_READ, IRP_MJ_WRITE, or IRP_MJ_DEVICE_CONTROL, you'll get support for IRP_MJ_CREATE (and therefore IRP_MJ_CLOSE). WDMWIZ.AWX doesn't generate skeleton dispatch functions for many types of IRP that are used only by file system drivers.

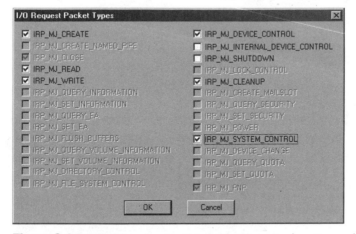

Figure C-2. *Dialog box for specifying the IRP major function codes for which you want dispatch functions .*

DEVICEIOCONTROL CODES

If you specified handling for IRP_MJ_DEVICE_CONTROL, the wizard will present a page (depicted in Figure C-3) to allow you to specify information about the control operations you support.

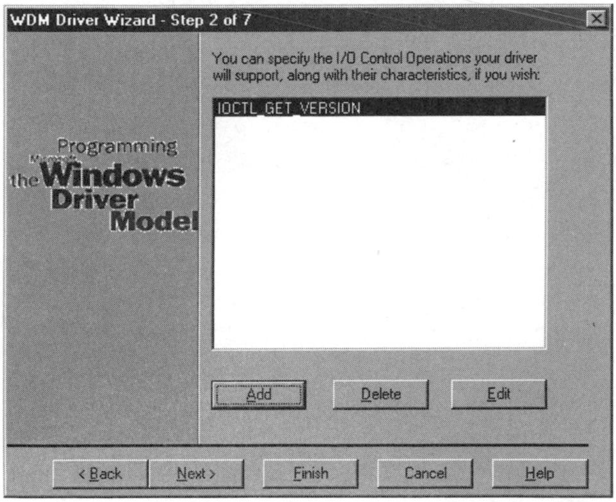

Figure C-3. *Page for specifying supported I/O control operations.*

Figure C-4 is an example of how you specify information about a particular **DeviceIoControl** operation. Most of the fields correspond directly to parameters in the CTL_CODE preprocessor macro and should therefore require no explanation. Setting the Asynchronous option generates support for an operation that you complete asynchronously, after the dispatch function returns STATUS_PENDING.

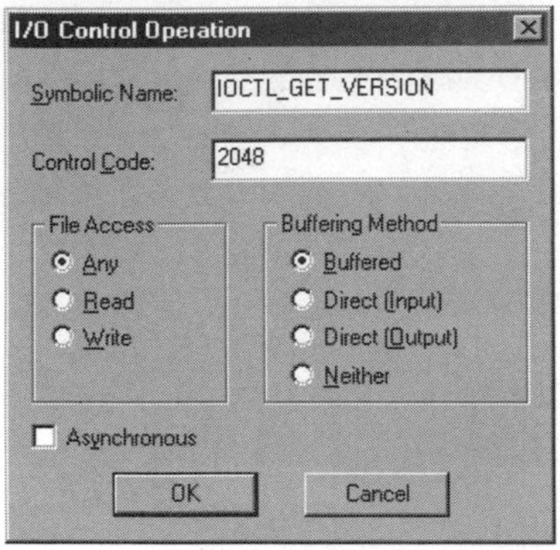

Figure C-4. *Dialog box for adding and editing an I/O control operation.*

I/O RESOURCES

If your device uses any I/O resources, you can fill in the third page with information about them, as Figure C-5 shows.

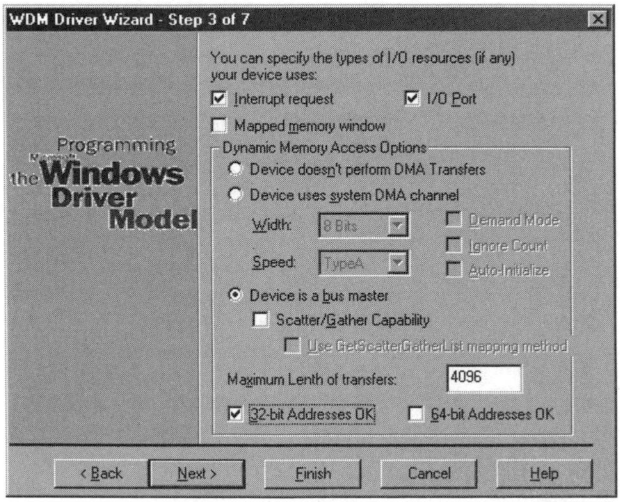

Figure C-5. *Page for specifying I/O resources.*

POWER CAPABILITIES

The fourth step in the wizard (shown in Figure C-6) allows you to specify some miscellaneous power management capabilities. With the exception of the Idle Detection option, I haven't debugged all the interactions between this page and the driver options on other pages. Be prepared to sort this out yourself if you set any option other than Idle Detection.

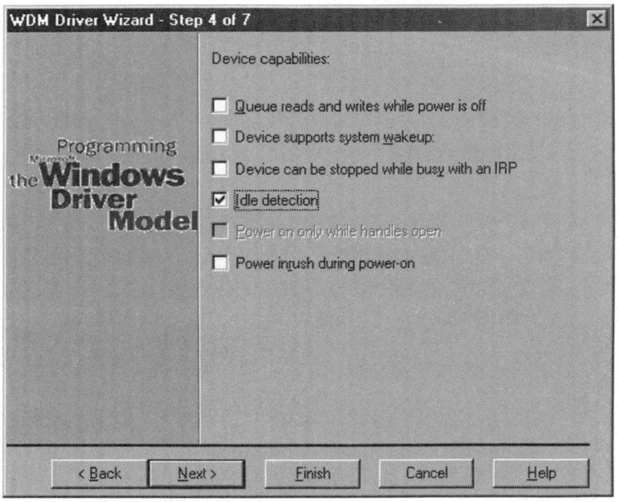

Figure C-6. *Page for specifying power management capabilities.*

The capabilities in this page are as follows:

- **Queue Reads And Writes While Power Is Off**   Set this option if your driver will accept and queue read and write IRPs even while your device is powered down. Clear this option if your driver will reject new read and write IRPs during such periods.

- **Device Supports System Wakeup**   Set this option if your device has system wake-up capability. Otherwise, clear the option. Setting the option generates skeletal support for generating IRP_MN_WAIT_WAKE requests at appropriate points.

- **Device Can Be Stopped While Busy With An IRP**   If your driver has some way to halt an active read or write IRP when an IRP_MN_STOP_DEVICE comes along, you can set this option if you want. Otherwise, leave the option clear.

- **Idle Detection**   Set this option if you want your device to automatically power down after a user-prescribed period of inactivity. If you're using GENERIC.SYS with your driver, you'll automatically get support for a set of IOCTLs that my POWCPL.DLL uses, thereby gaining a user interface for free.

- **Power On Only While Handles Open**   This option is available for USB devices only. Set it if you want your device powered on only while an application has an open handle.

■ **Power Inrush During Power-On**   Set this option if your device is an *inrush* device that demands a large spike of current when powering on.

USB ENDPOINTS

If you selected USB Function Driver in the first page, the wizard will present a page that allows you to describe the endpoints of your device, as Figure C-7 shows. This page lists the names of variables in your device extension that will hold pipe handles. The order of names corresponds to the order of endpoint descriptors on your device.

NOTE   This page isn't sufficiently complex to let you describe a device with multiple interfaces or with alternate settings for interfaces.

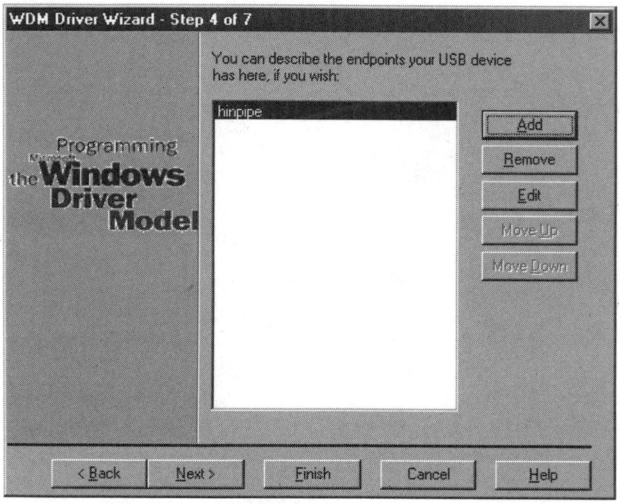

Figure C-7. *Page for defining USB endpoints.*

Refer to Figure C-8 for an illustration of the dialog box you can use to describe a single endpoint. The Description Of Endpoint group relates to the description of the endpoint in your device firmware and should be self-explanatory. Within the Resources In The Driver group, complete the fields as follows:

■ **Name Of Pipe Handle In Device Extension**   Supply the name of a DEVICE_ EXTENSION member to hold the pipe handle you'll use for operations on this endpoint.

■ **Maximum Transfer Per URB**   Specify here the maximum number of bytes you'll transfer in a single URB. In general, this value is much larger than the endpoint maximum.

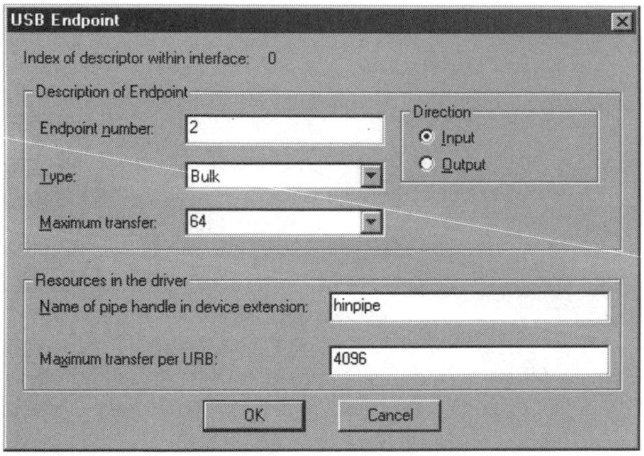

Figure C-8. *Dialog box for adding and editing a USB endpoint.*

WMI SUPPORT

If you've specified that you want to handle IRP_MJ_SYSTEM_CONTROL requests, the wizard will present the page shown in Figure C-9 to allow you to specify the elements of your custom WMI schema.

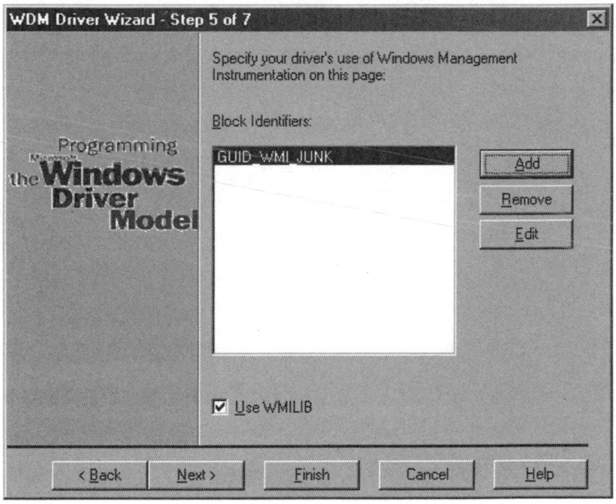

Figure C-9. *Page for specifying WMI options.*

In this page, you should always leave the Use WMILIB option checked because the generated code won't give you much help in handling WMI requests otherwise. The Block Identifiers list names the class GUIDs in your custom schema in the order they'll appear in the GUID list for WMILIB.

Figure C-10 illustrates how you can describe one class in your custom schema. The topmost (unlabelled) control is the symbolic name of a GUID that the wizard will generate for you automatically. You can specify the following attributes of this class:

- **Number Of Instances**   Indicates how many instances of the class your driver will create.

- **Expensive**   Indicates an expensive class that must be specifically enabled.

- **Event Only**   Indicates that the class is used only to fire an event.

- **Traced**   Corresponds to a WMI option that I don't currently understand. But if I ever do understand it, I'll be able to use this check box to influence its state.

You can choose between PDO-based instance naming or instance naming using a base name. Microsoft recommends you use PDO-based naming.

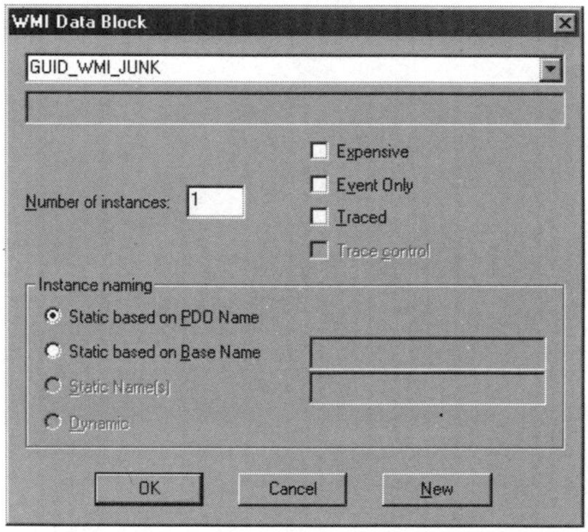

Figure C-10. *Dialog box for specifying a WMI class.*

PARAMETERS FOR THE INF FILE

The last page in the wizard (shown in Figure C-11) lets you specify information for the INF file that becomes part of your driver project.

The fields in this page are as follows:

- **Manufacturer Name**   Name of the hardware manufacturer.

- **Device Class**   The standard device class to which your device belongs. Sample is my own class for the driver samples in this book: you shouldn't use this class for a production device.

- **Hardware ID**   The hardware identifier for this device. I made up *WCO0C01 for this example. You should specify the identifier that will match one of the identifiers that the relevant bus driver will create. Refer to the section titled "Device Identifiers" in Chapter 12, "Installing Device Drivers," for more information.

- **Friendly Name For Device**   If you want to have a **FriendlyName** value inserted into the device's hardware key, specify that name here.

- **Auto-Launch Command**   If you want the AutoLaunch service to automatically start an application when your device starts, specify the command line here. For example, when I built the AutoLaunch sample for Chapter 12, I specified %windir%\altest.exe %s %s in this field.

- **Device Description**   Insert the description of your device here.

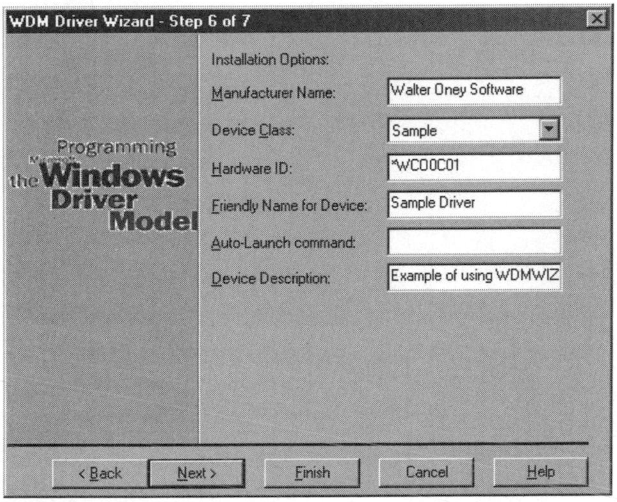

Figure C-11. *Page for specifying INF file options.*

NOW WHAT?

After you run through all the pages of the wizard, you'll have a project that you can use to finish crafting your driver. Because of limitations on the custom wizard support in Visual C++, you'll need to add some project settings by hand. Please refer to WDMBOOK.HTM on the companion disc for a description of these settings.

The generated code will contain a number of TODO comments that highlight areas where you need to write some code. I suggest you use the Find In Files command to locate these items.

Index

Note: Page numbers in italics refer to figures or tables.

WALTER ONEY

Walter Oney is a freelance software consultant based in Boston, Massachusetts. A member of the class of 1968, he holds S.B. and S.M. degrees in Electrical Engineering from the Massachusetts Institute of Technology. When not teaching programming seminars, he enjoys running, cycling, watching ballet, and playing the oboe.

About the Companion Disc

The companion disc for *Programming the Microsoft Windows Driver Model* contains more than 20 sample drivers and test programs to illustrate the topics covered by the book. Each sample also has an HTML file that describes the overall purpose of the sample and contains brief instructions about how to build and test the sample.

The companion disc also includes a wizard to help learn about creating drivers (WDMWIZ.AWX), a library to help handle Plug and Play and power management details (GENERIC.SYS), a utility to quickly install drivers in Windows 2000 (FASTINST), and a fully searchable electronic version of the book.

SYSTEM REQUIREMENTS

To test the samples, you must have either (preferably both) of the following operating systems:

- Microsoft Windows 98. (Some samples require Windows 98, Second Edition.)

- Microsoft Windows 2000. (The samples were tested with Windows 2000 RC1.)

To build the samples, you must have the following software installed:

- Microsoft Visual C++ 6.0, Professional or Enterprise Edition.

- Microsoft Platform Software Development Kit (SDK). (The samples were built and tested with the version that accompanied the RC1 release of Windows 2000.)

- Microsoft Windows 2000 Driver Development Kit (DDK). (The samples were built and tested with the version that accompanied the RC1 release of Windows 2000.)

- Microsoft Windows 98 Driver Development Kit (DDK). (Only some of the samples require this DDK.)

For information about Microsoft's SDKs, see *http://msdn.microsoft.com/developer/sdk/*. For information about Microsoft's DDKs, see *http://www.microsoft.com/ddk/*.

MICROSOFT LICENSE AGREEMENT

Book Companion CD

IMPORTANT—READ CAREFULLY: This Microsoft End-User License Agreement ("EULA") is a legal agreement between you (either an individual or an entity) and Microsoft Corporation for the Microsoft product identified above, which includes computer software and may include associated media, printed materials, and "on-line" or electronic documentation ("SOFTWARE PRODUCT"). Any component included within the SOFTWARE PRODUCT that is accompanied by a separate End-User License Agreement shall be governed by such agreement and not the terms set forth below. By installing, copying, or otherwise using the SOFTWARE PRODUCT, you agree to be bound by the terms of this EULA. If you do not agree to the terms of this EULA, you are not authorized to install, copy, or otherwise use the SOFTWARE PRODUCT; you may, however, return the SOFTWARE PRODUCT, along with all printed materials and other items that form a part of the Microsoft product that includes the SOFTWARE PRODUCT, to the place you obtained them for a full refund.

SOFTWARE PRODUCT LICENSE

The SOFTWARE PRODUCT is protected by United States copyright laws and international copyright treaties, as well as other intellectual property laws and treaties. The SOFTWARE PRODUCT is licensed, not sold.

1. GRANT OF LICENSE. This EULA grants you the following rights:

  a. Software Product. You may install and use one copy of the SOFTWARE PRODUCT on a single computer. The primary user of the computer on which the SOFTWARE PRODUCT is installed may make a second copy for his or her exclusive use on a portable computer.

  b. Storage/Network Use. You may also store or install a copy of the SOFTWARE PRODUCT on a storage device, such as a network server, used only to install or run the SOFTWARE PRODUCT on your other computers over an internal network; however, you must acquire and dedicate a license for each separate computer on which the SOFTWARE PRODUCT is installed or run from the storage device. A license for the SOFTWARE PRODUCT may not be shared or used concurrently on different computers.

  c. License Pak. If you have acquired this EULA in a Microsoft License Pak, you may make the number of additional copies of the computer software portion of the SOFTWARE PRODUCT authorized on the printed copy of this EULA, and you may use each copy in the manner specified above. You are also entitled to make a corresponding number of secondary copies for portable computer use as specified above.

  d. Sample Code. Solely with respect to portions, if any, of the SOFTWARE PRODUCT that are identified within the SOFTWARE PRODUCT as sample code (the "SAMPLE CODE"):

  i. Use and Modification. Microsoft grants you the right to use and modify the source code version of the SAMPLE CODE, *provided* you comply with subsection (d)(iii) below. You may not distribute the SAMPLE CODE, or any modified version of the SAMPLE CODE, in source code form.

  ii. Redistributable Files. Provided you comply with subsection (d)(iii) below, Microsoft grants you a nonexclusive, royalty-free right to reproduce and distribute the object code version of the SAMPLE CODE and of any modified SAMPLE CODE, other than SAMPLE CODE (or any modified version thereof) designated as not redistributable in the Readme file that forms a part of the SOFTWARE PRODUCT (the "Non-Redistributable Sample Code"). All SAMPLE CODE other than the Non-Redistributable Sample Code is collectively referred to as the "REDISTRIBUTABLES."

  iii. Redistribution Requirements. If you redistribute the REDISTRIBUTABLES, you agree to: (i) distribute the REDISTRIBUTABLES in object code form only in conjunction with and as a part of your software application product; (ii) not use Microsoft's name, logo, or trademarks to market your software application product; (iii) include a valid copyright notice on your software application product; (iv) indemnify, hold harmless, and defend Microsoft from and against any claims or lawsuits, including attorney's fees, that arise or result from the use or distribution of your software application product; and (v) not permit further distribution of the REDISTRIBUTABLES by your end user. Contact Microsoft for the applicable royalties due and other licensing terms for all other uses and/or distribution of the REDISTRIBUTABLES.

2. DESCRIPTION OF OTHER RIGHTS AND LIMITATIONS.

  - **Limitations on Reverse Engineering, Decompilation, and Disassembly.** You may not reverse engineer, decompile, or disassemble the SOFTWARE PRODUCT, except and only to the extent that such activity is expressly permitted by applicable law notwithstanding this limitation.

  - **Separation of Components.** The SOFTWARE PRODUCT is licensed as a single product. Its component parts may not be separated for use on more than one computer.

  - **Rental.** You may not rent, lease, or lend the SOFTWARE PRODUCT.

  - **Support Services.** Microsoft may, but is not obligated to, provide you with support services related to the SOFTWARE PRODUCT ("Support Services"). Use of Support Services is governed by the Microsoft policies and programs described in the user manual, in "on-line" documentation, and/or in other Microsoft-provided materials. Any supplemental software code provided to you as part of the Support Services shall be considered part of the SOFTWARE PRODUCT and subject to the terms and conditions of this EULA. With respect to technical information you provide to Microsoft as part of the Support Services, Microsoft may use such information for its business purposes, including for product support and development. Microsoft will not utilize such technical information in a form that personally identifies you.

- **Software Transfer.** You may permanently transfer all of your rights under this EULA, provided you retain no copies, you transfer all of the SOFTWARE PRODUCT (including all component parts, the media and printed materials, any upgrades, this EULA, and, if applicable, the Certificate of Authenticity), **and** the recipient agrees to the terms of this EULA.

- **Termination.** Without prejudice to any other rights, Microsoft may terminate this EULA if you fail to comply with the terms and conditions of this EULA. In such event, you must destroy all copies of the SOFTWARE PRODUCT and all of its component parts.

3. **COPYRIGHT.** All title and copyrights in and to the SOFTWARE PRODUCT (including but not limited to any images, photographs, animations, video, audio, music, text, SAMPLE CODE, REDISTRIBUTABLES, and "applets" incorporated into the SOFTWARE PRODUCT) and any copies of the SOFTWARE PRODUCT are owned by Microsoft or its suppliers. The SOFTWARE PRODUCT is protected by copyright laws and international treaty provisions. Therefore, you must treat the SOFTWARE PRODUCT like any other copyrighted material **except** that you may install the SOFTWARE PRODUCT on a single computer provided you keep the original solely for backup or archival purposes. You may not copy the printed materials accompanying the SOFTWARE PRODUCT.

4. **U.S. GOVERNMENT RESTRICTED RIGHTS.** The SOFTWARE PRODUCT and documentation are provided with RESTRICTED RIGHTS. Use, duplication, or disclosure by the Government is subject to restrictions as set forth in subparagraph (c)(1)(ii) of the Rights in Technical Data and Computer Software clause at DFARS 252.227-7013 or subparagraphs (c)(1) and (2) of the Commercial Computer Software—Restricted Rights at 48 CFR 52.227-19, as applicable. Manufacturer is Microsoft Corporation/One Microsoft Way/Redmond, WA 98052-6399.

5. **EXPORT RESTRICTIONS.** You agree that you will not export or re-export the SOFTWARE PRODUCT, any part thereof, or any process or service that is the direct product of the SOFTWARE PRODUCT (the foregoing collectively referred to as the "Restricted Components"), to any country, person, entity, or end user subject to U.S. export restrictions. You specifically agree not to export or re-export any of the Restricted Components (i) to any country to which the U.S. has embargoed or restricted the export of goods or services, which currently include, but are not necessarily limited to, Cuba, Iran, Iraq, Libya, North Korea, Sudan, and Syria, or to any national of any such country, wherever located, who intends to transmit or transport the Restricted Components back to such country; (ii) to any end user who you know or have reason to know will utilize the Restricted Components in the design, development, or production of nuclear, chemical, or biological weapons; or (iii) to any end user who has been prohibited from participating in U.S. export transactions by any federal agency of the U.S. government. You warrant and represent that neither the BXA nor any other U.S. federal agency has suspended, revoked, or denied your export privileges.

6. **NOTE ON JAVA SUPPORT.** THE SOFTWARE PRODUCT MAY CONTAIN SUPPORT FOR PROGRAMS WRITTEN IN JAVA. JAVA TECHNOLOGY IS NOT FAULT TOLERANT AND IS NOT DESIGNED, MANUFACTURED, OR INTENDED FOR USE OR RESALE AS ON-LINE CONTROL EQUIPMENT IN HAZARDOUS ENVIRONMENTS REQUIRING FAIL-SAFE PERFORMANCE, SUCH AS IN THE OPERATION OF NUCLEAR FACILITIES, AIRCRAFT NAVIGATION OR COMMUNICATION SYSTEMS, AIR TRAFFIC CONTROL, DIRECT LIFE SUPPORT MACHINES, OR WEAPONS SYSTEMS, IN WHICH THE FAILURE OF JAVA TECHNOLOGY COULD LEAD DIRECTLY TO DEATH, PERSONAL INJURY, OR SEVERE PHYSICAL OR ENVIRONMENTAL DAMAGE. SUN MICROSYSTEMS, INC. HAS CONTRACTUALLY OBLIGATED MICROSOFT TO MAKE THIS DISCLAIMER.

DISCLAIMER OF WARRANTY

NO WARRANTIES OR CONDITIONS. MICROSOFT EXPRESSLY DISCLAIMS ANY WARRANTY OR CONDITION FOR THE SOFTWARE PRODUCT. THE SOFTWARE PRODUCT AND ANY RELATED DOCUMENTATION ARE PROVIDED "AS IS" WITHOUT WARRANTY OR CONDITION OF ANY KIND, EITHER EXPRESS OR IMPLIED, INCLUDING, WITHOUT LIMITATION, THE IMPLIED WARRANTIES OF MERCHANTABILITY, FITNESS FOR A PARTICULAR PURPOSE, OR NONINFRINGEMENT. THE ENTIRE RISK ARISING OUT OF USE OR PERFORMANCE OF THE SOFTWARE PRODUCT REMAINS WITH YOU.

LIMITATION OF LIABILITY. TO THE MAXIMUM EXTENT PERMITTED BY APPLICABLE LAW, IN NO EVENT SHALL MICROSOFT OR ITS SUPPLIERS BE LIABLE FOR ANY SPECIAL, INCIDENTAL, INDIRECT, OR CONSEQUENTIAL DAMAGES WHATSOEVER (INCLUDING, WITHOUT LIMITATION, DAMAGES FOR LOSS OF BUSINESS PROFITS, BUSINESS INTERRUPTION, LOSS OF BUSINESS INFORMATION, OR ANY OTHER PECUNIARY LOSS) ARISING OUT OF THE USE OF OR INABILITY TO USE THE SOFTWARE PRODUCT OR THE PROVISION OF OR FAILURE TO PROVIDE SUPPORT SERVICES, EVEN IF MICROSOFT HAS BEEN ADVISED OF THE POSSIBILITY OF SUCH DAMAGES. IN ANY CASE, MICROSOFT'S ENTIRE LIABILITY UNDER ANY PROVISION OF THIS EULA SHALL BE LIMITED TO THE GREATER OF THE AMOUNT ACTUALLY PAID BY YOU FOR THE SOFTWARE PRODUCT OR US$5.00; PROVIDED, HOWEVER, IF YOU HAVE ENTERED INTO A MICROSOFT SUPPORT SERVICES AGREEMENT, MICROSOFT'S ENTIRE LIABILITY REGARDING SUPPORT SERVICES SHALL BE GOVERNED BY THE TERMS OF THAT AGREEMENT. BECAUSE SOME STATES AND JURISDICTIONS DO NOT ALLOW THE EXCLUSION OR LIMITATION OF LIABILITY, THE ABOVE LIMITATION MAY NOT APPLY TO YOU.

MISCELLANEOUS

This EULA is governed by the laws of the State of Washington USA, except and only to the extent that applicable law mandates governing law of a different jurisdiction.

Should you have any questions concerning this EULA, or if you desire to contact Microsoft for any reason, please contact the Microsoft subsidiary serving your country, or write: Microsoft Sales Information Center/One Microsoft Way/Redmond, WA 98052-6399.

Proof of Purchase

Do not send this card with your registration.
Use this card as proof of purchase if participating in a promotion or
rebate offer on *Programming the Microsoft® Windows® Driver Model*. Card must be used in conjunction
with other proof(s) of payment such as your dated sales receipt—see offer details.

Programming the Microsoft® Windows® Driver Model

WHERE DID YOU PURCHASE THIS PRODUCT?

CUSTOMER NAME

mspress.microsoft.com

Microsoft Press, PO Box 97017, Redmond, WA 98073-9830

OWNER REGISTRATION CARD   *Register Today!*   0-7356-0588-2

Return the bottom portion of this card to register today

Programming the Microsoft® Windows® Driver Model

FIRST NAME   MIDDLE INITIAL   LAST NAME

INSTITUTION OR COMPANY NAME

ADDRESS

CITY   STATE   ZIP

(   )

E-MAIL ADDRESS   PHONE NUMBER

U.S. and Canada addresses only. Fill in information above and mail postage-free.
Please mail only the bottom half of this page.

**For information about Microsoft Press®
products, visit our Web site at
mspress.microsoft.com**

Microsoft®Press

BUSINESS REPLY MAIL

FIRST-CLASS MAIL   PERMIT NO. 108   REDMOND WA

POSTAGE WILL BE PAID BY ADDRESSEE

MICROSOFT PRESS
PO BOX 97017
REDMOND, WA 98073-9830